THE WESTERN CANON

'Harold Bloom's large-minded and large-hearted book about
the great books has many of the virtues that it sees and shows
in the work he so fiercely admires. I can't imagine a reader who
would not learn something from every page.'
CHRISTOPHER RICKS, *Washington Times*

'The [book's] significance lies in Bloom's rage about what has
happened to the study of literature when students are encouraged
to value books that see the world as they themselves see it, instead
of yielding up to other deeper ways in which it can be seen.'
MALCOLM BRADBURY, *Daily Telegraph*

'This is a book to teach you how to read and how to love literature.'
JAMES WOOD, *Guardian*

'*The Western Canon* remains a wonderful and, indeed, invaluable
reaffirmation of the central literary tradition.'
PETER ACKROYD, *The Times*

'This is a book not only to be reckoned with but to be enjoyed.
Bloom is a writer with whom it is a pleasure to argue; his curiosity
is insatiable, his reading vast and deep, his enthusiasm infectious,
and his heart is undoubtedly in the right place.'
ALLAN MASSIE, *Daily Telegraph*

'To read Harold Bloom's commentaries (as Coleridge said about
the great tragic actor Edmund Kean) is like reading classics by
flashes of lightning.'
M. H. ABRAMS

'Harold Bloom brilliantly reanimates the concept of the western
canon and a dazzling array of works that best represent it. At a
time when the culture of reading seems close to extinction, this
book will be greatly prized by educated readers.'
RICHARD POIRIER

'Here is a book to enrage some, but to gratify many others. Harold Bloom is brilliant, outrageous, headstrong, witty, heterodox, full of charm, immense learning, and tremendous zest.'
ANTHONY HECHT

'We have for so long been educated by Harold Bloom that it comes as something of a surprise to realize all this time we were skimming the surface: he is our encyclopedist as well.'
RICHARD HOWARD

'A heroically brave, formidably learned, and often unbearably sad response to the present state of the humanities . . . a passionate demonstration . . . It inspires hope . . . that what humanity has long cherished, posterity will also.'
NORMAN FRUMAN, *New York Times Book Review*

'A vigorous criticism, devastating and salutary . . . Its abiding importance lies in the notion it frames of how the canonical comes about and what purposes it serves in our cultural lives. These notions richly deserve reflection.'
ROBERT ALTER, *The New Republic*

'This book is terribly important . . . Bloom asserts here what desperately needs to be asserted . . . Splendid.'
FRANK McCONNELL, *Boston Globe*

THE WESTERN CANON

The Books and School of the Ages

HAROLD BLOOM

PAPERMAC

First published 1994 by Harcourt Brace & Company, New York

First published in Great Britain 1995 by Macmillan

This edition published 1995 by Papermac
an imprint of Macmillan General Books
25 Eccleston Place, London SW1W 9NF
and Basingstoke

Associated companies throughout the world

ISBN 0 333 63952 9

Published by arrangement with Harcourt Brace & Company

1 3 5 7 9 8 6 4 2

A CIP catalogue record for this book is available from
the British Library

Printed and bound in Great Britain by
Mackays of Chatham plc, Chatham, Kent

For

ANNE FREEDGOOD

Acknowledgments

My editors, Anne Freedgood and Pat Strachan, and my literary agents, Glen Hartley and Lynn Chu, have made crucial contributions to this book. Richard Poirier, John Hollander, Perry Meisel, and Roberto González Echevarria have encouraged and advised me throughout its composition. My research assistant, Martha Serpas, made possible the entire process of revision, during which she helped determine the volume's final shape. The libraries of Yale University, my endless resource for more than forty years, stoically have endured my work habits.

—HAROLD BLOOM
Timothy Dwight College
Yale University

Contents

THE
WESTERN
CANON

Preface and Prelude

THIS BOOK studies twenty-six writers, necessarily with a certain nostalgia, since I seek to isolate the qualities that made these authors canonical, that is, authoritative in our culture. "Aesthetic value" is sometimes regarded as a suggestion of Immanuel Kant's rather than an actuality, but that has not been my experience during a lifetime of reading. Things have however fallen apart, the center has not held, and mere anarchy is in the process of being unleashed upon what used to be called "the learned world." Mimic cultural wars do not much interest me; what I have to say about our current squalors is in my first and last chapters. Here I wish to explain the organization of this book and to account for my choice of these twenty-six writers from among the many hundreds in what once was considered to be the Western Canon.

Giambattista Vico, in his *New Science,* posited a cycle of three phases—Theocratic, Aristocratic, Democratic—followed by a chaos out of which a New Theocratic Age would at last emerge. Joyce made grand seriocomic use of Vico in organizing *Finnegans*

Wake, and I have followed in the wake of the *Wake,* except that I have omitted the literature of the Theocratic Age. My historical quence begins with Dante and concludes with Samuel Beckett, though I have not always followed strict chronological order. Thus, I have begun the Aristocratic Age with Shakespeare, because he is the central figure of the Western Canon, and I have subsequently considered him in relation to nearly all the others, from Chaucer and Montaigne, who affected him, through many of those he influenced—Milton, Dr. Johnson, Goethe, Ibsen, Joyce, and Beckett among them—as well as those who attempted to reject him: Tolstoy in particular, along with Freud, who appropriated Shakespeare while insisting that the Earl of Oxford had done the writing for "the man from Stratford."

The choice of authors here is not so arbitrary as it may seem. They have been selected for both their sublimity and their representative nature: a book about twenty-six writers is possible, but not a book about four hundred. Certainly the major Western writers since Dante are here—Chaucer, Cervantes, Montaigne, Shakespeare, Goethe, Wordsworth, Dickens, Tolstoy, Joyce, and Proust. But where are Petrarch, Rabelais, Ariosto, Spenser, Ben Jonson, Racine, Swift, Rousseau, Blake, Pushkin, Melville, Giacomo Leopardi, Henry James, Dostoevsky, Hugo, Balzac, Nietzsche, Flaubert, Baudelaire, Browning, Chekhov, Yeats, D. H. Lawrence, and so many others? I have tried to represent national canons by their crucial figures: Chaucer, Shakespeare, Milton, Wordsworth, Dickens for England; Montaigne and Molière for France; Dante for Italy; Cervantes for Spain; Tolstoy for Russia; Goethe for Germany; Borges and Neruda for Hispanic America; Whitman and Dickinson for the United States. The sequence of major dramatists is here: Shakespeare, Molière, Ibsen, and Beckett; and of novelists: Austen, Dickens, George Eliot, Tolstoy, Proust, Joyce, and Woolf. Dr. Johnson is here as the greatest of Western literary critics; it would be difficult to find his rival.

Vico did not postulate a Chaotic Age before the *ricorso* or return of a second Theocratic Age; but our century, while pretending to continue the Democratic Age, cannot be better characterized than as Chaotic. Its key writers are Freud, Proust, Joyce, Kafka: they personify whatever literary spirit the era possesses. Freud called himself a scientist, but he will survive as a great essayist like Montaigne or Emerson, not as the founder of a therapy already discredited (or elevated) as another episode in the long history of shamanism. I wish that there were space for more modern poets here than just Neruda and Pessoa, but no poet of our century has matched *In Search of Lost Time, Ulysses,* or *Finnegans Wake,* the essays of Freud, or the parables and tales of Kafka.

With most of these twenty-six writers, I have tried to confront greatness directly: to ask what makes the author and the works canonical. The answer, more often than not, has turned out to be strangeness, a mode of originality that either cannot be assimilated, or that so assimilates us that we cease to see it as strange. Walter Pater defined Romanticism as adding strangeness to beauty, but I think he characterized all canonical writing rather than the Romantics as such. The cycle of achievement goes from *The Divine Comedy* to *Endgame,* from strangeness to strangeness. When you read a canonical work for a first time you encounter a stranger, an uncanny startlement rather than a fulfillment of expectations. Read freshly, all that *The Divine Comedy, Paradise Lost, Faust Part Two, Hadji Murad, Peer Gynt, Ulysses,* and *Canto general* have in common is their uncanniness, their ability to make you feel strange at home.

Shakespeare, the largest writer we ever will know, frequently gives the opposite impression: of making us at home out of doors, foreign, abroad. His powers of assimilation and of contamination are unique and constitute a perpetual challenge to universal performance and to criticism. I find it absurd and regrettable that the current criticism of Shakespeare—"cultural materialist" (Neo-Marxist); "New Historicist" (Foucault); "Feminist"—has abandoned the quest to meet that challenge. Shakespeare criticism is in full flight from his aesthetic supremacy and works at reducing him to the "social energies" of the English Renaissance, as though there were no authentic difference in aesthetic merit between the creator of Lear, Hamlet, Iago, Falstaff and his disciples such as John Webster and Thomas Middleton. The best living English critic, Sir Frank Kermode, in his *Forms of Attention* (1985) has issued the clearest warning I know about the fate of the canon, that is to say, in the first place, the fate of Shakespeare:

Canons, which negate the distinction between knowledge and opinion, which are instruments of survival built to be time-proof, not reason-proof, are of course deconstructible; if people think there should not be such things, they may very well find the means to destroy them. Their defense cannot any longer be undertaken by central institutional power; they cannot any longer be compulsory, though it is hard to see how the normal operation of learned institutions, including recruitment, can manage without them.

The means to destroy canons, as Kermode indicates, are very much at hand, and the process is now quite advanced. I am not concerned, as this book repeatedly makes clear, with the current debate between the right-wing defenders of the Canon, who wish to preserve it for its supposed (and nonexistent) moral values, and the academic-journalistic network I have dubbed the School of Resentment, who wish to overthrow the Canon in order to advance their supposed (and nonexistent) programs for social change. I hope that the book does not turn out to be an elegy for the Western Canon, and that perhaps at some point there will be a reversal, and the rabblement of lemmings will cease to hurl themselves off the cliffs. In the concluding catalog of canonical authors, particularly of our century, I have ventured a modest prophecy as to survival possibilities.

ONE MARK of an originality that can win canonical status for a literary work is a strangeness that we either never altogether assimilate, or that becomes such a given that we are blinded to its idiosyncrasies. Dante is the largest instance of the first possibility, and Shakespeare, the overwhelming example of the second. Walt Whitman, always contradictory, partakes of both sides of the paradox. After Shakespeare, the greatest representative of the given is the first author of the Hebrew Bible, the figure named the Yahwist or J by nineteenth-century biblical scholarship (the "J" from the German spelling of the Hebrew Yahweh, or Jehovah in English, the result of a onetime spelling error). J, like Homer, a person or persons lost in the dark recesses of time, appears to have lived in or near Jerusalem some three thousand years ago, well before Homer either lived or was invented. Just who the primary J was, we are never likely to know. I speculate, on purely internal and subjective literary grounds, that J may very well have been a woman at King Solomon's court, a place of high culture, considerable religious skepticism, and much psychological sophistication.

A shrewd reviewer of my *Book of J* chided me for not having the audacity to go the whole way and identify J as Bathsheba the queen mother, a Hittite woman taken by David the king after he arranged for her husband, Uriah, to die conveniently in battle. I am happy to adopt the suggestion belatedly: Bathsheba, mother of Solomon, is an admirable candidate. Her dark view of Solomon's catastrophic son and successor, Rehoboam, implied throughout the Yahwistic text, is thus highly explicable; so is her very ironic presentation of the Hebrew patriarchs, and her fondness both for some of their wives and for such female outsiders as Hagar and Tamar. Besides, it is a superb, J-like irony that the inaugural author of what eventually became the Torah was not an Israelite at all, but a Hittite woman. In what follows, I refer to the Yahwist alternately as J or Bathsheba.

The J writer was the original author of what we now call Genesis, Exodus, and Numbers, but what she wrote was censored, revised, and frequently abrogated or distorted by a series of redactors across five centuries, culminating with Ezra, or one of his followers, in the era of the return from Babylonian exile. These revisionists were priests and cultic scribes, and they seem to have been scandalized by Bathsheba's ironical freedom in portraying Yahweh. J's Yahweh is human—all too human: he eats and drinks, frequently loses his temper, delights in his own mischief, is jealous and vindictive, proclaims his justness while constantly playing favorites, and develops a considerable case of neurotic anxiety when he allows himself to transfer his blessing from an elite to the entire Israelite host. By the time he leads that crazed and suffering rabblement through the Sinai wilderness, he has become so insane and dangerous, to himself and to others, that the J writer deserves to be called the most blasphemous of all authors ever.

The J saga concludes, as far as we can tell, when Yahweh, with his own hands, buries his prophet Moses in an unmarked grave, after refusing the long-suffering leader of the Israelites more than a glimpse of the Promised Land. Bathsheba's masterpiece is her story of the relations between Yahweh and Moses, a narrative beyond irony or tragedy that moves from Yahweh's surprising election of the reluctant prophet to his motiveless attempt to murder Moses, and to the subsequent vexations that afflict both God and his chosen instrument.

Ambivalence between the divine and the human is one of J's grand inventions, another mark of an originality so perpetual that we can scarcely recognize it, because the stories Bathsheba told have absorbed us. The ultimate shock implicit in this canonmaking originality comes when we realize that the Western worship of God—by Jews, Christians, and Moslems—is the worship of a literary character, J's Yahweh, however adulterated by pious revisionists. The only comparable shocks I know come when we realize that the Jesus loved by Christians is a literary character largely invented by the author of the Gospel of Mark, and when we read the Koran and hear one voice only, the voice of Allah, recorded in detail and at length by the audacity of his prophet Mohammed. Perhaps some day, well on in the twenty-first century, when Mormonism has become the dominant religion of at least the American West, those who come after us will experience a fourth such shock when they encounter the daring of the authentic American prophet Joseph Smith in his definitive visions, *The Pearl of Great Price* and *Doctrines and Covenants*.

Canonical strangeness can exist without the shock of such audacity, but the tang of originality must always hover in an inaugural aspect of any work that incontestably wins the agon with tradition and joins the Canon. Our educational institutions are thronged these days by idealistic resenters who denounce competition in literature as in life, but the aesthetic and the agonistic are one, according to all the ancient Greeks, and to Burckhardt and Nietzsche, who recovered this truth. What Homer teaches is a poetics of conflict, a lesson first learned by his rival Hesiod. All of Plato, as the critic Longinus saw, is in the philosopher's incessant conflict with Homer, who is exiled from *The Republic,* but in vain, since Homer and not Plato remained the schoolbook of the Greeks. Dante's *Divine Comedy,* according to Stefan George, was "the book and school of the ages," though that was more true for poets than for anyone else and is properly assigned to Shakespeare's plays, as will be shown throughout this book.

Contemporary writers do not like to be told that they must compete with Shakespeare and Dante, and yet that struggle was Joyce's provocation to greatness, to an eminence shared only by Beckett, Proust, and Kafka among modern Western authors. The fundamental archetype for literary achievement will always be Pindar, who celebrates the quasi-divine victories of his aristocratic athletes while conveying the implicit sense that his victory odes are themselves victories over every possible competitor. Dante, Milton, and Wordsworth repeat Pindar's key metaphor of racing to win the palm, which is a secular immortality strangely at odds with any pious idealism. "Idealism," concerning which one struggles not to be ironic, is now the fashion in our schools and colleges, where all aesthetic and most intellectual standards are being abandoned in the name of social harmony and the remedying of historical injustice. Pragmatically, the "expansion of the Canon" has meant the destruction of the Canon, since what is being taught includes by no means the best writers who happen to be women, African, Hispanic, or Asian, but rather the writers who offer little but the resentment they have developed as part of their sense of identity. There is no strangeness and no originality in such resentment; even if there were, they would not suffice to create heirs of the Yahwist and Homer, Dante and Shakespeare, Cervantes and Joyce.

As the formulator of a critical concept I once named "the anxiety of influence," I have enjoyed the School of Resentment's repeated insistence that such a notion applies only to Dead White European Males, and not to women and to what we quaintly term "multiculturalists." Thus, feminist cheerleaders proclaim that women writers lovingly cooperate with one another as quilt makers, while African-American and Chicano literary activists go even further in asserting their freedom from any anguish of contamination whatsoever: each of them is Adam early in the morning. They know no time when they were not as they are now; self-created, self-begot, their puissance is their own. As assertions by poets, playwrights, and prose fiction writers, these are healthy and understandable, however self-deluded. But as declarations by supposed literary critics, such optimistic pronouncements are neither true nor interesting and go against both human nature and the nature of imaginative literature. There can be no strong, canonical writing without the process of literary influence, a process vexing to undergo and difficult to understand. I have never been able to recognize my theory of influence when it is under attack, since what is under attack is never even an apt travesty of my ideas. As the chapter on Freud in this book demonstrates, I favor a Shakespearean reading of Freud, and not a Freudian reading of Shakespeare or of any other writer. The anxiety of influence is not an anxiety about the father, real or literary, but an anxiety achieved by and in the poem, novel, or play. Any strong literary work creatively misreads and therefore misinterprets a precursor text or texts. An authentic canonical writer may or may not internalize her or his work's anxiety, but that scarcely matters: the strongly achieved work *is* the anxiety. This point has been well expressed by Peter de Bolla in his book *Towards Historical Rhetorics:*

> the Freudian family romance as a description of influence represents an extremely weak reading. For Bloom, "influence" is both a tropological category, a figure which determines the poetic tradition, and a complex of psychic, historical and imagistic relations . . . influence describes the relations between texts, it is an intertextual phenomenon . . . both the internal psychic defense—the poet's experience of anxiety—and the external historical relations of texts to each other are themselves the *result* of misreading, or poetic misprision, and not the cause of it.

Doubtless that accurate summary will seem intricate to those unfamiliar with my attempts to think through the problem of literary influence, yet de Bolla gives me a good starting point, here at the start of this examination of the now-threatened Western Canon. The burden of influence has to be borne, if significant originality is to be achieved and reachieved within the wealth of Western literary tradition. Tradition is not only a handing-down or process of benign transmission; it is also a conflict between past genius and present aspiration, in which the prize is literary survival or canonical inclusion. That conflict cannot be settled by social concerns, or by the judgment of any particular generation of impatient idealists, or by Marxists proclaiming, "Let the dead bury the dead," or by sophists who attempt to substitute the library for the Canon and the archive for the discerning spirit. Poems, stories, novels, plays come into being as a response to prior poems, stories, novels, and plays, and that response depends upon acts of reading and interpretation by the later writers, acts that are identical with the new works.

These readings of precursor writings are necessarily defensive in part; if they were appreciative only, fresh creation would be stifled, and not for psychological reasons alone. The issue is not Oedipal rivalry but the very nature of strong, original literary imaginings: figurative language and its vicissitudes. Fresh metaphor, or inventive troping, always involves a departure from previous metaphor, and that departure depends upon at least partial turning away from or rejection of prior figuration. Shakespeare employs Marlowe as a starting point, and such early Shakespearean hero-villains as Aaron the Moor in *Titus Andronicus* and Richard III are rather too close to Barabas, Marlowe's Jew of Malta. When Shakespeare creates Shylock, his Jew of Venice, the metaphorical basis of the farcical villain's speech is radically altered, and Shylock is a strong misreading or creative misinterpretation of Barabas, whereas Aaron the Moor is something closer to a repetition of Barabas, particularly at the level of figurative language. By the time that Shakespeare writes *Othello*, all trace of Marlowe is gone: the self-delighting villainy of Iago is cognitively far subtler and light years more refined imagistically than the self-congratulatory excesses of the exuberant Barabas. Iago's relation to Barabas is one in which Shakespeare's creative misreading of his precursor Marlowe has triumphed wholly. Shakespeare is a unique case in which the forerunner is invariably dwarfed. *Richard III* manifests an anxiety of influence in regard to *The Jew of Malta* and *Tamburlaine,* but Shakespeare was still finding his way. With the advent of Falstaff in *Henry IV, Part One* the finding was complete, and Marlowe became only the way not to go, on the stage as in life.

After Shakespeare there are only a few figures who fight relatively free of the anxiety of influence: Milton, Molière, Goethe, Tolstoy, Ibsen, Freud, Joyce; and for all of these except Molière, Shakespeare alone remained the problem, as this book seeks to demonstrate. Greatness recognizes greatness and is shadowed by it. Coming after Shakespeare, who wrote both the best prose and the best poetry in the Western tradition, is a complex destiny, since originality becomes peculiarly difficult in everything that matters most: representation of human beings, the role of memory in cognition, the range of metaphor in suggesting new possibilities for language. These are Shakespeare's particular excellences, and no one has matched him as psychologist, thinker, or rhetorician. Wittgenstein, who resented Freud, nevertheless resembles Freud in his suspicious and defensive reaction to Shakespeare, who is an affront to the philosopher even as he is to the psychoanalyst. There is no cognitive originality in the whole history of philosophy comparable to Shakespeare's, and it is both ironic and fascinating to overhear Wittgenstein puzzling out whether there is an authentic difference between the Shakespearean representation of thinking and thinking itself. It is true, as the Australian poet-critic Kevin Hart observes, that "Western culture takes its lexicon of intelligibility from Greek philosophy, and all our talk of life and death, of form and design, is marked by relations with that tradition." Yet intelligibility pragmatically transcends its lexicon, and we must remind ourselves that Shakespeare, who scarcely relies upon philosophy, is more central to Western culture than are Plato and Aristotle, Kant and Hegel, Heidegger and Wittgenstein.

I feel quite alone these days in defending the autonomy of the aesthetic, but its best defense is the experience of reading *King Lear* and then seeing the play well performed. *King Lear* does not derive from a crisis in philosophy, nor can its power be explained away as a mystification somehow promoted by bourgeois institutions. It is a mark of the degeneracy of literary study that one is considered an eccentric for holding that the literary is not dependent upon the philosophical, and that the aesthetic is irreducible to ideology or to metaphysics. Aesthetic criticism returns us to the autonomy of imaginative literature and the sovereignty of the solitary soul, the reader not as a person in society but as the deep self, our ultimate inwardness. That depth of inwardness in a strong writer constitutes the strength that wards off the massive weight of past achievement, lest every originality be crushed before it becomes manifest. Great writing is always rewriting or revisionism and is founded upon a reading that clears space for the self, or that so works as to reopen old works to our fresh sufferings. The originals are not original, but that Emersonian irony yields to the Emersonian pragmatism that the inventor knows *how* to borrow.

The anxiety of influence cripples weaker talents but stimulates canonical genius. What intimately allies the three most vibrant American novelists of the Chaotic Age—Hemingway, Fitzgerald, and Faulkner—is that all of them emerge from Joseph Conrad's influence but temper it cunningly by mingling Conrad with an American precursor—Mark Twain for Hemingway, Henry James for Fitzgerald, Herman Melville for Faulkner. Something of the same cunning appears in T. S. Eliot's fusion of Whitman and Tennyson, and Ezra Pound's blend of Whitman and Browning, as again in Hart Crane's deflection of Eliot by another turn toward Whitman. Strong writers do not choose their prime precursors; they are chosen by them, but they have the wit to transform the forerunners into composite and therefore partly imaginary beings.

I am not directly concerned in this book with the intertextual relations among the twenty-six authors under consideration; my purpose is to consider them as representatives of the entire Western Canon, but doubtless my interest in problems of influence emerges almost everywhere, sometimes perhaps without my own full awareness. Strong literature, agonistic whether it wants to be or not, cannot be detached from its anxieties about the works that possess priority and authority in regard to it. Though most critics resist understanding the processes of literary influence or try to idealize those processes as wholly generous and benign, the dark truths of competition and contamination continue to grow stronger as canonical history lengthens in time. A poem, play, or novel is necessarily compelled to come into being by way of precursor works, however eager it is to deal directly with social concerns. Contingency governs literature as it does every cognitive enterprise, and the contingency constituted by the Western literary

Canon is primarily manifested as the anxiety of influence that forms and malforms each new writing that aspires to permanence. Literature is not merely language; it is also the will to figuration, the motive for metaphor that Nietzsche once defined as the desire to be different, the desire to be elsewhere. This partly means to be different from oneself, but primarily, I think, to be different from the metaphors and images of the contingent works that are one's heritage: the desire to write greatly is the desire to be elsewhere, in a time and place of one's own, in an originality that must compound with inheritance, with the anxiety of influence.

PART I

ON THE CANON

1.

An Elegy
for the Canon

ORIGINALLY THE CANON meant the choice of books in our teaching institutions, and despite the recent politics of multiculturalism, the Canon's true question remains: What shall the individual who still desires to read attempt to read, this late in history? The Biblical three-score years and ten no longer suffice to read more than a selection of the great writers in what can be called the Western tradition, let alone in all the world's traditions. Who reads must choose, since there is literally not enough time to read everything, even if one does nothing but read. Mallarmé's grand line—"the flesh is sad, alas, and I have read all the books"—has become a hyperbole. Overpopulation, Malthusian repletion, is the authentic context for canonical anxieties. Not a moment passes these days without fresh rushes of academic lemmings off the cliffs they proclaim the political responsibilities of the critic, but eventually all this moralizing will subside. Every teaching institution will have its department of cultural studies, an ox not to be gored, and an aesthetic underground will flourish, restoring something of the romance of reading.

Reviewing bad books, W. H. Auden once remarked, is bad for the character. Like all gifted moralists, Auden idealized despite himself, and he should have survived into the present age, wherein the new commissars tell us that reading good books is bad for the character, which I think is probably true. Reading the very best writers—let us say Homer, Dante, Shakespeare, Tolstoy—is not going to make us better citizens. Art is perfectly useless, according to the sublime Oscar Wilde, who was right about everything. He also told us that all bad poetry is sincere. Had I the power to do so, I would command that these words be engraved above every gate at every university, so that each student might ponder the splendor of the insight.

President Clinton's inaugural poem, by Maya Angelou, was praised in a *New York Times* editorial as a work of Whitmanian magnitude, and its sincerity is indeed overwhelming; it joins all the other instantly canonical achievements that flood our academies. The unhappy truth is that we cannot help ourselves; we can resist, up to a point, but past that point even our own universities would feel compelled to indict us as racists and sexists. I recall one of us, doubtless with irony, telling a *New York Times* interviewer that "We are all feminist critics." That is the rhetoric suitable for an occupied country, one that expects no liberation from liberation. Institutions may hope to follow the advice of the prince in Lampedusa's *The Leopard,* who counsels his peers, "Change everything just a little so as to keep everything exactly the same."

Unfortunately, nothing ever will be the same because the art and passion of reading well and deeply, which was the foundation of our enterprise, depended upon people who were fanatical readers when they were still small children. Even devoted and solitary readers are now necessarily beleaguered, because they cannot be certain that fresh generations will rise up to prefer Shakespeare and Dante to all other writers. The shadows lengthen in our evening land, and we approach the second millennium expecting further shadowing.

I do not deplore these matters; the aesthetic is, in my view, an individual rather than a societal concern. In any case there are no culprits, though some of us would appreciate not being told that we lack the free, generous, and open societal vision of those who come after us. Literary criticism is an ancient art; its inventor, according to Bruno Snell, was Aristophanes, and I tend to agree with Heinrich Heine that "There is a God, and his name is Aristophanes." Cultural criticism is another dismal social science, but literary criticism, as an art, always was and always will be an elitist phenomenon. It was a mistake to believe that literary criticism could become a basis for democratic education or for societal improvement. When our English and other literature departments shrink to the dimensions of our current Classics departments, ceding their grosser functions to the legions of Cultural Studies, we will perhaps be able to return to the study of the inescapable, to Shakespeare and his few peers, who after all, invented all of us.

The Canon, once we view it as the relation of an individual reader and writer to what has been preserved out of what has been written, and forget the canon as a list of books for required study, will be seen as identical with the literary Art of Memory, not with the religious sense of canon. Memory is always an art, even when it works involuntarily. Emerson opposed the party of Memory to the party of Hope, but that was in a very different America. Now the party of Memory *is* the party of Hope, though the hope is diminished. But it has always been dangerous to institutionalize hope, and we no longer live in a society in which we will be allowed to institutionalize memory. We need to teach more selectively, searching for the few who have the capacity to become highly individual readers and writers. The others, who are amenable to a politicized curriculum, can be abandoned to it. Pragmatically, aesthetic value can be recognized or experienced, but it cannot be conveyed to those who are incapable of grasping its sensations and perceptions. To quarrel on its behalf is always a blunder.

What interests me more is the flight from the aesthetic among so many in my profession, some of whom at least began with the ability to experience aesthetic value. In Freud, flight is the metaphor for repression, for unconscious yet purposeful forgetting. The purpose is clear enough in my profession's flight: to assuage displaced guilt. Forgetting, in an aesthetic context, is ruinous, for cognition, in criticism, always relies on memory. Longinus would have said that pleasure is what the resenters have forgotten. Nietzsche would have called it pain; but they would have been thinking of the same experience upon the heights. Those who descend from there, lemminglike, chant the litany that literature is best explained as a mystification promoted by bourgeois institutions.

This reduces the aesthetic to ideology, or at best to metaphysics. A poem cannot be read *as a poem,* because it is primarily a social document or, rarely yet possibly, an attempt to overcome philosophy. Against this approach I urge a stubborn resistance whose single aim is to preserve poetry as fully and purely as possible. Our legions who have deserted represent a strand in our traditions that has always been in flight from the aesthetic: Platonic moralism and Aristotelian social science. The attack on poetry either exiles it for being destructive of social well-being or allows it sufferance if it will assume the work of social catharsis under the banners of the new multiculturalism. Beneath the surfaces of academic Marxism, Feminism, and New Historicism, the ancient polemic of Platonism and the equally archaic Aristotelian social medicine continue to course on. I suppose that the conflict between these strains and the always beleaguered supporters of the aesthetic can never end. We are losing now, and doubtless we will go on losing, and there is a sorrow in that, because many of the best students will abandon us for other disciplines and professions, an abandonment already well under way. They are justified in doing so, because we could not protect them against our profession's loss of intellectual and aesthetic standards of accomplishment and value. All that we can do now is maintain some continuity with the aesthetic and not yield to the lie that what we oppose is adventure and new interpretations.

FREUD FAMOUSLY DEFINED anxiety as being *Angst vor etwas,* or anxious expectations. There is always something in advance of which we are anxious, if only of expectations that we will be called upon to fulfill. Eros, presumably the most pleasurable of expectations, brings its own anxieties to the reflective consciousness, which is Freud's subject. A literary work also arouses expectations that it needs to fulfill or it will cease to be read. The deepest anxieties of literature are literary; indeed, in my view, they define the literary and become all but identical with it. A poem, novel, or play acquires all of humanity's disorders, including the fear of mortality, which in the art of literature is transmuted into the quest to be canonical, to join communal or societal memory. Even Shakespeare, in the strongest of his sonnets, hovers near this obsessive desire or drive. The rhetoric of immortality is also a psychology of survival and a cosmology.

Where did the idea of conceiving a literary work that the world would not willingly let die come from? It was not attached to the Scriptures by the Hebrews, who spoke of canonical writings as those that polluted the hands that touched them, presumably because mortal hands were not fit to hold sacred writings. Jesus replaced the Torah for Christians, and what mattered most about Jesus was the Resurrection. At what date in the history of secular writing did men begin to speak of poems or stories as being immortal? The conceit is in Petrarch and is marvelously developed by Shakespeare in his sonnets. It is already a latent element in Dante's praise of his own *Divine Comedy*. We cannot say that Dante secularized the idea, because he subsumed everything and so, in a sense, secularized nothing. For him, his poem was prophecy, as much as Isaiah was prophecy, so perhaps we can say that Dante invented our modern idea of the canonical. Ernst Robert Curtius, the eminent medieval scholar, emphasizes that Dante considered only two journeys into the beyond, before his own, to be authentic: Virgil's Aeneas in Book 6 of his epic and St. Paul's as recounted in 2 Corinthians 12:2. Out of Aeneas came Rome; out of Paul came Gentile Christianity; out of Dante was to come, if he lived to the age of eighty-one, the fulfillment of the esoteric prophecy concealed in the *Comedy,* but Dante died at fifty-six.

Curtius, ever alert to the fortune of canonical metaphors, has an excursus upon "Poetry as Perpetuation" that traces the origin of the eternity of poetic fame to the *Iliad* (6.359) and beyond to Horace's *Odes* (4.8, 28), where we are assured that it is the Muse's eloquence and affection that allow the hero never to die. Jakob Burckhardt, in a chapter on literary fame that Curtius quotes, observes that Dante, the Italian Renaissance poet-philologist, had "the most intense consciousness that he is a distributor of fame and indeed of immortality," a consciousness that Curtius locates among the Latin poets of France as early as 1100. But at some point this consciousness was linked to the idea of a secular canonicity, so that not the hero being celebrated but the celebration itself was hailed as immortal. The secular canon, with the word meaning a catalog of approved authors, does not actually begin until the middle of the eighteenth century, during the literary period of Sensibility, Sentimentality, and the Sublime. The *Odes* of William Collins trace the Sublime canon in Sensibility's heroic precursors from the ancient Greeks through Milton and are among the earliest poems in English written to propound a secular tradition of canonicity.

The Canon, a word religious in its origins, has become a choice among texts struggling with one another for survival, whether you interpret the choice as being made by dominant social groups, institutions of education, traditions of criticism, or, as I do, by late-coming authors who feel themselves chosen by particular ancestral figures. Some recent partisans of what regards itself as academic radicalism go so far as to suggest that works join the Canon because of successful advertising and propaganda campaigns. The compeers of these skeptics sometimes go farther and question even Shakespeare, whose eminence seems to them something of an imposition. If you worship the composite god of historical process, you are fated to deny Shakespeare his palpable aesthetic supremacy, the really scandalous originality of his plays. Originality becomes a literary equivalent of such terms as individual enterprise, self-reliance, and competition, which do not gladden the hearts of Feminists, Afrocentrists, Marxists, Foucault-inspired New Historicists, or Deconstructors—of all those whom I have described as members of the School of Resentment.

One illuminating theory of canon formation is presented by Alastair Fowler in his *Kinds of Literature* (1982). In a chapter on "Hierarchies of Genres and Canons of Literature," Fowler remarks that "changes in literary taste can often be referred to revaluation of genres that the canonical works represent." In each era, some genres are regarded as more canonical than others. In the earlier decades of our time, the American prose romance was exalted as a genre, which helped to establish Faulkner, Hemingway, and Fitzgerald as our dominant twentieth-century writers of prose fiction, fit successors to Hawthorne, Melville, Mark Twain, and the aspect of Henry James that triumphed in *The Golden Bowl* and *The Wings of the Dove*. The effect of this exaltation of romance over the "realistic" novel was that visionary narratives like Faulkner's *As I Lay Dying,* Nathanael West's *Miss Lonelyhearts,* and Thomas Pynchon's *The Crying of Lot 49* enjoyed more critical esteem than Theodore Dreiser's *Sister Carrie* and *An American Tragedy*. Now a further revision of genres has begun with the rise of the journalistic novel, such as Truman Capote's *In Cold Blood,* Norman Mailer's *The Executioner's Song,* and Tom Wolfe's *The Bonfire of the Vanities; An American Tragedy* has recovered much of its luster in the atmosphere of these works.

The historical novel seems to have been permanently devalued. Gore Vidal once said to me, with bitter eloquence, that his outspoken sexual orientation had denied him canonical status. What seems likelier is that Vidal's best fictions (except for the sublimely outrageous *Myra Breckenridge*) are distinguished historical novels—*Lincoln, Burr,* and several more—and this subgenre is no longer available for canonization, which helps to account for the morose fate of Norman Mailer's exuberantly inventive *Ancient Evenings,* a marvelous anatomy of humbuggery and bumbuggery that could not survive its placement in the ancient Egypt of *The Book of the Dead*. History writing and narrative fiction have come apart, and our sensibilities seem no longer able to accommodate them one to the other.

FOWLER GOES a long way toward expounding the question of just why all genres are not available at any one time:

we have to allow for the fact that the complete range of genres is never equally, let alone fully, available in any one period. Each age has a fairly small repertoire of genres that its readers and critics can respond to with enthusiasm, and the repertoire easily available to its writers is smaller still: the temporary canon is fixed for all but the greatest or strongest or most arcane writers. Each age makes new deletions from the repertoire. In a weak sense, all genres perhaps exist in all ages, shadowly embodied in bizarre and freakish exceptions. . . . But the repertoire of active genres has always been small and subject to proportionately significant deletions and additions . . . some critics have been tempted to think of the generic system almost on a hydrostatic model—as if its total substance remained constant but subject to redistributions.

But there is no firm basis for such speculation. We do better to treat the movements of genres simply in terms of aesthetic choice.

I myself would want to argue, partly following Fowler, that aesthetic choice has always guided every secular aspect of canon formation, but that is a difficult argument to maintain at this time when the defense of the literary canon, like the assault against it, has become so heavily politicized. Ideological defenses of the Western Canon are as pernicious in regard to aesthetic values as the onslaughts of attackers who seek to destroy the Canon or "open it up," as they proclaim. Nothing is so essential to the Western Canon as its principles of selectivity, which are elitist only to the extent that they are founded upon severely artistic criteria. Those who oppose the Canon insist that there is always an ideology involved in canon formation; indeed, they go farther and speak of the ideology *of* canon formation, suggesting that to make a canon (or to perpetuate one) is an ideological act *in itself*.

The hero of these anticanonizers is Antonio Gramsci, who in his *Selections from the Prison Notebooks* denies that any intellectual can be free of the dominant social group if he relies upon merely the "special qualification" that he shares with the craft of his fellows (such as other literary critics): "Since these various categories of traditional intellectuals experience through an 'esprit de corps' their uninterrupted historical qualification, they thus put themselves forward as autonomous and independent of the dominant social group."

As a literary critic in what I now regard as the worst of all times for literary criticism, I do not find Gramsci's stricture relevant. The esprit de corps of professionalism, so curiously dear to many high priests of the anticanonizers, is of no interest whatsoever to me, and I would repudiate any "uninterrupted historical continuity" with the Western academy. I desire and assert a continuity with a handful or so of critics before this century and another handful or so during the past three generations. As for "special qualification," my own, contra Gramsci, is purely personal. Even if "the dominant social group" were to be identified with the Yale Corporation, or the trustees of New York University, or of American universities in general, I can search out no *inner* connection between any social group and the specific ways in which I have spent my life reading, remembering, judging, and interpreting what we once called "imaginative literature." To discover critics in the service of a social ideology one need only regard those who wish to demystify or open up the Canon, or their opponents who have fallen into the trap of becoming what they beheld. But neither of these groups is truly *literary*.

The flight from or repression of the aesthetic is endemic in our institutions of what still purport to be higher education. Shakespeare, whose aesthetic supremacy has been confirmed by the universal judgment of four centuries, is now "historicized" into pragmatic diminishment, precisely because his uncanny aesthetic power is a scandal to any ideologue. The cardinal principle of the current School of Resentment can be stated with singular bluntness: what is called aesthetic value emanates from class struggle. This principle is so broad that it cannot be wholly refuted. I myself insist that the individual self is the only method and the whole standard for apprehending aesthetic value. But "the individual self," I unhappily grant, is defined only against society, and part of its agon with the communal inevitably partakes of the conflict between social and economic classes. Myself the son of a garment worker, I have been granted endless time to read and meditate upon my reading. The institution that sustained me, Yale University, is ineluctably part of an American Establishment, and my sustained meditation upon literature is therefore vulnerable to the most traditional Marxist analyses of class interest. All my passionate proclamations of the isolate selfhood's aesthetic value are necessarily qualified by the reminder that the leisure for meditation must be purchased from the community.

No critic, not even this one, is a hermetic Prospero working white magic upon an enchanted island. Criticism, like poetry, is (in the hermetic sense) a kind of theft from the common stock. And if the governing class, in the days of my youth, freed one to be a priest of the aesthetic, it doubtless had its own interest in such a priesthood. Yet to grant this is to grant very little. The freedom to apprehend aesthetic value may rise from class conflict, but the value is not identical with the freedom, even if it cannot be achieved without that apprehension. Aesthetic value is by definition engendered by an interaction between artists, an influencing that is always an interpretation. The freedom to be an artist, or a critic, necessarily rises out of social conflict. But the source or origin of the freedom to perceive, while hardly irrelevant to aesthetic value, is not identical with it. There is always guilt in achieved individuality; it is a version of the guilt of being a survivor and is not productive of aesthetic value.

Without some answer to the triple question of the agon—more than, less than, equal to?—there can be no aesthetic value. That question is framed in the figurative language of the Economic, but its answer will be free of Freud's Economic Principle. There can be no poem in itself, and yet something irreducible does abide in the aesthetic. Value that cannot be altogether reduced constitutes itself through the process of interartistic influence. Such influence contains psychological, spiritual, and social components, but its major element is aesthetic. A Marxist or Foucault-inspired historicist can insist endlessly that the *production* of the aesthetic is a question of historical forces, but production is not in itself the issue here. I cheerfully agree with the motto of Dr. Johnson—"No man but a blockhead ever wrote, except for money"—yet the undeniable economics of literature, from Pindar to the present, do not determine questions of aesthetic supremacy. And the openers-up of the Canon and the traditionalists do not disagree much on where the supremacy is to be found: in Shakespeare. Shakespeare *is* the secular canon, or even the secular scripture; forerunners and legatees alike are defined by him alone for canonical purposes. This is the dilemma that confronts partisans of resentment: either they must deny Shakespeare's unique eminence (a painful and difficult matter) or they must show why and how history and class struggle produced just those aspects of his plays that have generated his centrality in the Western Canon.

Here they confront insurmountable difficulty in Shakespeare's most idiosyncratic strength: he is always ahead of you, conceptually and imagistically, whoever and whenever you are. He renders you anachronistic because he *contains* you; you cannot subsume him. You cannot illuminate him with a new doctrine, be it Marxism or Freudianism or Demanian linguistic skepticism. Instead, he will illuminate the doctrine, not by prefiguration but by postfiguration as it were: all of Freud that matters most is there in Shakespeare already, with a persuasive critique of Freud besides. The Freudian map of the mind is Shakespeare's; Freud seems only to have prosified it. Or, to vary my point, a Shakespearean reading of Freud illuminates and overwhelms the text of Freud; a Freudian reading of Shakespeare reduces Shakespeare, or would if we could bear a reduction that crosses the line into absurdities of loss. *Coriolanus* is a far more powerful reading of Marx's *Eighteenth Brumaire of Louis Napoleon* than any Marxist reading of *Coriolanus* could hope to be.

Shakespeare's eminence is, I am certain, the rock upon which the School of Resentment must at last founder. How can they have it both ways? If it is arbitrary that Shakespeare centers the Canon, then they need to show why the dominant social class selected him rather than, say, Ben Jonson, for that arbitrary role. Or if history and not the ruling circles exalted Shakespeare, what was it in Shakespeare that so captivated the mighty Demiurge, economic and social history? Clearly this line of inquiry begins to border on the fantastic; how much simpler to admit that there is a *qualitative* difference, a difference in kind, between Shakespeare and every other writer, even Chaucer, even Tolstoy, or whoever. Originality is the great scandal that resentment cannot accommodate, and Shakespeare remains the most original writer we will ever know.

ALL STRONG literary originality becomes canonical. Some years ago, on a stormy night in New Haven, I sat down to reread, yet once more, John Milton's *Paradise Lost*. I had to write a lecture on Milton as part of a series I was delivering at Harvard University, but I wanted to start all over again with the poem: to read it as though I had never read it before, indeed as though no one ever had read it before me. To do so meant dismissing a library of Milton criticism from my head, which was virtually impossible. Still, I tried because I wanted the experience of reading *Paradise Lost* as I had first read it forty or so years before. And while I read, until I fell asleep in the middle of the night, the poem's initial familiarity began to dissolve. It went on dissolving in the several days following, as I read on to the end, and I was left curiously shocked, a little alienated, and yet fearfully absorbed. What was I reading?

Although the poem is a biblical epic, in classical form, the peculiar impression it gave me was what I generally ascribe to literary fantasy or science fiction, not to heroic epic. *Weirdness* was its overwhelming effect. I was stunned by two related but different sensations: the author's competitive and triumphant power, marvelously displayed in a struggle, both implicit and ex- plicit, against every other author and text, the Bible included, and also the sometimes terrifying strangeness of what was being pre- sented. Only after I came to the end did I recall (consciously anyway) William Empson's fierce book *Milton's God,* with its critical observation that *Paradise Lost* seemed to Empson as bar- barically splendid as certain African primitive sculptures. Empson blamed the Miltonic barbarism upon Christianity, a doctrine he found abhorrent. Although Empson was politically a Marxist, deeply sympathetic to the Chinese Communists, he was by no means a precursor of the School of Resentment. He historicized freestyle with striking aptitude, and he continually showed aware- ness of the conflict between social classes, but he was not tempted to reduce *Paradise Lost* to an interplay of economic forces. His prime concern remained aesthetic, the proper business of the lit- erary critic, and he fought free of transferring his moral distaste for Christianity (and Milton's God) to an aesthetic judgment against the poem. The barbaric element impressed me as it did Empson; the agonistic triumphalism interested me more.

THERE ARE, I suppose, only a few works that seem even more essential to the Western Canon than *Paradise Lost*—Shakespeare's major tragedies, Chaucer's *Canterbury Tales,* Dante's *Divine*

Comedy, the Torah, the Gospels, Cervantes' *Don Quixote,* Homer's epics. Except perhaps for Dante's poem, none of these is as embattled as Milton's dark work. Shakespeare undoubtedly received provocation from rival playwrights, while Chaucer charmingly cited fictive authorities and concealed his authentic obligations to Dante and Boccaccio. The Hebrew Bible and the Greek New Testament were revised into their present forms by redactionists who may have shared very little with the original authors whom they were editing. Cervantes, with unsurpassed mirth, parodied unto death his chivalric forerunners, while we do not have the texts of Homer's precursors.

Milton and Dante are the most pugnacious of the greatest Western writers. Scholars somehow manage to evade the ferocity of both poets and even dub them pious. Thus C. S. Lewis was able to discover his own "mere Christianity" in *Paradise Lost,* and John Freccero finds Dante to be a faithful Augustinian, content to emulate the *Confessions* in his "novel of the self." Dante, as I only begin to see, creatively corrected Virgil (among many others) as profoundly as Milton corrected absolutely everyone before him (Dante included) by his own creation. But whether the writer is playful in the struggle, like Chaucer and Cervantes and Shakespeare, or aggressive, like Dante and Milton, the contest is always there. This much of Marxist criticism seems to me valuable: in strong writing there is always conflict, ambivalence, contradiction between subject and structure. Where I part from the Marxists is on the origins of the conflict. From Pindar to the present, the writer battling for canonicity may fight on behalf of a social class, as Pindar did for the aristocrats, but primarily each ambitious writer is out for himself alone and will frequently betray or neglect his class in order to advance his own interests, which center entirely upon *individuation.* Dante and Milton both sacrificed much for what they believed to be a spiritually exuberant and justified political course, but neither of them would have been willing to sacrifice his major poem for any cause whatever. Their way of arranging this was to identify the cause with the poem, rather than the poem with the cause. In doing so, they provided a precedent that is not much followed these days by the academic rabble that seeks to connect the study of literature with the quest for social change. One finds modern American followers of this aspect of Dante and Milton where one would expect to find them, in our strongest poets since Whitman and Dickinson: the socially reactionary Wallace Stevens and Robert Frost.

Those who can do canonical work invariably see their writings as larger forms than any social program, however exemplary. The issue is containment, and great literature will insist upon its self-sufficiency in the face of the worthiest causes: feminism, African-American culturism, and all the other politically correct enterprises of our moment. The thing contained varies; the strong poem, by definition, refuses to be contained, even by Dante's or Milton's God. Dr. Samuel Johnson, shrewdest of all literary critics, concluded rightly that devotional poetry was impossible as compared to poetic devotion: "The good and evil of Eternity are too ponderous for the wings of wit." "Ponderous" is a metaphor for "uncontainable," which is another metaphor. Our contemporary openers-up of the Canon decry overt religion, but they call for devotional verse (and devotional criticism!) even if the object of devotion has been altered to the advancement of women, or of blacks, or of that most unknown of all unknown gods, the class struggle in the United States. It all depends upon your values, but I find it forever odd that Marxists are perceptive in finding competition everywhere else, yet fail to see that it is intrinsic to the high arts. There is a peculiar mix here of simultaneous over-idealization and undervaluation of imaginative literature, which has always pursued its own selfish aims.

Paradise Lost became canonical before the secular Canon was established, in the century after Milton's own. The answer to "Who canonized Milton?" is in the first place John Milton himself, but in almost the first place other strong poets, from his friend Andrew Marvell through John Dryden and on to nearly every crucial poet of the eighteenth century and the Romantic period: Pope, Thomson, Cowper, Collins, Blake, Wordsworth, Coleridge, Byron, Shelley, Keats. Certainly the critics, Dr. Johnson and Hazlitt, contributed to the canonization; but Milton, like Chaucer, Spenser, and Shakespeare before him, and like Wordsworth after him, simply overwhelmed the tradition and subsumed it. That is the strongest test for canonicity. Only a very few could overwhelm and subsume the tradition, and perhaps none now can. So the question today is: Can you compel the tradition to make space for you by nudging it from within, as it were, rather than from without, as the multiculturalists wish to do?

The movement from within the tradition cannot be ideological or place itself in the service of any social aims, however morally admirable. One breaks into the canon only by aesthetic strength, which is constituted primarily of an amalgam: mastery of figurative language, originality, cognitive power, knowledge, exuberance of diction. The final injustice of historical injustice is that it does not necessarily endow its victims with anything except a sense of their victimization. Whatever the Western Canon is, it is not a program for social salvation.

THE SILLIEST way to defend the Western Canon is to insist that it incarnates all of the seven deadly moral virtues that make up our supposed range of normative values and democratic principles. This is palpably untrue. The *Iliad* teaches the surpassing glory of armed victory, while Dante rejoices in the eternal torments he visits upon his very personal enemies. Tolstoy's private version of Christianity throws aside nearly everything that anyone among us retains, and Dostoevsky preaches anti-Semitism, obscurantism, and the necessity of human bondage. Shakespeare's politics, insofar as we can pin them down, do not appear to be very different from those of his Coriolanus, and Milton's ideas of free speech and free press do not preclude the imposition of all manner of societal restraints. Spenser rejoices in the massacre of Irish rebels, while the egomania of Wordsworth exalts his own poetic mind over any other source of splendor.

The West's greatest writers are subversive of all values, both ours and their own. Scholars who urge us to find the source of our morality and our politics in Plato, or in Isaiah, are out of touch with the social reality in which we live. If we read the Western Canon in order to form our social, political, or personal moral values, I firmly believe we will become monsters of selfishness and exploitation. To read in the service of any ideology is not, in my judgment, to read at all. The reception of aesthetic power enables us to learn how to talk to ourselves and how to endure ourselves. The true use of Shakespeare or of Cervantes, of Homer or of Dante, of Chaucer or of Rabelais, is to augment one's own growing inner self. Reading deeply in the Canon will not make one a better or a worse person, a more useful or more harmful citizen. The mind's dialogue with itself is not primarily a social reality. All that the Western Canon can bring one is the proper use of one's own solitude, that solitude whose final form is one's confrontation with one's own mortality.

WE POSSESS the Canon because we are mortal and also rather belated. There is only so much time, and time must have a stop, while there is more to read than there ever was before. From the Yahwist and Homer to Freud, Kafka, and Beckett is a journey of nearly three millennia. Since that voyage goes past harbors as infinite as Dante, Chaucer, Montaigne, Shakespeare, and Tolstoy, all of whom amply compensate a lifetime's rereadings, we are in the pragmatic dilemma of excluding something else each time we read or reread extensively. One ancient test for the canonical remains fiercely valid: unless it demands rereading, the work does not qualify. The inevitable analogue is the erotic one. If you are Don Giovanni and Leporello keeps the list, one brief encounter will suffice.

Contra certain Parisians, the text is there to give not pleasure but the high unpleasure or more difficult pleasure that a lesser text will not provide. I am not prepared to dispute admirers of Alice Walker's *Meridian,* a novel I have compelled myself to read twice, but the second reading was one of my most remarkable literary experiences. It produced an epiphany in which I saw clearly the new principle implicit in the slogans of those who proclaim the opening-up of the Canon. The correct test for the new canonicity is simple, clear, and wonderfully conducive to social change: it must not and cannot be reread, because its contribution to societal progress is its generosity in offering itself up for rapid ingestion and discarding. From Pindar through Hölderlin to Yeats, the self-canonizing greater ode has proclaimed its agonistic immortality. The socially acceptable ode of the future will doubtless spare us such pretensions and instead address itself to the proper humility of shared sisterhood, the new sublimity of quilt making that is now the preferred trope of Feminist criticism.

Yet we must choose: As there is only so much time, do we reread Elizabeth Bishop or Adrienne Rich? Do I again go in search of lost time with Marcel Proust, or am I to attempt yet another rereading of Alice Walker's stirring denunciation of all males, black and white? My former students, many of them now stars of the School of Resentment, proclaim that they teach social self-lessness, which begins in learning how to read selflessly. The author has no self, the literary character has no self, and the reader has no self. Shall we gather at the river with these generous ghosts, free of the guilt of past self-assertions, and be baptized in the waters of Lethe? What shall we do to be saved?

The study of literature, however it is conducted, will not save any individual, any more than it will improve any society. Shakespeare will not make us better, and he will not make us worse, but he may teach us how to overhear ourselves when we talk to ourselves. Subsequently, he may teach us how to accept change, in ourselves as in others, and perhaps even the final form of change. Hamlet is death's ambassador to us, perhaps one of the few ambassadors ever sent out by death who does not lie to us about our inevitable relationship with that undiscovered country. The relationship is altogether solitary, despite all of tradition's obscene attempts to socialize it.

My late friend Paul de Man liked to analogize the solitude of each literary text and each human death, an analogy I once protested. I had suggested to him that the more ironic trope would be to analogize each human birth to the coming into being of a poem, an analogy that would connect texts as infants are connected, voicelessness linked to past voices, inability to speak linked to what had been spoken to, as all of us have been spoken to, by the dead. I did not win that critical argument because I could not persuade him of the larger human analogue; he preferred the dialectical authority of the more Heideggerian irony. All that a text, let us say the tragedy of *Hamlet,* shares with death is its solitude. But when it shares with us, does it speak with the authority of death? Whatever the answer, I would like to point out that the authority of death, whether literary or existential, is not primarily a social authority. The Canon, far from being the servant of the dominant social class, is the minister of death. To open it, you must persuade the reader that a new space has been cleared in a larger space crowded by the dead. Let the dead poets consent to stand aside for us, Artaud cried out; but that is exactly what they will not consent to do.

If we were literally immortal, or even if our span were doubled to seven score of years, say, we could give up all argument about canons. But we have an interval only, and then our place knows us no more, and stuffing that interval with bad writing, in the name of whatever social justice, does not seem to me to be the responsibility of the literary critic. Professor Frank Lentricchia, apostle of social change through academic ideology, has managed to read Wallace Stevens's "Anecdote of the Jar" as a political poem, one that voices the program of the dominant social class. The art of placing a jar was, for Stevens, allied to the art of flower arranging, and I don't see why Lentricchia should not publish a modest volume on the politics of flower arranging, under the title *Ariel and the Flowers of Our Climate*. I still remember my shock, thirty-five years or so back, when I was first taken to a soccer match in Jerusalem where the Sephardi spectators were cheering for the visiting Haifa squad, it being of the political right, while the Jerusalem squad was affiliated with the labor party. Why stop with politicizing the study of literature? Let us replace sports writers with political pundits as a first step toward reorganizing baseball, with the Republican League meeting the Democratic League in the World Series. That would give us a form of baseball into which we could not escape for pastoral relief, as we do now. The political responsibilities of the baseball player would be just as appropriate, no more, no less, than the now-trumpeted political responsibilities of the literary critic.

Cultural belatedness, now an all-but-universal world condition, has a particular poignance in the United States of America. We are the final inheritors of Western tradition. Education founded upon the *Iliad*, the Bible, Plato, and Shakespeare remains, in some strained form, our ideal, though the relevance of these cultural monuments to life in our inner cities is inevitably rather remote. Those who resent all canons suffer from an elitist guilt founded

upon the accurate enough realization that canons always do indirectly serve the social and political, and indeed the spiritual,
concerns and aims of the wealthier classes of each generation of
Western society. It seems clear that capital is necessary for the
cultivation of aesthetic values. Pindar, the superb last champion
of archaic lyric, invested his art in the celebratory exercise of
exchanging odes for grand prices, thus praising the wealthy for
their generous support of his generous exaltation of their divine
lineage. This alliance of sublimity and financial and political power
has never ceased, and presumably never can or will.

There are, of course, prophets, from Amos to Blake and beyond
to Whitman, who rise up to cry out against this alliance, and
doubtless a great figure, equal to a Blake, will some day come
again; but Pindar rather than Blake remains the canonical norm.
Even such prophets as Dante and Milton compromised themselves
as Blake would or could not, insofar as pragmatic cultural aspirations may be said to have tempted the poets of the *Divine Comedy* and *Paradise Lost*. It has taken me a lifetime of immersion in
the study of poetry before I could understand why Blake and
Whitman were compelled to become the hermetic, indeed esoteric
poets that they truly were. If you break the alliance between wealth
and culture—a break that marks the difference between Milton
and Blake, between Dante and Whitman—then you pay the high,
ironic price of those who seek to destroy canonical continuities.
You become a belated Gnostic, warring against Homer, Plato, and
the Bible by mythologizing your misreading of tradition. Such a
war can yield limited victories; a *Four Zoas* or a *Song of Myself*
are triumphs I call limited because they drive *their* inheritors to
perfectly desperate distortions of creative desire. The poets who
walk Whitman's open road most successfully are those who resemble him profoundly but not at all superficially, poets as severely
formal as Wallace Stevens, T. S. Eliot, and Hart Crane. Those
who seek to emulate his apparently open forms all die in the
wilderness, inchoate rhapsodists and academic impostors sprawling in the wake of their delicately hermetic father. Nothing is got
for nothing, and Whitman will not do your work for you. A minor
Blakean or an apprentice Whitmanian is always a false prophet,
making no way straight for anyone.

I am not at all happy about these truths of poetry's reliance upon worldly power; I am simply following William Hazlitt, the authentic left-winger among all great critics. Hazlitt, in his wonderful discussion of Coriolanus in *Characters of Shakespeare's Plays,* begins with the unhappy admission that "the cause of the people is indeed but little calculated as a subject for poetry: it admits of rhetoric, which goes into argument and explanation, but it presents no immediate or distinct images to the mind." Such images, Hazlitt finds, are everywhere present on the side of tyrants and their instruments.

Hazlitt's clear sense of the troubled interplay between the power of rhetoric and the rhetoric of power has an enlightening potential in our fashionable darkness. Shakespeare's own politics may or may not be those of Coriolanus, just as Shakespeare's anxieties may or may not be those of Hamlet or of Lear. Nor is Shakespeare the tragic Christopher Marlowe, whose work and life alike seem to have taught Shakespeare the way not to go. Shakespeare knows implicitly what Hazlitt wryly makes explicit: the Muse, whether tragic or comic, takes the side of the elite. For every Shelley or Brecht there are a score of even more powerful poets who gravitate naturally to the party of the dominant classes in whatever society. The literary imagination is contaminated by the zeal and excesses of societal competition, for throughout Western history the creative imagination has conceived of itself as the most competitive of modes, akin to the solitary runner, who races for his own glory.

The strongest women among the great poets, Sappho and Emily Dickinson, are even fiercer agonists than the men. Miss Dickinson of Amherst does not set out to help Mrs. Elizabeth Barrett Browning complete a quilt. Rather, Dickinson leaves Mrs. Browning far behind in the dust, though the triumph is more subtly conveyed than Whitman's victory over Tennyson in "When Lilacs Last in the Dooryard Bloom'd," where the Laureate's "Ode on the Death of the Duke of Wellington" is overtly echoed so as to compel an alert reader's recognition of how far the Lincoln elegy surpasses the lament for the Iron Duke. I do not know whether Feminist criticism will succeed in its quest to change human nature, but I rather doubt that any idealism, however belated, will change the entire basis of the Western psychology of creativity, male and female, from Hesiod's contest with Homer down to the agon between Dickinson and Elizabeth Bishop.

As I write these sentences, I glance at the newspaper and note a story on the anguish of feminists forced to choose between Elizabeth Holtzman and Geraldine Ferraro for a Senate nomination, a choice not different in kind from a critic pragmatically needing to choose between the late May Swenson, something close to a strong poet, and the vehement Adrienne Rich. A purported poem may have the most exemplary sentiments, the most exalted politics, and may also be not much of a poem. A critic may have political responsibilities, but the first obligation is to raise again the ancient and quite grim triple question of the agonist: more than, less than, equal to? We are destroying all intellectual and aesthetic standards in the humanities and social sciences, in the name of social justice. Our institutions show bad faith in this: no quotas are imposed upon brain surgeons or mathematicians. What has been devalued is learning as such, as though erudition were irrelevant in the realms of judgment and misjudgment.

The Western Canon, despite the limitless idealism of those who would open it up, exists precisely in order to impose limits, to set a standard of measurement that is anything but political or moral. I am aware that there is now a kind of covert alliance between popular culture and what calls itself "culture criticism," and in the name of that alliance cognition itself may doubtless yet acquire the stigma of the incorrect. Cognition cannot proceed without memory, and the Canon is the true art of memory, the authentic foundation for cultural thinking. Most simply, the Canon is Plato and Shakespeare; it is the image of the individual thinking, whether it be Socrates thinking through his own dying, or Hamlet contemplating that undiscovered country. Mortality joins memory in the consciousness of reality-testing that the Canon induces. By its very nature, the Western Canon will never close, but it cannot be forced open by our current cheerleaders. Strength alone can open it up, the strength of a Freud or a Kafka, persistent in their cognitive negations.

Cheerleading is the power of positive thinking transported to the academic realm. The legitimate student of the Western Canon respects the power of the negations inherent in cognition, enjoys the difficult pleasures of aesthetic apprehension, learns the hidden roads that erudition teaches us to walk even as we reject easier pleasures, including the incessant calls of those who assert a

political virtue that would transcend all our memories of individual aesthetic experience.

Easy immortalities haunt us now because the current staple of
our popular culture has ceased to be the rock concert, which has
been replaced by the rock video, the essence of which is an in-
stantaneous immortality, or rather the possibility thereof. The
relation between religious and literary concepts of immortality has
always been vexed, even among the ancient Greeks and Romans,
where poetic and Olympian eternities mixed rather promiscuously.
This vexation was tolerable, even benign, in classical literature,
but became more ominous in Christian Europe. Catholic distinctions between divine immortality and human fame, firmly founded
upon a dogmatic theology, remained fairly precise until the advent
of Dante, who regarded himself as a prophet and so implicitly
gave his *Divine Comedy* the status of a new Scripture. Dante
pragmatically voided the distinction between secular and sacred
canon formation, a distinction that has never quite returned, which
is yet another reason for our vexed sense of power and authority.

The terms "power" and "authority" have pragmatically opposed meanings in the realms of politics and what we still ought
to call "imaginative literature." If we have difficulty in seeing the
opposition, it may be because of the intermediate realm that calls
itself "spiritual." Spiritual power and spiritual authority notoriously shade over into both politics and poetry. Thus we must
distinguish the aesthetic power and authority of the Western
Canon from whatever spiritual, political, or even moral consequences it may have fostered. Although reading, writing, and
teaching are necessarily social acts, even teaching has its solitary
aspect, a solitude only the two could share, in Wallace Stevens's
language. Gertrude Stein maintained that one wrote for oneself
and for strangers, a superb recognition that I would extend into
a parallel apothegm: one reads for oneself and for strangers. The
Western Canon does not exist in order to augment preexisting
societal elites. It is there to be read by you and by strangers, so
that you and those you will never meet can encounter authentic
aesthetic power and the authority of what Baudelaire (and Erich
Auerbach after him) called "aesthetic dignity." One of the in-
eluctable stigmata of the canonical is aesthetic dignity, which is
not to be hired.

Aesthetic authority, like aesthetic power, is a trope or figuration for energies that are essentially solitary rather than social. Hayden White long ago exposed Foucault's great flaw as being a blindness toward his own metaphors, an ironic weakness in a professed disciple of Nietzsche. For the tropes of the Lovejoyan history of ideas Foucault substituted his own tropes and then did not always remember that his "archives" were ironies, deliberate and undeliberate. So is it with the "social energies" of the New Historicist, who is perpetually prone to forget that "social energy" is no more quantifiable than the Freudian libido. Aesthetic authority and creative power are tropes too, but what they substitute for—call it "the canonical"—has a roughly quantifiable aspect, which is to say that William Shakespeare wrote thirty-eight plays, twenty-four of them masterpieces, but social energy has never written a single scene. The death of the author is a trope, and a rather pernicious one; the life of the author is a quantifiable entity.

All canons, including our currently fashionable counter-canons, are elitist, and as no secular canon is ever closed, what is now acclaimed as "opening up the canon" is a strictly redundant operation. Although canons, like all lists and catalogs, have a tendency to be inclusive rather than exclusive, we have now reached the point at which a lifetime's reading and rereading can scarcely take one through the Western Canon. Indeed, it is now virtually impossible to master the Western Canon. Not only would it mean absorbing well over three thousand books, many, if not most, marked by authentic cognitive and imaginative difficulties, but the relations between these books grow more rather than less vexed as our perspectives lengthen. There are also the vast complexities and contradictions that constitute the essence of the Western Canon, which is anything but a unity or stable structure. No one has the authority to tell us what the Western Canon is, certainly not from about 1800 to the present day. It is not, cannot be, precisely the list I give, or that anyone else might give. If it were, that would make such a list a mere fetish, just another commodity. But I am not prepared to agree with the Marxists that the Western Canon is another instance of what they call "cultural capital." It is not clear to me that a nation as contradictory as the United States of America could ever be the context for "cultural capital," except for those slivers of high culture that contribute to mass culture. We have not had an official high culture in this country since about 1800, a generation after the American Revolution. Cultural unity is a French phenomenon, and to some degree a German matter, but hardly an American reality in either the nineteenth century or the twentieth. In our context and from our perspective, the Western Canon is a kind of survivor's list. The central fact about America, according to the poet Charles Olson, is space, but Olson wrote that as the opening sentence of a book on Melville and thus on the nineteenth century. At the close of the twentieth century, our central fact is time, for the evening land is now in the West's evening time. Would one call the list of survivors of a three-thousand-year-old cosmological war a fetish?

The issue is the mortality or immortality of literary works. Where they have become canonical, they have survived an immense struggle in social relations, but those relations have very little to do with class struggle. Aesthetic value emanates from the struggle between texts: in the reader, in language, in the classroom, in arguments within a society. Very few working-class readers ever matter in determining the survival of texts, and left-wing critics cannot do the working class's reading for it. Aesthetic value rises out of memory, and so (as Nietzsche saw) out of pain, the pain of surrendering easier pleasures in favor of much more difficult ones. Workers have anxieties enough and turn to religion as one mode of relief. Their sure sense that the aesthetic is, for them, only another anxiety helps to teach us that successful literary works are achieved anxieties, not releases from anxieties. Canons, too, are achieved anxieties, not unified props of morality, Western or Eastern. If we could conceive of a universal canon, multicultural and multivalent, its one essential book would not be a scripture, whether Bible, Koran, or Eastern text, but rather Shakespeare, who is acted and read everywhere, in every language and circumstance. Whatever the convictions of our current New Historicists, for whom Shakespeare is only a signifier for the social energies of the English Renaissance, Shakespeare for hundreds of millions who are not white Europeans is a signifier for their own pathos, their own sense of identity with the characters that Shakespeare fleshed out by his language. For them his universality is not historical but fundamental; he puts their lives upon his stage. In his characters they behold and confront their own anguish and their own fantasies, not the manifested social energies of early mercantile London.

The art of memory, with its rhetorical antecedents and its magical burgeonings, is very much an affair of imaginary places, or of real places transmuted into visual images. Since childhood, I have enjoyed an uncanny memory for literature, but that memory is purely verbal, without anything in the way of a visual component. Only recently, past the age of sixty, have I come to understand that my literary memory has relied upon the Canon as a memory system. If I am a special case, it is only in the sense that my experience is a more extreme version of what I believe to be the principal pragmatic function of the Canon: the remembering and ordering of a lifetime's reading. The greatest authors take over the role of "places" in the Canon's theater of memory, and their masterworks occupy the position filled by "images" in the art of memory. Shakespeare and *Hamlet,* central author and universal drama, compel us to remember not only what happens in *Hamlet,* but more crucially what happens in literature that makes it memorable and thus prolongs the life of the author.

The death of the author, proclaimed by Foucault, Barthes, and many clones after them, is another anticanonical myth, similar to the battle cry of resentment that would dismiss "all of the dead, white European males"—that is to say, for a baker's dozen, Homer, Virgil, Dante, Chaucer, Shakespeare, Cervantes, Montaigne, Milton, Goethe, Tolstoy, Ibsen, Kafka, and Proust. Livelier than you are, whoever you are, these authors were indubitably male, and I suppose "white." But they are not dead, compared to any living author whomsoever. Among us now are García Márquez, Pynchon, Ashbery, and others who are likely to become as canonical as Borges and Beckett among the recently deceased, but Cervantes and Shakespeare are of another order of vitality. The Canon is indeed a gauge of vitality, a measurement that attempts to map the incommensurate. The ancient metaphor of the writer's immortality is relevant here and renews the power of the Canon for us. Curtius has an excursus on "Poetry as Perpetuation" where he cites Burckhardt's reverie on "Fame in Literature" as equating fame and immortality. But Burckhardt and Curtius lived and died before the Age of Warhol, when so many are famous for fifteen minutes each. Immortality for a quarter of an hour is now freely conferred and can be regarded as one of the more hilarious consequences of "opening up the Canon."

The defense of the Western Canon is in no way a defense of the West or a nationalist enterprise. If multiculturalism meant Cervantes, who could quarrel with it? The greatest enemies of aesthetic and cognitive standards are purported defenders who blather to us about moral and political values in literature. We do not live by the ethics of the *Iliad,* or by the politics of Plato. Those who teach interpretation have more in common with the Sophists than with Socrates. What can we expect Shakespeare to do for our semiruined society, since the function of Shakespearean drama has so little to do with civic virtue or social justice? Our current New Historicists, with their odd blend of Foucault and Marx, are only a very minor episode in the endless history of Platonism. Plato hoped that by banishing the poet, he would also banish the tyrant. Banishing Shakespeare, or rather reducing him to his contexts, will not rid us of our tyrants. In any case, we cannot rid ourselves of Shakespeare, or of the Canon that he centers. Shakespeare, as we like to forget, largely invented us; if you add the rest of the Canon, then Shakespeare and the Canon wholly invented us. Emerson, in *Representative Men,* got this exactly right: "Shakespeare is as much out of the category of eminent authors, as he is out of the crowd. He is inconceivably wise; the others, conceivably. A good reader can, in a sort, nestle into Plato's brain, and think from thence; but not into Shakespeare's. We are still out of doors. For executive faculty, for creation, Shakespeare is unique."

NOTHING that we could say about Shakespeare now is nearly as important as Emerson's realization. Without Shakespeare, no canon, because without Shakespeare, no recognizable selves in us, whoever we are. We owe to Shakespeare not only our representation of cognition but much of our capacity for cognition. The difference between Shakespeare and his nearest rivals is one of both kind and degree, and that double difference defines the reality and necessity of the Canon. Without the Canon, we cease to think. You may idealize endlessly about replacing aesthetic standards with ethnocentric and gender considerations, and your social aims may indeed be admirable. Yet only strength can join itself to strength, as Nietzsche perpetually testified.

PART II

THE ARISTOCRATIC AGE

2.

Shakespeare,
Center of the Canon

ACTORS IN Elizabethan England were, by statute, akin to beggars and similar lowlife, which doubtless pained Shakespeare, who worked hard to be able to go back to Stratford as a gentleman. Except for that desire, we know next to nothing about Shakespeare's social outlook, except what can be gleaned from the plays, where all of the information is ambiguous. As an actor-playwright, Shakespeare necessarily depended upon aristocrats for patronage and protection, and his politics—if pragmatically he had any— were appropriate for the pinnacle of the long Aristocratic Age (in the Viconian sense) that I have posited as going from Dante through the Renaissance and the Enlightenment and concluding with Goethe. The politics of the young Wordsworth and of William Blake are those of the French Revolution and herald the next age, the Democratic, that touches apotheosis in Whitman and the American canon and reaches its final expression with Tolstoy and Ibsen. At the origins of Shakespeare's art, we are given as a fundamental postulate an aristocratic sense of culture, though Shakespeare transcends that sense, as he does everything else.

Shakespeare and Dante are the center of the Canon because they excel all other Western writers in cognitive acuity, linguistic energy, and power of invention. It may be that all three endowments fuse in an ontological passion that is a capacity for joy, or what Blake meant by his Proverb of Hell: "Exuberance is beauty." Social energies exist in every age, but they cannot compose plays, poems, and narratives. The power to originate is an individual gift, present in all eras but evidently greatly encouraged by particular contexts, national surges that we still study only in segments, because the unity of a great era is generally an illusion. Was Shakespeare an accident? Are literary imagination and the modalities for embodying it just as quirky entities as the manifestation of a Mozart? Shakespeare is not one of those poets who need to undergo no development, who seem fully formed from the start, the rare handful that includes Marlowe, Blake, Rimbaud, Crane. These hardly seem even to unfold: *Tamburlaine Part One, Poetical Sketches,* the *Illuminations, White Buildings* are already upon the heights. But the Shakespeare of the early histories and farcical comedies and of *Titus Andronicus* is only distantly prophetic of the author of *Hamlet, Othello, King Lear,* and *Macbeth.* Reading *Romeo and Juliet* and *Antony and Cleopatra* together, I sometimes can scarcely persuade myself that the lyrical dramatist of the first has created the cosmological glories of the latter.

When is Shakespeare first Shakespeare? Which plays are canonical from the beginning? By 1592, when Shakespeare was twenty-eight, he had written the three parts of *Henry VI* and their sequel in *Richard III,* as well as *The Comedy of Errors. Titus Andronicus, The Taming of the Shrew,* and *The Two Gentleman of Verona* are no more than a year later. His first absolute achievement is the astonishing *Love's Labour's Lost,* possibly written in 1594. Marlowe, half a year older than Shakespeare, was murdered in a tavern on May 30, 1593, aged twenty-nine. At that point, had Shakespeare died, he would have compared poorly to Marlowe. *The Jew of Malta,* the two parts of *Tamburlaine,* and *Edward II,* even the fragmentary *Doctor Faustus,* are a far more considerable achievement than Shakespeare's was before *Love's Labour's Lost.* Five years after Marlowe's death, Shakespeare had gone beyond his precursor and rival with the great sequence of *A*

Midsummer Night's Dream, The Merchant of Venice, and the two parts of *Henry IV.* Bottom, Shylock, and Falstaff add to Faulconbridge of *King John* and Mercutio of *Romeo and Juliet* a new kind of stage character, light years beyond Marlowe's talents or his interests. These five, despite the disapproval of formalists, walk out of their plays into the space of what A. D. Nuttall rightly calls "a new mimesis."

In the thirteen or fourteen years after the creation of Falstaff, we are given the succession worthy of him: Rosalind, Hamlet, Othello, Iago, Lear, Edmund, Macbeth, Cleopatra, Antony, Coriolanus, Timon, Imogen, Prospero, Caliban, and so many others. By 1598 Shakespeare is confirmed, and Falstaff is the angel of the confirmation. No other writer has ever had anything like Shakespeare's resources of language, which are so florabundant in *Love's Labour's Lost* that we feel many of the limits of language have been reached, once and for all. Shakespeare's greatest originality is in representation of character, however: Bottom is a wistful triumph; Shylock, a permanently equivocal trouble to all of us; but Sir John Falstaff is so original and so overwhelming that with him Shakespeare changes the entire meaning of what it is to have created a man made out of words.

Falstaff involves Shakespeare in only one authentic literary debt, and it is certainly not to Marlowe or to the Vice of medieval morality plays or the braggart soldier of ancient comedy, but rather to Shakespeare's truest, because most inward, precursor, the Chaucer of the *Canterbury Tales.* There is a tenuous but vibrant link between Falstaff and the equally outrageous Alys, Wife of Bath, far worthier to cavort with Sir John than is Doll Tearsheet or Mistress Quickly. The Wife of Bath has outworn five husbands, but who could outwear Falstaff? Scholars have noted the curious semiallusions to Chaucer that Falstaff exemplifies: Sir John also, early on, is observed on the road to Canterbury, and both he and Alys play ironically upon the verse in First Corinthians where Saint Paul urges believers in Christ to hold fast to their vocation. The Wife of Bath proclaims her vocation for matrimony: "In such a state as god hath cleped us / I wol persever: I nam not precious."

Falstaff emulates her in his defense of being a highwayman: "Why, Hal, 'tis no sin for a man to labor in his vocation." Both

grand ironist-vitalists preach an overwhelming immanence, a justification of life by life, in the here and now. Each a fierce indi-
vidualist and hedonist, they join in denying commonplace morality
and in anticipating Blake's great Proverb of Hell: "One Law for
the Lion and Ox is oppression." Lions of passion, and doubtless
of solipsistic intensity, they offend only the virtuous, as Falstaff
says of the rebels against Henry IV. What Sir John and Alys give
us is the lesson of savage intelligence mitigated by runaway wit.
Falstaff, "not only witty in myself, but the cause that wit is in
other men," is matched by the Wife, whose subversion of male
authority is carried on both verbally and sexually. Talbot Donaldson in *The Swan at the Well: Shakespeare Reading Chaucer*
captures the most striking parallel between these endless solilo-
quists and monologists, a quality they share with Don Quixote,
childlike absorption in the order of play: "The Wife tells us that
her intent is only to play, and that is perhaps true most of the
time of Falstaff. But as with the Wife, we are often unsure where
his play begins or leaves off." Yes, we are unsure, but Alys and
Sir John are not. Falstaff could say, with her, "that I have had my
worlde as in my time," but he is so much more realized than even
she is that Shakespeare could spare what would have been a redundancy. Chaucer's burgeoning secret of representation, which
makes the Wife of Bath the precursor of Falstaff, and the Pardoner
a crucial forerunner of Iago and Edmund, relates the order of play
to both character and language. We are shown Alys and the Pardoner overhearing themselves and respectively beginning to fall
out of the orders of play and of deception through that overhearing. Shakespeare slyly caught the hint and from Falstaff onward vastly expanded the effect of self-overhearing upon his
greater characters, and particularly upon their capacity to change.

There I would locate the key to Shakespeare's centrality in the
Canon. Just as Dante surpasses all other writers, before or since,
in emphasizing an ultimate changelessness in each of us, a fixed
position that we must occupy in eternity, so Shakespeare surpasses
all others in evidencing a psychology of mutability. That is only
part of the Shakespearean splendor; he not only betters all rivals
but originates the depiction of self-change on the basis of self-
overhearing, with nothing but the hint from Chaucer to provoke

him to this most remarkable of all literary innovations. One can surmise that Shakespeare, clearly deeply read in Chaucer, remembered the Wife of Bath when it came to that extraordinary moment in which Falstaff was invented. Hamlet, the leading self-overhearer in all literature, addresses himself scarcely more than Falstaff does. We all of us go around now talking to ourselves endlessly, overhearing what we say, then pondering and acting upon what we have learned. This is not so much the dialogue of the mind with itself, or even a reflection of civil war in the psyche, as it is life's reaction to what literature has necessarily become. Shakespeare, from Falstaff on, adds to the function of imaginative writing, which was instruction in how to speak to others, the now dominant if more melancholy lesson of poetry: how to speak to ourselves.

Falstaff in the marvelous course of his stage fortunes has provoked a chorus of moralizing. Some of the finest critics and speculators have been particularly nasty; their epithets have included "parasite," "coward," "braggart," "corrupter," "seducer," as well as the merely palpable "glutton," "drunkard," and "whorer." My favorite judgment is George Bernard Shaw's "a besotted and disgusting old wretch," a reaction I generously attribute to Shaw's secret realization that he could not match Falstaff in wit, and so could not prefer his own mind to Shakespeare's with quite the ease and confidence he so frequently asserted. Shaw, like all of us, could not confront Shakespeare without a realization antithetical to itself, the recognition of both strangeness and familiarity at once.

Coming to Shakespeare after writing about Romantic and modern poets and after meditating on the issues of influence and originality, I experienced the shock of difference, the difference in kind as well as in degree, that is uniquely Shakespeare's. This difference has little to do with drama as such. A bad production of Shakespeare, dreadfully directed and performed by actors who cannot speak verse, also differs in kind as well as in degree from good or bad productions of Ibsen and Molière. There is the shock of a verbal art larger and more definitive than any other, so persuasive that it seems to be not art at all but something that was always there.

Writing it is, most certainly: Shakespeare is the Canon. He sets the standard and the limits of literature. But where are his limits? Can we locate a blindness in him, a repression, a failing in imagination or in thought? In Dante, probably his nearest rival, we cannot locate poetic limits, but human circumferences can certainly be discovered. Other poets, earlier and contemporary, do not move the poet Dante to storms of generosity. Poets throng the *Divine Comedy,* and each is put in his place, precisely where Dante wants him to be. Strangely absent, in his proper person, is Guido Cavalcanti, Dante's best friend in their mutual springtime but banished from Florence by Dante in an ironic prelude to his own exile. Cavalcanti's father and father-in-law, the formidable Farinata, appear vividly in the *Inferno,* where the father expresses his chagrin that Dante, not his son Guido, has the honor of being the Pilgrim of eternity. In *Purgatorio* 11 Dante hints that he himself has taken Guido's place as "the glory of our tongue." Shakespeare's Guido Cavalcanti is approximated by a blend of Christopher Marlowe and Ben Jonson. In his earthy comedy Shakespeare could hardly portray them directly, but, not being a Shakespeare scholar, I have no inhibition in surmising that Malvolio in *Twelfth Night* is a satire upon some Jonsonian moral stances, and that Edmund in *King Lear* is a nihilistic vision founded upon aspects of not only Marlovian heroes but Marlowe himself. Neither figure lacks appeal; Malvolio is a comic victim in *Twelfth Night,* yet we feel he has wandered into the wrong play. Elsewhere, he would prosper and retain his dignity and self-esteem. Edmund is where he belongs, out-Iagoing Iago in the abyss of Lear's ruined cosmos. You have to be Goneril or Regan to love him, but all of us might find him dangerously engaging, free of hypocrisy, and asserting his and our responsibility for whatever it is we become.

Edmund has drive, grand wit, enormous intellect, and an icy joy, carrying his high spirits into the ranks of death. He also has no warm affect whatsoever and may be the first figure in literature to manifest the qualities of such Dostoevskian nihilists as Svidrigailov in *Crime and Punishment* and Stavrogin in *The Possessed.* An immense advance over Barabas in *The Jew of Malta,* Edmund carries the Marlovian Machiavel to a new sublimity and is at once an ironic tribute to Marlowe and a triumphant overcoming of the great overreacher. Like Malvolio, Edmund is an equivocal tribute but ultimately a testimony to Shakespearean generosity, albeit ironical.

We know almost nothing factual about the inner life of Shakespeare, but if you give many years to reading him incessantly, you begin to know what he is not. Calderón is a religious dramatist and George Herbert, a devotional poet; Shakespeare is neither. Marlowe the nihilist antithetically manifests a religious sensibility, and *Doctor Faustus* can be read against itself. Shakespeare's darkest tragedies, *Lear* and *Macbeth,* do not yield to Christianization, nor do the great equivocal plays, *Hamlet* and *Measure for Measure.* Northrop Frye thought that *The Merchant of Venice* had to be understood as a serious exemplification of Christian argument, New Testament mercy against Old Testament supposed insistence on having one's bond and one's revenge. *The Merchant of Venice*'s stage Jew, Shylock, is intended as a comic villain, for Shakespeare evidently shared the anti-Semitism of his time; but I find nothing of Frye's theological allegory in the play. It is Antonio, whose true Christian nature is demonstrated by spitting and cursing at Shylock, who proposes that the Jew's survival include the condition that he instantly become a Christian, a forced conversion to which Shylock improbably consents. Antonio's suggestion is Shakespeare's own invention and no part of the "pound of flesh" tradition. Whatever can be made of this episode, even I hesitate to call it Christian argument. Even at his most morally dubious, Shakespeare at once confounds our expectation and yet does not forsake his universality, which clearly has its dangerous aspects.

A friend, who teaches at the Hebrew University in Jerusalem and who was born in Bulgaria, told me about a performance of *The Tempest,* in Petrov's Bulgarian version, which she had recently attended in Sofia. It was played as farce, successfully she thought, but left the audience discontented because, she said, the Bulgars identify Shakespeare with the classical or canonical. Students and friends have described for me Shakespeare as they have seen him in Japanese, Russian, Spanish, Indonesian, and Italian, and the general report has been that the audiences were as one in finding that Shakespeare represented *them* upon the stage. Dante has been the poets' poet, even as Shakespeare has been the peoples' poet; each is universal, though Dante is not for the groundlings. I am aware of no cultural criticism, no materialist dialectic, that can account for either Shakespeare's classless or Dante's elitist universalism. Neither is exactly an accident or a product of overdetermined Eurocentrism. Clearly the phenomenon of surpassing literary excellence, of such power of thought, characterization, and metaphor that it triumphantly survives translation and transposition and compels attention in virtually every culture, does exist.

Dante was as self-conscious a poet as Milton; each sought to leave behind a prophetic structure that the future would not willingly let die. Shakespeare puzzles us in his apparent indifference to the posthumous destiny of *King Lear;* we have two rather different texts of the play, and pushing them together into the amalgam we generally read and see acted is not very satisfactory. The only works Shakespeare ever proofread and stood by were *Venus and Adonis* and *The Rape of Lucrece,* neither of them worthy of the poet of the Sonnets, let alone of *Lear, Hamlet, Othello, Macbeth.* How can there have been a writer for whom the final shape of *King Lear* was a careless or throwaway matter? Shakespeare is like the Arabian moon in Wallace Stevens that "throws his stars around the floor," as though the profusion of Shakespeare's gifts was so abundant that he could afford to be careless. The Shakespearean exuberance or gusto is part of what breaks through linguistic and cultural barriers. You cannot confine Shakespeare to the English Renaissance any more than you can keep Falstaff within the limits of the *Henry IV* plays, or the Prince of Denmark within the action of his drama.

Shakespeare is to the world's literature what Hamlet is to the imaginary domain of literary character: a spirit that permeates everywhere, that cannot be confined. A freedom from doctrine and simplistic morality is certainly one element in that spirit's ease of transference, though the freedom made Dr. Johnson nervous and Tolstoy indignant. Shakespeare has the largeness of nature itself, and through that largeness he senses nature's indifference. Nothing crucial in this largeness is culture-bound or gender-confined. If you read and reread Shakespeare endlessly, you may not get to know either his character or his personality, but you will certainly learn to recognize his temperament, his sensibility, and his cognition.

The School of Resentment is compelled by its dogmas to regard aesthetic supremacy, particularly in Shakespeare's instance, as a prolonged cultural conspiracy undertaken to protect the political and economic interests of mercantile Great Britain from the eighteenth century until today. In contemporary America, the polemic shifts to a Shakespeare utilized as a Eurocentric center of power in order to oppose the legitimate cultural aspiration of various minorities, including academic Feminists, who are now scarcely a minority. One sees why Foucault has won such favor with apostles of Resentment; he replaces the canon with the metaphor he calls the library, which dissolves hierarchies. But if there is no canon, then John Webster, who wrote always in Shakespeare's shadow, might as well be read in Shakespeare's place, a substitution that would have amazed Webster.

There is no substitute for Shakespeare, not even in the handful of dramatists, ancient or modern, who can be read and played with him or against him. What matches the four great Shakespearean tragedies? Even Dante, as James Joyce confessed, lacks Shakespeare's richness, which means that the reading of character appears infinite in Shakespeare, but also suggests that the thirty-eight plays and attendant sonnets form a discontinuous *Earthly Comedy* far more comprehensive than Dante's and refreshingly free of Dante's allegory of the theologians. Shakespeare's multiplicity far exceeds Dante's or Chaucer's. The creator of Hamlet and Falstaff, Rosalind and Cleopatra, Iago and Lear, differs in degree as well as in kind. If that difference can be defined, we will be closer to seeing why Shakespeare of necessity recentered the Western Canon, and will go on recentering it, however much it is altered for the worse by political considerations.

Milton's first published poem, written in his early twenties, was printed anonymously as one of the prefatory tributes to the Shakespeare Second Folio (1632). Shakespeare had been dead for sixteen years, and though by no means eclipsed, he was yet to undergo the canonization that proceeded throughout the eighteenth century, from Dryden through Pope to Dr. Johnson and on to the earlier phases of Romanticism, a movement that deified Shakespeare. The young Milton rather possessively refers to his forerunner as "my Shakespeare," identifies him as a male Muse, "dear son of Memory," and subtly hints that Shakespeare, "great heir of fame," will be in some sense part of Milton's own legacy. Milton will be among those who

> *Hath from the heavens of thy unvalued book,*
> *These Delphic lines with deep impression took,*
> *Then thou our fancy of itself bereaving,*
> *Dost make us marble with too much conceiving.*

"Unvalued book" in 1632 meant "invaluable book," but that alone does not clear away the ambiguity or ambivalence of these lines. Milton and the other discerning readers have become Shakespeare's monument. Marble, their fancy no longer their own, they have yielded to the power of Shakespearean "conceiving." But so, with Miltonic cunning, has Shakespeare. Milton anticipates Borges in giving us a Shakespeare who, by becoming everyone, is no one in himself, as anonymous as nature. If your readers and audience as well as your characters and players have become your work, your book, then you live in them only. Nature's own artist, Shakespeare becomes an anonymous endowment given to Milton, a resource so much his own as to make citation redundant. Shakespeare *is* Milton's strength, which he in turn generously wills to Shakespeare, who was there before him but also somehow will come after him. Here, in his public beginning, Milton already heralds his canonical end as another monument without a tomb, who will live in his readers. Shakespeare, however, had been granted a very large audience, both fit and unfit, while Milton anxiously hints that his own audience, at least in comparison, will be fit though few. Intercanonical, the poem to Shakespeare is also pragmatically self-canonizing.

There is a sense in which "the canonical" is always the "intercanonical," because the Canon not only results from a contest but is itself an ongoing contest. Literary power is produced by the partial victories in this contest, and even with a poet as strong as Milton it becomes clear that the strength is agonistic and so cannot be entirely Milton's own. For me, the radical cases of what looks like a fuller autonomy are Dante and, even more, Shakespeare. Dante in a way is a stronger Milton, and his overcoming of all rivals, ancient and contemporary, is even more convincing than Milton's triumph, if only because Shakespeare always lingers on in Milton. Dante affects the way we read Virgil, and Shakespeare can severely alter our approach to Milton. But Virgil has little effect upon our understanding of Dante, because the actual Epicurean Virgil has been abrogated by Dante. Milton cannot help with our analysis of Shakespeare, because Milton's reduction of Shakespeare to anonymity merely repeats and distorts Shakespeare's own tactics of losing his selfhood in his work.

That Shakespearean procedure, more potent than any overt self-canonization before or since, takes us again to Shakespeare's neutrality as canonical center. There is a firm biographical tradition that William Shakespeare the man was not at all idiosyncratic, in contrast to such formidable personalities as Dante, Milton, and Tolstoy. His friends and acquaintances left testimony of an amiable, rather ordinary-seeming person: open, neighborly, witty, gentle, free of manner, someone with whom you could have a relaxed drink. All agree that he was good-natured and unassuming, though a touch sharp at business. In true Borgesian mode, it is as though the creator of scores of major characters and hundreds of frequently vivid minor figures wasted no imaginative energy in inventing a persona for himself. At the very center of the Canon is the least self-conscious and least aggressive of all the major writers we have known.

There is an inverse ratio, a little beyond our analytical skills, between Shakespeare's virtual colorlessness and his preternatural dramatic powers. His two quasi-rivals in his own time were men of extraordinary intensity: the violent and burly Ben Jonson and Christopher Marlowe, double agent and Faustian overreacher. They were great poets and are nearly as famous now for their lives as for their works. Shakespeare has his personal affinities with the subdued Cervantes, but Cervantes unwillingly led a life of extravagant action and catastrophic misfortune. Again, there are character traits that Shakespeare shares with Montaigne, but Montaigne's life of creative retirement was punctuated by high politics and civil war. Molière is perhaps Shakespeare's double in temperament and in comic genius, but Shakespeare was a minor actor professionally and Molière a major one, and despite *Don Juan*, Molière avoided tragedy, even as Racine would not touch comedy. Shakespeare is therefore peculiarly solitary among the greatest writers, despite his evident sociability. He *perceived* more than any other writer, *thought* more profoundly and originally than any other, and had an almost effortless mastery of language, far surpassing everyone, including Dante.

Part of the secret of Shakespeare's canonical centrality is his disinterestedness; despite all the flailings of New Historicists and other Resenters, Shakespeare is almost as free of ideology as are his heroic wits: Hamlet, Rosalind, Falstaff. He has no theology, no metaphysics, no ethics, and rather less political theory than is brought to him by his current critics. His sonnets show that he was hardly free of the superego, unlike Falstaff; hardly transcendent, unlike Hamlet at the end; hardly in perpetual command of every perspective relevant to his own life, unlike Rosalind. But since he imagined all of them, we can assume that he refused to will himself beyond his own limits. Refreshingly, he is not Nietzsche or King Lear, and he declined to go mad, though he had the imagination of madness, as of everything else. His wisdom transmutes endlessly in all our sages, from Goethe to Freud, even though Shakespeare declined to step forward as a sage.

Nietzsche memorably told us that we find words only for what is already dead in our hearts, so that there is always a kind of contempt in the act of speaking. The antithetical aphorist must have been aware that he was paraphrasing both Hamlet and the Player King, just as Emerson must have known that he echoed Lear when he stated the law of Compensation as "Nothing is got for nothing." Kierkegaard also discovered that it was impossible not to be post-Shakespearean, haunted as he was by his inimitable precursor as melancholy Dane whose relation to Ophelia presaged Kierkegaard's to Regina. "Great havoc makes he of our originalities" was Emerson's remark about Plato, but Emerson himself would have admitted that Shakespeare had first taught him to cry havoc in questions of originality.

THE MOST DISTINGUISHED resenter of Shakespeare was Count Leo Nikolayevich Tolstoy, one of the unacknowledged ancestors of the School of Resentment. Here he is in "Shakespeare and the Drama" (1906), a pungent postlude to his notorious *What Is Art?* (1898):

> The subject of Shakespeare's pieces, as is seen from the demonstrations of his greatest admirers, is that lowest, most vulgar view of life which regards the external elevation of the lords of the world as a genuine distinction, despises the crowd, i.e., the working class, repudiates not only all religions, but also all humanitarian strivings directed to the betterment of the existing order.

> The fundamental inner cause of Shakespeare's fame was and is this—that his dramas . . . corresponded to the irreligious and immoral frame of mind of the upper classes of his time and ours.

> . . . having freed themselves from this hypnotic state, men will understand that the trivial and immoral works of Shakespeare and his imitators, aiming merely at the recreation and amusement of the spectators, cannot possibly represent the teaching of life, and that, while there is no true religious drama, the teaching of life should be sought for in other sources.
>
> *(translated by V. Tchertfoff)*

Much of Tolstoy's essay is devoted to ridiculing *King Lear,* a sad irony since Tolstoy, when he came to the last station of his cross, had involuntarily turned into King Lear. A sophisticated Resenter will not bring forth Bertolt Brecht as true Marxist drama, or Paul Claudel as true Christian drama, in order to prefer either of them to Shakespeare. Yet Tolstoy's outcry has the poignance of his authentic moral outrage and all the authority of his own aesthetic splendor.

Palpably, Tolstoy's essay—like his *What Is Art?*—is a disaster, prompting the serious question of how so great a writer could have been so mistaken. Disapprovingly, Tolstoy quotes as idolaters of Shakespeare a distinguished company that includes Goethe, Shelley, Victor Hugo, and Turgenev. He could have added Hegel, Stendhal, Pushkin, Manzoni, Heine, and scores of others, indeed virtually every major writer capable of reading, with a few unsavory exceptions like Voltaire. The less interesting aspect of Tolstoy's rebellion against the aesthetic is creative envy. There is a particular fury in Tolstoy's denial of an eminence shared by Shakespeare with Homer, a sharing that Tolstoy reserved for his own *War and Peace*. Much more interesting is Tolstoy's spiritual revulsion against the immoral and irreligious tragedy of *King Lear*. I prefer such a revulsion to any attempts to Christianize Shakespeare's deliberately pre-Christian drama, and Tolstoy is quite accurate in seeing that Shakespeare, as a dramatist, is neither a Christian nor a moralist.

I remember standing in front of Titian's painting of the flaying of Marsyas by Apollo when it was shown in Washington, D.C. Appalled and overwhelmed, I could only nod agreement to the comment of my companion, the American painter Larry Day, that the picture had something like the power and effect of the final act of *King Lear*. The Titian was there in St. Petersburg for Tolstoy to see; I can recall no specific comment by him, but presumably he would have conceived Titian's image of that horror, the promised end, as well. *What Is Art?* discards not only Shakespeare but Dante, Beethoven, and Raphael. If one is Tolstoy, perhaps one can dispense with Shakespeare, but we owe something to Tolstoy for locating the true grounds of Shakespearean power and offense: freedom from moral and religious overdeterminations. Evidently Tolstoy did not mean this in any commonplace sense, since Greek tragedy, Milton, and Bach also failed the Tolstoyan test of popular simplicity that was passed by some works of Victor Hugo and of Dickens, by Harriet Beecher Stowe and some minor Dostoevsky, and by George Eliot's *Adam Bede*. These were examples of Christian and moral art, though "good universal art" was also acceptable in a curious secondary grouping that included Cervantes and Molière. Tolstoy demands "the truth," and the trouble with Shakespeare, in Tolstoy's perspective, is that he was not interested in the truth.

That certainly joins the issue: How relevant is Tolstoy's complaint? Is the center of the Western Canon a pragmatic exaltation of lies? George Bernard Shaw greatly admired *What Is Art?* and presumably preferred Bunyan's *Pilgrim's Progress* to Shakespeare in somewhat the same way that Tolstoy ranked *Uncle Tom's Cabin* above *King Lear.* But this kind of thinking is now drearily familiar to us; one of my younger colleagues told me she valued Alice Walker's *Meridian* over Thomas Pynchon's *Gravity's Rainbow* because Pynchon lied and Walker incarnated the truth. With political correctness replacing religious rightness, we are back in Tolstoy's polemic against difficult art. And yet Shakespeare, as Tolstoy refused to see, is virtually unique in simultaneously manifesting both difficult and popular art. There, I suspect, was the true Shakespearean offense and the ultimate explanation of why and how Shakespeare centers the Canon. To this day, multiculturally, Shakespeare will hold almost any audience, upper or lower class. What burned its way into the canonical center was a mode of representation universally available as far as I can tell, give or take a few French naysayers.

Was or is that way of representing men and women true? Is *Uncle Tom's Cabin* more sincere than the *Divine Comedy,* whatever that assertion may mean? Perhaps Walker's *Meridian* is more sincere than *Gravity's Rainbow.* Doubtless the later Tolstoy is more sincere than Shakespeare or anyone else. Sincerity has no royal road to the truth, and imaginative literature situates itself somewhere between truth and meaning, a somewhere I once compared to what ancient Gnostics called the *kenoma,* the cosmological emptiness in which we wander and weep, as William Blake wrote.

Shakespeare gives one a more persuasive representation of the *kenoma* than anyone else, particularly when he sets the backgrounds of *King Lear* and *Macbeth.* There, once again, Shakespeare centers the Canon, because we have to struggle hard to think of any representation that is not more convincing in

Shakespeare than anywhere else, be it in Homer, Dante, or Tolstoy. Rhetorically, Shakespeare has no equal; no more awesome panoply of metaphor exists. If your quest is for a truth that defies rhetoric, perhaps you ought to study political economy or systems analysis and abandon Shakespeare to the aesthetes and the groundlings, who combined to elevate him in the first place.

I keep circling back to the mystery of Shakespeare's genius, well aware that the very phrase "Shakespeare's genius" means that I am out of it as far as the School of Resentment is concerned. But the trouble with Foucault's Death of the Author is that it merely alters rhetorical terms without creating a new method. If "social energies" wrote *King Lear* and *Hamlet,* why exactly were social energies more productive in the son of the Stratford artisan than in the burly bricklayer Ben Jonson? The exasperated New Historicist or Feminist critic has a curious affinity with the exasperations that keep creating partisans for the idea of Sir Francis Bacon or the earl of Oxford as the true author of *Lear.* Sigmund Freud, the master of all who know, went to his death insisting that Moses was an Egyptian and that Oxford wrote Shakespeare. The marvelously named Looney, the founder of the Oxfordians, gained a disciple in the author of *The Interpretation of Dreams* and *Three Essays on the Theory of Sexuality.* Had Freud joined the Flat Earth Society, we could not be more chagrined, though there are depths beneath depths, and at least we can be grateful that Freud never wrote more than a few sentences on the Looney hypothesis.

It was somehow a great comfort to Freud to believe that his precursor Shakespeare was not a rather ordinary personality from Stratford, but an enigmatic and mighty nobleman. More than snobbery was involved. For Freud, as for Goethe, the works of Shakespeare were the secular center of culture, the hope for a rational glory in mankind still to come. There was more even than that for Freud. On some level, Freud understood that Shakespeare had invented psychoanalysis by inventing the psyche, insofar as Freud could recognize and describe it. This could not have been a pleasant understanding, since it subverted Freud's declaration that "I invented psychoanalysis because it had no literature." Revenge came with the supposed demonstration that Shakespeare was an impostor, which satisfied Freudian resentment though rationally it did not make the plays any less of a precursor. Shakespeare had played great havoc with Freud's originalities; now Shakespeare was unmasked and disgraced. We can be grateful that we do not have Freud's *Oxford and Shakespeareanism* to consort on our shelves with *Moses and Monotheism* and the various classics of New Historicist, Marxist, and Feminist Shakespeare. French Freud was silly enough; and now we have French Joyce, which is hard to take. But nothing can be as oxymoronic as French Shakespeare, which is what the New Historicism ought to be called.

The real Stratfordian wrote thirty-eight plays in twenty-four years and then went home to die. At forty-nine he composed his last play, *The Two Noble Kinsmen,* splitting the job with John Fletcher. Three years later he was dead, close to his fifty-second birthday. The creator of Lear and Hamlet died a not very momentous death after an uneventful life. There are no great biographies of Shakespeare, not because we do not know enough but because there is not enough to know. In our own time, among writers of the first order, only the life of Wallace Stevens seems as lackluster in outward event or excitement as Shakespeare's. We know that Stevens hated the graduated income tax and that Shakespeare was quick to bring suits in Chancery to protect his estate investments. We know, more or less, that neither Shakespeare's nor Stevens's marriage was particularly passionate, once past its origin. After that we work at knowing the plays, or at knowing Stevens's intricate variations on his meditative ecstasies of apprehension.

It is very satisfactory to the imagination to be compelled to fall back upon the work when no authorial maelstrom seems to be there. With Christopher Marlowe I brood upon the man, who can be meditated upon endlessly, as the plays cannot; with Rimbaud I brood over both, though the boy is even more enigmatic than the poetry. Stevens the man evaded himself so completely that we scarcely need seek him; the man Shakespeare can hardly be termed evasive, or much of anything else. He has no incontestable spokesperson in the plays: not Hamlet, not Prospero, certainly not the ghost of Hamlet's father, whom he is supposed to have played. Nor can even his most careful scholars definitively mark out the

boundaries between the conventional and the personal in the sonnets. Seeking to understand the work or the man, we are always
returned to the indisputably central eminence of the greater plays,
almost from the days when they were first enacted.

One way of dealing with the eminence of Shakespeare's primacy
is to deny it. From Dryden to the present, it is remarkable how
few have chosen this path. The novelty or intended scandal of the
current New Historicism purports to reside elsewhere, but in fact
it dwells in this denial, generally implicit but sometimes overt. If
the social energies (assuming that these are more than a histori-
cizing metaphor, which I doubt) of the English Renaissance somehow wrote *King Lear,* then the singularity of Shakespeare can be
called into question. It may be that in a generation or so "social
energy" as author of *King Lear* will seem about as enlightening
as the surmise that the earl of Oxford or Sir Francis Bacon wrote
the tragedy. The impulse involved is much the same. But it is as
easy to reduce Shakespeare to his context, whatever context, as
to reduce Dante to the Florence and Italy of his day. No one is
going to rise up, here or in Italy, to proclaim that Cavalcanti was
the aesthetic equal of Dante, and it would be equally vain to make
a case for even Ben Jonson or Christopher Marlowe as authentic
rivals to Shakespeare. Jonson and Marlowe, in very different ways,
were great poets and sometimes remarkable dramatists, but the
reader or player enters another order of art in encountering *King
Lear.*

What is the Shakespearean difference that demands Dante, Cervantes, Tolstoy, and only a few others as aesthetic companions?
To ask the question is to undertake the quest that is the final aim
of literary study, the search for a kind of value that transcends
the particular prejudices and needs of societies at fixed points in
time. Such a quest is illusory, according to all our current ideologies; but the purpose of this book is, in part, to combat the
cultural politics, both Left and Right, that are destroying criticism
and consequently may destroy literature itself. There is a substance
in Shakespeare's work that prevails and that has proved multicultural, so universally apprehended in all languages as to have
established a pragmatic multiculturalism around the globe, one
that already far surpasses our politicized fumblings toward such
an ideal. Shakespeare is the center of the embryo of a world canon,

not Western or Eastern and less and less Eurocentric; and so again I am thrown back to the great question: What is the singular excellence of Shakespeare, the difference in kind as well as in degree from all other writers?

Shakespeare's command of language, though overwhelming, is not unique and is capable of imitation. Poetry written in English becomes Shakespearean frequently enough to testify to the contaminating power of his high rhetoric. The peculiar magnificence of Shakespeare is in his power of representation of human character and personality and their mutabilities. The canonical praise of this magnificence was inaugurated by Samuel Johnson's preface to the Shakespeare of 1765, and is both revelatory and misleading: "Shakespeare is above all writers, at least above all modern writers, the poet of nature, the poet that holds up to his readers a faithful mirrour of manners and of life."

Johnson, in tribute to Shakespeare, echoes Hamlet's praise of the actors. Against his words, one sets Oscar Wilde's: "This unfortunate aphorism about art holding the mirror up to Nature is deliberately said by Hamlet in order to convince the bystanders of his absolute insanity in all art-matters."

Actually Hamlet was speaking of the actors as holding a mirror up to nature, but Johnson and Wilde assimilated the actors to the poet-playwright. Wilde's "nature" was a blocking agent vainly attempting to thwart art, while Johnson saw "nature" as a reality principle, submerging the idiosyncratic in the general, the "progeny of common humanity." Shakespeare, wiser than both of these genuinely wise critics, saw "nature" through clashing perspectives, those of Lear and Edmund in the most sublime of the tragedies, of Hamlet and Claudius in another, of Othello and Iago in yet another. You cannot hold a mirror up to any of these natures, or persuade yourself convincingly that your sense of reality is more comprehensive than that of Shakespearean tragedy. There are no literary works that go beyond Shakespeare's in reminding you that nothing can be like a play except another play, while at the same time intimating that a tragic idea is not just like another tragic idea (though it may be) but is also like a person, or like change in a person, or like the final form of personal change, which is death.

The meaning of a word is always another word, for words are

more like other words than they can be like persons or things, but Shakespeare hints frequently that words are more like persons than they are like things. Shakespearean representation of character has a preternatural richness about it because no other writer, before or since, gives us a stronger illusion that each character speaks with a different voice from the others. Johnson, noting this feature, attributed it to Shakespeare's accurate portrayal of general nature, but Shakespeare might have been prompted to question the reality of such a nature. His uncanny ability to present consistent and different actual-seeming voices of imaginary beings stems in part from the most abundant sense of reality ever to invade literature.

When we attempt to isolate Shakespeare's consciousness of reality (or the plays' version of reality, if you prefer), we are likely to become bewildered by it. When you stand back from the *Divine Comedy,* the poem's strangeness shocks you, but Shakespearean drama seems at once utterly familiar and yet too rich to absorb all at once. Dante interprets his characters for you; if you cannot accept his judgments, his poem abandons you. Shakespeare so opens his characters to multiple perspectives that they become analytical instruments for judging you. If you are a moralist, Falstaff outrages you; if you are rancid, Rosalind exposes you; if you are dogmatic, Hamlet evades you forever. And if you are an explainer, the great Shakespearean villains will cause you to despair. Iago, Edmund, and Macbeth are not motiveless; they overflow with motives, most of which they invent or imagine for themselves. Like the great wits—Falstaff, Rosalind, Hamlet—these monstrous malevolences are artists of the self, or free artists of themselves, as Hegel remarked. Hamlet, the most fecund among them, is endowed by Shakespeare with something that looks very much like an authorial consciousness, and one not Shakespeare's own. Interpreting Hamlet becomes as difficult as interpreting such aphorists as Emerson, Nietzsche, and Kierkegaard. "They lived and wrote," something in one wants to protest, but Shakespeare has found a way of giving us Hamlet, who wrote those additions that revised *The Murder of Gonzago* into *The Mousetrap.* The most bewildering of Shakespearean achievements is to have suggested more contexts for explaining us than we are capable of supplying for explaining his characters.

For many readers the limits of human art are touched in *King Lear,* which with *Hamlet* appears to be the height of the Shakespearean canon. My own preference is for *Macbeth,* where I never get over my shock at the play's ruthless economy, its way of making every speech, every phrase count. Still, *Macbeth* has only the one huge character, and even *Hamlet* is so dominated by its hero that all the lesser figures are blinded (as we are) by his transcendent brilliance. Shakespeare's power of individualization is strongest in *King Lear* and, oddly enough, in *Measure for Measure,* two plays in which there are no minor characters. With *Lear* we are at the center of centers of canonical excellence, as we are in particular cantos of the *Inferno* or the *Purgatorio,* or in a Tolstoyan narrative like *Hadji Murad.* Here, if anywhere, the flames of invention burn away all context and grant us the possibility of what could be called primal aesthetic value, free of history and ideology and available to whoever can be educated to read and view it.

Partisans of Resentment might stress that only an elite can be so educated. As our more truthful moments inform us, it has become harder and harder to read deeply as this century grows older. Whether the cause be media or other distractions of the Chaotic Age, even the elite tend to lose concentration as readers. Close reading may not have ended with my generation, but it has certainly been eclipsed in the generations after us. Is it irrelevant that I was nearly forty before I first owned a television set? I cannot be sure, yet I sometimes wonder if a critical preference for context over text does not reflect a generation made impatient with deep reading. The tragedy of Lear and Cordelia can be imparted to even superficial playgoers or readers, because it is Shakespeare's oddness that he will divert nearly every level of attention. But properly played, properly read, it will demand more than any single answering consciousness is able to provide.

Dr. Johnson famously could not endure Cordelia's death: "I was many years ago so shocked by Cordelia's death, that I know not whether I ever endured to read again the last scenes of the play till I undertook to revise them as an editor."

There is, as Johnson conveyed, a terrible desolation in the final scene of *The Tragedy of King Lear,* an effect surpassing anything else of its kind, in Shakespeare or in any other writer. Johnson perhaps took Cordelia's death as a synecdoche for that desolation, for the vision of the old king, driven mad again by his grief, entering with Cordelia dead in his arms. As a spectacle, it has the force of an image reversing all natural expectations and was famously misread by Sigmund Freud in his "Theme of the Three Caskets" (1913):

> "Enter Lear with Cordelia dead in his arms."
> Cordelia is Death. Reverse the situation, and it becomes intelligible and familiar to us—the Death-goddess bearing away the dead hero from the place of battle, like the Valkyr in German mythology. Eternal wisdom, in the garb of the primitive myth, bids the old man renounce love, choose death and make friends with the necessity of dying.

Freud, at fifty-seven, had twenty-six years still to live, yet he could not speak of "the hero" without casting himself for the part. To renounce love, choose death, and make friends with the necessity of dying is Prince Hamlet-like, but does not suit King Lear. Kings die hard, in Shakespeare and in life, and Lear is the greatest of all representations of a king. His precursor is no literary monarch but the model of all rulers: Yahweh, the Lord himself, unless you choose to regard Yahweh as a literary character, encountered by Shakespeare in the Geneva Bible. The Yahweh of the J writer, who dominates the primal strand of Genesis, Exodus and Numbers, is as irascible and sometimes as mad as Lear. Lear, image of paternal authority, is not a favorite of Feminist critics, who easily categorize him as the archetype of patriarchal coercion. His power, even in ruin, appears to be what they cannot forgive, since they interpret it as the union of god, king, and father in the one impatient temperament. What they neglect is the given of the play: Lear is not only feared and venerated by everyone on the side of goodness in the play, he is positively loved by Cordelia, the Fool, Gloucester, Edgar, Kent, Albany, and evidently his people in general. He owes much in personality to Yahweh, but he is considerably more benign. His principal fault in regard to Cordelia is an excessive love that demands excess in return. Of all Shakespeare's vast company of characters, Lear is much the most passionate, a quality attractive perhaps in itself but suiting neither his age nor his position.

Even the most resentful interpretations of Lear, which demystify the king's supposed capacity for social pity, leave untouched his passionate intensity, a quality shared by his daughters, Goneril and Regan, who lack his bewildered drive toward love. They are what their father would have been if he had not also possessed the qualities of his daughter Cordelia. Shakespeare makes no explicit attempt to account for Cordelia's difference from her sisters, or Edgar's equally startling contrast to Edmund. But he masterfully endows both Cordelia and Edgar with a recalcitrance that is much larger than their shared reticence. There is something against the grain in these two authentically loving characters, something stubborn, a strength whose undersong is willfulness. Cordelia, knowing both her father and her sisters well, could forestall the tragedy by a touch of initial diplomacy, but she will not. Edgar adopts a self-punishing disguise far lowlier and more degraded than is strictly necessary, and he maintains all his disguises long after they could have been discarded. His refusal to reveal himself to Gloucester until just before he anonymously goes forth to cut down Edmund is as curious as Shakespeare's refusal to dramatize the scene of revelation and reconciliation between father and son. We hear Edgar's narrative of the scene, but we are denied the scene itself. I think we sense that Edgar may be Shakespeare's personal representative in the play, in contrast to the Marlovian Edmund. Edmund is a genius, as brilliant as Iago but colder, the coldest figure in all of Shakespeare. It is in the antitheses between Edmund and Lear that I would locate one of the sources of surpassing aesthetic power in the play. Something at Shakespeare's core is in this antithesis, something the playgoer's or reader's heart misses in the play, and something which makes the play unable to bless either us or itself. At the center of the strongest literary work I have ever encountered there is a terrible and deliberate gap, a cosmological emptiness into which we are thrown. A sensitive apprehension of *The Tragedy of King Lear* gives us a sense of having been thrown outward and downward until we are left beyond values, altogether bereft.

There is no transcendence at the end of *King Lear,* as there somehow appears to be when Hamlet dies. The death of Lear is a release for him, but not for the survivors: Edgar, Albany, Kent. And it is no release for us either. Too much has been incarnated in Lear for the manner of his dying to be acceptable to his subjects, and our own investment in Lear's sufferings has become too large for a Freudian "making friends with death." Perhaps Shakespeare kept the death of Gloucester offstage so that the contrast between the dying Lear and the dying Edmund would retain all of its pungency. Edmund makes a supreme effort to avoid a meaningless death by attempting to rescind his order for the deaths of Cordelia and Lear. He is too late, and neither we nor Edmund know what to make of him as he is carried offstage to die.

The greatness of the play has everything to do with Lear's patriarchal greatness, an aspect of the human that is now severely devalued in a critical age of Feminism, literary Marxism, and the various related modes of our importation from Paris of an anti-bourgeois crusade. Shakespeare is too shrewd, however, to commit his art to a patriarchal politics, or to Christianity, or even to the royal absolutism of his patron, King James I, and Lear is resented now mostly on irrelevant grounds. The bewildered old king takes his stand on behalf of nature, an altogether different nature than the one invoked as goddess by the nihilizing Edmund. In this vast play, Lear and Edmund never speak a single word to each other, though they are on stage together for two major scenes. What could they say, what dialogue is possible between Shakespeare's most passionate character and his coldest, between one who cares too much and one who does not care at all?

In Lear's sense of nature, Goneril and Regan are unnatural hags, monsters of the deep, and so indeed they are. In Edmund's concept of nature, his two demon lovers are surpassingly natural. Shakespeare's drama does not allow us a middle ground. Rejecting Lear is not an aesthetic option, however exercised one may be against his excesses and his uncanny power. Here Shakespeare rejoins the J writer, whose all-too-human Yahweh is both incommensurate with us and impossible to evade. If we want a human nature that does not prey upon itself, we turn to the authority of Lear, however flawed, however compromised in its hurtful power. Lear cannot heal us or himself, and he cannot survive Cordelia. But very little in the play can survive him: Kent, who wishes only to rejoin his master in death; Albany, who emulates Lear in abdicating; Edgar, apocalyptic survivor, who speaks evidently both for Shakespeare and the audience to close the play:

> *The weight of this sad time we must obey,*
> *Speak what we feel, not what we ought to say:*
> *The oldest hath borne most; we that are young*
> *Shall never see so much, nor live so long.*

Nature as well as the state is wounded almost unto death, and the three surviving characters exit with a dead march. What matters most is the mutilation of nature, and our sense of what is or is not natural in our own lives. So overwhelming is the effect at the play's close that everything seems against itself. Why are we simultaneously so strongly and so ambivalently affected by Lear's death?

In 1815, aged sixty-six, Goethe wrote an essay on Shakespeare that attempted to reconcile his own antithetical attitudes about the greatest Western poet. He had begun as a Shakespeare idolater, had developed a supposed "classicism" that found Shakespeare not wholly adequate, and had "corrected" Shakespeare by a rather severe version of *Romeo and Juliet*. Although Goethe's ultimate judgment is made in favor of Shakespeare, the essay is a bafflement and an evasion. It helped enhance Shakespeare's reign in Germany, but Goethe's ambivalence about a poetic and dramatic genius beyond his own prevented him from achieving a clear statement about Shakespeare's unique and abiding interest. It remained for Hegel, in the lectures posthumously published as *The Philosophy of Fine Art*, to achieve the insight into Shakespearean representation of character that still needs to be developed by us, if we are ever to arrive at a criticism worthy of him.

Essentially, Hegel attempts to distinguish Shakespeare's kind of characters from those of Sophocles and Racine, Lope de Vega and Calderón. The Greek tragic hero must oppose a higher, ethical Power with an individuality, an ethical pathos, which blends into what confronts him, because it is already part of that higher pathos. In Racine, Hegel finds an abstract style of character-drawing in which specific passions are represented as pure personification, so that the opposition between the individual and the higher Power tends to be abstract. Lope de Vega and Calderón are rated somewhat higher by Hegel, who sees in them as well an abstract style of character-drawing, but also a certain solidity and sense of personality, however inflexible. The German tragedies are not rated even that high: Goethe, despite his early Shakespeareanism, falls away from characterization into an exaltation of passion, and Schiller is rejected for having substituted violence for reality. Against all of them, at a salutary height, Hegel places Shakespeare, in the best critical passage on Shakespearean representation yet written:

> The more Shakespeare on the infinite embrace of his world-stage proceeds to develop the extreme limits of evil and folly, to that extent . . . he concentrates these characters in their limitations. While doing so, however, he confers on them intelligence and imagination; and *by means of the image in which they, by virtue of that intelligence, contemplate themselves objectively, as a work of art, he makes them free artists of themselves,* and is fully able, through the complete virility and truth of his characterization, to awaken our interest in criminals, no less than in the most vulgar and weak-witted lubbers and fools. [Italics mine]
>
> *(translated by F. P. B. Osmaston)*

Iago and Edmund and Hamlet contemplate themselves objectively in images wrought by their own intelligences and are enabled to see themselves as dramatic characters, aesthetic artifices. They thus become free artists of themselves, which means that they are free to write themselves, to will changes in the self. Overhearing their own speeches and pondering those expressions, they change and go on to contemplate an otherness in the self, or the possibility of such otherness.

Hegel has seen what needs to be seen in and about Shakespeare, but the Hegelian gnomic lecturing style requires some unpacking. Consider the bastard Edmund, Marlovian Machiavel of Lear's tragedy, as our Hegelian instance. Edmund is the extreme limit of evil, the first absolute representation of a nihilist that Western literature affords, and still the greatest. And out of Edmund, more even than out of Iago, will come the nihilists of Melville and Dostoevsky. As Hegel says, Edmund excels in both imagination and intellect; much more than Iago, he might be almost be a match for the greatest of counter-Machiavels, Hamlet. By virtue of his supreme intellect—endlessly fertile, rapid, cold, and accurate— Edmund projects an image of himself as bastard follower of the goddess Nature, and by means of that image he contemplates himself objectively as a work of art. So does Iago before him, but Iago imagines negative emotions and then feels, even suffers those emotions. Edmund is a freer artist of himself: *he feels nothing*.

I have observed already that the tragic hero, Lear, and the principal villain, Edmund, are never allowed a single moment in which they address each other. They share the stage in two crucial scenes, at the start and close to the end, but they have nothing to say to each other. Indeed they cannot exchange a word, for neither could engage the other for even a moment. Lear is all feeling, Edmund none. When Lear rages at his "unnatural" daughters, Edmund, for all his intelligence, cannot understand, since to Edmund his behavior toward Gloucester, and Goneril's and Regan's toward Lear, are "natural." Most natural of bastards, Edmund inevitably becomes the object of the murderously rapacious passions of Goneril and Regan, both of whom he gratifies, and neither of whom moves him at all until he beholds both of their corpses carried in upon stage just as he himself lies slowly dying from the death-wound given him by his brother Edgar.

Contemplating the dead monsters of the deep, Edmund confronts the true image of himself and is freed by it into becoming the absolute artist of his self: "I was contracted to them both; all three / Now marry in an instant." The tone is stunningly without affect, the irony almost unique, though Webster and other Jacobeans attempted to imitate it. Edmund's contemplation passes from irony into a tonality I can experience but only barely categorize: "Yet Edmund was belov'd! / The one the other poison'd for my sake / And after slew herself." He is speaking not so much to Albany and Edgar as out loud in order to be overheard by himself. Shakespeare's language conveys the painfulness of this most brilliant of villains spelling it out for himself, sharpening the image so as to enlarge the freedom of his own artistry of self. We do not hear pride or wonder, and yet there is a bemusement at the sense of connection, if only to these terrible sisters.

Hazlitt, with whom I share my startled affection for Edmund, emphasized Edmund's refreshing lack of all hypocrisy. Here too there is no shamming or posturing on Edmund's part. He over-hears himself, and the will to change is his response, which he realizes will be a positive moral alteration, though he insists that his own nature is not changing: "I pant for life. Some good I mean to do, / Despite of mine own nature." Shakespeare's tragic irony demands that this reversal be too late to save Cordelia. We are left asking: Why then does Shakespeare represent this extraordi-nary metamorphosis in Edmund? Whether this question is an-swerable or not, let us consider the change in itself, even though Edmund is carried out still convinced that Nature is his goddess.

What is it, what can it be, that a fictive character should be termed "a free artist of himself"? I do not find this phenomenon in Western literature before Shakespeare. Achilles, Aeneas, Dante the Pilgrim, Don Quixote do not change by overhearing what they themselves have said and on that basis, through their own intellect and imagination, turn themselves about. Our naïve but aestheti-cally crucial conviction that Edmund, Hamlet, Falstaff, and scores of others can, as it were, get up and walk on out of their plays, perhaps even against Shakespeare's own desires, is connected to their being free artists of themselves. As a theatrical and literary illusion, as an effect of figurative language, this Shakespearean power remains beyond comparison, though it has been imitated universally for almost four centuries now. The power would not be possible except for the Shakespearean soliloquy, forbidden to Racine by French critical doctrine, which could not allow the tragic actor to address either himself or the audience directly. The Span-ish Golden Age playwrights, Lope de Vega in particular, form the soliloquy as a sonnet, in a kind of baroque triumph that works against inwardness. Yet you cannot make a character into a free artist of himself or herself by denying that character inwardness. Shakespeare is not possible in the baroque mode, but then tragic freedom is a Shakespearean oxymoron rather than a condition in Lope or Racine or Goethe.

One sees why Cervantes failed as a writer for the theater and triumphed as the author of *Don Quixote*. There is a hermetic affinity between Cervantes and Shakespeare: the Don and Sancho are neither of them free artists of themselves; they enter fully into the order of play. It is the singular strength of Shakespeare that, heroes and villains alike, his tragic protagonists dissolve the demarcations between the orders of nature and of play. Hamlet's peculiar authority, his persuasive assumption of an authorial consciousness all his own, goes beyond his shaping of *The Murder of Gonzago* into *The Mousetrap*. At every moment Hamlet's mind is a play within the play, because it is Hamlet, more than anyone else in Shakespeare, who is the free artist of himself. His exaltation and his torment alike stem from his continuous meditation upon his own image. Shakespeare is at the center of the Canon at least in part because Hamlet is. The introspective consciousness, free to contemplate itself, remains the most elitist of all Western images, but without it the Canon is not possible, and, to put it most bluntly, neither are we.

Molière, born just six years after Shakespeare's death, wrote and acted in a France not yet exposed to Shakespeare's influence. Shakespeare's mixed fortunes in France begin to establish a pattern in about the middle of the eighteenth century, almost three generations after Molière's death. Yet Shakespeare and Molière have an authentic affinity, unlikely as Molière was even to have heard of Shakespeare. They are allied by temperament and by freedom from ideology, even though their formal traditions of comedy are somewhat at variance. Voltaire begins the French tradition of resistance to Shakespeare in the name of neoclassicism and the tragedies of Racine. The belated arrival of French Romanticism brought about a strong Shakespearean influence on French literature, which was particularly vital in Stendhal and Victor Hugo; but by the final third of the nineteenth century, most of the mania for Shakespeare had spent itself. Although he is now performed in France not much less often than Molière and Racine, essentially the Cartesian tradition has reasserted itself, and France retains a literary culture relatively un-Shakespearean.

It is difficult to overestimate the continued effect of Shakespeare on the Germans, even on Goethe, who was so wary of being influenced. Manzoni, the principal novelist of nineteenth-century

Italy, is very much a Shakespearean writer, as was Leopardi. And despite Tolstoy's furious polemics against Shakespeare, his own art depends on a Shakespearean sense of character, both in his two great novels and in the late masterpiece, the short novel *Hadji Murad*. Dostoevsky manifestly owes his grand nihilists to their Shakespearean precursors, Iago and Edmund, while Pushkin and Turgenev are among the crucial Shakespearean critics of the nineteenth century. Ibsen worked prodigiously to evade Shakespeare but could not succeed, fortunately for him. Perhaps all that Peer Gynt and Hedda Gabler have in common is their Shakespearean intensity, their inspired capacity to change by overhearing themselves.

Spain, until the modern age, had little need for Shakespeare. The major figures of the Spanish Golden Age—Cervantes, Lope de Vega, Calderón, Tirso de Molina, Rojas, Góngora—brought to Hispanic literature a baroque exuberance that was already somehow Shakespearean and Romantic. Ortega's famous essay on Shylock and Madariaga's book on *Hamlet* are the initial texts that matter; both reach the conclusion that the era of Shakespeare is also the era of Spain. Unfortunately, we have lost the play *Cardenio,* in which Shakespeare and Fletcher worked together to translate a story by Cervantes for an English audience; but many critics have felt the affinities between Cervantes and Shakespeare, and one of my permanent longings is for the new dramatist of genius who could bring the Don, Sancho, and Falstaff onto the same stage.

The influence of Shakespeare on our Chaotic Age remains persuasive, particularly on Joyce and Beckett. Both *Ulysses* and *Endgame* are essentially Shakespearean representations, each evoking *Hamlet* with a difference. In the American Renaissance, Shakespeare was most overtly present in *Moby-Dick* and in Emerson's *Representative Men,* but worked more subtly upon Hawthorne. There is no confining Shakespeare's influence, but it is not the influence that causes the Western Canon to be centered on him. If Cervantes can be said to have invented the literary irony of ambiguity that triumphs again in Kafka, Shakespeare can as truly be seen as having invented the emotive and cognitive irony of ambivalence that governs Freud. It shocks me increasingly to observe the vanishing of Freud's originalities in the presence of Shakespeare, but it would not have shocked Shakespeare, who understood that literature and plagiarism were scarcely to be distinguished. Plagiarism is a legal distinction, not a literary one, just as the sacred and the secular form a political and religious distinction and are not literary categories at all.

Universality is the authentic aspect of only a handful of Western writers: Shakespeare, Dante, Cervantes, perhaps Tolstoy. Goethe and Milton have dimmed, because of cultural change; Whitman, so popular on the surface, is hermetic at the core; Molière and Ibsen still share the stage, but always after Shakespeare. Dickinson is astonishingly difficult because of her cognitive originality, and Neruda is less of a Brechtian and Shakespearean populist than he may have intended himself to be. The aristocratic universalism of Dante ushered in the era of the greatest Western writers, from Petrarch through Hölderlin; but only Cervantes and Shakespeare fully achieved universality, populist authors in the greatest of aristocratic eras. The nearest approach to universality in the Democratic Age is the flawed miracle of Tolstoy, at once aristocrat and populist. In our chaotic time, Joyce and Beckett come closest, but the baroque elaborations of the first and the baroque undoings of the second both work to impede universality. Proust and Kafka have the strangeness of Dante in their sensibilities. I find myself agreeing with Antonio García-Berrio when he makes universality the fundamental property of poetic value. Centering the Canon for other poets has been the unique role of Dante. Shakespeare, with *Don Quixote,* continues to center the Canon for more general readers. Perhaps we can go farther; for Shakespeare we need a more Borgesian term than universality. At once no one and everyone, nothing and everything, Shakespeare is the Western Canon.

3.

The Strangeness of Dante:
Ulysses and Beatrice

THE NEW HISTORICISTS and allied resenters have been attempting to reduce and scatter Shakespeare, aiming to undo the Canon by dissolving its center. Curiously, Dante, the second center as it were, is not under similar onslaught, either here or in Italy. Doubtless the assault will come, since the assorted multiculturalists would have difficulty finding a more objectionable great poet than Dante, whose savage and powerful spirit is politically incorrect to the highest degree. Dante is the most aggressive and polemical of the major Western writers, dwarfing even Milton in this regard. Like Milton, he was a political party and a sect of one. His heretical intensity has been masked by scholarly commentary, which even at its best frequently treats him as though his *Divine Comedy* was essentially versified Saint Augustine. But it is best to begin by marking his extraordinary audacity, which is unmatched in the entire tradition of supposedly Christian literature, including even Milton.

Nothing else in Western literature, in the long span from the

Yahwist and Homer through Joyce and Beckett, is as sublimely outrageous as Dante's exaltation of Beatrice, sublimated from being an image of desire to angelic status, in which role she becomes a crucial element in the church's hierarchy of salvation. Because Beatrice initially matters solely as an instrument of Dante's will, her apotheosis necessarily involves Dante's own election as well. His poem is a prophecy and takes on the function of a third Testament in no way subservient to the Old and the New. Dante will not acknowledge that the *Comedy* must be a fiction, *his* supreme fiction. Rather, the poem is the truth, universal and not temporal. What Dante the pilgrim sees and says in the narrative of Dante the poet is intended to persuade us perpetually of Dante's poetic and religious inescapability. The poem's gestures of humility, on the part of pilgrim or of poet, impress Dante scholars but are rather less persuasive than the poem's subversion of all other poets and its persistence in bringing forward Dante's own apocalyptic potential.

These observations, I hasten to explain, are directed against much Dante scholarship and not at all against Dante. I do not see how we can disengage Dante's overwhelming poetic power from his spiritual ambitions, which are inevitably idiosyncratic and saved from being blasphemous only because Dante won his wager with the future within a generation after his death. If the *Comedy* were not Shakespeare's only authentic poetic rival, Beatrice would be an offense to the church and even to literary Catholics. The poem is too strong to disown; for a neo-Christian poet like T. S. Eliot, the *Comedy* becomes another Scripture, a Newer Testament that supplements the canonical Christian Bible. Charles Williams—a guru for such neo-Christians as Eliot, C. S. Lewis, W. H. Auden, Dorothy L. Sayers, J. R. R. Tolkien, and others—went so far as to affirm that the Athanasian creed, "the taking of the Manhood into God," did not receive full expression until Dante. The Church had to wait for Dante, and for the figure of Beatrice.

What Williams highlights throughout his intense study, *The Figure of Beatrice* (1943), is the great scandal of Dante's achievement: the poet's most spectacular invention is Beatrice. No single personage in Shakespeare, not even the charismatic Hamlet or the godlike Lear, matches Beatrice as an exuberantly daring invention. Only the J writer's Yahweh and the Gospel of Mark's Jesus are more surprising or exalted representations. Beatrice is the signature of Dante's originality, and her triumphant placement well within the Christian machinery of salvation is her poet's most audacious act of transforming his inherited faith into something much more his own.

Dante scholars inevitably repudiate such assertions on my part, but they live so under the shadow of their subject that they tend to lose full awareness of the *Divine Comedy*'s strangeness. It remains the uncanniest of all literary works for the ambitious reader to encounter, and it survives both translation and its own vast learning. Everything that allows a common reader to read the *Comedy* ensues from qualities in Dante's spirit that are anything but what is generally considered pious. Ultimately Dante has nothing truly positive to say about any of his poetic precursors or contemporaries and remarkably little pragmatic use for the Bible, except for Psalms. It is as though he felt King David, ancestor of Christ, was the only forerunner worthy of him, the only other poet consistently able to express the truth.

The reader who comes freshly to Dante will see very quickly that no other secular author is so absolutely convinced that his own work is the truth, all of the truth that matters most. Milton and perhaps the later Tolstoy approximate Dante's fierce conviction of rightness, but they both reflect contending realities as well and show more of the strain of isolated vision. Dante is so strong—rhetorically, psychologically, spiritually—that he dwarfs their self-confidence. Theology is not his ruler but his resource, one resource among many. No one can deny that Dante is a supernaturalist, a Christian, and a theologian, or at least a theological allegorist. But all received concepts and images undergo extraordinary transformations in Dante, the only poet whose originality, inventiveness, and preternatural fecundity actually rival Shakespeare's. A reader working through Dante for the first time, in a terza rima translation as accomplished as Laurence Binyon's or in John Sinclair's lucid prose version, loses an immensity in not reading the Italian poem, and yet an entire cosmos remains. But it is the strangeness as well as the sublimity of what remains that matters most, the utter uniqueness of Dante's powers, with the single exception of Shakespeare's. As in Shakespeare, we find in Dante a surpassing cognitive strength combined with an inventiveness that has no merely pragmatic limits.

When you read Dante or Shakespeare, you experience the limits of art, and then you discover that the limits are extended or broken. Dante breaks through all limitations far more personally and overtly than Shakespeare does, and if he is more of a supernaturalist than Shakespeare, his transcending of nature remains as much his own as Shakespeare's unique and idiosyncratic naturalism. Where the two poets challenge each other most is in their representations of love—which returns us to where love begins and ends in Dante, the figure of Beatrice.

The Beatrice of the *Comedy* occupies a position in the heavenly hierarchy that is difficult to apprehend. We have no guidelines for understanding it; there is nothing in doctrine that calls for the exaltation of this particular Florentine woman with whom Dante fell eternally in love. The most ironic commentary on that falling is by Jorge Luis Borges in "The Meeting in a Dream" (*Other Inquisitions, 1937–1952*):

> To fall in love is to create a religion that has a fallible god. That Dante professed an idolatrous admiration for Beatrice is a truth that does not bear contradicting; that she once ridiculed him and another time rebuffed him are facts rendered by the *Vita nuova*. Some maintain that those facts are symbolic of others. If that were true, it would strengthen even more our certainty of an unhappy and superstitious love.
>
> *(translated by Ruth L. C. Simms)*

Borges at least restores Beatrice to her origin as an "illusory encounter" and to her enigmatic otherness for all readers of Dante: "Infinitely Beatrice existed for Dante; Dante existed very little, perhaps not at all, for Beatrice. Our piety, our veneration cause us to forget that pitiful inharmony, which was unforgettable for Dante."

It scarcely matters that Borges is projecting his own ironically absurd passion for Beatrice Viterbo (see his Kabbalistic story, "The

Aleph"). What he slyly emphasizes is the scandalous disproportion between whatever it was that Dante and Beatrice experienced together (next to nothing) and Dante's vision of their mutual apotheosis in the *Paradiso*. Disproportion is Dante's royal road to the sublime. Like Shakespeare, he can get away with anything, because both poets transcend other poets' limits. The pervasive irony (or allegory) of Dante's work is that he professes to accept limits even as he violates them. Everything that is vital and original in Dante is arbitrary and personal, yet it is presented as the truth, consonant with tradition, faith, and rationality. Almost inevitably, it is misread until it blends with the normative, and at last we are confronted by a success Dante could not have welcomed. The theological Dante of modern American scholarship is a blend of Augustine, Thomas Aquinas, and their companions. This is a doctrinal Dante, so abstrusely learned and so amazingly pious that he can be fully apprehended only by his American professors.

Dante's progeny among the writers are his true canonizers, and they are not always an overtly devout medley: Petrarch, Boccaccio, Chaucer, Shelley, Rossetti, Yeats, Joyce, Pound, Eliot, Borges, Stevens, Beckett. About all that dozen possesses in common *is* Dante, though he becomes twelve different Dantes in his poetic afterlife. This is wholly appropriate for a writer of his strength; there are nearly as many Dantes as there are Shakespeares. My own Dante deviates increasingly from what has become the eminently orthodox Dante of modern American criticism and scholarship, as represented by T. S. Eliot, Francis Fergusson, Erich Auerbach, Charles Singleton, and John Freccero. An alternate tradition is provided by the Italian line that commenced with the Neapolitan speculator Vico and proceeded through the Romantic poet Foscolo and the Romantic critic Francesco de Sanctis, culminating in the early-twentieth-century aesthetician Benedetto Croce. If one combines this Italian tradition with some observations by Ernst Robert Curtius, the distinguished modern German literary historian, an alternative to the Eliot-Singleton-Freccero Dante emerges, a prophetic poet rather than a theological allegorist.

Vico rather splendidly overstated his case when he averred of Dante that "had he been ignorant of Latin and scholastic philosophy, he would have been even greater as a poet, and perhaps the Tuscan tongue would have served to make Homer's equal." Nevertheless, Vico's judgment is refreshing when one wanders in the dark wood of the theological allegorists, where the salient characteristic of the *Comedy* becomes Dante's supposedly Augustinian conversion from poetry to belief, a belief that subsumes and subordinates the imagination. Neither Augustine nor Aquinas saw poetry as anything except childish play, to be set aside with other childish things. What would they have made of the *Comedy*'s Beatrice? Curtius shrewdly observes that Dante presents her not merely as his means of salvation but as a universal agency available to everyone of gentle heart. Dante's conversion is to Beatrice, not to Augustine, and Beatrice sends Virgil to Dante to be his guide, rather than sending Augustine.

Clearly Dante prefers Beatrice, or his own creation, to the allegory of other theologians, and just as clearly Dante does not desire to transcend his own poetry. Augustine and Aquinas have the same relation to Dante's theology that Virgil and Cavalcanti have to Dante's poetry: all forerunners are dwarfed by the poet-theologian, the prophet Dante, who is the author of the final testament, the *Comedy*. If you want to read the *Comedy* as an allegory of the theologians, start with the only theologian who truly mattered to Dante: Dante himself. The *Comedy*, like all of the greatest canonical works, destroys the distinction between sacred and secular writing. And Beatrice is now, for us, the allegory of the fusion of sacred and secular, the union of prophecy and poem.

Dante's outstanding characteristics as poet and as person are pride rather than humility, originality rather than traditionalism, exuberance or gusto rather than restraint. His prophetic stance is one of initiation rather than conversion, to adopt a suggestion of Paolo Valesio, who emphasizes the hermetic or esoteric aspects of the *Comedy*. You are not converted by or to Beatrice; the journey to her is an initiation because she is, as Curtius first said, the center of a private gnosis and not of the church universal. After all, Beatrice is sent to Dante by Lucia, a remarkably obscure Sicilian saint, so obscure that Dante scholars are unable to say why Dante chose her. John Freccero, the best living Dante critic, tells us that "In a sense, the purpose of the entire journey is to write the poem, to attain the vantage-point of Lucy, and of all the blessed."

Yes, but why Lucy? To which the answer certainly cannot be: Why not? Lucy of Syracuse lived and was martyred a thousand years before Dante and would now be totally forgotten if she had not had an esoteric importance for the poet and for his poem. But we know nothing about that importance; we do not even know who the greater female soul who sent Lucy to Beatrice was. This "lady in heaven" is usually identified as the Virgin Mary, but Dante does not name her. Lucy is called "the enemy of all cruelty," presumably an attribute shared by all the ladies of heaven. "Illuminating Grace" is the usual abstraction stuck onto Dante's Lucy by the commentators; but that, too, would hardly seem to be a unique quality of a particular Sicilian martyr whose name means "light." I labor this point to underline how sublimely arbitrary Dante insists on being. There is hidden matter in the *Comedy;* the poem undeniably has its hermetic aspects, and they can hardly be judged of secondary importance since Beatrice centers them. We always come back to the figure of Beatrice in reading the *Comedy,* not so much because she is somehow a type of Christ, but because she is the ideal object of Dante's sublimated desire. We do not even know whether Dante's Beatrice had a historical existence. If she did and can be identified with the daughter of a Florentine banker, it scarcely matters in the poem. The *Comedy*'s Beatrice matters not because she is an intimation of Christ, but because she is Dante's idealized projection of his own singularity, the point of view of his work as an author.

Let me be blasphemous enough to mingle Cervantes with Dante, so as to compare their two heroic protagonists: Don Quixote and Dante the Pilgrim. Don Quixote's Beatrice is the enchanted Dulcinea del Tobosa, his visionary transfiguration of the farm girl, Aldonza Lorenzo. The banker's daughter, Beatrice Portinari, has the same relation to Dante's Beatrice that Aldonza has to Dulcinea. True, Don Quixote's hierarchy is secular: Dulcinea takes her place in the cosmos of Amadis of Gaul, Palmerin of England, the Knight of the Sun, and similar worthies of a mythological chivalry, while Beatrice ascends into the realm of Saint Bernard, Saint Francis, and Saint Dominic. If one has a preference for poetry over doctrine, this is not necessarily a difference. Knights-errant, like saints, are metaphors for and in a poem, and the heavenly Beatrice, in terms of institutional and historical Catholicism, has no more or less status or reality than the enchanted Dulcinea. But Dante's triumph is to make my comparison seem somehow a blasphemy.

Perhaps Dante really was both pious and orthodox, but Beatrice is his figure and not the church's; she is part of a private gnosis, a poet's alteration of the scheme of salvation. A "conversion" to Beatrice can be Augustinian enough, but it is hardly a conversion to Saint Augustine, any more than a devotion to Dulcinea del Tobosa is an act of worship directed toward Iseult of the White Hands. Dante was brazen, aggressive, prideful, and audacious beyond all poets, before or since. He imposed his vision on Eternity, and he has very little in common with the flock of his piously learned exegetes. If it is all in Augustine or in Thomas Aquinas, then let us read Augustine or Aquinas. But Dante wanted us to read Dante. He did not compose his poem to illuminate inherited truths. The *Comedy* purports to be the truth, and I would think that detheologizing Dante would be as irrelevant as theologizing him.

When the dying Don Quixote repents his heroic madness, he falls back into his original identity of Alonso Quixano the Good, and he thanks God's mercy for his conversion to pious sanity. Every reader joins Sancho Panza in protesting, "Don't die! . . . Take my advice and live many years. . . . Perhaps we shall find the lady Dulcinea behind some hedge, disenchanted and as pretty as a picture." When Dante's poem ends, there is no Sancho to join the reader in hoping that the poet's power not fail the high fantasy of the Christian heaven. I suppose there are readers who go to the *Divine Comedy* as a conduit to the divine love that moves the sun and the other stars, but most of us go to it for Dante himself, for a poetic personality and dramatic character that not even John Milton can quite equal. No one wants to transmute the *Comedy* into *Don Quixote,* but a touch of Sancho might have softened even the Pilgrim of Eternity and perhaps reminded his scholars that a fiction is a fiction, even if it itself believes otherwise.

But what kind of a fiction is Beatrice? If she is, as Curtius insisted, an emanation from God, then Dante was up to something we cannot decipher, even though we sense that it is there. Dante's revelation can hardly be termed private, like William Blake's, but not because it is less original than Blake's. It is more original, and is public because it is so successful; nothing else in Western literature, except for Shakespeare upon his heights, is nearly so fully articulated. Dante, the most singular and savage of all superbly refined temperaments, made himself universal not by his absorption of tradition, but by bending tradition until it fitted his own nature. By an irony that transcends anything I know akin to it, Dante's strength of usurpation has resulted in his being weakly misread in one mode or another. If the *Comedy* is a truthful prophecy, then its scholars are tempted to read it by the illumination of Augustinian tradition. Where else shall the proper interpretation of Christian revelation be found? Even so subtle an interpreter as John Freccero sometimes falls into the conversion of poetics, as if only Augustine could present a paradigm for self-mastering. A "novel of the self" like the Comedy must thus take its origin from Augustine's *Confessions*. Far more powerful than the Romantics who worshiped and imitated him, Dante invents his own origin and masters his self with his own conversionary figure, Beatrice, who does not seem to me a very Augustinian personage. Can Beatrice be the object of desire, however sublimated, in an Augustinian conversion narrative? Freccero eloquently says that, for Augustine, history is God's poem. Is the history of Beatrice a lyric by God? Since I myself am partial to finding the voice of God in Shakespeare or Emerson or Freud, depending upon my needs, I have no difficulty in finding Dante's *Comedy* to be divine. I would not speak of the divine *Confessions*, however, and I do not hear the voice of God in Augustine. Nor am I persuaded that Dante ever heard God in any voice but his own. A poem that prefers itself to the Bible can, by definition, be said also to prefer itself to Augustine.

BEATRICE IS Dante's *knowing*, according to Charles Williams, who had no sympathy for Gnosticism. By knowing he meant the way from Dante the knower to God the known. Yet Dante did not intend Beatrice to be his knowing alone. His poem argues not that each of us is to find a solitary knowing, but that Beatrice is to play a universal role for all who can find her, since presumably her intervention for Dante, via Virgil, is to be unique. The myth of Beatrice, though it is Dante's central invention, exists only within his poetry. Its strangeness cannot truly be seen, because we know of no figure comparable to Beatrice. Milton's Urania, his heavenly muse in *Paradise Lost,* is not a person, and Milton qualifies her with the warning remark that it is the meaning, not the name he calls. Shelley, imitating Dante, celebrated Emilia Viviani in his *Epipsychidion*, but High Romantic passion did not prevail, and Signora Viviani eventually became "a little brown demon" for her disillusioned lover.

To recover something of Dante's strangeness we need to see his treatment of a universal figure. No Western literary character is so incessant as Odysseus, the Homeric hero better known by his Latin name of Ulysses. From Homer to Nikos Kazantzakis, the figure of Odysseus/Ulysses undergoes extraordinary modifications in Pindar, Sophocles, Euripides, Horace, Virgil, Ovid, Seneca, Dante, Chapman, Calderón, Shakespeare, Goethe, Tennyson, Joyce, Pound, and Wallace Stevens, among many others. W. B. Stanford in his fine study *The Ulysses Theme* (1963) sets the muted but negative treatment by Virgil against Ovid's positive identification with Ulysses, in a contrast that establishes two of the major stances that will probably always contend in the metamorphoses of this hero, or hero-villain. Virgil's Ulysses will become Dante's, but so transmuted as to make Virgil's rather evasive portrait tend to fade away. Unwilling to condemn Ulysses directly, Virgil transfers that work to his characters, who identify the hero of the *Odyssey* with guile and deceit. Ovid, an exile and an amorist, mingles himself with Ulysses in a composite identity, so bequeathing to us the now-permanent idea of Ulysses as the first of the great wandering womanizers.

In canto 26 of the *Inferno,* Dante created the most original version of Ulysses that we have, one who does not seek home and wife in Ithaca but departs from Circe in order to break all bounds and risk the unknown. Hamlet's undiscovered country from whose bourn no traveler returns becomes the pragmatic destination of this most impressive of all doom-eager heroes. There is an extraordinary passage in *Inferno* 26 that is difficult to absorb. Ulysses and Dante are in a dialectical relationship because Dante fears the deep identity between himself as poet (not as pilgrim) and Ulysses as transgressive voyager. This fear may not be fully conscious, yet Dante must on some level experience it, because he portrays Ulysses as being moved by pride, and no more prideful poet than Dante has ever existed, not even Pindar or Milton or Victor Hugo or Stefan George or Yeats. Scholars want to hear Beatrice or assorted saints speak for Dante, but she and they do not share his accent. The voice of Ulysses and that of Dante are dangerously close, which may be why Virgil's explanation hardly suffices when he says that the Greek may disdain the voice of the Italian poet. Nor does Dante allow himself any reaction whatsoever to the magnificent speech that he writes for Ulysses, as a voice speaking out of the flame (I use here and throughout John D. Sinclair's 1961 prose translation):

> When I parted from Circe, who held me more than a year near Gaeta before Aeneas so named it, not fondness for a son, nor duty to an aged father, nor the love I owed Penelope which should have gladdened her, could conquer within me the ardor I had to gain experience of the world and of the vices and the worth of men; and I put forth on the open deep with but one ship and with that little company which had not deserted me. The one shore and the other I saw as far as Spain, as far as Morocco, and Sardinia and the other islands which that sea bathes round. I and my companions were old and slow when we came to the narrow outlet where Hercules set up his landmarks so that men should not pass beyond. On my right hand I left Seville, on the other had already left Ceuta. "O brothers," I said, "who through a hundred thousand perils have reached the west, to this so brief vigil of the senses that remains to us choose not to deny experience, in the sun's track, of the unpeopled world. Take thought of the seed from which you spring. You were not born to live as brutes, but to follow virtue and knowledge." My companions I made so eager for the road with

these brief words that I could hardly have held them back, and with our poop turned to the morning we made of the oars wings for the mad flight, always gaining on the left. Night then saw all the stars of the other pole and ours so low that it did not rise from the ocean floor. Five times the light had been rekindled and as often quenched on the moon's under-side since we had entered on the deep passage, when there appeared to us a mountain, dim by distance, and it seemed to me of such a height as I had never seen before. We were filled with gladness, and soon it turned to lamentation, for from the new land a storm rose and struck the forepart of the ship. Three times it whirled her round with all the waters, the fourth time lifted the poop aloft and plunged the prow below, as One willed, until the sea closed again over us.

Even as English prose rather than as preternaturally strong Italian terza rima, does this extraordinary speech provoke in the common reader anything like the following reflection, written by the most gifted of Dante's critics? "What separates Ulysses' definitive death by water from Dante's baptism unto death and subsequent resurrection is the Christ event in history, or grace, the Christ event in the individual soul."

Surely an infinitely less powerful passage could prompt exactly that reflection with equal justice. There is a disproportion between a doctrine or a piety that voids every difference except assent, and a poetic text almost beyond rival. Something is plainly wrong with a way of reading Dante that yields all authority to Christian doctrine, even if Dante himself is partly responsible for such reductiveness. In Dante's arrangement of Hell, we are at the eighth level down of the eighth circle down, which is not too far away from Satan. Ulysses is a fraudulent counselor, primarily because of his craft and cunning in bringing down Troy, ancestor of Rome and so of Italy, as Virgil in particular recorded. Dante does not speak to Ulysses because in one sense he is Ulysses; to write the *Comedy* you set your course for an uncharted sea. And with great clarity Dante tells us what he will not have Ulysses recount: the death of Achilles, the Trojan horse, the theft of the Palladium, all of which are occasions for the wanderer's damnation.

The last voyage is not in that category, whatever its outcome. Himself inflamed, Dante bends toward the flame of Ulysses with desire, the longing for knowledge. The knowledge he receives is that of pure quest, made at the expense of son, wife, and father. The quest is, amid much else, a figuration for Dante's own pride and obduracy in prolonging his exile from Florence by refusing terms that would have returned him to his family. Eating another man's salt bread, going down stairs not your own, is one price paid for questing. Ulysses is willing to pay a more ultimate price. Whose experience is truly closer to Dante's—the triumphant conversion of Augustine or the last voyage of Ulysses? Legend tells us that Dante was pointed out in the streets as the man who had somehow returned from a voyage to Hell, as though he were a kind of shaman. We can assume that he believed in the reality of his visions; a poet of such force who judged himself to be a true prophet would not have regarded his descent into Hell as mere metaphor. His Ulysses speaks with absolute dignity and terrible poignancy: not the pathos of damnation, but the pride that knows how pride and courage do not suffice.

Virgil's Aeneas is something of a prig, and that is what many of his scholars turn Dante into, or would if they could. But he is no Aeneas; he is as savage, self-centered, and impatient as his Ulysses, and like his Ulysses he burns with the desire to be elsewhere, to be different. His distance from his double is greatest, presumably, when he has Ulysses speak so movingly of "this so brief vigil of the senses that remains to us." Even there we should remember that Dante, who died at fifty-six, wished to live another quarter-century, for in his *Convivio* he set the perfect age at eighty-one. Only then would he have been complete, and his prophecy perhaps fulfilled. Granted that Ulysses sets sail for the "unpeopled world," while Dante's cosmic voyages are to lands crowded with the dead, there is a distinction between these two questers, and Ulysses is certainly the more extreme. At the least, Dante's quester is a hero-villain, akin to Melville's Ahab, another ungodly, godlike man. A Gnostic or Neoplatonic hero is very different from a Christian hero, but Dante's imagination is not always moved by Christian heroism, unless he is celebrating his own crusader ancestor, Cassiaguida, who more than reciprocates with overwhelming praise of his descendant's courage and audacity. That is the undersong of Dante's vision of Ulysses: admiration, fellow-feeling, familial pride. A kindred spirit is saluted, even though he resides in the Eighth Circle of Hell. It is Ulysses who makes the judgment that his final voyage was a "mad flight," presumably in contrast to Dante's Virgil-guided flight.

Viewed strictly as a poem, no flight could be madder than that of the *Comedy,* which Dante does not wish us to view as a poem only. That is Dante's privilege, but not the privilege of his scholars, and it ought not to be the stance of his readers. If we are to see what makes Dante canonical, the very center of the Canon after Shakespeare, then we need to recover his achieved strangeness, his perpetual originality. That quality has very little to do with the Augustinian story of how the old self dies and the new self is born. Ulysses may be the old self and Beatrice the new, but Dante's Ulysses is his own, and so is Beatrice. What Augustine had done, Dante could not do better, and Dante saw to it that the *Comedy* became no more Augustinian than it was Virgilian. It is what he desired it to be: Dantean only.

JESUS BEN SIRA, author of the wonderful Ecclesiasticus, which is consigned forever to the noncanonical Apocrypha, says that he comes as a gleaner in the wake of famous men, our fathers who begot us. Perhaps that is why he is the first Hebrew writer to insist upon his own proper name as author of his book. One cannot say too often that Dante did not come as a gleaner in order to praise the famous men before him. He distributes them, according to his own judgment, in Limbo, Hell, Purgatory, and Heaven, because he is the true prophet and expects to be vindicated in his own time. His judgments are absolute, ruthless, and sometimes morally unacceptable, at least to many now among us. He has given himself the last word, and while you are reading him, you don't want to argue with him, mostly because you want to listen and to visualize what he has seen for you. He cannot have been an easy person with whom to quarrel while he lived, and he has proved fierce ever since.

Though dead, white, male, and European, he is the most alive of all the personalities on the page, contrasting in this with his only superior, Shakespeare, whose personality always evades us, even in the sonnets. Shakespeare is everyone and no one; Dante is Dante. Presence in language is no illusion, all Parisian dogmas to the contrary. Dante has stamped himself upon every line in the *Comedy*. His major character is Dante the Pilgrim, and after that Beatrice, no longer the girl of the *New Life,* but a crucial figure in the celestial hierarchy. What is missing in Dante is the ascension of Beatrice; one can wonder why, in his daring, he did not also illuminate the mystery of her election. Perhaps it was because all of the precedents he had were not only heretical, but belonged to the heresy of heresies, Gnosticism. From Simon Magus onward, heresiarchs had elevated their closest female followers to the heavenly hierarchies, even as the outrageous Simon, first of the Fausts, had taken Helena, a whore of Tyre, and proclaimed her to have been Helen of Troy in one of her previous incarnations. Dante, whose Eros had been sublimated and yet remained permanent, risked no comparisons.

Still, in a poetic rather than a theological sense, Dante's myth of Beatrice is closer to Gnosticism than to Christian orthodoxy. All evidence for what might be called the apotheosis of Beatrice is not merely personal (as it has to be) but comes out of a visionary world akin to the Gnosticism of the second century. Beatrice must be an uncreated spark of the divine or emanation of Godhood, as well as a Florentine girl who died at the age of twenty-five. She does not undergo the religious categories of judgment that lead to blessedness and sainthood but seems to go directly from death to being part of the hierarchy of salvation. There is no indication, either in the *New Life* or the *Comedy,* that Beatrice was subject to sin, or even to error. Instead she was, from the start, what her name indicated: "she who confers blessing." Dante says of her that, at nine, she was "the youngest of the Angels," a daughter of God, and after she dies her poet speaks "of that blessed Beatrice who now gazes continually on His countenance, who is blessed throughout the ages."

We cannot regard Dante as indulging himself in erotic hyperbole; the *Comedy* is inconceivable without a Beatrice whose joyous acceptance in the highest regions was always assured. Petrarch, seeking to distance himself from the more than formidable poet of his father's generation, invented (as he thought) poetic idolatry in regard to his beloved Laura, but what, beyond Dante's own, scandalous authority, restrains us from seeing Dante's worship of Beatrice as the most poetic of all idolatries? By his authority, Dante integrates Beatrice into Christian typology, or perhaps it would be more accurate to say that he integrates Christian typology into his vision of Beatrice. Beatrice, not Christ, is the poem; Dante, not Augustine, is the maker. This is not to deny Dante's spirituality but only to indicate that originality is not in itself a Christian virtue, and that Dante matters because of his originality. As much as any other poet except Shakespeare, Dante has no poetic father, even though he asserts that Virgil occupies such a place. But Virgil is summoned by Beatrice and vanishes from the poem when Beatrice triumphantly returns to it, in the concluding cantos of the *Purgatorio.*

That return, extraordinary in itself, is preceded by another of Dante's grand inventions, Matilda, who is seen gathering flowers in a restored earthly paradise. The vision of Matilda was crucial for Shelley's poetry, and it is appropriate that this passage of Dante was translated by Shelley, in what may be the best version of any part of the *Comedy* in English. Here is the climax of the passage as rendered by Shelley, who went on to compose a diabolic parody of the vision in his very Dantesque death poem, *The Triumph of Life:*

> *I moved not with my feet, but mid the glooms*
> *Pierced with my charmèd eye, contemplating*
> *The mighty multitude of fresh May blossoms*
>
> *Which starred that night, when, even as a thing*
> *That suddenly, for blank astonishment,*
> *Charms every sense, and makes all thought take wing,—*
>
> *A solitary woman! and she went*
> *Singing and gathering flower after flower,*
> *With which her way was painted and besprent.*

"Bright lady, who, if looks had ever power
To bear true witness of the heart within,
Dost bask under the beams of love, come lower

Towards this bank. I prithee let me win
This much of thee, to come, that I may hear
Thy song: like Proserpine, in Enna's glen,

Thou seemest to my fancy, singing here
And gathering flowers, as that fair maiden when,
She lost the Spring, and Ceres her, more dear."

In the previous canto, Dante had dreamed of "a lady young and beautiful going through a meadow gathering flowers and singing," but she identified herself as Leah, the Biblical Jacob's first wife, and contrasted herself to her younger sister, Rachel, who became the Patriarch of Israel's second wife. Leah foretells Matilda, and Rachel is the forerunner of Beatrice, but it is a little difficult to see them as a contrast between the active and the contemplative life:

Know, whoever asks my name, that I am Leah, and I go plying my fair hands here and there to make me a garland; to please me at the glass I here adorn myself, but my sister Rachel never leaves her mirror and sits all day. She is fain to see her own fair eyes as I to adorn me with my hands. She with seeing, and I with doing am satisfied.

Has time destroyed these metaphors? Have they yielded to feminism's critique? Or is it that, in a post-Freudian era, we recoil from the exaltation of narcissism? Certainly the commentary of the usually acute Charles Williams seems a touch embarrassing at our current moment: "Dante, for the last time, dreams: of Leah gathering flowers—what else is all action? and of Rachel looking in her glass—what else is all contemplation? for now the soul may justly take joy in herself and in love and beauty."

The vision of Leah or Matilda gathering flowers as an emblem of doing or action unfortunately calls to my mind a James Thurber cartoon in which two women observe a third picking flowers, and one says to the other, "She has the true Emily Dickinson spirit except that she gets fed up occasionally." The image of Rachel or Beatrice contemplating herself in the mirror tends to summon up Freud's unfortunate moment when he compared the narcissism of women to that of cats. My associations are doubtless arbitrary, but typology, with whatever learned explanations, does not always serve Dante well. That he intended the *Comedy* to be a poem "about" his conversion, "about" his becoming a Christian, I greatly doubt. If he did, it could only be in the etymological meaning of the English "about," which is: to be on the outside of something. On its inside, the *Comedy* is about Dante's being called to the work of prophecy.

You can become a Christian without accepting the mantle of Elijah, but not if you are Dante. The vision of Matilda replacing Proserpina in a restored earthly paradise does not come to the newly converted Christian, but to the prophet-poet whose vocation has been confirmed. Shelley, no Christian but a Lucretian poet-prophet, was transformed by the Matilda passage because it illuminated, for him, the passion of the poetic vocation, the restoration of the paradisal nature that had abandoned his great precursor, Wordsworth. Matilda is Beatrice's forerunner because Proserpina revivified makes possible the return of the Muse. And Beatrice is not an imitation of the Christ, but Dante's creativity lancing out to identify itself with an old love, whether real or largely imaginary.

The idealization of lost love is an almost universal human praxis; what is remembered across the years is a lost possibility for the self, rather than of the other. The association of Rachel and Beatrice works so beautifully not because each is a type of the contemplative life, but because each is a passionate image of lost love. Rachel matters to the Church because of its interpretation of her as contemplative emblem, but she matters to poets and their readers because a great narrator, the Yahwist or J writer, made her early death in childbirth the great sorrow of Jacob's life. In poetic typology, Rachel precedes Beatrice as the image of the early death of a beloved woman, while Leah is linked to Matilda as a vision of deferred fulfillment. Jacob served Laban in order to win Rachel and first received Leah instead. Dante longs for the return of Beatrice, but the journey to Beatrice through Purgatory takes him first to Matilda. Although it is the hour of the morning star, of the planet Venus, it brings Matilda, not Beatrice, to Dante. Matilda sings like a woman in love, and Dante walks with her, but it is only a preparation, even as Leah was a preparation for Rachel.

What bursts upon the poet is a triumphal procession rather shockingly centered upon the prophet Ezekiel's vision of "the wheels and their work," the Chariot and the Enthroned Man. Dante evades the shock by telling his readers to go to the text of Ezekiel for the more outrageous details, even as he follows the Revelation of Saint John the Divine in reading Ezekiel's Man as Christ. For Dante, the Chariot is the triumph of the Church, not as it was, but as it should be; and he surrounds this idealized militancy with the books of the two Testaments, again not to rely on them but to get them out of his way. All of this, even that Griffon symbolizing Christ, matters only because of the beauty that it heralds, the return of one's ancient love, no longer forever and irretrievably lost.

The actual advent of Beatrice in canto 20 of the *Purgatorio* involves the permanent vanishing of Virgil. She makes Virgil redundant, not because theology is replacing poetry, but because Dante's *Comedy* now wholly replaces Virgil's *Aeneid*. Although he explicitly insists otherwise, Dante (now named, by Beatrice herself, for the first and only time in his poem) celebrates his own powers as poet by enthroning Beatrice. Pragmatically, what else could he be doing? Even Charles Singleton, the most theological of major Dante exegetes, emphasizes that Beatrice's beauty "is said to surpass any created by nature or by art." If you are intent upon assimilating Dante to the allegory of the theologians (as Singleton invariably was), then only God, through the Church, could create and sustain a splendor beyond nature and art. But Beatrice, as we need to keep reminding ourselves, is altogether Dante's creation, in precisely the sense in which Dulcinea was Don Quixote's. If Beatrice is more beautiful than any other woman in literature or in history, Dante is celebrating his own power of representation.

The *Purgatorio,* in Dante's overt scheme, explores the Catholic argument that desire for God, having been displaced into wrong channels, must be restored through expiation. Dante's boldest assertion throughout his work is that his desire for Beatrice was not a displaced one but always led on to a vision of God. The *Comedy* is a triumph, and so presumably must be the supreme Western instance of religious poetry. It is certainly the supreme example of a wholly personal poem that persuades many of its readers to believe they are encountering ultimate truth. Thus even Teodolinda Barolini, in a book professedly written to detheologize Dante, allows herself to say that "the *Commedia,* perhaps more than any other text ever written, consciously seeks to imitate life, the conditions of human existence."

The judgment is puzzling. Do the *Inferno* and the *Purgatorio,* let alone the *Paradiso,* seek to "imitate life" more consciously than *King Lear* or even the Dante-influenced *Canterbury Tales?* Whatever Dante's realism may be, it does not give us what Chaucer and Shakespeare bestow upon us: characters who change, even as actual human beings change. Only Dante changes and develops in the *Comedy;* everyone else is fixed and immutable. Indeed they have to be, because the final judgment has been made upon them. As for Beatrice, as a character in a poem, which is truly all she can be, she is necessarily even more removed from an imitation of life, for what has she to do with the conditions of human existence? Charles Williams, despite his gurulike attitudes, is sounder on this issue than the Dante scholars begin to be, when he observes of the *Comedy*, "Even that poem was necessarily limited. It does not attempt to deal with the problem of Beatrice's own salvation, and Dante's function there."

I find that claim somewhat crazy, but better such craziness than smothering Dante with doctrine or mistaking his poem for an imitation of life. As far as Dante was concerned, as a poet, there was absolutely no problem of Beatrice's own salvation. She saved Dante by giving him his greatest image for poetry, and he saved her from oblivion, little as she may have wanted such salvation. Williams muses mystically on the "marriage" between Beatrice and Dante, but that is Williams and not Dante. When she enters *Purgatorio* she speaks to her poet neither as a lover nor as a mother, but as a deity speaks to a mortal, albeit a mortal with whom she has a very special relationship. Her harshness to him is another inverted self-compliment on his part, since she is the superb mark of his originality, the trumpet of his prophecy. In effect, his own genius chides him, for what other reproof could the proudest of all poets accept? I suppose he would not have resisted a direct descent of Christ, but even Dante would not go so far as to risk such a representation.

The muse intervenes, but he names her "blessedness" and asserts a role for her that could benefit everyone else. She will not descend for and to others, except for his poetry; and so he is her prophet, a function he had been preparing since the *New Life*. Despite his complex relations to many traditions—poetic, philosophical, theological, political—Dante owes Beatrice to none of them. She can be distinguished from Christ, but not from the *Comedy,* because she *is* Dante's poem, the single image of images that represents not God, but Dante's own achievement. I am growing accustomed to having scholars tell me that Dante was interested in his own achievement as a way to God, and I decline to believe them. An exile from his own city, a witness to the failure of the emperor upon whom he had set his best hopes, Dante at last had only his poem to shore against his ruin.

The philosopher George Santayana in his *Three Philosophical Poets* (1910) distinguished among Lucretius, Dante, and Goethe on the basis of their Epicurean naturalism, Platonic supernaturalism, and Romantic or Kantian idealism, respectively. Santayana said of Dante that "He became to Platonism and Christianity what Homer had been to Paganism," but then added that love, as Dante "feels and renders it, is not normal or healthy love." It seems sacrilege to judge Dante's passion for Beatrice to be abnormal and unhealthy only because it offers so little resistance to a mystical transformation of the beloved into part of the divine apparatus for redemption. Still, Santayana was shrewd and refreshing in this, as also in ironically praising Dante for being ahead of his time in sustained egotism.

When Santayana added that Dante was a Platonist unlike any other, he should have gone on to a more important formulation: Dante was also a Christian unlike any other, and Beatrice is the mark of that unlikeness, the sign of what Dante added to the faith of the Church. Pragmatically, at least for poets and critics, the *Comedy* became the third Testament prophesied by Joachim of Fiore. The subtlest stand against the pragmatic test is not that made by the school of Auerbach, Singleton, and Freccero, but that by A. C. Charity in his study of Christian typology, *Events and Their Afterlife* (1966), and by Leo Spitzer, acknowledged by Charity as forerunner. Charity insists that Beatrice is an image of Christ, but is not Christ, or the Church, and he cites Kenelm Foster as saying that "she does not replace Christ, she reflects and transmits him." That may be piety, but it is not the *Comedy,* in which when Dante looks upon Beatrice, he sees Beatrice and not Christ. She is not a mirror but a person, and even Leo Spitzer in his 1988 *Representative Essays* does not altogether meet the difficulty of her individualistic status, indeed, her uniqueness:

> That Beatrice is the allegory, not only of revelation, but of *personal* revelation, is proved both by the autobiographical origin of this figure and by her status in the Beyond: she is not an angel, but the blessed soul of a human being that, just as it influenced Dante's life on this earth, is called to perform for Dante in the course of his pilgrimage services of which she alone is capable; she is not a saint, but a *Beatrice,* not a martyr, but one who died young and was allowed to stay on earth only in order to show Dante the possibility of miracles. The dogmatic license here taken by Dante appears less daring if we consider the fact that revelation may come to the Christian in an individual form, suited to him personally. . . . She is . . . the counterpart of . . . those historical persons born before the Redeemer who foreshadow him.

Resourceful as Spitzer was, this will not do, and it in no way diminishes Dante's "daring." According to Dante, Beatrice is much more than a merely personal or individual revelation. She has come initially to her poet, Dante, but through him she comes to his readers. Virgil says to her in the *Inferno,* "O lady of virtue, through whom alone (*sola*) the human kind surpasses everything within the smallest circle of the heavens," which Curtius expounds as "Through Beatrice alone, mankind surpasses everything earthly, whatever this may mean: Beatrice has a metaphysical dignity for all men—Beatrice alone." Spitzer also gets too quickly from the difference between being a *prefiguration* of Christ and an *imitation* of Christ. Had Beatrice come *before* Christ, you might argue that she was another forerunner, but, of course, she comes after, and what Dante fell in love with, in her and as her, was not the imitation of Christ. At the least she is, as Santayana observed, a Platonizing of Christianity, which has never stopped being Platonized, before and since Dante. At the most she is what Curtius insisted she was: the center of a poetic gnosis, of the vision of Dante.

That returns us to her as the sign of Dante's originality, the heart of his power and his strangeness. Pride is not a Christian virtue, but it has always been a crucial virtue in the greatest poets. Shakespeare may be the grand exception, as he is in so many things. We never will know what his attitude was in regard to having written *Hamlet* or *King Lear* or *Antony and Cleopatra*. Perhaps he required no attitude, because he never lacked acknowledgment and commercial success. He must have known, quite consciously, how original and enormous his achievement was, but we search the plays in vain for self-compliments, and the sonnets, though they contain some, also express considerable modesty. Could Shakespeare unironically have spoken of any rival poet's gift or scope, or believed in the "proud sail" of George Chapman's "great verse"? Dante proudly sets sail for Paradise, and celebrates himself for celebrating Beatrice. In *Paradise Lost* Satan's pride, however it is related to Milton's, brings him down. In the *Comedy*, Dante's pride carries him up, to Beatrice and beyond.

Beatrice emanates from Dante's pride but also from his need. Scholars interpret what she stands for or represents; I suggest we begin to consider what it was that Beatrice enabled Dante to exclude from his poem. Vico charmingly deplored Dante's extensive knowledge of theology. Dante's spiritual erudition is not the problem; that of his exegetes is. Remove Beatrice from the *Comedy*, and Virgil would have to yield to one saint or another as Dante's guide from the Earthly Paradise up to the Celestial Rose. A reader's religious resistance, which can already be rather more considerable than the Anglo-American scholars of Dante ever want to acknowledge, would certainly be heightened if Saint Augustine took the place of Beatrice. More important, Dante's resistance to received doctrine would have been heightened also. There is more apparent than actual concurrence between Dante's vision and the Catholic faith, but Dante centers on Beatrice partly to avoid having to waste his imaginative energies on a needless quarrel with orthodoxy.

It is Beatrice whose presence and function transform Augustine and Aquinas into something figuratively much richer, adding strangeness to truth (if you think it is the truth) or to fiction (if you regard it as that). I myself, as a student of gnosis, whether poetic or religious, judge the poem to be neither truth nor fiction but rather Dante's *knowing,* which he chose to name Beatrice. When you know most intensely, you do not necessarily decide whether it is truth or fiction; what you know primarily is that the knowing is truly your own. Sometimes we call such knowing by the name of "loving," almost invariably with the conviction that the experience is permanent. Most often it departs and leaves us bewildered, but we are not Dante and cannot write the *Comedy,* so all we finally know is loss. Beatrice is the difference between canonical immortality and loss, for without her Dante would now be another pre-Petrarchan Italian writer who died in exile, a victim of his own pride and zeal.

I have considerable distaste for Charles Williams whether he writes Christian fantasy, rather grotesque poetry, or unabashed Christian apologetics as in *He Came down from Heaven* and *The Descent of the Dove.* Nor is Williams what I regard as a disinterested critic of literature. He is, in his way, as much an ideologue as the neo-Feminists, pseudo-Marxists, and Francophile reductionists who make up our current School of Resentment. But Williams has the almost solitary distinction of reading Dante as primarily the creator of the figure of Beatrice:

> The image of Beatrice existed in his thought; it remained there and was deliberately renewed. The word, image, is convenient for two reasons. First, the subjective recollection within him was of something objectively outside him, it was an image of an

exterior fact and not of an interior desire. It was sight and not invention. Dante's assertion was that he could not have invented Beatrice.

A poet's assertion is a poem, and Dante is neither the first nor the last great poet to insist that his invention was a clearing of sight. Perhaps Shakespeare might have said the same of Imogen in *Cymbeline*. Williams compares Beatrice to Imogen, but Beatrice, unlike Dante the Pilgrim and Virgil the Guide, unlike the Ulysses of the *Inferno*, is not quite a literary character. She has dramatic qualities, including some flashes of high scorn; but being herself more the whole poem than a personage in it, she can be apprehended only when the reader has read and absorbed the entire *Comedy*, which perhaps accounts for a curious opacity (by no means here an aesthetic flaw) in the figure of Beatrice. Her remoteness, even toward her poet-lover, is far greater than Williams acknowledges and is carefully orchestrated by Dante, culminating in the poignant moment in the *Paradiso* when he sees her, now from afar:

> I lifted up my eyes and saw her where she made for herself a crown, reflecting from her the eternal beams. From the highest region where it thunders no mortal eye is so far, were it lost in the depth of the sea, as was my sight there from Beatrice; but to me it made no difference, for her image came down to me undimmed by aught between.
>
> "O Lady in whom my hope has its strength and who didst bear for my salvation to leave thy footprints in Hell, of all the things that I have seen I acknowledge the grace and the virtue to be from bondage into liberty by all those ways, by every means for it that was in thy power. Preserve in me thy great bounty, so that my spirit, which thou hast made whole, may be loosed from the body well-pleasing to thee." I prayed thus; and she, so far off as she seemed, smiled and looked at me, then turned again to the eternal fount.

Commenting on this amazing passage in a previous book, I noted that Dante refused to accept his cure from the hand of any man, however saintly, but only from the hand of his own creation, Beatrice. One Catholic literary critic chided me for not understanding the faith, and at least one Dante scholar said that my observation was Romantic-Satanic (whatever that can mean, this late in the day). My reference was clearly to Freud's plangent and eloquent summa, "Analysis Terminable and Interminable," the lament of the founder of psychoanalysis that his patients would not accept their cure from him. Dante, prouder than any of us, would accept his cure only from Beatrice, and it is to Beatrice that Dante prays. His prophetic audacity is not Augustinian, just as his Imperial politics repudiates Augustine's sense that the church had replaced the Roman Empire. The *Comedy* is an apocalyptic poem, and Beatrice is an invention possible only for a poet who expected his prophecy's fulfillment before his own death. What would Augustine have thought of Dante's poem? I would guess that his largest objection would have been to Beatrice, a private myth that carries the heavens before it, even as Dante bears away the Kingdom of God.

What precedent, if any, was there for Beatrice? She is a Christian muse who enters the poem's action and so fuses herself with the poem that we cannot conceive of it without her. Dante's designated precursor was Virgil, and if there is a parallel to Beatrice in the *Aeneid,* it has to be Venus. Virgil's Venus, as Curtius emphasizes, is much more an Artemis or Diana figure than an Aphrodite. She is severely restrained, strangely Sibyl-like, and scarcely the mother of Eros, as compared to the half-god, Aeneas. Himself both Epicurean and Stoic, the actual Virgil (as opposed to Dante's strong misreading) hardly longs for grace and redemption, only for respite from the endless vision of suffering and its meaninglessness. If Dante had been more accurate, Virgil would be with the superb Farinata in the sixth circle of hell, reserved for the Epicureans and other heretics.

Virgil's own precursor was Lucretius, the most powerful of all materialist and naturalistic poets, and more Epicurean than Epicurus. Dante had never read Lucretius, who was not revived until the closing decades of the fifteenth century. I regret this enormously, as it would have given Dante an opponent altogether worthy of his strength. Whether Lucretius would have horrified

Dante, we cannot know, but Dante would have been outraged to learn that Virgil was far closer in spirit, if not in sensibility, to Lucretius than to Dante. Certainly Virgil's Venus is a deliberate swerve away from the Lucretian Venus, so we have the irony that Lucretius is Dante's wicked grandfather as it were, if I am at all correct in surmising that the Virgilian Venus is the direct ancestor of Beatrice. George Santayana has an apt characterization of the Venus of *On the Nature of Things* as an Empedoclean Love existing in dialectical tension with Mars:

> The Mars and Venus of Lucretius are not moral forces, incompatible with the mechanism of atoms; they are this mechanism itself, insofar as it now produces and now destroys life, or any precious enterprise, like this of Lucretius in composing his saving poem. Mars and Venus, linked in each other's arms, rule the universe together; nothing arises save by the death of some other thing.

The Empedoclean-Lucretian formula "dying each other's life, living each other's death" delighted W. B. Yeats, pagan mystagogue that he was, but it would have been rejected, with contempt, by Dante. Virgil's undoubted reaction, on the basis of his own Venus, was ambivalent. He took from Lucretius, whose poem he clearly studied closely, the idea that Venus's truest life-giving was to the Romans, through her son Aeneas, their ancestor and founder. But his Venus does not engage in perpetual embraces with Mars. Weirdly, for she is after all the goddess of love, Virgil's Venus is as chaste as Beatrice. Virgil himself, unlike Dante, was not passionate toward women and probably (in Dante's scheme) deserved to be not only in canto 10 of the *Inferno* with Farinata the Epicurean, but also in canto 15 with Brunetto Latini the sodomite, Dante's honored teacher.

It is an exquisite irony that Beatrice, the supreme Christian muse, may find her likely origin in a Venus figure who is Diana-like partly as a reaction-formation against the lustful Epicurean Venus and partly because Dante's forerunner did not desire women. The dominant female in Virgil's epic is the frightening Juno, a nightmare of a goddess and the counterpoise to Virgil's

Venus, indeed, a countermuse to Venus. Does Dante have a countermuse? Freccero locates her in the Medusa of *Inferno*, canto 9, and in turn relates this figure to the Lady Petra of Dante's "stony rhymes," including the great sestina that Dante Gabriel Rossetti translated so powerfully: "To the dim light and the large circle of shade." Freccero contrasts Dante to Petrarch, his dissenting successor in the next generation, whose Laura is in effect both muse and countermuse, Beatrice and Medusa, Venus and Juno. For Freccero, the comparison favors Dante, since Beatrice points beyond herself, presumably to Christ and God, and Laura remains strictly within the poem. Pragmatically, I would suggest that this is a difference that makes no difference, despite Freccero's Augustinian severities:

> Like Pygmalion, Petrarch falls in love with his own creation and is in turn created by her: the pun *Lauro/Laura* points to this self-contained process which is the essence of his creation. He creates with his poetry the Lady Laura who in turn creates his reputation as poet laureate. She is therefore not a mediatrix, pointing beyond herself, but is rather enclosed within the confines of his own being as poet, which is to say, the poem. This is precisely what Petrarch acknowledges when he confesses in his final prayer to the sin of idolatry, adoration of the work of his hands.

If one is not persuaded theologically by Dante, and most of us no longer are, what supports Freccero's sense that Dante is somehow free of Petrarch's inescapable aesthetic dilemmas? Is it that Petrarch, as ancestor of both Renaissance and Romantic poetry, and so of modern poetry as well, must share in the supposed sins of those who arrive after the medieval synthesis has dissolved? Dante, like Petrarch, falls in love with his own creation. What else can Beatrice be? And since she is the *Comedy*'s greatest originality, does she not in turn create Dante? Only Dante is our authority for the fiction that Beatrice points beyond herself, and she is certainly confined within the *Comedy*, unless you believe that Dante's personal gnosis is true not only for him, but for everyone else as well.

Does anyone pray to Beatrice, except Dante the Pilgrim of Eternity? Petrarch was happy to confess to idolatry because, as Freccero himself has splendidly shown, the confession helped to distance him from his overwhelming precursor. But does Dante not adore the finished *Comedy,* the astonishing work of his own hands? Idolatry is a theological category and a poetic metaphor; Dante, like Petrarch, is a poet and not a theologian. That Dante was a greater poet than Laura's victim, Petrarch doubtless recognized; but of the two it is Petrarch who has been even more influential on later poets. Dante vanished until the nineteenth century; he was scarcely esteemed during the Renaissance and the Enlightenment. Petrarch took his place, thus fulfilling his shrewd program of embracing poetic idolatry or inventing the lyric poem. Dante died when Petrarch was seventeen, in 1321. When Petrarch, about 1349, prepared the first version of his sonnets, he seems to have known that he was inaugurating a mode that transcended the sonnet form, and that shows no signs of waning six and a half centuries later. A second *Comedy* was not possible, any more than tragedy has been possible since Shakespeare ceased to write it. The canonical greatness of Dante, for a final time, has nothing to do with Saint Augustine, or with the truths, if they are truths, of the Christian religion. At our present bad moment, we need above all to recover our sense of literary individuality and of poetic autonomy. Dante, like Shakespeare, is an ultimate resource for that recovery, provided we can evade the sirens that sing to us the allegory of the theologians.

4.

Chaucer:
The Wife of Bath, The Pardoner,
and Shakespearean Character

Except for Shakespeare, Chaucer is foremost among writers in the English language. That assertion, which merely repeats traditional judgment, is very much worth making as we approach the end of our century. Reading Chaucer or his few rivals in literature since the ancients—Dante, Cervantes, Shakespeare—can have the happy result of restoring perspectives that all of us may be tempted to lose as we face the onslaught of instant masterpieces that threatens us at this moment when cultural justice is at work, enforcing the exile of aesthetic considerations. Turning from what is overpraised to what cannot be overpraised, the *Canterbury Tales* is a remarkable tonic. One passes from names on the page to what I am impelled to call the virtual reality of literary characters, convincingly persuasive women and men. What gave Chaucer the power so to represent his persons as to make them permanent?

There is a superb 1987 biography by the late Donald R. Howard that attempts to answer this well-nigh impossible question.

Howard acknowledges that we have no intimate knowledge of Chaucer beyond his works, but then reminds us of Chaucer's human context:

> Property and inheritance were abiding concerns—obsessions, really—in the late Middle Ages, especially among the merchant class to which the Chaucers belonged; and armed seizure, kidnapping, and trumped-up lawsuits were not uncommon ways to gain possession of them. Englishmen of Chaucer's day were not like the stereotypical stiff-upper-lip English of modern times, who are the children of the Enlightenment and the Empire; they were more like their Norman forebears, hot-tempered and given to extremes when among equals (they cultivated reserve before inferiors or superiors). They wept freely in public, flew into rages, swore copious and imaginative oaths, carried on almost operatic blood feuds and endless legal battles. The mortality rate was high in medieval times and life more precarious; we find more recklessness and terror, more resignation and despair, and more gambling with fortune. More violence, too, or violence of a more vengeful, ostentatious kind: decapitated heads displayed on spikes or bodies hanging from a gibbet was their style, where mug shots in the post office is ours.

Our style is alas changing rapidly, with letter bombs exploding at universities, fundamentalist Muslim terrorism erupting in New York City, and gunfire drifting across New Haven even as I sit here writing. Howard depicts Chaucer as living through wars, plagues, and rebellions, and none of these seems very remote in contemporary America, with Howard himself dead of our version of the plague just before his book was published. His general emphasis remains excellent: Chaucer's times were not serene, his fellow citizens were not placid, and his Canterbury pilgrims had much to pray for when they reached the shrine of Saint Thomas à Becket. The personality of Chaucer the man, not just of the ironically portrayed Chaucer the Pilgrim, is powerfully marked on all his poetry. Like his direct precursors—Dante and Boccaccio—his great originality emerges most strongly in both his characters and his own voice, his mastery of tone and figuration. Like

Dante, he invented new modes for the representation of the self, and he has something of the same relation to Shakespeare that Dante had to Petrarch, the difference being the unbelievable fecundity of Shakespeare, which transcended even what John Dryden meant when he said of the *Canterbury Tales:* "Here is God's plenty." No writer, neither Ovid nor "the English Ovid," Christopher Marlowe, influenced Shakespeare as crucially as Chaucer did. Chaucerian hints, by no means fully developed by Chaucer, are the starting points for the greatest of Shakespeare's originalities, his way of representing human personality. But Chaucer's greatness needs emphasis and expositions before its legacy in Shakespeare can be sketched.

My favorite Chaucer critic remains G. K. Chesterton, who remarked, "the Chaucerian irony is sometimes so large that it is too large to be seen," and expanded upon what is central in that irony:

> There is in it some hint of those huge and abysmal ideas connected with the very nature of creation and reality. It has in it something of the philosophy of a phenomenal world, and all that was meant by those sages, by no means pessimists, who have said that we are in a world of his own shadows, and when he is on a certain plane, finds himself equally shadowy. It has in it all the mystery of the relation of the maker with things made.

Chesterton, with a characteristic sense of paradox, traces Chaucer's extraordinary realism, his psychological penetration, to an ironic awareness of lost time, of a greater reality that has fled, abandoning its remnants to regrets and nostalgia. Goodwill exists, but is always compromised in Chaucer, and a falling away from chivalric generosity can be observed everywhere. Chesterton's preoccupation with a vanished romance world, learned from Chaucer, is confirmed by Donald Howard as the informing "idea" of the *Canterbury Tales*. They give us "a picture of a disordered Christian society in a state of obsolescence, decline, and uncertainty; we do not know where it is headed." Only an ironist could sustain such a picture.

In his biography, Howard locates the source of Chaucer's alienation or ambivalence in the tension between a mercantile upbringing and the aristocratic training subsequently given to a young courtier-poet. Dante inaugurated the Aristocratic Age of literature, despite his continued attachment to the allegory of the Theological Age. But Chaucer, unlike Dante, did not belong to even the minor nobility. I am always wary of social explanations for the ironic stance of a great poet in whom temperament and panache resist all overdeterminations. Chaucer's is so large a consciousness, so pervasive and individual an irony, that circumstances alone are unlikely to have been dominant. Chaucer's English precursor was his friend the poet John Gower, a dozen years his senior, and palpably minor in comparison to the rising writer. English is the language that Chaucer spoke as a child, but he also spoke Anglo-French (formerly Norman), and in his courtier education he learned to speak, read, and write Parisian French and Italian.

Sensing early that he had no strong enough precursors in English, he turned first to Guillaume Machaut, the major living French poet (and composer). But after this early phase culminated in his remarkable elegy, *The Book of the Duchess,* Chaucer went to Italy on the king's business, and by February 1373 was in pre-Renaissance Florence, even as its great age in literature ebbed. The exiled Dante had been dead for more than half a century, and his successors in the next generation, Petrarch and Boccaccio, were both old; both died during the next two years. For a poet of Chaucer's power and scope, these writers—or rather, Dante and Boccaccio—were the inevitable inspirations and consequent spur to anxieties. Petrarch meant something to Chaucer as a representative figure, but hardly as an actual writer. At thirty, Chaucer the poet knew what he wanted, and it was not to be found in Petrarch and only peripherally in Dante. Boccaccio, never mentioned by name in Chaucer's work, became the origin that Chaucer needed.

Dante, whose spiritual pride was overwhelming, had written a third Testament, a vision of truth, wholly unsuitable for Chaucer's ironical temperament. The differences between Dante the Pilgrim of Eternity and Chaucer the Canterbury Pilgrim are startling, and clearly deliberate on Chaucer's part. *The House of Fame* is inspired by the *Divine Comedy* but amiably mocks it, and the *Canterbury*

Tales constitute, on one level, a skeptical critique of Dante, particularly of his relationship with his own vision. Temperament distanced Chaucer from Dante; they are incompatible poetic personalities.

Boccaccio, Dante's great admirer and exegete, was quite another matter; he would not be very happy, off in the poet's paradise, to be called "the Italian Chaucer," just as Chaucer, evader of even the name Boccaccio, would have dreaded being termed "the English Boccaccio." But the affinities, quite aside from Chaucer's marvelous and enormous appropriations, were authentic, almost inevitable. The crucial work here is the *Decameron,* which Chaucer never mentions and perhaps never read thoroughly, but which is the likely model for the *Canterbury Tales.* Ironic storytelling *whose subject is storytelling* is pretty much Boccaccio's invention, and the purpose of this breakthrough was to free stories from didacticism and moralism, so that the listener or reader, not the storyteller, became responsible for their use, for good or for ill. Chaucer took from Boccaccio the notion that stories need not be true or illustrate truth; rather, stories are "new things," novelties as it were. Since Chaucer was a greater ironist and an even stronger writer than Boccaccio, his transformation of the *Decameron* into the *Canterbury Tales* was a radical one, a thorough revision of Boccaccio's design. Read side by side, there are relatively few resemblances; but Chaucer's mature mode of storytelling could not have come into existence without the unacknowledged mediation of Boccaccio.

CHAUCER THOUGHT that his masterwork was *Troilus and Criseyde,* one of the handful of great long poems in the language but rarely read now in comparison to the *Canterbury Tales,* which is certainly the more original and canonical work. Perhaps Chaucer undervalued his most astonishing achievement precisely because of its originality, though something in me fiercely resents that surmise. The work is unfinished, and technically it consists of giant fragments; but as one reads, one has little impression of something unfinished. Indeed it may be one of those books that the author never expects to finish, because it has become one with his life.

The image of life as a pilgrimage, not so much to Jerusalem but to judgment, fuses with Chaucer's organizing principle of the pilgrimage to Canterbury, with thirty pilgrims telling stories as they go. Yet the poem is immensely secular, and almost unfailingly ironic.

Its narrator is Chaucer himself reduced to a total simplicity: he has zest, endless good nature, believes everything he hears, and has an amazing capacity for admiring even the dreadful qualities displayed by some of his twenty-nine companions. E. Talbot Donaldson, the most worldly wise and humane of Chaucer critics, emphasizes that Chaucer the pilgrim tends to be "acutely unaware of the significance of what he sees, no matter how sharply he sees it," while at the same time he is constant in expressing "ungrudging admiration for efficient thievery." It may be that Chaucer the pilgrim is not so much a Lemuel Gulliver, which Donaldson suggests, as a more wicked parody of Dante the Pilgrim, fierce, judgmental, frequently consumed by hatred, and really a kind of apocalyptic moralist who tends to be only too aware of the significance of what he sees with such terrible sharpness. It would be a proper Chaucerian irony to execute so subtle a mockery upon the poet whose imaginative arrogance doubtless appalled the author of *The House of Fame*.

The actual Chaucer, the comic ironist manipulating the apparently bland pilgrim, manifests a detachment, an accepting disinterestedness that is already Shakespearean, insofar as we can ever isolate any of Shakespeare's own attitudes. The detachment in both poets helps create an art of exclusion: we are frequently puzzled to explain just why Chaucer the pilgrim remembers certain details as he describes each individual, while forgetting or censoring others. In the two most interesting figures, the Wife of Bath and the Pardoner, this art of selective memory helps produce Shakespearean reverberations. Howard shrewdly notes that Chaucer revises Boccaccio by seeing "that the tale each told could tell a tale about its teller," and that latter tale, one surmises, would fill in some of the gaps left by Chaucer the pilgrim. We are, sometimes at least, to trust the tale and not the teller, particularly when the teller is formidable, like the Wife of Bath and the Pardoner. But of course Chaucer the pilgrim is even more formidable, since we never can be sure that he is as naïve as he evidently wants to be seen as being. Some critics argue that the narrator is frighteningly sophisticated, that he himself really is Chaucer the poet, masking himself from his companions by a dangerously sly blandness that actually misses nothing.

I think one would have to go back to the Yahwist or forward to Jonathan Swift to read an ironist as complete and fascinating as Chaucer. One of my favorites among the attacks against me for *The Book of J* was by a biblical scholar who asked, "What makes Professor Bloom think that irony existed three thousand years ago?" Because Chaucer is not sacred text, there are fewer resistances to accepting the difficult truth that so universal a storyteller as the author of the tales of the Canterbury pilgrims rarely writes an unironic passage. It may be that Chaucer's true literary parent was the Yahwist and his true child, Jane Austen. All three writers make their ironies their principal instruments for discovery or invention, by compelling readers to discover themselves precisely what it is that they have invented. Unlike the ferocity of Swift's irony, which is a universal corrosive, Chaucer's irony is rarely inhumane, though we cannot be certain with regard to the depravity of the Pardoner, and virtually everyone supposedly on pilgrimage is revealed as being no pilgrim at all. "Honest Iago," the terrifying refrain throughout *Othello,* is a Chaucerian irony, as Shakespeare must have known. "Honest Iago's" direct ancestor is the "gentil Pardoner." Jill Mann, in the best analysis of Chaucerian irony that I have encountered, charts its ambiguities as centered on its mobility, always comically leaping on to another view of things and thus consistently refusing us the possibility of moral judgment, because illusion lurks within illusion. That returns me to my surmise that Chaucerian irony is a reaction against the arrogance of the prophetic stance that Dante took as his own.

Confronted by the Wife of Bath and the Pardoner along with a number of other Canterbury pilgrims, Dante (if he could be bothered) would not hesitate to assign them to their proper circles in the inferno. Their interest, if any, would have to include where and why they are stationed in eternity, for only final realities concern Dante. Fiction, for Chaucer, is not a medium for representing or expressing ultimate truth; it is wonderfully suited for portraying affection and everything else that has commerce with illusions. Perhaps Chaucer would be surprised at our common agreement that he is primarily an ironist; unlike Dante, who loved only his own creation, Beatrice, Chaucer seems to have entertained a wary love for the entire comedy of creation. Finally, we should not separate Chaucer the man, Chaucer the poet, and Chaucer the pilgrim: all combine in one loving ironist whose richest legacy is a roster of literary characters second only to Shakespeare's in the language. In them we can see burgeoning what will become Shakespeare's most original imaginative power: the representation of change within particular dramatic personalities.

Chaucer anticipates by centuries the inwardness we associate with the Renaissance and the Reformation: his men and women begin to develop a self-consciousness that only Shakespeare knew how to quicken into self-overhearing, subsequent startlement, and the arousal of the will to change. Incipient at moments in the *Canterbury Tales,* this anticipation of what, after Freud, we call depth psychology in contrast to moral psychology coursed on in Shakespeare to a fullness that Freud, as I have observed already, could do little more than prosify and codify. And so we return to Howard's question, though his interest was story and mine is character: What gave Chaucer the power to transcend his own ironies and so be able to render his characters with a vitality that only Shakespeare goes beyond, and that with Chaucer's aid? Speculative and difficult as the question is, I will try to sketch an answer.

IN VERY different ways, Chaucer's two most inward and individual characters are the Wife of Bath and the Pardoner, respectively a great vitalist and something close to an authentic nihilist. Moralizing critics are no fonder of the Wife of Bath than they are of her only child, Sir John Falstaff; while the Pardoner—like his somewhat more remote descendants, Iago and Edmund—is beyond moralizing, again like his ultimate descendants, Dostoevsky's rather Shakespearean nihilists, Svidrigailov and Stavrogin, whose attributes owe something to Shakespeare's Iago in particular. Certainly one gets considerably more insight into and pleasure from the Wife of Bath and the Pardoner by comparing them to Falstaff and Iago than by setting them against their possible sources in the *Roman de la Rose,* the leading medieval poem before Chaucer's own. Scholars derive the Wife of Bath's character from La Vieille, the aged bawd of that work, while they trace the Pardoner to False-Seeming, a hypocrite who enlivens the *Roman.* But La Vieille is more rancid than vitalistic, unlike the Wife of Bath and Falstaff; and False-Seeming has nothing of the dangerous intellect that distinguishes both the gentle Pardoner and honest Iago.

Why many scholarly critics of Chaucer and of Shakespeare are so desperately more moralistic than their poets is an unhappy puzzle, one that I suspect is related to the current disease of moral smugness that is destroying literary study in the name of socio-economic justice. Heirs of Platonism, even when ignorant of Plato, both traditional scholars and the clerks of resentment seek to banish the poetic from poetry. Chaucer's greatest creations are the Wife of Bath and the Pardoner, which Shakespeare evidently saw and benefited from, far more than he benefited from any other single literary stimulus. To apprehend what touched Shakespeare is to return to the true path of canonization, in which the major writers elect their inescapable precursors. It was Edmund Spenser who called Chaucer the "pure well of English undefiled," yet it was Shakespeare who was, as Talbot Donaldson has charmingly indicated, "the swan at the well," drinking most deeply of what was unique to Chaucer, a new kind of literary character, or per-haps a new way of portraying an old kind, whether in the moral ambiguity of the Wife of Bath's rage to live, or in the immoral ambivalence of the Pardoner's rage both to deceive and to be found out.

That Chaucer himself was proud of having created the Wife we know from his short, late poem to his friend Bukton, which speaks of "the sorwe and wo that is in mariage" and cites her as the authority:

> *The Wyf of Bathe I pray yow that ye rede*
> *Of this matere that we have on honde.*
> *God graunte yow your lyf frely to lede*
> *In fredam, for ful hard is to be bonde.*

When first we meet the "good Wife," in the General Prologue to the *Canterbury Tales,* we are necessarily impressed, but not altogether prepared for the firecracker we will encounter in the prologue to her own tale, despite the narrator's early hints about her exuberant sexuality. She is somewhat deaf, for reasons we will discover later; her stockings are scarlet; her countenance is bold, fair, and matches her stockings. Famously gap-toothed and so presumably lustful, she has survived five husbands, not to mention other company, and is a notorious pilgrim, nationally and internationally, pilgrimages being the equivalent of love-boat cruises in our fallen times. Yet all of this merely intimates someone well versed in "wandringe by the waye," an expert in "the olde daunce" of love. Her Falstaffian wit, her feminism (as we might now say), above all her fantastic will to live are not yet truly in evidence.

Howard reminds us that Chaucer was a widower when he invented the Wife of Bath and adds astutely that no writer since the ancients manifested so much insight into the psychology of women, or portrayed them so sympathetically. I agree with Howard that the Wife is an absolute delight, whatever moralists urge against her, though I am haunted by her most formidable adversary, William Blake, who found in her the Female Will (as he called it) incarnate. His commentary on his picture of the Canterbury Pilgrims is rather hard on the Wife, but she evidently frightened him: "she is also a scourge and a blight. I shall say no more of her, nor expose what Chaucer has left hidden; let the young reader study what he has said of her: it is as useful as a scare-crow. There are of such characters born too many for the peace of the world."

Yet without such characters, there would be less life in literature, and less literature in life. The Wife of Bath's prologue is a kind of confession, but even more a triumphant defense or apologia. And unlike the Pardoner's prologue, her stream-of-consciousness-like reverie does not tell us more about her than she herself knows. The first word of her prologue is "experience," which she cites as her authority. To be the widow of five successive husbands, whether six hundred years ago or now, gives a woman a certain aura, as the Wife is well aware; but she boisterously declares herself eager for a sixth, while envying the wise King Solomon his

thousand bed-partners (seven hundred wives, three hundred con-
cubines). What is awesome about the wife is her endless zest and
vitality: sexual, verbal, polemical. Her sheer exuberance of being
has no literary antecedent and could not be matched until Shakespeare created Falstaff. It is a legitimate literary fantasy to visualize
an encounter between the Wife and the fat knight. Falstaff is more
intelligent and witty than the Wife, but even he, with all his gusto,
could not have kept her quiet. Fascinatingly, it is the frightening
Pardoner who interrupts her in Chaucer, but mostly to cheer her
on, and on she does go. Shakespeare wrote a reported (not actual)
death scene for Falstaff in *Henry V;* not even Chaucer could have
managed a similar scene for the Wife. And that is the highest
tribute we should pay her, brushing aside the chorus of moralizing
scholars: she has only life in her, the perpetual blessing of yet
more life.

As the Friar says, the Wife's is a long preamble of a tale; it goes
on for more than eight hundred lines, while the tale itself is just
four hundred and (alas) something of an aesthetic disappointment
after the wife's strong revelation of selfhood. But the reader, unless
heaven-bent on moralizing, will wish her prologue even longer
and her story shorter. Chaucer plainly is fascinated by her, as in
another register he is enthralled by the Pardoner: he knows that
these two characters have broken loose and uncannily course on
by themselves, miracles of art representing grotesques of nature.
I do not know of a female character in Western literature who is
more unanswerable than the Wife when she protests the consequences of men having written almost all of the books:

> *By God, if wommen hadde writen stories,*
> *As clerkes han withinne hir oratories,*
> *They wolde han writen of men more wikkednesse*
> *Than all the mark of Adam may redresse.*

It is her potent blend of confessional honesty and powerful
sexuality that has appalled many of the male scholars who have
defamed the Wife. Her implied, purely pragmatic critique of the
Church's moral scale of perfection is as subtle as it is comic and
presages much that is in contention between the Church and Cath-

olic feminists even as I write. Partly the Wife has offended moralists simply because she has a very forceful personality, and Chaucer, like all great poets, believed in personality. Because the Wife is also a subverter of established harmonies, she is consigned by many to the category of the grotesque, where the Pardoner legitimately resides. Although the Wife accepts the structure of the Church's thought about morality, there is a deep impulse in her that dissents from the church's affect. A scale of perfection that sets widowhood over marriage, as Saint Jerome did, makes no sense to her; nor does she share the doctrine that marital sexual relations are sanctified only in order to produce children.

Despite her five late husbands, she appears to be childless and says nothing about the matter. Where she does cross into opposition to the ideology of the medieval church is on the issue of dominance in marriage. Her firm belief in female sovereignty is the center of her rebellion, and I dissent from Howard when he says that her tale "undercuts her feminist views, reveals something about her we could only have suspected, something she doesn't know herself." In this view, the wife wants only an outward or verbal submission on the husband's part, but that is to underestimate the Wife's own share of Chaucerian irony. Two lines do not a tale make, nor do they undo eight hundred lines of passionate prologue: "And she obeyed him in every thing / That mighte doon him pleasance or lyking."

I take it that the Wife intends the phrase "in every thing" to be exclusively sexual. The lines directly follow one in which the husband kisses the wife a thousand times in a row, and the Wife of Bath's idea of what might give a man pleasure is rather monolithic. She wants sovereignty all right, everywhere except in bed, as her inevitable sixth husband is going to learn. As she has told us, her first three husbands were good, rich, and old, whereas the fourth and fifth were young and troublesome. The fourth, having dared to take a mistress, suffered the just fate of being tormented to death by her; and the fifth, half her age, deafened her by boxing her ears, after she had ripped pages out of the antifeminist book he insisted upon reading to her. When he yielded at last, burned the book, and resigned sovereignty to her, they lived happily together, but not ever after. Chaucer's ironic implication is that the ferociously lustful Wife wore out the beloved fifth husband, even as she had used up the first four.

Her fellow pilgrims clearly understand what the Wife is saying. Whether the reader is male or female, only tone deafness or revulsion from life could resist the Wife's most sublime moments of yearning and self-celebration. In the midst of her account of her fourth husband, she muses upon her love of wine and its close relation to her love of love, and then suddenly cries out,

> *But Lord Crist! whan that it remembreth me°*   [*I think*]
> *Upon my yowthe, and on my jolitee,°*   [*gaiety*]
> *It tikleth° me aboute myn herte rote.°*   [*tickles/heart's root*]
> *Unto this day it dooth myn herte bote°*   [*good*]
> *That I have had my world as in my tyme.*
> *But age, allas! that al wol evenyme,°*   [*poison*]
> *Hath me biraft° my beautee and my pith.°*   [*bereft of/vigor*]
> *Lat go,° farewel! the devel go therwith!*   [*Let it go*]
> *The flour is gone, ther is namore to telle:*
> *The bren,° as I best can, now moste I selle;*   [*bran or husks*]
> *But yet to be right mery wol I fonde.°*   [*try*]

There are no fresh revelations here; nothing that will help complete the scope and structure of the *Canterbury Tales*. These eleven lines mix the Wife's memory and desire, while acknowledging that time has transfigured her. If there is a passage in Chaucer that breaks through his own ironies, it is this one, in which all the irony belongs to time, invincible enemy of all heroic vitalists. Against that irony, the still heroic Wife of Bath sets the grandest of all her lines: "That I have had my world as in my tyme." "*My* time" is the triumph; reduced to husks as her vitality may be, the true pith of the woman abides in her Falstaffian high spirits. Ruefulness abounds and authenticates her realistic sense of loss: the rancidity of an aging lust may not be far away, but her understanding that only deliberate cheerfulness is appropriate for her constitutes the secular or experiential wisdom that completes her critique of the churchly ideals that might condemn her. Chaucer, feeling old indeed in his later fifties, has given her an eloquence worthy of both the character and her creator.

Does the Wife of Bath change in the course of her long confession of a prologue? Chaucerian irony is hardly a mode by which change is represented. We listen to the Wife of Bath's monologue; so do the Pilgrims. Does she overhear herself? We are very moved to hear that she has had her world in her time. Is she not moved also? She does not have the brilliantly schooled self-awareness of the Pardoner, who generally is blind only to the effect that he has on himself. The Wife's deepest affinity to Falstaff is that she appreciates her own appreciation of herself. She has no desire to change and therefore manifests throughout her prologue a spirited resistance to aging and so to the final form of change, death. What does alter in her is the quality of her high spirits, which transmute from natural exuberance into highly self-conscious vitalism.

That change, as far as I call tell, is not treated ironically by Chaucer, perhaps because, unlike so many of his scholars, he has too great an affection for his remarkable creation and allows her to appeal directly to the reader. Her deliberate cheerfulness differs from forced heartiness; the nearest analogue to it is the buoyancy of Sir John Falstaff, who has been even more maligned by scholarly critics. Falstaff's wit does not decline in *Henry IV, Part Two*, but we feel there is a darkening in him as his rejection by Hal gradually approaches. The Falstaffian gusto is still there, but the gaiety begins to acquire an edge, as though the will to live takes on a touch of an ideology of vitalism. The Wife of Bath and Falstaff both become less like the Panurge of Rabelais. They are still bearers of the Blessing, and both still cry out for more life, but they have learned that there is no time without boundaries, and they accept the new role of being agonists, fighting for their waning share of the Blessing. Although the wife has a powerful command of rhetoric and a dangerous wit, she cannot compete with Falstaff in these regards. Her rugged consciousness of a diminishment in vitality and her strong will to maintain her high spirits are closer analogues to Shakespeare's greatest comic character.

The Wife and Falstaff are ironists, early and late, and they found their authority upon their self-confident personalities, as Donaldson has noted. With Don Quixote, Sancho Panza, and Panurge they make up a company or family devoted to the order of play, as opposed to the order of society or of the organized spirit. What the order of play confers, within its strict limits, is freedom, the inner freedom of ceasing to be badgered by one's own superego. I take it that this is why one reads Chaucer and Rabelais, Shakespeare and Cervantes. For a space, the superego ceases to whack one for supposedly harboring aggressivity. The rhetorical drive of the Wife and of Falstaff is nothing if not aggressive, but the pragmatic aim is freedom: from the world, from time, from the moralities of state and church, from whatever in the self impedes the self's triumphs of self-expression. Even some admirers of the Wife of Bath and Falstaff persist in calling them solipsists; but egocentricity is not solipsism. The Wife and Falstaff are perfectly aware of neighbors and the sun, but very few who come near them interest us much, compared to these enchanted vitalists.

Many scholars have pointed to the equivocal relation both the Wife and Falstaff have to the text in First Corinthians in which Paul calls on Christians to persist in their vocation. The Wife's version is, "In such a state as God hath cleped us / I wol persever: I nam not precious," and Falstaff both echoes and outdoes her: "Why, Hal, 'tis my vocation, Hal, 'tis no sin for a man to labor in his vocation." In mocking Paul, the Wife and Falstaff are not being primarily impious. As wits they are both disenchanters, but they remain believers. The Wife deftly keeps reminding the godly that perfection is not required of her, while Falstaff is haunted by the fate of Dives the glutton. Falstaff is more anxiety-ridden than the Wife, but she has not suffered the misfortune of regarding the future Henry V as a kind of adopted son. Being Shakespeare's rather than Chaucer's, Falstaff undergoes more change by internalization than the Wife is capable of experiencing. Both characters listen to themselves, but only Falstaff consistently overhears himself. I suspect that the crucial character in Chaucer for Shakespeare was not the Wife of Bath but the Pardoner, ancestor of all Western literary characters condemned to nihilism. I abandon the Wife of Bath and Falstaff reluctantly, but to go from them to the Pardoner and his Shakespearean progeny is only to forsake positive for negative vitalism. No one could love the Pardoner, or Iago; but no one resists their negative exuberance.

IT IS A CRITICAL commonplace to link the Wife of Bath and Falstaff, but I have seen no speculation on the highly possible descent of Shakespeare's great villains, Iago in *Othello* and Edmund in *King Lear,* from the Pardoner. Marlowe's hero-villains, Tamburlaine the Great and even more Barabas, the wily Jew of Malta, clearly made a deep impression on Shakespeare's portrayal of Aaron the Moor in his first tragedy, the charnelhouse *Titus Andronicus,* and on that of Richard III. Between Aaron and Richard on the one hand and Iago and Edmund on the other, a shadow intervenes, and it seems to belong to the antithetical Pardoner, who is the outcast of the *Canterbury Tales.* Even his prologue and tale are outside the apparent structure of Chaucer's all-but-finished major poem. As a kind of floater, the Pardoner's Tale is its own world; it resembles nothing else in Chaucer, yet it seems to me his high point as a poet and is in its way unsurpassable, at one of the limits of art. Donald Howard, musing on the difference between the Pardoner and his story and the rest of the *Canterbury Tales,* compares the Pardoner's intrusion to "the marginal world of medieval aesthetics, the lewd or quotidian drawings in the margins of serious manuscripts," forerunners of Hieronymus Bosch. So pungent are the Pardoner's presence and his narration that the marginal becomes central in Chaucer, inaugurating what Nietzsche was to call "the uncanniest guest," the representation of European nihilism. The link between the Pardoner and Shakespeare's grand negations, Iago and Edmund, seems to me as profound as Dostoevsky's reliance upon Shakespeare's intellectual villains as models for Svidrigailov and Stavrogin.

The Pardoner first appears with his horrible chum, the grotesque Summoner, toward the close of the General Prologue. The Summoner is the equivalent of the thought police who currently afflict Iran; he is a layman who drags supposed spiritual offenders into a religious court. A snooper into sexual relations, he rakes off a percentage of the earnings of all the prostitutes at work in his diocese and blackmails their customers. As narrator of the General Prologue, the Pilgrim Chaucer expresses appreciation for the Summoner's mildness at blackmail: a mere quart of strong red wine each year permits an ongoing sexual relation to continue. Irony for once seems overcome by Chaucer's reluctance to react to the Summoner's moral squalor, which merely helps to provide context for the far more spectacular Pardoner. The Summoner is just an amiable brute, a fit companion for the Pardoner, who plunges us into an inferno of consciousness more Shakespearean than Dantesque because mutable in the highest degree. Chaucer inherits the identity of pardoners and charlatans from the literature and reality of his own times, but the remarkable personality of his Pardoner seems to me his most extraordinary invention.

Pardoners traveled about selling indulgences for sins in defiance of canon law, but rather clearly with church connivance. As lay persons, pardoners were not supposed to preach, but they did, and Chaucer's Pardoner is a superb preacher, surpassing any televangelist currently on the American scene. Critics divide on the Pardoner's sexual nature: is he a eunuch, a homosexual, a hermaphrodite? None of the above, I venture; and in any case Chaucer has seen to it that we just don't know. Perhaps the Pardoner knows; we are not certain even of that. Of the twenty-nine pilgrims, he is much the most questionable, but also much the most intelligent, in that regard almost a rival to Chaucer, the thirtieth pilgrim. The Pardoner's gifts are indeed so formidable that we are compelled to wonder about his long foreground, of which he tells us nothing. A knowing religious hypocrite, trading in spurious relics and daring to traffic in the redemption open through Jesus, he is nevertheless an authentic spiritual consciousness with a powerful religious imagination.

The heart of darkness that is an obscurantist metaphor in Joseph Conrad is all too appropriate a figure for the demoniac Pardoner, who rivals his fictive descendants as a kind of problematic abyss, depraved yet imaginative in the highest degree. One critic of Chaucer, R. A. Shoaf, brilliantly observes of the Pardoner, "He sells himself, his act, every day in his profession; but, to judge from the pattern of his obsession, he knows because he regrets that he cannot buy himself back." What he knows is that his performances, however astonishing, cannot redeem him, and we begin to suspect, as we ponder his spiel and his tale, that something beyond greed and the pride of preaching with power has driven him to his life's work as a professional deceiver. We can never know what it was in Chaucer that could create this first nihilist, at least in literature, but I find suggestive a characteristic paradox of G. K. Chesterton's:

Geoffrey Chaucer was exactly what "the gentle Pardoner" was not—he was a gentle Pardoner. But we shall misunderstand all the men of that curious and rather complex society, if we do not realize that in a sense their eccentricities were connected with the same centre. The official venality of the bad Pardoner, and the very unofficial amiability of the good Pardoner, both came from the peculiar temptations and difficult diplomacies of the same religious system. They came because it was not, in the Puritan sense, a simple system. It was accustomed, even in minds much more serious than Chaucer's, to seeing (so to speak) two sides of a sin; now as a venial sin utterly and unutterably different in its ultimate direction from a mortal sin. It was out of the abuse of distinctions of that kind that the distortions and corruptions appeared, which are made vivid in the flagrant figure of the Pardoner; the practice of Indulgences which had degenerated from the theory of Indulgences. But it was out of the use of distinctions of that kind that a man like Chaucer had originally reached the sort of balanced and delicate habit of mind, the habit of looking at all sides of the same thing; the power to realize that even an evil has a right to its own place in the hierarchy of evils, to realize, at least, that in the abysmal relativities of Hell and Purgatory, there are even things more unpardonable than the Pardoner.

Chesterton attributes to Chaucer a perspectivism made possible only by the overwhelming reality of the medieval Catholic faith. Whatever the root, the perspectivism matters poetically more than the faith. The ambivalence of perspectivism breaks loose the Pardoner, a figure who marks the limit of Chaucerian irony. In general, Chaucer is a true comic poet, in our sense (the Shakespearean one) of comedy. The Pardoner's prologue and his tale are not comic, but lethal. He is, as he says, "a ful vicious man," but he is also a genius—a lesser term will not do, either for the Pardoner or for Iago after him. Like Iago, the Pardoner combines the gifts of dramatist or storyteller, actor, and director; and, again like Iago, the Pardoner is both a supreme moral psychologist and a pioneering depth psychologist. The Pardoner, Iago, and Edmund cast a spell over their victims, ourselves included. All of them overtly proclaim their deceptiveness, but only to us, or in the Pardoner's case, to the Canterbury pilgrims as our surrogates. Their exultation in their own intellectual powers and in their viciousness captivates us, as sublime literary outrageousness always does. The negative exuberance of the Pardoner, Iago, and Edmund is as engaging as the positive exuberance of the Wife of Bath, Panurge, and Falstaff. We respond to energy, as William Hazlitt emphasized in his essay "On Poetry in General":

> We see the thing ourselves, and show it to others as we feel it to exist, and as, in spite of ourselves, we are compelled to think of it. The imagination, by thus embodying and turning them to shape, gives an obvious relief to the indistinct and importunate cravings of the will.—We do not wish the thing to be so; but we wish it to appear such as it is. For knowledge is conscious power; and the mind is no longer in this case, the dupe, though it may be the victim of vice or folly.

Of Iago, Hazlitt wrote "He is quite or nearly as indifferent to his own fate as to that of others; he runs all risks for a trifling and doubtful advantage; and is himself the dupe and victim of his ruling passion"—all of which is equally apt in regard to the Pardoner. Iago and the Pardoner contaminate us, as Shakespeare and Chaucer well understood. We delight in the Pardoner's inventions, his "holy relics": glass cases full of rags and bones and magical mittens. And we share his zest at disowning any moral consequences of his preaching:

Myn hondes and my tonge goon so yerne°	[*rapidly*]
That it is joye to see my bisinesse.	
Of avaryce and of swich° cursednesse	[*such*]
Is al my preching, for° to make hem free°	[*in order/generous*]
To yeven hir pens, and namely unto me.	
For myn entente° is nat but for to winne,	[*intention, profit*]
And nothing° for correccioun of sinne:	[*not at all*]
I rekke° nevere, whan that they ben beried,°	[*care/buried*]
Though that hir soules goon a-blakeberied!	

It is a joy for us to hear this and to see it through our hearing. An even deeper joy comes from reading the Pardoner's masterpiece of a tale, in which three tavern revelers, roaring boys who would now be Hell's Angels bikers, set forth to slay Death himself, it being plague time and Death being very active. They encounter a poor, infinitely old man who seeks only to return to his mother, the earth:

> And on the ground, which is my modres° gate,   [mother's]
> I knokke with my staf bothe erly and late,
> And seye, "Leve moder, leet me in!"

Threatened by the thugs, the uncanny old man directs them to where they will find Death, in the shape of a pile of gold coins beneath an oak. Two conspire to stab the youngest, but not before he has thoughtfully poisoned their wine. The old man's prophecy is fulfilled, but we are left wondering just who he is. Evidently he was Chaucer's own invention, which means that, within the *Canterbury Tales*, he is the product of the Pardoner's genius. A wandering old man, in apparent league with death though he himself, despite his wish, cannot die, and who directs others to the wealth he either scorns or has abandoned—scholars sensibly identify such a figure with the legend of the Wandering Jew. Does the Pardoner, knowingly facing damnation, fear to become another such wanderer? As the projection of the Pardoner, the strange old man exposes the emptiness of the Pardoner's boasts that only financial greed constitutes his motive for his career of deception. His authentic drive is for self-exposure, self-destruction, self-condemnation. He is doom-eager, or else needs to defer despair and self-immolation through sustaining the little death of humiliation by the bluff Host before the other pilgrims.

The crossing over from doom-eagerness as a condition to self-destruction as an act takes place in the Pardoner because he overhears himself speaking, and wills negatively on that basis. I find this moment particularly exciting because I suspect that it was for Shakespeare a crucial moment of poetic revisionism, out of which issued much that was original in the way of representing human character, cognition, and personality. Pandarus, the tricky go-between of Chaucer's *Troilus and Criseyde,* was hardly a sufficient forerunner for Iago and Edmund; the wily Pandarus is too good-natured, more than benign in his intentions. But here is the Pardoner, reacting to his own eloquence at concluding his awesome tale, and offering his professional services to his fellow pilgrims:

> *"Peraventure° ther may falle oon or two*   [*By chance*]
> *Doun of his hors, and breke his nekke atwo.°*   [*in two*]
> *Look which a seuretee° is it to you alle*   [*what a security*]
> *That I am in youre felaweship y-falle,*
> *That may assoille yow, bothe more and lasse,°*   [*great and small*]
>
> *Whan that the soule shal fro the body passe.*
> *I rede° that oure Host heer shal biginne,*   [*advise*]
> *For he is most envoluped° in sinne.*   [*enveloped, wrapped up*]
> *Com forth, sire Hoste, and offre first anon,°*   [*first now*]
> *And thou shalt kisse the reliks everichon,°*   [*every one*]
> *Ye, for a grote:° unbokel° anon they purs."* [*groat (fourpence)/ unbuckle*]

The palpable outrageousness of this speech invites a violent response and actually demands one when the address turns to the Host, the likeliest of all the pilgrims to crush the obsessed Pardoner. At this moment the Pardoner is in a desperate vertigo, just out of control, carried away by his own power of evocation into an unstoppable need for punishment. When the Host brutally offers to slice off and carry away the Pardoner's testicles, the voluble lay-preacher is reduced to silence: "So wroth he was no word ne wolde he say." I cannot separate this from Iago's final vow of silence: "From this time forth I never will speak word." The two grand negations share a concept of dread with which they contaminate us, even though they themselves do not consciously know the dread. Iago's genius is weirdly out of place in a spirit that knows only warfare, even as the Pardoner is a displaced spirit, exulting in deception even as he neglects his genius for evoking the terrors of eternity. Like the extraordinary cognitive powers of Edmund or of Dostoevsky's Svidrigailov, the wounding element in the Pardoner and in Iago is preternatural intelligence bent only on violating trust. The canonical greatness of Chaucer, who alone had the strength to teach Shakespeare the secrets of representation, comes to rest finally in the grimly prophetic portrait of the Pardoner, whose progeny are with us still, in life as in literature.

5.

Cervantes:
The Play of the World

W<small>E KNOW</small> more about Cervantes the man than we do about Shakespeare, and doubtless there is still much to be learned about him, because his life was vivid, arduous, and heroic. Shakespeare was an immense financial success as a playwright and died affluent, his societal ambitions (such as they were) fulfilled. Despite the popularity of *Don Quixote,* Cervantes received no royalties on it and had little luck with patrons. He had few realistic ambitions, beyond supporting himself and his family, and he failed as a playwright. Poetry was not his gift; *Don Quixote* was. Shakespeare's contemporary (they died, it is thought, on the same day), he has in common with Shakespeare the universality of his genius, and he is the only possible peer of Dante and Shakespeare in the Western Canon.

One thinks of him in conjunction with Shakespeare and Montaigne because the three of them are wisdom writers; there is no fourth so sane, temperate, and benign unless it be Molière, and in some sense he was Montaigne born again, but in another genre.

In one respect, only Cervantes and Shakespeare occupy the highest eminence; you cannot get ahead of them, because they are always there before you.

Confronting the strength of *Don Quixote,* the reader is never lessened, only enhanced. That is not true in many moments of reading Dante or Milton or Jonathan Swift, whose *Tale of a Tub* always impresses me as the best prose in the language after Shakespeare's and yet reproves me incessantly. It is also not true of the experience of reading Kafka, the central writer of our chaos. Shakespeare is again the nearest analogue to Cervantes; we are sustained by the dramatist's well-nigh infinite capacity for disinterestedness. Although Cervantes is ceaselessly careful to be faithfully Catholic, we do not read *Don Quixote* as a pious work. Presumably Cervantes was an Old Christian, not descended from Jewish *conversos* or New Christians, yet we cannot be certain about his origins, just as we cannot hope to surmise his attitudes precisely. Characterizing his ironies is an impossible task; missing them is also impossible.

Despite his heroic war service (he permanently lost the use of his left hand at the great sea battle of Lepanto against the Turks), Cervantes had to be very wary of the Counter-Reformation and the Inquisition. Quixote's modes of madness grant him, and Cervantes, something of a fool's license, akin to that of the Fool in *King Lear,* a work staged simultaneously with the publication of the first part of *Don Quixote.* Cervantes was almost certainly a disciple of Erasmus, the Dutch humanist whose writing on Christian inwardness appealed greatly to the *conversos,* caught between a Judaism they had been forced to abandon and a Christian system that made them second-class citizens. Cervantes' ancestral family was crowded with physicians, a popular Jewish profession in Spain before the expulsions and forced conversions of 1492. A century later, Cervantes seems subtly haunted by that terrible year, which did much harm to Jews and Moors, as well as to Spain's well-being as an economy and a society.

No two readers ever seem to read the same *Don Quixote,* and the most distinguished critics have failed to agree on most of the book's fundamental aspects. Erich Auerbach thought it had no rival in the representation of ordinary reality as a continuous gaiety. Having just finished rereading *Don Quixote,* I blink at my inability to find what Auerbach called "so universal and multi-layered, so noncritical and nonproblematical a gaiety." "Symbolic and tragic terms," even when employed to categorize the hero's madness, seemed false to Auerbach. Against that claim I set the most poignant and Quixotic of all critical agonists, the Basque man of letters Miguel de Unamuno, whose "tragic sense of life" was founded upon his intimate relationship with Cervantes' masterpiece, which for Unamuno replaced the Bible as the authentic Spanish Scripture. "Our Lord Don Quixote," Unamuno called him, a Kafkan before Kafka, because his madness comes from a faith in what Kafka was to name "indestructibility." Unamuno's Knight of the Sorrowful Countenance is a quester for survival, whose only madness is a crusade against death: "Great was Don Quixote's madness, and it was great because the root from which it grew was great: the inextinguishable longing to survive, a source of the most extravagant follies as well as the most heroic acts."

In this view, the Don's madness is a refusal to accept what Freud called "reality testing," or the reality principle. When Don Quixote makes friends with the necessity of dying, he dies soon enough, thus returning to a Christianity conceived as the cult of death—and not just by Unamuno among Spanish visionaries. For Unamuno, the book's gaiety belongs solely to Sancho Panza, who purges his *daimon,* Don Quixote, and thus pleasurably follows the sad knight through every outrageous misadventure. This reading is again very close to Kafka's extraordinary parable, "The Truth about Sancho Panza," in which it is Sancho who has devoured all the romances of chivalry until his imagined demon, personified as the Don, departs upon his adventures with Sancho tagging along. Perhaps Kafka was making *Don Quixote* into one long and rather bitter Jewish joke, but that may be more faithful to the book than reading it with Auerbach as unalloyed gaiety.

Probably only *Hamlet* spurs as many variant interpretations as *Don Quixote* does. No one among us can purge Hamlet of his Romantic interpreters, and Don Quixote has inspired just as numerous and persistent a Romantic school of criticism, as well as books and essays opposing such a supposed idealization of Cervantes' protagonist. Romantics (myself included) see Quixote as hero, not fool; decline to read the book primarily as satire; and find in the work a metaphysical or visionary attitude regarding the Don's quest that makes the Cervantine influence upon *Moby-Dick* seem wholly natural. From the German philosopher-critic Schelling in 1802 down to the Broadway musical *Man of La Mancha* in 1966, there has been a continuous exaltation of the supposedly impossible dream-quest. The novelists have been the major proponents of this apotheosis of Don Quixote: exuberant admirers have included Fielding, Smollett, and Sterne in England; Goethe and Thomas Mann in Germany; Stendhal and Flaubert in France; Melville and Mark Twain in the United States; and virtually all modern Hispanic American writers. Dostoevsky, who might seem the least Cervantine of writers, insisted that Prince Myshkin in *The Idiot* was modeled on Don Quixote. Since Cervantes' remarkable experiment is credited by many as having invented the novel, as opposed to the picaresque narrative, the devotion of so many later novelists is understandable enough; but the enormous passions evoked by the book, in Stendhal and Flaubert in particular, are extraordinary tributes to its achievement.

I myself naturally gravitate to Unamuno when I read *Don Quixote,* because for me the heart of the book is its revelation and celebration of heroic individuality, both in the Don and in Sancho. Unamuno rather perversely preferred the Don to Cervantes, but there I refuse to follow, because no writer has established a more intimate relation with his protagonist than Cervantes did. We wish we could know what Shakespeare himself thought of Hamlet; we know almost too much about how Don Quixote affected Cervantes, even if our knowledge is often indirect. Cervantes invented endless ways of disrupting his own narrative to compel the reader to tell the story in place of the wary author. The wily and wicked enchanters who supposedly work without ceasing to frustrate the magnificently indomitable Don Quixote are also employed to make us into unusually active readers. The Don supposes the sorcerers to exist, and Cervantes pragmatically realizes them as crucial components of his language. Everything is transformed through enchantment, is the Quixotic lament, and the wicked sorcerer is Cervantes himself. His characters have read all of the stories about one another, and much of the novel's second part concerns itself with their reactions to having read the first. The reader is educated into considerably more sophistication of response, even when Don Quixote stubbornly refuses to learn, though that refusal has more to do with his own "madness" than with the fictive status of the chivalric romances that have crazed him. The Don and Cervantes together evolve toward a new kind of literary dialectic, one that alternates in proclaiming both the potency and the vanity of the narrative in its relation to real events. Even as the Don, in part one, gradually comes to understand the limitations of fiction, so Cervantes grows in his pride of authorship and in the particular joy of having invented the Don and Sancho.

The loving, frequently irascible relationship between Quixote and Sancho is the greatness of the book, more even than the gusto of its representations of natural and social realities. What unites the Don and his squire is both their mutual participation in what has been called "the order of play" and their equally mutual if rather grumpy affection for each other. I cannot think of a fully comparable friendship anywhere else in Western literature, certainly not one that relies so exquisitely upon hilarious conversation. Angus Fletcher, in his *Colors of the Mind,* catches the aura of these conversations:

> Where Quixote and Sancho meet is in a certain kind of animation, the spiritedness of their conversations. As they talk, and often debate vigorously, they enlarge the field of each other's thoughts. No thought on either side goes unchecked or uncritiqued. By mainly courteous disagreement, most courteous when most sharply in conflict, they gradually establish an area of free play, where thoughts are set free for us the readers to ponder.

My personal favorite among the many scores of Quixote-Sancho exchanges takes place in part two, chapter 28, after the knight has emulated Sir John Falstaff in the wisdom of discretion as the better part of valor. Unfortunately, his decision has involved abandoning a stunned Sancho to a furious village. After the incident, poor Sancho moans that he aches all over and receives rather pedantic comfort from the knight:

"The reason for that," remarked Don Quixote, "is undoubtedly the fact that the club they used was a long one and caught you all the way down your back where those aching parts are located; and if it had gone any farther down, you would ache still more."

"By God," exclaimed Sancho, "your Grace has taken a great load off my mind and made everything as clear as can be! Body of me! Is the cause of my pain such a mystery that it is necessary to explain to me that I ache wherever the club reached me?"

Hidden in this exchange is the bond between the two, who beneath the surface enjoy the intimacy of equality. We can defer the question of which is the more original figure, while noting that the allied figure that they constitute together is more original than either is alone. A loving but quarrelsome duo, Sancho and the Don are united by more than their mutual affection and their authentic respect for each other. At their best, they are companions in the order of play, a sphere with its own rules and its own vision of reality: Unamuno is again the useful Cervantine critic here, but the theoretician is Johan Huizinga in his subtle book, *Homo Ludens* (1944), which barely mentions Cervantes. Huizinga begins by asserting that his subject, play, is to be distinguished from both comedy and folly: "The category of the comic is connected with *folly* in the highest and lowest sense of that word. Play, however, is not foolish. It lies outside the antithesis of wisdom and folly."

Don Quixote is neither a madman nor a fool, but someone who plays at being a knight-errant. Play is a voluntary activity, unlike madness and foolishness. Play, according to Huizinga, has four principal characteristics: freedom, disinterestedness, excludedness or limitedness, and order. You can test all of these qualities upon the Don's knight-errantry, but not always upon Sancho's faithful service as squire, for Sancho is slower to yield himself to play. The Don lifts himself into ideal place and time and is faithful to his own freedom, to its disinterestedness and seclusion, and to its limits, until at last he is defeated, abandons the game, returns to Christian "sanity," and so dies. Unamuno says of Quixote that he went out to seek his true fatherland and found it in exile. As always, Unamuno understood what was most inward in the great book. The Don, like the Jews and the Moors, is an exile, but in the mode of the *conversos* and *moriscos,* an internal exile. Don Quixote leaves his village to seek his spirit's home in exile, because only exiled can he be free.

CERVANTES NEVER tells us explicitly why Alonso Quijano (the book gives the name several variant spellings) was first driven to craze himself by reading chivalric romances, until at last he went out upon the roads to become Don Quixote. A poor gentleman of La Mancha, Alonso has only one vice: he is an obsessive reader of the popular literature of his day, which crowds reality out of his mind. Cervantes describes Alonso as a pure case of the unlived life. He is single, close to fifty, presumably without sexual experience, confined to the company of a housekeeper in her forties, a nineteen-year-old niece, a field hand, and his two friends: the village curate and Nicholas the barber. Not far away lives a peasant girl, the robust Aldonza Lorenzo, who has unknowingly become the ideal object of his fantasies, renamed in them as the great lady, Dulcinea del Toboso.

Whether she is truly the object of the good man's quest is unclear. One critic has gone so far as to suggest that Quijano is impelled to become Don Quixote because of barely repressed lust for his own niece, a notion nowhere in Cervantes' text, but an indication of the desperation to which Cervantes has been known to drive his scholars. All Cervantes tells us is that his hero has gone mad, and we are given no clinical details whatsoever. Unamuno's reaction seems to me the best one on the Quixotic loss of his wits: "He lost them for our sake, for our benefit, so as to leave us an eternal example of spiritual generosity." That is to say, Don Quixote goes mad as a vicarious atonement for our drabness, our ungenerous dearth of imagination.

Sancho, a poor peasant, is persuaded to go along as squire on the knight's second sally, which turns into the glorious affair of the windmills. The inducement for the good and ostensibly slow-witted Sancho is that he will govern an island, which the knight will conquer for him. Cervantes is inevitably ironic when he first introduces us to Sancho, whose wit is extraordinary and whose true desire is to gain fame rather than wealth, as a governor. More fundamentally, an element in Sancho desires the order of play, uneasy as the rest of Sancho is with some of the consequences of Quixotic play. Like the Don, Sancho searches for a new ego, an idea that Alejo Carpentier, the Cuban novelist, believes Cervantes first invented. I would say that Shakespeare and Cervantes came at it simultaneously, the difference between the two being the modalities of change in their principal characters.

Don Quixote and Sancho Panza are each other's ideal conversationalist; they change by listening to each other. In Shakespeare change comes from self-overhearing and from pondering the implications of what one has heard. Neither the Don nor Sancho is capable of overhearing himself; the Quixotic ideal and the Panzaesque reality are too strong for their upholders to doubt, so they cannot absorb their own departures from their standards. They can speak blasphemies but not recognize them when they emerge. The tragic greatness of the Shakespearean protagonists extends to comedy, history, and romance; only in climactic recognition scenes are the survivors able to listen fully to what others are saying. Shakespeare's influence, and not just in English-speaking countries, has overcome that of Cervantes. Modern solipsism stems from Shakespeare (and from Petrarch before him). Dante, Cervantes, Molière—who depend on interchanges between their personae—seem less natural than Shakespeare's gorgeous solipsism, and perhaps they are indeed less natural.

Shakespeare has no parallel to the exchanges between the Don and Sancho, because his friends and lovers never quite listen to one another. Think of Antony's death scene, in which Cleopatra hears and overhears mostly herself, or the attempts at play between Falstaff and Hal in which Falstaff is forced into defense because the prince so perpetually attacks. There are gentler exceptions, like Rosalind and Celia in *As You Like It;* but they are not the norm. Shakespearean individuality is matchless, but it exacts enormous costs. Cervantine egoism, exalted by Unamuno, is always qualified by the free relationship between Sancho and the Don, who grant one another space for play. Both Cervantes and Shakespeare are supreme in the creation of personality, but the greatest Shakespearean personalities—Hamlet, Lear, Iago, Shylock, Falstaff, Cleopatra, Prospero—at last wither gloriously in the air of an inward solitude. Don Quixote is saved by Sancho, and Sancho, by the Don. Their friendship is canonical and changes, in part, the subsequent nature of the canon.

WHAT DOES MADNESS mean if its sufferer cannot be deceived by other men or women? No one exploits Don Quixote, not even Quixote himself. He takes windmills for giants and puppet shows for realities, but he is not to be mocked, because he will outwit you. His madness is a *literary* madness and can be contrasted usefully to the only partly literary madness of the speaker in Robert Browning's great chivalric romance, "Childe Roland to the Dark Tower Came." Don Quixote is mad because his great prototype, the Orlando (Roland) of Ariosto's *Orlando Furioso,* fell into an erotic madness. So, as the Don points out to Sancho, did Amadis of Gaul, another heroic precursor. Browning's Childe Roland wants only to be "fit to fail," even as the poet-knights one by one failed before him at the Dark Tower. Don Quixote is considerably healthier than that; he wants to win, no matter how many times he gets painfully flattened. His madness, as he makes clear, is a poetic strategy worked out by others before him, and he is nothing if not a traditionalist.

Cervantes was wary of too close a Spanish precursor; his deepest affinities were with the *converso* Fernando de Rojas, author of the great narrative drama *Celestina,* not exactly a Catholic work in its savage amoralism and its lack of theological suppositions. Cervantes remarked that it "would be a divine book, in my view, if it concealed more the human," clearly meaning the refusal of human sexuality to accept any moral constraints. Don Quixote, of course, imposes moral constraints upon his sexual desires to such an extent that he might as well be a priest, which according to Unamuno he truly was: a priest of the true Spanish church, the Quixotic. The Don's perpetual eagerness for battle against nearly all odds is rather clearly a sublimation of the sexual drive. The obscure object of his desire, the enchanted Dulcinea, is the emblem of glory to be attained in and through violence, always rendered by Cervantes as an absurdity. A survivor of Lepanto and other battles, as well as of long years of Moorish captivity and then of Spanish prisons (where *Don Quixote* may have been begun), Cervantes had firsthand knowledge of battle and of bondage. We are intended to regard Don Quixote's shocking heroism with both great respect and considerable irony, a Cervantine stance not too easy to analyze. Outrageous as its manifestations are, the Don's courage convincingly surpasses that of any other hero in Western literature.

Direct confrontation of the greatness of *Don Quixote* cannot proceed very far without the critic's courage. Cervantes, with all his ironies, is in love with Don Quixote and Sancho Panza, and so is any reader who loves reading. Explaining love is a vain exercise in life, where the word "love" means everything and nothing but ought to be a rational possibility in regard to the greatest literature. Here Cervantes may have touched the universal more surely even than Shakespeare, since I remain bewildered that my intense love for Don Quixote's only rival among knights-errant, Sir John Falstaff, is not necessarily shared by all of my students, let alone by most of my fellow teachers. No one goes about calling Don Quixote "a disgusting and besotted old wretch," which was G. B. Shaw's judgment against Falstaff, but there are always Cervantine critics who persist in labeling the Don a fool and a madman, and who tell us that Cervantes is satirizing his hero's "undisciplined egocentricity." If that were true, there would be no book, for who wants to read about Alonso Quijano the Good? Disenchanted at the very end, he dies religiously and sanely, always reminding me of those friends of my youth who went through decades of psychoanalysis interminable, to terminate shrunken indeed and dried out, all passion spent, fit to die analytically and sanely. Even part one of the great book is anything but a satire on the hero, and part two, as is generally recognized, is so designed as to cause the reader an even firmer identification with the Don, and with Sancho.

Herman Melville, with authentic American gusto, called Don Quixote "that sagest sage that ever lived," happily ignoring the hero's fictiveness. There were for Melville three prime originals among literary characters: Hamlet, Don Quixote, and the Satan of *Paradise Lost*. Ahab, alas, was not quite a fourth—perhaps because he blended all three—but his crew acquired a Cervantine atmosphere, directly prayed for by Melville in a wonderful peroration that stations Cervantes, memorably and insanely, in the middle between the visionary of *Pilgrim's Progress* and President Andrew Jackson, hero of all American Democrats:

> Bear me out in it, thou great democratic God! who didst not refuse to the swart convict, Bunyan, the pale, poetic pearl; Thou who didst clothe with doubly hammered leaves of finest gold, the stumped and pauperized arm of old Cervantes; Thou who didst pick up Andrew Jackson from the pebbles; who didst hurl him upon a war-horse; who didst thunder him higher than a throne! Thou who, in all Thy mighty, earthly marchings, ever cullest Thy selectest champions from the kingly commons; bear me out in it, O God!

That is an ecstasy of the American religion, having little in common with the wary Catholicism of Cervantes, but much that is parallel with the Spanish religion of Quixotism as expounded by Unamuno. The tragic sense of life, discovered by Unamuno in *Don Quixote*, is also the faith of *Moby-Dick*. Ahab is a monomaniac; so is the kindlier Quixote, but both are tormented idealists who seek justice in human terms, not as theocentric men but as ungodly, godlike men. Ahab seeks only Moby-Dick's destruction; renown is nothing to the Quaker captain, and revenge is everything.

No one, except a panoply of mythical enchanters, has done any harm to Don Quixote, who absorbs buffetings with endless stoicism. The Don's motive, according to Unamuno, is eternal fame, interpreted as "an expansion of the personality in space and time." I read that as the secular equivalent of the Blessing in the Yahwist: more life into a time without boundaries. Generosity and simple goodness are the Quixotic virtues. His vice, if there is one, is the Golden Age Spanish conviction that victory through arms is everything; but since he is so frequently defeated, this failing is transitory at worst.

As I do, Unamuno took most seriously the Don's sublimated desire for Aldonza Lorenzo and his subsequent Beatrice-like exaltation of her as the angelic if unfortunately enchanted Dulcinea, which allows us to see the knight in something close to his full complexity. He lives by faith while knowing, as his lucid outbursts show, that he believes in a fiction, and knowing—at least in flashes—that it is only a fiction. Dulcinea is a supreme fiction, and Don Quixote, an obsessed reader, is a poet of action who has created a grand myth. Unamuno's Quixote is a paradoxical agonist, the ancestor of the diminished questers who wander through our chaos in Kafka and Beckett. The hero of a secular "indestructibility" was perhaps unintended by Cervantes himself, but he achieves apotheosis in Unamuno's fiery commentary. This Quixote is a metaphysical actor, able to risk derision in order to keep idealism alive.

AGAINST THE IDEALISTIC knight of an essentially erotic faith, Cervantes sets the figure of the trickster, an extraordinary, quite Shakespearean character, Ginés de Pasamonte, who first appears in part one, chapter 22, as one of the prisoners bound for the galleys, and returns again in part two, chapters 25–27, as the illusionist Master Pedro, who divinates through a mystical monkey and then stages a puppet show so vivid that Don Quixote, mistaking it for his own reality, attacks and demolishes the puppets. In Ginés, Cervantes gives us an imaginary figure who would be as much at home in the Elizabethan underworld as in the lower depths of Golden Age Spain. When Don Quixote and Sancho first encounter him, he is being marched down a road together with a dozen other prisoners, all condemned by the king to service as galley slaves. The other culprits are handcuffed, and all are strung together by their necks on an iron chain. Ginés, the most formidable, is chained more extravagantly (unless otherwise indicated, I use here and throughout Samuel Putnam's translation):

Back of these came a man around thirty years of age and of very good appearance, except that when he looked at you his eyes were seen to be a little crossed. He was shackled in a different manner from the others, for he dragged behind him a chain so huge that it was wrapped all around his body, with two rings at the throat, one of which was attached to the chain while the other was fastened to what is known as a keep-friend or friend's foot, from which two irons hung down to his waist, ending in handcuffs secured by a heavy padlock in such a manner that he could neither raise his hands to his mouth nor lower his head to reach his hands.

Ginés, as the guards explain, is famously dangerous, so bold and cunning that even chained as he is, they fear his escape. His sentence is ten years in the galleys, which is equivalent to civil death. The cruel inability of Ginés' head and hands to reach one another is, as Roberto González Echevarria notes, an irony directed against the authors of picaresque novels, for the picaroon Ginés is at work composing his own history, as he boasts:

"If you want to know anything about my life, know that I am Ginés de Pasamonte whose life story has been written down by those fingers that you see here."

"He speaks the truth," said the commissary, "for he has himself written his story, as big as you please, and has left the book in the prison, having pawned it for two hundred reales."

"And I mean to redeem it," said Ginés, "even if it costs me two hundred ducats."

"Is it as good as that?" inquired Don Quixote.

"It is so good," replied Ginés, "that it will cast into the shade *Lazarillo de Tormes* and all others of that sort that have been or will be written. What I would tell you is that it deals with facts, and facts so interesting and amusing that no lies could equal them."

"And what is the title of the book?" asked Don Quixote.

"The Life of Ginés de Pasamonte."

"Is it finished?"

"How could it be finished," said Ginés, "when my life is not finished as yet?"

The outrageous Ginés has stated a grand principle of the picaresque, one that does not apply to *Don Quixote,* even though that work too ends with the death of the hero. But Don Quixote dies metaphorically before Alonso Quijano the Good dies literally. *Lazarillo de Tormes,* the anonymous archetype of the Spanish picaresque, first published in 1553, remains wonderfully readable and was beautifully rendered into English by the poet W. S. Merwin in 1962. If the story of the boastful Ginés had been better than that, it would have been very good indeed; but of course it is, because it is part of *Don Quixote.* Ginés has done a previous four-year term in the galleys but is saved from his ten-year sentence through the intervention of the sublimely mad Quixote. Ginés and the other convicts escape, despite poor Sancho's desperate warning to his master that his action directly defies the king. Cervantes, himself a captive of the Moors for five years and imprisoned again in Spain for his supposed derelictions as a tax collector, clearly expresses a personal passion beyond irony in the speech of the Don that includes the plangent "There will be no dearth of others to serve his Majesty under more propitious circumstances; and it does not appear to me to be just to make slaves of those whom God created as free men."

After a general melee the guards run off, and the knight instructs the freed convicts to present themselves to Dulcinea, so as to describe the adventure. Ginés, after trying to talk sense to the soon infuriated Quixote, leads the convicts in stoning and stripping their savior and Sancho, before running off, until

> They were left alone now—the ass and Rocinante, Sancho and Don Quixote: the ass, crestfallen and pensive, wagging its ears now and then, being under the impression that the hurricane of stones that had raged about them was not yet over; Rocinante, stretched alongside his master, for the hack also had been felled by a stone; Sancho, naked and fearful of the Holy Brotherhood, and Don Quixote, making wry faces at seeing himself so mishandled by those to whom he had done so much good.

The pathos of this passage seems to me exquisite; it is one of those Cervantine effects that never leave one. Unamuno, as sublimely crazy as his lord, Don Quixote, delightfully comments, "All of which should teach us to liberate galley slaves precisely because they will not be grateful to us for it." The rueful Quixote disagrees with his Basque exegete and vows to Sancho that the lesson is learned, to which the wise squire ripostes, "If your Grace takes warning, then I am a Turk." It was Cervantes who took warning, because of his affection for his minor but superb creation, Ginés de Pasamonte, "the famous rogue and thief." Ginés, confidence man and shamanistic imp of the perverse, is what might be called one of the canonical criminal characters in literature, like Shakespeare's Barnardine in *Measure for Measure* or Balzac's superb Vautrin. If Vautrin can reappear as Abbé Carlos Herréra, then Ginés can manifest himself as Master Pedro, the puppet master. An important question to ask is what, besides the pride of authorship, impelled Cervantes to bring back Ginés de Pasamonte in part two of *Don Quixote*.

Critics generally agree that the contrast between Ginés and the Don, picaroon trickster and chivalric visionary, is partly an opposition of two literary genres, the picaresque and the novel, which Cervantes essentially invented, in much the same way that Shakespeare (who did not know Greek tragedy, only its crippled remnant in the Roman Seneca) invented modern tragedy and modern tragicomedy as well. As in the Shakespearean protagonists, authentic inwardness incarnates itself in Don Quixote, whereas the scamp Pasamonte is all outwardness, despite his deep talents at duplicity. Ginés is a shapeshifter; he cannot change except in externals. The Don, like the great Shakespearean characters, cannot stop changing: that is the purpose of his frequently irascible but always finally loving conversations with the faithful Sancho. Bound together by the order of play, they are also united by the endless further humanization they bring about in each other. Their crises are innumerable; how could they not be, in the realm of the Quixotic? Sancho hesitates sometimes on the verge of abandoning the relationship, yet he cannot; partly he is fascinated, but in the end he is held by love, and so is the Don. The love cannot perhaps be distinguished from the order of play, but that is as it should be. Certainly one reason for Ginés de Pasamonte's return in part two is that he never participates in play, even as puppet master.

Every reader recognizes that the difference between the two parts of *Don Quixote* is that everyone who matters most in part

two is either explicitly credited with having read part one or knows
that he was a character in it. That provides a different frame for
the reappearance of the picaroon Ginés when we reach the moment
in part two, chapter 25 when we encounter a man clad in chamois
skin, hose, breeches, and a doublet, and with a patch of green
taffeta over one eye and that whole side of his face. This is Master
Pedro come, as he says, with the divining ape and the spectacle
of the freeing of Melisendra by her husband, the famous knight-
errant, Don Gaiferos, she being the daughter of Charlemagne held
captive by the Moors, and he being a principal vassal of Charlemagne.

The landlord at the inn where Master Pedro joins Don Quixote
and Sancho Panza says of the puppet master that "he talks more
than six men, and drinks more than a dozen." After he identifies
the Don and Sancho, at the advice of his divining ape (whose
divination goes only backward, from present to past), Ginés-Pedro
stages the puppet show, certainly one of the metaphorical splendors of Cervantes' masterpiece. The classic exegesis here is from
Ortega y Gasset, in his *Meditations on Quixote;* he compares
Master Pedro's puppet show to the Velázquez *Maids of Honor,*
where the artist in painting the king and queen simultaneously
places his studio in the picture. It is not a painting upon which
Don Quixote could safely have gazed, and he is certainly the worst
possible audience for the puppet show:

> Upon seeing such a lot of Moors and hearing such a din, Don
> Quixote thought that it would be a good thing for him to aid
> the fugitives; and, rising to his feet, he cried out, "Never so long
> as I live and in my presence will I permit such violence to be
> done to so famous a knight and so bold a lover as Don Gaiferos.
> Halt, lowborn rabble; cease your pursuit and persecution, or
> otherwise ye shall do battle with me!"
>
> With these words he drew his sword, and in one bound was
> beside the stage; and then with accelerated and unheard-of fury
> he began slashing at the Moorish puppets, knocking some of
> them over, beheading others, crippling this one, mangling that
> one. Among the many blows he dealt was one downward stroke
> that, if Master Pedro had not ducked and crouched, would have

sliced off his head more easily than if it had been made of almond paste.

That downward stroke, by no means unintended, may be the heart of this delightful intervention. Master Pedro has intruded in the order of play, where he has no place, and it moves to avenge itself upon the rogue. A while before, Don Quixote has said to Sancho that the puppet master must have made a bargain with the devil, because the divining ape "answers only questions about the past or the present, for that is as far as the devil's knowledge extends." The knight's suspicion of the trickster continues when he criticizes Master Pedro's mistakes in ascribing church bells to the Moorish mosques. Ginés-Pedro's defensive reply further prepares us for the Don's shattering of the show:

> "Don't be looking for trifles, Señor Don Quixote, or expect things to be impossibly perfect. Are not a thousand comedies performed almost every day that are full of inaccuracies and absurdities, yet they run their course and are received not only with applause but with admiration and all the rest? Go on, boy, and let him talk; for so long as I fill my wallet, it makes no difference if there are as many inaccuracies in my show as there are motes in the sun."

Don Quixote's reply is the grimly laconic: "You have spoken the truth." Here Master Pedro has become Cervantes' great literary rival, the monstrously productive and successful poet-playwright Lope de Vega, whose financial triumphs heightened Cervantes' sense of commercial failure as a stage dramatist. The knight's subsequent assault upon pasteboard illusions is at once a critique of public taste and a metaphysical manifestation of Quixotic or visionary will, making ghostlier the demarcations between art and nature. The humor of disjunction is salted by literary satire, hardly mitigated by the aftermath in which the chastened Don makes financial amends for his generous error and blames the usual wicked enchanters for having deceived him. Ginés de Pasamonte then vanishes from the story, for he has performed his function as picaroon foil to the visionary knight. We are left with not only delight, but an aesthetic fable that goes on reverberating as an epitome of the Quixotic enterprise, showing at once its limits and its heroic persistence at breaking beyond the normative boundaries of literary representation. Ginés, archetype of the picaresque, cannot compete with the Don, forerunner of the triumph of the novel.

READERS DIVIDE over their preference for part one or part two of *Don Quixote*, perhaps because these are not only very different works but curiously separate from each other, not so much in tone and attitude as in the relation of the Don and Sancho to their world. I do not hear any weariness in Cervantes in part two (which I prefer), but knight and squire alike have to sustain a new self-consciousness, and sometimes they seem to take this as an implicit burden. To know that you are a character in an ongoing book is not always a help in your adventures. Surrounded by readers of their earlier debacles, Don Quixote and Sancho nevertheless remain uninhibited. Sancho actually gains in zest, and there is an even greater closeness in friendship between the two characters. Best of all, there is Sancho on his own, during his ten days of being a wise and much-harried governor, until he sensibly resigns and returns to Don Quixote and to himself. What happens to Cervantes in this part moves me most, because his relation to his own writing changes. He is facing toward death, and something of him (as he knows) will die with Don Quixote, while something else, perhaps deeper, will live on in Sancho Panza.

Cervantes' relation to his enormous book is never easy to categorize. Leo Spitzer saw it as conferring a new if carefully limited authority on the literary artist:

High above this worldwide cosmos of his making ... Cervantes's artistic self is enthroned, an all-embracing creative self, Nature-like, God-like, almighty, all wise, all good—and benign ... this artist is God-like but not deified. ... Cervantes always bows before the supernal wisdom of God, as embodied in the teachings of the Catholic Church and the established order of the state and of society.

Whether or not he was descended from Jewish forced converts, Cervantes would have been suicidal not to so bow, as Spitzer surely knew. Whatever *Don Quixote* is or is not, it is scarcely a Catholic devotional novel, or a paean to "sovereign reason," as Spitzer also suggested. The book's continuous laughter is frequently melancholy, even painful, and Don Quixote is both a stalwart of humane affection and a man of sorrow. Can the "peculiarly Cervantean" ever be defined? Erich Auerbach said that it "cannot be described in words" but courageously tried anyway:

> It is not a philosophy; it is no didactic purpose; it is not even a being stirred by the uncertainty of human existence or by the power of destiny, as in the case of Montaigne and Shakespeare. It is an attitude—an attitude toward the world, and hence also toward the subject matter of his art—in which bravery and equanimity play a major part. Together with the delight he takes in the multifariousness of his sensory play there is in him a certain Southern reticence and pride. This prevents him from taking the play very seriously.

I confess that these eloquent sentences do not describe the *Don Quixote* I persist in rereading, if only because Cervantes seems to take the play of the world and the counterplay of Don Quixote and Sancho Panza very seriously as well as ironically. The Cervantean is as multivalent as the Shakespearean: it contains us, with all of our severe differences from one another. Wisdom is as much an attribute of the Don and Sancho, particularly when they are considered together, as intelligence and mastery of language are qualities of Sir John Falstaff, Hamlet, and Rosalind. Cervantes' two heroes are simply the largest literary characters in the whole Western Canon, except for their triple handful (at most) of Shakespearean peers. Their fusion of folly and wisdom and their disinterestedness can be matched only in Shakespeare's most memorable men and women. Cervantes has naturalized us as Shakespeare has: we can no longer see what makes *Don Quixote* so permanently original, so searchingly strange a work. If the play of the world can still be located in the greatest literature, then it must be here.

6.

Montaigne and Molière: The Canonical Elusiveness of the Truth

THERE APPEARS to be no single figure in French literature who is at the center of the national canon: no Shakespeare, no Dante, Goethe, Cervantes, Pushkin, Whitman. Instead there is a concourse of titans, any of whom might be nominated: Rabelais, Montaigne, Molière, Racine, Rousseau, Hugo, Baudelaire, Flaubert, Proust. Perhaps one could designate a composite author, Montaigne-Molière, for the greatest of essayists was the spiritual father of Shakespeare's only rival as a comic dramatist.

Molière considered his enterprise, the amusement of decent people, an odd venture, which Shakespeare, the most comprehensive of consciousnesses, presumably did not. His audience welcomed all his indecencies. Queen Elizabeth was certainly not the Sun King, Louis XIV; and even James I, the most intellectual of British monarchs, never quite became Shakespeare's crucial playgoer, as Louis XIV had to be for Molière. Perhaps that consideration restricted Molière, though certainly not much, since he is nearly as universal a dramatist as Shakespeare. He has a surprising affinity to Shakespeare, in which a mutual relation to Montaigne may play a part. Molière's Hamlet is Alceste, protagonist of *The Misanthrope*. Both characters stem from aspects of Montaigne, and both justify Nietzsche's savage, permanently disturbing apothegm: "That which we can find words for is something already dead in our hearts; there is always a kind of contempt in the act of speaking." Such contempt is surmounted by Hamlet only in act V, and never by Alceste. Nietzsche's vehement insight applies to speaking, not to writing, so it is antithetical to the art of Montaigne the essayist.

Emerson, like Nietzsche a professed disciple of Montaigne, famously said of the *Essays,* "Cut these words and they would bleed; they are vascular and alive." Montaigne's triumph was to fuse himself and his book in an overt act that has to be called originality, a word more positive in English than in French, where to be an original is to be peculiar. What may be least French in Montaigne is the strangeness of his radical originality, yet it was the strangeness that made him canonical, not just for France but for the West. I always return with fresh wonder to this unrealized truth about the Western Canon: works are appropriated by it for their singularity, not because they fit smoothly into an existing order. Like every major canonical author, Montaigne startles the common reader at each fresh encounter, if only because he is unlike any preconception we bring to him. He can be interpreted as skeptic, humanist, Catholic, Stoic, even Epicurean, very nearly what you will.

His scope and capaciousness sometimes approach Shakespearean dimensions, and one way to consider him, though he knew nothing of Shakespeare while Shakespeare knew something of him, is as the largest-scale of all Shakespearean characters, huger than Hamlet as a questing self. Montaigne changes as he rereads and revises his own book; more perhaps than in any other instance, the book is the man is the book. No other writer overhears himself so acutely as Montaigne perpetually does; no other book is so much an ongoing process. I cannot make myself familiar with it, though I reread it constantly, because it is a miracle of mutability. The only equivalent reading experience that I know is to reread endlessly in the notebooks and journals of Ralph Waldo Emerson, the American version of Montaigne. But Emerson's journals are necessarily a vast sprawl, not a book, and Montaigne's self-assays are a book. For an elegiac literary critic like myself, Montaigne's *Essays* have scriptural status, competing with the Bible, the Koran, Dante, and Shakespeare. Of all French authors, even Rabelais and Molière, Montaigne seems the least confined by a national culture, though paradoxically he had much to do with forming the mind of France.

Montaigne's mother, whom he scarcely mentions, came from a family of *conversos,* Spanish Jews who had converted but abandoned their second-class citizens' status in Spain and settled in Bordeaux. Although Montaigne remained a Catholic, some of his siblings became Calvinists, and whatever kind of writer Montaigne became, it would be grotesque to call him a religious one. There are about a dozen mentions and citations of Socrates for each appearance of Christ in the pages of Montaigne's book. Even M. A. Screech, the one scholar who insists upon regarding Montaigne as a liberal Catholic religious writer, concludes by emphasizing that, for Montaigne, "The divine never touches human life without upsetting that natural order in which man is most at home." As a public man (mostly despite his own desire), Montaigne refused to take sides in the civil wars of religion that raged around him in France for most of his adult life. His personal devotion was to Henry of Navarre, his fellow Gascon, the Protestant champion who as Henry IV converted to Catholicism in order to secure Paris and the kingdom. Montaigne, had he been in better health, would probably have accepted Henry IV's invitation to become one of his advisers; but fate had it otherwise, and the author of the *Essays* died a private citizen at the age of fifty-nine.

His book was already famous throughout Europe and has never diminished in its popularity and influence. If the reluctant prophecy I venture is correct, and we are only a decade or less away from the dawning of a new Theocratic Age, Montaigne will vanish, at least for a time. His power depends uniquely upon the male reader's inability not to identify with the author. Feminists are unlikely ever to forgive Montaigne, who far exceeds Freud in male chauvinism; Freud declared women to be an insoluble mystery, but for Montaigne there was no mystery at all. They were not quite human in the sense that he most valued the human; he identified them wholly with nature. And yet he was too wise, even in his own day, not to know who bore the culpability. That is the implicit conclusion of his late, highly sexual essay, "On Some Verses of Virgil":

> I say that males and females are cast in the same mold; except for education and custom, the difference is not great. Plato invites both without discrimination to the fellowship of all studies, exercises, functions, warlike and peaceful occupations, in his commonwealth. And the philosopher Antisthenes eliminated any distinction between their virtue and ours. It is much easier to accuse one sex than to excuse the other. It is the old saying: The pot calls the kettle black.

I quote, as I will throughout this chapter, from the eloquent translation of the late Donald M. Frame, who also seems to me Montaigne's best interpreter. Frame locates Montaigne's mutable center in his gradual realization that all of us, male humanists included, are of the common herd, hardly a sensational discovery as we stumble toward the close of the Democratic Age. "But it was pretty radical and unhumanistic for a learned writer in 1590," Frame adds.

To recover much else that was radical about Montaigne in 1590, I suggest that we juxtapose him with Blaise Pascal, the French scientist and religious writer born a third of a century later, in 1623. Pascal could rarely refer to Montaigne without anxiety and resentment and refused to understand that Montaigne's Catholicism was actually founded upon his prevalent skepticism. Since Montaigne encounters only mutability in a world of Platonic appearances, he has no trouble espousing a belief that the Catholic God is immutable and beyond our knowledge. His God is not hidden but is nevertheless unreachable, so that we are compelled to abide eternally in patience, waiting for God's gift of himself. Meanwhile we live as natural men, happily skeptical of the world we inhabit. Pascal's God, in contrast, is both hidden and reachable, a paradox that creates a context for tragedy, as in Racine, but does not suit the domain of comedy, as in Molière. What Montaigne may well have been for Molière, Pascal certainly was for Racine: the stimulus for a dramatic vision. Montaigne's skepticism may have helped to induce tragicomedy in *Hamlet,* but it would more easily have helped to inspire ironic comedy in *The Misanthrope.* The tragic vision in France, exemplified by Pascal and Racine, has not been as readily exportable as the French comic vision of Montaigne and Molière has proved to be.

T. S. Eliot's dogmatic neo-Christianity prompted him to prefer Pascal to Montaigne, a possible spiritual choice but an insupportable literary judgment. Eliot had the embarrassment of introducing Pascal's *Pensées,* which is a bad case of indigestion in regard to Montaigne, so bad that it borders on what many would condemn as outright plagiarism. Pascal, some have surmised, wrote his *Pensées* with his copy of Montaigne's *Essays* open before him. Whether or not this was literally true, it was an apt metaphor for Pascal's resentful and dyspeptic cannibalizing of Montaigne's work. We are almost in the situation of Borges' early story, "Pierre Menard, Author of the *Quixote,*" with Pascal as Menard and Montaigne as Cervantes. Here is one of my favorite juxtapositions, Pascal's pensée 358, followed by a great moment in Montaigne's culminating essay, "Of Experience":

Man is neither angel nor brute, and the unfortunate thing is that he who would act the angel acts the brute.

They want to get out of themselves and escape from the man. That is madness: instead of changing into angels, they change into beasts; instead of raising themselves, they lower themselves.

Montaigne has his sources, which he revises and transcends through the medium of his strong self. All Pascal has is Montaigne, whom he does not want, but with whom he is obsessed. The result is doubly unfortunate: Pascal merely chides all of us; Montaigne accuses some of us of an idealizing madness. Pascal reduces us to our acts; Montaigne is concerned with our essential being. Why was Pascal so obsessed with Montaigne? Eliot insists that Pascal studied Montaigne in order to demolish him but could not do so, because it was like flinging hand grenades into a fog. Montaigne, Eliot assures us, was "a fog, a gas, a fluid, insidious element," which must surely be the oddest description of Montaigne ever attempted. The intention of Eliot's invidious metaphor is revealed when the author of *Murder in the Cathedral* insists that Montaigne "succeeded in giving expression to the skepticism of *every* human being," Pascal and Eliot doubtless included.

I think that this is simply wrong, and it underestimates Montaigne, whose originality and power do not emanate from his limited skepticism, which after all takes care to remain a Catholic skepticism. For all his ironic modesty, Montaigne writes as a charismatic somewhat like Hamlet. What contaminates us is not Montaigne's derivative skepticism but his highly original personality, the first personality ever put forward by a writer as the matter of his work. Walt Whitman and Norman Mailer are indirect descendants of Montaigne, even as Emerson and Nietzsche are his direct progeny. Pascal, his would-be destroyer, is one of Montaigne's involuntary victims. Not a fog, a gas, or a fluid, Montaigne is complete, natural man, and as such an offense to desperate implorers for grace like Pascal and T. S. Eliot, neither of them a comic writer, though each is a considerable ironist.

Frame's study of Montaigne is usefully called *Montaigne's Discovery of Man,* and though the late sixteenth century might seem a delayed time for such a discovery, it is more difficult to nominate an authentic precursor for Montaigne than it is for Freud. Montaigne cheerfully ascribed everything to Seneca and Plutarch; and he does ransack them, but only for material. Montaigne certainly is an original; self-consciousness had never before been expressed so fully and so well. The miracle of Montaigne is that he is almost never "self-conscious" in our current, negative sense. We do not compliment anyone by saying, "She is a self-conscious person." Montaigne talks about himself for 850 large pages, and we want still more of him, because he represents—not everyman, and certainly no woman, but very nearly every man who has the desire, ability, and opportunity to think and to read.

That was his gift or charisma, and it is very difficult to explain. Emerson, who saw it so well, could not expound it, and Montaigne's scholars cannot either. The best clue I know of is Plato's

Socrates, who haunted Montaigne. The Swiss historian Herbert Lüthy thought that all of Montaigne was in one of the most casual of his sentences: "When I play with my cat who knows if she does not amuse herself more with me than I with her?" That is a step beyond perspectivism and, even better, a playful step and a Socratic one. Yet Plato's Socrates is a dualist, exalting the soul over the body, and Montaigne is a monist, refusing to bruise the body in order to pleasure the soul. Even Socrates is not clue enough; what gave Montaigne the clarity to see and write the truth about himself? Most readers agree that Montaigne's greatest essay is the one he stations carefully as the conclusion to his book, "Of Experience." I turn to it to seek the secret of Montaigne, if I am capable of finding it out.

EMERSON'S OWN best essay is naturally entitled "Experience," and it has a particular moment, my favorite among others, that demonstrates eloquently what he had learned from his master, Montaigne: "and we cannot say too little of our constitutional necessity of seeing things under private aspects, or saturated with our humors. And yet is the God the native of these bleak rocks. That need makes in morals the capital virtue of self-trust. We must hold hard to this poverty, however scandalous, and by more vigorous self-recoveries, after the sallies of action, possess our axis more firmly."

"Poverty" here is imaginative need, as it will also be in Wallace Stevens's poetry. What was Montaigne's "poverty," his imaginative need for the readers of his *Essays*? The need and the charisma were one and account for his designs upon us. He fears his melancholy and ours, and offers his wisdom as antidote for both. His melancholy is itself canonical, and his wisdom has become so. On canonical melancholy, I like best the summary by Maggie Kilgour, in her study *From Communion to Cannibalism:*

Associated with theories of stellar influence, the infusion of external powers into the body, melancholy looks forward to theories of poetic influence and from its beginning was identified with the artistic personality, which was seen as essentially ambivalent. Melancholy was seen as both a humor and a disease, and, through the merging of the originally opposed theories of Galen and Aristotle, as both curse and blessing. It was a sign of both a *genius* and of a vicious *daemon,* both in the older sense of good and bad presiding spirits and later in the modern sense of innate qualities.

Melancholy or artistic ambivalence has much to do with the aesthetic anguish at not being self-begotten, as in the case of a great poet and ruined angel, Milton's Satan, who was Lucifer until he fell. In Montaigne, melancholy is central early on, in book 1, essays 2 and 3—"Of Sadness" and "Our Feelings Reach out Beyond Us"—but these trials do not tell us much. Authentic or mature melancholy in Montaigne transcends the ambivalences of authorship and turns upon the great shadows of pain and of death. The major, almost the only friendship of Montaigne's life was with Étienne de La Boétie, two years older than himself. After six years of close relationship, La Boétie died suddenly, at the age of thirty-two. Perhaps because he wished never again to suffer such a loss, Montaigne allowed no more real friendships after this death. The Christian or Pauline view of death, which sees it as an abnormality brought on by the Fall, is not Montaigne's. As Hugo Friedrich observes, Montaigne does not bother to polemicize against the Christian stance but simply ignores it as being irrelevant to him. Despite Montaigne's devotion to Socrates, he does not share the Socratic sense of the soul's immortality, let alone the Christian doctrine of survival after death. Nothing could be less Christian (or much funnier) than Montaigne's advice about preparations for dying, from "Of Physiognomy," book 3, essay 12:

> If you don't know how to die, don't worry; Nature will tell you what to do on the spot, fully and adequately. She will do this job perfectly for you, don't bother your head about it.

> We trouble our life by concern about death, and death by concern about life. One torments us, the other frightens us. It is not against death that we prepare ourselves; that is too

momentary a thing. A quarter hour of suffering, without consequences, without harm, does not deserve any particular precepts.
To tell the truth, we prepare ourselves against the preparations
of death.

Telling the truth, for Montaigne, is at last the telling "Of Experience," the next and final essay after this dismissal of Christian
dying. Natural skepticism yields to natural knowledge, only to
return to the limits of the knowable, and to Socrates: "It is from
my experience that I affirm human ignorance, which is, in my
opinion, the most certain fact in the school of the world. Those
who will not conclude their own ignorance from so vain an example as mine, or as theirs, let them recognize it through Socrates,
the master of masters."

What goes beyond ignorance is what Freud was to call the
realization that the ego is always a bodily ego, a truth that Montaigne phrases more artfully:

In fine, all this fricassee that I am scribbling here is nothing but
a record of the essays of my life, which, for spiritual health, is
exemplary enough if you take its instruction in reverse. But as
for bodily health, no one can furnish more useful experience
than I, who present it pure, not at all corrupted or altered by
art or theorizing. Experience is really on its own dunghill in the
subject of medicine, where reason yields it the whole field.

Reason presumably concerns "being" and, as Montaigne insists,
he does not depict being; he depicts passage, and our bodily health
is a story only of passage. Experience is passage; that will become
the philosophy of all literature after Montaigne, from Shakespeare
and Molière to Proust and Beckett. Montaigne set out to represent
his own being, only to uncover the truth that the self is passage
or transition, a crossing. If self is motion, then the chronicler of
the self cannot always remember what he "had wanted to say."
Wisdom is not knowledge, because knowledge, illusory in itself,
falls into the "had wanted to say." To be wise is to speak the
passing, and though Montaigne always possesses a self, self is
always passing into self, as tone yields to tone:

We must learn to endure what we cannot avoid. Our life is composed, like the harmony of the world, of contrary things, also of different tones, sweet and harsh, sharp and flat, soft and loud. If a musician liked only one kind, what would he have to say? He must know how to use them together and blend them. And so must we do with good and evil, which are consubstantial with our life. Our existence is impossible without this mixture, and one element is no less necessary for it than the other. To try to kick against natural necessity is to imitate the folly of Ctesiphon, who undertook a kicking match with his mule.

I cannot say that I accept this advice easily, though I know it is wisdom. Still, it does not hurt me, as a kicker against natural necessity, that I am engaged in a kicking match with a mule and am bound to lose. In Montaigne, this is the prelude to an honest discussion of his endless suffering from kidney stones, and of the ironic solace spoken to him by his own mind: "But you do not die of being sick, you die of being alive. Death kills you well enough without the help of illness. And illnesses have put off death for some, who have lived longer for thinking that they were on their way out and dying."

How far the irony extends here is left uncertain, but as we approach the final pages of the essay, the experience of irony mounts:

I, who boast of embracing the pleasures of life so assiduously and so particularly, find in them, when I look at them minutely, virtually nothing but wind. But what of it? We are all wind. And even the wind, more wisely than we, loves to make a noise and move about, and is content with its own functions, without wishing for stability and solidity, qualities that do not belong to it.

Montaigne here simultaneously declares both limitation and freedom: for life's pleasures, for the self, for his *Essays*. We can be as wise as the wind by not insisting upon qualities we do not possess. However ironic, this essay remains a defense of the self, of natural pleasures, and of Montaigne's writing, while acknowledging that all of them are passing phenomena. But, as the essay goes on to insist, to live appropriately during that passage is enough:

> We are great fools. "He has spent his life in idleness," we say; "I have done nothing today." What, have you not lived? That is not only the most fundamental but the most illustrious of your occupations. . . . To compose our character is our duty, not to compose books, and to win, not battles and provinces, but order and tranquillity in our conduct. Our great and glorious masterpiece is to live appropriately.

These words had a particular poignance for Montaigne and his first readers, for their immediate context was a brutal, three-cornered civil war among the Catholic League, led by the Guises; the Protestants, led by Henry of Navarre; and the royalists, led by Henry III, the last of the Valois kings. Order and tranquility are nevertheless now permanently difficult to achieve, and the passage retains its pungency. As "Of Experience" rises to its culmination, wisdom competes with irony for rhetorical ascendancy. Socrates is invoked again for a full-scale tribute, introduced by a charming observation: "Nor is there anything more remarkable in Socrates than the fact that in his old age he finds time to take lessons in dancing and playing instruments, and considers it well-spent." On the final edge of his life, Montaigne emulates Socrates, with the motto, "The shorter my possession of life, the deeper and fuller I must make it." We have been building toward the exaltation of the common life that offended Pascal into revising it by pilfering, but in its full context we are overwhelmed by it and forget Pascal:

> They want to get out of themselves and escape from the man. That is madness: instead of changing into angels, they change into beasts; instead of raising themselves, they lower themselves. These transcendental humors frighten me, like lofty and inaccessible places; and nothing is so hard for me to stomach in the life of Socrates as his ecstasies and possessions by his daemon, nothing is so human in Plato as the qualities for which they say

he is called divine. And of our sciences, those seem to me most terrestrial and low which have risen the highest. And I find nothing so humble and so mortal in the life of Alexander as his fancies about his immortalization. Philotas stung him wittily by his answer. He congratulated him by letter on the oracle of Jupiter Ammon which had lodged him among the gods: "As far as you are concerned, I am very glad of it; but there is reason to pity the men who will have to live with and obey a man who exceeds and is not content with a man's proportions."

That passage seems to me to touch a limit of the essayist's art; its strength is sublime in its rejections of the best—Socrates and Alexander—at their worst. We are beyond the writer's melancholy and its ambivalences; there is no sense of belatedness as Montaigne confronts the ancients, whom he honors but judges by the human test of wisdom. As Frame says, Montaigne has humanized his humanism, and wisdom depends upon the only knowledge we are certain of being able to attain: how to live. But to phrase it like that is to lose Montaigne, and we need to keep returning to his own writing in order to renew a canonical wisdom not available to us elsewhere. The essay "Of Experience," wise as it is, matters most because its affirmations are grounded in a cognitive music not to be heard anywhere else:

It is an absolute perfection and virtually divine to know how to enjoy our being rightfully. We seek other conditions because we do not understand the use of our own, and go outside of ourselves because we do not know what it is like inside. Yet there is no use our mounting on stilts, for on stilts we must still walk on our legs. And on the loftiest throne in the world we are still sitting only on our own rump.

Pascal must have been reduced to considerable agony by this comic vision, which leaves no latitude for transcendental yearnings, wagers of faith, and the tragedy of a God who hides himself. As we tumble toward a new Theocratic Age, those four sentences of Montaigne's should serve us as an apotropaic talisman, warding off apocalypse mongers. Montaigne helps to center the Western

Canon because an individual reader can locate the self, however crumpled it may have become, by employing Montaigne as a guidebook. Until the advent of Freud, no other secular moralist gave us nearly so much, and it seems to me now that the accurate tribute we can make to Freud is to see him as the Montaigne of our Chaotic Age.

THE VICTORIAN poet-novelist George Meredith, who wrote a Molière-like high comedy in his best novel, *The Egoist,* also composed an *Essay on Comedy* that gives us a Molière rather precariously stationed between upper- and middle-class elements in his audience, playing at once to court and to town, but with his heart secretly centered on the town. That is probably an idealization, since Molière, son of an upholsterer, more even than Shakespeare, son of a glover, seems the comic dramatist of the Aristocratic Age. Montaigne, in his final phase, associated his stance regarding life with that of the common people; but Molière, like Shakespeare, rarely gives us an insight into his own deepest sympathies. Like Montaigne, he is a naturalist and perhaps even a skeptic, and certainly he is as secular as Shakespeare.

The pragmatic attitude of Aristophanes is shared by the commonsensical Molière, who otherwise represses the Aristophanic spirit, which would hardly have been appropriate for the court of Louis XIV. God, for Molière, pragmatically meant his benignly glorious monarch, without whose sympathy and frequent support Molière could not have survived his enemies, the bigots of Paris. The Sun King is one pillar of Molière's mature career; the other is a religious devotion to the theater, where his work as playwright, actor, and head of a repertory company finally consumed his life. Molière died a legendary death after the fourth performance of *The Imaginary Invalid* (1673), a farce he had written, staged, and acted the lead part in, despite being seriously ill. He was fifty years old, and had spent thirty of them in the life of the theater.

Canonical displacement is a simple enough operation in our dying academic world but more difficult to manage in the pragmatic sphere of the stage, where Molière is no more menaced than is Shakespeare, since a theatrical audience, unlike an academic one, can always vote with its feet. Molière is therefore likelier to survive in America than Montaigne is, even though Molière follows Montaigne in demonstrating the elusiveness of the truth, which is not a demonstration welcomed by the idealists and ideologues who have seized the academy in the name of social justice. New Puritans, like old ones, are not going to embrace Montaigne or Molière; but in Molière's case that hardly matters. Perhaps he will keep the spirit of Montaigne's skepticism alive in our drift toward another Theocratic Age, where few are likely to find the truth at all elusive, and where Montaigne himself is likely to vanish with Freud.

In the comedies of Molière, as in the essays of Montaigne, truth is always elusive, always relative, always warred over by opposing individuals or camps or schools. Insofar as we can get at Molière's own consciousness, setting aside his evident domestic unhappiness, a secure faith in theater may have given him a certain detachment or serenity, which we like to bestow upon Shakespeare also. With both supreme dramatists we just do not know, and perhaps that is as it should be. The high comic vision, when it misses nothing (as in Molière), is certainly upsetting and ultimately even dismaying. I cannot read Molière or attend a performance of *Tartuffe* or *The Misanthrope* without reflecting on my own worst qualities, as well as the dreadful qualities of my enemies. What I confront in Molière are obsessives; but unlike the powerful grotesques of Ben Jonson, Molière's zealots are not presented as caricatures. It is the all-but-unique genius of Molière to write what I call "normative farce," which is almost an oxymoron but may be a persuasive one.

Jacques Guicharnaud memorably remarked that Molière's plays "show that everyone's life is a romance, a farce, a disgrace" so that the spectator "is led into a state of bad faith to avoid doubting himself." With an accurate gusto, he then went further, saying that Molière's greatest plays prove that the soul "is essentially vice, accompanied by an illusion of freedom." That may be a touch severe, since enough of Montaigne lingers in Molière to give us a sense of something else in the soul that is neither vice nor illusory freedom. Whatever that more amiable quality is, its greatest difference from Montaigne is that the sense of "passing," so prevalent in the *Essays,* is replaced in Molière by the force of repetition. Montaigne changes, but Molière's characters cannot. They must go on being what they were before. Montaigne overhears himself, as do Hamlet and Iago; that is precisely what the protagonists of Molière will not do.

By common consent, Molière's masterpieces are *The Misanthrope, Tartuffe,* and the very ambivalent *Don Juan,* a play in prose rather than verse, and one not easy to construe as comedy, at least not now. I have seen *Don Juan* played as though Molière wholly admired his protagonist, which did not work, and as though he totally condemned him, which did not work either. *The Misanthrope* and *Tartuffe* are less problematical, though complex enough. Whether Shakespeare had a particularly intimate relation to *Hamlet* among all his plays, we will never know, though critics have conjectured this for centuries. There is a link between Alceste the misanthrope and Molière, who created, directed, and acted the part of the most interesting of all his characters; but that link, whatever it is, is hardly an identity. Where is the truth in *The Misanthrope;* what are we to think of and feel about Alceste? The elusiveness of the truth in Molière is partly the spiritual effect of Montaigne on Molière, but much more the product of Molière's own highly original temperament.

The Misanthrope is above all else a play of shocking vitality; Molière must have been possessed by daemonic force as he composed it. Each time I see it or reread it, I am startled again at its speed and energy; it is a kind of violent scherzo from beginning to end. Richard Wilbur's translation conveys this quality from the start:

> PHILINTE
> Now, what's got into you?
> ALCESTE, *seated*
> Kindly leave me alone.
> PHILINTE
> Come, come, what is it? This lugubrious tone . . .
> ALCESTE
> Leave me, I said; you spoil my solitude.

PHILINTE

Oh, listen to me, now, and don't be rude.

ALCESTE

I choose to be rude, Sir, and to be hard of hearing.

Alceste, fiercely rejecting his friend for having given a hearty greeting to an acquaintance, immediately establishes the comic excess that marks him throughout. His vigor of response at every point in the play could be called either "heroic" or "lunatic," since it is both; but to call it "Quixotic" does not help. Like Tartuffe and Don Juan, Alceste is too strong for his context, which is only a salon. Tartuffe is a sublime religious hypocrite, like Chaucer's Pardoner, but his zest is so outrageous that some critics have compared him to those heroically disreputable vitalists, the Wife of Bath and Falstaff. Don Juan's mode of energy is strangely like Iago's and is another prophecy of modern nihilism.

There is a curious dialectic in Molière that resembles Shakespeare's tendency to enrich personalities by alienating them from communion with others. Alceste, Tartuffe, and Don Juan resemble Hamlet, Iago, and Edmund in that the price of energetic ambivalence is a separation out and away from anyone else. Philinte is Alceste's Horatio, while Tartuffe and Iago have only their victims. Don Juan has his hard-tried valet, Sganarelle, while Edmund has only his "yours in the ranks of death" double-date with Goneril and Regan. I find it a little disconcerting that the two major dramatists since the Athenians both imply that we become more exuberant, however negatively, in separation from others rather than in sharing our beings; but I do not find this similarity between Shakespeare and Molière to be accidental.

What is the truth about Alceste, or does its elusiveness forever commit us to an ambivalent view of him? Richard Wilbur, who has accomplished the miracle of making Alceste speak American verse, has a subtly balanced estimate that seems to me a touch too severe:

If Alceste has a rage for the genuine, and he truly has, it is unfortunately compromised and exploited by his vast, unconscious egotism. . . . Like many humorless and indignant people, he is hard on everybody but himself, and does not perceive it when he fails his own ideal. . . . A victim, like all around him, of the moral enervation of the times, he cannot consistently be the Man of Honor—simple, magnanimous, passionate, decisive, true. It is his distinction that he is aware of that ideal, and that he can fitfully embody it; his comic flaw consists in a Quixotic confusion of himself with the ideal, a willingness to distort the world for his own self-deceptive and histrionic purposes. Paradoxically, then, the advocate of true feeling and honest intercourse is the one character most artificial, most out-of-touch, most in danger of that nonentity and solitude which all, in the chattery, hollow world of this play, are fleeing. He must play-act continually in order to believe in his own existence.

That is both brilliant and specific, and it does not give Alceste very much, yet it cannot be the whole truth, for the audience/readership of Molière/Wilbur will continue to prefer the perpetually outraged Alceste to everyone else in the play. Try substituting "Hamlet" for "Alceste" in the first sentence I have quoted from Wilbur and then go on to read the whole passage as though it commented upon Hamlet. Some points will not work: Hamlet is humorous, dreadfully hard on himself, and largely lacks a Quixotic aspect. But as the passage continues, Wilbur on Alceste could well be Wilbur on Hamlet. Whether Molière intended Alceste to be a critique of Molière himself we do not know, any more than we can say whether Shakespeare represented any of his own qualities in Hamlet. But Alceste does seem to me the one character in Molière who has the moral intelligence (though not the humor) that would enable him to write a play by Molière, and it is an old realization to observe that Hamlet, author of much of the play within the play, could conceivably have written *Hamlet*.

John Hollander remarks on the peculiarity of what happens when a play has a satirist as a protagonist. Even Tartuffe the hypocrite and Don Juan the libertine are satirists of a sort, and Alceste is one of the fiercest of satirists. It is part of Molière's extraordinary gift that his comedy is much larger than his satire, so Alceste necessarily becomes a critic of society, who in turn is criticized by *The Misanthrope*. Hollander's insight is that the play must defend itself against the satiric protagonist, so Shakespeare, to keep *Romeo and Juliet* a tragedy, must kill off Mercutio before he absorbs too much of our interest. Against Wilbur, who represents the best in the critical tradition concerning Alceste, I would urge us to see *The Misanthrope* partly as defending itself against Alceste, just as the play *Hamlet* is, in part, a defense against the ferocious intellect of Hamlet. Alceste has all of the comic flaws that Wilbur indicates, and more, but he also has the aesthetic dignity of an authentic social satirist and of a moral psychologist of considerable distinction.

Alceste, in spite of his comic failings, holds our sympathy and even our admiration because Molière, like Shakespeare, understood what I call the aesthetics of representing someone in the state of being outraged, made furious by intolerable provocations. The playgoer and reader cannot resist identifying with such a representation, perhaps because ultimately we are outraged by the necessity of dying. Alceste is as outrageous as he is outraged, and he is a comic triumph. But his continual playacting, like Hamlet's, is more than a desperate attempt "to believe in his own existence," as Wilbur says. Alceste's histrionic intensity is an outraged satire on compromised human existence, and, again like Hamlet, Alceste's mind is more never-resting than restless. Both figures think too well, rather than too much, and neither can survive in the context to which he is condemned. Hamlet passively courts death; Alceste flees into absolute solitude. In their rejection of the women they love, they have another affinity. The coquette Celimene is not the soft Ophelia, but each is rejected because the outraged satirists, Alceste and Hamlet, set impossible standards for the beloved, as for the world, and so insist upon criteria they themselves could never meet. That is a crucial element in Molière's comedy and in Shakespeare's tragedy, which converge in handling the satirist as hero.

W. G. Moore, who with Jacques Guicharnaud seems to me the most useful critic of Molière, warns against centering upon an analysis of Alceste, rather than of the play's structure, which is again to suggest that the comedy subsumes the satirist:

> . . . it is far more than Alceste's character that is here illumined; it is an issue, the issue of how principles fare in a hard world.

To make this great play a study of character is to limit the range of its drama. The whole question of the nature of sincerity, involving as it does vanity, fashion, spite, convention—it is the complex of questions that conditions the order and structure of the play.

Yet Moore also sees how enormously complex a character Alceste truly is, the play's fool, yet also its Hamlet, a figure we can never be done comprehending:

> Alceste is ridiculous, in a fine sense, not because he rebukes the society of his day of insincerity. He is anti-social because he recommends on grounds of principle courses of action by which he stands to gain. . . . Alceste is a symbol of something much more interesting and complicated.
>
> In order to bring out the range and depth of Molière's characterization, it is worthwhile trying to see what this elusive quality is. One might call it the confusion of the general and the personal. It is a natural human tendency to cover and defend one's actions by the appeal to a standard outside oneself. Conversely we often fail to see how much our adherence to such a general standard is a consequence of self-interest and vanity. . . . And what Alceste wanted, unbeknown to himself, was recognition, preference, distinction. . . . In the course of dramatizing his theme of the misanthropic lover, the intensity of Molière's creative power has led him to sketch a figure far beyond any intention and comparable to Hamlet in its wide range of suggestion, personal, social, ethical, political, even theological.

But don't all of us confuse the general and the personal? And didn't Molière, the actor-dramatist, desire recognition, preference, distinction? Even Moore falls into the error of moralizing against Alceste. Molière himself does not fall. Ramon Fernandez tells us that "Alceste is a Molière who has lost his awareness of the comic." As Fernandez indicates, Alceste suffers from excess: he is too virtuous, too reasonable, too strong, too aggressive on behalf of the truth, even too witty for anyone to stand. Alceste is antithetical to his poet: Molière, as a man of the theater, had no special status, no right even to a decent burial. And as the courtier of Louis XIV, his protector and patron, Molière had to dissimulate, disguise his real opinions, and always hint at more than he actually said.

Even as he acted the part of Alceste, the highly professional repertory manager Molière must have noticed the oddity that the three roles for women in the play were performed by his estranged wife, his mistress, and the actress who persisted in refusing him. The relation between Alceste and Molière is bewildering and should make us wary of all moralizing critics. I am surprised that literary critics do not love Alceste (as I do) because he speaks so pungently for all critics daily deluged by floods of bad verse:

> *Sir, these are delicate matters; we all desire*
> *To be told that we've the true poetic fire.*
> *But once, to one whose name I shall not mention,*
> *I said, regarding some verse of his invention,*
> *That gentlemen should rigorously control*
> *That itch to write which often afflicts the soul;*
> *That one should curb the heady inclination*
> *To publicize one's little avocation;*
> *And that in showing off one's works of art*
> *One often plays a very clownish part.*

The only case to be made against Alceste, in my judgment, is the failure of his love for the charming and altogether enigmatic Celimene; but satirists traditionally evade marriage. Even here, I am driven to defend Alceste against the moralizing critics, who associate him with Don Juan because both Alceste and the Don nominate themselves absolute judges in all realms, including the erotic. Sometimes I suspect that modern critics of Molière compound him with Racine, which is as peculiar as it would be to fuse Montaigne with Pascal. Thus Martin Turnell in *The Classical Moment* assimilates Molière to his age, which becomes the Age of Racine, and soon enough *The Misanthrope* is a play whose protagonist is in a state of perpetual hysteria. The ultimate reduction of moralizing criticism is heard when Turnell scolds that "it is idle to pretend that order is re-established and that a chastened buffoon is brought back to the norm of sanity." "What norm?" Alceste would explode, and the sane playgoer or reader would have to agree with him. The greatness of *The Misanthrope* would vanish utterly if society were sane and only Alceste was deranged. I resort to Montaigne against the critics, if we are to save Alceste from them.

WE ARE ACCUSTOMED to finding in some aspects of Hamlet a Montaigne-like skeptic, but our critics do not present us with a Hamlet who is a buffoon. To see Hamlet played by an actor who cannot (and should not) touch the sublime is a dreadful experience, but we generally expect a powerful and comprehensive actor to undertake the role. To see an inadequate actor playing Alceste as a self-deceived fool is an uncannily bad theatrical experience. The critics' moral fits have done real harm to the play, at least in English-speaking countries. Alceste demands a great actor, as Molière himself evidently was when he first triumphed in the role. Tradition indicates that, directed and played by Molière, Alceste was presented as considerably more than a self-destructive buffoon. The work requires both a director and an actor who can conceive of a moral satirist who retains force and dignity but also falls victim, not to a vengeful society, but to the spirit of comedy.

Albert Bermel, in his otherwise sensitive *Molière's Theatrical Bounty*, passes harsh judgment upon Alceste, not on the usual moralistic grounds but because Alceste is a loner, not a Jacobin or a reformer, and because he lacks the heart to accept Celimene when she at last offers herself in marriage. By the same arguments, Hamlet would warrant rejection. Alceste is not as intelligent as Hamlet, but neither is any other literary character, and Alceste, as Bermel grants, "has formidable intellectual and moral prowess" but not a very admirable personality. No one has ever fallen in love with Alceste except Jean-Jacques Rousseau, who discovered in Celimene's suitor a character as virtuous as himself. As far as one can tell, Celimene and Alceste are not in love with each other, which suits the comic spirit of the play. Like Rousseau, Alceste loves only himself, which doubtless increased his appeal for Rousseau.

Molière, as devious as he is deep, did not want to exalt his antithesis in Alceste, but I suspect that he would be amused by the moral disapproval his aristocratic misanthrope has provoked in our chaotic century. Montaigne taught Molière the pragmatic elusiveness of truth—a superb lesson for an actor to learn, and one that would have benefited Alceste if he could have borne it, but he could not. We say that Molière's gift was for comedy, not tragedy, but we recognize that his greatest comedies are very dark, even if they never become tragicomedies, which are not a French genre. Montaigne and Molière alike avoid the tragic vision that Lucien Goldmann ascribed to Pascal and Racine in *The Hidden God*. A religious sensibility is very different from a religious belief, particularly in an era when belief is still imposed and the lack of a religious sensibility may be the crucial link between the essayist who wrote "Of Experience" and the playwright of *The Misanthrope, Tartuffe,* and *Don Juan.*

That link had to remain hidden for safety's sake, but metaphorically its place was taken by the two writers' common disdain for the medical profession. Molière's satires on doctors slyly insinuate analogues between medicine and theology, an insinuation blandly implicit in Montaigne. The movement from humanism to celebration of the common life, which Frame traced in Montaigne, was thoroughly absorbed by Molière, whose ideal audience would have been the honest men with whom Montaigne had replaced the humanistic ideal. Montaigne's originality had been the self-portrait, hardly the stuff from which a comic playwright could fashion his work. Molière's originality was to progress from farce to a kind of critical comedy, and for that progress a nontheatrical catalyst was needed. I surmise that Molière took Montaigne's hint but inverted the self-portraiture or turned it inside out. Alceste is the largest of those antithetical inversions, but there are others, and they follow Montaigne's depiction of the whole man by deliberately representing great truncated figures. Montaigne teaches a husbanding of the will, leading to self-possession; Molière shows the dark comedy of indulging the will, leading to self-abdication and destructive passion. Alceste, forceful and admirable as I find him to be, is the direct consequence of not acting upon Montaigne's admonition that concludes "Of Experience." If you want to get out of yourself and escape from the man, you fall into madness. You do not raise yourself to an angel, you lower yourself to a beast. At the end, wishing to flee to a desert solitude (however metaphorical), Alceste is courting everything that Montaigne most feared.

7.

Milton's Satan
and Shakespeare

MILTON'S PLACE in the canon is permanent, even though he appears to be the major poet at present most deeply resented by feminist literary critics. In conversation with John Dryden, he once confessed rather too readily that Spenser was his "Great Original," a remark that I have come to understand as a defense against Shakespeare. Shakespeare was at once the source of Milton's authentic if hidden poetic anxiety and, paradoxically, the engenderer of Milton's canonicity. Of all post-Shakespearean writers it is Milton, rather than Goethe or Tolstoy or Ibsen, who best exploited the Shakespearean representation of character and its changes, even while working furiously to ward off the Shakespearean shadow. The most Shakespearean of all literary characters after Shakespeare's own creations is Milton's Satan, who is the heir of the great hero-villains—Iago, Edmund, Macbeth—and of the darker aspects of Hamlet the counter-Machiavel as well. Milton and Freud (who greatly esteemed Milton) have in common their mutual debt to Shakespeare and their equally mutual evasion of the debt. Yet to be able to bear the strength of Shakespeare and convert it to one's own purposes may be the truest alliance between Miltonic and Freudian ambivalence, between Satan's rebellion against God and the civil war in the psyche.

The hero-villain was invented largely by Christopher Marlowe in Tamburlaine, a Scythian shepherd become world conqueror, and even more in Barabas, the self-delighting Jew of Malta, a humorist of evil. It is a direct path from Marlowe's grand nihilists to the early Shakespearean monsters, Aaron the Moor in the tragic slaughterhouse *Titus Andronicus,* and the hunchbacked Richard III. All of these figures are too unrefined to have affected the sensibility of John Milton. The intellectual nihilism of *Paradise Lost*'s Satan properly begins with the abyss within Hamlet's capacious consciousness; but the nihilistic accents of Milton's ruined angel are first heard in Iago, the original sufferer from a sense of injured merit, of having been passed over by his godlike general.

Milton's overt myth was that Shakespeare stood for "nature," meaning an inclusive wildness or natural freedom, whereas he, Milton, stood for the purer or better way of transcending nature in order to reach heaven, or at least the representation of heaven. But no one can stand Milton's heaven for very long at a time; Milton himself, a party or sect of one, could scarcely have endured it for a moment. *Paradise Lost* is magnificent because it is persuasively tragic as well as epic; it is the tragedy of the fall of Lucifer into Satan, though it declines to show us Lucifer, light-bearer and son of the morning, chief of the stars that will fall. We see only the fallen Satan, though we behold Adam and Eve before, at the very moment of, and after the fall. In another sense of "the tragic," *Paradise Lost* is the tragedy of Eve and Adam, who like Satan have their inevitably Shakespearean qualities and yet seem somewhat less persuasive representations than Satan, who is granted more of a Shakespearean growing inner self. This may be one clue to Milton's troubled relationship with the dramatist of *Othello* and *Macbeth,* the plays that seem to have contaminated *Paradise Lost* most intensively. In rejecting Shakespearean inclusiveness, Milton was still able to appropriate it for his villain more readily than for his hero and heroine, while fatally avoiding it altogether in his portraits of God and Christ, who owe nothing to Shakespeare and perhaps consequently are impoverished as dramatic characters. All you can say accurately about Milton's God is that he is pompous, defensive, and self-righteous, while Milton's Christ, as I once remarked, is reduced to the leader of an armored attack, a kind of heavenly Rommel or Patton.

When Milton was a boy of seven, Shakespeare died. In 1632, when Milton's poem, "On Shakespeare," was published, Shakespeare had been dead for sixteen years. We always need to recall this chronology in thinking about Milton's anxious relationship to the greatest poet in the language, perhaps in any language. It will soon be forty years since Wallace Stevens died (in 1955), yet his presence continues to haunt contemporary American poetry. Shakespeare was dangerously close in time to Milton, whose poem of tribute is truly a warding-off gesture, particularly here:

> *Dear son of memory, great heir of fame,*
> *What need'st thou such weak witness of thy name?*
> *Thou in our wonder and astonishment*
> *Has built thyself a life-long monument.*

Shakespeare, as the son of memory and mother of the muses, is himself a male muse inspiring Milton, but not to a transcendental vision. "Wonder and astonishment" is empirically right, then and now, for Shakespeare's effect upon any other poet whatsoever, but these qualities were secondary in Milton's aspirations. Like Dante, Milton wanted to write the divine poem or, pragmatically, a third Testament. Wonder and astonishment are very different from truth and reverence, while Shakespearean "nature" is a long way from scriptural or Miltonic "revelation." Macbeth and Satan are both victims of their own imaginations; the first may represent a latent anxiety in Shakespeare, who perhaps thus chastised his own power of imagining, but the second clearly reflects Milton's distrust of fantasy and its discontents.

As a Protestant prophet, indeed *the* Protestant poet, Milton would be very unhappy that *Paradise Lost* now reads like the most powerful science fiction. I reread the poem constantly and am moved primarily by wonder and astonishment, by the strangeness of the Miltonic achievement. What makes *Paradise Lost* unique is its startling blend of Shakespearean tragedy, Virgilian epic, and Biblical prophecy. The terrible pathos of *Macbeth* joins itself to the *Aeneid*'s sense of nightmare and to the Hebrew Bible's assertion of authority. That combination should have sunk any literary work nine fathoms deep, but John Milton, blind and battered by political defeat, was unsinkable. There may be no larger triumph of the visionary will in Western literature. We can sense Milton taking his losses rather hard in *Samson Agonistes* and *Paradise Regained,* but in *Paradise Lost* he wins out over every opponent except for the concealed agonist, Shakespeare.

The reader's center in *Paradise Lost* has to be Satan, the whipping boy of nearly all scholarly exegetes and yet clearly the greatest glory of the poem, only partly balanced by Milton's extraordinary expansion of the Hebraic accounts of Creation in book 7. Satan is, of course, defeated, but so are Iago and Macbeth at last, after the hero-villain's work is done, or as Mephistopheles in Goethe's poem is defeated by Faust's ascension. Such defeats are dialectical and depend upon who is left in control of the reader's perspective. Iago, baffled that Emilia should have given her life to rescue Desdemona's reputation, will die under torture rather than reveal his motives, even to himself: "From this time forth I never shall speak word." Satan, when last we see him, is a serpent hissing on the floor of Hell.

We do not altogether credit the perspective, which is Milton's most ruthless act of editorializing, and a self-wounding one. It makes Milton look bad, because it seems to be his own revenge upon Satan for having usurped too much of the poet's energy and power of desire. Shakespeare does not revenge himself upon Iago or Macbeth, or anyone else in any of the thirty-eight plays.

More than the dramatic genre determines the Shakespearean difference here. A miracle of disinterestedness, Shakespeare neither believes nor disbelieves, neither moralizes nor endorses nihilism. We delight in Iago even as he compels us to shudder. Milton makes our pleasure in Satan a guilty one, ostensibly insisting upon belief and an overt morality. Whether the later Milton of *Samson Agonistes* believed anything at all, I tend to doubt; I can make little sense of the figure of Christ in Milton's poetry anyway. Like the Jesus of American religionists, Milton's Christ is barely crucified and gets off the cross with extraordinary celerity. The American Jesus, resurrected upon this earth for infinitely more than forty days and neither crucified nor ascended, would have suited Milton as the European Jesus never could.

Magnificent and Miltonic, Satan is at home in *Paradise Lost,* as secure in his own role and identity as the master manipulator Iago is in *Othello,* until each crashes down at the last. We remember Iago progressing from one degree of control over all of the characters to another, until he can exult over the ruined Othello as his own negative creation, just as we recall Satan in the grandeur of his defiance and the cunning of his staging of our Fall. Their mutual pride, a Shakespearean refinement of Marlowe, is best expressed by Shakespeare's disciple John Webster in *The White Devil,* when one of the hero-villains, himself dying on a final scene's stage strewn with corpses, cries out in exultation, "I limned this night-piece, and it was my best!" As a limner of night pieces, Satan owes everything to Iago and Macbeth, Hamlet and Edmund.

We must assume that Milton did not consciously recognize the debt, though it is baffling that he did not. The Miltonic representation of Satan's ambivalence toward God, like the Freudian account of primal ambivalence, is wholly Shakespearean, founded upon Iago's ambivalence toward Othello, Macbeth's toward his own Oedipal ambition, and Hamlet's toward everything and everyone, himself most of all. Ambivalence, in its Freudian definition, is the essence of all relationship between the superego, that which is above the "I," and the id or "it," below the "I." Mingled and equal affects of love and hatred simultaneously flow back and forth between these psychic agencies or fictions, and the ebb and flow alternately desiccates and drowns the "I," the unhappy ego. Iago, Macbeth, and Satan are so dominated by this ambivalence that they can scarcely be distinguished from it.

Recognizing no differences between battle and civil existence, Iago in the long, unstated foreground of *Othello* has identified himself with his general, the war-god Othello, even as Lucifer identified himself with Milton's God. Satan suffers what he calls "a sense of injured merit" when he is passed over for Christ, even as Iago suffers one when passed over for Cassio, an outsider chosen by Othello as second in command in preference to Iago, the battle-tried ensign or flag officer who has had Othello's colors, and so his captain's honor, in his keeping. Presumably the experienced Othello, whose greatness is that he knows the boundaries between war and peace, recognizes that his devoted ensign or "ancient" cannot be trusted never to cross those lines. The case of Satan, being theologically overdetermined, is more problematical than that of Iago. Why does Milton's God proclaim Christ as son rather than Lucifer, chief of angels? And how precisely does Lucifer first fall into becoming Satan? If Lucifer has been passed over from the beginning, why does he know nothing about it until God's decree announcing the higher status of Christ?

It cannot be said that Milton's God enlightens us upon these matters:

> *Hear all ye angels, progeny of light,*
> *Thrones, dominations, princedoms, virtues, powers,*
> *Hear my decree, which unrevoked shall stand.*
> *This day I have begot whom I declare*
> *My only Son, and on this holy hill*
> *Him have anointed, whom ye now behold*
> *At my right hand; your head I him appoint;*
> *And by my self have sworn to him shall bow*
> *All knees in Heaven and shall confess him Lord:*
> *Under his great vicegerent reign abide*
> *United as one individual soul*
> *For ever happy: him who disobeys*
> *Me disobeys, breaks union, and that day*
> *Cast out from God and blessed vision, falls*
> *Into utter darkness, deep engulfed, his place*
> *Ordained without redemption, without end.*

This is certainly traditional Christian doctrine, but is it poetically acceptable? I cannot read this harsh, arbitrary declaration without recalling the late Sir William Empson's sensible observation that God thus causes all of the trouble in the first place, just as he does in the Book of Job, when he boasts to Satan of his servant Job's obedience and righteousness. The imaginative lapse here is that only God's menacing power prevents our hearing his threats as bluster. Disobedience, long before anyone ever disobeyed, appears to have been an obsession of the Hebraic God. The early history of Yahweh, which is not wholly recoverable, suggests that the anxiety about potential disobedience has much to do with the hidden story of how a solitary warrior-god, apparently one among many godlings, established himself as the supreme figure. But for the poet Milton there is no such early history, which would be akin to the romantic tales of a younger self with which the war-god Othello first won his bride Desdemona.

The republican Milton would presumably have rejected our feeling that we hear the rhetoric of tyranny when his God speaks, since the Protestant God was the only legitimate monarch for the poet of *Paradise Lost*. Still, Milton has made God sound more like James I or Charles I than like David or Solomon, let alone than like the Yahweh of the J writer. Something is very wrong with Milton's God, as with his warlike Messiah who leads the heavenly charge in the Chariot of Paternal Deity. Othello's rhetoric of authority is more persuasive than that of Milton's God: "Keep up your bright swords, for the dew will rust them." *That* is what Iago is up against, and it makes his triumph all the grander and more ruinous, against the far more equivocal triumph of Satan.

I am not suggesting that the tragic Satan is a "little Iago," more akin, say, to the Iachimo of *Cymbeline* than to Iago or Macbeth. What is poetically flawed about Satan (and it is minor, compared to his aesthetic eminence) results rather surprisingly from Milton's refusal or inability to dramatize the Christian argument of his poem properly. He could have benefited, as the non-Christians Goethe and Shelley did, by giving some attention to Spanish Golden Age drama and to Calderón in particular, although doubtless the Catholicism involved prevented him. It is difficult not to surmise that God and Christ, at least in *Paradise Lost*, inhibited Milton's genius, a surmise in which I have been anticipated by William Blake in *The Marriage of Heaven and Hell*.

What his great poem evidences is that Milton remained Shakespearean despite himself. His Satan integrates Iago's ontological nihilism with Macbeth's anticipatory fantasies, lacing the blend with Hamlet's contempt for the act of speaking. Anything he finds words for is already dead in Satan's heart, as it is in Hamlet's. Satan is driven on by a version of Iago's aesthetic pride in plotting a tragedy and by something like Macbeth's augmenting sense of being outraged that each usurpation should result only in another missed cue for a poor player. The superbly dramatic elements in Satan's predicament are all Shakespearean inventions, as is Satan's tendency to suffer change only after first overhearing himself and then brooding upon his own language. Yet Milton avoids representing for us the crucial change by which Satan ensues from Lucifer. If we search the text, that most crucial of metamorphic moments is simply missing. All we get is a curiously elliptical moralizing from Raphael, the not altogether affable archangel:

> *. . . but not so waked*
> *Satan, so call him now, his former name*
> *Is heard no more in heaven; he of the first,*
> *If not the first archangel, great in power,*
> *In favour and pre-eminence, yet fraught*
> *With envy against the Son of God, that day*
> *Honoured by his great Father, and proclaimed*
> *Messiah king anointed, could not bear*
> *Through pride that sight, and thought himself impaired.*

This is a most un-Shakespearean evasion; we want to hear it dramatized, just as we want to see Lucifer before he dwindles forever. In flight from Shakespeare, Milton represses the dramatic moment of his hero-villain's transformation. After all, Raphael is wrong; it is Lucifer who thinks himself impaired, and we are irked by the party line that tells us Lucifer is now an unperson named Satan. Shakespeare unfolds Iago and Macbeth before us, whereas Milton simply assumes that the reader, being Christian, will accept the story as told entirely from the perspective of the winning side. Many such moments would sink even *Paradise Lost*, which recuperates soon enough with the return of the Shakespearean Satan, given the chance to reveal his own perspective:

That we were formed then say'st thou? And the work
Of secondary hands, by task transferred
From Father to his Son? Strange point and new!
Doctrine which we would know whence learned: who saw
When this creation was? Remember'st thou
Thy making, while the maker gave thee being?
We know no time when we were not as now;
Know none before us, self-begot, self-raised
By our own quickening power, when fatal course
Had circled his full orb, the birth mature
Of this native heaven, ethereal sons,
Our puissance is our own.

It is a perspective insinuating pragmatic realities, poetic and human, that the supposed truths of Christianity cannot so easily smother. Granted that Satan indulges himself in a dramatic irony, there is more than irony in those rhetorical questions. They adopt the pattern of Iago's ferocious ones and make the reader of *Paradise Lost* into a momentary Othello, overwhelmed by a diction whose tendentiousness, though overt, can scarcely be resisted. What Satan has learned from Iago and Macbeth and, more subtly, from Hamlet is a negative energy that is persuasive because it transcends mere persistence and intimates a permanent drive beyond the pleasure principle. Shakespeare, who may not have created everything but who certainly invented us (such as we are), created Western nihilism in the movement from Hamlet through Iago and Edmund on to Macbeth.

Satan, gorgeous as his eloquence is, is nevertheless a repetition of Shakespeare's discovery of the nothingness at our center. Hamlet tells us that he is at once nothing and everything in himself, while Iago goes deeper into the abyss: "I am not what I am," which deliberately reverses Saint Paul's "by the grace of God, I am what I am." "We know no time when we were not as now," and yet we are nothing now. Ontologically, Iago knows he is a hollow man because the only bestower of being, the war-god Othello, has passed him over. Satan, passed over, insists he is self-created and sets out to undo the creation intended to replace him. Iago, far more potent, undoes his god, reducing to chaos the only reality and value he recognizes. Poor Satan, in contrast, can only attempt to pique God, not to destroy him.

That Iago dwarfs Satan in Satanic prowess is palpable and might have caused Milton despair had he allowed himself to confront directly the Shakespearean contamination. Long before *Paradise Lost* was conceived, Milton had contemplated writing not an epic but a tragedy, under the alternate titles of *Paradise Lost* or *Adam Unparadised*. What now appears in the poem as book 4, lines 32–41, would have opened the tragedy. Satan, on top of Mount Niphates at the origin of the Tigris River, has a prospect of the Garden of Eden and directly addresses the blazing sun, in the accents of a Jacobean hero-villain remembering the pathos of the Marlovian overreachers:

> *O thou that with surpassing glory crowned,*
> *Look'st from thy sole dominion like the God*
> *Of this new world; at whose sight all the stars*
> *Hide their diminished heads; to thee I call,*
> *But with no friendly voice, and add thy name*
> *O sun, to tell thee how I hate thy beams*
> *That bring to my remembrance from what state*
> *I fell, how glorious once above thy sphere;*
> *Till pride and worse ambition threw me down*
> *Warring in heaven against heaven's matchless king.*

In the surviving drafts of an outline for *Adam Unparadised*, there is no character named Satan; there is only Lucifer. This passage is our one clue to the character from whom Satan fell away. On the basis of these ten lines, Lucifer was as Marlovian as Satan became Shakespearean; we could be listening here to Tamburlaine, but not to Iago or Macbeth. Like Tamburlaine's, Lucifer's rhetoric is hyperbolical; the sublime is the standard of measurement, and everything is judged by either heightening or diminishment. The sun has replaced the morning star, and Lucifer initially disdains to name his usurper. When he adds the name, it is in professed hatred of what provokes the torment of nostalgia. We are returned to the great change that Milton declined to represent: precisely when, and how, did Lucifer become Satan?

Thirty-five or so lines on, presumably added to the original speech, seems the likeliest answer:

> *Which way I fly is hell; my self am hell;*
> *And in the lowest deep a lower deep*
> *Still threatening to devour me opens wide,*
> *To which the hell I suffer seems a heaven.*

The first line overtly revises Marlowe's Mephistopheles: "Why this is hell, nor am I out of it," but the three remaining lines are beyond Marlowe. Without the Iago-instigated torments of Othello, without Macbeth's negative journey into the interior of his fantasies, the great image of an authentic mouth of hell would not have been available to Milton. Lucifer, had *Adam Unparadised* been composed, would have been a role out of Marlowe; Satan ensued from Shakespeare's triumph within Milton's spirit. Marlowe was a caricaturist, and Lucifer, like Tamburlaine and Barabas, would have been a grand cartoon. Shakespeare invented the perpetually changing, endlessly growing inner self, the deepest self, all-devouring, the self first perfected in Hamlet and still ravening on in Satan. In *The Changing Nature of Man,* the Dutch psychiatrist J. H. Van den Berg credits Martin Luther as the discoverer of the growing inner self. There is certainly a new inwardness in Luther, but it differs only in degree, not in kind, from Jeremiah's prophecy that God henceforth would write the Law upon our inner parts. I would not venture to characterize Shakespeare's sensibility as being either Protestant or recusant Catholic. As always with Shakespeare, it is both and neither, and so perhaps the Lutheran inwardness broadly affected the Shakespearean sense of human consciousness. But Shakespearean inward selves seem to me different from Luther's in kind and not just in degree, and different indeed in kind from the entire history of Western consciousness up to Luther. Hamlet's radical self-reliance leaps over the centuries and joins itself to Nietzsche's and Emerson's, then goes beyond their outermost limits, and keeps on going beyond ours.

Emerson's observation on Shakespeare remains true: "His mind is the horizon beyond which, at present, we do not see."

Reductionists who insist upon reminding us that Shakespeare was primarily a professional playwright receive a fine Emersonian irony: "These tricks of his magic spoil for us the illusions of the green-room." What Emerson would have said to our current Cultural Materialists and New Historicists I can only surmise, but the proper reproof is there already in "Shakespeare; Or, The Poet" from *Representative Men* (1850): "Shakespeare is the only biographer of Shakespeare; and even he can tell nothing, except to the Shakespeare in us." The Shakespeare in Milton was Satan's lowest deep, his anxiety about being devoured by something in his own self. How did Milton derive that vision of the devourer?

The complexity of the derivation is that Satan is *both* Iago and the ruined Othello, *both* Edmund and the maddened Lear, *both* the exalted and the debased Hamlet, *both* Macbeth poised on the verge of regicide and Macbeth lost in the ensuing web of murder. By excising Lucifer and giving us only Satan, the mature Milton chose, perhaps unknowingly, to be more Shakespearean than he wanted to be. Lucifer, whatever his frustrations, would not have suffered from temporal anxieties and sexual jealousy, the negative intensities at the center of Satan. Satan's obsession with time derives from Macbeth's; after Shakespeare no grand sufferers from sexual envy—whether in Milton, Hawthorne, or Proust—can be wholly un-Shakespearean. The representation of negative energy scarcely exists before Shakespeare. After him, it pulsates in Dostoevsky's nihilists as vibrantly as it does in *Paradise Lost*'s Satan, but never again on anything like the Miltonic or sublime scale.

Compare two moments in which Iago and Satan study nostalgias, both moments constituting subtle variations on the principle of "I limned this night-piece, and it was my best." The first is from Iago, in act 3, scene 3, lines 321–33, a magnificent reverie that begins with the exit of Emilia, dispatched to fetch Desdemona's handkerchief, and that is sublimely interrupted by the entrance of the already ruined Othello:

> *I will in Cassio's lodging lose this napkin,*
> *And let him find it. Trifles light as air*
> *Are to the jealous confirmations strong*
> *As proofs of holy writ; this may do something.*

The Moor already changes with my poison:
Dangerous conceits are in their natures poisons,
Which at the first are scarce found to distaste,
But with a little act upon the blood
Burn like the mines of sulfur.

Enter *Othello*

I did say so.
Look where he comes! Not poppy, nor mandragora,
Nor all the drowsy syrups of the world
Shall ever medicine thee to that sweet sleep
Which thou ow'dst yesterday.

Contrast to this a parallel moment of Iago's disciple Satan in book 4, lines 366–85, where as a Peeping Tom he ogles the unsuspecting Adam and Eve:

Ah, gentle pair, ye little think how nigh
Your change approaches, when all these delights
Will vanish and deliver ye to woe
More woe, the more your taste is now of joy;
Happy, but for so happy ill secured
Long to continue, and this high seat your heaven
Ill fenced for heaven to keep out such a foe
As now is entered; yet no purposed foe
To you whom I could pity thus forlorn
Though I unpitied: league with you I seek,
And mutual amity so strait, so close,
That I with you must dwell, or you with me
Henceforth; my dwelling haply may not please
Like this fair Paradise, your sense, yet such
Accept your maker's work; he gave it me,
Which I as freely give; hell shall unfold,
To entertain you two, her widest gates,
And send forth all her kings; there will be room,
Not like these narrow limits, to receive
Your numerous offspring.

Whether or not "the inner man" was born in Luther's conception of "Christian Freedom" in 1520, Iago's triumph is that he
has caused Othello's inner man to collapse by the play's midpoint,
while Satan savors his own imminent triumph as he gloats over
the final moments of inward freedom for Adam and Eve. Without
the inner as well as outward splendor of their victims, Iago and
Satan could not exult on so grand and frightening a scale. Both
passages present the sublime of nihilistic power, associating aesthetic pride in the night piece one has limned with a sadomasochistic nostalgia for the integral greatness one has ruined or is
about to ruin. Iago, Satan's precursor, takes an unalloyed delight
in his achievement, whereas Satan verges upon merely hypocritical
regrets. The advantage is necessarily Iago's, because his handiwork
is closer to that of the pure aesthete. You can hear John Keats
and Walter Pater in Iago's crooning:

> *Not poppy, nor mandragora*
> *Nor all the drowsy syrups of the world*
> *Shall ever medicine thee to that sweet sleep*
> *Which thou ow'dst yesterday.*

Whereas in Satan you hear a parody of all the forced marriages
of statecraft: "mutual amity so strait, so close."

The movement from dramatic critic to politician saddens us and
makes us realize that we want Satan to share more even than he
does in Iago's genius and nihilism. But what was Milton to do?
There is authentic spiritual nihilism in Chaucer's Pardoner, but
the trait was not fully developed until Shakespeare shrewdly saw
how to trump the Marlovian hero-villains with a more inward
mode of savage amoralism. Social and historical energies were just
as available to Shakespeare's contemporaries as they were to the
dramatist of *Othello, King Lear,* and *Macbeth,* but rather clearly
more inward energies were available to him as well. Shakespeare
knew precisely how to use and transform Chaucer and Marlowe,
but no one, not even Milton or Freud, has known precisely how
to use Shakespeare rather than be used by him, or how to transform anything so large and universal into something altogether
one's own.

8.

Dr. Samuel Johnson, the Canonical Critic

ONE CAN TRACE Western literary criticism back to a number of origins, including Aristotle's *Poetics* and Plato's attack upon Homer in *The Republic*. I myself tend to follow Bruno Snell's *Growth of the Mind,* which gives the honor to Aristophanes' fierce assault upon Euripides. It seems grimly appropriate that an intellectual activity should have emerged from deliberate farce and now is dying into the unintentional farce acted out by the swarm of contemporary "political" and "cultural" critics who are sinking our educational institutions. No elegy for the Western Canon could be complete without an appreciation of the canonical critic proper, Dr. Samuel Johnson, unmatched by any critic in any nation before or after him.

Johnson has less in common with Montaigne and Freud, the other two essayists studied in this book, than they have with each other. A skeptical or Epicurean temper aroused Johnsonian ire; he was authentically royalist, Christian, and classicist—unlike T. S. Eliot, who aspired to that triple identity with considerable bad faith. There is no bad faith in or about Dr. Johnson, who was as good as he was great, yet also refreshingly, wildly strange to the highest degree. By that, I mean more than his singular or odd (though magnificent) personality, as conveyed to us in what is still the best of all literary biographies, Boswell's *Life of Johnson*. Johnson was a powerful poet and wrote a superb prose-romance in *Rasselas,* but all of his work—the literary criticism particularly—is essentially wisdom literature.

Like his true precursor, whoever it was that wrote Ecclesiastes in the Hebrew Bible, Johnson is disturbing and unconventional, a moralist altogether idiosyncratic. Johnson is to England what Emerson is to America, Goethe to Germany, and Montaigne to France: the national sage. But Johnson as much as Emerson is an original writer of wisdom, even though he insists that his morality follows Christian, classical, and conservative ideologies. Again like Emerson, or Nietzsche, or the tradition of French moralists, Johnson is a great aphorist, fusing the ethical and the prudential, as M. J. C. Hodgart observed. Perhaps the precise term for Johnson is experiential critic, both of literature and of life. More than any other critic, Johnson demonstrates that the only method is the self, and that criticism is therefore a branch of wisdom literature. It is not a political or social science or a cult of gender and racial cheerleading, its present fate in Western universities.

All critics, great and small, err sometimes, and even Dr. Johnson was not infallible. "*Tristram Shandy* did not last" is the most unfortunate of all Johnsonian pronouncements, but there are others, such as his praise of a passage of poetry in Congreve's *Mourning Bride* as superior to anything in Shakespeare. Johnson, more than Coleridge or Hazlitt, A. C. Bradley or Harold Goddard, seems to me the best interpreter of Shakespeare in the language, so this particular lapse is very odd. It is mitigated by the plain badness of the Congreve, which has nothing in common with his great prose comedies. Congreve describes a temple that is a tomb and seems to have provoked something of Johnson's awe in regard to death, which was scarcely less than his awe in considering God. There is a famous passage in Boswell's *Life* that is central in understanding Johnson:

his thoughts upon this awful change were in general full of dismal apprehensions. His mind resembled the vast amphitheatre, the Colisaeum at Rome. In the center stood his judgment, which, like a mighty gladiator, combated those apprehensions that, like the wild beasts of the *Arena,* were all around in cells, ready to be let out upon him. After a conflict, he drove them back into their dens, but not killing them, they were still assailing him. To my question, whether we might not fortify our minds for the approach of death, he answered, in a passion, "No, Sir, let it alone. It matters not how a man dies, but how he lives. The act of dying is not of importance, it lasts so short a time." He added, with an earnest look, "A man knows it must be so, and submits. It will do him no good to whine."

Pragmatically, Johnson's stance recalls Montaigne's, but the affect is altogether different: there is nothing in Montaigne like Johnson's anxious passion or terrible earnestness. A thinker for himself (part of the praise he gave Milton), Johnson avoided theological speculation but not the anxieties attendant upon human limitations in apprehending the last things. "Hope and fear" is a frequent Johnsonian linkage; few writers have been so sensitive to endings of every sort: of enterprises, literary works, human lives. There is a complex relationship between Johnson's ultimate anxieties and his critical outlook upon literature. Unlike T. S. Eliot, he does not make aesthetic judgments on religious grounds. Johnson was very unhappy with both Milton's politics and Milton's spirituality, yet the power and originality of *Paradise Lost* persuaded him, despite their ideological differences.

On Milton, on Shakespeare, on Pope, Johnson is everything a wise critic should be: he directly confronts greatness with a total response, to which he brings his complete self. I can think of no other major critic nearly so aware as Johnson was of what he called "the treachery of the human heart," particularly the heart of the critic. The phrase I have quoted is from *The Rambler* 93, where Johnson first rather grimly observes that "there is indeed some tenderness due to living writers," but then warns that this tenderness is not "universally necessary; for he that writes may be considered as a kind of general challenger, whom everyone has a right to attack." This canonical sense of literature as agon is, as Johnson knew, wholly classical, and prompts a marvelous statement that is Johnson's credo as a critic:

> But whatever be decided concerning contemporaries, whom he that knows the treachery of the human heart, and considers how often we gratify our own pride or envy under the appearance of contending for elegance and propriety, will find himself not much inclined to disturb; there can surely be no exemptions pleaded to secure them from criticism, who can no longer suffer by reproach, and of whom nothing now remains but their writings and their names. Upon these authors the critick is, undoubtedly, at full liberty to exercise the strictest severity, since he endangers only his own fame, and, like Æneas when he drew his sword in the infernal regions, encounters phantoms which cannot be wounded. He may indeed pay some regard to established reputation; but he can by that shew of reverence consult only his own security, for all other motives are now at an end.

The agon here is traced to its origins, and a brilliant irony reminds the critic that he draws his sword against phantoms in Hades, authors who cannot be wounded. But what about the greatest of phantoms: Shakespeare, Milton, Pope? "There is always an appeal open from criticism to nature"; Johnson intended Shakespeare as the "nature" of that sentence, and Walter Jackson Bate sees it as the motto or starting point of all Johnson's critical writings, thus emphasizing that Johnson is an experiential critic. Wisdom, not form, is the ultimate standard for judging imaginative literature, and Shakespeare provides Johnson with the critic's supreme test: how can one's response be adequate to the central writer in the Western Canon?

JOHNSON ON SHAKESPEARE may be said to commence with a famous sentence early in the "Preface" (1765): "Nothing can please many, and please long, but just representations of general nature." To establish the justice of Shakespearean imitation of nature is Johnson's quest, and no one has done better in that enterprise: "In the writings of other poets a character is too often an individual; in those of Shakespeare it is commonly a species." Clearly Johnson does not mean that Hamlet and Iago are not individual representations; rather, their individuality is verified and enhanced because they center a system of life, an extension of design, so that we can scarcely conceive of a charismatic intellectual, in life or literature, who does not have a touch of Hamlet; or a genius of evil, an aesthete who delights in composing with people rather than words, who will not have Iago as a bad eminence against which he or she must be judged. Molière evidently knew nothing of Shakespeare, yet Alceste in *The Misanthrope* evokes Hamlet. Ibsen most certainly knew Shakespeare, and Hedda Gabler is a worthy descendant of Iago. Shakespeare's hold upon human nature is so sure that all post-Shakespearean characters are to some degree Shakespearean. Johnson shrewdly notes that every other dramatist tends to make love a universal agent, but not Shakespeare:

> but love is only one of many passions, and as it has no great influence upon the sum of life, it has little operation in the dramas of a poet, who caught his ideas from the living world, and exhibited only what he saw before him. He knew, that any other passion, as it was regular or exorbitant, was a cause of happiness or calamity."

Who is more accurate about the place of the drive in Shakespeare, Johnson or Freud? Freud's comments on *Hamlet, Lear,* and *Macbeth* give the struggle for sexual fulfillment, however repressed, at least an equal place in those plays with the struggle for power. Johnson and Shakespeare would not agree with Freud, and the drive or passion in Shakespeare is far more comprehensive—an amalgam of many exorbitant passions—than Freud would allow for, particularly in the three greatest tragedies. We may observe that Johnson's own drive, though allied with fiercely repressed sexuality, was altogether Shakespearean, informed as it was by the poetic will to immortality, memorably, negatively, and ironically understated by Johnson in a letter to Boswell (8 December, 1763):

There lurks, perhaps, in every known heart a desire of distinction which inclines every man first to hope, and then to believe, that Nature has given him something peculiar to himself. This vanity makes one mind nurse aversions and another actuate desires, till they rise by art much above their original state of power and as affectation, in time, improves to habit, they at last tyrannize over him who at first encouraged them for show.

This was certainly intended to be a self-critique; is it not also a just account of Shakespearean character, say, of Macbeth? The desire for distinction is certainly the motive for metaphor, the drive that makes poets. Does it not also animate heroes and heroines, villains, and hero-villains in Shakespeare? Johnson, in his preface to Shakespeare, says: "Characters thus ample and general were not easily discriminated and preserved, yet perhaps no poet ever kept his personages more *distinct* from each other" (my italics). The individuation of speech, the appropriateness of speech to character, is one of the Shakespearean miracles, deftly appropriated by Johnson for self-analysis in his desire for distinction. What I find curious is Johnson's belief that Shakespeare was essentially a comic writer who imposed tragedy upon himself, presumably in search of yet more distinction:

In tragedy he is always struggling after some occasion to be comick, but in comedy he seems to repose, or to luxuriate, as in a mode of thinking congenial to his nature. In his tragick scenes there is always something wanting, but his comedy often surpasses expectation or desire. His comedy pleases by the thoughts and the language, and his tragedy for the greater part by incident and action. His tragedy seems to be skill, his comedy to be instinct.

Shakespeare's development, essentially from comedy and history through tragedy to romance (to use our terms), both confutes and supports Johnson. Is *Lear* skill, and *As You Like It* instinct? Partly, Johnson tells us here as much about Johnson as about Shakespeare, but as Johnson has insisted that Shakespeare was "the mirror of nature," this is not inappropriate. It is more interesting that Johnson evidently prefers Falstaff to Lear, which must be related to Johnson's anxiety that Shakespeare "seems to write without any moral purpose," hardly an anxiety that we now share. As Bate shows, however, Johnsonian anxieties have real critical power. That Shakespeare would not indulge in "poetic justice" is a Johnsonian sorrow, because Johnson himself is profoundly benign and authentically fearful of tragedy and of madness. Shakespeare, like Jonathan Swift, unnerved Johnson, who may well have read King Lear's madness as a prophecy of what could become his own derangement. A great natural satirist, Johnson largely avoided writing satire, which may have crippled him as a poet, where we have all too little of him. The fury of Lear engaged Johnson despite himself, and his general observation upon the play is disturbingly intense:

> The tragedy of Lear is deservedly celebrated among the dramas of Shakespeare. There is perhaps no play which keeps the attention so strongly fixed; which so much agitates our passions and interests our curiosity. The artful involutions of distinct interests, the striking opposition of contrary characters, the sudden changes of fortune, and the quick succession of events, fill the mind with a perpetual tumult of indignation, pity, and hope. There is no scene which does not contribute to the aggravation of the distress or conduct of the action, and scarce a line which does not conduce to the progress of the scene. So powerful is the current of the poet's imagination, that the mind, which once ventures within it, is hurried irresistibly along.

We hear a powerful mind resisting the most powerful of minds, but vainly, as Johnson is swept into the current of Shakespeare's imagination. Johnson is never so strong and authentic a critic as when he is most divided against himself, and one finds here again the troubled metaphor of "distinct" in the "artful involutions of *distinct* interests." To be distinct is both achievement and vanity for Johnson; in Shakespeare's dramatic cosmos, it is achievement only, beyond poetic justice, beyond good and evil, beyond madness and vanity. No one before him had expressed Shakespeare's unique and overwhelming strength of representation as Johnson was able to do, and with his wonderful sense of diction he located the essence of Shakespeare as the art of division, of making it distinct, of creating differences. Tragedy is hardly alien to that art, as Johnson certainly knew. The most capacious of souls, Shakespeare's, found in Johnson's soul the most capacious of critical mirrors, a mirror with a voice. I would locate the center of Johnson on Shakespeare, the canonical critic interpreting the canonical poet, in a particular, brief passage of the "Preface," where "distinctions" again repeat another form of the crucial metaphor linking the critic to his poet:

> Though he had so many difficulties to encounter, and so little assistance to surmount them, he has been able to obtain an exact knowledge of many modes of life, and many cast of native dispositions; to vary them with great multiplicity; to mark them by nice distinctions; and to shew them in full view by proper combinations. In this part of his performance he had none to imitate, but has himself been imitated by all succeeding writers; and it may be doubted, whether from all his successors more maxims of theoretical knowledge, or more rules of practical prudence, can be collected, than he alone has given to his country.

So much is packed in here that we need to stand back from it, to see what Johnson has seen and to hear the reverberations of his praise of Shakespeare. "Theoretical knowledge" is what we might call "cognitive awareness"; "practical prudence" is wisdom. If Shakespeare obtained "exact knowledge" and showed it in full view, he is beyond what philosophers could achieve. With no inherited contingencies, Shakespeare as originator establishes a contingency that all writers after him must sustain. Johnson realizes, and tells us, that Shakespeare has established the standard for measuring representation ever after. Knowing many modes of life and many casts of native dispositions is not knowing apart from representing. Shakespeare varies with multiplicity, marks by nice distinctions, and shows in a full prospect. To vary, mark, and show *is* the knowing, and what is known is what we have learned to call our psychology, of which Shakespeare, as Johnson intimates, is the inventor. If this is holding a mirror up to nature, it is a very active mirror indeed.

ONE OF JOHNSON'S small masterpieces is "On the Death of a Friend," *The Idler* 41. It is dated 27 January 1759, only a few days after the death of his mother. Johnson, a Christian, speaks of the hope of reunion, but the tone and dark pathos of his writing shows as full an acceptance of the reality principle, of making friends with the necessity of dying, as we more naturally expect to find in the skeptical Montaigne and in Freud, for whom religion was an illusion. On the psychology of being a survivor, Johnson can hardly be bettered:

> These are the calamities by which Providence gradually disengages us from the love of life. Other evils fortitude may repel, or hope may mitigate, but irreparable privation leaves nothing to exercise resolution or flatter expectation. The dead cannot return, and nothing is left us here but languishment and grief.

Compared to this extraordinary prose, Johnson's assertions of faith seem not so much weak as divided, even forced. An empiricist and a naturalist, fierce in his common sense, Johnson never came easily to belief. There is a passion for consciousness itself in Johnson that nothing could assuage; he wanted more life, down to the end. Even if Boswell had never written the *Life,* we would remember Johnson's personality, which is the undersong of everything he wrote and said. The personality of the critic is much deprecated in our time, by various formalisms, or by the current cultural materialists. Yet when I think of the modern critics I most admire—Wilson Knight, Empson, Northrop Frye, Kenneth Burke—what I remember first is neither theories nor methods, let alone readings. What return first are expressions of vehement and colorful personalities: Wilson Knight straightforwardly quoting from seances; Empson proclaiming the almost Aztec or Benin high barbarism of *Paradise Lost;* Frye cheerfully characterizing T. S. Eliot's neo-Christian account of civilization's decline as the Myth of the Great Western Butterslide; Burke compounding I, aye, and eye in Emerson's vision of the transparent eyeball. Dr. Johnson is stronger than all other critics, not only in cognitive power, learning, and wisdom, but in the splendor of his literary personality.

Offsetting the somber contemplator of death is Johnson the critical humorist, who teaches the critic not to be solemn, smug, or superior. In *The Lives of the Poets,* his major critical achievement, Johnson found himself introducing fifty poets, chosen mostly by the booksellers (publishers), including such noncanonical worthies as Pomfret, Sprat, Yalden, Dorset, Roscommon, Stepney, and Felton, fit precursors for many of our prematurely canonized poetasters and inchoate rhapsodists. Yalden may stand for the others, then and now. Johnson remarked that Yalden attempted Pindaric odes in the manner of Abraham Cowley (himself now forgotten, except by specialists): "Having fixed his attention on Cowley as a model, he has attempted in some sort to rival him, and has written a *Hymn to Darkness,* evidently as a counterpart to Cowley's *Hymn to Light."*

The unhappy Yalden would not be remembered at all, even for that, except that the *Life of Yalden* concludes with a superb Johnsonian sentence: "Of his other poems it is sufficient to say that they deserve perusal, though they are not always exactly polished, though the rhymes are sometimes very ill sorted, and though his faults seem rather the omissions of idleness than the negligence of enthusiasm."

That would not appear to have left much of the unfortunate Yalden, and yet it is not the finest observation the minor bard provoked in the major critic. Yalden also attempted his own *Hymn to Life* in which, in response to the sudden advent of the newly created Light, he has God somewhat at a loss: "Awhile th' Almighty wondering stood." Upon this line, Johnson comments, "He ought to have remembered that Infinite Knowledge can never wonder. All wonder is the effect of novelty upon Ignorance."

The great *Lives of the Poets* is most powerful on Alexander Pope, Johnson's own precursor; on Richard Savage, a poor poet but great talker, with whom Johnson had shared his early London years as a Grub Street Bohemian; on Milton, whom Johnson both disliked and overwhelmingly admired; and on Dryden, in some respects his critical forerunner. But there are also important and famous moments in the essays devoted to Cowley, Waller, Addison, Prior, Swift, Young, Gray, and even in the handful of pages given to Johnson's friend, the mad poet William Collins. As a body of poetic criticism and literary biography, it has no rival in the language. Like the remainder of Johnson's criticism—much of the *Rambler* and *Idler* periodical essays, aspects of *Rasselas,* the preface and notes to Shakespeare, and indeed much of what is quoted in Boswell's *Life*—the distinction between interpretation and biography can rarely be sustained.

Johnson may not have believed (as I do) with Emerson that "there is properly no history; only biography," but pragmatically Johnson wrote biographical criticism. When almost no biography was available, as with Shakespeare, Johnson shows how subtle a mode an essentially biographical history can be. For Johnson, the prime biographical emphasis is always upon individuality, so that the crucial issues for him are originality, invention, and imitation, both of nature and of other poets. Critics like myself whose concern is influence necessarily learn from Johnson, who implicitly understood why he confined his important poems to *London* and *The Vanity of Human Wishes,* both wonderful works, but hardly adequate to his potential. His sense of the perfection of Pope blocked him from further achievement; he celebrates Pope but avoids creatively misreading this elegant poetic father, whose temperament was hardly Johnsonian.

T. S. Eliot, a minor critic compared to Johnson, became a strong poet by revising Tennyson and Whitman in *The Waste Land.* Johnson deliberately refrained from giving the neoclassic tradition of Ben Jonson, Dryden, and Pope stronger continuators than Oliver Goldsmith and George Crabbe, both of whom Johnson supported. It remains a mystery to me why the pugnacious Johnson refused to enter into the contest with Pope, for which he was so supremely fitted. Johnson's relation to Pope is more like Anthony Burgess's to Joyce than like Beckett's to his one-time master. I have a passion for Burgess's *Nothing Like the Sun,* but it lovingly repeats *Ulysses* without revising it. Even the early Beckett, in his hilarious novel *Murphy,* presents a highly creative misreading of *Ulysses,* swerving away from it to his own purposes and beginning the long evolution that will lead him through *Watt* and the great trilogy (*Molloy, Malone Dies, The Unnameable*) to the very un-Joycean triumph of *How It Is,* as well as to his three major plays. As a poet Johnson refused greatness, though he certainly touched it in *The Vanity of Human Wishes.* As a critic Johnson was more uninhibited, and he surpassed everyone who had come before him. Boswell does not explain this conundrum for us. The issue is not the strength of the *Vanity,* but its singularity; Johnson knew how good it was. Why did he not go on from it?

I cannot think of another poet in English of Johnson's powers who so consciously declined to be a major poet. Emerson had the same relation to Wordsworth's poetry that Johnson had to Pope's, and like Johnson, Emerson chose the other harmony of prose. But even Emerson's best poems—"Bacchus," "Days," the "Channing" ode, and a few more like "Uriel"—are not of the weight and splendor of Johnson's *Vanity of Human Wishes.* After the *Vanity* Johnson's genius went to criticism and to conversation, but not to poetry. Shakespeare was the poet whom Johnson loved despite himself, and in partial contradiction of his deep yearning for "poetical justice" and the moral betterment of mankind. But Pope—more even than Dryden—Johnson loved absolutely; he gave his heart away to Pope, even affirming that Pope's translation of the *Iliad* was "a performance which no age or nation can pretend to equal," a performance indeed that "may be said to have tuned the English tongue," including Johnson's own.

Against this scandalous overpraise of a version now dead for nearly all of us must be set Johnson's brilliant preference for *The Dunciad,* one of Pope's greatest achievements, over the vastly overvalued *Essay on Man,* which Johnson crushes: "Never was penury of knowledge and vulgarity of sentiment so happily disguised. The reader feels his mind full, though he learns nothing; and when he meets it in its new array, no longer knows the talk of his mother and his nurse."

Johnson had little doubt as to his superiority over Pope in wisdom, learning, and intellect. What was it then that shadowed him, so that he would not give his deepest energies to a sustained career as a poet? His account of Pope's poetic strength must be part of the answer:

Pope had, in proportions very nicely adjusted to each other, all the qualities that constitute genius. He had *Invention,* by which new trains of events are formed, and new scenes of imagery displayed, as in the *Rape of the Lock;* and by which extrinsick and adventitious embellishments and illustrations are connected with a known subject, as in the *Essay on Criticism.* He had *Imagination,* which strongly impresses on the writer's mind, and enables him to convey to the reader, the various forms of nature, incidents of life, and energies of passion, as in his *Eloisa, Windsor Forest,* and the *Ethick Epistles.* He had *Judgement,* which selects from life or nature, what the present purpose requires, and by separating the essence of things from its concomitants, often makes the representation more powerful than the reality: and he had colours of language always before him, ready to decorate his matter with every grace of elegant expression, as when he accommodates his diction to the wonderful multiplicity of Homer's sentiments and descriptions.

I question only the last virtue, *Judgment,* and its manifestations in Pope's *Iliad,* but heartily agree with the praise of *Invention* in *The Rape of the Lock,* and of *Imagination* in the *Epistles.*

Where Johnson, in his passion for Pope, risks hyperbole is in his summation of the case for his poet:

New sentiments and new images others may produce; but to attempt any further improvement of versification will be dangerous. Art and diligence have now done their best, and what shall be added will be the effort of tedious toil and needless curiosity.

After all this, it is surely superfluous to answer the question that has once been asked, Whether Pope was a poet? otherwise than by asking in return, If Pope be not a poet, where is poetry to be found? To circumscribe poetry by a definition will only shew the narrowness of the definer, though a definition which shall exclude Pope will not easily be made. Let us look round upon the present time, and back upon the past; let us enquire to whom the voice of mankind has decreed the wreath of poetry; let their productions be examined, and their claims stated, and the pretensions of Pope will be no more disputed. Had he given the world only his version, the name of poet must have been allowed him: if the writer of the *Iliad* were to class his successors, he would assign a very high place to his translator, without requiring any other evidence of Genius.

Here one faces a certain bafflement. One side of Johnson takes the dogmatic view that the neoclassical couplet is the final, normative perfection of poetic form. Why so skeptical an experiential critic, so learned a scholar, should have made such a fetish of Pope's admitted technical perfection I cannot hope to understand. Johnson had literally thousands of lines of Pope and Dryden by heart, and relatively few of Milton, but he knew (as they did) that they were not of Milton's eminence, let alone of Shakespeare's. Johnson raised Milton by merit to rather a bad eminence, but no similar ambivalence colored his vision of Shakespeare. Certainly, Johnson never identified himself with the Homer-Pope Achilles, as he beautifully identified with Sir John Falstaff. It is not even clear that *The Vanity of Human Wishes* is not a technical advance over Pope. Emphatically Johnson was what he praised Milton for being, a thinker for himself, and the prestige of Pope hardly factors into Johnson's generous overpraise. Pope is a great poet, but you cannot say of him, as you can of Shakespeare and Dante, that one is reading poetry itself; and it is peculiar to assert that Homer would have approved of Pope's *Iliad*. That almost invites the furious rejoinder of William Blake, attacking his Popean patron, the bad poet William Hayley, and Pope together:

> Thus Hayley on his Toilette seeing the Sope
> Cries Homer is very much improvd by Pope.

It was Pope's artistry that most engaged Johnson, or what Johnson oddly called Pope's *poetical prudence,* defined by Robert Griffin as "Pope's peculiar combination of natural faculties with a disposition to labor." One of Johnson's myths about himself was that he was indolent, in contrast to Pope's diligence; but what he meant was the difference between his own restlessness and impatience of mind and Pope's deliberateness. Johnson notoriously feared his own mind, almost as though he might be victimized by his imagination, as Macbeth had been in Shakespeare's most striking vision of the dangerous prevalence of the imagination. Johnson was too good a son to his poetic father Pope, and the Muse requires ambivalence in the family romance of poets. The underlying sorrow, implied throughout but rarely expressed, of *The Lives of the Poets* is what Laura Quinney calls a quest for "the Oedipalization of literary space." Confronted by Alexander Pope as his Laius, Johnson fled the crossroads rather than risk impiety. Perhaps Johnson was too good a man to become a great poet, but we need not regret his scruples, for we know him now as both a great man and the greatest of literary critics.

CANONICAL CRITICISM, which is what Johnson consciously writes, has its religiopolitical and socioeconomic motivations in Johnson, but it fascinates me to watch the critic push aside his own ideologies in his *Life of Milton*. Our current apostles of "criticism and social change" ought to try reading, in sequence, Johnson and Hazlitt on Milton. On all issues of religion, politics, society, and economics, the Tory Johnson and the Radical Dissenter Hazlitt are totally opposed, but they praise Milton for the same qualities, Hazlitt as memorably as Johnson, particularly here:

> Milton has borrowed more than any other writer, and exhausted every source of imitation, sacred or profane; yet he is perfectly distinct from every other writer. He is a writer of cantos, and yet in originality scarcely inferior to Homer. The power of his mind is stamped on every line. . . . In reading his works, we feel ourselves under the influence of a mighty intellect, that the nearer it approaches to others, becomes more distinct from them. . . . Milton's learning has the effect of intuition.

Shakespeare is the one exception to the truth of this, as I tried to show in tracing the Shakespearean influence that persisted in Milton's Satan. Hazlitt, who seems to me second only to Johnson among English critics, disliked Johnson. But Johnson on Milton anticipates Hazlitt:

> The highest praise of genius is original invention . . . of all the borrowers from Homer, Milton is perhaps the least indebted. He was naturally a thinker for himself, confident of his own abilities, and disdainful of help or hindrance: he did not refuse admission to the thought or images of his predecessors, but he did not seek them.

Both critics accurately find in Milton a power that converts learning into intuition: the power of invention, which Johnson considered the essence of poetry. Johnson's melancholia, which alienated Hazlitt, taught him to value invention all the more highly, because the cure for melancholia involves a continual discovery and rediscovery of the possibilities of life. More than anyone else I have read, Johnson understood how little we can bear any anticipation of death, especially our own death. It is not excessive to say that his criticism is founded upon this understanding. The basic law of human existence, for Johnson, cannot vary: human nature declines to confront death head on. When Johnson praises Shakespeare by observing that his characters act and speak under the influence of the general passions that agitate all mankind, the critic is thinking in the first place of the passion to evade the consciousness of dying. There is a splendidly grim conversation reported by Boswell, April 15, 1778, when Johnson was sixty-nine:

> BOSWELL. "Then, Sir, we must be contented to acknowledge that death is a terrible thing."
> JOHNSON. "Yes, Sir. I have made no approaches to a state which can look on it as not terrible."
> MRS. KNOWLES. (seeming to enjoy a pleasing serenity in the persuasion of benignant divine light,) "Does not St. Paul say, 'I have fought the good fight of faith, I have finished my course; henceforth is laid up for me a crown of life!' "
> JOHNSON. "Yes, Madam; but here was a man inspired, a man who had been converted by supernatural interposition."

BOSWELL. "In prospect death is dreadful; but in fact we find that people die easy. Few believe it certain they are then to die; and those who do, set themselves to behave with resolution, as a man does who is going to be hanged. He is not the less unwilling to be hanged."

MISS SEWARD. "There is one mode of the fear of death, which is certainly absurd; and that is the dread of annihilation, which is only a pleasing sleep without a dream."

JOHNSON. "It is neither pleasing, nor sleep; it is nothing. Now mere existence is so much better than nothing, that one would rather exist even in pain, than not exist."

Johnson ends the exchange by remarking that "The lady confounds annihilation, which is nothing, with the apprehension of it, which is dreadful. It is in the apprehension of it that the horror of annihilation consists." The critic's realism associates that horror with both the fear of madness and the hope of salvation, but the horror itself transcends both the fear and the hope. To go on living, we retreat from the consciousness that induces the horror.

Johnson on Shakespeare is never subtler than in his comment on the Duke's astonishing "Be absolute for death" speech in act 3, scene 1 of *Measure for Measure:* "Thou hast nor youth, nor age; / But as it were an after-dinner's sleep, / Dreaming on both." Johnson remarks,

This is exquisitely imagined. When we are young we busy ourselves in forming schemes for succeeding time, and miss the gratifications that are before us; when we are old we amuse the languor of age with the recollection of youthful pleasures or performances; so that our life, of which no part is filled with the business of the present time, resembles our dreams after dinner, when the events of the morning are mingled with the designs of the evening.

Dinner for Shakespeare and Johnson was the midday meal we call lunch. What Johnson sees is that Shakespeare's exquisite imagining reveals our total inability to live in the present moment; either we are prospective, or we recollect. What Johnson refuses to say, but implies, is that we forsake the present because we must die at a present moment. The horror of annihilation is the motive for metaphor; what Nietzsche called "the desire to be different, the desire to be elsewhere" is activated by a refusal to accept dying. And the heart's desire to win distinction, including literary distinction, according to Johnson has the same drive: to evade the consciousness that is reduced to vertigo by the thought of ceasing to be.

Bate, in the finest insight on Johnson I know, emphasized that no other writer is so obsessed by the realization that the mind is an *activity*, one that will turn to destructiveness of the self or of others unless it is directed to labor. The heart's hunger for survival, displaced into a rainbow of forms, is exposed by Johnson as the de-idealized drive for literary canonization. Johnson's gloom, which offended Hazlitt as unnatural, might be called a negative empiricism opposed to Hazlitt's positive naturalism. Both critics exalted Falstaff as Shakespeare's finest representation of the comic spirit, but Johnson's greater need for the relief provided by humor led him to an amazing identification with Falstaff, wholly against his moral will. Hazlitt is totally delighted by Falstaff, as all of us should be; Johnson, like lesser moralists down to the present, disapproves of Falstaff but cannot hold out against him.

Though morally inhibited, Johnson is so moved by Falstaff that he becomes rhapsodic until he checks himself:

> But Falstaff unimitated, unimitable Falstaff, how shall I describe thee? Thou compound of sense and vice; of sense which may be admired but not esteemed, of vice which may be despised, but hardly detested. Falstaff is a character loaded with faults, and with those faults which naturally produce contempt. He is a thief, and a glutton, a coward, and a boaster, always ready to cheat the weak, and prey upon the poor; to terrify the timorous and insult the defenceless. At once obsequious and malignant, he satirises in their absence those whom he lives by flattering. He is familiar with the Prince only as an agent of vice, but of this familiarity he is so proud as not only to be supercilious and haughty with common men, but to think his interest of importance to the Duke of Lancaster. Yet the man thus corrupt,

thus despicable, makes himself necessary to the prince that despises him, by the most pleasing of all qualities, perpetual gaiety, by an unfailing power of exciting laughter, which is the more freely indulged, as his wit is not of the splendid or ambitious kind, but consists in easy escapes and sallies of levity, which make sport but raise no envy. It must be observed that he is stained with no enormous or sanguinary crimes, so that his licentiousness is not so offensive but that it may be borne for his mirth.

The moral to be drawn from this representation is, that no man is more dangerous than he that with a will to corrupt, hath the power to please; and that neither wit nor honesty ought to think themselves safe with such a companion when they see Henry seduced by Falstaff.

As a fierce Falstaffian, I disagree with much of this, preferring Johnson's contemporary, Maurice Morgann, who in *An Essay on the Dramatic Character of Sir John Falstaff* (1777) vindicated the finest comic character in all literature. Johnson's reaction to Morgann, according to Boswell, was to mutter that Morgann would next demonstrate the moral virtue of Iago. Yet one forgives Johnson for his moving observation that Falstaff manifests "the most pleasing of all qualities, perpetual gaiety."

Johnson's great need of that quality was constant, and his references to Falstaff, in conversation as in his writings, were frequent. He liked to portray himself as Falstaff, old but light-hearted, with an indomitable vitality though gradually darkened by impending loss. The vitality abides in Johnson's own writing, as it does in the figure of Johnson, within and without Boswell. Whether that strength of being will continue to haunt us, I cannot prophesy. If canonical values are exiled completely from the study of literature, will Johnson still have an audience?

If there are to be no more generations of common readers, free of ideological cant, then Johnson will vanish, together with much else that is canonical. Wisdom does not die so easily, however. If criticism expires in the universities and colleges, it will reside in other places, since it is the modern version of wisdom literature. I cannot bear to be elegiac about Dr. Johnson, my hero since my boyhood, and so I close this chapter by giving him the last word, from the "Preface to Shakespeare," so that we hear again the greatest of critics on the strongest of poets:

> The irregular combinations of fanciful invention may delight a-while, by that novelty of which the common satiety of life sends us all in quest; but the pleasures of sudden wonder are soon exhausted, and the mind can only repose on the stability of truth.

9

Goethe's *Faust, Part Two:*
The Countercanonical Poem

Of all the strongest Western writers, Goethe now seems the least available to our sensibility. I suspect that this distance has little to do with how badly his poetry translates into English. Hölderlin translates poorly also, but his appeal to most of us dwarfs Goethe's. A poet and wisdom writer who is his language's equivalent of Dante can transcend inadequate translation but not changes in life and literature that render his central attitudes so remote from us as to seem archaic. Goethe is no longer our ancestor, as he was Emerson's and Carlyle's. His wisdom abides, but it seems to come from some solar system other than our own.

Goethe had no German poetic precursors of anything like comparable strength; Hölderlin came after him, and he has had no rival since, not even in Heine, Mörike, Stefan George, Rilke, Hofmannsthal, or the astonishing Trakl and Celan. But though he stands at the true beginning of imaginative literature in German, Goethe is, from a Western perspective, an end rather than a beginning. Ernst Robert Curtius, to me the most distinguished of modern German literary critics, has observed that European literature formed a continuous tradition from Homer through Goethe. The step beyond was taken by Wordsworth, the inaugurator of modern poetry and also of that line of introspection which goes from Ruskin through Proust into Beckett, until recently the major living writer. Goethe's dates were 1749–1832, while Wordsworth's were 1770–1850, which makes the English Romantic a younger contemporary of the German sage. But British and American poets continue to rewrite Wordsworth involuntarily, and one cannot say that Goethe is a vital influence on German poetry at this time.

Nevertheless, it should be argued that Goethe's remoteness is part of his enormous value for us now, particularly at a time when French speculators have proclaimed the death of the author and the hegemony of texts. Every Goethe text, however divergent from the others, bears the mark of his unique and overwhelming personality, which cannot be evaded or deconstructed. To read Goethe is to know again that the death of the author is merely a belated Gallic trope. Goethe's daemon or daemons—he appears to have commanded as many as he wanted—is always present in his work, aiding the perpetual paradox that the poetry and prose alike are at once exemplary of a Classical, almost universal *ethos,* and a Romantic, intensely personal *pathos.* The *logos,* or in Aristotelian terms the *dianoia* (thought content) of Goethe's work, is the only vulnerable aspect, since the eccentric Goethean Science of Nature today seems an inadequate conceptualizing of his formidable daemonic apprehension of reality. That hardly matters, for Goethe's literary power and wisdom survive the evaporation of his rationalizations.

Curtius adroitly remarks that "Predominance of light over darkness is the condition that suits Goethe best," and reminds us that Goethe's word for this condition is *heiter,* not so much "joyous" as the equivalent of the Latin *serenus,* a cloudless sky, whether night or day. Like Shelley after him, Goethe found his personal emblem in the morning star, but not for its moment of exquisite waning into the dawn, as Shelley did. The serene Goethe is now a temperamental burden for us; neither we nor our writers are tranquil. Goethe's Faust lives to be one hundred years old, and Goethe ardently desired the same for himself. Nietzsche taught us a poetics of pain; only the painful, he brilliantly insisted, could truly be memorable. Curtius ascribes to Goethe a poetics of pleasure in an old tradition, but a poetics of serenity, of unclouded skies, is even closer to the Goethean vision.

"Error about life is necessary for life," a crucial Nietzschean insight, is part of Nietzsche's large (and acknowledged) debt to Goethe, whose idea of poetry centered upon a complex awareness that poetry essentially was trope, and that trope was a kind of creative error. Curtius in his masterwork, *European Literature and the Latin Middle Ages* (1948; 1953 in English), brings together two splendid statements on trope by Goethe. In the "Notes and Essays" attached to the *West-Östlicher Divan,* Goethe comments on metaphor in Arabic poetry:

> to the Oriental, all things suggest all things, so that, accustomed to connecting the most remote things together, he does not hesitate to derive contrary things from one another by very slight changes in letters or syllables. Here we see that language is already productive in and of itself, and indeed, in so far as it coincides with the imagination, is poetic. If, then, we should begin with the first, necessary, primary tropes and then mark the freer and bolder, until we finally reached the most daring and arbitrary, and even the inept, conventional, and the hackneyed, we should have obtained a general view of Oriental poetry.

Clearly this would constitute a general metaphor for poetry, where "all things suggest all things." In his *Maxims and Reflections,* Goethe says of his true precursor (the only one he could accept, because he wrote in a different modern language): "Shakespeare is rich in wonderful tropes which stem from personified concepts and which would not suit us at all, but which in him are perfectly in place because in his time all art was dominated by allegory."

This reflects Goethe's unfortunate distinction between "alle-gory, where the particular serves only as an example of the general" and "symbol" or "the nature of poetry; it expresses something particular, without thinking of the general or point-ing to it." But Goethe goes on to observe that Shakespeare "finds images where we would not go for them, for example in the book . . . still regarded as something sacred." To trope a book as something sacred is hardly allegory in Goethe's rather unin-teresting sense, but it is allegory as an authentically symbolic mode in which all things again suggest all things. Such a metaphor of the book opens Goethe to his own largest ambitions as a poet, to embody and extend the European tradition of literature without being overcome by its contingencies, and so without losing the image of oneself.

This aspect of Goethe has been best illuminated by his principal twentieth-century heir, Thomas Mann. With loving irony (or per-haps ironic love), Mann composed a series of remarkable portraits of Goethe, from the essay on "Goethe and Tolstoy" (1922) through a triad of essays in the 1930s (on the man of letters, the "representative of the Bourgeois Age," and *Faust*) to the novel *Lotte in Weimar* (1939), concluding with the "Fantasy on Goethe" of the 1950s. Setting *Lotte in Weimar* aside, the most remarkable of these Goethean performances is the speech on the hundredth anniversary of the poet's death: "Goethe as Representative of the Bourgeois Age." For Mann, Goethe is "this great man in poet's form," the prophet of German culture and idealistic individualism, but above all "this miracle of personality," and Carlyle's "godlike man." As bourgeois Representative Man, Goethe himself speaks of a "free trade of conceptions and feelings," which Mann inter-prets as "a characteristic transference of liberal economic prin-ciples to the intellectual life."

Mann emphasizes that Goethe's serenity was an aesthetic achievement rather than a natural endowment. In the late "Fantasy on Goethe," Mann commends Goethe for his "splendid narcis-sism, a contentment with self far too serious and far too concerned to the very end with self-perfection, lightening, and distillation of personal endowment, for a petty-minded word like 'vanity' to be applicable." The charm of this characterization is that Mann describes himself as much as Goethe, both here and in the splendid essay of 1936 on "Freud and the Future":

> The *imitatio* Goethe, with its Werther and Wilhelm Meister stages, its old-age period of *Faust* and *Divan,* can still shape and mythically mould the life of an artist—rising out of his unconscious, yet playing over—as is the artist way—into a smiling, childlike, and profound awareness.

Mann's *imitatio* Goethe gives us Tonio Kröger as Werther, Hans Castorp as Wilhelm Meister, *Dr. Faustus* for *Faust,* and *Felix Krull* for the *Divan.* There are deliberate echoes in Mann's remarks of Goethe's "even perfect models have a disturbing effect in that they lead us to skip necessary stages in our *Bildung,* with the result, for the most part, that we are carried wide of the mark into limitless error." Mann quotes, in several places, Goethe's cruel and central question, phrased in his old age as, "Does a man live when others also live?" Implicit in the question are two superb Goethean aphorisms that between them form a dialectic of belated creation: "Only by making the riches of the others our own do we bring anything great into being," and "What can we in fact call our own except the energy, the force, the will!"

E. R. Curtius's Goethe is the perfecter and final representative of the literary culture that goes from Homer through Virgil to Dante and that achieved later sublimity in Shakespeare, Cervantes, Milton, and Racine. Only a writer with Goethe's daemonic force could have summed up so much without falling into the perfection of death. Our puzzle now is that Goethe, despite his vitality and wisdom, confronts us in his strongest lyric poetry with too undivided a consciousness for us to believe we can be found by that poetry, palpably as powerful as Wordsworth's, yet infinitely less moving. The *Trilogies der Leidenschaft,* or "Passion Trilogies," despite their extraordinary rhetorical intensity, are not poems of the center of our being like "Tintern Abbey" and the "Intimations" ode. The *Prelude* cannot be judged poetry of a higher order than *Faust,* yet it seems by far the more normative work. The great aesthetic puzzle of Goethe is not his lyric and narrative achievements, both of which are unquestionable, but *Faust,* the most grotesque and unassimilable of major Western poems in dramatic form.

ERICH HELLER cunningly writes, "What is Faust's sin? Restlessness of spirit. What is Faust's salvation? Restlessness of spirit." This is either a Goethean confusion or Goethe's personal version of the Gnostic idea of salvation through sin; it seems fair to call it a confusion. Heller sees it as more a kind of illicit ambiguity:

> What he could not write was the tragedy of the human *spirit*. It is here that the tragedy of Faust fails and becomes illegitimately ambiguous, because there is for Goethe in the last analysis no specifically *human* spirit. It is fundamentally at one with the spirit of nature.

Hermann Weigand, although he concedes that "Faust's salvation is a highly unorthodox affair," ascribes the heretical redemption to the hero's "ceaseless striving to expand his personality," which was certainly the quest of Goethe himself. But I am afraid that Heller is accurate and Faust has no personality or specifically human spirit, which is one of our difficulties with the poem. Nothing in Goethe is more Homeric (or more a grotesque parody of Homer) than the absence of any notion of a human spirit apart from the forces and drives of nature. Faust, like the Homeric heroes, is a battleground where contending forces collide. This is his largest difference from Hamlet, who is in the Biblical tradition of a *human* spirit. Faust could never say, with Hamlet, that in his heart there was a kind of fighting. Rather, his heart, his mind, and his perceptions are strictly divided from one another, and he is the more or less arbitrary site where they clash.

Goethe is, however, writing not Homeric epic but the German tragedy, though "tragedy" has a peculiar meaning in regard to *Faust*. Heller says that Faust's tragedy is that he is incapable of tragedy. Is Homer's Achilles a tragic hero? Bruno Snell, E. R. Dodds, and Hans Fraenkel show us that even Achilles, the best of the Achaeans, is essentially childlike, because there is no integration of his intellect, his emotions, and his sense impressions.

There is a positive Homeric quality in Goethe himself, but Faust seems Homeric only in being childlike. Oedipus and Hamlet become mature in their tragedies; Faust is a baby in comparison.

This is scarcely an aesthetic defect. It adds to the extraordinary strangeness that makes *Faust* the most grotesque masterpiece of Western poetry, the end of the Classical tradition in what could be called a vast, cosmological satyr-play. *Part One* is crazy enough, but *Part Two* makes Browning and Yeats seem tame and Joyce straightforward. It was fortunate for Goethe that Shakespeare was English, because the linguistic distance allowed him to absorb and imitate Shakespeare without crippling anxieties. *Faust* cannot be called truly Shakespearean, but it almost incessantly parodies Shakespeare.

Benjamin Bennett finds the poem's project to be no less than "the regeneration of language," which I might reduce to "an attempt to regenerate German as Shakespeare regenerated English." Bennett considers the weird nongenre of *Faust* an "antipoetic" that seeks to purge irony from poetic language and restore a kind of visionary pathos. With a grand (and deliberate) critical irrealism, Bennett proclaims that the size of *Faust* is "infinite in the sense of being as large as one pleases." Sometimes in reading *Faust* I wish that the poem and I could join in a strict diet, but the suggestiveness of Bennett's point abides.

The impossible critical question is: Can one define the aesthetic achievement—its range and its limitations—of Goethe's *Faust*? Bennett has perhaps foreclosed the question of range, but the matter of limitations cannot be evaded, particularly at a time and in a country where *Faust* seems to be an uncanny redundancy, a snowy white elephant of the central poetic tradition. As I have said, we read Wordsworth's *Prelude* or even Blake's epics more readily than we learn to read *Faust*. Are we baffled by the apparent serenity of Goethe's poetic personality and the squalid intensities of *Faust*? Or is it just that we cannot locate ourselves in relation to Goethe's world theater, so we wonder what is going on and ask why we should be involved at all?

To argue for the greatness of *Faust* on the basis of its lyrical variety and rhetorical power, or even its mythological inventiveness, no longer seems sufficient. We tend to prefer Goethe's *Roman*

Elegies, the *West-Östlicher Divan,* and sometimes even the *Venetian Epigrams,* to *Faust.* I have heard the very unkind remark that *Faust* is to Goethe what *Thus Spake Zarathustra* is to Nietzsche (and all Nietzscheans), a gorgeous disaster. It is true that a summary of *Faust* is about as inedible as a summary of *Zarathustra.* Reading *Faust* closely is quite another matter. It becomes a banquet of sense, though doubtless too replete with scarcely healthy viands. As a sexual nightmare or erotic fantasy, it has no rival, and one understands why the shocked Coleridge declined to translate the poem. It is certainly a work about what, if anything, will suffice, and Goethe finds myriad ways of showing us that sexuality by itself will not. Even more obsessively, *Faust* teaches us that, without an active sexuality, absolutely nothing will suffice.

Bennett very usefully reminds us that the peculiar art of *Faust* is that the poem systematically cancels out all of the perspectives from which we might wish to view it. You block out perspectivism only by deliberate ambiguity, of which Goethe seems to have invented some seventy-seven types. Nietzsche's Goethe incarnates Dionysus rather than Apollo, just as Freud's Goethe embodies Eros, not Thanatos. The only god or godling in *Faust* seems to me to be Goethe himself, for this extraordinary poet was neither Christian nor Epicurean, neither Platonist nor empiricist. Perhaps the Spirit of Nature rather than Mephistopheles speaks for Goethe, but we are bored or irritated now by Goethe's Spirits, so the persuasive figure in *Faust* has to be Mephistopheles, rightly hailed by Erich Heller as the legitimate precursor to Nietzsche's vision of the nihilistic void. Heller thinks that Nietzsche was a Faustian after all; but that is to evade Nietzsche's own ironies.

I do not know a more surprising poetry than the grotesque and sublimely absurd final utterances of the heroically ridiculous Mephistopheles as he fights a solitary rearguard action against the heavenly floods of floating roses and angelic buttocks that prevent his snatching away the soul that Faust has pledged to him. What are we to do with so astonishingly outrageous a scene? Directly Faust has cried out, "I now enjoy my highest moment," he sinks back and is gone, and what follows is both beyond and beneath literary criticism. Low farce that courts a dreadful bathos overwhelms us as Mephistopheles leads on his cowardly legions of fat devils with short, straight horns, and lean devils with long, curved horns, only to see them all run away when the delicious bevy of boy angels appears. Overcome by his exuberant lust for these charmers, Mephistopheles still battles gallantly, then hilariously compares himself to Job and ends up conceding defeat, winning our final rueful affection by his confession of all-too-human lust.

"Poor old devil," we think, yet "tough old devil" too, who accurately accuses himself. That is a crucial part of Goethe's perpetually surprising achievement: Faust doesn't have a human spirit or personality, but Mephistopheles delightfully does. When he wrote of Mephistopheles, Goethe was a true poet, and of the Devil's party while knowing it, because Goethe seems to have known everything.

ALTHOUGH FAUST is more an opera than a stage play, it still receives performances in Germany. I haven't seen one and would prefer not to, unless a gifted director brings to it all the resources of cinema. *Faust, Part Two* is already a nightmare of a movie, which one directs in one's head even as one struggles with the weirdness of the text. Curious as *Part One* most certainly is, it is *Part Two* that constitutes the most peculiar yet canonical work of Western literature.

Goethe started to compose what became *Faust* in 1772, when he was about twenty-three, and finished sixty years later, just before he died in 1832. A poetic drama composed during six decades is bound to be a monster, and Goethe labored at making *Part Two* as monstrous as possible. His critics have argued endlessly for the supposed "unity" of the play and tend to find *Part Two* at least implicit in *Part One*. Aside from a few mechanical links, all that the two *Fausts* possess in common are Faust himself and the comic Devil, Mephistopheles, who is not a very Satanic figure, whether we think of the Satan of popular tradition or the hero-villain of Milton's *Paradise Lost*. As Faust is without personality and Mephistopheles has no single personality, they provide little continuity to the two parts of the drama.

This scarcely matters, since the poet of *Part Two* was happy to be as enigmatic as possible. Acclaimed as a literary messiah almost from the start of his career, Goethe shrewdly evaded stultification by becoming an endless experimenter, and *Faust, Part Two* may well be more of an experiment than a poem. Editions of *Faust* frequently present an analytical table of dates of composition and verse forms that reminds me of the charts devoted to the Pentateuch in works of Biblical scholarship, except that Goethe himself is at once Yahwist, Elohist, Deuteronomist, Priestly Writer, and grand Redactor. Like the plays of Shakespeare, Dante's *Divine Comedy,* and Cervantes' *Don Quixote, Faust* is another secular scripture, a vast book of absolute ambition. Unlike Shakespeare and Cervantes—whose interests were not cosmological—but parodistically like Dante and Milton, Goethe aspires to a total vision. Being Goethe, that should be plural: visions. The mix of mythologies, histories, speculations, and earlier poets' imaginings in *Part Two* cannot even be termed "eclectic." Whatever it is, Goethe will use it, because everything can be folded into "fragments of a great confession," the literary works of Goethe, *Faust* in particular.

Shakespeare, whom Goethe genially (and realistically) set above himself, is not quite as dominant an influence upon *Part Two* as he is upon *Part One,* which doubtless helps to account for the flood of classical characters, stories, and forms that surges through *Part Two.* Goethe's opening to the ancients is in part a defensive movement against Shakespeare, though as an evasion of Shakespeare it does not succeed. How could it? The crucial Goethean pronouncement on Shakespeare is the 1815 essay, "Schäkespear und kein Ende!" translated by Randolph S. Bourne under the title "Shakespeare ad Infinitum." Despite his continued ambivalence about the greatest of writers, Goethe's aesthetic sensibility triumphed over his own vulnerability:

No one has shown perhaps better than he the connection between Necessity and Will in the individual character. The person, considered as a character, is under a certain necessity; he is constrained, appointed to a certain particular line of action; but as a human being he has a will, which is unconfined and universal in its demands. Thus arises an inner conflict, and Shakespeare is superior to all other writers in the significance with which he endows this. But now an outer conflict may arise, and the individual through it may become so aroused that an insufficient will is raised through circumstance to the level of irremissible necessity. These motives I have referred to earlier in the case of Hamlet.

Goethe's interpretation of Hamlet is set forth in *Wilhelm Meister's Apprenticeship* (1796), where Wilhelm gives us his famous but absurdly misdirected idealization of Shakespeare's most comprehensive character. Can we recognize Hamlet in his words?

A lovely, pure, noble, and most moral nature, without the strength of nerve which forms a hero, sinks beneath a burden which it cannot bear, and must not cast away. All duties are holy for him; the present is too hard. Impossibilities have been required of him; not in themselves impossibilities, but such for him. He winds, and turns, and torments himself; he advances and recoils; is ever put in mind, ever puts himself in mind; at last does all but lose his purpose from his thoughts; yet still without recovering his peace of mind.

One hardly knows what play Goethe/Wilhelm Meister was reading; certainly not Shakespeare's tragedy in which Hamlet casually slaughters Polonius, cheerfully sends Rosencrantz and Guildenstern to their deaths, and acts toward Ophelia with a brutality so obscene as to be beyond forgiveness. But then, nothing could be unkinder to Goethe's *Faust*—whether *Part One* or *Part Two*—than comparing the play to *Hamlet,* or indeed to any major Shakespearean tragedy. The Prince of Denmark is a dramatic character whose personality is universally compelling and uncannily capacious. Hamlet's is the only *authorial consciousness* among all fictive characters, by which I do not mean that Hamlet is Shakespeare's self-representation. Rather, Hamlet is a miracle of inwardness; Shakespeare found ways of suggesting a psychological richness that confounds us, until we begin to want to hear Hamlet speak on every matter in the cosmos that perplexes us. Long as the play is, the fascinated reader (rather than the playgoer) wants it longer; we wish every observation by Hamlet that we can hope to get.

By that impossible standard, Goethe's Faust, and even his Mephistopheles, scarcely seem characters at all. Goethe, wary of challenging Shakespeare, turned to the Baroque drama of Spain's Golden Age, to Calderón in particular, for a rival model. In Calderón's greater plays, as in *Faust,* the protagonists move and have their being somewhere in the indeterminate realm between character and idea; they are extended metaphors for a complex of thematic concerns. This works wonderfully for Calderón as for Lope de Vega, but Goethe wanted to have the opposition between personalities and thematic metaphors both ways and felt free to drop the mode of Calderón and reenter the Shakespearean cosmos almost at will.

A master of caprice, Goethe frequently gets away with it, but not always; and his cosmological drama suffers whenever Shakespeare is evoked. The reader experiences the oddity that the vast play, particularly its bizarre second part, truly is "saturated with life" as the old Gide said, except where its supposedly tragic hero is concerned. Mad mythologies and the endlessly plotting Mephistopheles swarm by us, always lively, but Faust himself can be passive, colorless, long-winded, or just plain asleep. The problem is not that there is too much of the multiselved Goethe in his Renaissance quester transmuted into a German, but that there is very little messiah in his principal figure. Goethe's exuberance is lavished upon the marvelous monsters of *Part Two,* but not upon poor Faust himself. It cannot be accidental, yet it remains an aesthetic misfortune. Goethe was evidently so stubbornly determined not to allow Faust to be mistaken for him that he forgot his greatest, preternatural strength, which was the incommensurate nature of his own personality. There is a similar problem with *Wilhelm Meister's Apprenticeship* (Carlyle's title for the best of Goethe's prose fictions), where I am fascinated by nearly every character except the wooden Wilhelm Meister himself.

Goethe so enchanted himself and everyone he ever encountered that no character he created could possibly live up to its creator. Shakespeare scarcely interested himself and was evidently quite colorless in comparison to Christopher Marlowe and Ben Jonson, or even to such lesser figures as George Chapman or John Marston. The puzzle and glory of Goethe's works, and of *Faust, Part Two* in particular, is the way in which the writing becomes so totally imbued with the seductive personality of the poet that it is the poet himself, and not his representations, that we most value. What happens in Byron happens on a grander scale in Goethe, as the canny author of *Faust* certainly understood.

Charismatics who become great writers are not numerous; Goethe is the major example in all of Western literature. What mattered most about him was his personality; he is to authors what Hamlet is to literary characters. His definitive biographer, Nicholas Boyle, begins the first volume of *Goethe: The Poet and the Age* (1991) with an indisputable assertion: "More must be known, or at any rate there must be more to know, about Goethe than about almost any other human being." Even Napoleon, Goethe's contemporary, cannot challenge that judgment, nor can Byron or Oscar Wilde or any other aesthetic luminary. About Shakespeare we know next to nothing that matters, and we learn to be skeptical about how much more there is to know, about the man as opposed to the plays. About Goethe, Boyle seems to know everything, and it all does seem to matter.

As both Nietzsche and Curtius observed in very different ways, Goethe is in himself an entire culture, the culture of literary humanism in the long tradition that goes from Dante to *Faust, Part Two,* the canonical achievement of Vico's Aristocratic Age. In the memory of Goethe, the classics of the Theological Age—Homer, the Athenian tragedies, the Bible—are crossed by Dante, Shakespeare, Calderón, and Milton, and what issues from this crossing is a culture that, in Goethe's era and nation, belonged to Goethe alone. Nor has the amalgam flourished in any great poet since. As he seems to have known, Goethe is an end and not a fresh beginning. Sages were to rise in his wake for nearly a century after his death, but he died with them, and he lives on today not in any poet who is with us but only in the dead and in scholars who feast on the dead.

The enigma of Goethe resides in the mystery of his personality, the aura of which survived the Democratic Age, only to fade away at last into our common Chaos. Thomas Mann is the final great writer to emerge from Goethe, and Mann is sadly dimmed now, even as his master Goethe has darkened, although not forever.

Humanistic irony is not a fashionable stance in the early 1990s and will hardly gain currency in what will be the apocalyptic forebodings of the later Nineties. Goethe, never a Christian, found himself acclaimed as a messiah while still in his youth and defended himself with formidable irony against his own deification. The only theist in *Faust, Part Two* is Mephistopheles; Faust himself prefigures Nietzsche by urging us to think of the earth rather than of a transcendental authority.

Shakespeare became a mortal god for Victor Hugo and many after him (myself included), and Goethe had the mixed satisfaction of achieving the status of a divine being among his own generation of German aesthetes. But the immense contrast between Shakespeare and Goethe remains what might be called the charisma of the word and of the writer. His contemporaries all but universally (the aphorist Lichtenberg is the only exception I can think of) found in Goethe a prodigy of nature and a luminosity that seemed to surpass mere nature. Goethe, however, declined to be a prophet, let alone a god, and liked to refer to himself as a *Weltmensch,* a child of this world. A total iconoclast, Goethe inherits everything that is wildest and most idiosyncratic in Western aesthetic culture, little as we seem to understand this fact today. His superb self-centeredness is the model for what Emerson was to convert into the American religion of self-reliance, and in some complex but very real sense the United States of our time is more Goethean (without knowing it) than modern Germany can be. At the center of Goethe's charismatic intensity of spirit is a restless self-regard, and *Faust* is a religious poem only insofar as it is the epic drama of the self that knows no limits.

THE RELIGION of the self has no more sublime monument than *Faust, Part Two. Part One* is a remarkable poem but only a shadowy foretaste of what comes rushing upon us in the second part. The figure of Faust goes back to the apparent origins of Christian heresy in the supposed first Gnostic, Simon Magus of Samaria, who when he went to Rome took on the name of Faustus, "the favored one." Earlier in his rather lurid career, Simon had discovered a prostitute in Tyre, Helen, whom he proclaimed the fallen Thought of God, in one of her previous incarnations Helen of Troy. This heretical scandal is the distant source of the Faust legend, which became attached to an actual Georg or Johann Faust, an early-sixteenth-century wandering confidence man and astrologer, who died about 1540.

The earliest Faust Chapbook (1587) contains the basic incidents exploited first by Christopher Marlowe in *Doctor Faustus* (1593) and then by Goethe, among many others. Both popular and poetic versions of the Faust story showed an early inclination to associate Faust with the libertine Don Juan. The two legends have clear affinities: both hero-villains quest for hidden knowledge, whether occult or sexual; both go from one erotic delusion to another; both evolve through desire and excess into damnation. Byron, as poet and as charismatic celebrity, brings both legends to culmination in himself, as Goethe shrewdly came to realize. The dying fall of the linked legends, Faust and Don Juan, is accomplished in *Faust, Part Two,* when Euphorion (Byron), the child of Faust and Helen, suffers the fate of Icarus.

Part One gives us a sadly inadequate Don Juan in its protagonist, whose wretched affair with the innocent Margaret leads directly to her earthly destruction and her rather unconvincing heavenly salvation. But Goethe was properly more concerned in giving us the most adequate of all possible Fausts, though the lyric success overwhelms the dramatic achievement in the Goethean Faust. We do not remember this greatest of all Fausts as the representation of a potential person, but as the history of a consciousness fundamentally detached from both action and passion, however much he aspires to them. Goethe's own mind was never-resting; his Faust's mind is merely perpetually restless. Goethe was clearly aware of the difference and cheerfully assumed the aesthetic risk involved. No one rereads *Faust*—either part—because she or he becomes engrossed with Faust, as most of us become obsessed with Hamlet. I reread *Faust* to see what Goethe can do with his somewhat un-Goethean protagonist. When I reread *Hamlet,* it is much more a question of what Hamlet can do with Hamlet.

It comes down to Erich Heller's point again: Goethe avoids tragedy while Shakespeare captures the genre forever or, as Heller grimly summed it up, "If it can be said that Goethe's limitations have their origin in the apparently limitless scope of his genius, then what is meant is his *genius,* not his talents; on the contrary, he always used his talents to defend himself against his genius."

I would modify that only by remarking that *Part One* is Goethe's defense against his own genius, but the much more powerful *Part Two* is Goethe's more interesting defense against the genius of others: the Greek tragedies, Homer, Dante, Calderón, Shakespeare, and Milton. *Part Two* no more confronts the reality of evil than *Part One* does, but the reader impatient for tragedy ceases to care, indeed cannot care, for a preternatural energy of response is demanded by the tidal waves of Goethean mythmaking that roll in upon us. Lyric does not translate, but monster films do, and *Faust, Part Two* is the grandest monster movie ever directed at us. The same endowment in me that sends me out to every fresh *Dracula* always returns me to *Part Two,* where Mephistopheles becomes the most imaginative of all vampires. Goethe, supposedly renouncing desire, nevertheless allows Mephistopheles to write most of *Part Two,* with superb poetic results.

Part One ends with a perfect cauldron of sin, error, and remorse, fit only for Faust to drown in; but the first scene of *Part Two* takes all that away. Goethe's most profound debt to Shakespeare was the pragmatic realization that apotheosis can be dramatically persuasive. The Hamlet of act 5 has transcended everything that he brought about in the first four acts, and from the second scene of *Part Two* onward, Faust is completely free of the Margaret tragedy. Hamlet may protest the intensity of his past love for the dead Ophelia, but we rightly do not believe him, and Faust does not even bother to protest nostalgia for his version of Ophelia. Goethe was evidently not addicted to remorse, particularly in erotic matters. A lost woman was an achieved poem, and Margaret was now *Part One,* even as Helen would be *Part Two.* I shudder to contemplate feminist readings of Goethe, or of Dante or Yeats, since more even than Milton these are the poets who idealized and therefore demonized women. When the Chorus Mysticus concludes *Part Two* by chanting, "Woman, eternally, / shows us the way," a woman now is likely to ask, "To what?"

Goethe was following Dante, but that could hardly be taken now for a defense. Whether the ostensible object was Margaret or Helen, Faust remained the subject and finally the true object of his own quest, since Goethe knowingly quested only for himself. Like Berowne in *Love's Labour's Lost,* Goethe sought in women's eyes the right Promethean fire, as a reflection of his own creative flame. Shakespeare is wildly and deliberately humorous on this subject, but Goethe is as narcissistic as Berowne. One sees why feminist criticism is best off with Shakespeare; his stance is for all sexes and for none. Goethe is so vulnerable to a feminist critique that the results could be of little interest, unless the critique were directed to the feminization of the grotesque in the monstrous mythology that is just ahead of us.

The only contemporary rival to Goethe as poetic mythmaker was William Blake, who had no public and whose engraved "brief epics" (a Miltonic notion) are still available to only a small, instructed, almost obsessive readership. Since I have read Blake's more esoteric poems from childhood on and published extensive commentaries on them while I was still young, it is natural for me to think of Blake in contrast as I read *Faust, Part Two.* Blake's mythopoeic creations are systematic and very much in the service of his apocalyptic argument with canonical tradition. Goethe's inventions are freestyle, profoundly playful, and work to subsume the tradition. I surprise myself by choosing *Faust, Part Two* over *The Four Zoas, Milton,* and *Jerusalem.*

The same judgment must be made when Shelley, Keats, and Byron are juxtaposed to *Part Two,* nor would Shelley and Byron have disputed the verdict if those admirers of Goethe had survived to read his greatest poem. Shelley's translation of parts of *Part One* is still the best in English, while the Byron-Goethe relationship is one of the crucial, only partly hidden centers of *Part Two.* The spirit of Byron appears as the Boy Charioteer and as the unfortunate Euphorion, child of the union between Faust and Helen. Even more weirdly, the Byronic, which for Goethe is the same as the daemonic, works its way into the figure of Homunculus, a much livelier being than either the Boy Charioteer or Euphorion. Goethe and Byron never met and had only a brief exchange of epistolary compliments before Byron went to his death in Greece, but it is not too much to say that Goethe developed a kind of infatuation for Byron, whom he weirdly ranked above Milton and just below Shakespeare. Goethe's somewhat imperfect English doubtless affected these judgments, which nevertheless were not uncommon throughout Europe in the Romantic period. Despite all of Goethe's classical yearnings, *Faust, Part Two* is the central work of European Romanticism, and Byronism inevitably had to play itself out in this German tragedy that is not a tragedy.

Shakespeare and Dante, Goethe, Cervantes, and Tolstoy destroy all genre distinctions by and in their work. Goethe takes the risk of explicitly mocking genre, rather in the mode of Hamlet's ironies. I cannot think of another work of *Faust*'s eminence that so aggressively refuses any clear perspective to its reader. Perhaps that is why Goethe appealed so immensely to the perspectivizing Nietzsche, but it makes any reader (myself included) very uneasy to confront a poem that does not allow itself, at any moment, to be taken either wholly seriously or altogether ironically. There is a certain lack of authorial good faith on Goethe's part, though from another perspective that lack is enormously (and deliberately) charming. *Finnegans Wake,* as great a literary white elephant as *Faust,* is a very humorous book, once you've learned to read it, but it abounds in Joycean good faith. Devote an inordinate part of your lifetime to *Finnegans Wake,* and it will reward your labors; that is its design. *Faust, Part Two* is a scandalous pleasure for the exuberant reader, but it is also a trap, a Mephistophelean abyss in which you will never touch bottom.

Joyce takes the *Wake* with heartfelt if amiable seriousness; its reader is to be neither mocked nor exploited. Goethe as ambitiously attempts world literature and a remaking of language, but somewhat at the reader's expense. Though a Viconian heroic bard of the Chaotic Age, Joyce is democratic in his literary elitism, as Blake was before him. Work through the set difficulties, and there will be fair pay. The knowingly last bard of the Aristocratic Age, Goethe is delightedly content to abandon us to ultimate contradiction and confusion. This hardly lessens the aesthetic splendor of *Part Two,* but it does leave us a touch exasperated, particularly at our present moment. Perhaps that only means that the time of Faustian man has finally passed in the age of feminism and allied ideologies. But it may also mean that Goethe reproves us for wanting from poems what they do not have to give. Still, the question abides: What, besides authorial flamboyance and endless exuberance of language, does *Part Two* possess? Are lyric magnificence and mythopoeic inventiveness enough to sustain so bizarre and baroque an extravaganza at twice the length of *Faust, Part One*? Are we truly deluded if we ask for more from much the strongest writer ever to compose in German?

There is an extraordinary audacity in Goethe's attempt to exalt desire and renunciation simultaneously in a single poetic drama, even if it is 12,111 lines long and was sixty years in the making. Although he became a national sage, Goethe was refreshingly devoid of both normative religion and middle-class morality, nor was he intimidated by societal considerations of good taste. Just about anything goes in *Faust,* particularly in the second part. Most educated readers have read some version of *Part One,* so I will comment upon it here only insofar as *Part Two* can be said to depend on it as foreground. As I have said before, the two parts are so different as actually to constitute two separate poems, but since Goethe thought otherwise, his authorial intentions must prevail.

A complete performance of *Faust,* both parts, would presumably take twenty-one or twenty-two hours, using an uncut *Hamlet* as a model and multiplying by about four. Of such a possibility, I would cry out with the Lorca who laments the death of the bullfighter, "I don't want to see it!" Goethe had the odd notion that Shakespeare did not write for the stage, and certainly the complete *Faust* is best performed in the afterlife (though it has been done in Germany). Emerging as he did from storm and stress, or the German version of the English Age of Sensibility, Goethe naturally associated an authentically sublime drama with the theater of mind, which is not at all to assert that *Faust* is a philosophical play. Rather, this dramatic poem obsessed with sexual desire has very little to do with a realistic representation of love in any social context, despite the eminent Georg Lukacs' Marxist attempt at analyzing the Faust-Margaret affair. As a giant fantasy, *Faust* inhabits the domain of Freud's drives, Eros and Thanatos, with Faust himself an uneasy Eros and Mephistopheles a Thanatos uneasily at ease.

Let us break into *Faust, Part One* on Walpurgis Night, sparing

ourselves the charmingly painful early stages of Faust's catastrophic seduction of poor Margaret. Goethe's Walpurgis Night,
as every reader rapidly recognizes, is not to be taken as an evil
orgy celebrating a witches' sabbath on the Brocken in the Harz
mountains. This is, after all, not exactly a Christian poem, and
Goethe's soul prefers the Brocken to a cathedral. So do we, when
we contrast Walpurgis Night to the scene just before it, when
Margaret (let us call her Gretchen, as Goethe now begins to do)
encounters her Evil Spirit in the cathedral and swoons at the
persecution inflicted on her by this highly Christian gaseous vapor,
which has nothing in common with the lively Mephistopheles. A
more crucial contrast is between Walpurgis Night and the earlier
scene, Forest and Cave, which interrupts Faust's courtship of
Gretchen.

Goethe shares with Walt Whitman (unlikely duo!) the oddity
that they are the only major poets before the twentieth century
to deal overtly with masturbation; Whitman celebrates it, and
Goethe is ironical. Mephistopheles comes upon Faust, in "Forest
and Cave," interrupting a solitary reverie in which Faust finds
bliss "ever nearer to the gods" and unfairly blames Mephistopheles
for the lust the scholar now feels for Gretchen. The devil's reply
is crushing (here and subsequently I quote from the translation of
Stuart Atkins, which seems to me much the most accurate English
version):

> *Superterrestrial delights—*
> *to lie on mountain tops in dew and darkness,*
> *embracing earth and sky ecstatically,*
> *to be puffed up so as though you were a god,*
> *to probe the earth with urgent intimations,*
> *to feel your heart at one with all six days creation,*
> *enjoying who knows what in your great arrogance*
> *and, now no more an earthbound mortal,*
> *blissfully merging with the All—*
> *and then to let your lofty intimations*
> *(he makes an expressive gesture)*
> *end in a way that I can't mention.*

Whether Faust has been prevented from losing himself in masturbation is not really open to doubt. Suggestions that intimate self-gratification are found elsewhere in *Part One* and throughout *Part Two*. Walpurgis Night—following this rejection of sublimation and the subsequent seduction of Margaret, followed by her Christian self-torment—comes upon us as an overwhelming relief. Faust himself experiences an exuberant sense of release as he goes off on a spring romp, an opening into realms of dreaming, erotic and liberating, mixing with naked young witches galore, including the splendid Lilith, Adam's first wife. The climax of the dance-orgy that follows is in the contradictory visions of Faust and Mephistopheles, who see the same figure, interpreted by the devil as Medusa and by Faust as his victimized Gretchen. The pathos of Gretchen's fate will center the remainder of *Faust, Part One,* all of which is contaminated by the witches' sabbath and its pragmatic exaltation of erotic appetite. Gretchen may be saved as far as heaven is concerned, but the reader runs away from the scene of her agony with Faust and Mephistopheles, all too glad to abandon Ophelia-like suffering for the visionary world of *Part Two.*

Because this book concerns itself with the canonical question, my interest in *Faust, Part Two* is limited here to precisely that: What makes so strange a poem permanent and universal? I have neither the space nor the specialized knowledge to offer a commentary upon the entire work. Faust's wager with Mephistopheles is a traditional crux for critics of both parts of the drama, but it seems a minor matter to me. His lack of personality makes me indifferent to whether he achieves a beautiful moment, and so begs it to tarry for a while. The theme of his endless striving also seems to me of little consequence, whether as stimulus to a devil's bargain or as supposed salvation from such a pact. The power of Goethe's work does not reside in these now-exhausted commonplaces, which would have long since sunk *Faust* if they mattered as much as they are said to do. The mythopoeic strength of *Part Two* is centered on very different inventions: Faust's descent to the Mothers and subsequent vision of Helen; the genesis and career of Homunculus; the classical Walpurgis Night; the idyll of Faust, Helen, and Euphorion; finally, the struggle for the dead Faust's soul and the rather equivocal depiction of heaven that concludes the poem. Out of these curious imaginings, Goethe shapes a composite myth that makes a difference to any reader willing and able to struggle with a poetry as difficult as it is rhapsodic.

Goethe's sublime bad taste returns with his memorable episode of the Mothers where the "key" given to Faustus by Mephistopheles is all too clearly phallic:

MEPHISTOPHELES. *Here, take this key!*
FAUST.   *That tiny thing!*
MEPHISTOPHELES. *Just grasp it, and remember what it's worth!*
FAUST. *It's a growing in my hand—it shines and flashes!*
MEPHISTOPHELES. *You're quick to see that it has special properties.*
    It has an instinct for the place one wants to be;
    Follow its lead down to the Mothers.

This descent evidently involves a quasi-incestuous, shadowy, multiple encounter with one's female forebears. When Mephistopheles tells Faust that he will be crowded by strange shapes below, the questing scholar is urged to "brandish your key and keep them at a distance!" Faust enthusiastically replies, "I hold it tight and feel new strength, new courage." The "great enterprise" of the mythic descent is palpably a masturbation, heroic in its prolongation and highly poetic in its result, the vision of Paris's initial rape of Helen. The jealous Faust, himself mad with desire for the classical enchantress, cries out that his hand still holds the key. He points the key at Paris until it touches that apparition, and he seizes Helen. There is an orgasmic explosion, Faust faints away, and the phantoms dissolve as vapors.

That concludes act 1; Benjamin Bennett demonstrates that the four remaining acts of *Part Two* all conclude with progressively subtler suggestions of masturbatory climaxes. At the end of act 2, Homunculus performs an Onanistic suicide at the feet of Galatea. Euphorion ends act 3 by throwing himself into the air with fierce erotic intensity, even as he declines female comfort. Goethe's satire of Christianity enters into the closures of acts 4 and 5 with clear hints that the context of masturbation is still relevant. In 4, a triumphant archbishop envisions a cathedral soaring upward from "the place that sin has so defiled," while the entire poem ends with a pseudo-Dantesque epiphany in which Gretchen becomes Beatrice and Faust takes on the role of Dante. Yet amid this outburst of proto-Catholic jubilation, Goethe remains quietly outrageous. The final scene is replete with "divine surges of rapture," as one Father is transpierced by arrows and another observes all-potent Love in the movement of a tree rising straight to the sky. In the midst of all this heavenly ecstasy, the "more Perfect Angels" rather nastily decline to bear, "even cremated," any impure remainders of earth, as if they insist upon the separation between spirit and body. Spiritual brooding throughout the poem, as Bennett reminds us, remains erotic but confines its eroticism to the sphere of self-excitation and self-gratification.

The descent to the Mothers, which would not be possible for the awed Faust without the phallic key, is in effect the invocation of the muses of mythology for *Part Two*. Mephistopheles won Faust away from self-gratification with the victimized Gretchen; it is a merely ironic advance and human defeat that Faust is returned to autoeroticism throughout *Part Two* by his projected union with an ectoplasmic Helen. The dilemma of perspectivism is again summed up for us by Goethe, and is never resolved in *Part Two*. Once again a witches' sabbath, this time classical rather than Germanic, gives us more exuberant images of Eros than do either solitary Romantic strivings or communal Christian promptings. Goethe adds the further irony that Mephistopheles, a Christian devil, is frequently uncomfortable when confronted by the realism of the classical Walpurgis Night. "Nakedness everywhere," he mutters at shameless Sphinxes, unembarrassed Griffins, and all sorts of creatures "offering us both rear and frontal views."

It is mildly hilarious when the devil wishes "in modern fashion" for a figleaf or two. Faust, longing for his classical Helen, feels more at home among the ancient monsters, while Homunculus is the most venturesome of the trio. This peculiar being, one of *Part Two*'s most glorious inventions, has been created by Wagner the alchemist, once Faust's faithful assistant. A charming little man, or miniature adult, compelled to live inside the glass phial where he was created, Homunculus in no way resembles Mephistopheles, whose presence in Wagner's laboratory contributed the infernal energy that transformed flame into more than human mind. Homunculus is neither sardonic nor nihilistic, nor is he a kind of tiny-scaled Faust, as some critics have suggested. Too amiable to be a Goethean satire, the Hermetic Homunculus surpasses us all in knowledge and understanding. A flame of consciousness not incarnated but manifested as mind, he seems to enjoy more of Goethe's affection than nearly anyone else in the poem. Endlessly humorous and entertaining, he has the tragic flaw of longing for love, which will bring about his desperate self-destruction when he encounters Galatea.

Homunculus, despite being confined to act 2, makes so strong an impression as a personality because the Faust of *Part Two* is unfortunately beyond personality, at least so far as Goethe is concerned. Faust in *Part One* was a poor-man's version of Hamlet, but he had strong emotions, idiosyncratic fierceness, and the ability to be very negative indeed. In *Part Two* he is tediously noble, abstracted, and incapable of elemental reactions of any kind. Goethe consciously idealized this later Faust into an allegory of the classical poetic temperament, so that even his passion for Helen becomes a version of Goethe's own passion for Greek poetry and sculpture. Inevitably, this rather cold heightening of Faust brings about a parallel change in Mephistopheles, who almost ceases to be the Devil, so hard is he compelled to work at being a kind of High Romantic Christian, vainly deprecating the splendor of the classical, or at least seeking somehow to reconcile Greece and Germany. Poor Mephisto! He becomes a reasoner and a comparer, even a historicist, rather than a schemer who seeks to return us to the negations of a Primal Abyss.

This must be why the very idea of flying Faust off to the classical Walpurgis Night emanates from Homunculus, not from the Devil. The little man makes clear that the expedition's purpose is therapy for Faust by bringing him nearer to Helen, while the personal motive is the drive that will culminate at the feet of Galatea. All of these details are incidental to Goethe's motive, which is to stage the great set-piece of his poetic career, the fifteen hundred lines of an ancient Greek witches' sabbath that never was, on land or sea, but is now because Goethe desires it to come into being.

If the essence of poetry is invention, as Dr. Johnson rightly maintained, then the classical Walpurgis Night shows us what poetry essentially is: a controlled wildness, a radical originality that subsumes previous strength, and, most of all, the creation of new myth. Goethe confirms his place in the literary canon by adding more strangeness to beauty (Pater's formula for the Romantic) than any Western poet has accomplished since. Goethe's sublime extends the grotesque further than I would have thought it could go. So peculiarly outrageous is this achievement that criticism has been unable to accommodate it, particularly German criticism, Goethe worship being so solemn a secular religion.

Goethe excludes nearly everything we might expect to find in normal classicism: the Olympian gods, the Homeric warriors, the heroic slayers of monsters. The Goethean gods themselves are monsters: the Phorkyads, formless lurkers in primeval Night. Metamorphic and fecund, they inspire an uneasiness in us that is crucial to Goethe's purpose here. Oddly enough, the only contemporary equivalent I can think of is the long nightmare that opens Norman Mailer's *Ancient Evenings,* where we are carried back to the world of the Egyptian *Book of the Dead.* Mailer is at his strongest in those grim pages and suggestively conveys the *otherness* of his ancient evenings. His lapses come later in his Egyptian novel, but death, like bumbuggery, never fails to activate Mailer's imagination.

Life in death is more Goethe's specialty, and his tour of the dark side cheerfully surpasses Mailer's. We start in Thessaly at Pharsalus, where Caesar defeated Pompey. The witch Erichto, a creation of the poet Lucan, is converted by Goethe from a corpse despoiler to a chronicler of vain battles. Rather than confront the odd trio of Homunculus, Faust, and Mephistopheles she runs off, leaving them free to explore the thousand campfires, around which are gathered primeval gods and monsters, resurrected for this one night of the year. Goethe manipulates so many classical models in his mythopoeic counterpoint that to select one as his guiding genius is bound to be deceptive, yet *The Frogs* of Aristophanes does seem the nearest precursor. Aristophanes was a cruel parodist, particularly of Euripides, but no parodist in literary history is as comprehensive as the Goethe of *Faust, Part Two.* The peculiar range of tonalities begins to be established when

Mephistopheles comes upon the Griffins, whom I would certainly not care to encounter. These unamiable beasts, whose job was treasureguarding, have the heads and wings of eagles and the body and paws of lions. Multicolored, sharp-eyed, fearfully quick, they are the ultimate watch animals, ferocious in temper. But in Goethe they are only rancid old misers, who, when greeted by Mephistopheles as "sage graybeards," reply like somewhat daffy dictionary editors, rolling their guttural r's:

> *Not graybeards! Griffins! —no one likes to hear*
> *himself called gray. The sound of words reflects*
> *the origins from which their sense derives:*
> *gray, grieving, grungy, gruesome, graves, and groaning,*
> *that have one etymology,*
> *all put us out of sorts.*

No reader is going to be terrified of an heraldic beast that utters a line like

> *Grau, grämlich, griesgram, greulich, Gräber, grimmig.*

As soon as Goethe's monsters have begun to speak, even their ill-temper is no more awesome than the verbal bad manners of the fantastics in *Through the Looking Glass.* The classical Walpurgis Night is childlike enough to convert every demonic being into another grotesque. So the sphinxes are not primarily granite eminences with girls' faces and lions' bodies but manifest themselves instead as talkative old storytellers, superstitious busybodies who still ask clever riddles. The fabled Sirens deceive no one and cannot sing very well, while the Lamiae, who ought to be crazed vampires, are merely tightly laced, overpainted provincial whores who still retain the capacity to turn into very unpleasant entities when embraced.

None of Goethe's monsters is reduced by him; their grotesquerie retains splendor and intensity, but we, after all, are there only as Faust, wholly obsessed with the absent Helen, or as the disembodied Mephistopheles, more rancid than anything he encounters. We see as Mephistopheles sees because only he, of the three, is in search of not fulfillment but just whatever sensation he can secure. He secures nothing, of course, and wanders off to get lost until he blunders on Homunculus, who takes him to hear a debate between the pre-Socratic philosophers Thales and Anaxagoras.

Thales, serene and apparently wise, argues for water as the first principle, while remaining blind to the catastrophes of Walpurgis Night. Anaxagoras, apostle of fire, is a revolutionary apocalyptic like Blake's Orc or the actual visionaries who helped bring on the French Revolution. Since Anaxagoras is left prostrate upon the ground, adoring Hecate while blaming himself for disasters, the palm is clearly awarded to the sweet-tempered if rather too Panglossian Thales.

By the time the classical Walpurgis Night has worked through many more complexities to its conclusion, our three aeronauts have met very diverse fates. Mephistopheles, the most ill-natured of German tourists, has had a terrible revel at the Greek witches' sabbath. Frustrated by each devious Lamia, the poor Devil stumbles on until he encounters the really hideous Pharkyads, three hags with but a single eye and a single tooth between them. They are so ghastly that Mephistopheles cannot bear to gaze upon them, until he realizes that they are his sisters, children of Night and Chaos as he himself is. Acknowledging them, he merges with one of the three, and it is in the formless form of a Greek goddess of the Abyss that he leaves Pharsalus, going off to Sparta to wait for the return of Helen.

Faust meanwhile has fallen in with Chiron the Centurion, a benign skeptic who seeks to cure him of his obsession with Helen by taking him to Manto, daughter of the archetypal physician Aesculapius. But she is an Orphic Romantic, not a rational reductionist, and, recognizing in Faust another Orpheus, she takes him, as she once took Orpheus, down to Persephone, this time to bring up Helen rather than Eurydice. With enormous cunning, Goethe decided not to write the scene between Faust and Persephone, and we are left to imagine it for ourselves.

Instead, Goethe invested his creative energies in the story of Homunculus, whose destiny does not allow him to survive the classical Walpurgis Night. Seeking to achieve a proper existence outside of his phial, the little fellow endures the debate of Thales and Anaxagoras but receives no useful advice from it. Instead, he goes off with the benign Thales to observe Goethe's most beautiful invention, a kind of baroque water-carnival, featuring Sirens (now somewhat redeemed), Nereids, and Tritons. We have left Pharsalus with its monsters and are in the moonlit world of Aegean Sea islets.

At Samothrace we are in the realm of the Cabiri, peculiar little gods: "constantly self-generating, / but can't discover who they are." Goethe does not make clear whether these ignorant dwarfs are only terra-cotta pots, exalted by ignorant scholars, or potent deities, capable of saving the shipwrecked. But whoever they are, the celebratory procession of sea beings courses on in their honor, and that aesthetic spectacle is what matters. Its glory is the oceanic grace, Galatea, drawn by dolphins from her home in Paphos, sacred to Aphrodite. At once the occasion of self-transcendence and self-destruction for Homunculus, Galatea is for Goethe a wholly positive figure.

More ambiguous is Proteus, master of deceptions and evasions, yet also a truthful foreteller with a total knowledge of time and its secrets. A mocker of all human aspirations, this old man of the sea is childlike and cheerful and, by one of the best of all Goethean ironies, at once the best and most dangerous philosopher of the art of advising Homunculus how to live, what to do. Plunge into the sea, is the advice of Proteus, in order to join in an endless metamorphosis, but not with the view of rising up to human status. The best of humans, Achilles and Hector, end by going down into Hades. Better to circulate as the sea circulates, to accept life without the individual death that afflicts the human.

Do we hear an aspect of the aged Goethe himself in Proteus, since the poet was a lifelong psychic shapeshifter? Or does Goethe invest himself in the next philosopher-prophet, Nereus, who preaches renunciation yet still employs the accents of Eros? When his daughters the Dorides, presided over by Galatea, urge him to grant immortality to the young sailors they have rescued and loved, he refuses, uttering what sounds distinctly like Goethe's own, lifelong erotic wisdom: "when affection's spell has ended, / tenderly put them back on land." Renunciation is extolled again when Nereus and Galatea, like Lear and Cordelia sharers in an overwhelming father-daughter love, exchange only a single glance and a shout of recognition and joy before the dolphins carry Galatea away for another year's absence.

This exaltation of renunciation, so crucial to the old Goethe, provides the equivocal background for the passion of Homunculus. Weary of his enclosed existence, the alchemical daemon decides he must choose between fire, his native element, and the otherness of water. Refused definitive guidance by Nereus, he rides out on Proteus to meet the procession of Galatea. Goethean irony pervades the masturbatory climax of the erotic quest, as Homunculus leaps up to expire at Galatea's feet: "now mounts high and strong, now burns sweet and long / though it were stirring with pulsations of love." Galatea is the object, but poor Homunculus is the only lover, until at last his vial shatters on her throne. The flame that is his life breaks into the waves, momentarily transfiguring them. The Sirens lead all the sea beings in a hymn of triumph, proclaiming that the victory belongs to Eros. Goethe doubtless agrees, but the classical Walpurgis Night closes with an act that goes well beyond renunciation. The occult representation of detached human intellect destroys mind as another tribute to Eros. Goethe's characteristic ambivalence refuses us any absolute perspective on this loss, and the remainder of *Faust, Part Two* will only reinforce the ambiguous stance of the old poet toward his own doctrine of renunciation.

I AM ABOUT to leap over three thousand lines, mostly magnificent, of *Part Two* in order to concentrate on Faust's death scene and the subsequent seriocomic struggle for his soul between Mephistopheles and the angels. The largest omission resulting from my clumsy but desperate leap is Goethe's extraordinary Helen fantasy, a marvelously outrageous transposition of Germany into Greece. With his customary audacity, Goethe parodies Homer and the Athenian tragedies in order to give us one of the most singular poems ever written: the resurrection of Helen of Troy, her union with Faust, the birth and death of their son Euphorion, and the return of Helen to the shades. Like the classical Walpurgis Night, and like the heavenly choruses at the close of *Part Two*, the Helen that Goethe gives us is a countercanonical poem, an unthinkable revision of Homer, Aeschylus, and Euripides, even as the classical Walpurgis Night turns the origins of Greek mythology inside out, and the final choruses parody Dante's *Paradiso* with a subtly savage gusto.

None of this was wholly new for Goethe; *Faust, Part One* is a continuous parody of Shakespeare, with touches of Calderón and Milton added on. I cannot think of any other poet who inherited as much of the Western Canon as Goethe did. From Homer through Byron, the entire procession is taken into *Faust,* emptied out, and then filled anew, but with the large difference that parody, however dignified, necessarily constitutes. I argue throughout this book that to become canonical, any new work must have the countercanonical built into it, but hardly in Goethe's extreme sense. Ibsen repeats something of Goethe's stance, and *Peer Gynt* parodies *Faust* even as it does Shakespeare. The other great writers of the Democratic Age—Whitman, Dickinson, and Tolstoy among them—do not attempt to gather the Western tradition together as Ibsen, however flintily, does. There are versions of Ibsen in our era of Chaos—Joyce looms largest among them—but the last traces of Goethe's piety regarding what is parodied do not abide in figures of comparable strength. Beckett's relation to Shakespeare is like Joyce's and somewhat like Ibsen's, but it is not at all Goethean. Curtius, in his *Essays on European Literature* (translated by Michael Koval, 1973), quotes from a letter that Goethe wrote in 1817: "We epigone poets must revere the legacy of our ancestors—Homer, Hesiod, *et al.*—as the authentic canonical books; we bow before these men whom the Holy Spirit has inspired and dare not ask, when or whither."

That is not the accent of Ibsen or of Joyce. Curtius, writing in 1949, was accurate: Goethe marked an end to one aspect of tradition. Perhaps my appropriation of Vico gets in the way here, but if "aristocratic" refers to an elitism of the spirit, to the sense of a gnosis, then Goethe is indeed the last great writer of the era that Dante inaugurated. To write a countercanonical epic or cosmological drama like *Faust, Part Two,* you need a more intimate relation to the Canon than anyone since Goethe has suffered (or enjoyed). That gives a particular poignance to the death of Faust, because more than the character Faust is dying.

How would Peer Gynt have died if Ibsen had been willing to abandon him to the Button-Molder? Can we imagine the death of Poldy Bloom? Faustian man dies a classical death, as we are about to see, because the continuity with tradition, however parodistic or ironic, remains unbroken. After Goethe, everything that can be broken has been. Emerson, Carlyle, Nietzsche all revered Goethe, and all realized that he had been very much an ending. Faust's death rehearses that ending. Freud, seeking an image for his therapy, came up with "Where it was, there I shall be." The ambition is Faust's final project, the reclamation of the shore, the making of a new Netherlands.

A Goethean ironist, despite his Goethean scientism, Freud knew what Faust is still learning at the end, which is the mentality of reversal: "Where I am, there it shall be." In the reversal, Mephistopheles and his thugs commit murder on Faust's ecological behalf, and Faust endures Oedipal blunders in remorse, even as he fights off Care. Casting out magic, resolving to stand up against magic, resolving to stand up against nature by himself, rejecting every possibility of transcendence, the dying Faust (though he does not know he is dying) begins to become Freudian man, embracing the reality principle. With that embrace comes the final idealistic illusion, to drain the last swamp, so that where it was, there Faust shall be.

Mephistopheles intervenes with his final insult: ghoulish Lemures replace the workmen, and the blind Faust, hearing the sound of their shovels, does not know they are at work digging his grave and not his final improvement of nature. Virgilian spirits of the night and the dead, the Lemures are mere skeletons, indeed mummies, and they pirate the gravedigger's song in *Hamlet* as he digs Ophelia's grave. To this ghoulish music, the sound of shovels, and Hamletian melancholy, Faust incongruously utters his final delusion: "I now enjoy my highest moment." With that, he falls backward into the arms of the Lemures, who lay him on the ground and inter him. By Faust's own language, his soul ought to be forfeit, his and God's wager lost.

What follows is dreadful and famous comedy, flavored by the aged Goethe's deliberately outrageous bad taste. As the wretchedly anxious Mephistopheles laments that agreements are worthless nowadays, he and his cowardly devils are pelted by a storm of angelic roses. Fighting on alone, abandoned by his lesser fiends, the unhappy devil loses self-control and is overcome by divinely induced lust for the buttocks of the boy angels. The soul of Faust is borne heavenward by these enticing youths, and Mephistopheles rightly laments the manner of his defrauding. This is all good, unclean fun, and perhaps Goethe should have ended it there. Instead, he loots and parodies Dante's *Paradiso*, presenting all readers since with an ultimate problem in perspectivizing. What are we to do with this apparently Catholic conclusion to an altogether non-Christian poetic drama? The Blessed Boys and various grades of Angels are one sort of entity, but how is the reader to react to the heavenly battery of Doctor Marianus and all the Penitent women who attended Jesus? Is Faust really going to take up residence in Dantesque heavens as the loving teacher of a bevy of Blessed Boys? Is Oscar Wilde somehow writing this conclusion in advance, or is all this Goethe's final blasphemy, his ultimate outrage to normative sensibilities?

If we read closely, we are not likely to judge Goethe's final vision as uncharacteristically Christian. Rather, it is Hermetic and personal, and heterodox to the highest degree; but so was Dante's vision until the Church yielded to its excellence and canonized it. Very slyly, Goethe emulates Dante and simultaneously outdoes him by enthroning more than one personal Beatrice in heaven. Even Doctor Marianus is not precisely orthodox: he salutes the Virgin as "one coequal of the gods; / Queen we have elected!" And poor Gretchen, who repented on earth and still repents in heaven, is accepted only by the Mater Gloriosa so that Faust may be instructed, when he follows his beloved to higher spheres.

But when did we hear Faust repent? True, Faust has died, but being a century old, it was certainly about time. Unrepentant, unforgiven, after a lifetime in league with the Devil, Faust rises to instant salvation, as befits a name meaning "the favored one." It is unjust, certainly not Catholic, and not Christian in any orthodox sense whatsoever. Goethe has brazenly subsumed Catholic mythology and Dantesque structures into his own mythopoeic system, as personal as Blake's but much more cheerfully courting, indeed inviting self-contradictions. If Faust is in the higher spheres, it is because the religion of esoteric Goetheism has reached out to redeem him. Christianity and Christ are only another strand in a mythopoeic counterpoint as *Faust, Part Two* achieves conclusion.

The last words, as shrewdly translated by Atkins, are pure Goethean erotic High Romanticism: "Woman, eternally, / Shows us the way." What way is that? Faust has not been shown the way by the Virgin, but by Margaret and by Helen. Goethe was shown the way by his grand sequence of Muses, immortalized in his lyric poetry. The Catholic colorings as *Part Two* closes are yet another instance of the countercanonical, no more, no less, in Goethe's lifelong triumph of language and of personality.

PART III

THE DEMOCRATIC AGE

10.

Canonical Memory in Early Wordsworth and Jane Austen's *Persuasion*

T HERE ARE musicologists who assert that the three great innovators in our musical history were Monteverdi, Bach, and Stravinsky, though the assertion is disputable. Western, canonical lyric poetry seems to me to have only two such figures: Petrarch, who invented Renaissance poetry, and Wordsworth, who can be said to have invented modern poetry, which has been a continuum for two full centuries now. To employ Vico's terms, since I have used them to organize this book, Petrarch created the lyric poetry of the Aristocratic Age, which culminated in Goethe. Wordsworth inaugurated the blessing/curse of poetry in the Democratic/Chaotic Eras, which is that poems are "about" nothing. Their subject is the subject herself or himself, whether manifested as a presence or as an absence.

Petrarch invented what John Freccero termed the poetry of idolatry; Wordsworth started anew on a tabula rasa of poetry, as William Hazlitt observed, and filled that blank slate with the self, or more precisely with the memory of the self. In the second

Theocratic Age, which I anxiously follow Vico in prophesying as imminent, I assume that poetry will cast aside aristocratic idolatry and democratic memory alike and return to a more restricted, devotional function, though I wonder if the object of devotion will always be called God. Wordsworth in any case is a beginning, though like all great writers he was haunted by heroic precursors, Milton and Shakespeare beyond all others.

Jane Austen may seem an odd choice to share a chapter with Wordsworth, yet she was his younger contemporary, born five years after him; and though he outlived her by a third of a century, all of his most vital poetry had been composed before she started to publish. Austen's literary cosmos centered upon her forerunners in the novel, Samuel Richardson and Henry Fielding, and upon Dr. Johnson. We have no evidence that she read Wordsworth, any more than we do that Emily Dickinson ever read Walt Whitman; but there are concerns that Austen's later novels, the posthumous *Persuasion* (1818) in particular, share with Wordsworth, so I have chosen to juxtapose the later Austen with the earlier Wordsworth, and with three poems in particular: "The Old Cumberland Beggar" (1797), *The Ruined Cottage* (1798), and "Michael" (1800).

Wordsworth wrote more influential and even more sublime poetry in his epic *Prelude,* and in the triad of great crisis-lyrics, the "Intimations of Immortality" Ode, "Tintern Abbey," and "Resolution and Independence." But there is a terrifying poignance in the three poems I have chosen that even Wordsworth does not match elsewhere, and as I go into old age, they move me more than virtually any other poems, by their exquisitely controlled pathos and their aesthetic dignity in representing individual human suffering. They have an aura that the early Wordsworth shares only with the later Tolstoy and with certain moments in Shakespeare, a universally common sorrow presented with stark simplicity and no taint of ideology of any kind. After the turn into the nineteenth century, Wordsworth became a more Miltonic poet, but in his late twenties he was very Shakespearean, rewriting *Othello* in *The Borderers* and capturing in beggars, peddlers, children, and mad people something of the Jobean quality of *King Lear.* Here is the extraordinary opening of "The Old Cumberland Beggar":

I saw an aged Beggar in my walk;
And he was seated, by the highway side,
On a low structure of rude masonry
Built at the foot of a huge hill, that they
Who lead their horses down the steep rough road
May thence remount at ease. The aged Man
Had placed his staff across the broad smooth stone
That overlays the pile; and, from a bag
All white with flour, the dole of village dames,
He drew his scraps and fragments, one by one;
And scanned them with a fixed and serious look
Of idle computation. In the sun,
Upon the second step of that small pile,
Surrounded by those wild unpeopled hills,
He sat, and ate his food in solitude:
And ever, scattered from his palsied hand,
That, still attempting to prevent the waste,
Was baffled still, the crumbs in little showers
Fell on the ground; and the small mountain birds,
Not venturing yet to peck their destined meal,
Approached within the length of half his staff.

I recall writing about this passage in a book published a third of a century ago (*The Visionary Company,* 1961), saying that the Old Cumberland Beggar differed from the other destitute solitaries in Wordsworth because he is not the agent of a revelation; he does not startle the poet into a privileged moment of vision. It now seems to me that I was too young to understand, though I was slightly older than Wordsworth was when he wrote the passage. The entire poem, nearly two hundred lines of it, is secular revelation, an uncovering of last things. If there can be the oxymoron of a revealed yet natural piety, it must be this: the aged beggar and the small mountain birds, the sun on the pile of masonry, the shower of crumbs falling from the shaking hand. This is an epiphany because it intimates to Wordsworth, and to us, a supreme value, the dignity of the human being at its most outrageously reductive, the immensely old beggar scarcely conscious of his condition. Against a refrain of "He travels on, a solitary

Man," the poem portrays the Beggar as so old and decrepit that "on the ground / His eyes are turned, and, as he moves along, / *They* move along the ground."

Here, and later, Wordsworth gives almost ecstatic emphasis to the Beggar's bodily decay and helplessness, in order to make yet stronger the poem's fierce argument for not confining the old man in a "HOUSE, misnamed of INDUSTRY," which is a protest prophetic of Dickens's attack against society for its poorhouses. The old man "creeps" from door to door and constitutes "a record which together binds / Past deeds and offices of charity, / Else unremembered." Wordsworth allows the perspective to remain our choice: do we see this as grotesque, or as one of the works of love, or as both? The poet's own perspective is difficult to share and impossible not to admire (with a certain shudder):

> *Then let him pass, a blessing on his head!*
> *And while in that vast solitude to which*
> *The tide of things has borne him, he appears*
> *To breathe and live but for himself alone,*
> *Unblamed, uninjured, let him bear about*
> *The good which the benignant law of Heaven*
> *Has hung around him: and, while life is his,*
> *Still let him prompt the unlettered villagers*
> *To tender offices and pensive thoughts.*
> *—Then let him pass, a blessing on his head!*
> *And, long as he can wander, let him breathe*
> *The freshness of the valleys; let his blood*
> *Struggle with frosty air and winter snows;*
> *And let the chartered wind that sweeps the heath*
> *Beat his grey locks against his withered face.*

This is acceptable, to most of us, only if the old man is now taken to be process as much as person. Wordsworth does not let up, exulting in the paradox that the old man must be open to nature, whether or not he himself apprehends it:

> *Let him be free of mountain solitudes;*
> *And have around him, whether heard or not,*

The pleasant melody of woodland birds.
Few are his pleasures: if his eyes have now
Been doomed so long to settle upon earth
That not without some effort they behold
The countenance of the horizontal sun,
Rising or setting, let the light at least
Find a free entrance to their languid orbs,
And let him, where and when he will, sit down
Beneath the trees, or on a grassy bank
Of highway side, and with the little birds
Share his chance-gathered meal; and, finally,
As in the eye of Nature he has lived,
So in the eye of Nature let him die!

This sublime and peculiar passage moves from "Let him be free" to "let him die," and pragmatically the freedom cannot be more than the freedom to suffer and to die out in the open. The shock of this conclusion is considerable, when we ponder it, until we allow the metaphor of "the eye of Nature" its full range and strength. It cannot be just the sun, nor can it be available only through the senses, for the old man is past hearing and sees only the ground beneath his feet. To exalt the old man's will seems fantastic, yet that is exactly what Wordsworth is doing, even though the exercise of the will is reduced to where and when the Beggar rests and eats. But this is highly deliberate in the early Wordsworth: human dignity is indestructible, the will endures, the eye of Nature is on you from life to death. In no danger of sentimentality, the poem courts the possibility of brutality in its quest for a natural piety that stands at the border of the preternatural. Wordsworth's originality can hardly be overestimated here; the *otherness* of the poet's mind is the largest figure that the poem makes, and it is the otherness that I have carried in my head these past thirty-three years whenever my memory drifts back to "The Old Cumberland Beggar." Robert Frost and Wallace Stevens, in their spookier poems of old age, like Frost's "An Old Man's Winter Night" and Stevens's "Long and Sluggish Lines," recapture

something of Wordsworth's otherness, but not its full reverberations.

MOST READERS who know *The Ruined Cottage,* Wordsworth's
tale of Margaret, have read it in its final, revised form as book 1 of
The Excursion (1815), a frigid long poem except for poor Margaret. Wordsworth worked on *The Ruined Cottage* from 1797; the
best version is clearly the one known to scholars as Manuscript
"D" (1798), now easily available in both the Oxford and Norton
anthologies of English literature, and the text I will use here. The
poem's greatest admirer remains its first, Samuel Taylor Coleridge,
who wanted to separate it from *The Excursion* and return it to an
independent existence as one of the most beautiful poems in the
language. *The Ruined Cottage,* two hundred years later, remains a
poem of superlative beauty and almost unbearable poignance.
There is a current fashion in Anglo-American criticism of the
materialist and New Historicist varieties—odd mixtures of Marx
and Foucault—to condemn Wordsworth for not having remained
political enough, once he had given up his early support for the
French Revolution. By 1797 Wordsworth had surmounted a long
political and psychic crisis, and his poems ceased to urge political
solutions for social distress. "The Old Cumberland Beggar," *The
Ruined Cottage,* "Michael," and Wordsworth's other poems that
depict the sufferings of the English lower classes are masterpieces
of compassion and profound feeling, and only shallow ideologues
could reject them on political grounds. Our new breed of academic
moralists should reflect upon the reception of Wordsworth's
poems by Shelley, politically the Leon Trotsky of his day, or by
radicals like Hazlitt and Keats. What Shelley, Hazlitt, and Keats
marvelously realized was that Wordsworth had a miraculous genius for teaching one how to feel sympathy for those in all manner
of distress. If our academic commissars knew how to read, Wordsworth might humanize them, which is the great program of his
poems like *The Ruined Cottage.*
    The tale of Margaret is told to Wordsworth by an old wandering
peddler, the poet's friend, at the site of a ruined cottage, "four
naked walls / That stared upon each other," with "a plot / Of

garden ground now wild." Once the home of Margaret, her husband Robert, and their two young children, it has become a desolation. The Wanderer (as he comes to be called in *The Excursion*,
so I will use it here) finds in the ruined scene a very personal
sorrow, for he and Margaret had loved each other like a father
and daughter. Stopping to drink at what had been Margaret's
spring, the Wanderer confronts loss directly:

> *When I stopped to drink*
> *A spider's web hung to the water's edge,*
> *And on the wet and slimy footstone lay*
> *The useless fragment of a wooden bowl.*
> *It moved my very heart.*

Strong yet stoical in its grief, this yields to an eloquent outburst
of paternal mourning, Biblical in its dignity and intensity, as suits
the Wanderer, a patriarchal figure. (The aura of "patriarchal" in
our universities is now so negative that I hasten to explain that I
use the word in the context of what Jewish tradition called "the
virtues of the fathers," and of Abraham and Jacob in particular.)
What we hear is at once lament for and celebration of Margaret:

> *The day has been*
> *When I could never pass this road but she*
> *Who lived within these walls, when I appeared,*
> *A daughter's welcome gave me, and I loved her*
> *As my own child. Oh Sir, the good die first,*
> *And they whose hearts are dry as summer dust*
> *Burn to the socket. Many a passenger*
> *Has blessed poor Margaret for her gentle looks*
> *When she upheld the cool refreshment drawn*
> *From that forsaken spring, and no one came*
> *But he was welcome, no one went away*
> *But that it seemed she loved him. She is dead,*
> *The worm is on her cheek, and this poor hut,*
> *Stripped of its outward garb of household flowers,*
> *Of rose and sweetbriar, offers to the wind*
> *A cold bare wall whose earthy top is tricked*

With weeds and the rank spear grass. She is dead,
And nettles rot and adders sun themselves
Where we have sate together while she nursed
Her infant at her breast. The unshod colt,
The wandring heifer and the Potter's ass,
Find shelter now within the chimney wall
Where I have seen her evening hearthstone blaze
And through the window spread upon the road
Its cheerful light. You will forgive me, sir,
But often on this cottage do I muse
As on a picture, till my wiser mind
Sinks, yielding to the foolishness of grief.

Few passages in Wordsworth, plangent and searching as he often is, reverberate as austerely as

Oh Sir, the good die first,
And they whose hearts are dry as summer dust
Burn to the socket.

These lines burned into Shelley's memory and became the epigraph to his long poem, *Alastor,* where they are implicitly turned against Wordsworth, who was Shelley's poetic father. In *The Ruined Cottage* they serve as epitaph for Margaret, who dies early of her goodness, of the power of her hope, which is the best part of her, and which is nurtured by her memory of goodness, of her life with her husband and children before disaster came.

Failed harvests, a war economy, destitution, despair drive Margaret's husband away, and her perpetual will to hope for his return becomes the destructive passion that destroys her and her household. I cannot find, anywhere else in Western literature, anything like Wordsworth's understanding that the apocalyptic power of hope, drawing its strength from benign memory, becomes more dangerous than despair could be. Perhaps Lear dies blasted by the mad hope that Cordelia lives, rather than by realistic despair that she is dead; but Shakespeare seems content to leave the matter equivocal. Poor Malvolio in *Twelfth Night,* victimized by cruel practical jokers, is reduced to crude farce by the strength of his absurd erotic and social hopes. These are imperfect analogues to Wordsworth's enterprise in *The Ruined Cottage* and elsewhere. Wordsworth made his particular myth of memory canonical by his frightening insight into the dangers of a hope that could destroy nature in us. Her hope is larger than Margaret, and larger than most of us.

You could argue that Margaret's hope is a secularization of Protestant hope, which was a function of the Protestant will. That will turned upon the individual soul's self-esteem and on the allied right of private judgment in spiritual realms, including the assertion of the inner light, by which each man and woman read and interpreted the Bible for himself or herself. In high literature, I doubt that secularization has ever taken place. Calling a work of sufficient literary power either religious or secular is a political decision, not an aesthetic one. Margaret is tragic because she is destroyed by what is best in her: hope, memory, faith, love. The Protestant temper in her, like the exercise of the Protestant will in Jane Austen's heroines, can be called either religious or secular, but the calling will describe you rather than *The Ruined Cottage* or *Persuasion*. What matters about Margaret is akin to the reason why we are so moved by Wordsworth's stance vis-à-vis the Old Cumberland Beggar, or by the majestic, covenantal suffering of the old shepherd in "Michael," the poem named for him.

In his Shakespearean play, *The Borderers* (1795–96), a mixed success at best, Wordsworth rather strangely gives the drama's Iago figure, Oswald, some extraordinary lines that form the credo of all of Wordsworth's own early poetry. Speaking to the hero, his Othello-like dupe, Oswald transcends the situation, the play, and his own vision in a Jacobean outburst that Shakespeare would have been glad to appropriate:

> *Action is transitory—a step, a blow,*
> *The motion of a muscle—this way or that—*
> *'Tis done, and in the after-vacancy*
> *We wonder at ourselves like men betrayed:*
> *Suffering is permanent, obscure and dark,*
> *And shares the nature of infinity.*

Shakespeare might have found the lines more appropriate for Macbeth than for Iago, but the implicit nihilism suits both hero-villains, and Edmund as well. Wordsworth would have rejected my association of these lines with his depictions of suffering innocence, yet the poetic power of his earlier work has little to do with consolation or concern for the meaningfulness of sorrow. *The Ruined Cottage* is harrowing because it eschews comfort, as here at the climax of Margaret's story:

> *Meanwhile her poor hut*
> *Sunk to decay; for he was gone, whose hand*
> *At the first nippings of October frost*
> *Closed up each chink, and with fresh bands of straw*
> *Chequered the green-grown thatch. And so she lived*
> *Through the long winter, reckless and alone,*
> *Till this reft house, by frost, and thaw, and rain,*
> *Was sapped; and when she slept, the nightly damps*
> *Did chill her breast, and in the stormy day*
> *Her tattered clothes were ruffled by the wind*
> *Even at the side of her own fire. Yet still*
> *She loved this wretched spot, nor would for worlds*
> *Have parted hence; and still that length of road,*
> *And this rude bench, one torturing hope endeared,*
> *Fast rooted at her heart. And here, my friend,*
> *In sickness she remained; and here she died,*
> *Last human tenant of these ruined walls.*

Like the Old Cumberland Beggar, Margaret dies open to the eye of Nature, with the harsh wind free to come in upon her. The poem's greatness gathers itself together in Wordsworth's strong reaction to the Wanderer's tale of Margaret:

> *The old Man ceased: he saw that I was moved.*
> *From that low bench rising instinctively,*
> *I turned aside in weakness, nor had power*
> *To thank him for the tale which he had told.*
> *I stood, and leaning o'er the garden gate*
> *Reviewed that Woman's sufferings; and it seemed*

> *To comfort me while with a brother's love*
> *I blessed her in the impotence of grief.*

This is not a Biblical blessing, since that carried the promise of more life, of ongoing generations, and it would be difficult to say what kind of a blessing "the impotence of grief" can bestow. Wordsworth is so original a poet that he risks the oxymoron of an impotent blessing, knowing that it seems a contradiction. *The Borderers* is Shakespearean, even as *The Prelude* is Miltonic, but there are no poems before Wordsworth as strange and naked as "The Old Cumberland Beggar" and *The Ruined Cottage*. Destruction by hope is the pervasive Wordsworthian anxiety, and we still hesitate when we have to interpret so antithetical a ruin.

Wordsworth invented modern or democratic poetry as surely as Petrarch inaugurated Renaissance poetry. There are always shadows, even on the strongest and most original poets; Petrarch was haunted by Dante, even as Wordsworth, in his major phase, could never evade Milton. Here Vico's prophecy is again illuminating; the Theocratic Age exalts the gods, the Aristocratic Age celebrates heroes, the Democratic Age mourns and values human beings. There was for Vico no Chaotic Age, only a Chaos during which the recourse to a Theocratic Age would commence. In my own view, our century has enshrined chaos in our long postponement (may it last!) of a new Theocratic Era. After gods, heroes, humans, there remain only cyborgs, and I gaze in rapt alarm at muscular Terminators crowding out the human. *The Ruined Cottage* is a very dark poem in itself, but here in the 1990s it seems a blessed consolation, a human cry against chaos and any recourse to Theocratic rigidities.

What could Wordsworth have been trying to do for himself, as a poet, by writing *The Ruined Cottage*? I modify the question from Kenneth Burke, who taught us to ask always: What was the writer trying to do for herself or himself, as a person, by writing this poem, play, or story? As a poet, Wordsworth sought to create the taste by which he could be appreciated, for no central writer—not even Dante—was so determined to universalize his own highly individual temperament. Wordsworth's spirit was open to both human and natural otherness, as perhaps no other poet's was, before or since. Hazlitt caught this truth perfectly in an 1828 comparison of Wordsworth and Byron, four years after Byron's death and many years into Wordsworth's dreadful poetic dotage (which went on drearily from 1807 to 1850, the longest dying of a major poetic genius in history). After asking a shrewdly wicked question about the late Lord Byron ("With his pride of ancestry, had he no curiosity to explore the heraldry of intellect?"), Hazlitt contrasts Wordsworth and Byron, who never ceased to prefer Pope to Wordsworth: "The author of the *Lyrical Ballads* describes the lichen on the rocks, the withered fern, with some peculiar feeling that he has about them: the author of *Childe Harold* describes the stately cypress, or the fallen column, with the feeling that every schoolboy has about them."

At the origins of "The Old Cumberland Beggar" and *The Ruined Cottage* are some very peculiar feelings, difficult to translate into normative terms. It is Wordsworth's uniqueness that he made of these curious feelings a universally available poetry in a mode analogous to what the later Tolstoy desired. The rightness of allowing an immensely old beggar to die as he has lived, in the eye of Nature; the terrible pathos of Margaret, a peasant woman wholly humane and lovable, who is destroyed by her powers of memory and hope; these are matters available to every human consciousness in every age, regardless of gender, race, social class, ideology. To condemn Wordsworth for not writing verse of political and social protest, or for having forsaken the revolution, is to cross the final divide between academic arrogance and moral smugness. Beyond that divide, we need a new Dickens to depict hypocrisy, and a new Nietzsche to chronicle the man or woman of *ressentiment*, whose "soul *squints*."

"MICHAEL" (1800) is Wordsworth's great pastoral and the archetype of the best and most characteristic poems that we associate with Robert Frost. The poet of "The Death of the Hired Man" has his own power of representing a primordial human pathos, but not on the Wordsworthian scale, which challenges even the Yahwist's ability to touch the limits of art. Wordsworth's Michael, at eighty years of age still a Biblical patriarch of force and vigor, is a shepherd who has "learned the meaning of all winds, / Of blasts of every tone." Storms send him up to the mountains to rescue his flocks, and his solitude memorably exalts him: "he had been alone / Amid the heart of many thousand mists, / That came to him, and left him, on the heights."

His only child, the son of his old age, Luke, bred as a shepherd, is the center of his father's existence. Financial need compels him to send the boy away for a time, to earn his living with a kinsman in the city. To tell the poem's plot like this is to invite the satire of my favorite cinematic work, W. C. Fields's demonic *Fatal Glass of Beer,* in which Fields's son, the dreadful Chester, goes to the big town and is seduced by college boys into drinking the fatal glass of beer. Immediately intoxicated, Chester breaks the tambourine of a Salvation Army girl, herself a reformed high-kicker from a chorus line. Much affronted, she has recourse to experience and stuns Chester with a single high-kick. Inexorably the incident leads Chester to a life of crime and to eventual extinction at the hands of Paw and Maw Snavely, or W. C. Fields and spouse. Luke is not far from Chester, but the sublime Michael, before Luke's departure, requests that the boy place a single stone to start a new sheepfold, to be completed by his father in the boy's absence, as a covenant between them. After the boy has fallen from virtue and fled to a remote country, we are left, most memorably, with a vision of grief and yet of chiding strength.

> *There is a comfort in the strength of love;*
> *'Twill make a thing endurable, which else*
> *Would overset the brain, or break the heart:*
> *I have conversed with more than one who well*
> *Remember the old Man, and what he was*
> *Years after he had heard this heavy news.*
> *His bodily frame had been from youth to age*
> *Of an unusual strength. Among the rocks*
> *He went, and still looked up to sun and cloud,*
> *And listened to the wind; and, as before,*
> *Performed all kinds of labour for his sheep,*
> *And for the land, his small inheritance.*
> *And to that hollow dell from time to time*

Did he repair, to build the Fold of which
His flock had need. 'Tis not forgotten yet
The pity which was then in every heart
For the old Man—and 'tis believed by all
That many and many a day he thither went,
And never lifted up a single stone.

The final line of that passage has been admired from Matthew Arnold on to the Wordsworthians who survive the present fall of the academies; but while it is a remarkable line, I prefer the poem's final verse paragraph, which challenges our memory with a single oak:

There, by the Sheep-fold, sometimes was he seen
Sitting alone, or with his faithful Dog,
Then old, beside him, lying at his feet.
The length of full seven years, from time to time,
He at the building of his Sheep-fold wrought,
And left the work unfinished when he died.
Three years, or little more, did Isabel
Survive her husband: at her death the estate
Was sold, and went into a stranger's hand.
The Cottage which was named THE EVENING STAR
Is gone—the ploughshare has been through the ground
On which it stood; great changes have been wrought
In all the neighbourhood:—yet the oak is left
That grew beside their door; and the remains
Of the unfinished Sheep-fold may be seen
Beside the boisterous brook of Green-head Ghyll.

When I was younger, I believed that memory was divided equally between pleasure and pain, and I thought that I remembered verbatim the poems that were most inevitable in their phrasings and most pleasurable in their incantatory qualities. In early old age, I find myself agreeing with Nietzsche, who tended to equate the memorable with the painful. A more difficult pleasure can be painful, as I now think Wordsworth explicitly understood. There is a way that leads from the Protestant will to Wordsworth's sympathetic imagination and that accounts for some of the curious affinities with Wordsworth that this chapter explores in Austen's *Persuasion*. Michael's covenant, unbroken with nature but broken by Luke, is an exercise of the Protestant will, seeking to impress itself upon memory. Its emblems at the end of "Michael" are the solitary oak and the unhewn stones of the unfinished sheepfold.

Wordsworth, unlike Austen (who was a throwback), did not favor happy endings, for in him the metaphor for marriage has more to do with the rapport between what he calls "nature" and his own "adverting mind" than with the union of man and woman. Nature, in Wordsworth, is the great persuader, and the persuasion is one in which experiential loss is bartered for imaginative gain. The gain in "The Old Cumberland Beggar" is an exultation not easy to accommodate, but also not easy to forget. *The Ruined Cottage* concludes with a blessing that is all loss but fearfully memorable, while "Michael" also concludes with a vision of utter loss.

All that Wordsworth's grim but sublime pastorals give us is canonical memory, "canonical" because Wordsworth has practiced the selection for us. He offers himself to us as a Hermes who will tell us what and how to remember, not so that we will be saved or become prudentially wiser, but because only the myth of memory can redress our experiential losses. His lesson, once learned, was canonical: it survived in George Eliot, in Proust (through the mediating figure of Ruskin) and in Beckett, whose *Krapp's Last Tape* may be regarded as Wordsworth's last stand. And it survives still, even in this bad time when canonical memory is threatened by aggressive moralizations and by learned ignorance.

"PERSUASION" is a word derived from the Latin for "advising" or "urging," for recommending that it is good to perform or not perform a particular action. The word goes back to a root meaning "sweet" or "pleasant," so that the good of performance or non-performance has a tang of taste rather than of moral judgment about it. Jane Austen chose it as the title for her last completed novel. As a title, it recalls *Sense and Sensibility* or *Pride and*

Prejudice rather than *Emma* or *Mansfield Park*. We are given not the name of a person or house and estate, but of an abstraction, a single one in this case. The title's primary reference is to the persuasion of its heroine, Anne Elliot, at the age of nineteen, by her godmother, Lady Russell, not to marry Captain Frederick Wentworth, a young naval officer. This was, as it turns out, very bad advice, and, after eight years, it is mended by Anne and Captain Wentworth. As with all of Austen's ironic comedies, matters end happily for the heroine. And yet each time I finish a rereading of this perfect novel, I feel very sad.

This does not appear to be my personal vagary; when I ask my friends and students about their experience of the book, they frequently mention a sadness which they also associate with *Persuasion,* more even than with *Mansfield Park*. Anne Elliot, a quietly eloquent being, is a self-reliant character, in no way forlorn, and her sense of self never falters. It is not *her* sadness we feel as we conclude the book: it is the novel's somberness that impresses us. The sadness enriches what I would call the novel's canonical persuasiveness, its way of showing us its extraordinary aesthetic distinction.

Persuasion is among novels what Anne Elliot is among novelistic characters—a strong but subdued outrider. The book and the character are not colorful or vivacious; Elizabeth Bennett of *Pride and Prejudice* and Emma Woodhouse of *Emma* have a verve to them that initially seems lacking in Anne Elliot, which may be what Austen meant when she said that Anne was "almost too good for me." Anne is really almost too subtle for us, though not for Wentworth, who has something of an occult wavelength to her. Juliet McMaster notes "the kind of oblique communication that constantly goes on between Anne Elliot and Captain Wentworth, where, though they seldom speak to each other, each constantly understands the full import of the other's speech better than their interlocutors do."

That kind of communication in *Persuasion* depends upon deep "affection," a word that Austen values over "love." "Affection" between woman and man, in Austen, is the more profound and lasting emotion. I think it is not too much to say that Anne Elliot, though subdued, is the creation for whom Austen herself must have felt the most affection, because she lavished her own gifts upon Anne. Henry James insisted that the novelist must be a sensibility upon which absolutely nothing is lost; by that test (clearly a limited one) only Austen, George Eliot, and James himself, among all those writing in English, would join Stendhal, Flaubert, and Tolstoy in a rather restricted pantheon. Anne Elliot may well be the one character in all of prose fiction upon whom nothing is lost, though she is in no danger of turning into a novelist. The most accurate estimate of Anne Elliot that I have seen is by Stuart Tave:

> Nobody hears Anne, nobody sees her, but it is she who is ever at the center. It is through her ears, eyes, and mind that we are made to care for what is happening. If nobody is much aware of her, she is very much aware of everyone else and she perceives what is happening to them when they are ignorant of themselves . . . she reads Wentworth's mind, with the coming troubles he is causing for others and himself, before those consequences bring the information to him.

The aesthetic dangers attendant upon such a paragon are palpable: how does a novelist make such a character persuasive? Poldy, in Joyce's *Ulysses,* is overwhelmingly persuasive because he is so complete a person, which was the largest of Joyce's intentions. Austen's ironic mode does not sanction the representation of completeness: we do not accompany her characters to the bedroom, the kitchen, the privy. What Austen parodies in *Sense and Sensibility* she raises to an apotheosis in *Persuasion:* the sublimity of a particular, inwardly isolated sensibility. Anne Elliot is hardly the only figure in Austen who has an understanding heart. Her difference is in her almost preternatural acuteness of perception of others and of the self, which are surely the qualities that most distinguish Austen as a novelist. Anne Elliot is to Austen's work what Rosalind of *As You Like It* is to Shakespeare's: the character who almost reaches the mastery of perspective that can be available only to the novelist or playwright, lest all dramatic quality be lost from the novel or play. C. L. Barber memorably emphasized this limitation:

The dramatist tends to show us one thing at a time, and to realize that one thing, in its moment, to the full; his characters go to extremes, comical as well as serious; and no character, not even a Rosalind, is in a position to see all around the play and so be completely poised, for if this were so the play would cease to be dramatic.

I like to turn Barber's point in the other direction: more even than Hamlet or Falstaff, or than Elizabeth Bennet, or than Fanny Price in *Mansfield Park,* Rosalind and Anne Elliot are almost completely poised, nearly able to see all around the play and the novel. Their poise cannot transcend perspectivizing completely, but Rosalind's wit and Anne's sensibility, both balanced and free of either excessive aggressivity or defensiveness, enable them to share more of their creators' poise than we ever come to do.

Austen never loses dramatic intensity; we share Anne's anxiety concerning Wentworth's renewed intentions until the novel's conclusion. But we rely upon Anne as we should rely upon Rosalind; critics would see the rancidity of Touchstone as clearly as they see the vanity of Jacques if they placed more confidence in Rosalind's reactions to everyone else in the play, as well as to herself. Anne Elliot's reactions have the same winning authority; we must try to give the weight to her words that is not extended by the other persons in the novel, except for Wentworth.

Stuart Tave's point, like Barber's, is accurate even when turned in the other direction; Austen's irony is very Shakespearean. Even the reader must fall into the initial error of undervaluing Anne Elliot. The wit of Elizabeth Bennet or of Rosalind is easier to appreciate than Anne Elliot's accurate sensibility. The secret of her character combines Austenian irony with a Wordsworthian sense of deferred hope. Austen has a good measure of Shakespeare's unmatched ability to give us persons, both major and minor, who are each utterly consistent in her or his separate mode of speech, and yet completely different from one another. Anne Elliot is the last of Austen's heroines of what I think we must call the Protestant will, but in her the will is modified, perhaps perfected, by its descendant, the Romantic sympathetic imagination, of which Wordsworth, as we have seen, was the prophet. That is perhaps what helps to make Anne so complex and sensitive a character.

Jane Austen's earlier heroines, of whom Elizabeth Bennet is the exemplar, manifested the Protestant will as direct descendants of Samuel Richardson's Clarissa Harlowe, with Dr. Samuel Johnson hovering nearby as moral authority. Marxist criticism inevitably views the Protestant will, even in its literary manifestations, as a mercantile matter, and it has become fashionable to talk about the socioeconomic realities that Jane Austen excludes, such as the West Indian slavery that is part of the ultimate basis for the financial security most of her characters enjoy. But all achieved literary works are founded upon exclusions, and no one has demonstrated that increased consciousness of the relation between culture and imperialism is of the slightest benefit whatsoever in learning to read *Mansfield Park*. *Persuasion* ends with a tribute to the British navy, in which Wentworth has an honored place. Doubtless Wentworth at sea, ordering the latest batch of disciplinary floggings, is not as pleasant as Wentworth on land, gently appreciating the joys of affection with Anne Elliot. But once again, Austen's is a great art founded upon exclusions, and the sordid realities of British sea power are no more relevant to *Persuasion* than West Indian bondage is to *Mansfield Park*. Austen was, however, immensely interested in the pragmatic and secular consequences of the Protestant will, and they seem to me a crucial element in helping us appreciate the heroines of her novels.

Austen's Shakespearean inwardness, culminating in Anne Elliot, revises the moral intensities of Clarissa Harlowe's secularized Protestant martyrdom, her slow dying after being raped by Lovelace. What removes Clarissa's will to live is her stronger will to maintain the integrity of her being. To yield to the repentant Lovelace by marrying him would compromise the essence of her being, the exaltation of her violated will. What is tragedy in *Clarissa* is converted by Austen into ironic comedy, but the will's drive to maintain itself scarcely alters in this conversion. In *Persuasion* the emphasis is on a willed exchange of esteems, where both the woman and the man estimate the value of the other to be high. Obviously outward considerations of wealth, property, and social standing are crucial elements here, but so are the inward

considerations of common sense, amiability, culture, wit, and affection. In a way (it pains me to say this, as I am a fierce Emersonian) Ralph Waldo Emerson anticipated the current Marxist
critique of Austen when he denounced her as a mere conformist
who would not allow her heroines to achieve the soul's true freedom from societal conventions. But that was to mistake Jane
Austen, who understood that the function of convention was to
liberate the will, even if convention's tendency was to stifle individuality, without which the will was inconsequential.

Austen's major heroines—Elizabeth, Emma, Fanny, and Anne
—possess such inward freedom that their individualities cannot
be repressed. Austen's art as a novelist is not to worry much about
the socioeconomic genesis of that inner freedom, though the anxiety level does rise in *Mansfield Park* and *Persuasion*. In Austen,
irony becomes the instrument for invention, which Dr. Johnson
defined as the essence of poetry. A conception of inward freedom
that centers upon a refusal to accept esteem except from one upon
whom one has conferred esteem, is a conception of the highest
degree of irony. The supreme comic scene in all of Austen must
be Elizabeth's rejection of Darcy's first marriage proposal, where
the ironies of the dialectic of will and esteem become very nearly
outrageous. That high comedy, which continued in *Emma*, is
somewhat chastened in *Mansfield Park*, and then becomes something else, unmistakable but difficult to name, in *Persuasion*, where
Austen has become so conscious a master that she seems to have
changed the nature of willing, as though it, too, could be persuaded
to become a rarer, more disinterested act of the self.

No one has suggested that Jane Austen becomes a High Romantic in *Persuasion;* her poet remained William Cowper, not Wordsworth, and her favorite prose writer was always Dr. Johnson. But
her severe distrust of imagination and of "romantic love," so prevalent in the earlier novels, is not a factor in *Persuasion*. Anne and
Wentworth maintain their affection for each other throughout
eight years of hopeless separation, and each has the power of imagination to conceive of a triumphant reconciliation. This is the material for a romance, not for an ironical novel. The ironies of

Persuasion are frequently pungent, but they are almost never directed at Anne Elliot and only rarely at Captain Wentworth.

There is a difficult relation between Austen's repression of her characteristic irony about her protagonists and a certain previously unheard plangency that hovers throughout *Persuasion*. Despite Anne's faith in herself she is very vulnerable to the anxiety, which she never allows herself to express, of an unlived life, in which the potential loss transcends yet includes sexual unfulfillment. I can recall only one critic, the Australian Ann Molan, who emphasizes what Austen strongly implies, that "Anne . . . is a passionate woman. And against her will, her heart keeps asserting its demand for fulfillment." Since Anne had refused Wentworth her esteem eight years before, she feels a necessity to withhold her will, and thus becomes the first Austen heroine whose will and imagination are antithetical.

Although Austen's overt affinities remained with the Aristocratic Age, her authenticity as a writer impelled her, in *Persuasion*, a long way toward the burgeoning Democratic Age, or Romanticism, as we used to call it. There is no civil war within Anne Elliot's psyche, or within Austen's; but there is the emergent sadness of a schism in the self, with memory taking the side of imagination in an alliance against the will. The almost Wordsworthian power of memory in both Anne and Wentworth has been noted by Gene Ruoff. Since Austen was anything but an accidental novelist, we might ask why she chose to found *Persuasion* upon a mutual nostalgia. After all, the rejected Wentworth is even less inclined to will a renewed affection than Anne is, and yet the fusion of memory and imagination triumphs over his will also. Was this a relaxation of the will in Jane Austen herself? Since she returns to her earlier mode in *Sanditon*, her unfinished novel begun after *Persuasion* was completed, it may be that the story of Anne Elliot was an excursion or indulgence for the novelist. The parallels between Wordsworth and *Persuasion* are limited but real. High Romantic novels in England, whether of the Byronic kind like *Jane Eyre* and *Wuthering Heights* or of a Wordsworthian sort like *Adam Bede,* are a distinctly later development. The ethos of the Austen heroine does not change in *Persuasion*, but she is certainly a more problematic being, tinged with a new sadness concerning life's limits. It may be that the elegant pathos *Persuasion* sometimes courts has a connection to Jane Austen's own ill health, her intimations of her early death.

Stuart Tave, comparing Wordsworth and Austen, shrewdly noted that both were "poets of marriage" and both also possessed "a sense of duty understood and deeply felt by those who see the integrity and peace of their own lives as essentially bound to the lives of others and see the lives of all in a more than merely social order." Expanding Tave's insight, Susan Morgan pointed to the particular affinity between Austen's *Emma* and Wordsworth's great "Ode: Intimations of Immortality from Recollections of Earliest Childhood." The growth of the individual consciousness, involving both gain and loss for Wordsworth but only gain for Austen, is the shared subject. Emma's consciousness certainly does develop, and she undergoes a quasi-Wordsworthian transformation from the pleasures of near solipsism to the more difficult pleasures of sympathy for others. Anne Elliot, far more mature from the beginning, scarcely needs to grow in consciousness. Her long-lamented rejection of Wentworth insulates her against the destructiveness of hope, which we have seen to be the frightening emphasis of the earlier Wordsworth, particularly in the story of poor Margaret. Instead of hope, there is a complex of emotions, expressed by Austen with her customary skill:

> How eloquent could Anne Elliot have been,—how eloquent, at least, were her wishes on the side of early warm attachment, and a cheerful confidence in futurity, against that over-anxious caution which seems to insult exertion and distrust Providence! —She had been forced into prudence in her youth, she learned romance as she grew older—the natural sequel of an unnatural beginning.

Here learning romance is wholly retrospective; Anne no longer regards it as being available to her. And indeed Wentworth returns, still resentful after eight years, and reflects that Anne's power with him is gone forever. The qualities of decision and confidence that make him a superb naval commander are precisely what he condemns her for lacking. With almost too meticulous a craft, Austen traces his gradual retreat from this position, as the power of memory increases its dominance over him and as he learns that his jilted sense of her as being unable to act is quite mistaken. It is a beautiful irony that he needs to undergo a process of self-persuasion while Anne waits, without even knowing that she is waiting or that there is anything that could rekindle her hope. The comedy of this is gently sad, as the reader waits also, reflecting upon how large a part contingency plays in the matter.

While the pre-Socratics and Freud agree that there are no accidents, Austen thinks differently. Character is fate for her also, but fate, once activated, tends to evade character in so overdetermined a social context as Austen's world. In rereading *Persuasion,* though I remember the happy conclusion, I nevertheless feel anxiety as Wentworth and Anne circle away from each other in spite of themselves. The reader is not totally persuaded of a satisfactory interview until Anne reads Wentworth's quite agonized letter to her:

"I can listen no longer in silence. I must speak to you by such means as are within my reach. You pierce my soul. I am half agony, half hope. Tell me not that I am too late, that such precious feelings are gone for ever. I offer myself to you again with a heart more your own, than when you almost broke it eight years and a half ago. Dare not say that man forgets sooner than woman, that his love has an earlier death. I have loved none but you. Unjust I may have been, weak and resentful I have been, but never inconstant. You alone have brought me to Bath. For you alone I think and plan.—Have you not seen this? Can you fail to have understood my wishes?—I had not waited even these ten days, could I have read your feelings, as I think you must have penetrated mine. I can hardly write. I am every instant hearing something which overpowers me. You sink your voice, but I can distinguish the tones of that voice, when they would be lost on others.—Too good, too excellent creature! You do us justice indeed. You do believe that there is true attachment and constancy among men. Believe it to be most fervent, most undeviating in

F. W.

"I must go, uncertain of my fate; but I shall return hither, or follow your party, as soon as possible. A word, a look will be enough to decide whether I enter your father's house this evening or never."

I cannot imagine such a letter in *Pride and Prejudice,* or even in *Emma* or *Mansfield Park.* The perceptive reader might have realized how passionate Anne was, almost from the start of the novel, but until this there was no indication of equal passion in Wentworth. His letter, as befits a naval commander, is badly written and not exactly Austenian, but it is all the more effective thereby. We come to realize that we have believed in him until now only because Anne's love for him provokes our interest. Austen wisely has declined to make him interesting enough on his own. Yet part of the book's effect is to persuade the reader of the reader's own powers of discernment and self-persuasion; Anne Elliot is almost too good for the reader, as she is for Austen herself, but the attentive reader gains the confidence to perceive Anne as she should be perceived. The subtlest element in this subtlest of novels is the call upon the reader's own power of memory to match the persistence and intensity of the yearning that Anne Elliot is too stoical to express directly.

The yearning hovers throughout the book, coloring Anne's perceptions and our own. Our sense of Anne's existence becomes identified with our own consciousness of lost love, however fictive or idealized that may be. There is an improbability in the successful renewal of a relationship devastated eight years before which ought to work against the texture of this most "realistic" of Austen's novels, but she is very careful to see that it does not. Like the author, the reader becomes persuaded to wish for Anne what she still wishes for herself. Ann Molan has the fine observation that Austen "is most satisfied with Anne when Anne is most dissatisfied with herself." The reader is carried along with Austen, and gradually Anne is also persuaded and catches up with the reader, allowing her yearning a fuller expression.

Dr. Johnson, in *The Rambler* 29, on "The folly of anticipating misfortunes," warned against anxious expectations of any kind, whether fearful or hopeful:

because the objects both of fear and hope are yet uncertain, so we ought not to trust the representations of one more than the other, because they are both equally fallacious; as hope enlarges happiness, fear aggravates calamity. It is generally allowed, that no man ever found the happiness of possession proportionate to that expectation which incited his desire, and invigorated his pursuit; nor has any man found the evils of life so formidable in reality, as they were described to him by his own imagination.

This is one of a series of Johnsonian pronouncements against the dangerous prevalence of the imagination, some of which his disciple Austen had certainly read. If you excluded such representations, on the great critic's advice, then Wordsworth could not have written at all, and Austen could not have written *Persuasion*. Yet it was a very strange book for her to write, this master of the highest art of exclusion that we have known in the Western novel. Any novel by Jane Austen could be called an achieved ellipsis, with everything omitted that could disturb her ironic though happy conclusions. *Persuasion* remains the least popular of her four canonical novels because it is the strangest, but all her work is increasingly strange as we approach the end of the Democratic Age that her contemporary Wordsworth did so much to inaugurate in literature. Poised as she is at the final border of the Aristocratic Age, she shares with Wordsworth an art dependent upon a split between a waning Protestant will and a newly active sympathetic imagination, with memory assigned the labor of healing the divide. If the argument of my book has any validity, Austen will survive even the bad days ahead of us, because the strangeness of originality and of an individual vision are our lasting needs, which only literature can gratify in the Theocratic Age that slouches toward us.

11.

Walt Whitman as Center
of the American Canon

IF ONE ATTEMPTS to list the artistic achievements of our nation against the background of Western tradition, our accomplishments in music, painting, sculpture, architecture tend to be somewhat dwarfed. It is not a question of using Bach, Mozart, and Beethoven as the standard; Stravinsky, Schoenberg, and Bartók are more than enough to place our composers in a somewhat sad perspective. And whatever the splendors of modern American painting and sculpture, there has been no Matisse among us. The exception is in literature. No Western poet, in the past century and a half, not even Browning or Leopardi or Baudelaire, overshadows Walt Whitman or Emily Dickinson. And in our century the principal poets—Frost, Stevens, Eliot, Hart Crane, Elizabeth Bishop, among others—rival Neruda, Lorca, Valéry, Montale, Rilke, Yeats. Our major novelists—Hawthorne, Melville, James, Faulkner—can similarly stand with their Western peers.

Perhaps only James can sustain the company of Flaubert, Tolstoy, George Eliot, Proust, and Joyce, but we have single books that matter in world terms: *The Scarlet Letter, Moby-Dick, Huck-leberry Finn, As I Lay Dying.* The book that matters most is the 1855 original *Leaves of Grass.* Whitman is to be sure more than the poet of 1855, with his triumphs in the then-untitled long poems that were eventually to be called *Song of Myself* and "The Sleepers." In 1856, the second *Leaves of Grass* introduced the "Sun-Down Poem" we now know as "Crossing Brooklyn Ferry." The 1860 third edition gave us "As I Ebb'd with the Ocean of Life" and "Out of the Cradle Endlessly Rocking," and 1865 trag-ically added the American elegy that sustains comparison with "Lycidas" and "Adonais," the great lament for the martyred Abra-ham Lincoln: "When Lilacs Last in the Dooryard Bloom'd."

These six major poems, *Song of Myself* and the five lesser but still extraordinary meditations, are what matter most in Whitman. To find their aesthetic equivalent in the West one must go back to Goethe, Blake, Wordsworth, Hölderlin, Shelley, and Keats. Nothing in the second half of the nineteenth century or in our now almost completed century matches Whitman's work in direct power and sublimity, except perhaps for Dickinson. It is an un-happy paradox that we have never got Whitman right, because he is a very difficult, immensely subtle poet who is usually at work doing almost the precise opposite of what he asserts himself to be doing.

For many current readers, Whitman is the passionate populist, precursor of Allen Ginsberg and other professional rebels. His actual authentic descendants are the strong American poets who tried to flee him but could not: T. S. Eliot and Wallace Stevens. One should add the magnificent Hart Crane, who wrote in the rhetoric of Eliot and Stevens but with Whitmanian aspiration and stance. The English poet-prophet D. H. Lawrence is the fourth true Whitmanian poet in the language; Pound, William Carlos Williams, and other nominees are something else, while John Ash-bery seems to me the fifth and most Whitmanian of those who actually learn from and extend *Song of Myself.* Hispanic poets, culminating in Neruda, take Whitman's influence in another di-rection, one that has more to do with Walt Whitman as symbolic figure than with the actual text of the poetry.

Whitman's originality has less to do with his supposedly free verse than it does with his mythological inventiveness and mastery of figurative language. His metaphors and meter-making arguments break the new road even more effectively than his innovations in metrics. Even very brief, slight poems manifest the shock of his originality.

> This is thy hour O Soul, thy free flight into the wordless,
> Away from books, away from art, the day erased,
>   the lesson done.
> Thee fully forth emerging, silent, gazing, pondering
>   the themes thou lovest best,
> Night, sleep, death and the stars.

That is "A Clear Midnight," a very late poem, which lingered on in Wallace Stevens's consciousness. "The stars" at the lyric's close are a substitution for the absent, oceanic mother or mothering ocean, which are always the fourth and fifth presences when Whitman evokes "Night, sleep, death." Stevens praised the little poem because of the strength it manifested of Whitman's stance in relation to his subject, his clear sense of his world. Midnight is Whitman's point of epiphany, when revelation is undisturbed by the distractions of day. His great poem of that point is "The Sleepers," perhaps the most neglected of his six major pieces. In 1855, like the rest of *Leaves of Grass*, it carried no title; in 1865 it was "Night Poem," and in 1860, "Sleep Chasings." As was often the case, Whitman's first thought was the best; this is indeed his "Night Poem." Entering into the night, Whitman self-consciously incarnates himself as the American Jesus, an audacity that repeats a crucial moment of death and resurrection in *Song of Myself*, but it is better to start with "The Sleepers" and move through aspects of *Song of Myself*, on toward the explicitly elegiac Whitman.

· We know that, as American religious prophet, Whitman was responding to the stimulus of Emerson as well as to the traditions Emerson represented, Eastern as well as Western heretical strains. His starting point in 1854 seems to have been Emerson's famous essay on "The Poet," with its declaration that the poets are "liberating gods." The notebook fragments that are the earliest drafts of *Song of Myself* record an even closer identification with the American Jesus than does their revised form in section 38 of the completed poem:

In vain were nails driven through my hands.
I remember my crucifixion and bloody coronation
I remember the mockers and the buffeting insults
The sepulchre and the white linen have yielded me up
I am alive in New York and San Francisco,
Again I tread the streets after two thousand years.
Not all the traditions can put vitality in churches
They are not alive, they are cold mortar and brick,
I can easily build as good, and so can you:—
Books are not men——

The Jesus of the American religion is neither the crucified man nor the God of the Ascension, but rather the resurrected man who passes forty days with the disciples, forty days about which the New Testament tells us virtually nothing. The poet of the last fifteen sections of *Song of Myself* is our largest literary representation of resurrected man. "The Sleepers" is the prehistory of that resurrection and depicts Whitman's version of the mystery of the Incarnation, in which the man-god and the poetical character merge. The poem necessarily, like most of the strongest Whitman, addresses much else, since the evocation of messianic election is inconsistent; yet here and elsewhere it is never far from Whitman.

I think that critics generally do not discuss it because it embarrasses them, just as Whitman's frank autoeroticism is difficult to discuss. There is very little evidence that Whitman ever had sexual relations with anyone except himself, and on the basis of what I understand of both his life and his poetry, I suspect that there was only one abortive attempt at relationship, presumably homosexual, in the winter of 1859–60. Perhaps Whitman discovered again that to touch his body to someone else's was just about as much as he could bear. Yet whatever his quasi-autistic psychosexual sufferings, he had the genius and the heroism to write his half-dozen major longer poems. "The Sleepers" counts the cost of confirmation and is the most Blakean of Whitman's poems, although Whitman had not yet read Blake. Like Blake, Whitman adapts the visionary stance of a Hebrew prophet:

> *I wander all night in my vision,*
> *Stepping with light feet, swiftly and noiselessly stepping and*
> * stopping,*
> *Bending with open eyes over the shut eyes of sleepers,*
> *Wandering and confused, lost to myself, ill-assorted,*
> * contradictory,*
> *Pausing, gazing, bending, and stopping.*

Despite his own condition, he confronts the sleepers, dead and undead, suffering and placid, and makes a difference to the afflicted:

> *I stand in the dark with drooping eyes by the worst-suffering*
> * and the most restless,*
> *I pass my hands soothingly to and fro a few inches from*
> * them,*
> *The restless sink in their beds, they fitfully sleep.*

After a remarkable series of identifications, some of which implicitly menace him, the poem's speaker begins to undergo a reintegration, which I am reluctant to interpret in Freudian terms, let alone Jungian. Forces outside the prophetic self that will strengthen it threaten at first to inundate it, so that Whitman fears for himself the death by water suffered by his surrogate in section 3 of the poem, "a beautiful gigantic swimmer swimming naked through the eddies of the sea." This titan, or "courageous giant," is flanked in the original poem by two passages Whitman later suppressed, a dream episode in which he is thrust out, naked and ashamed, into the world, and a nightmare identification with a Lucifer-like figure that climaxes in a curious, dark analogue with Melville's snowy Leviathan:

> Now the vast dusk bulk that is the whale's bulk, it seems mine;
> Warily, sportsman! Though I lie so sleepy and sluggish, the tap
> of my flukes is death.

Fantasies of being an outcast alternate with diabolical negations: that is a pattern of ordeals and temptations attendant upon election as a deliverer. The beautiful final section of Whitman's poem of night begins with what could serve as the description of a painting by William Blake:

The sleepers are very beautiful as they lie unclothed,
They flow hand in hand over the whole earth from east to west
    as they lie unclothed.

The magical word for Whitman at night is "pass," and salvation for him is to be a passerby. All of the distressed sleepers wake in a quasi-resurrection: "They pass the invigoration of the night and the chemistry of the night, and awake." Confronted by that vision, Whitman grants his poem and himself a majestic reconciliation as closure:

I too pass from the night,
I stay a while away O night, but I return to you again and love
    you,
Why should I be afraid to trust myself to you?
I am not afraid, I have been well brought forward by you,
I love the rich running day, but I do not desert her in whom
    I lay for so long,
I know not how I came of you and I know not where I go with
    you, but I know I came well and shall go well.
I will stop only a time with the night, and rise betimes,
I will duly pass the day O my mother, and duly return to you.

Only the mother and the night are mentioned, but death is implicit throughout. There are still reservations and fears in this passage, but how could it be otherwise? In the vocabulary of the ancient Gnostics, which Whitman so curiously approaches here, the abyss of night is the foremother, and the creation out of that abyss constituted the fall. Professing much less than full knowledge, at this point Whitman takes the conscious risk of cyclic death and cyclic resurrection. His gnosis is that he came well, shall go well, and then shall rise again. The dark contrast to Whitman's wavering faith is in Lear's despairing declarations to Gloucester: "Thou must be patient; we came crying hither. / Thou know'st, the first time that we smell the air / We wawl and cry," and "When we are born, we cry that we are come / To this great stage of fools." Whitman's pathos is that his still imperfect gnosis is not yet that far from Lear's tragic outcries. *Song of Myself,* from section 38 on, tries to offer a more perfected knowing. Section 41 builds on Whitman's accurate insight that all the gods, Jehovah included, were once men, rising into superb blasphemy:

Magnifying and applying come I,
Outbuilding at the start the old cautious hucksters,
Taking myself the exact dimensions of Jehovah,
Lithographing Kronos, Zeus his son, and Hercules his grandson,
Buying drafts of Osiris, Isis, Belus, Brahma, Buddha,
In my portfolio placing Manito loose, Allah on a leaf,
With Odin and the hideous-faced Mexitli and every idol
*   and image,*
Taking them all for what they are worth and not a cent more,
Admitting they were alive and did the work of their days.

Against them, Whitman pledges the work of his days: "The supernatural of no account, myself waiting my time to be one of the supremes." In section 43, accepting Jesus is placed in the context of accepting a multiplicity of gods, and the concluding sections of the poem cast off all spiritual anxieties. The notebook fragments make Whitman's ambitions clearer: "I am myself waiting my time to be a God; / I think I shall do as much good and be as pure and prodigious as ever." No more extreme statement of Whitman's project could be imagined than his notebook draft of what became section 49: "Mostly this we have of God; we have man," and again: "I can comprehend no being more wonderful than man." What Joseph Smith proclaimed as the Mormon doctrine of man perfected into God is independently visualized in Whitman's hermeticism.

Whitman's version of the American religion relies upon *Song of Myself*'s most original aspect, its psychic cartography of three components in each of us: soul, self, and real me or me myself. I employ here Whitman's own terms, which do not reduce to Freudian or any other psychological categories. Whitman's initial distinction is between soul and self, in which the soul, like the body, is very much part of nature, a somewhat alienated nature. By the soul, Whitman means character or ethos as opposed to the self, by which he means personality or pathos. Character *acts,* but personality *suffers,* even if it is the pleasurable suffering of passion, high or low. So when Whitman writes "my soul" he means his own dark side, the estranged or alienated component in his nature. When he writes "my self," as in the title, *Song of Myself,* he means what he calls Walt Whitman, an American, one of the roughs, palpably an aggressive male.

But Whitman's self, as he freely admits, is split in two. There is also a nuanced, feminine self, which he calls "the real me" or "me myself" and identifies with the powerful quartet of night, death, the mother, and the sea. The Whitmanian soul is unknown nature, a kind of blank, while the rough self is a persona or mask, an endlessly shifting series of identifications. But the real me, the me myself, is not only a known realm but the faculty of knowing, something close to the Gnostic capacity to know even as one is known.

Whitman's mythology of the soul and two selves is quite coherent, even if complex. He could have called his major poem *Song of the Soul* but was in no way tempted to do so, just as he would not entitle it *Song of the Real Me.* There are great songs of the real me or me myself by Whitman, and they include "The Sleepers" and "As I Ebb'd with the Ocean of Life." Even the "Lilacs" elegy is overwhelmingly the song of the me myself, though it drives toward what it calls "the tally of my soul" or revelation of my unknown nature.

It is in *Song of Myself,* his most ambitious poem, that Whitman gives his fullest, if still incomplete, account of the relations between his soul and his two selves. "I celebrate myself," he begins, meaning that his hero is Walt Whitman, or as he called the poem in 1856: "Poem of Walt Whitman, an American." In his fourth line, he invites his soul—an invitation taken up in section 6, but only after the "me myself," who *never* invites the soul, receives a beautiful portrayal in section 5. I frequently find these the best lines in *Song of Myself,* or at least the most seductive, presaging as they do the poetic personae of T. S. Eliot and John Ashbery. Here, Whitman suddenly says, is the real me, not the rough Walt:

> *Apart from the pulling and hauling stands what I am,*
> *Stands amused, complacent, compassionating, idle, unitary,*
> *Looks down, is erect, or beds an arm on an impalpable certain*
> *   rest,*
> *Looking with side-curved head curious what will come next,*
> *Both in and out of the game and watching and wondering*
> *   at it.*

Withdrawn from both competition and too easy an Eros, the real me stands apart yet not isolated, incredibly graceful in stance, open to immediacy but detached from it, at once a player and a fan, as it were. The entire passage is endlessly charming and memorable. For once, Whitman does not try to evade us, and we begin to understand him a little better.

But then he swiftly and powerfully darkens our understanding: "I believe in you my soul, the other I am must not abase itself to you, / And you must not be abased to the other."

We are at the center of Whitman's genius here, and it is the genius he shares with his mentor, Emerson. The rough self, the persona Walt Whitman, is capable of free relations with the soul or unknown nature, but the other I am, the real or Hermetic me, has a tendency to enter into only a master–slave relationship with the soul. Whitman's language needs very close reading here: the poet's personality evidently has a masochistic urge toward his unfathomable character, and the character could in turn be compelled to be subservient to the detached, turned-away authentic self, though we are not told what the agent of that compulsion would be. What in him is at once in and out of the game, for all its stance of freedom, would abase itself to what cannot know or be known, and that alienated nature could suffer the reverse abasement.

Both postures of the spirit are rejected by Walt Whitman, American poet, and both abasements are handled elsewhere in the poem in its two great passages of acute crisis and partial resolution. The soul's virtual rape of the me myself in sections 28–30 is followed by the soul's humiliation toward the otherness within the self in section 38. Both crises are meant to contrast with the metaphorical semiunion of the soul and the rough, outered self in section 5 of the poem. Whitman humorously portrays an absurdly impossible embrace, which has not prevented many solemn exegetes from literalizing the poet's comedy. It is wonderfully grotesque to visualize one's soul holding onto one's self's beard with one hand while reaching for the self's feet with the other. Where Whitman baffles us most by mingling the literal and the figurative helter-skelter is in his evocations of autoeroticism. There is the startling close of the curious chant, "Spontaneous Me":

The wholesome relief, repose, content,
And this bunch pluck'd at random from myself,
It has done its work—I toss it carelessly to fall where it may.

Even more startling is the first crisis of *Song of Myself*, where the image, perhaps the represented act as well, is a successful though reluctant masturbation. One of the many current ironies of Whitman's reception is that he is acclaimed as a gay poet. Beyond doubt, his deepest drive was homoerotic, and his poems of heterosexual passion have convinced no one, including Whitman himself. But for whatever reason, in his poetry as probably in his life, his erotic orientation was onanistic. A prevalent image in his poetry is that of spilling one's seed upon the ground after self-excitation. More even than sadomasochism, autoeroticism appears to be the last Western taboo, at least in terms of literary representation, yet Whitman acclaims it in some of his most important poems.

If someone in 1855 had announced that the canonical American writer had just appeared with a book called *Leaves of Grass*, rather awkwardly printed and with no subject except himself, we might have expressed a modest skepticism. That our national poet should be an egotistical onanist, who proclaimed his own divinity in a series of untitled, unrhymed, apparently prosy verses, would probably have moved us to amiable pity at best. After all, the young Henry James, arguably the most organized critical sensibility we have produced, reviewed *Drum Taps* a full decade later with the confident dismissal that Whitman, a prosaic mind, was only, as it were, the Arnold Schwarzenegger of his day, lifting himself by muscular exertion into a vain attempt at sublimity.

James repented later; but we would have done no better, and we would have repented also. The grand exception is Ralph Waldo Emerson, who received the book in the post, read it, and wrote to Whitman telling him that he had brought forth the greatest piece of wit and wisdom yet composed by an American. Emerson's judgment is still true. Emerson aged prematurely and added some severe qualifications, but his early verdict remains the high point of American pragmatic literary criticism. Emerson had been doing his best, and that was very good indeed, but he recognized immediately that this was the poet he had prophesied, the literary Messiah for whom he had served as an Elijah or John the Baptist.

In his letter to Whitman, Emerson remarked of the 1855 *Leaves of Grass,* "I am very happy in reading it, as great power makes us happy." Five years later, in his last great work, *The Conduct of Life,* he gave his definition of power:

All power is of one kind, a sharing of the nature of the world. The mind that is parallel with the laws of nature will be in the current of events, and strong with their strength. One man is made of the same stuff of which events are made; is in sympathy with the course of things, can predict it. Whatever befalls, befalls him first, so that he is equal to whatever shall happen.

I think that Emerson was correct in his first impression of Whitman as the American shaman. The shaman is necessarily self-divided, sexually ambiguous, and difficult to distinguish from the divine. As shaman, Whitman is endlessly metamorphic, capable of being in several places at once, and a knower of matters that Walter Whitman, Jr., the carpenter's son, scarcely could have known. We begin to read Whitman adequately when we see in him a throwback to ancient Scythia, to strange healers who were demonic, who knew themselves to possess or be possessed by a magical or occult self. That is why Whitman is the poet of the American religion to this day. When I read the ancient, quasi-

Gnostic Gospel of Thomas, I am compelled to think of Whitman, and when I read Southern Baptist hymns about walking and talking with Jesus, the dissident Quaker Whitman again comes to mind. This is the Whitman, as Richard Poirier has shown, of "The Last Invocation," the one American lyric that is worthy to have been written by St. John of the Cross, another celebratory lament of the Obscure Night of the Soul:

> At the last, tenderly,
> From the walls of the powerful fortress'd house,
> From the clasp of the knitted locks,
>   from the keep of the well-closed doors,
> Let me be wafted.
>
> Let me glide noiselessly forth;
> With the key of softness unlock the locks—with a whisper,
> Set open the doors O soul.
>
> Tenderly—be not impatient,
> (Strong is your hold O mortal flesh,
> Strong is your hold O love.)

It is the last invocation, for even the shaman must know that the final form of change is death. The soul, or one's own unknown nature, opens the doors to the real me's embrace by death. As in the dark night of John of the Cross, the lyric model is the Song of Songs which was Solomon's, echoed earlier by Whitman in the "Lilacs" elegy, particularly in the hermit thrush's Song of Death. Yet there death and the mother are still an identity; at the end in Whitman's vision the self's erotic destiny returns to its own domain and to its adventures with its own soul. This means that Whitman's ultimate romance is with Whitman, and we are returned to what seems to trouble some of us, the Eros of autoeroticism in our national poet.

The muse of masturbation is not highly valued among us, or among anyone else as far as I know, but the permanent scandal of Whitman has a vital autoerotic component. I would suggest that Whitman's universality, his immense capacity for transcending linguistic boundaries, is not impeded by his comprehensive sexuality, including this component. Whitman's poetry refuses to acknowledge any sexual demarcations, just as it refuses to accept any fortified lines dividing the human and the divine. Clearly Whitman, a Free Soil New York State Democrat in his own day, is a permanent party of one, even as John Milton is a sect of one; but, like Milton, he knew the secret of making his solitary idiom into a permanently relevant voice.

Whitman's canonicity depends upon his achievement in permanently altering what might be called the American image of voice. One can hear Whitman's image of voice in Hemingway, probably without intention on Hemingway's part, almost as overwhelmingly as one can hear it in poets who otherwise have nothing in common. The voice raised in solitude, wounded or stoic, in our imaginative literature now tends to have Whitmanian overtones. Stevens scarcely desires to have his singing girl at Key West evoke Whitman, yet his poem ends with

> The maker's rage to order words of the sea,
> Words of the fragrant portals, dimly-starred,
> And of ourselves and of our origins,
> In ghostlier demarcations, keener sounds.

The words of the portals belong to Keats, but words of the sea, words of ourselves, words of our origin are Whitman's, whose "Out of the Cradle Endlessly Rocking" was originally called "A Word Out of the Sea," the word being death, sane and sacred death. I can never quite absorb the fact that Wallace Stevens, who was contemptuous of Whitman's tramp persona, of the rough, American Walt, wrote the most magnificent tribute to Whitman that our literature affords:

> In the far South the sun of autumn is passing
> Like Walt Whitman walking along a ruddy shore.
> He is singing and chanting the things that are part of him,
> The worlds that were and will be, death and day.
> Nothing is final, he chants. No man shall see the end.
> His beard is of fire and his staff is a leaping flame.

How happy Whitman would have been with this as an appropriate evocation of his Emersonian power! Stevens packs it all in: Whitman as the lion sun, autumnal and elegiac, a passerby, refusing finalities, denying the promised end. Always in the sun, sunset and sunrise, singing and chanting the divided self and the unknowable soul, Stevens's Whitman is no divinity, but he kindles with a flame that surpasses natural fire. And without actually echoing the "each and all" intertwining chant that ends the "Lilacs" elegy, Stevens intimates its rhapsodic intensities, its confidence that there are indeed "retrievements out of the night." I hear no ironies in Stevens's celebratory ecstasy, nor any ideologies, no social energies working themselves through and out. What I hear is the sounding of an image, the image of a voice, a voice singing, chanting, passing, in an absolute conviction that origin and end, for the sake of life, can be kept apart.

In his old age, nursing his memories of his mentor, Whitman reported a consoling remark made to him by Emerson, that in the end the world would come round to the poet of *Leaves of Grass* because it would have to, because it was indebted to him. Whatever the later misunderstandings between Emerson and Whitman—and they were many—we remember that accurate prophecy, even as we remember Whitman's remark at Emerson's grave: "A just man, poised on himself, all-loving, all-inclusive, and sane and clear as the sun." What links Whitman and Emerson is far more vital than what divides them, and Whitman caught it in that "all-inclusive," the image of the sun as a self-sufficient orb.

The sage of the American religion, for all his reticences, revealed himself totally in his writings. The poet of the American religion, shouting his confidences, concealed almost everything. Emerson is a wisdom writer, like Nietzsche, Kierkegaard, Freud, and his precursor, Montaigne. Prudentially shrewd, Whitman has no wisdom to impart, and we do not miss it. He gives us his torment and his division and the weird faculty of a self that is both the knower and the known. You cannot distinguish between the ontological and empirical selves in his best poetry. By the standards of continental dialectics, that ought to render even his best poems incoherent, to make them forerunners of Pound's *Cantos*. There is a complex relationship between Whitman and Pound, but you don't get much light on *Song of Myself* or "Lilacs" by finding intimations of the *Cantos* in them, whereas backward glances from *The Waste Land* and *Notes Towards a Supreme Fiction* will at least partially illuminate Whitman. What replaces wisdom or philosophical insight in him is what Blake called "vision." Blake, being more urgent, as suited an apocalyptic, meant by "vision" a program for restoring the human. Whitman's vision is more modest, despite his American bravura: integrating the Whitmanian psyche was project enough. The project was unfinished, and unfinishable; but the American God, as I understand the American religion, is also unfinished, being another project in perpetual process.

One needs to be circular in trying to center Whitman, in order to account for his absolute centrality in the American literary canon. We have had remarkable women poets: Dickinson, Moore, Bishop, Swenson. Even if a dozen of that eminence yet spring up among us, they will not decenter Walt, because as a writer he was no more a male phenomenon than was Shakespeare, or Henry James. Shakespeare seems to me bisexual, James epicene, and Whitman autoerotic, but however they manage it, none of the three is gender-restricted or male-oriented. Some of the greatest writers have been: Milton, Wordsworth, Yeats, and above all Dante. They have characteristics not easily accepted by our more militant feminist critics, and some of those characteristics are not particularly amiable. For a time, these great poets may seem vulnerable to new cultural critiques, but eventually the poets will modify the critiques.

The strength of the canonical is manifested in the quiet persistence of the strongest writers. Their fecundity is endless because they represent the heart and the head rather than the loins or the privileges of caste or sect or race. You can protest, if you are so inclined, the ethos of Dante or of Milton, but they are close to invulnerable when it comes to logos or pathos. Trotsky, hardly an uncommitted intellectual, refused to consider Dante's *Comedy* a "mere historical document" and urged Russian writers to see a "directly aesthetic relationship" between themselves and Dante's poem. In Trotsky's judgment the power and intensity of Dante's work, its intellect and depth of feeling, made it essential to Marxist writers. A direct *aesthetic* relationship is enforced upon us by the

Comedy and *Paradise Lost*—Christian poems perhaps, but each of a strangeness and barbaric splendor (as William Empson observed of Milton's poem) hardly to be equaled elsewhere in literature.

Whitman, who was precisely what D. H. Lawrence judged him to be, the greatest of modern poets, of poets born in the nineteenth century and after, shares in the strangeness and even in the barbaric power, a curious survival in the strongest writers of the Democratic Age: Whitman, Tolstoy, Ibsen. Compared to the central writers of our Chaotic Era—Joyce, Proust, Kafka, Beckett, Neruda—there is something archaic that Whitman retrieves, as do Tolstoy and Ibsen. There is so much extravagance and generosity in *Song of Myself,* as in Tolstoy's *Hadji Murad* and Ibsen's *Peer Gynt,* that it makes sense to call all three truly Homeric in contrast to Joyce's *Ulysses,* which despite its armory of carefully organized analogues remains closer to Flaubert than to Homer. *Song of Myself, Hadji Murad,* and *Gynt,* like their makers, have heroic stature, whatever their opacities and their childlike failings. Achilles after all was childlike too, and though Odysseus is certainly a grown-up, he does not seem the oldest of the Greeks, whereas Joyce's Poldy, scarcely middle-aged, seems two thousand years older than anyone else in Dublin.

The protagonist of *Song of Myself* is indeed like Emerson, of whom his admirer Nietzsche wonderfully remarked, "He does not know how old he is already, or how young he is still going to be." Nietzsche alas suffers aesthetically when we read *Song of Myself* and *Thus Spake Zarathustra* side by side. Compared to Whitman's, the dithyrambs of Zarathustra suffer precisely because Nietzsche knows all too well how old he is already and is too certain about how young he will attempt to be. Trying to live as though it is perpetually morning is a very dangerous aesthetic quest, which sank Zarathustra without trace. Sometimes the Walt of *Song of Myself* plays Adam early in the morning, but quite often he is as deliberately old as Chaos and Night.

From Emerson, Whitman had learned the difficult notion that the American poet to come was to be at once the namer and the unnamer of everything he encountered. Confronted by this dialectical dilemma, Whitman shrewdly chose evasion as his mode:

he simply refused to name anything, or to unname it. Emily Dickinson, whose relation to Emerson was still subtler, perfected an art of unnaming and renaming; but her cognitive powers, as far as I can tell, were unmatched in Western imaginative literature since Shakespeare. Whitman had a canny mind, cunning and resourceful, but no more than Tennyson (whom he admired) did he manifest any cognitive originality. What was original in him lay elsewhere: innovations in form, stance, style, psychic cartography, visionary perspective. As in Tennyson, what frequently matters most in Whitman is the quality of his anguish, upon which so much of his poetry's power depends. That anguish produced the two crises of *Song of Myself,* in sections 28 and 38, the first sexual and therefore autoerotic, the second religious and Christ-like but with the American difference.

The early notebook fragments that were the starting point of *Song of Myself,* and of Whitman's breakthrough into his own poetic voice, include a draft of what was to become section 38. The image of "the headland," which occurs in each, seems to me the essential emblem of Whitman's emergence as a poet. A headland, in common naming, is a promontory, extending above and out into the water and so featuring the menace of a sheer drop. Neither naming nor unnaming it, as usual, Whitman makes the headland a metaphor for his antithetical relationship to his own sexuality, as here in the notebook, where "It" is a touch, his own touch:

> *It brings the rest around it, and they all stand on a headland*
>   *and mock me*
> *They have left me to touch, and taken their place on a*
>   *headland.*
> *The sentries have deserted every other part of me*
> *They have left me helpless to the torrent of touch*
> *They have all come to the headland to witness and assist*
>   *against me.——*
> *I roam about drunk and stagger*
> *I am given up by traitors,*
> *I talk wildly I am surely out of my head,*
> *I am myself the greatest traitor.*
> *I went myself first to the headland*

Song of Myself adds to that last line: "my own hands carried me there." Why criticism has not addressed itself to the image of masturbation in Whitman I scarcely know. Richard Chase and Kenneth Burke noted it before me, and I have meditated upon it several times. Whitman's senses, except for touch, desert him and stand on the headland to mock him, to witness against him, and even to assist touch against him. Yet the treacherous senses merely emulate Whitman, who went first to the headland.

Which Whitman is this "I . . . myself"? And why "the headland"? It must be the "me myself" or "real me" abasing itself to the otherness of the unknown soul, while the headland, rising above the maternal waters, is palpable enough. Although he exuberantly celebrates male sexuality, Whitman visualizes the phallus as a place of danger with a sheer drop into death, the mother, the ocean, the primal night. Gerard Manley Hopkins, in full flight from his own homoeroticism, remarked on the closeness of his soul to Whitman's, admired the metrics and diction of some passages of *Song of Myself,* and whether consciously or not, alluded to a line from "The Sleepers" ("Onward we move! a gay gang of blackguards") in the "gay-gangs" of clouds at the start of his poem "That Nature Is a Heraclitean Fire and of the Comfort of the Resurrection."

In one of his most intense sonnets, "No Worst, There Is None," Hopkins has a metaphor, "cliffs of fall," that has something of the Jobean anguish of Whitman's "headland," but with more concealed sexual reference: "O the mind, mind has mountains; cliffs of fall / Frightful, sheer, no-man-fathomed." The mind, in Whitman, finds its cliff of fall in the headland, emblem of a psychic extravagance that Whitman both celebrates and fears. It is Emersonian of Whitman to convert his personal obsessions into poetic strengths, and the image of the headland transforms the pathos of masturbation into aesthetic dignity. One can contrast Whitman here to Norman Mailer, who like Allen Ginsberg stems rather more from Henry Miller than from Whitman. Mailer's trope for masturbation is "bombing yourself," which is less impressive as an image than the possibility of falling off a headland and also collides with Whitman's celebration of a successfully completed autoerotic act. It is only until climax that Whitman stands upon the headland; afterward, he exults in the exuberantly masculine landscapes he has brought forth. Like an ancient Egyptian god, Whitman creates a world through masturbation, yet we tend to find his headlands more memorable than his harvests.

The crisis is more acute in section 38, where Whitman suffers an agony of overidentification with all the outcasts of humanity and cries out against his own attempt to atone for everyone: "Enough! enough! enough! Somehow I have been stunn'd. Stand back! / Give me a little time. . . ." He will recover with astonishing celerity and force, despite the terrible bitterness he turns on his Passion, the suffering of the Me Myself as the American Christ: "That I could look with a separate look on my own crucifixion and bloody crowning." And when he rises up, when "fastenings roll from me," we are given the crucial literary manifestation of the American religion's obsession with Resurrection, in one of the strangest passages in all of Whitman:

> I troop forth replenished with supreme power, one of an average
>   unending procession,
> Inland and sea-coast we go, and pass all boundary lines,
> Our swift ordinances on their way over the whole earth,
> The blossoms we wear in our hats the growth of thousands
>   of years.

Whitman is so considerable a humanist that the irony here cannot be uncalculated, yet it remains difficult to apprehend. The bard of *Song of Myself* is Christ-like and also "one of an average unending procession." The image is one of a general American Resurrection, in which the preparatory blossoms have been growing for millennia. "This was a great defeat," Emerson said of Golgotha, and then added that as Americans, we demand victory, a victory of the senses as well as of the soul. *Song of Myself* celebrates the Resurrection as a great American victory, precisely in Emerson's spirit. In the "Divinity School Address," Emerson had proclaimed that Jesus "saw that God incarnates himself in man, and evermore goes forth anew to take possession of his world." That going forth anew is magnified into Whitman's trooping off replenished with supreme power, in the American religion's mode of treating the United States itself as the greatest poem, or as the general Resurrection.

That is what the astonishing last quarter of *Song of Myself* is, the poem of a Resurrection that demands no last judgment, no days of finality. Mormon and Southern Baptist, black Baptist and Pentecostal, whatever persuasion or denomination, or secular lover of poetry—all of us are free to identify the Whitman of the final, miraculous tercets of *Song of Myself* as the American Jesus with whom the American walks and talks in the perpetually extended forty days between Resurrection and Ascension:

> *You will hardly know who I am or what I mean,*
> *But I shall be good health to you nevertheless,*
> *And filter and fibre your blood.*
>
> *Failing to fetch me at first keep encouraged,*
> *Missing me one place search another,*
> *I stop somewhere waiting for you.*

It may be that Whitman, like all great writers, was an accident of history. It may be that there are no accidents, that everything, including what we take to be a supreme work of art, is overdetermined. But history is more than the history of class struggle, or of racial oppression, or of gender tyranny. "Shakespeare makes history" seems to me a more useful formula than "history makes Shakespeare." History is no more a god or demiurge than language is, but *as a writer* Shakespeare was a sort of god. Shakespeare centers the Western Canon because he changes cognition by changing the representation of cognition. Whitman centers the American canon because he changes the American self and the American religion by changing the representation of our unofficial selves and our persuasive if concealed post-Christian religion.

A political reading of Shakespeare is bound to be less interesting than a Shakespearean reading of politics, just as a Shakespearean reading of Freud is more productive than Freudian reductions of Shakespeare. Whitman is admittedly not Shakespeare, or Dante, or Milton, but he compares very powerfully with any Western writer from Goethe and Wordsworth to the present.

What does it mean to write the poems of our climate, or of anyone's climate? Goethe, highly exportable throughout the entire nineteenth century, is scarcely read now outside of Germany. Yet more than any other German-language poet, he wrote the poems of his climate. Whitman, exportable almost from the start, remains a worldwide figure today, but will he eventually become language-confined, like Goethe? Whitman's peculiar status as poet of the American religion may seem to argue his perpetual relevance overseas, but then one remembers that the young Goethe appeared to be nothing less than a Messiah to many of his contemporaries. I suspect that to center a national canon is to guarantee a perpetual currency within a language, but that an eminence beyond a particular language is very rare as a permanent phenomenon. Whitman may yet fade abroad, though never, I think, in these states. The poet of *Leaves of Grass* emerged from a desperate family, replete with dark inertia and passion, haunted by demons and ghosts. A miracle of survival, Whitman seems to have known that his poetic vocation depended upon keeping himself open to all of the familial torment.

The second *Leaves of Grass* (1856) contained one new poem, now known as "Crossing Brooklyn Ferry." Originally called "Sun-Down Poem," it has the distinction of having been Thoreau's favorite among Whitman's works and of having fostered Hart Crane's *The Bridge* (1930), where the great span of Brooklyn Bridge replaces the Brooklyn–Manhattan ferry of Whitman's day, a replacement both empiric and symbolic. Like *Song of Myself,* the sundown poem is essentially celebratory, but its sixth section is one of Whitman's most negative litanies of the self:

It is not upon you alone the dark patches fall,
The dark threw its patches down upon me also,
The best I had done seem'd to me blank and suspicious,
My great thoughts as I supposed them, were they not in reality
*   meagre?*
Nor is it you alone who know what it is to be evil,
I too knitted the old knot of contrariety.

Celebration and anguish coexist in many superb poets, but self-celebration and self-anguish are a startling, ever-present juxtaposition in Whitman. Elegies for the self are the characteristic genre of American poetry because of Whitman's example; the puzzle is not why Whitman invented the mode, but why it was so inevitably transmitted after him. The two great "Sea-Drift" poems that crowned the third *Leaves of Grass* in 1860, "Out of the Cradle Endlessly Rocking" and "As I Ebb'd with the Ocean of Life," have engendered an endless progeny as varied as Eliot's "Dry Salvages," Stevens's "Idea of Order at Key West," Elizabeth Bishop's "End of March," John Ashbery's "A Wave," and A. R. Ammons's "Corsons Inlet." Since my prime subject is the canonical, the acute critical question for me becomes what makes these two poems so central.

Part of the answer is the sea's melodious hissing of "death" in "Out of the Cradle," since any consideration of death in our national literature must always circle back to Walt Whitman. Night, death, the mother, and the sea triumphantly blend in "Out of the Cradle," but are held off and almost overcome in "As I Ebb'd with the Ocean of Life," the more powerful of the two poems. Whereas "Out of the Cradle" traces the incarnation of the poetic character in Whitman, "As I Ebb'd" obliquely represents an obscure but traumatizing personal crisis that Whitman appears to have suffered in the winter of 1859–60. Presumably sexual, the sense of failure fills "As I Ebb'd" with a new pathos, richer than any before in Whitman. Nothing in him until the "Lilacs" elegy is so perfectly expressive of the American family romance as the extraordinary moment when he falls in anguish on the beach and creates out of that gesture our strongest image of reconciliation with the father:

> *I throw myself upon your breast my father,*
> *I cling to you so that you cannot unloose me,*
> *I hold you so firm till you answer me something.*
>
> *Kiss me my father,*
> *Touch me with your lips as I touch those I love,*

*Breathe to me while I hold you close the secret of the
  murmuring I envy.*

The secret of the ocean's murmuring and motherly moaning is
that, despite the ferocity of the ebbing, the flow will always return.
For Whitman, this is a religious secret, part of a gnosis, a knowing
in which the self itself is known. Whitman had a profound understanding that his country required its own religion as well as
its own literature. Part at least of his place as center of the American canon is his still unacknowledged function and status as the
national religious poet. The sages and theologians of the American
religion are a weirdly varied company: Ralph Waldo Emerson,
the Mormon prophet Joseph Smith, the belated visionary of the
Southern Baptists Edgar Young Mullins, William James, Ellen
Harmon White who founded the Seventh Day Adventists, and
Horace Bushnell, subtlest of the American theologians.

The poet of the American religion is a solitary, even as he keeps
proclaiming that he is a multitude. And when he walks in company, it is either with Jesus or with death:

*Solitary at midnight in my back yard, my thoughts gone from
  me a long while,
Walking the old hills of Judea with the beautiful gentle god
  by my side.*

Those old hills are of Judea, but they are *in* America, like the
shadowy swamp where Whitman hears the song of the hermit
thrush in the "Lilacs" elegy. The bird sings a carol of death and
reconciliation in which the taboo of mother-incest is figuratively
broken apart. Whitman is a great religious poet, though the religion is the American religion and not Christianity, just as Emerson's transcendentalism is post-Christian. Like Thoreau, Whitman
has a touch of the *Bhagavad-gita*, but the Hindu vision is mediat-
ed by Western hermeticism with its Neoplatonic and Gnostic
elements.

In Whitman, knowing is called "tallying" or "keeping tally"
and is associated with both autoeroticism and the writing of
poems. When Whitman tallies he reminds himself, following

Emerson, that he is no part of creation, or rather that what is best and oldest in him goes back before the creation. The "tally" becomes Whitman's metaphor for gnosis, the timeless knowing of the American religion. By extension, Whitman's tally is his prime canonical trope, centering our national literature. Hart Crane understood this in his invocation to Whitman in the "Cape Hatteras" canto of *The Bridge:* "O, upward from the dead / Thou bringest tally, and a pact, new bound / Of living brotherhood!" Whitman's new covenant, in Crane's vision, is Orphic, with the "tally" a substitute for Eurydice. Crane's interpretation of the elegiac Whitman seems to me unsurpassed, for the tally is indeed what the poet of "When Lilacs Last in the Dooryard Bloom'd" brings back from his descent into death, but only after offering the tally's emblem up to Lincoln's coffin:

> *Here, coffin that slowly passes,*
> *I give you my sprig of lilac.*

The forty-second saying of Jesus in the ancient, proto-Gnostic Gospel of Thomas is "Be passersby." Perhaps Jesus is telling his disciples to be wanderers like the Cynic sages, but I prefer a more Whitmanian reading. "Passing" is the verbal metaphor for the "Lilacs" elegy, even as "tally" is its substantive figuration, and it is the genius of Whitman's poem that its knowing is a kind of passing, a journeying or questioning to where inwardness is fully tallied:

> *Yet each to keep and all, retrievements out of the night,*
> *The song, the wondrous chant of the gray-brown bird,*
> *And the tallying chant, the echo arous'd in my soul,*
> *With the lustrous and drooping star with the countenance full*
> * of woe,*
> *With the holders holding my hand nearing the call of the*
> * bird,*
> *Comrades mine and I in the midst, and their memory ever to*
> * keep, for the dead I loved so well,*
> *For the sweetest, wisest soul of all my days and lands—and*
> * this for his dear sake,*

Lilac and star and bird twined with the chant of my soul.
There in the fragrant pines and the cedars dusk and dim.

This extraordinary closure, probably the finest in Whitman or indeed in American poetry, is intricately woven from the many strands of imagery that have made up the poem. It twines together more than the elegy's dominant emblems. All of Whitman's major poetry comes together here, even as the poet confidently chants a tally that is at one with his canonical centrality.

If you think of the major American writers, you are likely to remember Melville, Hawthorne, Twain, James, Cather, Dreiser, Faulkner, Hemingway, and Fitzgerald among the novelists. Nathanael West, Ralph Ellison, Thomas Pynchon, Flannery O'Connor, and Philip Roth would be among those I would add. The poets who matter most begin with Whitman and Dickinson and include Frost, Stevens, Moore, Eliot, Crane, and perhaps Pound and William Carlos Williams. Of more recent figures, I would list Robert Penn Warren, Theodore Roethke, Elizabeth Bishop, James Merrill, John Ashbery, A. R. Ammons, May Swenson. The dramatists are less illustrious: Eugene O'Neill now makes for unsatisfactory reading, and perhaps only Tennessee Williams will gain by the passage of time. Our major essayists remain Emerson and Thoreau; no one has matched them since. Poe is too universally accepted around the world to be excluded, though his writing is almost invariably atrocious.

Of these thirty-odd writers (including anyone you would add) there is no question who has had the largest influence, at home and abroad. Eliot and Faulkner may be Whitman's nearest rivals in their effect upon other writers, but they are not of his almost worldwide significance. Dickinson and James may have an aesthetic eminence equal to Whitman's, but they cannot compete with his universality. American literature abroad is always, in the first place, Whitman, whether it be in Spanish-speaking America, Japan, Russia, Germany, or Africa. Here I want only to note Whitman's influence on two poets, D. H. Lawrence and Pablo Neruda.

Neruda can be regarded as the canonical center of all Latin American literature, while Lawrence, though now distinctly out of fashion in our age of social dogmatics, remains a permanent novelist, essayist, poet, indeed a prophet, whose honor and influence will always return. Like Shelley and Hardy before him, Lawrence will go on burying his own undertakers, even as Whitman buried several generations of dismissive morticians.

Lawrence saw Whitman as possessing something of the aura that devout Mormons confer upon Brigham Young, the American Moses. Lawrence's more figurative Moses would have pleased Whitman:

> Whitman, the great poet, has meant so much to me. Whitman, the one man breaking a way ahead. Whitman, the one pioneer. And only Whitman. No English pioneers, no French. No European pioneer-poets. In Europe the would-be pioneers are mere innovators. The same in America. Ahead of Whitman, nothing. Ahead of all poets, pioneering into the wilderness of unopened life, Whitman. Beyond him, none.

Lawrence helped foster the American critical tradition of always rediscovering the actual Whitman, the great artist of delicacy, nuance, subtle evasiveness, hermetic difficulty, and, above all else, canonical originality. Whitman founded what is uniquely American in our imaginative literature, even if rival camps among us claim him as ancestor. Among poets I honor in my own generation, James Wright caught up one Whitman, John Ashbery quite another, A. R. Ammons still another, and there are doubtless more authentic Whitmans to come.

I remember one summer, in crisis, being at Nantucket with a friend who was absorbed in fishing, while I read aloud to both of us from Whitman and recovered myself again. When I am alone and read aloud to myself, it is almost always Whitman, sometimes when I desperately need to assuage grief. Whether you read aloud to someone else or in solitude, there is a peculiar appropriateness in chanting Whitman. He is the poet of our climate, never to be replaced, unlikely ever to be matched. Only a few poets in the language have surpassed "When Lilacs Last in the Dooryard Bloom'd": Shakespeare, Milton, perhaps one or two others. Whether even Shakespeare and Milton have achieved a more poignant pathos and a darker eloquence than Whitman's "Lilacs,"

I am not always certain. The great scene between the mad Lear and the blind Gloucester; the speeches of Satan after he has rallied his fallen legions—these epitomize the agonistic Sublime. And so does this, but with preternatural quietness:

> In the dooryard fronting an old farm-house near the
>   white-wash'd palings,
> Stands the lilac-bush tall-growing with heart-shaped leaves
>   of rich green,
> With many a pointed blossom rising delicate, with the per-
>   fume strong I love,
> With every leaf a miracle—and from this bush in the
>   dooryard,
> With delicate-color'd blossoms and heart-shaped leaves of
>   rich green,
> A sprig with its flower I break.

12.

Emily Dickinson:
Blanks, Transports, the Dark

If one borrowed the title of Eric Bentley's *The Playwright as Thinker* for a book to be called *The Poet as Thinker*, Emily Dickinson would have to be one of the volume's particular concerns. Except for Shakespeare, Dickinson manifests more cognitive originality than any other Western poet since Dante. Her nearest rival might be Blake, who also reconceptualized everything for himself. But Blake was a systematic mythmaker, and his system helps to organize his speculations. Dickinson rethought everything for herself, but she wrote lyrical meditations rather than stage dramas or mythopoeic epics. Shakespeare has hundreds of personae and Blake, dozens of what he called Giant Forms. Dickinson kept to the capital letter *I* while practicing an art of singular economy.

What her critics almost always underestimate is her startling intellectual complexity. No commonplace survives her appropriations; what she does not rename or redefine, she revises beyond easy recognition. Whitman sent his work to Emerson; Dickinson characteristically chose Thomas Wentworth Higginson, a brave man but no critic. He was baffled, but we differ from him only in degree; we too are baffled, not by her extraordinary eminence but by the power of her mind. I do not believe that any critic has been adequate to her intellectual demands, and I do not expect to be either. But I hope to establish further her surpassing cognitive originality and the consequent difficulty of her work, so as to help us see what is there in some of her strongest poems.

Strangeness, as I keep discovering, is one of the prime requirements for entrance into the Canon. Dickinson is as strange as Dante or Milton, who imposed their idiosyncratic visions upon us so that our scholars find them far more orthodox than they are. Dickinson is too sly to impose anything, but she is as individual a thinker as Dante. Her contemporary, Whitman, stays ahead of us by nuance and by metaphoric evasiveness. Dickinson waits for us, perpetually up the road from our tardiness, because very few of us can emulate her by rethinking everything through for ourselves.

About a decade ago, in a little book called *The Breaking of the Vessels,* I traced some of the fortunes of the metaphor of the blank in English and American poetry, from Milton through Wordsworth, Coleridge, Emerson, Whitman, and Stevens. I had thought of brooding on Dickinson's blanks as well, but I retreated before their formidable intensity. They figure in nine of her poems, all of them remarkable, but the one I like best is number 761, dated about 1863 when the poet was thirty-two:

> *From Blank to Blank—*
> *A Threadless Way*
> *I pushed Mechanic feet—*
> *To stop—or perish—or advance—*
> *Alike indifferent——*
>
> *If end I gained*
> *It ends beyond*
> *Indefinite disclosed—*
> *I shut my eyes—and groped as well*
> *'Twas lighter—to be Blind——*

To pack this much into forty-one words and ten lines ought not to be possible. This minute gnome of a lyric takes us all the way from Theseus, archetype of the ungrateful hero, who abandons the woman who gives him the thread to the labyrinth, to Milton, who dominates male poets' use of his metaphor of the universal blank that nature presented to his blindness. There is no Ariadne to give Dickinson the thread to find the way out, even if she surmises what she dreads to approach, presumably her own nightmare of a Minotaur, an emblem of male force, perhaps including male sexuality. The dread induces the indifference of hopelessness, the necessity to push mechanical feet as one goes threadlessly from blank to blank. Kafka's burrow is prophesied, and one remembers Paul Celan's fascination with Dickinson, which resulted in some remarkable translations. All of this is contained in the nineteen words of the first stanza; and there is more, for how can we confine the reverberations of "From Blank to Blank"?

The ruin or blank that we see in nature, Emerson had written, is in our own eye. His allusion was presumably to Coleridge's "Dejection" ode, where the protagonist gazes "with how blank an eye," a further allusion, as both Coleridge and Emerson knew, to Milton's lament for his blindness. "To be Blind" by choice is to give up seeing the Blank, which, in Dickinson as in her male precursors, is a figure for poetic crisis. Certainly, Stevens's incessant blanks are closer to Dickinson's than to Milton's or Coleridge's, and in Stevens the association with poetic crisis is incessant. If you glance back at the first stanza of "From Blank to Blank," its governing verb is past tense: "pushed." Where then is she now? The second stanza doesn't disclose the answer: "If end I gained / It ends beyond / Indefinite disclosed—." That is very tough writing and hard thinking. The movement from "gained" to the present tense of "ends" hints that she did gain an end, one that goes on ending beyond a revelation that remains indefinite.

The stubborn word is the transcendentalizing "beyond," which gives a different value tone to the conditional "end" and reminds us of the wordplay of "end" and "ends." An end that ends *beyond* whatever is already no end at all and prepares for the poem's resolute act that contrasts with pushing mechanical feet: "I shut my eyes." You are out of the ruin or labyrinth of nature when you cease to behold the blank, but your gain is equivocal: "and groped as well / 'Twas lighter."

Should that be read "and groped as well as if it were lighter"? Possibly, but only at the expense of an appalling irony, which broadens into the concluding phrase within dashes: "to be Blind." Is it lighter to be blind? Milton's lament in this metaphoric revision loses its heroic pathos, the pathos upon which Coleridge, Wordsworth, and Emerson founded their own tropes of the blank. All of Dickinson's quest poems have Kafkan, labyrinthine aspects: they are journeys to nowhere, rather like Stevens's beach wandering in *The Auroras of Autumn* and Whitman's in the *Sea-Drift* poems. That her "From Blank to Blank" poem empties out a certain tradition of the male poet's heroic pathos seems to me evident. Her blank *is* Milton, and/or Emerson, in a very Shakespearean meaning of blank: the bull's-eye or white spot at the center of the target, "the true blank of thine eye." That bull's-eye may have suggested Theseus and Ariadne's thread to the threadless Dickinson, but the sly chance of associating the classical (not the Shakespearean) Theseus with the patriarchal Milton may have been too good to miss. "From Blank to Blank" is then a movement from bull's-eye to bull's-eye, from Theseus to Milton, and Dickinson's tiny gnome carries a subtle menace indeed.

What I have outlined so far is an instance of an unnaming, rather like Ursula Le Guin's parable in which Eve unnames the beasts. Le Guin's title might have been Dickinson's, had Dickinson ever deigned to use a title: "She Unnames Them." If I could, I would use that as the title instead of *The Complete Poems of Emily Dickinson*. She never does stop unnaming them as she sublimely and outrageously unnames even the blanks. Emerson urged the poet to unname and rename. Whitman shrewdly evaded naming or unnaming. Dickinson was not much interested in renaming, since that comes after the reconceptualizing, which is so akin to unnaming. I am no more interested in making Dickinson into the Wittgenstein of Amherst than I am in seeing her as the precursor of Adrienne Rich and similar rebels against patriarchal poetic traditions. The mode Dickinson invented is very difficult to emulate and has not had much effect on our best women poets of this century: Marianne Moore, Elizabeth Bishop, May Swenson. Dickinson's influence can be more substantially traced in Hart Crane and Wallace Stevens, who inherited her passion for unnaming, throwing away the lights and the definitions, but who cannot match her intricate intellect.

The late Sir William Empson was thinking of Hart Crane when he said that poetry in our time had become a mug's game, an act of desperation virtually suicidal in its implications. Except for Kafka, I cannot think of any writer who has expressed desperation as powerfully and as constantly as Dickinson. We all sense that Kafka's desperation is primarily spiritual; Dickinson's seems essentially cognitive. She was Emersonian enough to exalt her own whim, and Miltonic enough to become a sect of one, in the manner though not the mode of William Blake. Her anguish is intellectual but not religious, and all attempts to read her as a devotional poet have crashed badly. The entity named "God" has a very rough career in her poetry and is treated with considerably less respect and understanding than the rival entity she names "Death." Dickinson fell in love with a clergyman or two, and with a judge, but she never wasted her affections on a lover who she said was too distant and too stately for her. A poet who addresses God as father only after first calling him burglar and banker is up to something other than piety.

Literary originality achieves scandalous dimensions in Dickinson, and its principal component is the way she thinks through her poems. She begins before she begins, by the implicit act of unnaming she performs upon the Miltonic-Coleridgean-Emersonian blank, with her hidden Shakespearean substitution. She next unpacks the trope by restoring its diachronic aspect; she knows implicitly more than we do about the temporal inadequacy of metaphor. Some of it she learned by reading Emerson, but more of it is her own; he did not manifest anything like her suspicion of the historical tyranny of metaphors for poetic immortality or for spiritual survival. And though she is High Romantic enough to seek what Stevens was to call an ever-early candor, her sense of her White Election was again more mistrustful of the cost of a reachieved earliness. If you are the major Western woman poet ever, you can afford to revere Mrs. Browning, who isn't actually capable of inhibiting you. Like Whitman, Dickinson is the most dangerous of direct influences. Whitman's truest followers are his most covert: the Eliot of *The Waste Land* and Stevens. Similarly, Dickinson's best effect is upon Elizabeth Bishop and May Swenson, who took care not to resemble her on the poetic surface. Her own obvious affinity is with Emerson's poetry, but her immediate precursors, like his, are the English High Romantics, and her underground affiliations are surprisingly Shakespearean. The immense legacy of the male tradition was a singular advantage for her, since she had an original relation to that literary cosmos. Feminist criticism, unable or unwilling to see that agon is the iron law of literature, continues to treat Dickinson as a comrade rather than as the rather forbidding figure she necessarily is.

THERE ARE GREAT poets one can read when one is exhausted or even distraught, because in the best sense they console. Wordsworth and Whitman are certainly among them. Dickinson demands so active a participation on the reader's part that one's mind had better be at its rare best. The various times I have taught her poems have left me with fierce headaches, since the difficulties force me past my limits. My late teacher, William K. Wimsatt, used to take grim pleasure in my accounts of my Dickinson seminars, which confirmed (he said) my status as a monument to what he had termed the Affective Fallacy. Certainly, Dickinson is a menace to anyone who believes that sublime literature is an invitation to what once was called "transport." Dickinson wickedly liked that word, whether as verb or as substantive. We can tell from her manuscripts that she regarded both "terror" and "rapture" as alternative words for "transport." In such a compounding of terror and rapture, she at first seems very much a throwback to a sensibility current a century before her, in the literary age of Sentimentalism and the Sublime. But her "transport" is something utterly different, indeed the difference that makes a difference of Emersonian pragmatism, as here in poem 1109, composed about 1867:

> *I fit for them—*
> *I seek the Dark*

Till I am thorough fit.
The labor is a sober one
With this sufficient sweet
That abstinence of mine produce
A purer food for them, if I succeed,
If not I had
The transport of the Aim——

Forty-five words in nine lines to break our heads upon, but I rarely get out of my mind Angus Fletcher's recasting of Shelley on the Sublime, which is that the Sublime persuades us to give up easier pleasures for more difficult and painful ones. Freud might not have been happy with that formulation, which appears to raise what he termed the "incitement premium" by sadomasochistic measures. The five words centering this strong, brief poem are the two "fits," and the triad of "Dark," "transport," and "Aim." The poem's crucial question is "Who are the Dark?" rather than "What is the Dark?"—a distinction I base upon "them" in "I fit for them," where "them" appears to be the antecedent for "the Dark." "The Dark" in Dickinson, as opposed to "Darkness," sometimes appear to be what you and I would call "the dead."

Most strong poets implicitly demand that we learn their language by reading all or nearly all of their poems. In Dickinson, the demand might as well be explicit, so I turn to poem 419, of about 1862:

We grow accustomed to the Dark—
When Light is put away—
As when the Neighbor holds the Lamp
To witness her Goodbye——

A Moment—We uncertain stop
For newness of the night—
Then—fit our Vision to the Dark—
And meet the Road—erect——

And so of larger—Darknesses—
Those Evenings of the Brain—

When not a Moon disclose a sign—
Or Star—come out—within——

The Bravest—grope a little—
And sometimes hit a Tree
Directly in the Forehead—
But as they learn to see——

Either the Darkness alters—
Or something in the sight
Adjusts itself to Midnight—
And Life steps almost straight.

The wonderful humor of the bravest hitting a tree, directly in the forehead, helps save the poem from too simplistic an allegory. I take it that the poem centers upon "fit our Vision to the Dark," which prophesies the poem of five years later, "I fit for them— / I seek the Dark / Till I am thorough fit." The earlier poem is about the surmounting of our fear of the dead and so of our own death, while the later "I fit for them—" starts somewhere far beyond trepidation. Making oneself fit for the dead, fitting oneself to the dark, comes about through sustained, highly deliberate meditation upon one's own dead. What follows begins to be very rugged thinking: what can Dickinson mean when she terms this meditation her abstinence, and says that if she is successful, a purer food will be produced for the dark, for her dead?

Unless one reads this occultly, we appear to have here an equivalent to what Freud called in a great figuration "the work of mourning." Dickinson anticipates Rilke and her translator Celan by associating a thorough fitting of mourner to mourned with the purer food that replaces the less fitting food of a mourning that becomes melancholia. Despite her poem's superb confidence, Dickinson warily adds "if I succeed." What remains is a consolation that is a fierce irony: "If not I had / the transport of the Aim." That hollows out "transport" by suggesting that it is a synecdoche for failure in the discipline of mourning, and relates it to what the earlier poem, "We grow accustomed to the Dark—" gives as the easier alternative of the darkness altering, rather than the adjustment of one's sight to Midnight, the proper achievement of growing accustomed to the Dark, to one's own dead.

Dickinson was no worshiper of Midnight, as Yeats was to be. When Yeats wrote that at the stroke of midnight God will win, he meant death would triumph, God and death being near equivalents in Yeats's variety of Gnostic vision. Neither God nor death wins in Dickinson, and she takes care to keep them apart. She wanted poetry, "this loved Philology," to win, and so her poetry eventually has won, in the strictly limited way that moves in a continuous tradition from Petrarch to the present. Her Petrarchan Lauras are surmised by different scholars to have been different men, and her internalized passion for them, whatever relation it had to reality, certainly rewarded her with metaphors for poetry.

Here is another of her incredibly brief lyrics of transport, the blank, and dying, thirty-six words in eight short lines, poem 1153, perhaps written in 1874, a dozen years before her own death:

> *Through what transports of Patience*
> *I reached the stolid Bliss*
> *To breathe my Blank without thee*
> *Attest me this and this——*
>
> *By that bleak exultation*
> *I won as near as this*
> *Thy privilege of dying*
> *Abbreviate me this——*

Unpacking the ironies here is a bleak exultation in itself. "Transports of Patience" is oxymoronic even for Dickinson, who tends to follow Keats in being addicted to a rhetoric of seeming contradictions. Jane Austen would have admired "transports of Patience" as being her kind of irony. "Stolid Bliss" is even better as a preparation for the grim process of breathing one's Blank, which transfers the ruin we confront in nature to vitality itself, rather than to the Emersonian bodily eye. From that point on it is all difficulty, centering on the fourfold "this." The poem turns upon the contrast between its fourth and eighth lines, "Attest me this and this—" playing off against "Abbreviate me this."

It is the dead beloved (or perhaps lover) who is called upon to attest and to abbreviate. Paraphrase of Dickinson is dangerous but sometimes useful, and I will attempt one here. Bereft and sick unto death of mere survival, the poet ironically reverses all her hard-won victories of endurance and stoicism in regard to her several losses. Ecstasy has dwindled into patience; contentment has become stolid; to breathe is to accept a ruined vision. Going on without the lost one is an achievement in attestation by the deed, which is the first "this." The second "this" gathers up the state wonderfully termed "bleak exultation," a Shakespearean condition akin to what we might feel at the end of Hamlet's death scene. With the third "this" ("as near as this") we reach the poem's present moment and move to its one positive oxymoron, "The privilege of dying." The final "this" is life's remnant, a death-in-life. "Abbreviate me this" is neither prayer nor request, but an assertion of merit, a movement toward what has been earned, release from the despair of living on. Is there a more distinguished brief lyric of profound despair in the language, British or American?

What do "transports," "blanks," and "the dark" have in common for Dickinson? She is not her nation's first post-Christian poet; that would have to be Emerson. And she certainly gets slantwise at her highly original spiritual stance, unlike Whitman, who seems direct in this, and in this alone. But she had the best mind of all our poets, early and late, and she illuminates the American religion as no other writer does. The aesthetic equivalent of our national blend of Orphism, Enthusiasm, and Gnosticism is originality, and not even Emerson thought through originality as subtly as Dickinson did. She wanted originality even in her mode of despair, and she achieved it. For her, despair is also an ecstasy or transport, and blanks cannot be distinguished from the dark, not because of blindness but because she powerfully distrusts whatever can be categorized as a feeling. Love, she knows, is not a feeling, while pain is altogether a feeling. Somewhere there is a Wittgensteinian aphorism that is pure Dickinson:

Love is not a feeling. Love, unlike pain, is put to the test. One does not say: "That was not a true pain because it passed away so quickly."

Whatever Dickinson's psychosexual preferences may have been, she did not have a taste for pain as such, because she had thought her way to the other side of feeling. Despair, for her, is not a feeling; like love, despair is put to the test. Her most original poems frequently constitute that test and are rightly among her most famous, as in poem 258:

> *There's a certain Slant of light,*
> *Winter Afternoons—*
> *That oppresses, like the Heft*
> *Of Cathedral Tunes——*
>
> *Heavenly Hurt, it gives us—*
> *We can find no scar,*
> *But internal difference,*
> *Where the Meanings, are——*
>
> *None may teach it—Any—*
> *'Tis the Seal Despair—*
> *An Imperial affliction*
> *Sent us of the Air——*
>
> *When it comes, the Landscape listens—*
> *Shadows—hold their breath—*
> *When it goes, 'tis like the Distance*
> *On the look of Death——*

I surmise that, for Dickinson, transports were as much affairs of the light as were blanks and the dark. Her best biographer, Richard Sewall, remarks in a fine understatement that "she was something of a specialist on light" and quotes her charming condescension to her precursor Wordsworth, in a letter of March 1866, about five years after the great "Slant of Light" lyric:

February passed like a Skate and I know March. Here is the "light" the Stranger said "was not on land or sea." Myself could arrest it but we'll not chagrin Him.

Wordsworth is the Stranger because Dickinson identified him with Coleridge's expectation of a desired stranger in "Frost at Midnight." Both nature and consciousness are famously alluded to as Strangers in Dickinson's poetry, and the composite form of the master or male precursor is sometimes addressed by her as Stranger. When Wordsworth, in the "Elegiac Stanzas" on Peele Castle, sadly recanted and wrote that the visionary light never was on land or sea but was rather only the poet's dream, he had not the benefit of observing the final stages of a New England winter, "when afternoons return," to cite Wallace Stevens's rewriting of Dickinson's "certain slant of light" in his revisionary "The Poems of Our Climate."

"What is there here except the weather?"—a grand Stevensian question—is answered proleptically (as Stevens knew) in Dickinson's superb lyric of despair. Her poem is a transport of negations, sublimely catching the blank of blanks in a bull's-eye of vision, an oxymoronic "Heavenly Hurt" or "imperial affliction." The substantives are "Hurt" and "affliction"; the light conveys the pain of despair, and yet the modifiers, "Heavenly" and "imperial," suggest that the light ought to be welcomed, that it conveys something admirable. To be oppressed by the Heft of Cathedral Tunes is after all a peculiar mode of oppression, available only to an aroused and heightened sensibility. Emersonian pragmatist that she was, Dickinson discovered the "internal difference" that does make a difference, an alternation of meanings beyond the possibility of further instruction.

The particular slant of light, "certain" in a double sense, is identified as the "Seal Despair," not one of the seven Seals of Revelation, but something closer to an inversion of the erotic seal set upon the heart in the *Song of Songs:*

Set me as a seal upon thine heart, as a seal upon thine arm: for love is strong as death; jealousy is cruel as the grave; the coals thereof are coals of fire, which hath a most vehement flame.

Dickinson finds no scar, yet a seal has been set upon her. The despair, as so often in her strongest poems, is overtly ontological but covertly erotic, and the particular slant of light intimates a melancholia of loss. This is part of the hidden meaning of the unmentioned "in between," as it were, of the final stanza, where we are told about the coming and going of the slant of light, while the brief interval in which the slant prevails is evaded. The listening landscape and breath-holding shadows are among Dickinson's finest figurations, but her ellipsis is finer still. We have been given the effect of the light throughout the poem, but no description of the light itself except that it comes down at a certain slant. Every word is a bias or inclination, Nietzsche said, and so every word, as a prejudgment, is already a slant, even as all truth should be told slant, according to Dickinson. The word slant is thus a word of words, and by using it Dickinson makes it another metaphor for her despair.

I do not think that the standard interpretation of this poem is at all Dickinsonian; the poem hardly concerns the fear of mortality. What the slant of light adds to her "internal difference" is quite another apprehension, one that involves further erotic loss, which will set another seal upon her heart. Even the most negative or blank of transports in Dickinson is still part of the American Sublime, still a celebration of the uncanniness of a self that is no part of nature. And I take it that her slant of light is also no part of nature. It is a synecdoche for a particular slant in Dickinson's own consciousness. Blake says that we become what we behold, but Dickinson is close to Emerson, who says that which we are, that only can we see. What oppresses Dickinson is not wholly external to her; the imperial affliction is to some degree already hers, as is the heaven of the hurt. Her consciousness, rarely passive, is subtly represented in this poem as answering the wintry light with an auxiliary gleam. Against the Stranger, Wordsworth, she rightly asserted that she had arrested his light that never was, on land or sea.

The most mysterious element in the "Slant of light" poem is its deferral of meaning, a deferral enhanced well beyond Dickinson's already extreme general praxis. In a lyric of "internal difference," a hush follows the light and constitutes its deepest significance. A year later, in poem 627, she achieved her greatest work while developing a similar insight. Except for Whitman's "Lilacs," this seems to me the height of American poetry and, with Whitman's poem, the authentic American Sublime:

> The Tint I cannot take—is best—
> The Color too remote
> That I could show it in Bazaar—
> A Guinea at a sight——
>
> The fine—impalpable Array—
> That swaggers on the eye
> Like Cleopatra's Company—
> Repeated—in the sky——
>
> The Moments of Dominion
> That happen on the Soul
> And leave it with a Discontent
> Too exquisite—to tell——
>
> The eager look—on Landscapes—
> As if they just repressed
> Some Secret—that was pushing
> Like Chariots—in the Vest——
>
> The Pleading of the Summer—
> That other Prank—of Snow—
> That Cushions Mystery with Tulle,
> For fear the Squirrels—know,
>
> Their Graspless manners—mock us—
> Until the cheated Eye
> Shuts arrogantly—in the Grave—
> Another way—to see——

There, packed together, we have her poetics, at once Emersonian and counter-Emersonian, a new and wholly personal Self-Reliance and a grand unnaming, an act of negation as dialectical and profound as any essayed by Nietzsche or Freud. Dickinson's "Tint I cannot take" poem knows, as no other poem in her century knows, that we are always besieged by perspectives. Dickinson's entire art at its outer limits, as in this poem, is to think and write her way out of that siege. Yet she knows that we are governed by the contingency of living within the primordial poem of our precursors' perspectives. Nietzsche's *Will to Power* aphorisms, written a generation after Dickinson's major phase, can be read as comments on "The Tint I cannot take—is best." Here is a cento from section 1046 (circa 1884) of *The Will to Power:*

> *We want to hold fast to our senses and to our faith in them*
>   *—and think their consequences through to the end!*
> *The existing world, upon which all earthly living things have*
>   *worked so that it appears as it does (durable and changing*
>   *slowly), we want to go on building—and not criticize it*
>   *away as false!*
> *Our valuations are a part of this building; they emphasize*
>   *and underline.*
> *One must understand the artistic basic phenomenon that is*
>   *called "life"——*
>   *(translated by Walter Kaufmann and R. J. Hollingsdale)*

Nietzsche proposes a double stance, which Emerson and Dickinson had already fulfilled. We need simultaneously to recognize the contingency of our own perceptions, and yet find a new direction for those perceptions, as though no one had perceived and described them before us.

The entire emphasis of Dickinson's "Tint" poem is on what cannot be taken, an ungraspable secret, a trope or metaphor not to be expressed. The famous closing line, "another way—to see——" has been weakly misread by feminist critics as a gendered alternative of vision. But this is a very difficult poem, as tough as it is distinguished, and it will yield only to preternaturally close reading, not to ideology or polemical zeal, however benign in social purpose. We confront, at the height of her powers, the best mind to appear among Western poets in nearly four centuries. Whatever our own policies or purposes, we must be very wary not to confuse our stances with hers. Emerson, Nietzsche, and Rorty alert us to the bewilderments of perspectivism, while Dickinson, in doing the same, also has the poetic strength to hint at a beyond, another way to bring selfhood and the contingencies of canonical tradition into a dialectical relation.

In 1862, when Dickinson was thirty-one, she began her correspondence with the benign if baffled Thomas Wentworth Higginson, a hero in both peace and war but not exactly an Emerson in intellect. Higginson was one of Dickinson's handful of reachings out for an audience but, like the others, he represented a highly qualified quest on her part. He provided still another confirmation that the tint or color she aspired to was so remote that showing it in the bazaar of publication was absurd. Yet her first stanza is no boast; the prime emphasis is not on the bazaar but on the limits of her art, on what she would catch or take, but cannot. Four tropes (or colors) are offered successively to adumbrate "the Tint I cannot take": a skyscape, a discontent resulting from the soul's experience of dominion, a certain light or "eager look" on landscape, the seasons' difference of summer and winter. All four take the Tint as antecedent, but they are more subtly allied or unified by a mounting urgency of representation, the need to portray the negativity of what "I cannot take" even as the recognition of a presence is vividly intimated.

This fourfold of Sublime negations begins with the swaggering finery of Cleopatra's company of courtiers, repeated via a Keatsian finer tone in an "impalpable Array," visible in the sky. "Impalpable" is not a very Dickinsonian word; she uses it only one other time in all her 1,775 poems and fragments, when she observes that "affliction feels impalpable / Until Ourselves are struck—" (poem 799). Perhaps what she cannot take, and so cannot render, has not struck her, so that the tint or array seems purely visionary even when actually seen. This would be consonant with the next stanza, where "the Moments of Dominion . . . happen *on* the Soul" (emphasis mine), rather than in it, or by it.

When the transition is made to landscape, we are placed even more in the realm of the impalpable:

> *The eager look—on Landscapes—*
> *As if they just repressed*

> *Some Secret—that was pushing*
> *Like Chariots—in the Vest*

What is palpable is the charm, in all senses of that word. "Repressed" enters only here in all of Dickinson's poetry, and in our post-Freudian age we need to remember the word's older meaning, which has to do with voluntary rather than involuntary concealment or forgetfulness. The eager Landscapes, humanized to a degree unusual for Dickinson, can barely hold in their secret, presumably manifested in some slant of light. That secret is partly elucidated in the next stanza, the poem's penultimate revelation:

> *The Pleading of the Summer—*
> *That other Prank—of Snow—*
> *That Cushions Mystery with Tulle,*
> *For fear the Squirrels—know.*

The snow is a veil or gown of tulle, starched white silk; but what is the mystery that it cushions or conceals, what is the secret? What does the summer plead, only to have the winter reveal that even a season's pleading is only another prank? Pleading, playing pranks, cushioning, are all evasions instigated by a humanized and perspectivized nature's suspicion that the squirrels know the secret, have penetrated the mystery. Yet the squirrels themselves are the poem's most mysterious component. How are we to read the startling line that says of them, "Their Graspless manners—mock us—"?

In the great, still undated poem 1733, there is perhaps a clue:

> *No man saw awe, nor to his house*
> *Admitted he a man*
> *Though by his awful residence*
> *Has human nature been.*
>
> *Not deeming of his dread abode*
> *Till laboring to flee*
> *A grasp on comprehension laid*
> *Detained vitality.*

Awe is Jehovah (or perhaps even the beloved Judge Lord), and his awful, dread house is presumably eternity, not to be entered without yielding up vitality to death. The grasp laid on comprehension is a knowing defense against the reality principle, or what Freud called making friends with the necessity of dying. When the squirrels' manners are termed "Graspless," and are said to mock us, it may mean that no grasp has been laid on their comprehension of reality testing, unlike our own. We go on being mocked by them:

> *Until the Cheated Eye*
> *Shuts arrogantly—in the Grave—*
> *Another way—to see*

The eye of each of us has been cheated because a grasp has been laid upon our comprehension, and the eye shuts arrogantly in the false expectation that it will open again, wherever. What is "another way—to see," in the context of the Grave? Unless the final line is pure, harsh irony, and I do not think it is, we are returned to the perspectivism that Dickinson learned from Emerson and then developed beyond that learning into her own negative poetics. Her new perspectivism is another way to see because it sees what cannot be seen, the forces that propel landscapes and seasons into human meanings. Hers is not the cheated eye, because she has forsaken plunder or appropriation for herself. What she cannot take is indeed best, and the consequent receptivity of her will compensates her with a unique power of unnaming.

The will to power in Emerson and in Nietzsche is also receptive, but its reaction is interpretation, so that, in them, every word becomes an interpretation either of the human or of nature. Dickinson's way, whether to see or to will, favors questioning over interpretation and intimates a kind of othering, both of human stance and of natural processes. Her originality is unmatched even by the strength of her poetic descendants: Wallace Stevens, Hart Crane, Elizabeth Bishop. Her canonicity results from her achieved strangeness, her uncanny relation to the tradition. Even more, it ensues from her cognitive strength and rhetorical agility, not from her gender or from any gender-derived ideology. Her unique transport, her Sublime, is founded upon her unnaming of all our certitudes into so many blanks; and it gives her, and her authentic readers, another way to see, almost into the dark.

13.

The Canonical Novel:
Dickens's *Bleak House,*
George Eliot's *Middlemarch*

IT MAY BE that the new Theocratic Age of the twenty-first century, whether Christian or Muslim or both or neither, will amalgamate with the Computer Era, already upon us in early versions of "virtual reality" and "the hypertext." Combined with universal television and the University of Resentment (already well along in consolidation) into one rough beast, this future would cancel the literary canon once and for all. The novel, the poem, and the play might all be replaced. This brief chapter is a nostalgic confrontation with the canonical novel at its strongest. The novel, child of the now-archaic genre of romance, itself became archaic after its ultimate limits were touched in Joyce, Proust, Kafka, Woolf, Mann, Lawrence, Faulkner, Beckett, and the South American heirs of Sterne and Faulkner. At its most flourishing, in the Democratic Age, the novel's masters were astonishingly numerous: Austen, Scott, Dickens, Eliot, Stendhal, Hugo, Balzac, Manzoni, Tolstoy, Turgenev, Goncharov, Dostoevsky, Zola, Flaubert, Hawthorne, Melville, James, Hardy, with an epilogue in Conrad. After Conrad, the shadow of the object fell across the ego, and narrative prose fiction entered the era that is closing now.

No nineteenth-century novelist, not even Tolstoy, was stronger than Dickens, whose wealth of invention almost rivals Chaucer and Shakespeare. *Bleak House,* most critics now tend to agree, is his central work; Dickens had enormous affection for *David Copperfield,* but this was his Portrait of the Artist as a Young Man. The Dickens cosmos, his phantasmagoric London and visionary England, emerges in *Bleak House* with a clarity and pungency that surpasses the rest of his work, before and after. No other novel in English invents so much, though perhaps more in the mode of Ben Jonson than of Shakespeare. A Dickens protagonist frequently cannot change and tends to be diminished by action, observations in which I follow G. K. Chesterton, my favorite critic of Dickens, as he is also of Chaucer and of Browning. We do not expect Uriah Heep and Pecksniff and Squeers to change any more than we could confront mutations of consciousness in Volpone or Sir Epicure Mammon. But Esther Summerson certainly does keep changing; in his subtle creation of her first-person narrative as of her character and personality, Dickens is often underestimated.

I must admit that each time I reread the novel, I tend to cry whenever Esther Summerson cries, and I don't think I am being sentimental. The reader must identify with her or simply not read the book in the old-fashioned sense of reading, which is the only sense that matters. We are, insofar as we are traumatized, versions of Esther; like her, we "recollect forwards." Esther weeps at every mark of kindness and love that she encounters; at our best, when we are not caught in death in life, we are tempted to weep also. Trauma recollects forward; every remission from it brings on tears of relief and joy.

Esther's trauma is universal because it derives from the burden of parentlessness, and sooner or later we are all condemned to be without living parents. Feminist critics have been exercised by the notion that Esther is the victim of a patrilinear society, and they tend not to admire John Jarndyce, much against Dickens's entire art of representation. Dickens, as a great literary artist, is no more patriarchal than Shakespeare, and the creator of Rosalind and

Cleopatra does not seem to me ideologically patriarchal. Whatever ideology Shakespeare the man had we do not know. Dickens the husband, father, and prophet of household wisdom certainly was an ideologue of patriarchy, which John Stuart Mill properly resented; but the creator of Esther Summerson, the novelist Dickens, is no ideologue. Esther, who cannot stop deprecating herself, is one of the most intelligent characters in the history of the novel and seems to me a much more authentic portrait of essential elements in Dickens's spirit than David Copperfield ever is. Dickens would never have said what Flaubert said of his relation to Emma Bovary; how odd it would be if he had confessed, "I am Esther Summerson." I suggest, however, that he is.

Esther is the unifying figure in *Bleak House*'s double plot; only she brings together the Kafkan labyrinth of Chancery and the tragedy of her mother, Lady Dedlock. Her link to Chancery is not the fall of Richard Carstone and his marriage to Ada, but rather the negation of Chancery by her guardian John Jarndyce, a negation in which she participates. The prime function of John Jarndyce in *Bleak House* is not that he be the most amiable and ultimately selfless of patriarchs (and he is), but that his absolute dismissal of Chancery be maintained consistently, so as to prove that a labyrinth made by man can be dissolved by man. One of the blessings of Dickens's powerful influence upon Kafka is the altogether Borgesian impact of Kafka upon our understanding of Dickens. Chancery, like the Trial and the Castle in Kafka, is a Gnostic vision: the Law has been usurped by the Cosmocrator, the Demiurge. Blake had no effect upon Dickens, yet *Bleak House* reads like a very Blakean book thanks to a shared Gnostic perspective, though Dickens's heretical impulse is anything but conscious. Chancery in *Bleak House* cannot be reformed; it is burned up only when you cease to behold it, as John Jarndyce and Esther refuse to behold it. That seems to be the apocalyptic meaning of poor Mr. Krook's spontaneous combustion, the most notorious weirdness of *Bleak House* (though there are many others, all to the enhancement of a novel that is also a fantasy-romance). Mad but rather kind, Krook goes up like a bonfire because of his self-admitted symbolic identity with the Lord Chancellor.

Esther Summerson has always divided critics, from Dickens's

day until ours; I don't think she has divided common readers, or critics who have remained intuitive readers. *Bleak House*'s rhetorical ironies are mostly crowded into the anonymous narrator's chapters. Dickens excludes overt irony from Esther's narrative until she is strong and healed enough to make her own ironical judgments, as she finally does against Skimpole and others. She seems less Dickens's experiment in representing selflessness or even trauma than she is his one extended attempt, necessarily Shakespearean, at depicting psychological change. In some ways Dickens creates her against the grain of his own genius, as he perhaps realized. Although phantasmagoria overwhelms her in her mysterious illness and its aftermath, she is less of the Dickens world than her parents are, since both Nemo and Lady Dedlock emerge from the characteristic turbulence of Dickensian drives. Esther stands apart, so different from Dickens's flamboyance that he sometimes seems lovingly in awe of her. She is his contribution to the British tradition of heroines of the Protestant will, descended from Clarissa Harlowe and concluding in Lawrence's women in love, Ursula and Gudrun Brangwen; in Forster's sisters, Margaret and Helen in *Howard's End;* and in Woolf's Lily Briscoe in *To the Lighthouse.*

Esther seems less solitary when we contrast her with *Middlemarch*'s Dorothea Brooke or with Hardy's Marty South in *The Woodlanders.* A selfless will is very nearly an oxymoron, but Esther is in her way a formidable rhetorician, and her characteristic mode is understatement. She is a survivor, and her mildness is a defense against trauma. Her entire personality is a highly purposeful mechanism for outlasting trauma and resisting the maniac society that attributes guilt to illegitimacy. Although she never wastes energy by fighting back against her society, she never once yields to its obscene moral judgments, even when she is a little girl compelled to endure her godmother's tirades about her perpetual shame. Even the child Esther knows that she is innocent and that her salvation from societal madness depends on her own moral intelligence and her preternatural capacity for patience. Her overt rhetoric of self-deprecation is a powerful defense against not only an abominable system but, more crucially, against her own traumatization, of which she is deeply aware. "Silence, exile, cunning"—the only weapons that Joyce's Stephen would allow himself—Joyce derived not from David Copperfield but from Esther Summerson, who in her oceanic passivity remains the most formidable consciousness in all of Dickens, indeed in all of British literature of the Democratic Age.

Disliking Esther is an easy option for the "materialist" critics of the School of Resentment. Esther is not exactly a feminist ideal or a Marxist exemplar of rebellion. Their heroine in *Bleak House* should be the splendid Hortense, a forerunner of the even more superb Madame DuFarge of *A Tale of Two Cities*, written seven years later. Hortense, like the still fiercer Madame DuFarge, stimulates Dickens's and the reader's masochism but is overmatched by the healthily resistant Inspector Bucket, the most curious of surprising Dickensian visionaries. Expressionistic, impatient, talkative, and murderous, the attractive Hortense is not a surrogate for Lady Dedlock (as feminist critics assert) but a foil for Esther, highlighting her quietude and her Wordsworthian wise passivity.

Is Esther the victim of a patriarchal society? Her trauma is far too individual to ascribe to the greater stigma attached to an illegitimate girl as opposed to a bastard boy. Nor do I consider her stubborn patience a failure in self-esteem. Here again, in a Borgesian way, Kafka aids the interpretation of *Bleak House,* because he is the master of what I would call canonical patience. For Kafka the only sin is impatience, and there is something awesomely Kafkan about Esther Summerson, by which I mean Franz Kafka the person, rather than his characters or his fictive cosmos. Kafka's personal trauma is strikingly parallel to Esther's (and to Kierkegaard's). All three are adept at Kierkegaardian forward recollection. It is almost as though Esther Summerson had awaited, from her birth onward, the appearance of the strong, benign father, John Jarndyce, as compelling a figure as Dickens creates in *Bleak House,* except for Esther herself. Esther essentially being Dickens, or what Walt Whitman would have called Dickens's "real me" or "me myself," John Jarndyce is the idealized father Dickens longed for, rather than his Micawber-like actual father.

In these days, critics of the newer persuasions mutter darkly that Dickens never tells us the source of Jarndyce's clearly substantial income. That is to mistake the nature of *Bleak House* and to forget that it is as much fantasy-romance as social novel. The benign Jarndyce belongs to romance; perhaps little elves labor for him in a happy valley somewhere, minting faery gold. His names for Esther all point toward making her the little old woman, Dame Durden or Cobweb or whoever, of faery tales, and his careful love for her is almost as maternal as paternal. But mixed with this mother-father of romance there is the pathos of wasted life, of a great refusal doubtless allied to Jarndyce's total aversion to the labyrinth of Chancery. Dickens does not intimate what it was that displaced this fountain of benignity into early retirement at Bleak House.

It is worth noting that most of the important figures in *Bleak House* are based upon prototypes: Skimpole notoriously upon the Romantic essayist Leigh Hunt; Boythorn upon the poet Walter Savage Landor; Bucket upon a noted London police inspector; Hortense upon the Belgian murderess Maria Manning, whose public execution both Dickens and Melville attended. Mrs. Jellyby, Miss Flute, poor Jo, and others all have their models, while Esther herself certainly appears to be very like Dickens's favorite sister-in-law, Georgina Hogarth, who ran his household. Sir Leicester Dedlock has been traced to the sixth duke of Devonshire, while Lady Dedlock, like John Jarndyce, is pure invention. Something of Dickens, perhaps whatever does not become part of Esther, finds expression in Jarndyce; but what matters most in Esther's guardian belongs to romance, as Lady Dedlock does altogether. Jarndyce flees from gratitude, not out of any self-destructiveness but because it is not a romance virtue. Lady Dedlock's flight into death is a pure romance narrative, a parabolic punishment of female transgressiveness by a male society. If there is expiation, it is not for having mothered an illegitimate daughter, but for having abandoned the child to others and to much initial lovelessness.

That, again, is closer to romance and has little to do with patriarchal politics. Dickens's largest decision against romance in the novel is when he breaks the pattern of renunciation by having Jarndyce realize that his true responsibility to Esther is paternal. In marrying Woodcourt rather than Jarndyce, Esther is freed of over-determination: she will not repeat her mother's story. Her trauma is not wholly lifted from her, the haunting continues, and yet we feel that she will never again be persuaded by her own self-negations. It is astonishing how much of her consciousness Dickens is able to make available to us.

Jarndyce is another matter, and if we are left in relative darkness, we understand that much of Jarndyce is not available to Jarndyce, let alone to Dickens. Jarndyce was never truly in search of a wife, whatever he may have thought about it, but of two daughters and a son. He loses the son, Rick, to the madness induced by Chancery, and he ends with Ada returned to him and Esther close by. The puzzle left unexplained is why he ever dreamed of marrying Esther, since he is not a sexual being, and she (like her mother) decidedly is. Perhaps his authentic anxiety was that she would turn into Lady Dedlock and thus despair, but their dwelling together at Bleak House must have cured him of that fear.

The truth may be quite simple; he is not as strong as Esther, as he must see, and he fights loneliness, the spirit of solitude that torments the romance world, by active benevolence. No reader of the novel would believe that Jarndyce lusts after Esther; if the projected marriage can be called semi-incestuous, it must be from her perspective, not from his. Neither Dickens nor the reader wants the marriage, and at last we come to see that neither Esther nor Jarndyce much wanted it either.

The puzzle involved is larger than *Bleak House;* the question of the will in Dickens seems to me to account for much of the strangeness and the fascination of his fictive world. In George Eliot, the reader encounters a moral clarity that may be unmatchable in fiction of such distinction, but the self stands clear. The teeming turbulence of Dickens's stage exalts the drive above the will and makes us wonder at times if there are not separate kinds of wills in Dickens's characters. In Shakespeare, as in what we have agreed to call reality, human wills differ from one another in degree but scarcely in kind. In Dickens the really mean persons have one sort of will, the great grotesques another, and the more amiable a third variety. Although critics usefully regard Jonson and Molière as Dickens's precursors, and Jonson in particular shares the enormous Dickensian gusto, Dickens did not become a dramatist. His stage plays did not answer his expectations; as a one-man show, acting all of the parts in his own novels, he was overwhelming, and his enormous expenditure of energy in these performances before adoring and enormous audiences undoubtedly helped to kill him at the age of fifty-eight.

Although Dostoevsky and Kafka frequently shadow him, Dickens has no true heir in his own language. How can you achieve again an art in which fairy tales are told as though they were sagas of social realism? Northrop Frye found the Dickensian center in the novels' insistence that what ought to be never be annihilated by the prevailing state of things. Critics who quarrel with the happy conclusion of *Bleak House* always seem out of court: Mr. Pickwick remains the archetypal Dickens character, and Dickens's most sublime moment may well be the recitation, in *Pickwick Papers,* by Mrs. Leo Hunter of her own "Ode to an Expiring Frog." *Bleak House* has several sublime epiphanies, as befits Dickens's most powerful work, including one double moment when the two narrative strands of the book come together in Lady Dedlock's flight. The narrator's chapter 56 ends with Inspector Bucket experiencing a vision:

> There, he mounts a high tower in his mind, and looks out far and wide. Many solitary figures he perceives, creeping through the streets; many solitary figures out on heaths, and roads, and lying under haystacks. But the figure that he seeks is not among them. Other solitaries he perceives, in nooks of bridges, looking over; and in shadowed places down by the river's level; and a dark, dark, shapeless object drifting with the tide, more solitary than all, clings with a drowning hold on his attention.
>
> Where is she? Living or dead, where is she? If, as he folds the handkerchief and carefully puts it up, it were able, with an enchanted power, to bring before him the place where she found it, and the night landscape near the cottage where it covered the little child, would he descry her there? On the waste, where the brick-kilns are burning with a pale blue flare; where the straw-roofs of the wretched huts in which the bricks are made, are being scattered by the wind; where the clay and water are hard frozen, and the mill in which the gaunt blind horse goes round all day, looks like an instrument of human torture;— traversing this deserted blighted spot, there is a lonely figure

with the sad world to itself, pelted by the snow and driven by the wind, and cast out, it would seem, from all companionship. It is the figure of a woman, too; but it is miserably dressed, and no such clothes ever came through the hall, and out at the great door, of the Dedlock mansion.

Bucket here is clearly Dickens's representative, and what he sees is the truth: the impending self-destruction of Lady Dedlock. This vision yields to a nightmare image, strikingly akin to Browning's "Childe Roland to the Dark Tower Came," written in 1852, the same year that *Bleak House* was begun, although it was not published until 1855. It is unlikely that Dickens had seen the poem when he recorded Bucket's vision, but not impossible, since John Forster sometimes lent Browning manuscripts to Dickens. But the analogue is more interesting here than any direct influence might be. Exact contemporaries (each born in 1812), Browning and Dickens composed parallel visions in their fortieth year. Bucket beholds: "where . . . the mill in which the gaunt blind horse goes round all day, looks like an instrument of human torture" while Browning's quester regards first "One stiff blind horse, his every bone a-stare, / Stood stupefied, however he came there." And then, after that red gaunt horse, he sees an infernal instrument, akin to Dickens's "instrument of human torture":

> And more than that—a furlong on—why, there!
>   What bad use was that engine for, that wheel,
>   Or brake, not wheel—that harrow fit to reel
> Men's bodies out like silk? with all the air
> Of Tophet's tool, on earth left unaware,
>   Or brought to sharpen its rusty teeth of steel.

Browning and Dickens are the two great English masters of the grotesque, but this is the only point where they come so close to each other. This visionary mode, common to both, has the nightmare of mortality dominant here, perhaps because they both touch meridian and become middle-aged. Esther Summerson's vision, the chapter after Bucket's, begins when she accompanies Bucket in his vain pursuit to save her fleeing mother:

The transparent windows with the fire and light, looking so bright and warm from the cold darkness out of doors, were soon gone, and again we were crushing and churning the loose snow. We went on with toil enough; but the dismal roads were not much worse than they had been, and the stage was only nine miles. My companion smoking on the box—I had thought at the last inn of begging him to do so, when I saw him standing at a great fire in a comfortable cloud of tobacco—was as vigilant as ever; and as quickly down and up again, when we came to any human abode or any human creature. He had lighted his little dark lantern, which seemed to be a favourite with him, for we had lamps to the carriage; and every now and then he turned it upon me, to see that I was doing well. There was a folding-window to the carriage-head, but I never closed it, for it seemed like shutting out hope.

The "crushing and churning" represent the breaking of a repressive shield, allowing Esther to acknowledge her mother more fully and leading on to another Browning-like vision of the demonic water mill: "We were again upon the melancholy road by which we had come; tearing up the miry sleet and thawing snow, as if they were torn up by a waterwheel." But where Browning and Inspector Bucket see an instrument of torture, Esther Summerson sees a return of the repressed, tearing up the barrier that trauma has imposed upon her. Here, as at so many crisis points in his fiction, Dickens's imagery is uncannily profound, accurate, suggestive. There is an occult rightness to his boldest imaginings. The same doubtless could be said of Edgar Allan Poe, who sometimes seems a ghostly presence in *Bleak House;* but Poe's phantasmagoria rarely found language adequate to its intensities. Dickens's diction and metaphors are a seemingly inevitable match for his inventiveness, and the canonical strangeness of *Bleak House* thereby triumphs.

THE EXPERIENCE OF reading *Middlemarch* has almost nothing in common with an immersion in the Dickens world, where "reading" sometimes seems too traditional a term for the total yielding that *Bleak House* invites. Between Shakespeare and Dickens only Byron had anything like the immediate public that Dickens enjoyed by the time that he was twenty-five. The novelist's lifelong popularity differs in kind as well as in degree from that of all other writers, including Goethe and Tolstoy, who did not have a universal effect on all social classes in so many nations. It may be that Dickens, more than Cervantes, is Shakespeare's only rival as a worldwide influence and so represents, with Shakespeare, the Bible, and the Koran, the authentic multiculturalism already available to us.

That Shakespeare should be a kind of Bible for secularists is not surprising; it is more startling to realize that Dickens, translated and read everywhere, has also become something close to a cosmic mythology. His canonical largeness transcends the genre of prose fiction, even as Shakespeare, stageable and staged everywhere, cannot be confined to the theater. In that sense, Dickens by himself is a dangerous instance of the canonical novel in the Democratic Age. Balzac, Hugo, and Dostoevsky have something at least of Dickens's breadth in them, though they take us closer to the limits of the canonical novel as an achievement. Stendhal, Flaubert, James, and George Eliot seem the inevitable canonical novelists who essentially keep to genre; in choosing Eliot's *Middlemarch* I am guided not only by the book's indisputable eminence, but by its particular usefulness at this bad moment, when inchoate moralists appropriate literature for purposes they assert to be conducive to social change. If there is an exemplary fusion of aesthetic and moral power in the canonical novel, then George Eliot is its best representative, and *Middlemarch* is her subtlest analysis of the moral imagination, possibly the subtlest ever achieved in prose fiction.

Middlemarch's pleasures begin with the strength of its stories and the depth and vividness of its characterization, both in turn dependent upon George Eliot's rhetorical art, her control of the resources of her language, even though she is not a great stylist. Yet she is more than a novelist; she advances the novel into the mode of moral prophecy in a new way that was strenuously developed by D. H. Lawrence, who had little resemblance to Eliot on the surface but was her disciple nevertheless. The line of descent from Dorothea Brooke of *Middlemarch* to Ursula Brangwen of *Women in Love* is direct; fullness of being is the goal of the quest, and the evidence of the quester's election is a particular variety of moral consciousness, almost wholly displaced from its Protestant origins.

Nietzsche professed to despise George Eliot for her supposed conviction that you could get rid of the Christian God while holding onto Christian morality, but for once Nietzsche was guilty of a rather weak misreading. Eliot is not a Christian moralist, but a Romantic or Wordsworthian one; her sense of the moral life emanates from "Tintern Abbey," "Resolution and Independence," and the "Intimations of Immortality" ode. There is both a gentle irony and a recognition when she responds to her publisher's having "felt the want of brighter lights" in the pastoral *Silas Marner*:

> I don't wonder at your finding my story, as far as you have read it, rather sombre: indeed, I should not have believed that anyone would have been interested in it but myself (since William Wordsworth is dead) if Mr. Lewes had not been strongly arrested by it. But I hope you will not find it at all a sad story, as a whole, since it sets—or is intended to set—in a strong light the remedial influences of pure, natural human relations.

Silas Marner returns us to *The Ruined Cottage,* "Michael," "The Old Cumberland Beggar"—to the vision of pastoral man and woman as a primordial good. That Wordsworthianism always remained fundamental to Eliot; her morality of renunciation is meaningful only because its object is to treat others not just as if their interest transcended one's own, but as if they could be encouraged to practice the same renunciation. Isolated, that now seems an archaic idealism; in her it is the pragmatic manifestation of a stance at once moral and aesthetic, since by "the good" both she and Wordsworth do not necessarily intend a conventional goodness. They urge us toward a moral Sublime: agonistic, antithetical to nature and to what we call "human nature," solitary, yet open to communion with others.

But one does not visualize Wordsworth writing novels. *Mid-*

dlemarch is a huge, intricate representation of an entire provincial society set in the recent past; that hardly seems to allow for a Wordsworthian vision as such. Still, Wordsworth rather than any novelist remains George Eliot's precursor in her major achievement (if we exempt the Gwendolen Harleth part of *Daniel Deronda*), or perhaps we might speak of a composite precursor, the Bunyan of *Pilgrim's Progress* combined with Wordsworth, a linkage in which I follow Barry Qualls.

Middlemarch is set in the early 1830s, the age of Reform that began the Victorian era, and the idea of a societal hope is counterpointed throughout the novel with the painful moral education of the protagonists, Dorothea Brooke and Lydgate. As Qualls notes, when they belatedly learn to surrender their fictions of the self, they are already exiled or alienated from any communal context. The visions of Bunyan and of Wordsworth, though they always move the narrator, seem estranged from the resigned fates of Dorothea and of Lydgate; yet they remain just beneath the appearances of choice. Martin Price, brooding upon Lydgate's entrapment by Rosamond Vincy, observes that "George Eliot attempted work of great subtlety, the study of how a man's virtues are implicated in and in some measure promote his errors." On the more sublime scale of *The Ruined Cottage,* that is the pathos of Margaret, who destroys herself and her children through the power of her apocalyptic hope for her husband's return. The subtlety is there in both the inventor of modern poetry and the most intelligent of all novelists, and one can see again what George Eliot owed to Wordsworth.

Cognitive power is generally not a quality we consciously seek in a novelist, or in a lyric poet or dramatist. George Eliot, like Emily Dickinson and Blake, and like Shakespeare, rethought everything through for herself. She is the novelist as thinker (not as philosopher), and we frequently mistake her because we underestimate the cognitive strength she brings to her perspectivizings. There is certainly an alliance between that strength and her capacity for moral insight, but she also has an unallied directness as a moralist that frees her from any excessive self-consciousness that would inhibit her willingness to judge her own characters, implicitly and explicitly.

Her descendant in this regard is Iris Murdoch, who cannot often sustain direct comparison with George Eliot, but Eliot's moral authority could scarcely be attained by any novelist more than a century later. We no longer have sages or sybils, literary or spiritual, and we experience both nostalgia and puzzlement when we read accounts of Eliot's reception as an oracle. The most famous is by F. W. H. Myers, describing the novelist's visit to Cambridge University in 1873:

> I remember how at Cambridge I walked with her once in the Fellows' Garden of Trinity, on an evening of rainy May; and she, stirred somewhat beyond her wont, and taking as her text the three words which had been used so often as the inspiring trumpet-call of men—the words God, Immortality, Duty—pronounced with terrible earnestness how inconceivable was the first, how unbelievable was the second, and yet how peremptory and absolute the third. Never, perhaps, have sterner accents confirmed the sovereignty of impersonal and unrecompensing Law. I listened, and night fell; her grave, majestic countenance turned towards me like a sybil's in the gloom; it was as though she withdrew from my grasp, one by one, the two scrolls of promise and left me the third scroll only, awful with inevitable fates. And when we stood at length and parted, amid that columnar circuit of forest trees, beneath the last twilight of starless skies, I seemed to be gazing, like Titus at Jerusalem, on vacant seats and empty halls—on a sanctuary with no Presence to hallow it, and heaven left empty of God.

The high rhetoric here, if we wrote it, would be ironical, but that would be an irony to little purpose. An ironist when she wished to be, George Eliot was the least comic of canonical novelists, yet also the most difficult to satirize; there are only involuntary parodies of her work. Moral sublimity makes us impatient if it is unsponsored, whether by institution or by cause. Something of George Eliot's aura has survived for us; we glimpse it but want to put it aside, to talk instead about her ideas or her art. Still, it does not altogether vanish, because it is founded upon the novels, and upon *Middlemarch* in particular.

Henry James, evading the role of disciple, while brooding on her posthumously published letters and notes, had to fall into the same rhetoric of beholding sublimity: "But there rises from them a kind of fragrance of moral elevation; a love of justice, truth, and light; a large, generous way of looking at things; and a constant effort to hold high the torch in the dusky spaces of man's conscience."

James was being elegiac and not wicked, but we wonder how any novelist could survive that kind of praise. A canonical novel is not supposed to be wisdom literature, and very few are; perhaps only *Middlemarch* is. We recoil from Saul Bellow's *The Dean's December*. I read it and agreed with every observation, yet suffered from its incessant tendentiousness. In *Middlemarch* I rarely agree with the novelist's frequent interventions, and yet they are as welcome as everything else in the book. The aesthetic secret of George Eliot is her mastery of what James, reviewing her in 1866, called "a certain middle field where morals and aesthetics move in concert." Perhaps it is not so much a secret as it is George Eliot herself, since I can think of no other major novelist, before or since, whose overt moralizings constitute an aesthetic virtue rather than a disaster. Even if one passionately agreed with the crusade against male human beings urged by Doris Lessing and Alice Walker, their rhetoric of exclusion gives no pleasure. Some close scrutinies of *Middlemarch* should aid in seeing something more of how Eliot manages her harmonizing of morals and aesthetics.

Middlemarch, like Eliot's final novel, *Daniel Deronda,* is ambitiously conceived as a large structure with an implicit but clear relation to Dante's *Comedy.* Alexander Welsh has shown this in regard to *Middlemarch,* and Welsh and Qualls have both noted the influence in *Deronda.* The Dantean desire to know and finally to be known, to be remembered, Welsh sees as the driving motive of *Middlemarch*'s two impressive questers: Dorothea, who in some ways is the author's surrogate, and Lydgate, for whom Eliot seems to feel a keen but wary sympathy. Dante, the most ambitious of great writers, dared a vision of judgment in which all of the characters necessarily have achieved finality. They unfold before us, but they can no longer change; they have had their chance. George Eliot, as a humane freethinker, made a curious choice in employing

Dante as a paradigm, but her capacity for severe moral judgment presumably helps to account for her initially surprising affinities with the creator of the *Divine Comedy*, who presumably would have placed her in canto 5 of the *Inferno*, difficult as it is for us to visualize George Eliot and George Henry Lewes as a nineteenth-century Francesca and Paolo. Her own sympathies in the *Inferno* must have been with Ulysses, whose destructive quest for knowledge is the heroic archetype that the major characters in *Middlemarch* follow.

Welsh remarks of Lydgate that "It is he whose stature and whose punishment are most Dantean of all," so I start here with Lydgate and the dark contrast between chapter 15, where he is introduced, and chapter 76, where he acknowledges defeat, thus abandoning all hope of further knowledge. First we are given the twenty-seven-year-old Lydgate, a promising surgeon with an intellectual passion for medical research:

We are not afraid of telling over and over again how a man comes to fall in love with a woman and be wedded to her, or else be fatally parted from her. Is it due to excess of poetry or of stupidity that we are never weary of describing what King James called a woman's "makdom and her fairnesse," never weary of listening to the twanging of the old Troubadour strings, and are comparatively uninterested in that other kind of "makdom and fairnesse" which must be wooed with industrious thought and patient renunciation of small desires? In the story of this passion, too, the development varies: sometimes it is the glorious marriage, sometimes frustration and final parting. And not seldom the catastrophe is bound up with the other passion, sung by the Troubadours. For in the multitude of middle-aged men who go about their vocations in a daily course determined for them much in the same way as the tie of their cravats, there is always a good number who once meant to shape their own deeds and alter the world a little. The story of their coming to be shapen after the average and fit to be packed by the gross, is hardly ever told even in their consciousness; for perhaps their ardour in generous unpaid toil cooled as imperceptibly as the ardour of other useful loves, till one day their earlier self walked like a ghost in its old home and made the new furniture ghastly. Nothing in the world more subtle than the process of their gradual change! In the beginning they inhaled it unknowingly: you and I may have sent some of our breath towards infecting them, when we uttered our conforming falsities or drew our silly conclusions: or perhaps it came with the vibrations from a woman's glance.

Lydgate did not mean to be one of those failures, and there was the better hope of him because his scientific interest soon took the form of a professional enthusiasm: he had a youthful belief in his breadwinning work, not to be stifled by that initiation in makeshift called his 'prentice days; and he carried to his studies in London, Edinburgh, and Paris, the conviction that the medical profession as it might be was the finest in the world; presenting the most perfect interchange between science and art; offering the most direct alliance between intellectual conquest and the social good. Lydgate's nature demanded this combination: he was an emotional creature, with a flesh-and-blood sense of fellowship which withstood all the abstractions of special study. He cared not only for "cases," but for John and Elizabeth, especially Elizabeth.

"King James" here is not the English Bible but James I himself, speaking of a lady's "makdom and her fairnesse" or composure and beauty. Poor Lydgate, who was to die defeated at fifty, becomes one of the multitude of middle-aged men who do not shape their own deeds and who alter the world not at all. Substitute the name of Dr. Dick Diver for Dr. Tertius Lydgate, and you could insert these two paragraphs into *Tender Is the Night,* where they would fit precisely for their matter, though scarcely for their manner. Like Lydgate, Fitzgerald's Diver fails because of a ruinous marriage, as well as through other actions that ensue from both characters' "commonness," as George Eliot calls it. Frank Kermode remarks that "*Middlemarch* is as much a book about marriage in its social aspects as *The Rainbow* is about marriage in its spiritual aspects." Fitzgerald seems to have intended both aspects; lacking Eliot's extraordinary intelligence and Lawrence's prophetic insight, he failed, though *Tender Is the Night* remains a gorgeous failure. Diver could well be the subject of George Eliot's wonderful statement that Lydgate quests for "the imagination that reveals subtle actions inaccessible by any sort of lens, but tracked in that outer darkness through long pathways of necessary sequence by the inward light which is the last refinement of Energy, capable of bathing even the ethereal atoms in its ideally illuminated space."

That is George Eliot's version of Dante's paradise, expressed as an idealized secular pilgrimage, and this is the vision that Lydgate and Diver fail. In his defeat, Lydgate again anticipates the protagonist of *Tender Is the Night*, who ends up practicing medicine in one or another Finger Lakes town in the western reserve of New York State. We hear the collapse of Lydgate in chapter 76, when he tells Dorothea,

It is very clear to me that I must not count on anything else than getting away from Middlemarch as soon as I can manage it. I should not be able for a long while, at the very best, to get an income here, and—and it is easier to make necessary changes in a new place. I must do as other men do, and think what will please the world and bring in money; look for a little opening in the London crowd, and push myself; set up in a watering-place, or go to some southern town where there are plenty of idle English, and get myself puffed,—that is the sort of shell I must creep into and try to keep my soul alive in.

That is the fall of Lydgate, from a paradisal quest for knowledge to a place where the soul cannot be kept alive, nor soon enough, the body either. The opposite fate is earned by Dorothea, who endures a purgatorial marriage to the impotent Casaubon and survives to marry Ladislaw, in a match that most critics insist is inadequate to her, but that is neither Dorothea's nor George Eliot's judgment. Impressive and poignant as Lydgate is, particularly in his fall, the novel is nevertheless Dorothea's and could legitimately have been called *Dorothea Brooke* rather than *Middlemarch*. Virginia Woolf insisted that Dorothea spoke for all of Eliot's heroines:

That is their problem. They cannot live without religion, and they start out on the search for one when they are little girls. Each has the deep feminine passion for goodness, which makes the place where she stands in aspiration and agony the heart of the book—still and cloistered like a place of worship, but that she no longer knows to whom to pray. In learning they seek their goal; in the ordinary tasks of womanhood; in the wider service of their kind. They do not find what they seek, and we cannot wonder. The ancient consciousness of woman, charged with suffering and sensibility, and for so many ages dumb, seems in them to have brimmed and overflowed and uttered a demand for something—they scarcely know what—for something that is perhaps incompatible with the facts of human existence. George Eliot had far too strong an intelligence to tamper with those facts, and too broad a humour to mitigate the truth because it was a stern one. Save for the supreme courage of their endeavour, the struggle ends, for her heroines, in tragedy, or in a compromise that is even more melancholy.

Again, George Eliot would not have been happy with Virginia Woolf's judgment that Dorothea ended in a compromise even more melancholy than tragedy, which does seem too severe a judgment on Dorothea's second husband, the well-meaning if somewhat feckless Will Ladislaw. Richard Ellmann, in an acute biographical speculation upon "Dorothea's Husbands," finds no single prototype for the wretched Casaubon, pseudo-scholar of all mythologies, but he suggests that the ultimate model was a darker side of Eliot herself, the consequence of protracted early sexual repression and consequent unhealthy fantasies. As compelling is Ellmann's suggestion that the tiresome, idealized Will Ladislaw is not only a version of George Henry Lewes, Eliot's first husband, but also of John Cross, more than twenty years her junior and her second husband during the last seven months of her life. Like Dorothea, Eliot cannot be said to have found her own equal in a husband; but then, short of John Stuart Mill (who was not available), where was such an intellectual and spiritual peer to be found? The extraordinary "Prelude" to *Middlemarch* contrasts Saint Theresa of Avila to "later-born Theresas . . . helped by no coherent social faith and order which could perform the function of knowledge for the ardently willing soul." In the prelude's final paragraph, Eliot utters a powerfully ironic, somber, and aggressive lament for herself and her Dorothea:

> Some have felt that these blundering lives are due to the inconvenient indefiniteness with which the Supreme Power has fashioned the natures of women: if there were one level of feminine incompetence as strict as the ability to count three and no more, the social lot of women might be treated with scientific certitude. Meanwhile the indefiniteness remains, and the limits of variation are really much wider than any one would imagine from the sameness of women's coiffure and the favourite love-stories in prose and verse. Here and there a cygnet is reared uneasily among the ducklings in the brown pond, and never finds the living stream in fellowship with its own oary-footed kind. Here and there is born a Saint Theresa, foundress of nothing, whose loving heart-beats and sobs after an unattained goodness tremble off and are dispersed among hindrances, instead of centering in some long-recognisable deed.

What place in the *Paradiso* would Dante have selected for a "foundress of nothing"? Fierce as George Eliot was, she is not a convenient figure for our current Feminist critics, any more than Jane Austen is. An essay of 1972 by Lee Edwards was prophetic of many judgments to come. Lucidly aware that "*Middlemarch* is a novel about imaginative energy," Edwards made a powerful protest against Eliot's refusal to endow Dorothea with more of the novelist's energy and will:

> . . . George Eliot did not finally create a woman who knew before the fact that she neither liked nor needed husbands since such liking would force her either to submit or to destroy. Had George Eliot been able to find some system of values by which such a woman could live, she might have succeeded in breathing life again into Saint Theresa's desiccated image.

Dorothea, like her creator, was not prepared to give up marriage; perhaps *Middlemarch* might have been an even stronger novel if Eliot had been a radical feminist; perhaps not. But Eliot was unique, not in her degree of emancipation, or even in her energy and will, but in the range and strength of her intellect. Was she to endow Dorothea with a mind comparable in conceptual originality to Blake's or Emily Dickinson's? *Middlemarch* is not a *Portrait of the Artist as a Young Woman;* it is the portrait of Dorothea Brooke, a Protestant Saint Theresa in her potential, but living in a time and place that gave inadequate scope to so saintly a woman.

Lydgate quests for scientific knowledge and the fame it might bring, but Dorothea's urge to know is purely spiritual. Contemplative by nature, Dorothea cannot be a social crusader or a political reformer. Like Jane Austen, George Eliot was too great an artist and too acute an ironist to be crippled by the societal structures of her day. Both novelists pursued the novel's good, the difference between them being that Eliot fused aesthetic and moral purposes more overtly than Austen did, and both had a more informed moral sense than is now common among us. Eliot's deft control as a narrator forbids her to choose possibilities for Dorothea that are barely available to Eliot herself. Mordecai, the exalted Jewish prophet, says to Daniel Deronda that "The divine principle of our race is action, choice, resolved memory." Eliot was sublimely gifted enough not only to write that sentence but to live it, though only in part. Perhaps Feminist criticism is justified in its yearning for a more feminist George Eliot, but the justification is not in itself literary. Henry James prophesied the ambivalence of Feminist critics when he protested the waste of the superb heroine and insisted that the reader's imagination demanded more for Dorothea than George Eliot had chosen to provide. Eliot, endlessly astute, had anticipated all such complaints in her novel's final paragraphs:

Certainly those determining acts of her life were not ideally beautiful. They were the mixed result of young and noble impulse struggling amidst the conditions of an imperfect social state, in which great feelings will often take the aspect of error, and great faith the aspect of illusion. For there is no creature whose inward being is so strong that it is not greatly determined by what lies outside it. A new Theresa will hardly have the opportunity of reforming a conventual life, any more than a new Antigone will spend her heroic piety in daring all for the sake of a brother's burial: the medium in which their ardent deeds took shape is for ever gone. But we insignificant people with our daily words and acts are preparing the lives of many Dorotheas, some of which may present a far sadder sacrifice than that of the Dorothea whose story we know.

Her finely-touched spirit had still its fine issues, though they were not widely visible. Her full nature, like that river of which Cyrus broke the strength, spent itself in channels which had no great name on the earth. But the effect of her being on those around her was incalculably diffusive: for the growing good of the world is partly dependent on unhistoric acts; and that things are not so ill with you and me as they might have been, is half owing to the number who lived faithfully a hidden life, and rest in unvisited tombs.

I know of few sentences as wise and admonishing as "For there is no creature whose inward being is so strong that it is not greatly determined by what lies outside it." Partisans of resentment do not need that sentence; I do. But "greatly" is very precise, and Eliot implies that the strength of inward being also determines what the extent of that "greatly" will be. Overdetermination is a dark truth, in life as in literature, and the agon of individual will and energy with societal and historical forces is endless in both realms. Dorothea has chosen not to be an agonist, believing (with her creator) that "the growing good of the world is partly dependent on unhistoric acts."

James may have been right: my own imagination as a reader sometimes longs for a Dorothea whose acts might have been historic. But James may have been wrong; what are the historic acts of his most fascinating heroines, Isabel Archer and Milly Theale? The canonical novel, in the summer of its existence, may have reached its Sublime in *Middlemarch,* whose effect upon its readers remains "incalculably diffusive."

14.

Tolstoy and Heroism

THE BEST INTRODUCTION to Tolstoy I have found is Maxim Gorky's *Reminiscences* (1921), based upon his visits to the seventy-two-year-old novelist who, early in 1901, was living in the Crimea, in poor health and recently excommunicated from the Russian Orthodox Church. Gorky expresses directly the ambivalences that flowed between Tolstoy and himself, ambivalences that heighten the sense of Tolstoy's uncanniness that keeps breaking through:

> In his diary which he gave me to read, I was struck by a strange aphorism: "God is my desire." To-day on returning him the book, I asked him what it meant.
> "An unfinished thought," he said, glancing at the page and screwing up his eyes. "I must have wanted to say: God is my desire to know him. . . . No, not that. . . ." He began to laugh, and rolling up the book into a tube, he put it into the big pocket of his blouse. With God he has very suspicious relations; they

sometimes remind me of the relation of "two bears in one den."
(translated by S. S. Koteliansky and Leonard Woolf)

Gorky's shrewdness in citing the proverb catches the hidden truths of Tolstoy's nihilism and his inability to abide nihilism. The prophet-novelist's finished thought identified God with the desire not to die. Immensely courageous as he was, Tolstoy was moved not so much by a commonplace fear of dying or death as by his own extraordinary vitality and vitalism, which could not accommodate any sense of ceasing to exist. Gorky again is very good on this:

> All his life he feared and hated death, all his life there throbbed in his soul the "Arsamasian terror"—must he die? The whole world, all the earth looks towards him; from China, India, America, from everywhere living, throbbing threads stretch out to him; his soul is for all and forever. Why should not nature make an exception to her law, give to one man physical immortality?"

We might call Tolstoy's longing an apocalyptic wistfulness, rather than a religious desire. There are still some Tolstoyans scattered about the world, but they are now difficult to distinguish from many other varieties of spiritualized rationalism. Tolstoy loved what he called God with a cold passion, needy rather than ardent. His Christ was the preacher of the Sermon on the Mount and nothing more, perhaps less a god than Tolstoy himself. Reading Tolstoy on religion one encounters a severe, sometimes savage moralist who does not edify, unless like Gandhi you set nonviolence above every other value. Tolstoy fathered thirteen children on his wife, but his views on marriage and family are painful, and his stance in regard to human sexuality is misogynistic to a frightening degree. Of course, all this is true of the discursive Tolstoy, not of the fiction writer, even in the late novel *Resurrection,* or in later short novels like *The Devil* and the notorious *Kreutzer Sonata.* So powerful and sustained is Tolstoy's narrative gift that his sermonizing digressions do not disfigure his fiction much or render it tendentious.

Russian critics have emphasized that his novels and stories portray the familiar with such strangeness that everything seems new-minted. What Nietzsche called "the primordial poem of mankind," the cosmos as we have agreed to see it, is reperspectivized by Tolstoy. Reading him incessantly, you don't so much begin to see what he sees, you start to realize how arbitrary your own seeing tends to be. Your world is much less abundant than his, since he somehow manages to suggest that what he sees is at once more natural and yet more strange. It takes a while to understand just how metaphorical his concept of nature is, since its apparent simplicity is a rhetorical triumph. The clearest analogue in English is early Wordsworth, before "Tintern Abbey," poems like "Guilt and Sorrow," *The Ruined Cottage,* and "The Old Cumberland Beggar." In them, Wordsworth requires no myth of memory or Coleridgean sense of a reciprocal exchange between the human mind and nature. Harrowing in its vision of the sorrows of natural man and women, Wordsworth's first major poetry is Tolstoyan before Tolstoy, simplified through an intensity so artful as almost to conceal its art from us. George Eliot at her most Wordsworthian, in *Adam Bede,* seems curiously Tolstoyan, a seeming confirmed by Tolstoy's admiration for that novel.

Wordsworth's intimations of what he called immortality came to him from memories of his own earliest childhood, and though they were to fade in the light of common day, they sustained his natural piety. Tolstoy had no similar intimations, and he sought the equivalent of natural piety in the Russian peasant. Whatever it was he found could hardly have been the reassurance he sought. Too tough a rationalist to share in the people's faith, he nevertheless strove to achieve their love of God. Since he rejected all miracles, it is more than a little difficult to define what a loving God might have meant for him. Gorky wrote that Tolstoy "went on to say that truth is the same for all—love of God. But on this subject he spoke coldly and wearily." Another time, Tolstoy told Gorky that faith and love required courage and daring, which comes closer to the Tolstoyan ethos. If the love of God is itself an audacity, who will save the fearful? What compels admiration, here as elsewhere in Tolstoy, is his originality or strangeness of temperament. His motives are rarely ours. Courage and daring are epic virtues, and Tolstoy's religion (to call it that) takes on the qualities of his art, which has epic tendencies at every point. When Tolstoy compares himself to Homer we are persuaded, as no other post-Homeric writer could persuade us. Whether as prophet or as moralist, Tolstoy remains both an epic figure and a creator of epic.

Do Tolstoy's beliefs—moral, religious, aesthetic—matter? If the question pertains to the beliefs in themselves, the answer would be positive in terms of the past, when there were so many Tolstoyans, but not now, when he must be read in the company of Homer, the Yahwist, Dante, and Shakespeare, as perhaps the only writer since the Renaissance who can challenge them. How unhappy he would have been at this destiny; he valued himself more as prophet than as storyteller. Even as a writer, he would have welcomed the *Iliad* and Genesis as companions, but doubtless would have continued in his scorn for Dante and Shakespeare. He had a particular fury against *King Lear*, although his final days were spent involuntarily playing the part of Lear when he fled his home in a desperate lunge toward an outcast freedom. He overwhelmingly wanted martyrdom, perpetually denied to him by the shrewdness of the Tsar's government, which persecuted his followers but refused to touch the world-famous sage and epic novelist, acknowledged almost from the start as Pushkin's true inheritor and fulfiller, and so as the greatest of all writers in Russian, an eminence he is unlikely ever to lose. Perhaps something in him never got away from the desire to match and even outdo Homer and the Bible, though agonistic intensity in him generally expressed itself as a distrust of literature, even a repudiation of the aesthetic sphere of value.

Yet *What Is Art?* (1896)—his fierce denunciation of Greek tragedy, Dante, Michelangelo, Shakespeare, and Beethoven—is contravened by the astonishing *Hadji Murad,* the short novel he wrote between 1896 and 1904 but left unpublished when he died. Although he sometimes deprecated *Hadji Murad* as a self-indulgence, he wrote draft after draft of the story and knew very well that it was a masterpiece, one that contradicted almost all of his principles for Christian and moral art. One hesitates to value *Hadji Murad* over all of Tolstoy's other achievements in the short novel,

a genre in which he excelled, and which includes works as remarkable as *The Death of Ivan Ilyich, Master and Man, The
Devil, The Cossacks, The Kreutzer Sonata,* and *Father Sergius.*
Still, not even the first two in that listing haunt me as *Hadji
Murad* has since I first read it more than forty years ago. It is
my personal touchstone for the sublime of prose fiction, to me
the best story in the world, or at least the best that I have ever
read.

I have argued throughout this book that originality, in the sense
of strangeness, is the quality that, more than any other, makes a
work canonical. Tolstoy's strangeness is itself strange, because it
so paradoxically seems not strange at all at first. You always hear
Tolstoy's voice acting as the narrator, and that voice is direct,
rational, confident, and benign. Victor Shklovsky, a major modern
Russian critic, noted that "the most common strategy in Tolstoy
is one of refusing to recognize an object, of describing it as if it
were seen for the first time." This technique of strangeness, combined with Tolstoy's tonality, results in the reader's happy conviction that Tolstoy enables him to see everything as if for the
first time, while also giving him the sense that he has seen everything already. To be both estranged and at home seems unlikely,
but that is Tolstoy's all but unique atmosphere.

How can fiction be at once uncanny and natural? I suppose it
could be argued that the highest fictions—the *Divine Comedy,
Hamlet, King Lear, Don Quixote, Paradise Lost, Faust, Part Two,
Peer Gynt, War and Peace, In Search of Lost Time*—fuse such
antithetical attributes. They open themselves to a wilderness of
perspectives, perhaps even create those perspectives. But there are
not many short novels capable of accommodating bewildering
antinomies. *Hadji Murad* is as strange as the *Odyssey* and as
familiar as Hemingway. When Tolstoy's story concludes with
Hadji Murad's heroic last fight, he and a literal handful of devoted
supporters against a host of enemies, we are bound to be reminded
of what seems to me the most memorable episode in *For Whom
the Bell Tolls,* El Sordo's last stand with his little knot of partisans
against the vastly more numerous and more heavily armed Fas-
cists. Hemingway, always Tolstoy's eager student, brilliantly im-
itates his great original. Yet Hadji Murad also lives and dies as

the archaic epic hero, combining in himself all of the virtues and none of the flaws of Odysseus, Achilles, and Aeneas.

About all that Ludwig Wittgenstein and Isaak Babel may be said to have in common are their very different Jewish origins, but it fascinates me that they also share a reverence for *Hadji Murad*. Wittgenstein gave a copy of it to his disciple Norman Malcolm to accompany Malcolm into military service, telling him that there was a lot to be got out of it. Babel, rereading the book as he continued on in his time of troubles, in 1937, became virtually rhapsodic: "Here the electric charge went from the earth, through the hands, straight to the paper, with no insulation at all, quite mercilessly stripping off all outer layers with a sense of truth."

A book that stimulated Babel and Wittgenstein to their unique tributes clearly touches the universal, which was always Tolstoy's desire. Henry James, who vastly preferred Turgenev to Tolstoy, would scarcely have been able to refer to *Hadji Murad* as a "loose, baggy monster," his peculiar description of *War and Peace*. A close examination of it demonstrates what it is that makes Tolstoy the most canonical of all nineteenth-century writers, an almost solitary figure even in that immensely rich era of democratic art.

Hadji Murad is first of all history, though it would be odd to regard it as historical fiction, even in the sense that *War and Peace* could be called an historical novel. There are no meditations on history in *Hadji Murad*, which is pure storytelling; and yet what happens in the book is, strictly speaking, not Tolstoy's invention, at least in its core. Reading the short novel side by side with J. F. Baddeley's *Russian Conquest of the Caucasus* (1908) I find myself confronting again the paradox that Tolstoy seems to follow the facts even as he seems to follow nature, and yet his *Hadji Murad* is uncanny, belonging to mythical epic and not to chronicle. Throughout the first half of the nineteenth century, the Russian Empire battled incessantly to conquer the Muslims of the Caucasian mountains and forests. Unified in a holy war against the Russians, the Caucasians were ultimately led by the imam Shamil, whose most effective military subordinate was Hadji Murad, legendary long before his death in battle. In December 1851, having fallen out with Shamil, Hadji Murad went over to the Russians. Four months later, in April 1852, he attempted to break away, was pursued, and died fighting in a desperate last stand.

Tolstoy's biographer and translator, Aylmer Maude, finds the ultimate origin of the story in a letter Tolstoy wrote on December 23, 1851, just before he began to serve as an artillery officer in the war against Shamil:

> If you wish to show off with news from the Caucasus, you may recount that a certain Hadji Murad (the second man in importance to Shamil himself) surrendered a few days ago to the Russian Government. He was the leading daredevil and "brave" in all Circassia, but was led to commit a mean action.

Half a century later, Tolstoy renders not the slightest judgment that any of Hadji Murad's actions are mean, or even could be mean. Compared to anyone else in the novel, particularly the rival leaders, Shamil and the Tsar, Nicholas I, Hadji Murad is wholly heroic. Although Tolstoy never complained of any aspect of Homer, Hadji Murad constitutes, in Tolstoy's vision of him, a powerful critique of the Homeric hero. The admirable qualities that Homer divides between Achilles and Hector are brought together in Tolstoy's hero, who manifests neither the murderous rage of Achilles against mortality nor Hector's collapse into a passive acceptance of the end.

Magnificent in his sense of force, like Achilles, Hadji Murad is mature, unambiguous, potent without savagery. More sublimely vital than Achilles, he equals Odysseus in craft and in diplomacy. Like Odysseus, he desires to get home to his women and children. He fails in his quest, as Odysseus did not, but Tolstoy gives us an apotheosis of the hero, not a lament for his defeat. No other central figure in Tolstoy receives so loving and full an accounting as Hadji Murad, and I am not persuaded that there is an equivalent to the Tartar chief anywhere else in Western literature. Who else has given us the natural man as triumphant protagonist, rich in courage and guile alike? Conrad's Nostromo, man of the people, is a grand figure, but far less imaginatively conceived than Hadji

Murad. Tolstoy's daredevil is as cunning as Tolstoy himself and dies a worthy death, as gorgeously heroic as Nostromo's death is ironic.

It cannot be irrelevant that Tolstoy came close to dying early in 1902. His illness retreated by early April and allowed him to return to the revision of *Hadji Murad,* a reprieve reflected in the death of his protagonist, who dies his author's death for him, as it were. As the novelist perhaps understood, on some level he *was* Hadji Murad, or rather the hero is a Shakespearean version of Tolstoy in an ironic triumph of the dramatist over the writer who most maligned him.

Hadji Murad is certainly Tolstoy's most Shakespearean story in its gallery of rich characterizations, in the extraordinary range of its dramatic sympathies, above all in the representation of change in its central protagonist. Like Shakespeare, the Tolstoy who narrates Hadji Murad's story is at once everyone and no one, both interested and disinterested, profoundly moved yet dispassionate. Tolstoy has learned from Shakespeare (though he would have denied it) the art of juxtaposing highly diverse scenes in order to achieve more complex continuities than a simpler progression could provide. We encounter Hadji Murad in contexts he has never known, and we delight in his mastery of situations and persons.

Tolstoy absurdly attacked Shakespeare for being unable to endow his characters with individuality of language, which is rather like saying that Bach could not compose a fugue. Knowing more English would not have enlightened Tolstoy; his fury at Shakespeare was defensive, though presumably he was unaware of it. Only Falstaff pleased him, and Lear in particular drove him wild with disdain. It is painful to speak of Tolstoy's limitations, but they exist only if one compares him to Shakespeare. His strongest character, Anna Karenina, has profound strains of Shakespeare in her, for which Tolstoy, who loves her, will not forgive her. Since it is not hyperbolical to observe that Tolstoy actually hated Shakespeare, it is only just to add that he also feared him. Thomas Mann thought that Tolstoy secretly identified Shakespeare with nature, and himself with spirit. Moralism is back in fashion in our academies, and we will yet have acclaim for Tolstoy's choice of Harriet Beecher Stowe over Shakespeare. New Historicists, Feminists, and Marxists ought to prefer *Uncle Tom's Cabin* to *King Lear*, as Tolstoy pioneered in doing.

Hadji Murad is the grandest exception in late Tolstoy, for here the old shaman rivals Shakespeare. Shakespeare's extraordinary faculty for endowing even the most minor characters with exuberant being, for ramming them with life, is slyly absorbed by Tolstoy. Everyone in *Hadji Murad* is vividly individualized: Shamil; Tsar Nicholas; Avdeev, the hapless Russian soldier slain in a skirmish; Prince Vorontsov, to whom Hadji Murad surrenders; Poltoratsky, a company commander; and Hadji Murad's faithful little band of followers: Eldar, Gamzalo, Khan Mahoma, and Khanefi. The catalog seems endless, as in a major Shakespearean play. There are also the elder Vorontsov, head of the Russian army, and his aide-de-camp, Loris-Melikov, who is placed in charge of Hadji Murad, as well as Butler, a heroic officer able to appreciate the Tartar chief's qualities. Also glowing in their persuasiveness are the two women who figure most in the story: Princess Marya Vasilevna, wife of the younger Vorontsov, and Marya Dmitrievna, the mistress of a minor officer.

These fifteen characters and a dozen more minor ones are all sketched with a Shakespearean precision and gusto that provide a frame to enhance Hadji Murad, whom we come to know as we know Shakespeare's great warriors: Othello, Antony, Coriolanus, or the bastard Faulconbridge in *King John*. Indeed, we come to know Hadji Murad more fully than we can know Anna Karenina, who is too close to Tolstoy. For once, like Shakespeare, Tolstoy speaks through a voice not at all his own and enacts the great role of Hadji Murad, the natural man as epic hero.

The historical Hadji Murad both is and is not Tolstoy's. In J. F. Baddeley's account the Tartar hero is perhaps even more daring and courageous, but rather more darkly inhumane. An Avar of Dagestan, a mountain nation, Hadji Murad initially fought against the Murids, the mass movement of Muslim mystical revivalism that sparked a sixty-year war between the Russians and the Avars. Baddeley's chronicle of Hadji Murad's career, though merely factual, reads like fantasy fiction. After killing the leader of the Murids, Imam Hamyad, the hero joined the Russians, then was betrayed by the leader of the Avars and falsely denounced to the Russians as a follower of Shamil, the new imam. Escaping from the Russians by leaping from a high precipice, Hadji Murad survived to go over to the Murids, where his abilities soon made him Shamil's principal subordinate. Magnificent at raids and pitched battles alike, the hero's fame in time provoked the envy of Shamil, who condemned his best soldier to death in order to safeguard the interests of dynastic succession. With no other option, Hadji Murad again defected to the Russians, as he does at the outset of Tolstoy's novella. Careful as Tolstoy was to be factually accurate, he took Hadji Murad at his word, and allowed no shadows of ambition or cruelty to mingle with the fierce light of the hero's glory.

TOLSTOY'S NOVEL opens with a brief prelude in which, returning from a walk, the narrator with great difficulty picks "a beautiful thistle plant of the crimson variety, which in our neighborhood they call 'Tartar.' " Already the thistle is the implicit emblem of Hadji Murad: "But what energy and tenacity! With what determination it defended itself, and how dearly it sold its life!" Each time I read this prelude, I marvel again that the too-obvious symbolism of the thistle does not seem to me an aesthetic blemish. But then I reflect that everything in *Hadji Murad* is finely obvious. There are no surprises or unexpected turns anywhere in the story; indeed Tolstoy frequently lets us know in advance everything that is going to happen. This technique reaches the height of narrative subversion when we are shown the severed head of the hero before the story concludes with a detailed account of Hadji Murad's last stand. It is as though Tolstoy assumes we know the history already, and yet the novella abstains from reflecting upon the story's meanings; no morals are drawn, and no polemic is urged. What matters is evidently neither action nor pathos but only the hero's ethos, the revelation we receive of the character of Hadji Murad.

Despite his shrewdness and daring, the hero is doomed from the start, caught as he is between two vicious despots, Shamil and Tsar Nicholas. His ultimate fate is therefore overdetermined; the Russians will not trust him enough to let him lead an uprising against Shamil, yet he must attempt to rescue his family, held hostage by the imam. So he, too, like Tolstoy and the reader, knows how his story must end, how all stories must end if they concern the final destiny of the hero. But Hadji Murad is neither the Ulysses of Dante nor any other epic hero trapped in a belatedly moral universe. He is a Shakespearean protagonist whose deepest ethos is the capacity for inner change, strengthened by opposing what must destroy him, as Antony finally is humanized when the god Hercules abandons him. Tolstoy, telling the story of Hadji Murad, becomes so fascinated by the art of the storyteller that he frees himself of the Tolstoyan doctrines and takes on instead the purity of art and its praxis.

On a cold November evening, Hadji Murad, wrapped in hood and cape and attended only by his *murid* Eldar, rides into a Tartar village some fifteen miles outside of the Russian lines. He is there to await word whether the Russians will receive him, now that he is in flight from Shamil, an imam who, according to Baddeley, went everywhere accompanied by an ax-wielding executioner. The aura established by the opening paragraphs of Tolstoy's narrative helps to persuade us of what I suspect Wittgenstein most admired about *Hadji Murad,* a tragic hero who both arouses and appeases our skepticism about the truth of tragedy to nature.

A fine study by Laura Quinney, *The Grimness of the Truth,* applies Wittgenstein's dialectical attitude toward the tragic sense of life to both Dr. Johnson and Shelley. Wittgenstein, who was fascinated by Tolstoy and Dostoevsky, antithetical as they are to each other, seems to have found in both of them something of his ambivalence about tragedy. Shakespeare upset Wittgenstein, who apparently feared the playwright of *Hamlet* and *King Lear* almost as much as Tolstoy did. If you are skeptical about tragedy yet crave it, as Tolstoy and Wittgenstein did in spite of themselves, Shakespeare will be your largest problem, because you resent the fact that tragedy seems to come to him as easily as comedy or romance. Tolstoy in particular could not forgive what happened in *King Lear,* and it may be that *Hadji Murad,* for all its unconscious Shakespeareanism, is a critique of the way in which the tragic hero in Shakespeare lets loose forces that are beyond human acquaintance. Hadji Murad, since he must go on as himself, bravest of all Tartars, cannot save himself, but he does not combat or evoke daemonic forces. He is tragic only because he is heroic and natural and yet must confront impossible odds. Gorky comes to mind here because his dialogue with Tolstoy makes me marvel how Tolstoy, at that very moment, could have been working to finish *Hadji Murad*:

> I said that all writers are to some extent inventors, describing people as they would like to see them in life. I also said that I liked active people who desire to resist the evil of life by every means, even by violence.
>
> "And violence is the chief evil," he exclaimed, taking me by the arm. "How will you get out of that contradiction, inventor? Now your Mr. Traveling Companion isn't invented—it's good just because it isn't invented. But when you think, you beget knights, all Amadises."

Tolstoy's knight-errant, his Amadis of Gaul, is, of course, the magnificent and very violent (when he has to be) Hadji Murad, the hero whom the novelist both has and has not invented. As the prophet of nonviolence, Tolstoy is simply absent in the fierce narrative he writes for the Tartar leader. Which is the truer Tolstoy, the storyteller of *Hadji Murad* or the moral visionary of *Confession* and *What Is Art*? One hesitates to declare that there were two Tolstoys, each the antithesis of the other. How can the following passage (in the Aylmer Maude translation) not be the Tolstoy who matters most, the canonical Tolstoy?

> The eyes of the two men met, and expressed to each other much that could not have been put into words and that was not at all what the interpreter said. Without words they told each other the whole truth. Vorontsov's eyes said that he did not believe a single word Hadji Murad was saying, and that he knew he was and always would be an enemy to everything Russian and had surrendered only because he was obliged to. Hadji Murad understood this and yet continued to give assurances of his fidelity. His eyes said, "That old man ought to be thinking of his death and not of war, but though he is old he is cunning,

and I must be careful." Vorontsov understood this also, but nevertheless spoke to Hadji Murad in the way he considered necessary for the success of the war.

Tolstoy is also the old man who fights off thinking of his own death and thinks of war instead. Like Homer, Tolstoy neither celebrates nor deplores battle; each of them accepts battle as the basic law of life. Again one wonders about Tolstoy and nonviolence, but what could nonviolence have to do with the Caucasus of Vorontsov and Hadji Murad? Battle is release in *Hadji Murad,* the only way out in a world balanced between the allied treacheries of Shamil and Nicholas. Clearly, writing *Hadji Murad* was a release, the best of all indulgences for the old Tolstoy, who nevertheless told Gorky, "Heroes—that's a lie and invention; there are simply people, people and nothing else."

Who then is Hadji Murad, if he is not a hero? Perhaps in part he is a surrogate for Tolstoy's long-lost youth, but that alone would not account for the varied excellences of the Tartar warrior. Compared to him, the protagonists of Tolstoy's major novels are at once less vivid and less totally sympathetic. Something in every reader searches for a fictive character who is as fit for his world as Hadji Murad is. More than any other writer since Shakespeare, Tolstoy had the gift of representing the struggle for power in a warring world, and Hadji Murad is worthy of comparison to Antony in *Antony and Cleopatra* or to Conrad's Nostromo. Like Shakespeare, Tolstoy is at once dispassionate about the agon of his hero and profoundly sympathetic to the hero's impending fate.

There is an added element in Tolstoy's relation to Hadji Murad, something wonderfully personal, edging toward true identification. Circumstances have compelled Hadji Murad to become an outcast, albeit a dignified and even honored fugitive. Though superbly suited to his context, he is aware that the context is dissolving for him, leaving him alone except for his handful of men. The tang of finality hovers throughout Tolstoy's story, just as it pervades every appearance of the hero in *Antony and Cleopatra.* Caught between Shamil and the Tsar, Hadji Murad has only the last freedom of dying courageously, his identity not only unimpaired but enhanced.

It cannot be accidental that the two literary characters Tolstoy himself most resembled were the Yahweh of the J writer and Shakespeare's Lear, but he would rather have resembled his own Hadji Murad, a resourceful and valiant warrior, not an irascible god-king. Thomas Mann, in an odd essay on "Goethe and Tolstoy," confirms this point, but in a way that he cannot have intended:

> We have noted the same excess of animal spirits in Tolstoy; in whom, indeed, they persisted up to an old age lacking in the dignity, stateliness, and formal gravity of Goethe's latest period. Which need surprise nobody. For we cannot doubt that Goethe led a more earnest, laborious, exemplary life than the Slavic Junker; or that his cultural activities presupposed far more genuine self-abnegation, restraint, and discipline than Tolstoy's uttermost ineffectual efforts at spiritualization, sticking fast as these always did in a bag of fantastic absurdity. Tolstoy's aristocratic charm was, and Gorky so depicts it, that of a noble animal. He never managed to arrive at the dignity of man the civilized, man the triumpher over odds.

One sound answer to this was made by John Bayley, who remarked that both Goethe and Tolstoy were gigantic egoists, but of very different kinds: "If Goethe cared for nothing but himself, Tolstoy *was* nothing but himself; and his sense of what awaited him and of what life had come to mean for him is correspondingly more intimate and more moving."

Tolstoy, like his Hadji Murad, was nothing but himself. Mann presumably would have regarded Hadji Murad as another noble animal, devoid of civilized dignity, whatever the odds. As a great ironist, Mann confronted here what was beyond his own artistic powers. What matters most about Hadji Murad is his aesthetic dignity, which transcends anything we can discover in any of Mann's characters. With the question of aesthetic dignity, we move to the last stand and death of Hadji Murad, perhaps the finest of Tolstoy's fictive epiphanies.

ONE DIFFERENCE between Tolstoy and Hadji Murad is that the Chechen hero loves his son and his wives, and dies in a desperate attempt to position himself so that he may save them from Shamil's vengeance. It is questionable whether Tolstoy ever loved anyone, including his children. Not even Wordsworth or Milton, not even Dante could match Tolstoy as a great solipsist. Tolstoy's religious and moral writings are nothing but confessions of his solipsism; yet what reader of *War and Peace* or *Hadji Murad* would wish that Tolstoy had been less self-obsessed? Nothing is got for nothing, and certain strong writers (women as well as men) cannot achieve their aesthetic splendor without solipsism. Shakespeare, as far as we can tell, may have been one of the least solipsistic of poets; Chaucer appears to rival Shakespeare in this happy regard, and I am sometimes tempted to play a parlor game in which one divides up the major writers on the basis of their degree of solipsism. Does it make a difference? Not at all as to the relative eminence of their achievements, but it does seem to be related to a difference in kind. Joyce was a monumental solipsist, while Beckett appears to have been one of the most selfless of men. The contrast between *Finnegans Wake* and Beckett's trilogy of *Molloy, Malone Dies,* and *The Unnameable* has something to do with Beckett's evasion of his precursor, but more to do with their strikingly different senses of other selves.

Unlike some of Tolstoy's other male protagonists, Hadji Murad has a preternatural sense of the reality of other selves. Without it he long since would have been dead; but his awareness is much more than a mere wariness, as is shown by his affectionate relationship with Butler, whose Romantic vision and compulsive gambling have overtones of the young Tolstoy's military service in the Caucasus. If in one respect Hadji Murad's tragic isolation projects Tolstoy's own dilemma, the Tartar warrior's generosity of affection introjects a quality that the novelist understood to be lacking in himself. Undoubtedly, the military prowess of his hero was also an attribute with which Tolstoy sought to identify. John Bayley sums up Tolstoy's army service as "consisting almost entirely in talking and trying to compose stories, shooting hares and pheasants, having affairs with Cossack girls, and getting treated for gonorrhea at the local spa." As Bayley charmingly adds, this experience is akin to the active military exploits of Hemingway, whose entire career was a self-conscious agon with Tolstoy's. Both novelists carried their self-idolatry into the farthest regions of their art by investing their selves in the nature of things, so that they entered massively into the realm of what Freud called "reality testing," though without the final Freudian wisdom of making friends with the necessity of dying.

Hadji Murad, magnificent in his last stand as in his entire life, manifests that wisdom as only Shakespeare's tragic heroes and heroines do, fighting to the end and dying defiantly but with grace. On his last morning, when it is already light but before the sun has risen, he calls for his horse and rides out accompanied by his five henchmen and a guard of five Cossacks. Killing and driving off these Cossacks, he and his men are still not able to escape the mass of other Cossacks, as well as Tartar militia serving the Russians, who surround them. After a fierce firefight, the end comes for Hadji Murad:

> Another bullet hit Hadji Murad in the left side. He lay down in the ditch and again pulled some cotton wool out of his *beshmét* and plugged the wound. This wound in the side was fatal, and he felt that he was dying. Memories and pictures succeeded one another with extraordinary rapidity in his imagination. Now he saw the powerful Abu Nutsal Khan, dagger in hand and holding up his severed cheek he rushed at his foe; then he saw the weak, bloodless old Vorontsóv with his cunning white face, and heard his soft voice; then he saw his son Yusúf, his wife Sofíat, and then the pale, red-bearded face of his enemy Shamil with its half-closed eyes. All these images passed through his mind without evoking any feeling within him—neither pity nor anger nor any kind of desire: everything seemed so insignificant in comparison with what was beginning, or had already begun, within him.
>
> Yet his strong body continued the thing that he had commenced. Gathering together his last strength he rose from behind the bank, fired his pistol at a man who was just running towards him, and hit him. The man fell. Then Hadji Murad got quite out of the ditch, and limping heavily went dagger in hand straight at the foe.
>
> Some shots cracked and he reeled and fell. Several militia men

with triumphant shrieks rushed toward the fallen body. But the body that seemed to be dead suddenly moved. First the uncovered, bleeding, shaven head rose; then the body with hands holding to the trunk of a tree. He seemed so terrible, that those who were running towards him stopped short. But suddenly a shudder passed through him, he staggered away from the tree and fell on his face, stretched out at full length like a thistle that had been mown down, and he moved no more.

He did not move, but still he felt.

When Hadji Aga, who was the first to reach him, struck him on the head with a large dagger, it seemed to Hadji Murad that someone was striking him with a hammer and he could not understand who was doing it or why. That was his last consciousness of any connexion with his body. He felt nothing more and his enemies kicked and hacked at what had no longer anything in common with him.

Aside from the objective, almost dispassionate power of this passage, we are moved to wonder that Tolstoy, despite his identification with the hero, abstains from any shock, elegiac regret, or metaphysical horror over Hadji Murad's departure from consciousness. The corpse "had no longer anything in common with him," and we remember Natasha's outcry in *War and Peace,* when she hears of the death of Prince Andrew: "Where is he and who is he now?" I quote John Bayley's suggested literal version, upon which Bayley makes the fine comment, considering Tolstoy's power of identity: "Solipsism is an index of immortality."

The death of Hadji Murad, who was the aged Tolstoy's escape from solipsism, provokes nothing like Natasha's anguished, double question. Instead, Tolstoy gives us "The nightingales, that had hushed their songs while the firing lasted, now started their trills once more: first one quite close, then others in the distance."

We are left with the crushed thistle, called the Tartar, in the ploughed field, and with the threnody of the nightingales. The subtle power of Tolstoy's narrative, Homeric in its ambiance, Shakespearean in its characterization, compensates us above all with its image of heroism. Hadji Murad is the best there is in his universe—whether Caucasian or Russian—at every attribute that matters: daring, horsemanship, resourcefulness, leadership, vision of reality. No other hero of epic or saga, ancient or modern, is quite equal to him, or nearly as likable. As Hadji Murad dies, he is purged of pity, anger, and desire. And so is Tolstoy. And so are we. That Tolstoy, of all writers, could imagine a death at once so appropriate and so unlike his own dread of death is an unexpected and reassuring triumph for aesthetic dignity. Whatever we take the canonical to be, *Hadji Murad* centers it in the Democratic Age.

15.

Ibsen: Trolls and *Peer Gynt*

I FOUND MYSELF recently on the stage of the American Repertory Theatre at Harvard, supposedly discussing Ibsen's *Hedda Gabler*. My fellow performers were an eminent Ibsen scholar (male), an acclaimed Harvard Feminist, and the distinguished and beautiful actress who had just played Hedda. I achieved the success of being hissed by much of the audience when I mildly and amiably observed that Hedda's true precursors were Shakespeare's Iago and Edmund, so that even if the Norwegian society of her day had allowed her to rise to Chief Executive Officer of the firearms industry, Hedda would still have been sadomasochistic, manipulative, murderous, and suicidal, that is to say, her dreadfully fascinating self.

With perhaps some mischief, I added that it made no difference therefore whether Hedda was a woman or a man, and just as actresses have played Hamlet, perhaps some actor would yet play Hedda. The audience was much happier when the scholarly Feminist replied that Hedda was a victim of society and of nature, being both unhappily married and unwillingly pregnant. "She is trapped in a woman's body" became a refrain, as did the notion that society victimized Hedda by giving her nothing to do.

My Feminist opponent was not particularly original; nor was I. Brigid Brophy had anticipated us both back in 1970 by saying that Hedda's tragedy could have been avoided had she "become commander-in-chief of the Norwegian armed forces," but I think the formidable author of *Black Ship to Hell* (one of my favorite books) was mistaken. Whether commanding an army or arms factory, Hedda would have acted like her forerunners Iago and Edmund. Her genius, like theirs, is for negation and destruction. Again like them, she is a playwright who writes with the lives of others. Her intelligence is malign, not because of social circumstances but for her pleasure, for the exercise of her will. If she resembled anyone that Ibsen had ever known, it was Ibsen himself, as he was aware.

It is no accident that *Hedda Gabler,* written in Munich in 1890, is the masterpiece of the Aesthetic Age, that perilous transition between the Democratic and Chaotic. Iago, pridefully savoring his debasement of Othello, and Edmund, detachedly contemplating the gullibility of his father Gloucester and his brother Edgar, are in league with Hedda hoping ardently that Løvberg has shot himself, at her urging and with her pistol, in proper style. Elevating Iago to Othello's second in command and Edmund to Gloucester's heir would only have delayed the tragedies they animate; other starting points would have been generated. Hedda as armaments minister or as field marshal would still have found another impetus for destroying Løvberg, and herself.

All this is intended as a prelude to the most crucial element in Ibsen's canonicity: his social colorings are only a mask for his conversion of Shakespearean tragedy and Goethean fantasy into a new kind of Northern tragicomedy, a dramatic poem overtly High Romantic in *Brand* and *Peer Gynt,* yet subtly just as High Romantic in *Hedda Gabler* and *The Master Builder.* The shadows of *Hamlet* and of *Faust* fall upon all of Ibsen throughout the half-century of his career as dramatist. His canonicity, as well as his playwright's stance, have everything to do with his struggle to individuate his own poetic will and almost nothing to do with the

social energies of his age. Irritable and cranky, ruthless in devotion
to his gift, the not very charismatic Ibsen resembles Goethe only
to the degree that both renounced some of their most vital impulses
in order to practice their art without impediment. Ibsen charmed
almost no one; Goethe charmed everyone, himself included. Like
Shakespeare, Ibsen had the mysterious endowment of the true
dramatist, which is to be able to lavish more life on a character
than one possesses oneself. Goethe's only persuasive dramatic creation is his own personality, or Mephistopheles insofar as he is
Goethe. There is no one in Goethe's plays or dramatic poems like
Brand, Peer Gynt, Emperor Julian, Hedda Gabler, Solness. Demoniac or trollish beings, they are intensely rammed with life, a
Shakespearean panoply of roles without rival in modern literature.
But they carry an un-Shakespearean burden, which is the playwright's disapproval. Eric Bentley, nearly half a century ago, isolated this central peculiarity in Ibsen: "he wrote works which were
more and more subjective and difficult and which bore within
them a concealed condemnation of modern men, including the
poet himself."

This condemnation is directed even more, as Bentley implied,
at the public, who suffer through their stage surrogates precisely
what Ibsen wishes them to suffer. Kierkegaard, who had a strong
if oblique effect on Ibsen, distinguished between two despairs: that
of having failed to become oneself, and the greater one, of having
indeed become oneself. Ibsen's protagonists quite definitely have
become themselves. Except for Peer Gynt, they end in despair.
Ibsen labored mightily to make Peer Gynt despair, but this is the
one character who got completely away from him and entered the
literary space inhabited by Hamlet, Falstaff, Lear's Fool, Barnardine (of *Measure for Measure*), Don Quixote and Sancho Panza,
and only a few others.

Part of the odd comedy of *Peer Gynt* as dramatic poem ensues
from watching Ibsen working hard but vainly to make himself,
and us, disapprove of or dislike Peer. Falstaff's wit justifies his
every fault, mitigates his life, until we reflect upon it; and who
has time for such reflection while Falstaff is on stage? Peer's endless
energy and insouciance keep him going against adversaries as
preternaturally formidable as the troll king, the Great Boyg, the

Button-Molder, and the Strange Passenger, as well as against all merely human opponents. Whether in the theater or in the study, we side with Peer, indeed are absorbed into the great Gyntian self.

Ibsen is the exemplary dramatist of the Aesthetic period because, far more subtly even than Chekhov, let alone Strindberg, Wilde, and Shaw, he intuited how to perspectivize his characters through aspects of our perceptions and sensations. He is the democratic heir of the aristocratic Goethe, and though he could not equal *Faust, Part Two* as a dramatic poem, he possessed the secret that Goethe never learned, how to revive poetic drama in the post-Enlightenment. The mythologies of *Faust, Part Two* were too remote for dramatic immediacy; Ibsen relied instead upon an occult Norwegian folk mythology that functioned for him the way the Freudian mythology works for many of the writers of our Chaotic Age.

Ibsen's dramatic psychology centers upon the figure of the troll, suddenly popular again in children's dolls. The wild-haired little imps that I pass in the storefronts have, however, a rather more benign aura than Ibsen's trolls, who are authentic demons. In an early essay on folk ballads (1857), Ibsen noted that popular writing in his nation had favored "fantastic travels to the home of the trolls . . . war with trolls," which puts us into the world of *Peer Gynt.* Reading Ibsen and watching him performed, I am overwhelmed by the impression that Ibsen's trolls are not, to him, ancient fantasies or modern metaphors. Like Goethe, Ibsen believes in his *daimones,* in the preternatural sources of his own genius. Trolls are not, as some critics have suggested, Ibsen's equivalent of the Freudian unconscious. They are closer to the later Freudian mythology of the drives, Eros and Thanatos, and since *we* possess the drives, we are partly trollish in our nature. But Ibsen is a monist where Freud tries to be a dualist; our alternating desires for life and death, in Ibsen's view, are not the human element in us. Since the drives are nevertheless universal (or at least a universal mythology), trolls cannot be simply ogres, as, say, the mountain trolls are in *Peer Gynt.* Peer himself is a borderline troll, and Hedda Gabler and Solness, as we will see, are trolls except for their merely societal timidities. In *Brand,* the girl Gerd is someone we both admire and abhor, because the human in her, all that is not troll, is an authentic spiritual prophetess. Something fundamental in Ibsen, a sly uncanniness uneasily allied to his creativity, is pure troll.

I do not think Ibsen would have agreed with some of his modern scholars in their definitions of trolls. Muriel Bradbrook called the troll "the animal version of man," but the healthy animal in the endlessly active Peer Gynt rejects the trolls. Rolf Fjelde, whose version of *Peer Gynt* is the one I will use, goes beyond Bradbrook by saying of the troll, "in recent history he ran the death camps." Ibsen's trolls are personally very nasty indeed, particularly in *Peer Gynt,* but they are closer to sadistic, disturbed children than to systematic technocrats of genocide. Most simply, trolls are *before* good and evil, rather than beyond it.

The most formidable humanized troll in Ibsen is Hedda Gabler, and Hedda cannot be called evil. That would be as uninteresting as saying her precursors Iago and Edmund are wicked fellows. Doubtless Ibsen thought of Shakespeare's hero-villains, Macbeth included, as being trolls; but that is not a very Shakespearean myth. In Iago and Edmund, as in Hedda, there is a playfulness gone rancid, and insofar as the sublime Falstaff yields to a certain rancidity, a trollishness appears in him also. The opposite of troll-ishness is wit and the high spirits that sheer wit can engender. Sir John, witty to the end, never transmutes into a troll, whereas the sadistic clown of *As You Like It,* Touchstone, is little better than one.

Trollishness, whether in Ibsen or, as he partly teaches us to find it, in Shakespeare, is a dialectical matter. Like the Goethean dae-monic, it is destructive of most human values, yet it seems the inevitable shadow side of energies and talents that exceed the human measure. Hedda Gabler, whose ambiguous sexuality in-cludes sadistic desires for Thea Elfstead, ultimately descends from Lilith, Adam's first wife according to Jewish esoteric tradition. In one account, Lilith abandoned Adam in Eden because she declined further sexual intercourse in the missionary posture, as we have come to call it. When Ibsen noted that Hedda desired to live altogether as a man, he implied that his tragic protagonist was in Lilith's line, since Norwegian folklore traced hidden female trolls (huldres) as the daughters of Adam's first wife. Again the point is not Hedda's supposed evil nature, but her preternatural allure. Properly directed and acted, Hedda should be as coldly fascinating and nihilistically seductive as Edmund, and should have the power of turning something in each of us into a Goneril or a Regan. Her trollishness is her glory, however sinister.

Criticism or performance that converts Ibsen into a social re-former or moralist is destructive of his aesthetic achievement and threatens his authentic place in the Western dramatic canon, one second only to Shakespeare and perhaps Molière. More even than the later Shakespeare, Ibsen is an occult or visionary playwright. From start to finish he writes romance, even if the flamboyance of *Brand, Peer Gynt,* and *Emperor and Galilean* seems to vanish in the bourgeois, democratic tragedies that became Ibsen's char-acteristic work. In abandoning poetry for prose, Ibsen says he was yielding to modernity; but nothing in his nature was at all yielding. George Bernard Shaw deceived himself and others in proclaiming a social Ibsen; I cannot think of any other Western dramatist of true magnitude who is as consistently weird as Ibsen. A strangeness that refuses domestication, an eccentric vision, really a baroque art—Ibsen manifests these qualities as does every other titan of the Western Canon. As with Milton or Dante or Dickinson or Tolstoy, so it is with Ibsen: we have lost sight of his originality because we are contained by that individuality; we have been partly formed by Ibsen. Shakespeare is necessarily the largest in-stance of this phenomenon. But Ibsen, early and late, remained more Shakespearean than he cared to recognize.

CRITICS GENERALLY agree that Ibsen's first canonical play is the ferocious *Brand,* composed in Italy in 1865, when the dramatist was thirty-seven. More even than *Peer Gynt,* which followed it, *Brand* seems a play for the theater of the mind and not for any actual stage. It now has a peculiar glory in English, because the version by the poet Geoffrey Hill (1978) is much the finest Ibsen available to us as poetry. Hill, a master of savage eloquence, is a martyrologist, and his temperament, as manifested in his own poems, is peculiarly Brandian. He declines to call his *Brand* a translation, but it surpasses any purported translation we have.

What Hill demonstrates sublimely is that Brand is sublimely unbearable; when he dies at the end, in an avalanche, the audience or readers can only be relieved that the doom-eager priest will not be able, following the highest of principles, to destroy anyone else. On this central issue of his tragedy, Ibsen is hidden or equivocal: is Brand's God only a magnified Brand? If one believes (as I do) that every god, Yahweh included, was once a man (the central insight of Joseph Smith, the Mormon prophet), one reflects on the truth of the mad girl Gerd's final conviction that Jesus never died but instead became Brand. Brand is the Norwegian or Viking Jesus, even as American religionists worship not Jesus of Nazareth, but the American Jesus. W. H. Auden, striving for an eminent Christian orthodoxy, condemned Brand as an idolater, hardly an Ibsenite judgment:

> . . . our final impression of Brand is of an idolator who worships not God, but *his* God. It makes no difference if the God he calls his happens to be the true God; so long as he thinks of him as his, he is as much an idolater as the savage who bows down to a fetish.

Gerd's reading of Brand is not Ibsen's and yet remains more relevant to the play than Auden's interpretation does. Brand's God is his only to the extent that any prophet's or mystic's God is his own. Whatever Brand's relation to his God, it isn't the relation that renders him unbearable. His human relations, starting with his mother, are hopeless, including his marriage, since Agnes is shown as falling in love not with the man but with the hero of faith.

However Norwegian Brand is or was, his religion seems very American and post-Christian to me. We learn little about Brand's God, but there is just enough to show us that Brand and God exist together in a mutual solitude, whether of one self or of two. Auden sees in Brand the not wholly successful representation of an apostle, but Ibsen's Brand is no apostle of anyone. Like Ibsen himself, like Peer Gynt, Brand is a trollish self. Ibsen is a dramatic genius, and Brand a very persuasive representation of that fearful phenomenon, a religious genius. Peer Gynt, like Don Quixote and

Sir John Falstaff, is something else, a genius of play, what Huizinga called *homo ludens.* Brand's nearest parallel in Ibsen is Julian the Apostate, another fascinating but ultimately unloving and unbearable genius of the spirit.

In both figures, as in nearly all of Ibsen's major protagonists, there are qualities that remind us of oddities in Ibsen's own trollish nature. I have a good many friends who are authentic poets, novelists, and playwrights, and many possess a considerable number of eccentricities; but none of them keeps a poisonous scorpion under glass upon his or her writing desk, plying it with fruit. Ibsen was neither Brand nor Emperor Julian, but he was a master builder knowingly in league with trolls. And while he evidently intended Peer Gynt to be only a self-parody at best, the universalism of Peer is very nearly a full brother to Hamlet, Falstaff, Don Quixote, Sancho Panza.

Far more than Goethe's Faust (whom Ibsen greatly admired), Peer is the one nineteenth-century literary character who has the largeness of the grandest characters of Renaissance imaginings. Dickens, Tolstoy, Stendhal, Hugo, even Balzac have no single figure quite so exuberant, outrageous, vitalistic as Peer Gynt. He merely *seems* initially to be an unlikely candidate for such eminence: what is he, we say, except a kind of Norwegian roaring boy, marvelously attractive to women (in his youth), a kind of bogus poet, a narcissist, absurd self-idolater, a liar, seducer, bombastic self-deceiver? But this is paltry moralizing, all too much like the scholarly chorus that rants against Falstaff. True, Peer, unlike Falstaff, is not a great wit (though Peer can be very funny). But in the Yahwistic Biblical sense, Peer the scamp bears the Blessing: more life. Brand is doom-eager, a Viking death-ship in himself. Peer is a warmth bringer, though not exactly a light bearer. Ibsen makes this palpable in the wonderful pathos of the death scene of Peer's fierce and loving mother, who is comforted by Peer's playful tenderness as she expires, a scene that overtly contrasts with Brand's obnoxious and principled refusal to ease the dying of his own miserly and miserable mother.

Much of the critical reaction to *Peer Gynt* consists simply of seeing Peer as Brand turned upside down. Since Brand's essence is "No compromise!" the Gyntian self is identified with trimming, in a weak interpretation of the Great Boyg's injunction: "Go round about." Peer is a multiplicity of self-indulgences, but hardly a compromiser as such. As befits the Democratic Age, Peer is the natural man—all too natural. He is also, like Brand and Julian the Apostate, the preternatural man, driven by trollishness and by the need of transcending trollishness. We don't much like Peer toward the end on shipboard, being wolfish about the crew; or the shipwrecked Peer, drowning the cook with a touch of gusto. But for the most part Peer provokes our affection. His violent side reflects not only his trollishness, but his mythological origin and status as troll killer.

Ibsen professedly derived his Peer Gynt from a quasi-historical hunter, Per Gynt, who is the hero of a Norwegian folktale. The hunter encounters the Great Boyg, a mysterious and invisible troll who is a bent, snakelike presence; but unlike Ibsen's Gynt, who has to follow the Boyg's injunction to go around it, the folktale hero slays the Boyg. Subsequently, this ferocious hunter slaughters the trolls who make love to the herd girls, the same passionate women who entice Ibsen's Peer Gynt. The playwright softens the violence of the original Per, while retaining the hero's reputation as yarnspinner and storyteller. Ibsen's Peer is a nineteenth-century Norwegian peasant, child of a declining family, not an uncanny hunter, except in his fantastifications. These yearnings are hardly to be taken as an indication that Peer is what W. H. Auden interpreted him as being, the artist-genius as a new kind of dramatic hero. Ibsen's Peer is neither artist nor genius, and Auden brilliantly insisted on getting this wrong:

> the Peer we see on stage has no appetites or desires in the ordinary sense; he plays at having them. Ibsen solves the problem of presenting a poet dramatically by showing us a man who treats nearly everything he does as a role, whether it be dealing in slaves or idols or being an Eastern Prophet. A poet in real life would have written a drama about slave trading, then another drama about a prophet but, on the stage, play acting stands for making.

The Peer we encounter in Ibsen's pages is consumed by wonderfully ordinary appetites and desires and is certainly much more a natural man than a poet. Yet Auden's insight remains; Solness in *The Master Builder* is an architect, while Rubek in *When We Dead Awaken* is a sculptor. As for Løvberg's burnt-up manuscript in *Hedda Gabler,* neither we nor Ibsen estimate the cultural cost to be very great. Auden looks for the nonexistent poet in Peer Gynt because Ibsen seems to have an intimate relation to this protagonist, more than to Brand or to Emperor Julian. Part of the mystery of human and aesthetic Ibsen is that among all his characters he seems most heavily invested in Peer Gynt and Hedda Gabler. He *is* Hedda, as Flaubert is Emma Bovary. The relation to Peer Gynt is very different and abides in the slash mark between identity/nonidentity. If one winds around again to Shaw's association of Peer Gynt with Don Quixote and Hamlet, the phenomenon is aesthetic universalism, transcending national canons. Hamlet is probably not a representation of Shakespeare's own imagination; Macbeth is closer to that prophetic intensity. The Don and Cervantes no one need speculate upon, for Cervantes memorably ends his epic romance with an overt declaration: "For me alone Don Quixote was born, and I for him. He knew how to act, and I knew how to write. We two alone are as one."

It would startle us to substitute "Peer Gynt" for "Don Quixote," and Ibsen would never have done so. Yet truly for Ibsen alone was Peer Gynt born, and Ibsen for him, even though neither perhaps (in Cervantes' sense) knew how to act. Other plays by Ibsen achieve tragic eminence, but nothing else is so fecund. Eric Bentley, nearly half a century ago, accurately termed *Peer Gynt* "a masterpiece and a delight" and encouraged us to interpret this grand dramatic poem with a little sympathy. I like best Bentley's word "delight."

Ibsen's contemporaries did not appreciate acts 4 and 5, which are the glory of the work, never surpassed by Ibsen as invention, the essence of poetry. The last two acts together are considerably longer than the first three together and transcend the saga of the young Peer. Acts 1 through 3 show us Peer at twenty, vitalistic and unstoppable, contending with neighbors and with trolls. Judging himself unworthy of Solveig because of his trollish amours, and isolated by the death of his mother, Peer goes into exile, and the play becomes surrealistic, perhaps irrealistic, closer to Beckett than to Strindberg. The gorgeous and hilarious act 4 opens on the coast of Morocco, proceeds into the Sahara Desert, and ends in a Cairo madhouse. Peer is now a splendidly corrupt middle-aged Americanized slave trader, hosting an outdoor dinner for equally corrupt cronies—British, French, Prussian, and Swedish—to whom he expounds the Gyntian moral philosophy:

> *The Gyntian self—it's an army corps*
> *Of wishes, appetites, desires,*
> *The Gyntian self is a mighty sea*
> *Of whim, demand, proclivity—*
> *In short, whatever moves my soul*
> *And makes me live to my own will,*
> *But just as our Lord had need of clay*
> *To be creator of the universe,*
> *So I need gold if I'm to play*
> *The emperor's part with any force.*

The troll in Peer has triumphed, since pragmatically he has followed the Troll King's injunction: "Troll, to yourself be—enough!" rather than the human motto: "Man, to yourself be true!" In trollish consistency, the Greek revolt against the Turks being under way, Peer reverses Byronic heroism and proposes financing the Turks. When his associates flee with his gold-laden yacht and then explode with it, he praises God, while lamenting that the Deity is scarcely economical.

The hero of the first three acts is now more clearly a hero-villain, but he is also consistently funnier and even more likable, because his rueful misadventures touch so tellingly on a universal strain in human fantasies. Knowing still that he somehow remains elect, the scamp Peer clambers up a tree, where we see him fighting off monkeys as if they were so many trolls. With his customary insouciance he next wanders through the desert and meditates on improving it. Peer, we suddenly see, is the link between Goethe's Faust and Joyce's Poldy Bloom. Each dreams of a new domain, reclaimed from ruined nature; and Faust's seaside kingdom, Gyntiana, and Poldy's New Bloomusalem in the Nova Hibernia of the future are all best summed up by Peer:

In the midst of my sea, on a rich oasis,
I'll reproduce the Nordic races.
The dalesman's blood is royal almost;
Arabian crossings will do the rest.
Within a cove, on a shelving strand,
I'll found Peeropolis, my capital.
The world's obsolete! Now the ages call.
For Gyntiana, my Virgin land!

Ibsen mingles farce, fantasy, and a yearning pathos when Peer goes on to cry out for a crusade against Death, a presage of the marvelous quest of act 5. Fate (and Ibsen) bring Peer the stolen horse and robes of the emperor of Morocco. Sublimely mounted and attired, he goes off to become a prophet, surrounded by dancing girls led by Anitra, a particularly attractive celebrator of the Gyntian self. As prophet, Peer is very nearly fulfilled but falls into the quotidian when he attempts a more secular satisfaction with the wily Anitra, who runs off with the horse and the prophet's wealth, while gratifying poor Peer not at all. We like Peer all the better for his quick bounce back from his latest erotic humiliation:

To try to stop time by skipping and dancing;
To fight the current by preening and mincing!
To strum the lute, take love for a fact,
Then end like a hen—by getting plucked.
That's conduct to call prophetic frenzy—
Plucked! Oh Lord, I've been plucked all right!

His prophetic career over, Peer sets himself to be an old historicist, a skimmer-off of history's cream. As a new Vico, he seeks "the sum of the past" and goes to Egypt to hear the Statue of Memnon welcome sunrise. Peer's impulse is a parody of Faust's in *Part Two* of Goethe's poem, which haunts Ibsen's acts 4 and 5. Instead of Goethe's extraordinary revivification of the classic, with Faust as the lover of Helen, we get Peer as Norwegian tourist, who writes in his notebook,

The statue sang. Heard definite tones,
But can't figure what it all means.
A hallucination, obviously.
Nothing else worthy of note today.

Instead of carrying Peer into the dark backward abyss of classical history, Memnon reminds him only of the Troll King. What
ought to be an even more imposing confrontation with the Great
Sphinx at Giza again fails as world history and seems to Peer only
another encounter with the Great Boyg. The Oedipal answer to
the riddle "What is Man?" is given not by Peer but by Begriffinfeldt, head of the Cairo madhouse, who is also visiting the Sphinx
in search of understanding (as Begriffinfeldt's name literally
means). The search is over when Begriffinfeldt proclaims Peer the
Emperor of Interpreters, who has solved the riddle of life by saying
of the trollish Sphinx, "He's *himself.*" Baffled but forever willing,
Peer finds himself in the Scholar's Club or madhouse where Begriffinfeldt locks the keepers in a cage and releases the inmates,
making a grand anti-Hegelian pronouncement: "Absolute Reason
/ Died last night at eleven o'clock."

Reason is dead, and the shocked Peer reigns in its place and
receives the demented homage of Huhu, a language reformer; of
a fellah, who carries the mummy of King Apis on his back; and
best of all, of Hussein, a cabinet minister who lives in the illusion
that he is a pen. For Ibsen, these were brutal contemporary political satires, but they live now in their own inspired lunacy. Peer
sends Huhu off to interpret the Moroccan apes with whom he
had struggled earlier, and instructs the fellah to hang himself in
order to become like King Apis. Amiably as the Huhu matter turns
out, the actual suicide of the fellah horrifies Peer, and a second
suicide, by the penman Hussein, is too much altogether and causes
Peer to pass out. In a sublimely sordid apotheosis, Begriffinfeldt
crowns the unconscious Peer with a wreath of straw, and all hail
the Emperor of Self as act 4 ends.

I cannot think of a twentieth-century play that equals *Peer Gynt*
act 4 as a revival of the tradition of Aristophanes and of *Faust,*
Part Two. Ibsen's verve is unfailing as he surges from one outrageous invention to another. Whatever it is that Peer represents,

we do him wrong to invoke Augustinian moralizings, as some of the best Ibsen critics have done. Ibsen is more of a scorpion than a moralist and, in this play, more of a Dionysiac than we have understood. Eric Bentley is perhaps a touch too harsh on Peer, harsher than Ibsen was:

> *Peer Gynt* is a counter-Faust. It shows the other side of Faustian striving, the striving of modern careerism with all its vast implications. In his gay unscrupulousness, his adventurous egoism, and his amiable immorality, Peer Gynt is the Don Quixote of free enterprise and should be the patron saint of the National Association of Manufacturers.

Peer, in one phase, was indeed a great robber baron, but ultimately he is too vitalistic and metamorphic to abide in any role, and his self-absorption produces a pragmatic disinterestedness. Peer is a genius of play, trollish and manic play. Ibsen, like Cervantes and Shakespeare, is not interested in the Fall of Man. Trollishness is not a rebellion against God, even when it manifests itself in men rather than in trolls. Act 4 of *Peer Gynt* is as anti-Christian as it is anti-Hegelian; absolute reason and absolute spirituality die together at midnight, while the battered Peer lives on.

Whatever his critics think, Ibsen does not regard Peer as a failure or a hollow man. *Faust, Part Two* is an even greater dramatic poem than *Peer Gynt,* but unlike Faust, Peer is the triumphant representation of a personality. What Ibsen values in Peer is what we should value: the idiosyncratic that refuses to be melted down into the reductive or the commonplace, which is the agon of act 5 of the play. I dissent strongly from a view now held by many, expressed most forcefully by Michael Meyer in his *Ibsen on File* (1985):

> Whether one regards Peer as having died in the madhouse or in the shipwreck, Act V surely represents either the unreeling of his past life in his mind at the moment of death or (which is perhaps the same thing) the wandering of his soul in purgatory.

Ibsen's Peer Gynt does not die, either in the madhouse or in the shipwreck; he is still very much alive when the final curtain falls. Peer, like Odysseus and Sancho Panza and unlike Don Quixote and Falstaff and Faust, is a survivor, as befits the precursor of Leopold Bloom. Ibsen cheerfully buries Brand under an avalanche, but he cannot bear to kill Peer Gynt. The great trolls, Hedda Gabler and Solness and Rubek, must all die; trollish Peer, who is Ibsen's sense of life, must live. All of act 5 is a refusal of death by water, of meltdown, of purgatorial suffering. Not for Peer Gynt the Faustian apotheosis into an angelic and womanly sphere; instead Ibsen provides a return to the woman who becomes at once mother and much belated bride.

Critics and directors need not fear that this is melodramatic and sentimental; it is rather Ibsen's final outrage in an endlessly outrageous drama. The trolls could not destroy Peer because he had women backing him, and the Strange Passenger and the Button-Molder are thwarted by the same Byronic and Goethean enigma. Peer's relation to Aase, his mother, and the saintly Solveig is knowingly obscured by Ibsen, since we are far likelier to remember the protagonist's erotic adventures, human and trollish. The connecting element is gusto, for which Ibsen forgives Peer almost everything.

Act 5 darkens Peer, giving him his first ugly moments in the play. Part of the lasting strangeness of *Peer Gynt* is that it is more a trilogy of dramas than a single work. The twenty-year-old Peer of the first three acts is a heroic vitalist, uncanny enough to be part troll in his energies and desires. Act 4's middle-aged Peer is both a matured humorist and a scoundrelly scamp, and his fantastic adventures just barely stay within natural bounds. The supernatural pervades the final act, in which the aged Peer, at some cost to his humor, is at once more rancid and more poignant than ever before. Although *Peer Gynt* is Ibsen's most original and least Shakespearean play, this double development in Peer parallels Falstaff's fortunes as the second part of *Henry IV* ebbs to its conclusion.

The return to the sea and to the mountain valleys of Norway has much, but not all, to do with the changed atmosphere of the final act. Old age—Peer's and, by a prolepsis, Ibsen's—sets the bleakness of a cosmos where death is a constant intimation. Like Goethe in *Faust, Part Two* (to whom he is again indebted), Ibsen has a frankly elitist vision of immortality. The great mass of souls are melted down into a common fund, from which fresh life can receive its spirit; but the great, creative souls retain their individuality after death. This concept goes back to Petrarch, but Goethe and Ibsen enliven it with a desperate twist into literalism. The question then becomes: What is the greatness of Peer Gynt, now at his most savagely trollish, that justifies his holding off the Strange Passenger and the Button-Molder? It is one thing for Gretchen (and Goethe) to save Faust, but why is it even more persuasive that Solveig (and Ibsen) save Peer Gynt?

Ibsen, to his dramatic credit, does not make this problem easy for us. Peer for the first time is unpleasant to confront, unless one happens to be the rather grisly Strange Passenger, who requests the gift of Peer's corpse for the purposes of unsavory research, and who utters the memorable comfort to the hero: "No one dies halfway through the last act." But two-thirds of the way through the last act Peer meets the Button-Molder, who shapes the rest of the play. Ibsen's debt to Goethe here was shrewdly worked out in 1942 by A. E. Zucker, who rightly compared the Button-Molder's tone to that of Mephistopheles. Ibsen's inventiveness matches Goethe's in sardonic and macabre humor and has the added force of a lifelong obsession going back to Ibsen's own childhood. As a boy, Ibsen had used a casting ladle in a game of button molding, just as Aase, early in the play, says that the childish Peer had done the same. When the Button-Molder tells Peer, "You know the craft," he touches a source where early fascination mingles with terror. The metaphor involved is Biblical and prophetic, implying purification more than punishment, though this "purification" ironically consists in the loss of self-identity, a particular horror for Peer (and for Ibsen).

"Friend, it's melting time" is the Button-Molder's wry remark to Peer, and part of the Button-Molder's curious charm is his patience, his willingness to be postponed until the next crossroads. He knows that Peer will encounter the haggard and deposed Troll King before that rendezvous and will again hear the trollish word: *enough.* "Troll, to yourself be enough" pragmatically ensues in

"Friend, it's melting time." At their second meeting, the dialogue between Peer and the Button-Molder takes a turn that Ibsen's critics sometimes tend to Christianize. Peer, in honest confusion, asks what is it "to be yourself," and the Button-Molder replies with too easy a paradox: "To be yourself is to slay yourself."

But why should we think that the Button-Molder speaks for Ibsen, or rather for the play? There is no protagonist anywhere in Ibsen who achieves selfhood by suicide, including Rubek at the end of *When We Dead Awaken* and Hedda Gabler. No literary artist was less interested in slaying his own self than Ibsen, and I take it that the true point of the Button-Molder is that he is wise enough to accept perpetual deferment. For how can you melt Peer Gynt down into the communal? So much does Peer fear so unlikely an end that he offers himself up to a curious character called the Lean One, Ibsen's version of Mephistopheles; but the Lean One thinks that Peer is not worth damnation, at least incognito. The famed Peer Gynt, Quixotic emperor of himself, is another matter, and the Lean One goes off southward in search, misdirected by the unrevealed Peer.

The increasing separation between the actual and the legendary Peer begins to seem the play's final center. For a third time the Button-Molder yields, and the advent of Solveig, at once Gretchen and Beatrice, transforms the situation. Still, the drama ends in an antiphony of voices, Solveig's and the Button-Molder's, moving to cancel each other out. The Button-Molder promises a meeting at the final crossroads, while Solveig embraces Peer, promising an endless regressiveness. There is little reason to associate Ibsen with the endorsement of either promise. For him, and for us, the play concludes in irony, that is to say, meaninglessness. Peer is neither saved nor doomed to a final meltdown. Instead, he is to sleep and dream. Certainly, he will not be enough to and in himself, and he will have been purged; but will he be himself when asleep in Solveig's lap?

Peer Gynt is about five hundred lines longer than the uncut *Hamlet,* though compared to *Faust* it is a brief work. Clearly, *Peer Gynt* is Ibsen's *Hamlet* and his *Faust,* the play or dramatic poem in which the full range of an imagination is exposed. With *Brand* as its prelude and *Emperor and Galilean* as its huge epilogue, *Peer Gynt* is the center of Ibsen, containing everything he had, everything he quarried for the prose plays of his supposedly major phase. The canonicity of *Peer Gynt* is to me one with its trollishness, even as the best of the prose plays are the most trollish, *Hedda Gabler* in particular.

To return to Ibsen's trollishness is to return to Ibsen the dramatist, for the true quintessence of Ibsenism is the troll. Whatever it meant in Norse folklore, the troll in Ibsen is the figure for his own originality, the signature of his spirit. Trolls mattered most to Ibsen because it can be so difficult to tell them from people, a difficulty augmented in Ibsen's later plays. The difficulty, at least for Ibsen, was neither a moral nor a religious matter. Is Brand a troll? The question is irksome but hardly meaningless, and it ceases to be irksome when we ask it concerning Hilde Wangel, Rebecca West, Hedda Gabler, Solness the Builder, and Rubek, among others.

Trollishness, for and in Ibsen, is a question of psychic cartography. The daemonic is its own category in Goethe, but it does not pervade everything. With Ibsen there are no boundaries, and we do not know who is altogether human and who is contaminated by the Northern demons. We tend, however, to be most interested when the characters are trollish, and the formula in Ibsen therefore becomes something close to the hidden principle that the dramatic is another name for the preternatural. That is very unlike what Ibsen is supposed to be; but the actual Ibsen, as a playwright, resembles his own serpentine troll, the Great Boyg. That should teach us, at the least, to stop terming Peer Gynt a moral weakling, an evasive compromiser, an unrealized self. He is a borderline troll, fascinating and vitalizing, and so is Ibsen. Eric Bentley long ago emphasized that the later Ibsen was a realist outside, a vast phantasmagoria within. Bentley, of course, was right: in *Brand* and *Peer Gynt* and *Hedda Gabler* the inside and the outside cannot be distinguished, and we are given ghostlier demarcations, keener sounds, than in any dramas since.

PART IV

THE CHAOTIC AGE

16.

Freud: A Shakespearean Reading

EVERY CRITIC has (or should have) her or his own favorite critical joke. Mine is to compare "Freudian literary criticism" to the Holy Roman Empire: not holy, not Roman, not an empire; not Freudian, not literary, not criticism. Freud bears only part of the blame for the reductiveness of his Anglo-American followers; he need share no responsibility for the Franco-Heideggerian psycholinguistics of Jacques Lacan and company. Whether you believe that the unconscious is an internal combustion engine (American Freudians), or a structure of phonemes (French Freudians), or an ancient metaphor (as I do), you will not interpret Shakespeare any more usefully by applying Freud's map of the mind or his analytical system to the plays. Freudian allegorization of Shakespeare is as unsatisfactory as current Foucaultian (New Historicist), Marxist and Feminist allegorizations or past Christian and moral views of the plays through ideological lenses.

For many years I have taught that Freud is essentially prosified Shakespeare: Freud's vision of human psychology is derived, not

altogether unconsciously, from his reading of the plays. The founder of psychoanalysis read Shakespeare in English throughout his
life and recognized that Shakespeare was the greatest of writers.
Shakespeare haunted Freud as he haunts the rest of us; deliberately
and unintentionally, Freud found himself quoting (and misquot-
ing) Shakespeare in conversation, in letter-writing, and in creating
for psychoanalysis a literature of its own. I don't think it is accurate
to say that Freud loved Shakespeare as he loved Goethe and Milton. Whether he could even be called ambivalent about Shakespeare seems to me doubtful. Freud did not love the Bible or show
any ambivalence toward it, and Shakespeare, much more than the
Bible, became Freud's hidden authority, the father he would not
acknowledge.

Whether consciously or not, Freud on some level weirdly associated Shakespeare with Moses, as in his essay on Michelangelo's Moses. This remarkable meditation upon Michelangelo's
sculpture was published anonymously in 1914 in the psychoanalytic journal *Imago,* as though Freud wished to disavow it even
as he made it known to his disciples. He begins by remarking on
the bewildering or riddling effect of certain masterpieces of literature and of sculpture, and before he mentions the Moses of
Michelangelo he speaks of *Hamlet* as a problem that psychoanalysis has solved. A very unattractive dogmatism pervades this
pronouncement, shielded as it is by anonymity:

> Let us consider Shakespeare's masterpiece, *Hamlet,* a play now
> over three centuries old. I have followed the literature of psy-
> choanalysis closely, and I accept its claim that it was not until
> the material of the tragedy had been traced back analytically to
> the Oedipus theme that the mystery of its effect was at last
> explained. But before this was done, what a mass of differing
> and contradictory interpretative attempts, what a variety of
> opinions about the hero's character and the dramatist's design!
> Does Shakespeare claim our sympathies on behalf of a sick man,
> or an ineffectual weakling, or of an idealist who is only too
> good for the real world? And how many of these interpretations
> leave us cold—so cold that they do nothing to explain the effect
> of the play and rather incline us to the thoughts in it and the

splendour of its language. And yet, do not those very endeavours speak for the fact that we feel the need of discovering in it some source of power beyond these alone?

Rather than argue with this view, I prefer to ask why Freud should have chosen to use *Hamlet* in connection with Michelangelo's Moses. Oddly, he is far more suggestive and imaginative in his interpretation of the marble statue than in his reduction of Shakespeare's most complex character to a victim of an Oedipal fixation. Perhaps identifying with Moses activated Freud's imagination, but I am inclined to believe that Shakespeare induced a considerable anxiety in Freud, while Michelangelo provoked none. Eventually, Freud was to link Moses and Shakespeare indirectly in a troubling way; both figures were not who they seemed to be, and Freud refused to accept any traditional account of either. In Freud's final phase, *Moses and Monotheism* replaced the Bible's Hebrew prophet of God with an Egyptian, while William Shakespeare was given his historical existence as an actor, but not as a writer.

Freud went to his death insisting that Moses had been an Egyptian and that the Earl of Oxford had written the plays and poems falsely ascribed to Shakespeare. The latter notion, invented by J. Thomas Looney in his *Shakespeare Identified* (1921), is even crazier than the former. Nevertheless, the Looney hypothesis became Freudian truth within a few years and was still being affirmed in his final work, the posthumously published *Outline of Psychoanalysis*. Nothing, of course, could be loonier: Edward de Vere, seventeenth Earl of Oxford, was born in 1550 and died in 1604. He was thus dead before the composition of *King Lear, Macbeth, Antony and Cleopatra,* and the late Shakespearean romances. To be a Looneyite you have to begin by arguing that these plays were left in manuscript at Oxford's death, and then go on from there. How could Freud, possibly the best mind of our century, have fallen into such zaniness?

Freud's desire that Shakespeare not be Shakespeare took a variety of forms before his gladsome discovery of the Looney hypothesis. One feels that Freud was open to every possible suggestion that the son of a Stratford glover, the actor William

Shakespeare, was an impostor. Ernest Jones, Freud's hagiographer, tells us that Meynert, who taught the young Freud the brain's anatomy, believed in the theory that Sir Francis Bacon had written Shakespeare. Despite his admiration for Meynert, Freud declined to become a Baconian, but for a revealing reason: Bacon's cognitive achievement added to Shakespeare's eminence would give us an author with "the most powerful brain the world has ever borne."

Rejecting the Baconian thesis, Freud picked up every other weird notion circulated about and against Shakespeare, including an Italian academic's suggestion that the name was a version of Jacques Pierre! If anyone had hinted at any exposure of the true identity of the actor from Stratford, one feels that Freud would have been receptive. When he encountered Looney's book in 1923, he swallowed it without skepticism. It did not matter that the Earl of Oxford was dead before *Lear* was composed; it mattered enormously that Oxford, like Lear, had three daughters. Oxford's friends finished his plays for him after his death, and anyway the actor from Stratford had only two daughters. What was working in Freud's subtle and powerful mind that allowed such literalism serious consideration? The Oedipus complex, imposed upon Hamlet decades before by Freud, was now the Oxford complex. As the author of *Hamlet,* Oxford lost his father while he was still a boy and eventually estranged himself from his mother, who had remarried. It would have done no good to tell Freud that such a practice was common to Elizabethan high aristocrats; he wanted, he *needed* the poet of *Hamlet, Lear, Macbeth* to be a wealthy and powerful nobleman.

If, as I argue, Freud indeed owed Shakespeare much too much, how did it lessen the burden if Oxford and not the provincial actor was the precursor? Was this merely Freud's Viennese social snobbery? My surmise is that Freud desperately wanted to read the great tragedies as autobiographical revelations. The actor from Stratford would do well enough as the dramatist of *The Merry Wives of Windsor,* but not as the creator of domestic tragedies of those in high estate: Hamlet, King Lear, Othello, Macbeth. In a letter to his old friend, Arnold Zweig (April 2, 1937), Freud comes close to losing his composure at his inability to convert the baffled Zweig to Looneyism:

He seems to have nothing at all to justify his claim, whereas Oxford has almost everything. It is quite inconceivable to me that Shakespeare should have got everything secondhand— Hamlet's neurosis, Lear's madness, Macbeth's defiance and the character of Lady Macbeth, Othello's jealousy, etc. It almost irritates me that you should support the notion.

(translated by Ernst L. Freud)

I read these words with amazement: this is a powerful and sophisticated mind, still at the height of its powers; indeed it is the mind of our age, as Montaigne was the mind of Shakespeare's. Shakespeare's mind, as Freud knows but refuses to acknowledge, was the mind of all the ages, and the centuries to come will never catch up with it. Freud, hardly an unimaginative consciousness, calls the Shakespearean imagination a getting of "everything secondhand."

The Freudian defensiveness is awesome. It is as though he badly needs to have *Hamlet* written by Hamlet, *Lear* by Lear, *Macbeth* by Macbeth, *Othello* by Othello. The inference would seem to be that Freud himself has written his *Hamlet* in *The Interpretation of Dreams;* his *Lear* in the *Three Essays on the Theory of Sexuality;* his *Othello* in *Inhibitions, Symptoms, Anxieties;* and his *Macbeth* in *Beyond the Pleasure Principle*. The "man from Stratford" could not have invented Freudian psychology; the Earl of Oxford, a proud and wayward peer, could not have invented it either, but he could have lived it, unlike the humble actor.

Unless one is a religious Freudian, this is the ancient story of literary influence and its anxieties. Shakespeare is the inventor of psychoanalysis; Freud, its codifier. But misreading Shakespeare's works was not enough for Freud; the threatening precursor had to be exposed, dismissed, disgraced. The actor from Stratford was a forger and a plagiarist at best. Oxford, the great unknown, was the tragic protagonist who was somehow able to write down what he had suffered. In relation to Freud, Oxford is only an Elijah to Freud's Messiah, a roarer in the wilderness of the psyche who cries out to prophesy the coming of the true interpreter. The Egyptian Moses of Freud's fantasy will be murdered by the Jews and will then become the totemic father more powerful than the living prophet had been. Shakespeare, in Freud's Looney fantasy, is obliterated, to be replaced by a titanic aristocrat less powerful than the living poet-playwright had been.

OBVIOUSLY I AM HERE discussing Freud as a writer, and psychoanalysis as literature. This is a book on the Western Canon of what, in a better time, we called imaginative literature, and Freud's greatness as a writer is his actual achievement. As a therapy, psychoanalysis is dying, perhaps already dead: its canonical survival must be in what Freud wrote. One could object that Freud is an original thinker as well as a powerful author, to which I would reply that Shakespeare is an even more original thinker. One does not need to add the achievement of Sir Francis Bacon to Shakespeare's in order to confront the major psychologist in the world's history.

I do not mean that Shakespeare was merely a moral psychologist while Freud invented depth psychology. Hamlet did not have an Oedipus complex, but Freud certainly had a Hamlet complex, and perhaps psychoanalysis is a Shakespeare complex! As a student of literary influence, I do not know how to overestimate the influence of Shakespeare upon Freud. It does not differ in kind, only in degree, from Shakespeare's influence upon Goethe, Ibsen, Joyce, and so many others who are the subject of this book. But I want to go further: Shakespeare influences Freud the way Emerson influences Whitman; we are speaking of the prime precursor, as we would speak of Wordsworth in regard to Shelley, or Shelley in relation to Yeats, or Yeats to all Anglo-Irish poets after him, the superb Seamus Heaney included. Freud's anxiety in the matter of Shakespeare we have seen already; had Looney never existed, Freud would have invented an earl of Oxford for himself.

Freudian literary criticism of Shakespeare is a celestial joke; Shakespearean criticism of Freud will have a hard birth, but it will come, since Freud as a writer will survive the death of psychoanalysis. Transference to a shaman is an ancient, worldwide technique of healing, widely studied by anthropologists and scholars of the history of religion. Shamanism preceded psychoanalysis and will survive it; it is the purest form of dynamic psychiatry. Freud's work, which is the description of the totality of human nature, far transcends the faded Freudian therapy. If there is an essence of Freud, it must be found in his vision of civil war within the psyche. That division presupposes a view of how the personality is organized and a number of myths or metaphors to render that organization dynamic (or in a more literary term, dramatic). These Freudian figurations include psychic energy, the drives, the mechanisms of defense. Although Freud, as befits a founder, carried out a self-analysis in order to discover or invent his drama of the self, he explicitly forbade all those who came after him to emulate their leader.

This premier self-analysis depended for its coherence upon a dramatic paradigm, and Freud found it where European Romanticism generally has found it, in Hamlet. Oedipus, I suggest, was hauled in by Freud and grafted onto Hamlet largely in order to cover up an obligation to Shakespeare. The Freudian analogies between the two tragedies represent strong misreadings and cannot be sustained by an analysis that evades Freud's overvaluation of what he called the Oedipus complex. A Hamlet complex is a very rich affair, since there is no more intelligent character in all of Western literature. The Oedipus of Sophocles may have a Hamlet complex (which I define as thinking not too much but much too well), yet the Hamlet of the man from Stratford most definitely does not have an Oedipus complex.

Shakespeare's Hamlet certainly loves and honors the memory of his father and harbors considerable reservations regarding his mother. Freud's contention is that Hamlet unconsciously desires his mother and unconsciously harbors murderous thoughts about his father, of the kind actually carried out by Claudius. Shakespeare is rather subtler; his Oedipal tragedies are *King Lear* and *Macbeth,* but not *Hamlet.* Queen Gertrude, recently the recipient of several Feminist defenses, requires no apologies. She is evidently a woman of exuberant sexuality, who inspired uxurious passion first in King Hamlet and later in King Claudius. Freud would not bother to notice it, but Shakespeare was careful to show that Prince Hamlet was a rather neglected child, at least by his father. Nowhere in the play does anyone, including Hamlet and the Ghost, tell us that the uxurious father loved the son. A basher in battle, like Fortinbras, the fractious king seems to have had no time for the child between the demands of state, war, and husbandly lust. Thus, when the Ghost urges Hamlet to revenge, it cries out, "If thou didst ever thy dear father love—," but says nothing about its own affection for the prince. Similarly Hamlet, in his first soliloquy, emphasizes the devotion between his father and mother while excluding their regard, if any, for him. His own memories of love, taken and given, center entirely upon poor Yorick, his father's jester, who took the place of the parents so smitten with one another:

> Alas, poor Yorick! I knew him, Horatio, a fellow of infinite jest, of most excellent fancy. He hath bore me on his back a thousand times, and now how abhorr'd in my imagination it is! my gorge rises at it. Here hung those lips that I have kiss'd I know not how oft.

Hamlet, in the graveyard of act 5, is virtually beyond affect, even when he disputes with Laertes as to who felt more love for the dead Ophelia. The sadness of his cold elegy for Yorick might have made Freud reflect that there were no other lips—not Ophelia's, Gertrude's, King Hamlet's—that the hero had kissed he knew not how oft. Freud's concept of the Oedipal complex is the masterpiece of what Freud called emotional ambivalence, which he thought he had first formulated. I have dismissed the Oedipal complex as largely irrelevant to Hamlet, but where had Freud encountered extraordinary affective and cognitive ambivalence in literature? Where else but in Hamlet, the character in whom Shakespeare first fully invested his genius for representing ambivalence? Hamlet has taught Europe and the world the lesson of ambivalence for almost four centuries now, and Freud was a latecomer in Hamlet's wake. As an interpreter of Hamlet, Freud does not warrant a passing grade, but as a commentator upon Freudian concerns, Hamlet surpasses all rivals. Here is the starting point in Freud's celebrated letter (October 15, 1897) to Wilhelm Fliess:

> Since then I have got much further, but have not yet reached any real resting-place. Communicating the incomplete is so laborious and would take me so far afield that I hope you will

excuse me, and content yourself with hearing the parts which are established for certain. If the analysis goes on as I expect, I shall write it all out systematically and lay the results before you. So far I have found nothing completely new, but all the complications to which by now I am used. It is no easy matter. Being entirely honest with oneself is a good exercise. Only one idea of general value has occurred to me. I have found love of the mother and jealousy of the father in my own case too, and now believe it to be a general phenomenon of early childhood, even if it does not always occur so early as in children who have been made hysterics. (Similarly with the "romanticization of origins" in the case of paranoiacs—heroes, founders of religion). If that is the case, the gripping power of *Oedipus Rex,* in spite of all the rational objections to the inexorable fate that the story presupposes, becomes intelligible, and one can understand why later fate dramas were such failures. Our feelings rise against any arbitrary, individual fate such as shown in the *Ahnfrau,* etc., but the Greek myth seizes on a compulsion which everyone recognizes because he has felt traces of it in himself. Every member of the audience was once a budding Oedipus in phantasy, and this dream-fulfillment played out in reality causes everyone to recoil in horror, with the full measure of repression which separates his infantile from his present state.

The idea has passed through my head that the same thing may lie at the root of *Hamlet.* I am not hinting of Shakespeare's conscious intentions, but supposing rather that he was impelled to write it by a real event because his own unconscious understood that of his hero. How can one explain the hysteric Hamlet's phrase "So conscience doth make cowards of us all," and his hesitation to avenge his father by killing his uncle, when he himself so casually sends his courtiers to their death and despatches Laertes so quickly? How better than by the torment roused in him by the obscure memory that he himself had meditated the same deed against his father because of passion for his mother—"use every man after his desert, and who should 'scape whipping?" His conscience is his unconscious feeling of guilt. And are not his sexual coldness when talking to Ophelia, his rejection of the instinct to beget children, and finally his transference of the deed from his father to Ophelia, typically hysterical? And does he not finally succeed, in just the same remarkable way as my hysterics do, in bringing down his punishment on himself and suffering the same fate as his father, being poisoned by the same rival?

(translated by Eric Mosbacher and James Strachey)

The peculiar badness of the second paragraph, when taken as a reading of *Hamlet,* causes me to blink and wince, but its literary power survives its weak misreading of a rival who had poisoned Freud and went on poisoning him. How different these two paragraphs are: *Oedipus Rex* is viewed abstractly and at a great distance from the text, while Hamlet is up close, and details and verbal reminiscences abound. The remarks about *Oedipus* could be made about absolutely any literary work that turned upon a tragic fate; there is nothing there that is specific to Sophocles' play. But *Hamlet* is an intimate matter for Freud: the play reads him, and allows him to analyze himself as a Hamlet. Hamlet is not a hysteric, except for brief lapses, but Freud has his hysterics, his patients, and he assimilates Hamlet to them. Far more interestingly, he has assimilated himself to Hamlet, and to Hamlet's ambivalence. The assimilation continued in Freud's dream book, as he liked to call it—*The Interpretation of Dreams* (1900)—where the Oedipus complex is first overtly formulated, though not named as such until 1910.

By 1900, Freud had learned to mask his Shakespearean indebtedness; in the dream book he gives a very full (if curiously dry) account of *Oedipus Rex* before going on to Hamlet the person. We have the puzzle that *Hamlet* and not *Oedipus Rex* is Freud's true concern and interest, and yet the term chosen is not "the Hamlet complex." Few figures in cultural history have had anything like Freud's success at insinuating concepts into our consciousness. "Why, of course, it is the Oedipus complex, and we all have it," we learn to mutter, but in fact it is the Hamlet complex, and only writers and other creators necessarily possess it.

Why didn't Freud call it the Hamlet complex? Oedipus unknowingly cuts down his father while Hamlet had no such impulses at all toward the rightful king, though as the prince of ambivalences he doubtless had counterimpulses toward everyone at every level of his multiform consciousness. But the Hamlet complex would have drawn the menacing Shakespeare too closely into the matrix of psychoanalysis; Sophocles was far safer and also offered the prestige of classical origins. In *The Interpretation of Dreams*, Hamlet enters only in a long footnote in the Oedipus discussion, and it was not until the 1934 edition that the anxious Freud elevated the discussion of *Hamlet* into his text, as one long, dense paragraph (unless otherwise noted, I use here and throughout James Strachey's translations of Freud):

Another of the great creations of tragic poetry, Shakespeare's *Hamlet*, has its roots in the same soil as *Oedipus Rex*. But the changed treatment of the same material reveals the whole difference in the mental life of these two widely separated epochs of civilization: the secular advance of repression in the emotional life of mankind. In the *Oedipus* the child's wishful phantasy that underlies it is brought into the open and realized as it would be in a dream. In *Hamlet* it remains repressed; and—just as in the case of a neurosis—we only learn of its existence from its inhibiting consequences. Strangely enough, the overwhelming effect produced by the more modern tragedy has turned out to be compatible with the fact that people have remained completely in the dark as to the hero's character. The play is built up on Hamlet's hesitations, and an immense variety of attempts at interpreting them have failed to produce a result. According to the view which was originated by Goethe and is still the prevailing one today, Hamlet represents the type of man whose power of direct action is paralysed by an excessive development of his intellect. (He is "sicklied o'er with the pale cast of thought.") According to another view, the dramatist has tried to portray a pathologically irresolute character which might be classed as neurasthenic. The plot of the drama shows us, however, that Hamlet is far from being represented as a person incapable of taking any action. We see him doing so on two occasions: first in a sudden outburst of temper, when he runs his sword through the eavesdropper behind the arras, and secondly in a premeditated and even crafty fashion, when, with all

the callousness of a Renaissance prince, he sends the two courtiers to the death that had been planned for himself. What is it,
then, that inhibits him in fulfilling the task set him by his father's
ghost? The answer, once again, is that it is the peculiar nature
of the task. Hamlet is able to do anything—except take vengeance on the man who did away with his father and took that
father's place with his mother, the man who shows him the
repressed wishes of his own childhood realized. Thus the loath-
ing which should drive him on to revenge is replaced in him by
self-reproaches, by scruples of conscience, which remind him
that he himself is literally no better than the sinner whom he is
to punish. Here I have translated into conscious terms what was
bound to remain unconscious in Hamlet's mind; and if anyone
is inclined to call him a hysteric, I can only accept the fact as
one that is implied by my interpretation. The distaste for sexuality expressed by Hamlet in his conversation with Ophelia fits
in very well with this: the same distaste which was destined to
take possession of the poet's mind more and more during the
years that followed, and which reached its extreme expression
in *Timon of Athens*. For it can of course only be the poet's own
mind which confronts us in Hamlet. I observe in a book on
Shakespeare by Georg Brandes (1896) a statement that *Hamlet*
was written immediately after the death of Shakespeare's father
(in 1601), that is, under the immediate impact of his bereave-
ment and, as we may well assume, while his childhood feelings
about his father had been freshly revived. It is known, too,
that Shakespeare's own son who died at an early age bore the
name "Hamnet," which is identical with "Hamlet." Just as
Hamlet deals with the relation of a son to his parents, so *Macbeth* (written at approximately the same period) is concerned
with the subject of childlessness. But just as all neurotic symptoms, and, for that matter, dreams, are capable of being "over-
interpreted" and indeed need to be, if they are to be fully
understood, so all genuinely creative writings are the product
of more than a single motive and more than a single impulse in
the poet's mind, and are open to more than a single interpretation. In what I have written I have only attempted to interpret
the deepest layer of impulses in the mind of the creative writer.

"Repression in the emotional life of mankind" is a curious expression, since Freud cannot be talking about Oedipus and Hamlet, but only about Sophocles and Shakespeare. Oedipus has after all no idea of whom he has slain at the crossroads, and Hamlet would not have agreed with Freud that his ambivalence about cutting down Claudius represented guilt at having wished the murder of his own father. One might repeat at this point that Hamlet's powers of self-analysis not only match Freud's, but provide Freud with a paradigm for emulation. It is not Hamlet who lies upon the famous couch in Dr. Freud's office, but Freud who hovers with the rest of us in a miasma of corruption in the halls at Elsinore, and Freud has no special privilege as we jostle one another in the corridors: Goethe, Coleridge, Hazlitt, A. C. Bradley, Harold Goddard, and all the rest of us, since everyone who reads *Hamlet* or attends its performance is compelled to become an interpreter.

Freud tells us that a healthy Hamlet would murder Claudius, and since Hamlet evades the act, he must be a hysteric. I turn again to the Nietzschean refinement of Goethe's view, which is that Hamlet thinks not too much but much too well, and at the frontiers of human consciousness declines to become his father, who would certainly have skewered *his* uncle in the same circumstances. Young Fortinbras is old Fortinbras come again, another bully boy, but Prince Hamlet is hardly just his father's son. To say gently that Freud crudely misreads and underestimates Hamlet is not, alas, to divest Freud's misreading of its permanent strength.

Freud declines to see how intellectually formidable Hamlet and Shakespeare are, but I do not underestimate Freud. We all of us now believe we possess (or are possessed by) *libido,* but there is no such entity: there is, in fact, no separate sexual energy. Had Freud decided to fuel the death drive with *destrudo,* a notion that once engaged him, we would all of us go about now carrying with us not only our Oedipus complex and our *libido* but our *destrudo* as well. Fortunately, Freud decided against *destrudo,* but our near miss should be instructive. Freud, as Wittgenstein warned, is a powerful mythologist, the great mythmaker of our time, fit rival to Proust, Joyce, and Kafka as the canonical center of modern literature. His rallying cry is the final sentence of the long paragraph on *Hamlet* quoted above; after an unconvincing gesture of interpretive modesty, supposedly granting that authentic creative writing is produced by "more than a single motive and more than a single impulse," Freud charmingly suggests that his "single interpretation" attempts to reach bedrock: "the deepest layer of impulses in the mind of the creative writer." "Deepest" strata do not exist in the mind; Milton's Satan, a great poet, rightly laments that in every deep a lower deep opens and threatens to devour him. Freud, himself a Miltonic rather than a Satanic figure, understood the metaphor of "the deepest" as well as anyone has ever understood it.

The issue, I insist, is not the Oedipus complex but the Hamlet complex, and Freud worried it once more in a sketch for an essay, "Psychopathic Characters on the Stage," written in 1905 or 1906, but published only posthumously:

The first of these modern dramas is *Hamlet*. It has as its subject the way in which a man who has so far been normal becomes neurotic owing to the peculiar nature of the task by which he is faced, a man, that is, in whom an impulse that has hitherto been successfully suppressed endeavors to make its way into action. *Hamlet* is distinguished by three characteristics which seem important in connection with our present discussion. (1) The hero is not psychopathic, but only *becomes* psychopathic in the course of the action of the play. (2) The repressed impulse is one of those which are similarly repressed in all of us, and the repression of which is part and parcel of the foundations of our personal evolution. It is this repression which is shaken up by the situation in the play. As a result of these two characteristics it is easy for us to recognize ourselves in the hero: we are susceptible to the same conflict as he is, since "a person who does not lose his reason under certain conditions can have no reason to lose." (3) It appears as a necessary precondition of this form of art that the impulse that is struggling into consciousness, however clearly it is recognizable, is never given a definite name; so that in the spectator too the process is carried through with his attention averted, and he is the grip of his emotions instead of taking stock of what is happening. A certain amount of resistance is no doubt saved in this way, just as, in an analytic treatment, we find derivatives of the repressed material reaching consciousness, owing to a lower resistance, while the repressed material itself is unable to do so. After all, the conflict in *Hamlet* is so effectively concealed that it was left to me to unearth it.

We are a great distance from *Hamlet* here, barred from it by Freud's system and by his burst of "unearthing" dogmatism. What is clear is that there is now absolutely no distinction between Hamlet and a Freudian patient, even in degree of interest! The hero of Western consciousness is one more psychopath, and a Shakespearean tragedy is reduced to a case for analytic treatment. We might call this rather dreary paragraph "The Passing of the Hamlet Complex," except that I do not believe it. What actually happened was that Hamlet was replaced by Lear and by Macbeth, and Freud's struggle with Shakespeare was transferred to different battlegrounds, since the handling of *Hamlet* in five later contexts added nothing but Oedipal repetitions, unworthy of Freud as agonist.

FREUD FOUND his first Cordelia in Martha Bernays, before she became his wife, and his second and more authentic Cordelia in his daughter Anna, his great favorite among all his children and his worthy continuator in her strong book on the ego and its mechanisms of defense. The Freudian reading of *King Lear* is to be found partly in a fascinating essay, "The Theme of the Three Caskets" (1913), and partly in a late letter to one Bransom (March 25, 1934), printed in an appendix to the *Life and Work* of Freud by Ernest Jones. Bransom had written an unfortunate book on *King Lear,* which found the play's hidden meaning in Lear's repressed incestuous lust for Cordelia, an insane view with which Freud happily concurred. This is the mythologically impressive conclusion of "The Theme of the Three Caskets":

Lear is an old man. We said before that this is why the three sisters appear as his daughters. The paternal relationship, out of which so many fruitful dramatic situations might arise, is not turned to further account in the drama. But Lear is not only an old man; he is a dying man. The extraordinary project of dividing the inheritance thus loses its strangeness. The doomed man is nevertheless not willing to renounce the love of women; he insists on hearing how much he is loved. Let us now recall that most moving last scene, one of the culminating points reached in modern tragic drama: "Enter Lear with Cordelia dead in his arms." Cordelia is Death. Reverse the situation and it becomes intelligible and familiar to us—the Death-goddess bearing away the dead hero from the place of battle, like Valkyr in German mythology. Eternal wisdom, in the garb of the primitive myth, bids the old man renounce love, choose death and make friends with the necessity of dying.

The poet brings us very near to the ancient idea by making the man who accomplishes the choice between the three sisters aged and dying. The regressive treatment he has thus undertaken with the myth, which was disguised by the reversal of the wish, allows its original meaning so far to appear that perhaps a superficial allegorical interpretation of the three female figures in the theme becomes possible as well. One might say that the three inevitable relations man has with woman are here represented: that with the mother who bears him, with the companion of his bed and board, and with the destroyer. Or it is the three forms taken on by the figure of the mother as it proceeds: the mother herself, the beloved who is chosen after her pattern, and finally the Mother Earth who receives him again. But it is vain that the old man yearns after the love of woman as once he had it from his mother; the third of the Fates alone, the silent goddess of Death, will take him into her arms.

I am baffled by Freud's judgment that "The paternal relationship . . . is not turned to further account in the drama." *King Lear* concerns itself with two paternal relationships, Lear to Cordelia, Goneril, and Regan, and Gloucester to Edgar and Edmund. What is Freud repressing? Lear, though immensely old, is not a dying man until the final scene, and the loyal Cordelia is hardly Death; but who would want to quarrel with the magnificent sentence that ends the first paragraph? Few moments even in Proust, Joyce, and Kafka are more memorable than the Freudian wisdom that bids us "renounce love, choose death and make friends with the necessity of dying." The reverberations of that line echo on in the eloquent prose poem of the final paragraph, where Lear and Freud blend together into a larger mystic figure, almost a dying god.

Alas, twenty-one years later we are given a jumble of psychoanalytic reductiveness and Looneyite Oxfordism! Bransom is assured that he is right as to Lear, and then Cordelia-Anna is added to the incestuous muddle:

> Your supposition illuminates the riddle of Cordelia as well as that of Lear. The elder sisters have already overcome the fateful love for the father and become hostile to him; to speak analytically, they are resentful at the disappointment of their early love. Cordelia still clings to him; her love for him is her holy secret. When asked to reveal it publicly she has to refuse defiantly and remain dumb. I have seen just that behavior in many cases.

This is too absurd to refute; when had Freud last read or seen the play? Rather than belabor him, let us pore over his more interesting errors or inventions. He says that there is no mention of the mother of Lear's daughters; there is one, though it is not crucial. But what gave Freud the idea that Goneril is pregnant? And how could he believe that Lear's madness ensued not from the old king's fury, but from his barely repressed desire for Cordelia? These objections pale besides the information imparted to Bransom, and to us, that Albany in *King Lear,* as well as Horatio in *Hamlet,* are to be equated with Lord Derby, the Earl of Oxford's first son-in-law! "O, matter and impertinency mix'd / Reason in madness!" The resistance to Shakespeare, pronounced enough in the Freudian reading of Hamlet as Oedipus, has achieved awesome complexity in this blend of Lear, Oxford, and Freud into one. What has happened to the apocalyptic tragedy that Shakespeare wrote, and where is Sigmund Freud, who once knew how to read? Both the drama and Freud's interpretive strength vanish into the terrible need to fend off the untutored actor from Stratford.

King Lear was too close for Freud; *Macbeth* allowed him to return to himself, particularly in the essay "Some Character-Types Met with in Psychoanalytic Work" (1916), where we are reminded why Freud is indeed a canonical author. He had remarked long before that the childlessness of Macbeth and Lady Macbeth was a key to the tragedy's meaning. In the 1916 essay, he centers on Lady Macbeth as a character "wrecked by success" and by subsequent remorse:

> It would be a perfect example of poetic justice in the manner of the talion if the childlessness of Macbeth and the barrenness of his Lady were the punishment for their crimes against the sanctity of geniture—if Macbeth could not become a father because he had robbed children of their father and a father of his children, and if Lady Macbeth had suffered the unsexing she had demanded of the spirits of murder. I believe one could without more ado explain the illness of Lady Macbeth, the transformation of her callousness into penitence, as a reaction to her childlessness, by which she is convinced of her impotence against the decrees of nature, and at the same time admonished that she has only herself to blame if her crime has been barren of the better part of its results.

How many children had Lady Macbeth? The question, asked facetiously by a formalist critic, is not by any means a silly one, though it cannot be answered with any certitude. Freud speaks of her "barrenness," but why then does she say that she has given suck? As the wife of a powerful thane who is the king's cousin, she is too highly placed to have nursed any child but her own. We must conclude that there was at least one child, but it died. Nor can she have been left barren; Macbeth in praise of her resolution urges her to bring forth men-children only. And yet Macbeth has his Herod-like aspect. He tries to have Fleance, Banquo's son, murdered, and he orders the slaughter of Macduff's children. There is a horror of generation in Macbeth's almost Gnostic hatred of time, and both he and Lady Macbeth are haunted by the prophecy that Banquo's descendants (the Stuart line that began in England with James I, son of Mary

Queen of Scots) will come to rule Scotland. Freud is therefore prag-matically right to assert that *Macbeth* is a play "about childless-ness," and he impressively concedes that he cannot give a total interpretation of the play, a concession that would have been equally relevant in his accounts of *Hamlet* and *King Lear,* but his intimate reaction to Hamlet and Lear presumably excluded such a disclaimer:

What, however, these motives can have been which in so short a space of time could turn the hesitating, ambitious man into an unbridled tyrant, and his steely-hearted instigator into a sick woman gnawed by remorse, it is, in my view, impossible to divine. I think we must renounce the hope of penetrating the triple obscurity of the bad preservation of the text, the unknown intention of the dramatist, and the hidden purport of the legend. But I should not admit that such investigations are idle in view of the powerful effect which the tragedy has upon the spectator. The dramatist can indeed, during the representation, overwhelm us by his art and paralyse our powers of reflection; but he cannot prevent us from subsequently attempting to grasp the psycho-logical mechanism of that effect. And the contention that the dramatist is at liberty to shorten at will the natural time and duration of the events he brings before us, if by the sacrifice of common probability he can enhance the dramatic effect, seems to me irrelevant in this instance. For such a sacrifice is justified only when it merely affronts probability, and not when it breaks the causal connection; besides, the dramatic effect would hardly have suffered if the time-duration had been left in uncertainty, instead of being expressly limited to some few days.

This paragraph begins as one of interpretive modesty and pro-ceeds to a fecund testiness on questions of dramatic representation, particularly of time. Again, I suspect repression in Freud explains his discontent, and I assume that his Hamlet complex is at work here. If ambivalence (or rather its representation) is a Shake-spearean and not a Freudian concept, indeed became Freudian only because of Freud's experience of Shakespeare, then Freud is

compelled to resent and misread the strongest Shakespearean representations of ambivalence, and those are the four great domestic
tragedies: *Hamlet, Othello, King Lear,* and *Macbeth.* I know of
no other instances in literature, Dante included, in which we are
placed so persuasively in an equivocal cosmos, where emotional
ambivalence governs nearly all relationships and where cognitive
ambivalence—in Hamlet, Iago, Edmund—helps to overdetermine
those murderous intensities that are Freud's truest subject. Neither
Hamlet nor Othello manifests the Hamlet complex, and neither
do Cordelia, Desdemona, Ophelia, and Edgar, but Iago, Edmund,
Goneril, Regan, Macbeth, and Lady Macbeth are immortal masterpieces of ambivalence carried to the heights of the sublime.
Freud, as prose-poet of the post-Shakespearean, sails in Shakespeare's wake; and the anxiety of influence has no more distinguished sufferer in our time than the founder of psychoanalysis,
who always discovered that Shakespeare had been there before
him, and all too frequently could not bear to confront this hu-
miliating truth.

In *Macbeth,* the ambivalence is so prevalent that time itself
becomes its representation, as Freud obscurely senses. What Freud
called *Nachträglichkeit,* a sense of always being after the event,
like a bad actor who invariably misses his cues, is the peculiar
condition of Macbeth himself. Freud is shrewd to question the
only apparent motivations of Macbeth and Lady Macbeth, since
the fruit of their ambition is so dismal, and since Shakespeare
enigmatically avoids defining the precise nature of their desires.
They have nothing in them of Marlowe's Tamburlaine or Shakespeare's own Richard III: the sense of glory attendant upon the
sweet fruition of an earthly crown. Why, after all, do they wish
to become king and queen of Scotland? The joyless dinner at which
Banquo's ghost appears is doubtless typical of court life under
Macbeth, as drab as it is menacing. What Freud hints at is the
essence of the play: childlessness, empty ambition, the butchery
of the fatherly Duncan, so mild and good that neither of the
Macbeths feels even a touch of *personal* ambivalence about him.
But however they became childless, their revenge against time is
usurpation, murder, and an attempt to cancel the future: all of
those tomorrows and tomorrows and tomorrows whose petty pace

so oppresses Macbeth. On this tragedy at least, by reining in his interpretive dogmatism, Freud has been profoundly suggestive.

WHAT, BESIDES his sense of the primacy of ambivalence and its apex in the Hamlet/Oedipus complex, did Freud owe most (knowingly or not) to Shakespeare? Shakespeare is everywhere in Freud, far more present when unmentioned than when he is cited. Freud's fundamental stance toward Shakespeare is what he called "negation" (*Verneinung*), which is the formulation of a previously repressed thought, feeling, or desire, one that enters consciousness only by being disowned, so that defense or repression continues. The repressed is accepted intellectually but not emotionally; Freud accepted Shakespearean ideas, even as he denied their source. Freud's drive for self-preservation made it necessary for him to negate Shakespeare, yet he never ceased to identify himself with Hamlet, not always consciously, and to a lesser extent with *Julius Caesar*'s Brutus, who was in Shakespeare's development a kind of pre-Hamlet. Identification with Hamlet is, of course, hardly unique to Freud; it has been universal, transcending dead white European males and appearing in an amazing variety of persons at diverse times and places. Ernest Jones notes that Freud's favorite quotation, in conversation or in writing, was Hamlet's admonition to Horatio: "There are more things in heaven and earth, Horatio, / Than are dreamt of in your philosophy." One sees why Freud made this an implicit motto for psychoanalysis, and it is even more apt when the context is restored. Directly preceding it is this exchange:

> *Horatio.* O day and night, but this is wondrous strange.
> *Hamlet.* And therefore as a stranger give it welcome.

This is the miniature representation, for Freud, of the initial situation of psychoanalysis: Horatio stands for the public, and Hamlet for Freud, urging the courteous welcome that strangers deserve. I cannot recall any place in Freud's letters or other writings, or any reported conversations, what may well have struck him as an invidious contrast: the resistance to psychoanalysis as compared to the almost universal acceptance of Shakespeare, from his own day and nation onward until his worldwide apotheosis in our time. I do remember that when Freud analyzed one of his own dreams, he found a comparison for his relation to Shakespeare in Prince Hal's unconscious usurpation of kingship: "Wherever there is rank and promotion the way lies for wishes that call for suppression. Shakespeare's Prince Hal could not, even at his father's sick-bed, resist the temptation of trying on the crown."

There is an old tradition that Shakespeare himself acted the part of the ghost of Hamlet's father when *Hamlet* was first produced. Psychoanalysis, in many ways a reductive parody of Shakespeare, continues to be haunted by Shakespeare's ghost because Shakespeare could be judged as a transcendental kind of psychoanalysis. When his characters change, or will themselves to change upon self-overhearing, they prophesy the psychoanalytic situation in which patients are compelled to overhear themselves in the context of their transference to their analysts. Before Freud, Shakespeare was our prime authority on love and its vicissitudes, or on the vicissitudes of the drive, and it is clear that he remains our best instructor still, and never ceased to guide Freud. Comparing Freud's two theories of anxiety, the revised account seems to me more Shakespearean than the earlier, rejected hypothesis. Before his *Inhibitions, Symptoms, and Anxiety* (1926) Freud believed that neurotic and realistic anxiety could be rigidly distinguished from each other: Realistic anxiety was caused by true danger, while neurotic anxiety resulted from dammed-up libido or unsuccessful repression, and was therefore not involved in the civil wars of the psyche.

After 1926, Freud abandoned the notion that libido can be transformed into anxiety. Instead, anxiety was seen as being prior to repression, and thus the motive for repression. In the earlier theory, repression preceded anxiety, which appeared only if repression failed. In the revised notion, Freud abandoned forever the causal distinction between real fear and neurotic anxiety. Translated into Shakespeare's dramatic cosmos, the older theory is very much at home, particularly in the high tragedies that Freud preferred, where anxiety is as primal as ambivalence.

Hamlet's Elsinore, Iago's Venice, Lear's and Edmund's Britain,

Macbeth's Scotland: in all of these, playgoers and readers confront an atmosphere of anxiety that is antecedent to character and event. If the masterpiece of ambivalence is the Hamlet/Oedipus complex, the masterpiece of anxiety is what I want to call the Macbeth complex, because that hero-villain is Shakespeare's most anxious. In the Macbeth complex, dread cannot be distinguished from desire, and imagination becomes both invulnerable and malign. For Macbeth, to fantasize is to have leaped the gap over the will and be on the other side of having performed the act. The time is not free until Macbeth is slain, because temporal forebodings are always realized in his realm, even before he has usurped power. If the Hamlet/Oedipus complex conceals the wish to father oneself, the Macbeth complex barely hides the desire for self-destruction. Freud named it the death drive in *Beyond the Pleasure Principle,* but I prefer the doom-eagerness and atmospheric intensity conveyed by the Macbeth complex.

Although Freud never identified as fully with Macbeth as with Hamlet, there are some startling analogies that he cited, as when he prophesied the nearly thirty years of labor remaining for him, in a letter of 1910: "What is one to do on a day when thoughts cease to flow and the proper words won't come? One cannot help trembling at this possibility. That is why, despite the acquiescence in fate that becomes an upright man, I secretly pray: no infirmity, no paralysis of one's powers through bodily distress. We'll die with harness on, as King Macbeth said." The affect there, with its noble humor, is rather different than in the usurper Macbeth's apocalyptic desperation:

> *I gin to be a-weary of the sun,*
> *And wish th' estate o' th' world were now undone.*
> *Ring the alarum-bell! Blow wind, come wrack,*
> *At least we'll die with harness on our back.*

Freud indeed died in full armor, thinking and writing virtually to the end. That his identification with Macbeth, however slight, has its positive aspect, is intimated by "as *King* Macbeth said." More than once, Freud asserted that his vision of his own published works startled him, even as Macbeth cried out at the spectral line of Banquo's royal Stuart descendants: "What, will the line stretch out to the crack of doom?" Again, the identification is light but proud, testifying to the contaminating power of Macbeth's imagination. Freud might say that the theme of *Macbeth* was childlessness, but on a deeper level he associated his own strength of imagination with Macbeth's, finding in the bloody tyrant and in himself both a heroic persistence and an image-making fecundity.

Shakespeare is the apotheosis of aesthetic freedom and originality. Freud was anxious about Shakespeare because he had learned anxiety from him, as he had learned ambivalence and narcissism and schism in the self. Emerson was freer and more original about Shakespeare because he had learned wildness and strangeness from him. It is appropriate that Emerson, rather than the equally canonical Freud, have the last word here: "Now, literature, philosophy, and thought, are Shakespearized. His mind is the horizon beyond which, at present, we do not see."

17

Proust: The True Persuasion
of Sexual Jealousy

Proust's greatest strength, amid so many others, is his charac-terization: no twentieth-century novelist can match his roster of vivid personalities. Joyce has the single, overwhelming figure in Poldy, but Proust has a portrait gallery: Charlus, Swann, Alber-tine, Bloch, Bergotte, Cottard, Françoise, Elstir, Gilberte, Bathilde the Grandmother, Oriane Guermantes, Basin Guermantes, the Mama of the Narrator/Marcel, Odette, Norpois, Morel, Saint-Loup, Madame Verdurin, the marquise de Villeparisis, and above all the dual figure of the Narrator and his earlier self, Marcel. Probably I have neglected some of equal importance with many of those listed, but that is already a score of characters I cannot forget.

In Search of Lost Time (herein called *Search* for short), which unfortunately may always be known in English by the beautiful but misleading Shakespearean title, *Remembrance of Things Past,* actually challenges Shakespeare in its powers of representing per-sonalities. Germaine Brée observed that Proust's personages, like

Shakespeare's, resist all psychological reductions. Again like
Shakespeare, Proust is a master of tragicomedy: I wince as I laugh,
but I have to agree with Roger Shattuck that the comic mode is
central to Proust because it allows him representational distance
in exploring the then partly forbidden matter of homosexuality.
Because of Proust's preternatural comic genius, he also rivals
Shakespeare at portraying sexual jealousy, one of the most canonical of human affects for literary purposes, handled by Shakespeare as catastrophic tragedy in *Othello* and near-catastrophic
romance in *The Winter's Tale*. Proust gives us three magnificent
sagas of jealousy: the ordeals, in sequence, of Swann, Saint-Loup,
and Marcel (I will call him Marcel, even though the Narrator gives
him that name only once or twice in the enormous novel). These
three tragicomic, obsessive anguishes are only one strand in an
encyclopedic work, yet Proust, like Freud, can be said to join both
Shakespeare and the Hawthorne of *The Scarlet Letter* in confirm-
ing the canonicity of sexual jealousy. It is hell in human life but
purgatorial splendor as *materia poetica*. Shelley affirmed that in-
cest was the most poetical of circumstances; Proust teaches us that
sexual jealousy may be the most novelistic.

In 1922, the year of Proust's death (he was just fifty-one), Freud
published a powerful, brief essay on sexual jealousy, "Certain
Neurotic Mechanisms in Jealousy, Paranoia, and Homosexuality." There is an opening association between jealousy and grief,
and Freud assures us that persons who seem not to manifest these
two universal affects have undergone severe repression, so that
jealousy and grief become even more active in the unconscious.
With grim irony, Freud divides jealousy into three parts: competitive, projected, delusional. The first is narcissistic and Oedipal;
the second imputes to the loved one a guilt, whether real or imagined, that belongs to the self; the third, over the border into paranoia, takes as its usually repressed object someone of one's own
sex. As is customary with Freud, the analysis is highly Shakespearean, though more in the mode of *The Winter's Tale*, which
Freud did not mention, than in the tragic darkness of *Othello*,
where Freud once specifically located projected jealousy. Leontes
in *The Winter's Tale* almost systematically works through Freud's
three varieties of jealousy. Proust's three grand cases of jealousy
leap over the normal or competitive variety, dally briefly with the

projected sort, and center themselves ferociously in the delusional mode. But Freud is Proust's rival, not his master, and the Proustian account of jealousy is very much Proust's own. Applying Freud to Proust on jealousy is as reductive and misleading as analyzing *Search*'s vision of homosexuality in a Freudian way.

There is no subtler ironist than Proust in our century, and his novel's mythological likening of Jews to homosexuals does not exactly dispraise either group. Proust was neither an anti-Semite nor a homophobe. His love for his Gentile father was real, but his passion for his Jewish mother was overwhelming, and his love affairs with the composer Reynaldo Hahn and with Alfred Agostinelli, the prototype for Albertine, were very authentic relationships. The refugees from Sodom and Gomorrah are compared by Proust to the Jews of the Diaspora, and more explicitly to Adam and Eve exiled from Eden. J. E. Rivers emphasizes that this parallel of Sodom, Jerusalem, and Eden is at the heart of Proust's novel and fuses the Jewish power of survival with homosexual endurance throughout the ages, so that both Jews and homosexuals achieve representative status as instances of the human condition since, as Proust says, "the true paradises are the paradises we have lost." Proust's humor can seem harsh in regard to the masochistic homosexuality of Charlus or the Jewish insecurities of the unpleasant Bloch, but we do Proust violence if we judge him to be chagrined by either his Jewish ancestry or his homosexual orientation.

Judging him does him violence in any case; *Search* is so meditative a work that it transcends Western canons of judgment. Its temper, as I recall Roger Shattuck observing, is curiously Eastern: Proust, the Narrator, and Marcel fuse in the implicit conviction that we are never fully formed but always go on slowly evolving in consciousness. I am aware that Proust is an apotheosis of French culture, not of Hindu thought. Perhaps Ruskin, mad as he was, imbued Proust with something of his secular mysticism; or, more likely, Proust's mastery of reverie carried him to the borders of an inward transformation. I wonder sometimes why Proust is unique in seeing and representing the high comedy, rather than the low farce, of sexual jealousy. The meditative process of *Search* carried him to a perspective in which Marcel's jealous sufferings can be seen as exquisitely, if still painfully, comic.

This does not mean that Proust in the solitude and silence of his cork-lined room immersed himself in as unlikely a work as the *Bhagavad-gita,* but *Search* is wisdom literature, even as Montaigne, Dr. Johnson, Emerson, and Freud are finally authors who touch a border between meditation and contemplation. Roger Shattuck says of *Search:* "We can read as far into it as our age and understanding allow." At the very close of the novel we don't necessarily believe that the Narrator has come to *know* a truth or a reality, but we sense that he is on the verge of *becoming* a kind of consciousness different from anything else that I at least have encountered in Western fiction. It is from the stance of that barely emergent consciousness that sexual jealousy and passionate love become ludicrously, if sublimely, indistinguishable from one another.

SAMUEL BECKETT near the conclusion of his *Proust* (1931) says that Proust's men and women "seem to solicit a pure subject, so that they may pass from a state of blind will to a state of representation." For Beckett, Proust becomes the pure subject: "He is almost exempt from the impurity of the will." I assume that Beckett here means neither the Narrator nor Marcel, but rather Marcel Proust, who suffers from asthma, reads Schopenhauer, and strives to attain the condition of music. Walter Pater, who had the same relation to Ruskin that Proust had, is the critic who would have best understood Proust. Pater's "privileged moment," a secularized and materialistic epiphany, is what Proust's jealous lovers—Swann and Marcel—seek when they anxiously conduct their historical and scholarly searches into the erotic past. Proust's high and terrifying comedy makes his protagonists into veritable art historians of jealousy, who pursue their researches long after their love has lapsed and even, in Marcel's case, after the beloved is dead. Sexual jealousy, Proust suggests, is a mask for the fear of mortality: the jealous lover becomes obsessed with every detail of the space and time of betrayal because he dreads that there will not be enough space and time for himself. Like the art historian, the bereft lover is seeking the truth of a past illumination, but the researcher of jealousy finds the illumination a darkness.

Proust himself thought that the crucial part of *Swann's Way,* the first volume of *Search,* was the extraordinary account of Swann's jealous sufferings. And indeed when I think of Swann, I recall first the trajectory of his descent into the inferno of jealousy. J. E. Rivers says that "Proust's vision is not feminine; it is androgynous," which is sometimes true of Shakespeare also. My own experience of *Search,* particularly of its major or Albertine sequence (*The Captive* and *The Fugitive*), is that the narrator's stance could only be called that of a male lesbian, which is itself a variant of the androgynous imagination Proust both manifests and celebrates. Proust's Narrator in *Cities of the Plain* invokes the transsexual world of Shakespearean comedy (I will use throughout Terrence Kilmartin's revision of C. K. Scott Moncrief's translation): "The young man whom we have been attempting to portray was so evidently a woman that the women who looked upon him with desire were doomed (failing a special taste on their part) to the same disappointment as those who in Shakespeare's comedies are taken in by a girl disguised as a youth."

In the comedies, Shakespeare tends to link sexual disguise and sexual jealousy in ways that evade obsessiveness. Proustian comedy swerves away from Shakespeare into the audacity that allows compulsiveness its free play. Jealousy is never allowed a literary ancestry by Proust; Othello and Leontes are light years away from Swann and Marcel. No jealous lover in Proust would become murderous: the spirit of *Search*'s comedy forbids it. That is why the governing metaphor for Swann and Marcel is the scholarly researcher, particularly the Ruskinian art historian. Torture by fact finding is Proust's comic formula, since this is self-torment, and the facts themselves are essentially imaginative surmises. The pattern is set by Swann:

> But in this strange phase of love the personality of another person becomes so enlarged, so deepened, that the curiousity which he now felt stirring inside him with regard to the smallest details of a woman's daily life, was the same thirst for knowledge with which he had once studied history. And all manner of actions from which heretofore he would have recoiled in shame, such as spying, to-night, outside a window, to-morrow perhaps, for all he knew, putting adroitly provocative questions to casual

witnesses, bribing servants, listening at doors, seemed to him now to be precisely on a level with the deciphering of manuscripts, the weighing of evidence, the interpretation of old monuments—so many different methods of scientific investigation with a genuine intellectual value and legitimately employable in the search for truth.

Later, Swann's passion for reconstructing the petty details of Odette's social life is compared to the passion of "the aesthete who ransacks the extant documents of fifteenth-century Florence in order to penetrate further into the soul of the Primavera, the fair Vanna, or the Venus of Botticelli." Odette's soul is impenetrable, as Swann discovers, which becomes a perpetual provocation to fresh onslaughts of the torments of jealousy, mixed with the "nobler" desire to know the truth. In one of Proust's loveliest ironies Swann finds that "it was another of the faculties of his studious youth that his jealousy revived, the passion for truth, but for a truth which, too, was interposed between himself and his mistress, receiving its light from her alone." Such a truth, at the matrix of all jealousies, receives only darkness from the gloom that the lover emanates. Freud's ironic description of being in love, "the over-estimation of the object," is inadequate to the passion that jealousy initially augments and then replaces. Here the genius of Proust goes beyond Shakespeare, beyond Freud, as an insight into erotic obsession:

> Certainly, of the extent of this love Swann had no direct awareness. When he sought to measure it, it happened sometimes that he found it diminished, shrunk almost to nothing; for instance, the lack of enthusiasm, amounting almost to distaste, which, in the days before he was in love with Odette, he had felt for her expressive features, her faded complexion, returned on certain days. "Really, I'm making distinct headway," he would tell himself next day. "Looking at things quite honestly, I can't say I got much pleasure last night from being in bed with her. It's an odd thing, but I actually thought her ugly." And certainly he was sincere, but his love extended a long way beyond the province of physical desire. Odette's person, indeed, no longer

held any great place in it. When his eyes fell upon the photograph of Odette on his table, or when she came to see him, he had difficulty in identifying her face, either in the flesh or on the pasteboard, with the painful and continuous anxiety which dwelt in his mind. He would say to himself, almost with astonishment, "It's she!" as though suddenly we were to be shown in a detached, externalised form one of our own maladies, and we found it bore no resemblance between love and death, far more striking than those which are usually pointed out, that they make us probe deeper, in the fear that its reality may elude us, into the mystery of personality. And this malady which Swann's love had become had so proliferated, was so closely interwoven with all his habits, with all his actions, with his thoughts, his health, his sleep, his life, even with what he hoped for after his death, was so utterly inseparable from him, that it would have been impossible to eradicate it without almost entirely destroying him; as surgeons say, his love was no longer operable.

Freud remarks on the heightening of passion by "incitement premiums," but he meant societal and related barriers as well as the inward process of repression. Proust pragmatically tells us that sexual jealousy is the greatest of incitement premiums, with the comic consequence that the sexual itself becomes devalued: "Odette's person, indeed, no longer held any great place in it." Her photograph, even her actual face, refuses identity "with the painful and continuous anxiety which dwelt in his mind." Love and death have come dangerously close, and the debonair Swann approaches the abyss, but to us it is exquisitely funny:

Sometimes he hoped that she would die, painlessly, in some accident, since she was out of doors, in the streets, crossing busy thoroughfares, from morning to night. And as she always returned safe and sound, he marvelled at the strength and the suppleness of the human body, which was able continually to hold at bay, to outwit all the perils that beset it (which to Swann seemed innumerable since his own secret desire has strewn them in her path), and almost with impunity, to its career of mendacity, to the pursuit of pleasure. And Swann felt a very cordial sympathy with the sultan Mahomet II whose portrait by Bellini he admired, who, on finding that he had fallen madly in love with one of his wives, stabbed her to death in order, as his Venetian biographer artlessly relates, to recover his peace of mind. Then he would be ashamed of thinking thus only of himself, and his own sufferings would seem to deserve no pity now that he himself held Odette's very life so cheap.

The climax of "Swann in Love," one of the most famous passages in all of Proust, follows a colorful dream that compounds Forcheville, Swann's rival for Odette, with Napoleon III, again in a comic register for us, but not for poor Swann, who at last believes that he has had enough:

But while, an hour after his awakening, he was giving instructions to the barber to see that his stiffly brushed hair should not become disarranged on the journey, he thought of his dream again, and saw once again, as he had felt them close beside him, Odette's pallid complexion, her too thin cheeks, her drawn features, her tired eyes, all the things which—in the course of those successive bursts of affection which had made of his enduring love for Odette a long oblivion of the first impression that he had formed of her—he had ceased to notice since the early days of their intimacy, days to which doubtless, while he slept, his memory had returned to seek their exact sensation. And with the old, intermittent caddishness which reappeared in him when he was no longer unhappy and his moral standards dropped accordingly, he exclaimed to himself: "To think that I've wasted years of my life, that I've longed to die, that I've experienced my greatest love, for a woman who didn't appeal to me, who wasn't even my type."

Caddishness reappears when unhappiness ceases, and this allows our morality to sink to its normal level. That delicious observation is preamble to Swann's immortal lament, fit medicine for all of us, of whatever gender or sexual persuasion. Odette certainly was not Swann's mode, genre, type, being neither high enough nor low enough for an aesthete and dandy with so brilliant a social life. Swann, alas, is caught; in Proust's cosmos you cannot say "Goodbye, Odette, and I forgive you for everything I ever did to you" (the American mode) or "Falling out of love is one of the great human experiences; you seem to see the world with newly awakened eyes" (Anglo-Irish style). For Swann love dies, but jealousy endures longer; so he marries Odette, not despite but because she has betrayed him, with women as well as with men. Proust's explanation for the marriage is worthy of him:

> Almost everyone was surprised at the marriage, and that in itself is surprising. No doubt very few people understand the purely subjective nature of the phenomenon we call love, or how it creates, so to speak, a supplementary person, distinct from the person whom the world knows by the same name, a person most of whose constituent elements are derived from ourselves.

Long after Swann's jealousy in regard to his wife has followed his love for her into oblivion, his memory of jealousy still torments him, and his researches continue:

> He went on trying to discover what no longer interested him, because his old self, though it had shrivelled to extreme decrepitude, still acted mechanically, in accordance with preoccupations so utterly abandoned that Swann could not now succeed even in picturing to himself that anguish—so compelling once that he had been unable to imagine that he would ever be delivered from it, that only the death of the woman he loved (though death, as will be shown later on in this story by a cruel corroboration, in no way diminishes the sufferings caused by jealousy) seemed to him capable of smoothing the path of his life which then seemed impassably obstructed.

The presage of the Albertine-Marcel hell belongs here because Swann is Marcel's forerunner, the John the Baptist who prophesies the jealous crucifixion of the Narrator's younger self. Proust provides a double transition between the two martyrdoms, the ordeal by jealousy that afflicts Saint-Loup in his affair with Rachel, and Swann's direct, prophetic warning to the unheeding Marcel.

Before examining this crossing, it seems appropriate to confront two unfair criticisms currently aimed at Proust. Why is the Narrator not half-Jewish, as Proust was, and, doubtless now more important, why is the Narrator heterosexual when Proust was bisexual, with the homoerotic impulse stronger in him? One prevalent defense stresses Proust's desire for universality, but that seems hardly relevant. Another points out that even in 1922, while the aftermath of the Dreyfus affair was still fresh, homosexuality carried a stigma. This is not altogether convincing either; Proust is so great an artist that his aesthetic dignity deserves our seeking aesthetic motives for what were essentially aesthetic decisions. Is it a better novel if the Narrator is a Christian heterosexual?

Biographical scholars have cleared away the nonsense that allegorizes Marcel's affair with Albertine into Proust's relationship with Alfred Agostinelli. *Within a Budding Grove* is an ingenious translation of *À l'Ombre des jeunes filles en fleur,* though it does not catch all of *In the Shadow of Young Girls in Blossom.* Ironize that into a budding grove of young boys and you destroy the aesthetic wistfulness that Proust achieves. Albertine's lesbianism, a haunting splendor as Proust handles it, allegorizes very crudely as Agostinelli's lapses into heterosexuality. Proust knew precisely what he was doing: Swann and Marcel are contrasts to the homosexual Charlus and the bisexual Saint-Loup. The torments of love and jealousy transcend gender and sexual orientation, and it would spoil the novel's mythology of the Cities of the Plain if the Narrator could not distance himself from homosexuals and Jews alike.

Proust's main concern is not social history or sexual liberation or the Dreyfus affair (though he was consistently an active supporter of Dreyfus). Aesthetic salvation is the enterprise of his vast novel; Proust challenges Freud as the major mythmaker of the Chaotic Era. The story he creates is a visionary romance depicting how the Narrator matures from Marcel into the novelist Proust, who in the book's final volume reforms his consciousness and is able to shape his life into a new form of wisdom. Proust rightly judged that the Narrator would be most effective if he could assume a dispassionate stance regarding the mythology that raises the narrative into a cosmological poem, Dantesque as well as Shakespearean. Balzac, Stendhal, Flaubert are left behind in Proust's leap into a vision that compounds Sodom and Gomorrah, Jerusalem, and Eden: three abandoned paradises. The Narrator, as a Gentile heterosexual, is more persuasive as a seer of this new mythology.

BETWEEN SWANN and Marcel, sufferers in the breathless air of jealousy, the Narrator inserts Saint-Loup, who will marry Gilberte, Swann's daughter and Marcel's first love, and who will die all too soon, a victim of World War I. Embedded in the waning affair between Saint-Loup and Rachel is what may be Proust's most pungent apothegm on jealousy: "Jealousy, which prolongs the course of love, is not capable of retaining many more ingredients than the other products of the imagination."

I reflect, as I read this, that Proust is the true doctor for all those unhappily in love, which means, sooner or later, all those in love. Unfortunately, his medicine, like all remedies for love, works only after the illness—even in its pure form of jealousy—is over. He provides retrospective comfort, the only kind we can accept. It is a belated delight to be told that jealousy is a weak poem, unable to develop even the three or four images that it harbors. In the novels that we write with our lives, the jealousy that consumes us at a particular time fades into the seriocomic pathos of all deceased Eros. Saint-Loup is neither an art historian of jealousy, like his father-in-law, nor its novelist, like his friend Marcel. Love, kept falteringly alive by jealousy, dies with it, and Saint-Loup gently suffers the curious comfort of having become a familiar and reassuring relic for Rachel:

> Sometimes Rachel came in so late at night that she could ask her former lover's permission to lie down beside him until the morning. This was a great comfort to Robert, for it reminded him how intimately, after all, they had lived together, simply to see that even if he took the greater part of the bed for himself it did not in the least interfere with her sleep. He realised that

she was more comfortable, lying close to his familiar body, than she would have been elsewhere.

It is difficult to establish the priorities between humor and sadness here; what matters most is that neither Saint-Loup nor Rachel feels either sadness or regret as they fall asleep together in the emptiness that has replaced passion. His former jealousy has fallen away from Saint-Loup into this quasi-familial interchange. Swann, as he acknowledges to Marcel, is not capable of even that much of a retrospective ghostliness of ancient attachments:

> "People are very inquisitive. I've never been inquisitive, except when I was in love, and when I was jealous. And a lot I ever learned! Are you jealous?" I told Swann that I had never experienced jealousy, that I did not even know what it was. "Well, you can count yourself lucky. A little jealousy is not too unpleasant, for two reasons. In the first place, it enables people who are not inquisitive to take an interest in the lives of others, or of one other at any rate. . . . Even when one is no longer attached to things, it's still something to have been attached to them; because it was always for reasons which other people didn't grasp. The memory of those feelings is something that's to be found only in ourselves; we must go back into ourselves to look at it."

In his aesthetic solipsism, Swann seems more than ever a parody of Ruskin, whose idolatry of art is transmuted into the collector's self-idolatry. In Proust's fine irony, Swann's word "inquisitive" simply means "caring," and we abandon Swann with a sense of great chill. The metaphor or transference that Freud called "love," Proust calls "jealousy," so that when Marcel tells the invalid Swann that he has never felt jealous, he implicitly confesses that he did not love Gilberte. Time's revenges are about to descend upon him in the novel's great affair of jealousy, the demonic parody of its search for lost time. The Albertine-Marcel saga of possession, jealousy, death, and subsequent augmented jealousy begins as it should, with jealousy, which, according to the Narrator, *precedes* Marcel's love for Albertine. Early in *The Captive* the pattern is made clear: the excitation of his jealousy is what motivates Marcel, in a contest with Albertine's lesbian lovers that he can never hope to win:

> In leaving Balbec, I had imagined that I was leaving Gomorrah, plucking Albertine from it; in reality, alas, Gomorrah was disseminated all over the world. And partly out of jealousy, partly out of ignorance of such joys (a case which is extremely rare), I had arranged unawares this game of hide and seek in which Albertine would always elude me.

If Freudian love is the overestimation of the object, then Proustian jealousy, far more dialectical and ambivalent, is at once the underestimation of the object and the lunatic hyperbolization of her appeal for everyone else. And as Proust emphasizes, it can contain total contradictions:

> I should not have been jealous if she had enjoyed her pleasures in my vicinity, with my encouragement, completely under my surveillance, thereby relieving me of any fear of mendacity; nor should I have been jealous if she had moved to a place so unfamiliar and remote that I could not imagine, had no possibility of knowing, and no temptation to know, her manner of life. In either case, my uncertainty would have been eliminated by a knowledge or an ignorance equally complete.

Certainty and knowledge alike destroy the romance of jealousy, which in Proust's interpretation is all romance, literary and experiential. But what can we ever be certain of except death, and what at last can we know, except the incommunicable experience of death? Why does Proust, the artist of jealousy, produce so unrelenting a tragicomedy of the lover's compulsiveness? It is Proust—not Ruskin, Pater, Wilde, and their heirs in Yeats, Joyce, Beckett—who is the uncontested high priest of the religion of art. Art, and not sexual possession, is Proust's only escape from the experiential romance of jealousy, and *Search*'s final volume, *Time Regained,* rescues the novel from the literary romance of jealousy. However Proust acquired his quasi-Hindu stance of the self, he hugely enjoys his apocalypse of jealousy in *The Captive* and *The Fugitive,* and so do we. But we wince at it also, and Proust is preparing us for a very different vision of reality, one for which there is a past and perhaps even a future, whereas for jealousy there is only present time, however retrospective the jealousy may be.

Albertine diagnoses Marcel's jealousy not at all, assuring him that her lies result only from her love for him. The Narrator never solves the reader's wonder about why Albertine holds onto Marcel as long as she does; she is the Muse and does not yield her secrets. When she flees, her farewell letter ends, "I leave you the best of myself," a statement as true and as false as everything else in the affair. After her accidental death horseback riding, Marcel receives two notes from her in response to his lying letter that he will marry her friend Andrée; the first congratulates him on his choice, while the second offers to return to him. This perfect contradiction, abrogated only by Albertine's death, prepares Marcel and the reader for the well-nigh Napoleonic campaign of research that the survivor mounts into the erotic life of the lost beloved, mostly by his inquisition of Andrée, once her lover and now, for a time, his.

Only an inadequate reader would dare to make moralizing observations against Proust's *Search;* the book's grandeur and its irony defend it from fools. But Proust's wisdom is very hard; love is authentic among grandmother, mother, and Marcel, but between no one else in the novel. Even friendship seems as impossible as love; the true persuasion is jealousy, which is bewilderingly complex among those of the truest persuasion, the hardy exiles of Sodom and Gomorrah:

> Some—those no doubt who have been most timid in childhood—are not greatly concerned with the kind of physical pleasure they receive, provided that they can associate it with a masculine face. Whereas others, whose sensuality is doubtless more violent, feel an imperious need to localise their physical pleasure. These latter, perhaps, would shock the average person with their avowals. They live perhaps less exclusively beneath the sway of Saturn's outrider, since for them women are not entirely excluded as they are for the former sort, in relation to

whom women have no existence apart from conversation, flirtation, loves not of the heart but of the head. But the second sort seek out those women who love other women, who can procure for them a young man, enhance the pleasure they experience in his company; better still, they can, in the same fashion, enjoy with such women the same pleasure as with a man. Whence it arises that jealousy is kindled in those who love the first sort only by the pleasure which they may enjoy with a man, which alone seems to their lovers a betrayal, since they do not participate in the love of women, have practised it only out of habit and to preserve for themselves the possibility of eventual marriage, visualising so little the pleasure that it is capable of giving that they cannot be distressed by the thought that he whom they love is enjoying that pleasure; whereas the other sort often inspire jealousy by their love-affairs with women. For, in their relations with women, they play, for the woman who loves her own sex, the part of another woman, and she offers them at the same time more or less what they find in other men, so that the jealous friend suffers from the feeling that the man he loves is riveted to the woman who is to him almost a man, and at the same time feels his beloved almost escape him because, to these women, he is something which the lover himself cannot conceive, a sort of woman.

The tone of this passage defies description: there is irony of course, and a certain detachment, but the primary aura seems to be a kind of wonder. Proust has had distinguished critics—Beckett, Brée, Benjamin, Girard, Genette, Bersani, Shattuck (whom I prefer) among them—but more than Joyce, Proust defeats his critics. A novel of 3,300 pages, sinuous beyond comparison, is almost an *Arabian Nights* in itself. Samuel Richardson's *Clarissa* seems to me the only Western novel as strong (or as long!), but *Clarissa* centers on only two personages, the martyred Clarissa and her despoiler, Lovelace. Marcel and Albertine are the enigmas of *Search,* but it is hardly their novel alone. Nor is it the Narrator's, the now-matured Marcel; uncannily it is Proust's novel, and he is not quite either the Narrator or Marcel. I know the Narrator's views on jealousy; I am not certain that I know Proust's, for the

Narrator is neither homosexual nor Jewish. When wisdom speaks most powerfully, in the closing volume of the novel, the Narrator almost imperceptibly fuses into the novelist Proust, and the mordant humor of jealousy is set aside. That will come later, but we are not done with that true persuasion as yet.

There is an ecstatic passage in *The Captive* that pretends to assail jealousy and instead ironically celebrates it:

one's jealousy, ransacking the past in search of a clue, can find nothing; always retrospective, it is like the historian who has to write the history of a period from which he has no documents; always belated, it dashes like an enraged bull to the spot where it will not find the dazzling, arrogant creature who is tormenting it and whom the crowd admires for his splendour and cunning. Jealousy thrashes around in the void.

A disabled historian and a deceived bull: as metaphors for jealousy, these are not complimentary, and yet the Narrator, recalling Marcel's investigations of Albertine's exuberantly active career of lesbian Eros, is moved to analogize jealousy and the desire for posthumous fame:

When we try to consider what will happen to us after our own death, is it not still our living self which we mistakenly project at that moment? And is it much more absurd, when all is said, to regret that a woman who no longer exists is unaware that we have learned what she was doing six years ago than to desire that of ourselves, who will be dead, the public shall still speak with approval a century hence? If there is more real foundation in the latter than in the former case, the regrets of my retrospective jealousy proceeded none the less from the same optical error as in other men the desire for posthumous fame.

The specific other men are the precursors: Flaubert, Stendhal, Balzac, Baudelaire, Ruskin, but they certainly include Proust the novelist, into whom the Narrator will merge. The "optical error" is a sickness not ignoble, as Keats would have said, and the link between jealousy and literary art is overt. Earlier though, the

Narrator has made a parenthetical remark: "It is astonishing what a want of imagination jealousy, which spends its time making petty suppositions that are false, shows when it comes to discovering what is true." The limitations of jealousy are another preamble to the emergence of Proustian vocation. Thrashing about in his void, Marcel found, "There is no idea that does not carry in itself its possible refutation, no word that does not imply its opposite."

Paralysis ensues; Marcel is little better off when he affirms that "Lying is essential to humanity. It plays as large a part perhaps as the quest for pleasure, and is moreover governed by that quest." Such an observation might perhaps help to make a moralist, but not a novelist. A good contrast comes when the Narrator, in *Time Regained,* is able to see how useful Albertine had been to him, from a literary point of view: "The happy years are the lost, the wasted years, one must wait for suffering before one can work." We perceive that the Narrator has become one with Proust the novelist when the long-deceased Albertine receives her just tribute:

And in a sense I was right to trace them back to her, for if I had not walked on the front that day; if I had not got to know her, all these ideas would never have been developed (unless they had been developed by some other woman). But I was wrong too, for this pleasure which generates something within and which, retrospectively, we seek to place in a beautiful feminine face, comes from our senses: but the pages I would write were something that Albertine, particularly the Albertine of those days, would quite certainly never have understood. It was, however, for this very reason (and this shows that we ought not to live in too intellectual an atmosphere), for the reason that she was so different from me, that she had fertilized me through unhappiness and even, at the beginning, through the simple effort which I had to make to imagine something different from myself.

There is the essence of why the Narrator, who had been Marcel, is now enabled to become Proust the novelist and not merely another Swann, reduced to examining his collection of jealous memories. What saves Proust from being the snob and the jealous paranoiac he might have been is an enormous labor, at once therapeutic, aesthetic, and (what else can I call it?) mystical. All of Proust's readers hear at last in *Search* the reverberations that Roger Shattuck aptly compares to Hindu conceptions of the self. *Search* is the product of a discipline that has cast aside what Krishna in the *Bhavagad-gita* calls "dark inertia." It may be another irony, not necessarily Proustian, that the novelist of *In Search of Lost Time* is our truest modern multiculturalist, transcending some of the distinctions between the Western and Eastern Canons.

18.

Joyce's Agon
with Shakespeare

JAMES JOYCE, who rarely lacked audacity, conceived of Shakespeare as Virgil to himself as Dante. This ambition was so large that not even Joyce could fulfill it. *Ulysses* and *Finnegans Wake,* by general consent, have only Proust's *In Search of Lost Time* as a rival during our long ebbing that—if Vico and Joyce were right—will bring us to the verge of a new Theocratic Age. Perhaps Joyce and Proust also both came close to matching Dante's achievement in the *Divine Comedy,* even though Kafka, who did not come close, seems more the Dante of this age. But no one who has read Shakespeare deeply, and who has attended Shakespeare properly directed and adequately acted, would consider Joyce the fulfillment of which Shakespeare was the forerunner. Joyce knew this, and there is a certain anxiety in his obsessive references to the earlier poet that crowd both *Ulysses* and the *Wake.* Had there been no Shakespeare, Joyce and Freud would probably never have felt the anguish of contamination that only Shakespeare seems to have provoked in both of them.

Joyce was more genial than Freud about this influence and never joined in the Looney hypothesis, though in *Finnegans Wake* he plays with the Baconian theory. Primarily, Joyce gave us the hypothesis set forth by Stephen Dedalus in the library scene of *Ulysses*, a theory that attacks not so much paternalism as paternity itself, and that certainly does not attack Shakespeare. In response to the hoary question of which book to take to a desert island if you could take only one, Joyce told Frank Budgen: "I should hesitate between Dante and Shakespeare, but not for long. The Englishman is richer and would get my vote." "Richer" is a fine word there; alone on a desert island one would want more people, and Shakespeare is wealthier in characters than his nearest competitors, Dante and the Hebrew Bible. Joyce, despite the Dickensian vigor of the minor characters in *Ulysses*, has only a rather inadequate Hamlet in Stephen, and a rival for the Wife of Bath in Molly. Poldy can challenge Shakespeare, or attempt to, the act being impossible to perform because the larger entity, in all literary agons, swallows up the smaller. While Stephen says that he does not believe his own theory about Shakespeare and Hamlet, Richard Ellmann tells us that, according to friends, Joyce took it very seriously and never recanted it. It is the necessary starting point for considering Joyce's canonical struggle with Shakespeare, in both *Ulysses* and *Finnegans Wake*.

Joyce's courage in founding *Ulysses* simultaneously upon the *Odyssey* and *Hamlet* was remarkable since, as Ellmann notes, the two paradigms of Odysseus/Ulysses and the Prince of Denmark have virtually nothing in common. One clue to Joyce's designs might be that the literary character after Hamlet (and Falstaff) who seems most intelligent is the hero of the *Odyssey*, even though Joyce commends him for completeness rather than for mental resources. But the first Ulysses wants to get home, while Hamlet has no home, in Elsinore or anywhere else. Joyce manages to compound Ulysses with Hamlet only by doubling: Poldy is both Ulysses and the ghost of Hamlet Senior, while Stephen is both Telemachus and young Hamlet, and Poldy and Stephen together form Shakespeare and Joyce. This sounds a little bewildering, yet it fits Joyce's purpose, which is to absorb Shakespeare into himself. Like Joyce, Shakespeare is secular, replacing Scripture with the writings of common humanity, and Joyce defends Shakespeare against Freud by rightly refusing an identity between Hamlet and Oedipus. A better critic of *Hamlet* than Freud was, Joyce found no trace of lust for Gertrude or murderousness toward King Hamlet in their son. Stephen and Bloom (Poldy, that is) also seem free of Oedipal ambivalence, and if Joyce harbored it about Shakespeare (he had, in the past), he overtly works at not manifesting it in *Ulysses*.

Joyce's theory of *Hamlet* is expounded by Stephen in the National Library scene in *Ulysses* (part 2, 9). Frank Budgen's *James Joyce and the Making of "Ulysses"* (1934), still the best guide to the book because it has so much of the personal Joyce in it, tells us that "Shakespeare the man, the lord of language, the creator of persons, occupied [Joyce] more than Shakespeare the maker of plays." It is certainly Stephen's Shakespeare who follows a well-attested tradition by coming on stage at the Globe Theatre in the role of the ghost of Hamlet's father:

—The play begins. A player comes on under the shadow, made up in the castoff mail of a court buck, a wellset man with a bass voice. It is the ghost, the king, a king and no king, and the player is Shakespeare who has studied *Hamlet* all the years of his life which were not vanity in order to play the part of the spectre. He speaks the words to Burbage, the young player who stands before him beyond the rack of cerecloth, calling him by a name:
>   *Hamlet, I am thy father's spirit,*
bidding him list. To a son he speaks, the son of his soul, the prince, young Hamlet and to the son of his body, Hamnet Shakespeare, who has died in Stratford that his namesake may live for ever.
   Is it possible that that player Shakespeare, a ghost by absence, and in the vesture of buried Denmark, a ghost by death, speaking his own words to his own son's name (had Hamnet Shakespeare lived he would have been Prince Hamlet's twin), is it possible, I want to know, or probable that he did not draw or foresee the logical conclusion of these premises: you are the dispossessed

son: I am the murdered father: your mother is the guilty queen, Ann Shakespeare, born Hathaway?

Ann Hathaway as Gertrude, the deceased Hamnet as Hamlet, Shakespeare as the ghost, his two brothers as a composite Claudius—it is all outrageous enough to be permanently compelling, and it fostered Anthony Burgess's best novel, *Nothing like the Sun* (1964), which is also the only successful novel ever written about Shakespeare. Burgess, a loving disciple of Joyce, provides so Joycean an extension of Stephen's theory that I long ago jumbled the library scene and Burgess's imaginings together in my mind and am startled always, rereading Joyce, not to find much that I wrongly expect to find, which is gorgeously present in Burgess. That is partly because Joyce's Stephen is so subtly suggestive, condensing a total vision of Shakespeare's life and work into a handful of eloquent throwaways that conceal their finer intimations and bewilderments. Earlier, Malachi "Buck" Mulligan, in whom Joyce travestied Oliver St. John Gogarty, poet-physician and general roustabout, explained the theory: "He proves by algebra that Hamlet's grandson is Shakespeare's grandfather and that he himself is the ghost of his own father." A shrewd parody, this is also a palpable hit, since Stephen's purpose is to dissolve the authority of fatherhood itself.

> Fatherhood, in the sense of conscious begetting, is unknown to man. It is a mystical estate, an apostolic succession, from only begetter to only begotten. On that mystery and not on the madonna which the cunning Italian intellect flung to the mob of Europe the church is founded and founded irremovably because founded, like the world, macro and microcosm, upon the void. Upon incertitude, upon unlikelihood. *Amor matris,* subjective and objective genitive, may be the only true thing in life. Paternity may be a legal fiction. Who is the father of any son that any son should love him or he any son?

Stephen rapidly mocks this view, but it is not easily mocked, and not easily understood, for its implications are endless. The Church and all of Christianity dissolve if it is to be believed, and

Joyce neither withdraws nor argues the point. The late Sir William Empson protested what he charmingly named the Kenner smear, though he might have called it the Eliot smear, since T. S. Eliot preceded Hugh Kenner in baptizing Joyce's imagination as "eminently orthodox." Empson, of course, was right: Christianizing Joyce is a pitiful critical procedure. If there is a Holy Ghost in *Ulysses* it is Shakespeare, and if there is any paternity that is a valid fiction, then Joyce would like to see himself as Shakespeare's son. But where is Joyce in *Ulysses*? Certainly he is represented in the book, but strangely split between Stephen and Poldy, Joyce as the young artist and Joyce as the humane, curious man who has refused violence and hatred. The strangeness of the division defies critical solution; at this final novelistic stance of personality in English, before persuasive characters dissolve into the mythologies of *Finnegans Wake* and the negations of Samuel Beckett, we are given a desperately amiable demonstration that paternity is a pure fiction, an aesthetic concept, but only an uncertain one.

The reader accurately senses that the novel *Ulysses* has more to do with *Hamlet* than with the *Odyssey,* but what are the relations between the fourfold of Shakespeare, Joyce, Dedalus, and Bloom? *Ulysses* has enough verbal splendor to furnish a legion of novels, yet we sense that the book's central position in the Canon transcends Joyce's styles, masterful as all of them are. Proust's aesthetic mysticism is not Joyce's way, and Beckett, who inherits from both Joyce and Proust, shows something like an ascetic's refusal of Proust's triumph. Joyce remains enigmatic; his engagement with Shakespeare seems to me one of the few ways he opens into the enigma.

Stephen extends his Shakespearean excursion into the warfare between heresy and Church theology: "Sabellius, the African, subtlest heresiarch of all the beasts of the field, held that the Father was Himself his Own Son. The bulldog of Aquin, with whom no word shall be impossible, refutes him. Well: if the father who has not a son be not a father can the son who has not a father be a son?"

It follows, Stephen adds, that the poet who wrote *Hamlet* "was not the father of his own son merely but, being no more a son, he was and felt himself the father of all his race, the father of his own grandfather, the father of his unborn grandson who, by the same token, never was born." Out of this emerges a Godlike Shakespeare, but he is presumably only Stephen's portrait of the artist; and Stephen, Shakespeare-obsessed as he is, is in Poldy's book, not his own.

If there is a mystery in *Ulysses* it resides in Leopold Bloom, who has his own puzzling relation to Shakespeare, that mortal god. Stephen's Shakespeare is a prophecy of Poldy. Shakespeare is the father who is himself his own father. He has no precursor and no successor, which is clearly Joyce's idealized vision of himself as author. Poldy's father, the Jewish side of his ancestry, was self-slain, and Poldy has no living son, unless one somehow construes Stephen as a son in spirit. The only spirit in *Ulysses* is Shakespeare, ghostly father and ghostly son, and we begin to see that his spirit has settled not upon the more or less Dantesque Stephen but upon the Joyce-like Bloom, whose favorite scene in Shakespeare is the conversation between Hamlet and the gravediggers in act 5.

What can we find in Poldy that is Shakespearean? I suspect that the answer must have something to do with Joyce's complete representation of a personality, which could be regarded as Shakespeare's last stand, or the final episode in the long history of Shakespearean mimesis in the literature of the English language. Whether or not you believe that Shakespeare held a mirror up to nature, you will have difficulty finding a fuller portrait of the natural man than Joyce renders in Poldy. It may be considered an eccentric judgment on Joyce's part, but his archetype of the natural man would seem to have been Shakespeare, a Joycean Shakespeare to be sure.

Joyce's Shakespeare was not a dramatist; Joyce weirdly judged Ibsen's *When We Dead Awaken* to be far more dramatic than *Othello.* Joyce's notion of drama is not easy to apprehend, and his Shakespeare was evidently not a poet of action but a creator of men and women. If we are to uncover the Shakespeareanism of Poldy, we dispense with drama and concentrate upon the representation of change. When I think about *Ulysses,* I think first of Poldy, but rarely as a figure in an exchange or a relationship. What counts about Mr. Bloom, because of his comprehensiveness, is as much his ethos or character as is his pathos or personality,

and even his logos or thought, divinely commonplace as that tends
to be. What is not commonplace about Poldy is the wealth of his
consciousness, his capacity to transmute his feelings and sensations
into images. And there, I think, is bedrock: Poldy has a Shakespearean inwardness, far more profoundly manifested than the
interior life is in Stephen, or Molly, or anyone else in the novel.
The heroines of Jane Austen, George Eliot, and Henry James are
more refined social sensibilities than Poldy, but even they cannot
compete with his inward turn. Nothing is lost upon him, even
though his reactions to what he perceives can be humdrum. Joyce
favors him as he favors no one else in his work, a point that
Richard Ellmann pioneered in stressing.

Joyce admired Flaubert, but Poldy's consciousness does not
resemble Emma Bovary's. It is a curiously ancient psyche for a
man barely middle-aged, and everyone else in the book seems
much younger than Mr. Bloom. Presumably that has something
to do with the riddle of his Jewishness. From a Jewish perspective,
Poldy is not and yet is a Jew. Both his mother and her mother
were Irish Catholics; his father, Virag, was a Jew who converted
to Protestantism. Poldy himself has been both a Protestant and a
Catholic, but he identifies with his dead father and clearly regards
himself as being Jewish, though his wife and daughter are not.
Dublin uneasily considers him to be a Jew, though his isolation
seems self-imposed. He has many acquaintances, apparently
knows everybody, yet we would be startled if we were asked who
his friends were, because he is perpetually inside himself, surprisingly so for a truly amiable man.

Having once been enchanted by watching Zero Mostel perform
in *Ulysses in Nighttown*, half-dancing nimbly through the role in
a very strong misreading of it, I have to fight against the image
of Mostel as I reread the book. Joyce is not Mel Brooks, yet
sometimes he did invest Poldy with what looks like a touch of
Jewish humor. Mostel was charming, Poldy is not; but Poldy
moves Joyce and moves us because amid so many Irish, only he
does not display what Yeats called "a fanatic heart." Hugh Kenner, who in his first book on Joyce saw Poldy as a kind of Eliotic
Jew (the anti-Semitic T. S. Eliot, not the humane George Eliot),
after twenty years of further study ceased to find Mr. Bloom an

example of modern depravity and eloquently made the more Joycean judgment that Joyce's protagonist was "fit to live in Ireland without malice, without violence, without hate." How many among us now are fit to live, in Ireland or the United States, without malice, without violence, without hate? Who among us is tempted to condescend to Poldy, as though so persuasive a representation of a thoroughly benign human being, who remains so interesting to us, were available anywhere else?

Quirky, cheerful enough, self-possessed and endlessly kind, though masochistic even in his curiosity, Poldy does seem to be Joyce's version, not of any Shakespearean character, but of the ghostly Shakespeare himself, at once everyman and no man—a somewhat Borgesian Shakespeare perhaps. This, of course, is not Shakespeare the poet but citizen Shakespeare, wandering about London as Poldy wanders about Dublin. Stephen, in one particularly madcap moment of his library discourse, goes so far as to suggest that Shakespeare was a Jew, presumably on Poldy's model, though Stephen cannot know that except as a mystical prolepsis. The climax of Stephen's theory comes in its most extraordinary and haunting evocation of Shakespeare's life as a universal completion:

—Man delights him not nor woman neither, Stephen said. He returns after a life of absence to that spot of earth where he was born, where he has always been, man and boy, a silent witness and there, his journey of life ended, he plants his mulberrytree in the earth. Then dies. The motion is ended. Gravediggers bury Hamlet *père* and Hamlet *fils*. A king and a prince at last in death, with incidental music. And, what though murdered and betrayed, bewept by all frail tender hearts for, Dane or Dubliner, sorrow for the dead is the only husband from whom they refuse to be divorced. If you like the epilogue look long on it: prosperous Prospero, the good man rewarded, Lizzie, grandpa's lump of love, and nuncle Richie, the bad man taken off by poetic justice to the place where the bad niggers go. Strong curtain. He found in the world without as actual what was in his world within as possible. Maeterlinck says: *If Socrates leave his house today he will find the sage seated on his doorstep. If*

Judas go forth tonight it is to Judas his steps will tend. Every life is many days, day after day. We walk through ourselves, meeting robbers, ghosts, giants, old men, young men, wives, widows, brothers-in-love, but always meeting ourselves. The playwright who wrote the folio of this world and wrote it badly (He gave us light first and the sun two days later), the lord of things as they are whom the most Roman of catholics call *dio boia*, hangman god, is doubtless all in all in all of us, ostler and butcher, and would be bawd and cuckold too but that in the economy of heaven, foretold by Hamlet, there are no more marriages, glorified man, an androgynous angel, being a wife unto himself.

Stephen's emphasis, certainly as Joyce's mouthpiece here, is as much against the hangman god of Christianity as it is final praise for the poet of *Hamlet*. There are two playwrights, the Catholic God and Shakespeare, both of them gods; but Shakespeare's prophet, Hamlet, foretells Joyce's vision of "glorified man, an androgynous angel, being a wife unto himself," a vision incarnated in both Shakespeare and poor Poldy. Of the two folios, this world and Shakespeare's, the Joycean preference is for his ghostly father, who returns after a life of absence, as Joyce did not live to do. The rest is silence, exile being over and all cunning also at an end. Few sentences, even in *Ulysses,* are as inescapable as "We walk through ourselves, meeting robbers, ghosts, giants, old men, young men, wives, widows, brothers-in-love, but always meeting ourselves." That could be condensed (with some loss) as Joyce chanting, "I walk through myself, meeting the ghost of Shakespeare, but always meeting myself." Such a confession of influence, and of a self-confidence at having the strength to internalize Shakespeare, could be called *Ulysses*'s finest compliment to its own canonical splendor.

A STUDY OF the Western Canon that organizes itself by Vico's cycles could hardly neglect *Finnegans Wake,* which relies upon Vico for some of its structural principles. Since the *Wake,* more than *Ulysses,* is the only authentic rival our century has produced for Proust's *In Search of Lost Time,* it takes a place here as well. The movement misnamed "multiculturalism," which is altogether anti-intellectual and anti-literary, is removing from the curriculum most works that present imaginative and cognitive difficulties, which means most of the canonical books. *Finnegans Wake,* Joyce's masterpiece, presents so many initial difficulties that one has to be anxious about its survival. I suspect that it will find company in Spenser's great poetic romance, *The Faerie Queene,* and that both works will be read, for the rest of time, by only a small band of enthusiastic specialists. That is a sadness, but we are moving toward a time when Faulkner and Conrad may have to endure the same fate. One of my closest friends, a follower of Adorno and his Frankfurt School, defended her university's decision to drop Hemingway from a required course in favor of a rather inadequate Chicano short-story writer, by telling me that her students would thus be better prepared to live in the United States. Aesthetic standards, she implied, were for our private pleasures of reading but were now wicked in the public sphere.

It is a considerable leap from a Hemingway short story, superb as the best of them are, to *Finnegans Wake,* and our new anti-elitist morality will consign the book to fewer and fewer readers, which is an immense aesthetic loss. Here, in a few pages, I can scarcely do justice to the *Wake,* beyond observing that if aesthetic merit were ever again to center the canon, the *Wake,* like Proust's *Search,* would be as close as our chaos could come to the heights of Shakespeare and Dante. My concern in what follows is only to continue the story of Joyce's agon with Shakespeare, whom he somehow found to be the greatest of writers (at least before Joyce) but dramatically inferior to Ibsen (an outrageous judgment from which Joyce never wavered; but one forgives him in gratitude for his grand remark: "There are some who think Ibsen was a feminist in *Hedda Gabler,* but he was no more a feminist than I am an archbishop").

Finnegans Wake, all critics agree, begins where *Ulysses* ends: Poldy goes to sleep, Molly broods magnificently, and then a larger Everyman dreams the book of the night. This new Everyman, Humphrey Chimpden Earwicker, is too huge to have a personality, any more than Albion, the Primordial Man of Blake's epics, is a human character. That is always my only sadness in turning from *Ulysses* to the *Wake;* the *Wake* is richer, but I lose Poldy though I gain what Joyce called a "history of the world." It is a very peculiar and powerful history, including literary history, and takes all of literature as its model, unlike *Ulysses,* which founded itself upon a curious amalgam of *Hamlet* and *The Odyssey.* Since Shakespeare and the Western Canon are one and the same, that necessarily returns Joyce to Shakespeare, the principal source (together with the Bible) of the concealed allusions and quotations that flood the pages of the book. For these I am indebted to James S. Atherton's *The Books at the Wake* (1960), still the most useful of the several fine studies that the *Wake* has provoked, and to Matthew Hodgart's pioneering essay, "Shakespeare and *Finnegans Wake*" (1953) in *The Cambridge Journal.*

Adaline Glasheen, in her *Third Census of "Finnegans Wake"* (1977), remarked that Shakespeare, the man and his works, was the matrix of the *Wake,* that is, "the rock mass in which metal, fossils, gems are enclosed or embedded." That, of course, is only one perspective on a book whose readers need absolutely every perspective that they can get, but it has always guided my reading of the *Wake.* The largest difference between the Shakespeare of *Ulysses,* holy ghost as I found him to be, and of *Finnegans Wake* is that Joyce for the first time is willing to express envy of his precursor and rival. He does not so much desire Shakespeare's gifts and his scope—Joyce believed that he was equal to Shakespeare in those—but is rightly jealous of Shakespeare's audience. That jealousy makes the *Wake* a tragicomedy rather than the comedy that Joyce intended. The reception of the book discouraged the dying Joyce, yet how could it have been otherwise? No literary work in the language since Blake's Prophecies presents so many initial obstacles to even the eager, generous, and informed reader. Only a few pages into the great "Anna Livia Plurabelle" section of the *Wake,* Joyce keens, *"By earth and the cloudy but I badly want a brandnew bankside, bedamp and I do, and a plumper at that!"*

Bankside puns on "backside," *bedamp* on "bedammed," and since this is the Liffey River speaking as well as Earwicker's wife, Atherton's comment is apt: "What Joyce is saying is that he wishes the Liffey had a South Bank where literature was appreciated as it was by Shakespeare's Thames." Shakespeare had the Globe Theatre and its audience; Joyce has only a coterie.

Staring at the pages of the *Wake*, even the generous reader must wonder whether Joyce was alert to how high he had raised the Freudian "incitement premium" if one is to vault into his greatest work. Tentatively, but after mulling the matter for some years, I think that Shakespeare's challenge to Joyce was part of the stimulus for the *Wake*'s desperate audacity. *Ulysses* tries to absorb Shakespeare on his own ground: *Hamlet*. Dublin is a large context but not large enough to swallow up Shakespeare, as a climactic moment of the "Circe" section, set in the inferno of Nightown, rather clearly indicates. Directly after poor Poldy suffers the squalor of being a Peeping Tom at the keyhole, watching Blazes Boylan plough Molly, the drunken Lynch, Stephen's sidekick, points to a mirror and cries out, "The mirror up to nature." We are then given a confrontation between Shakespeare and the two components of Joyce, Stephen and Bloom:

(*Stephen and Bloom gaze in the mirror. The face of William Shakespeare, beardless, appears there, rigid in facial paralysis, crowned by the reflection of the reindeer antler hatrack in the hall.*

SHAKESPEARE
(*in dignified ventriloquy*) 'Tis the loud laugh bespeaks the vacant mind. (*to Bloom*) Thou thoughtest as how thou wastest invisible. Gaze. (*he crows with a black capon's laugh*) Iagogo! How my oldfellow chokit his Thursdaymornun. Iagogo!

BLOOM
(*smiles yellowly at the three whores*) When will I hear the joke?

The cuckolded Shakespeare (on Stephen's theory) gazes on the cuckolded Poldy and the intoxicated Stephen after Lynch quotes Hamlet's admonishment to the players, reminding them that their purpose "was and is, to hold as it were, a mirror up to nature." Beardless, and rigid in facial paralysis, Shakespeare is crowned by his cuckold's horns, yet is still dignified as he misquotes from Oliver Goldsmith's poem, *The Deserted Village* (1770): "And the loud laugh that spoke the vacant mind," where "vacant mind" has the positive meaning of "leisurely" or "rested." Here Shakespeare reproves not only Lynch's empty mind, but also the vacancy of Boylan and of the whores as they mock poor Poldy. But to Poldy, Shakespeare directs the warning not to become a second Othello, spurred on by Iago-Boylan to murder Molly as my "Oldfellow" or "father" murdered my "Thursday mother."

Since Stephen was born on Thursday, we have two amalgamations (at least): Stephen and Bloom fuse, while Shakespeare is again the ghost of Hamlet's father warning the Joycean fusion not to add a further fusion of Hamlet and Othello, thus making Molly Bloom into an amalgam of Stephen's dead mother, Gertrude, and Desdemona. That is quite a joke on the wretched Poldy but still does not elucidate the main point: why is Shakespeare transformed so that he is not just a capon, but beardless and frozen-faced? Ellmann remarked that "Joyce warns us that he is working with near-identities, not perfect ones," but I hold to my earlier judgment that Joyce finally admits to his case of influence anxiety. Shakespeare the precursor mocks his follower, Stephen-Bloom-Joyce, in effect saying: "You stare in the mirror, trying to see yourself as me, but you behold what you are: only a beardless version, lacking my onetime potency, and rigid in facial paralysis, devoid of my ease of countenance." In *Finnegans Wake,* Joyce, recalling this as Shakespeare's farewell to him in *Ulysses,* determines to do better in the struggle with Shakespeare in the final round.

The end of *Finnegans Wake,* the monologue of the dying Anna Livia—mother, wife, and river—is frequently and rightly esteemed by critics as the most beautiful passage in all of Joyce. Going on fifty-eight, Joyce wrote his final fiction, evidently in November 1938. A little more than two years later he was dead, just before he turned sixty. Patrick Parrinder sensitively remarks that "Death, which has been faced with curiosity, anguish, mockery and farce in Joyce's earlier work, is here the subject of a painful excitement, a terrible rapture." If one substituted "Shakespeare's" for "Joyce's" in that eloquent sentence, the "here" would be the death of the king at the very close of *King Lear.* The river going home to the sea at the end of Joyce would be a version of dead Cordelia in the arms of her mad father, very soon to die himself.

Can one live the whole of literary history in a night's sleep?

Finnegans Wake says yes and asserts that all of human history can pass through one in a long, discontinuous dream. Anthony Burgess, Joyce's devoted disciple—in contrast to Samuel Beckett, who broke loose—says that "it is the most natural thing in the world to see Dr. Johnson and Falstaff, as well as the woman next door, waiting in Charing Cross railway station." I recall a Bloomian dream of my own in which I arrived too late at the New Haven railway station to keep a rendezvous with Mr. Zero Mostel, my double, and woke to decide it was my usual anxiety dream at not getting to a *Ulysses* class on time. Waiting at the station was everyone I had never wanted to meet again, from life and literature alike.

That dream was no fun; the *Wake* is, and is sometimes very funny, as funny as Rabelais or Blake in his Notebook. The Shakespeare it turns to, however, is mostly not the comic dramatist but the tragedian of *Macbeth, Hamlet, Julius Caesar, King Lear, Othello,* or the late romancer, the exception being that greatest of comic creations, Sir John Falstaff. That Joyce should compound Shakespeare and history is wholly natural, but either the *Wake* is a darker book than it intended to be, or else Shakespeare insinuated himself where he would. Earwicker or Everyman is also God, Shakespeare, Leopold Bloom, the mature James Joyce, King Lear (also King Leary), as well as Ulysses, Caesar, Lewis Carroll, the ghost of Hamlet's father, Falstaff, the sun, the sea, and the mountain, among many others.

There is a marvelous list in Glasheen's *Third Census* under the grand Joycean title, "Who Is Who When Everybody is Somebody Else." Joyce intended reconciliation and inclusion, as only Proust among our century's other writers might have intended it, though not on quite so cosmological a scale. But the tragic Shakespeare is not a reconciler, and *Macbeth* in particular is a very dark work to have cut its way into the *Wake*. If Joyce was Lear in his Celtic form as Old Man of the Sea, then his Cordelia was his tragically mad daughter Lucia, and the will to comedy doubtless sometimes faltered in him. He remembers himself as a young artist, Shem the Penman, at once Hamlet and Stephen Dedalus (Macbeth sneaks in there too), and what Harry Levin wisely called "the outcry of the great writer who has come too late" is heard:

You were bred, fed, fostered and fattened from holy childhood up in this two easter island on the piejaw of hilarious heaven and roaring the other place (plunders to night of you, blunders what's left of you, flash as flash can!) and now, forsooth, a nogger among the blankards of this dastard century, you have become of twosome twinminds forenenst gods, hidden and discovered, nay, condemned fool, anarch, egoarch, hiersiarch, you have reared your disunited kingdom on the vacuum of your own most intensely doubtful soul. Do you hold yourself then for some god in the manger, Shehohem, that you will neither serve nor let serve, pray nor let pray? And here, pay the piety, must I too nerve myself to pray for the loss of selfrespect to equip me for the horrible necessity of scandalisang (my dear sisters, are you ready?) by sloughing off my hope and tremors while we all swin together in the pool of Sodom?

Sniffer of carrion, premature gravedigger, seeker of the nest of evil in the bosom of a good word, you, who sleep at our vigil and fast for our feast, you with your dislocated reason, have cutely foretold, a jophet in your own absence, by blind poring upon your many scalds and burns and blisters, impetiginous sore and pustules, by the auspices of that raven cloud, your shade, and by the auguries of rooks in parlament, death with every disaster, the dynamitisation of colleagues, the reducing of records to ashes, the levelling of all customs by blazes, the return of a lot of sweetempered gunpowdered didst unto dudst but it never stphruck your mudhead's obtundity (O hell, here comes our funeral! O pest, I'll miss the post!) that the more carrots you chop, the more turnips you slit, the more murphies you peel, the more onions you cry over, the more bullbeef you butch, the more mutton you crackerhack, the more potherbs you pound, the fiercer the fire and the longer your spoon and the harder you gruel with more grease to your elbow the merrier fumes your new Irish stew.

There is humor about the situation of Joyce's youth here, but that scarcely seems to be the primary affect. There is deep bitterness toward Ireland, the Church, Joyce's entire context, and a ferocious investment in his own autonomy as a writer. I suspect that just as Beckett was to turn to writing in French so as to surmount Joyce's influence on his early work, so Joyce broke with the English of Shakespeare in *Finnegans Wake*. The break was dialectical, partly inspired by Shakespearean wordplay and punning; the feast of language in *Love's Labour's Lost* is already Joycean. In the passages above, beyond the parody of Tennyson's Light Brigade directed against the Church and the echo of Stephen in the *Portrait* answering that "I will not serve," there is the fiercest of parodies of Saint Paul in Corinthians ("O death, where is thy sting? O grave, where is thy victory?") in the parenthesis of belatedness that Levin pointed to: "(O hell, here comes our funeral! O pest, I'll miss the post!)." Whether *Finnegans Wake* has missed the post is still not clear, but the death of the serious study of literature *as literature* probably dooms Joyce's greatest achievement. Shakespeare is the *Wake*'s principal instance of a writer who made the post, who indeed has become the postal service itself. Shem, we are told, was

> aware of no other shaggspick, other Shakhisbeard, either preexactly unlike his polar andthisishis or procisely the seem as woops (parn!) as what he fancied or guessed the sames as he was himself and that, greet scoot, duckings and thuggery, though he was foxed fux to fux like a bunnyboy rodger with all the teashop lionses of Lumdrum hivanhoesed up gagainst him, being a lapsis linquo with a ruvidubb shortartempa, bad cad dad fad sad mad nad vanhaty bear, the consciquenchers of casuality prepestered crusswords in postposition, scruff, scruffer, scruffumurraimost andallthatsortofthing, if reams stood to reason and his lanka-livline lasted he would wipe alley english spooker, multaphon-iaksically spuking, off the face of the erse.

There is controlled aggressiveness toward Shakespeare and a profound desire to play at replacing English with the dialect of the *Wake*, the language of the outlaw, as Joyce would have put it, who negates the nineteenth-century English novelists (scoot, duckings, and thuggery: Scott, Dickens, Thackeray) and is at once Shakespeare's antithesis and Shakespeare in a Viconian recoursing.

The echo of Swinburne on Villon ("Villon our sad bad glad mad brother's name") is appropriate for Joyce's rather unpersuasive presentation of his mild, Poldian self as a literary outlaw, Rimbaud or Villon. Slips of the tongue are raised here, and throughout the *Wake,* to a Shakespearean obsessiveness, as though Joyce could be confounded with the language-mad Shakespeare of *Love's Labour's Lost.* As with so much of the *Wake,* the freshness of the effect more than compensates for the obscurity, even if Joyce does not always mount to paradise by the stairway of surprise.

If you cannot exorcise Shakespeare (who can?) and cannot absorb him (the lesson of his mirror epiphany in Nightown), then you must transform him into yourself, or confront the ruinous quest of transmuting yourself into him, what Hodgart, Glasheen, and Atherton have shown is a delightfully strenuous Joycean effort to turn Shakespeare into the creator of the *Wake.* As an obsessive student of literary influence, I celebrate this effort as the most successful metamorphosis of Shakespeare in literary history. The only possible rival is Beckett, who in *Endgame* appropriates *Hamlet* with audacity and skill. But Beckett, an early and close student of the *Wake,* was warily indebted to his former friend and master, at least for example.

There is still a kind of genial desperation evidenced by the grand scale on which "Great Shapesphere" is employed in the *Wake,* and I am uncertain what would happen to the book if all of Shapesphere were withdrawn from it. Hodgart identifies a significant allusion on almost every other page. All in all there are three hundred of them, many so significant as to transcend what we would normally call "allusions." Earwicker—God, father, and sinner—is the ghost in *Hamlet* but also the wicked Claudius and Polonius. In addition, Earwicker contains the martyred King Duncan in *Macbeth,* Julius Caesar, Lear, the hideous Richard III, and two sublimities: Bottom and Falstaff. Shem or Stephen Dedalus is more than ever Prince Hamlet, but also Macbeth, Cassius, and Edmund, so that Joyce, with interpretive cunning, makes Hamlet into another pragmatically murderous hero-villain. Shaun, Shem's brother, is at once Joyce's own brother, the long-suffering and loyally supportive Stanislaus, and the recalcitrant Shakespearean fourfold of Laertes, Macduff, Brutus, and Edgar.

These Shakespearean identities more than firm up Joyce's plot (if one may call it that); they provide roles for Earwicker and his family, including Anna Livia as Gertrude, and Isabella (the daughter for whom Earwicker feels an incestuous and guilty desire) as Ophelia. Hodgart has a useful description of this role playing:

> A character appears in a particular aspect by being reincarnated into one of the "types," speaking with his voice like a "control" taking possession of a medium during a seance. . . . When a "type" has become the main channel for the narrative, the allusions to him are thickened. . . . Hence it is to be expected that Shakespearean quotations will come not in single spies but in battalions, spread out over passages of varying length, and each group announcing the presence of a corresponding character from the play.

The biggest battalions march forth from *Hamlet, Macbeth,* and *Julius Caesar,* in decreasing order. *Hamlet* by now is no surprise, but the difficult question of why *Macbeth,* let alone *Julius Caesar,* remains. These are all plays of killing the king, whereas Lear dies only by agonized degrees, stretched on the rack for five increasingly apocalyptic acts, which may be why Joyce saves him for last, to help close the *Wake.* The king being killed is, of course, Earwicker, that is to say, Joyce/Shakespeare, and despite Shem's Hamlet complex it is never clear who is doing the killing.

I suggest that this is the reason *Macbeth* is so important to *Finnegans Wake.* Joyce, a superb reader of Shakespeare, as well as a powerful misreader, builds through the *Macbeth* allusions to suggest that the Joycean, Shakespearean, Earwickian imagination is the killer, just as Macbeth's extraordinary and proleptic strength of imagination has a murderousness all its own, which it imposes upon the rest of the play. The earliest Shakespearean allusion in the *Wake* is to *Macbeth,* just as the final one is to *King Lear.* Hodgart observes that quotations from *Macbeth* appear wherever Earwicker endures enormous emotional stress in the *Wake* and when his self-destructive drive emerges most visibly, as in the hero's agitation at the end of book 1:

Humph is in his doge. Words weigh no no more to him than raindrops to Rethfernhim. Which we all like. Rain. When we sleep. Drops. But wait until our sleeping. Drain Sdops.

"Duncan is in his grave; / After life's fitful fever he sleeps well." Rathfernham is a Dublin district, "doge" puns on "doze," and "sdoppiare" in Italian means something like "disconnect" or "open outward." The subsequent battle between Macduff the avenger and Macbeth the murderer duly takes place about twenty-five pages later, and the three witches or Weird Sisters as well as the three murderers of Banquo put in several appearances each. Hodgart demonstrates that the Macbeth act 5, scene 5 soliloquy, the famous "Tomorrow and tomorrow and tomorrow," is echoed almost entire, as is Hamlet's "To be or not to be" monologue, but each is scattered and strung out through the text of the *Wake,* an act of dispersal that is both useful to Joyce's purposes and something of a revenge on the prevalence of Shapesphere! But Shakespeare's revenge recoils upon Joyce:

> *Yet's the time for being now, now, now.*
> *For a burning would is come to dance inane.*
> *Glamours hath moidered's lieb and herefore*
> *Coldours must leap no more. Lack breath must leap*
> *no more.*

Lewis Carroll, Jonathan Swift, and Richard Wagner are all drawn on throughout the *Wake* (though not as extensively as Shakespeare is), but they never strike back or get away from Joyce as Shakespeare does. One could say that Shakespeare in the *Wake* has the same relation to Joyce that Hamlet, Iago, and Falstaff have to Shakespeare: the creation breaks free from the creator. Shakespeare is no one's creation, or he is everyone's; and Joyce, though he fights brilliantly, in my judgment loses the contest. But even as he loses, he achieves the Sublime in Anna Livia's dying return to childhood as the *Wake* ends:

But I'm loothing them that's here and all I lothe. Loonely in me loneness. For all their faults. I am passing out. O bitter ending!

I'll slip away before they're up. They'll never see. Nor know. Nor miss me. And it's old and old it's sad and old it's sad and weary I go back to you, my cold father, my cold mad father, my cold mad feary father, till the near sight of the mere size of him, the moyles and moyles of it, moananoaning, makes me seasilt saltsick and I rush, my only, into your arms. I see them rising! Save me from those therrble prongs! Two more. Onetwo moremens more. So. Avelaval. My leaves have drifted from me. All. But one clings still. I'll bear it on me. To remind me of. Lff! So soft this morning, ours. Yes. Carry me along, taddy, like you done through the toy fair! If I seen him bearing down on me now under whitespread wings like he'd come from Arkangels, I sink I'd die down over his feet, humbly dumbly, only to washup. Yes, tid. There's where. First. We pass through grass behush the bush to. Whish! A gull. Gulls. Far calls. Coming, far! End here. Us then. Finn, again! Take. Bussoftlhee, mememoremee! Till thousendsthee. Lps. The keys to. Given! A way a lone a last a loved a long the

The Celtic sea-god Manannán Mac Lir, who makes a singular appearance in the Nightown phantasmagoria of *Ulysses,* is also *King Lir* or Lear, "my cold father, my cold mad father, my cold mad feary father," to whom Anna Livia-Cordelia returns in death, as the Liffey floats out to the sea. Since Lear, in the *Wake,* stands for three other fathers—Earwicker, Joyce, Shakespeare—as well as for the sea, this beautiful death-passage might have been Joyce's deliberate hint that another great work lay ahead of him, an epic he had projected on the sea. Keats wrote his splendid sonnet "On the Sea" when he reread *King Lear* and came to "Hark! do you hear the sea" (4.6.4). We can regret Joyce not living on into his sixties in order to write his *On the Sea,* where doubtless his endless agon with Shakespeare would have taken yet another turn, as canonical as those that came before.

19.

Woolf's *Orlando:*
Feminism as the Love
of Reading

Sainte-Beuve, to me the most interesting of French critics, taught us to ask as a crucial question of any writer in whom we read deeply: What would the author think of us? Virginia Woolf wrote five remarkable novels—*Mrs. Dalloway* (1925), *To the Lighthouse* (1927), *Orlando* (1928), *The Waves* (1931), and *Between the Acts* (1941)—which are very likely to become canonical. These days she is most widely known and read as the supposed founder of "Feminist literary criticism," particularly in her polemical *A Room of One's Own* (1929) and *Three Guineas* (1938). Since I am not yet competent to judge Feminist criticism, I will center here upon only one element in Woolf's feminist writing, her extraordinary love for and defense of reading.

Woolf's own literary criticism seems to me very mixed, especially in her judgment of contemporaries. To regard Joyce's *Ulysses* as a "disaster," or Lawrence's novels as lacking "the final power which makes things entire in themselves," is not what we expect from a critic as erudite and perceptive as Woolf. And yet one could argue that she was the most complete person-of-letters in England in our century. Her essays and novels expand the central traditions of English literature in ways that freshen beyond any possible reach of her polemics. The preface to *Orlando* begins by expressing a debt to Defoe, Sir Thomas Browne, Sterne, Sir Walter Scott, Lord Macaulay, Emily Brontë, De Quincey, and Walter Pater, "to name the first that come to mind." Pater, the authentic precursor, or "absent father," as Perry Meisel calls him, might have headed the list, since *Orlando* is certainly the most Paterian narrative of our era. Like Oscar Wilde's and the young James Joyce's, Woolf's way of confronting and representing experience is altogether Paterian. But other influences are there as well, with Sterne perhaps the most crucial after Pater. Only Pater seems to have provoked Woolf to some anxiety; she very rarely mentions him and ascribes the model for her "moments of being" not to Pater's "privileged moments" or secularized epiphanies but rather oddly to Thomas Hardy, or to Joseph Conrad at his most Paterian. Perry Meisel has traced the intricate ways in which Pater's crucial metaphors inform both Woolf's fiction and her essays. It is an amiable irony that many of her professed followers tend to repudiate aesthetic criteria for judgment, whereas Woolf herself founded her feminist politics upon her Paterian aestheticism.

There may be other major writers of our century who loved reading as much as Woolf did, but no one since Hazlitt and Emerson has expressed that passion so memorably and usefully as she did. A room of one's own was required precisely for reading and writing in. I still treasure the old Penguin edition of *A Room of One's Own* that I purchased for ninepence in 1947, and I go on musing about the passage I marked there, which brings together Jane Austen and Shakespeare as a kind of wished-for, composite precursor:

> and, I wondered, would *Pride and Prejudice* have been a better novel if Jane Austen had not thought it necessary to hide her manuscript from visitors? I read a page or two to see; but I could not find any signs that her circumstances had harmed her work in the slightest. That, perhaps, was the chief miracle about it. Here was a woman about the year 1800 writing without hate,

without bitterness, without fear, without protest, without preaching. That was how Shakespeare wrote, I thought, looking at *Antony and Cleopatra;* and when people compare Shakespeare and Jane Austen, they may mean that the minds of both had consumed all impediments; and for that reason we do not know Jane Austen and we do not know Shakespeare, and for that reason Jane Austen pervades every word that she wrote, and so does Shakespeare. If Jane Austen suffered in any way from her circumstances it was in the narrowness of life that was imposed upon her. It was impossible for a woman to go about alone. She never travelled; she never drove through London in an omnibus or had luncheon in a shop by herself. But perhaps it was the nature of Jane Austen not to want what she had not. Her gift and her circumstances matched each other completely. But I doubt whether that was true of Charlotte Brontë, I said. . . .

Was Woolf, in this respect, more like Austen or more like Charlotte Brontë? If we read *Three Guineas* with its prophetic fury against the patriarchy, we are not likely to decide that Woolf's mind had consumed all impediments; yet when we read *The Waves* or *Between the Acts* we may conclude that her gift and her circumstances matched each other completely. Are there two Woolfs, one the precursor of our current critical maenads, the other a more distinguished novelist than any woman at work since? I think not, although there are deep fissures in *A Room of One's Own.* Like Pater and like Nietzsche, Woolf is best described as an apocalyptic aesthete, for whom human existence and the world are finally justified only as aesthetic phenomena. As much as any writer ever, be it Emerson or Nietzsche or Pater, Virginia Woolf declines to attribute her sense of self to historical conditioning, even if that history is the endless exploitation of women by men. Her selves, to her, are as much her own creation as are *Orlando* and *Mrs. Dalloway,* and any close student of her criticism learns that she does not regard novels or poems or Shakespearean dramas as bourgeois mystifications or as "cultural capital." No more a religious believer than Pater or Freud, Woolf follows her aestheticism to its outer limits, to the negativity of a pragmatic nihilism and of suicide. But she cared more for the romance of the journey than for its end, and she located what was best in life as her reading, her writing, and her conversations with friends, preoccupations not those of a zealot.

Will we ever again have novelists as original and superb as Austen, George Eliot, and Woolf, or a poet as extraordinary and intelligent as Dickinson? Half a century after Woolf's death, she has no rivals among women novelists or critics, though they enjoy the liberation she prophesied. As Woolf noted, if ever there has been Shakespeare's sister, it was Austen, who wrote two centuries ago. There are no social conditions or contexts that necessarily encourage the production of great literature, though we will be a long time learning this uncomfortable truth. We are not being flooded with instant masterpieces these days, as the passage of even a few years will show. No living American woman novelist, of whatever race or ideology, compares in aesthetic eminence to Edith Wharton or to Willa Cather, nor have we a current poet within range of Marianne Moore or Elizabeth Bishop. The arts are simply not progressive, as Hazlitt noted in a wonderful fragment of 1814, where he remarks that "The principle of universal suffrage . . . is by no means applicable to matters of taste"; Woolf is Hazlitt's sister in sensibility, and her immense literary culture shares little with the current crusade mounted in her name.

IT IS DIFFICULT, at this time, to maintain any kind of balance or sense of proportion in writing about Woolf. Joyce's *Ulysses* and Lawrence's *Women in Love* would seem to be achievements well beyond even *To the Lighthouse* and *Between the Acts,* and yet many current partisans of Woolf would contest such a judgment. Woolf is a lyrical novelist: *The Waves* is more prose poem than novel, and *Orlando* is best where it largely forsakes narrative. Herself neither a Marxist nor a feminist, according to the informed testimony of her nephew and biographer, Quentin Bell, Woolf is nevertheless an Epicurean materialist, like her precursor Walter Pater. Reality for her flickers and wavers with every fresh perception and sensation, and ideas are shades that border her privileged moments.

Her feminism (to call it that) is potent and permanent precisely because it is less an idea or composite of ideas and more a formidable array of perceptions and sensations. Arguing with them is to sustain defeat: what she perceives and what she experiences by her sensibility is more finely organized than any response I can summon. Overwhelmed by her eloquence and her mastery of metaphor, I am unable—while I read it—to dispute *Three Guineas,* even where it makes me wince. Perhaps only Freud, in our century, rivals Woolf as a stylist of tendentious prose. *A Room of One's Own* has a design on its reader, and so does *Civilization and Its Discontents,* but no awareness of the design will save the reader from being convinced while he or she undergoes the polemical magnificence of Freud and of Woolf. They are two very different models of persuasive splendor: Freud anticipates your objections and at least appears to answer them, while Woolf strongly insinuates that your disagreement with her urgency is founded upon imperceptiveness.

I am puzzled each time I reread *A Room of One's Own,* or even *Three Guineas,* as to how anyone could take these tracts as instances of "political theory," the genre invoked by literary Feminists for whom Woolf's polemics have indeed assumed scriptural status. Perhaps Woolf would have been gratified, but it seems unlikely. Only by a persuasive redefinition of politics, one that reduced it to "academic politics," could these works be so classified; and Woolf was not an academic, nor would she be one now. Woolf is no more a radical political theorist than Kafka is a heretical theologian. They are writers and have no other covenant. The pleasures they give are difficult pleasures, which cannot be reduced to categorical judgments. I am moved, even awed, by Kafka's aphoristic circlings of "the indestructible," yet it is the resistance of "the indestructible" to interpretation that becomes what needs to be interpreted. What most requires interpretation in *A Room of One's Own* are its "irreconcilable habits of thought," as John Burt put it back in 1982.

Burt showed that the book presents both a "feminist" central argument—the patriarchy exploits women economically and socially in order to bolster its inadequate self-esteem—and a Romantic underargument. The underargument gives us women not as looking glasses for male narcissism but (Woolf says) as "some renewal of creative power which it is in the gift only of the opposite sex to bestow." This gift has been lost, Woolf adds, but not because of the depredations of the patriarchy. The First World War is the villain, but what then has happened to the book's overt argument? Was the Victorian Period the bad old days or the good old days?

Burt's summary seems to me eminently just:

The two arguments of A Room of One's Own are not reconcilable, and any attempt to reconcile them can be no more than an exercise in special pleading. A Room of One's Own, however, is not an argument but, as Woolf proclaims in its opening pages, a portrayal of how a mind attempts to come to terms with its world.

Woolf comes to terms only as Pater and Nietzsche did: the world is reconceived aesthetically. If A Room of One's Own is characteristic of Woolf, and it is, then it is almost as much a prose poem as The Waves, and as much a Utopian fantasy as Orlando. To read it as "cultural criticism" or "political theory" is possible only for those who have dismissed aesthetic concerns altogether, or who have reserved reading for pleasure (difficult pleasure) for another time and place, where the wars between women and men, and between competing social classes, races, and religions, have ceased. Woolf herself made no such renunciation; as a novelist and literary critic she nurtured her sensibility, which included a strong propensity for comedy. Even the tracts are deliberately very funny, and thereby still more effective as polemics. To be solemn about Woolf, to analyze her as a political theorist and cultural critic, is to be not at all Woolfian.

Clearly this is an odd time in literary studies: D. H. Lawrence actually was a rather weird political theorist in The Crown essays, in his Mexican novel The Plumed Serpent, and his Australian Kangaroo, another Fascist fiction. No one would wish to substitute the political Lawrence, or the somewhat more interesting cultural moralist Lawrence, for the novelist of The Rainbow and Women in Love. Yet Woolf is now more often discussed as the author of

A Room of One's Own than as the novelist who wrote *Mrs. Dalloway* and *To the Lighthouse. Orlando*'s current fame has nearly everything to do with the hero-heroine's sexual metamorphosis and owes very little to what most matters in the book: comedy, characterization, and an intense love of the major eras of English literature. I cannot think of another strong novelist who centers everything upon her extraordinary love of reading as Woolf does.

Her religion (no lesser word would be apt) was Paterian aestheticism: the worship of art. As a belated acolyte of that waning faith, I am necessarily devoted to Woolf's fiction and criticism, and I therefore want to take up arms against her feminist followers, because I think they have mistaken their prophet. She would have had them battle for their rights, certainly, but hardly by devaluating the aesthetic in their unholy alliance with academic pseudo-Marxists, French mock philosophers, and multicultural opponents of all intellectual standards whatsoever. By a room of one's own, she did not mean an academic department of one's own, but rather a context in which they could emulate her by writing fiction worthy of Sterne and Austen, and criticism commensurate with that of Hazlitt and Pater. Woolf, the lover of the prose of Sir Thomas Browne, would have suffered acutely confronting the manifestos of those who assert that they write and teach in her name. Herself the last of the high aesthetes, she has been swallowed up by remorseless Puritans, for whom the beautiful in literature is only another version of the cosmetics industry.

Of Shelley, whose spirit haunts her works, particularly in *The Waves,* Woolf observed that "his fight, valiant though it is, seems to be with monsters who are a little out of date and therefore slightly ridiculous." That seems true of Woolf's fight also: where are those Edwardian and Georgian patriarchs against whom she battled? Approaching millennium, we have been abandoned by the monsters of the patriarchy, though Feminist critics labor at conjuring them up. Yet Shelley's greatness, as Woolf rightly saw, prevailed as "a state of being." The lyrical novelist, like the lyrical poet, abides now as the re-imaginer of certain extraordinary moments of being: "a space of pure calm, of intense and windless serenity."

Woolf's quest to reach that space was more Paterian than Shelleyan, if only because the erotic element in it was so much reduced. The image of heterosexual union never abandoned Shelley, though it turned demonic in his death poem, the ironically entitled *Triumph of Life*. Woolf is Paterian or belated Romantic, with the erotic drive largely translated into a sublimating aestheticism. Her feminism once again cannot be distinguished from her aestheticism; perhaps we should learn to speak of her "contemplative feminism," really a metaphorical stance. The freedom she seeks is both visionary and pragmatic and depends upon an idealized Bloomsbury, hardly translatable into contemporary American terms.

The Penguin American edition in which I first read *Orlando*, in the autumn of 1946, begins its back cover by saying, "No writer was ever born into a more felicitous environment." Woolf, like her feminist followers, would not have agreed with that judgment, but it possesses considerable truth nevertheless. It did not retard her development to have John Ruskin, Thomas Hardy, George Meredith, and Robert Louis Stevenson trooping through her father's house, or to count the Darwins and Stracheys among her relatives. And though her polemics urge otherwise, the intricately organized Virginia Stephen would have broken down even more often and thoroughly at Cambridge or Oxford, nor would she have received there the literary education provided for her by her father's library and by tutors as capable as Walter Pater's sister.

Her father, Leslie Stephen, was not the patriarchal ogre portrayed by her resentment, though one would not know this by reading many of our current Feminist scholars. I am aware that they follow Woolf herself, for whom her father was a selfish and lonely egotist who could not surmount his own consciousness of failure as a philosopher. Her Leslie Stephen is the Mr. Ramsay of *To the Lighthouse*, a last Victorian who is more of a grandfather than a father to his children. But Leslie Stephen's particular difference from his daughter centers upon her aestheticism and his empiricism and moralism, indeed his violent repudiation of the aesthetic stance, including a virulent hatred for its great champion, Pater.

In reaction to her father, Woolf's aestheticism and feminism (again, to call it that) were so fused that they could never again be pulled apart. Probably an ironic perspective is best these days in contemplating how Woolf's disciples have converted her purely literary culture into a political *Kulturkampf.* This transformation cannot work, because Woolf's most authentic prophecy was unwilled by her. No other twentieth-century person-of-letters shows us so clearly that our culture is doomed to remain a literary one in the absence of any ideology that has not been discredited. Religion, science, philosophy, politics, social movements: are these live birds in our hands or dead, stuffed birds on the shelf? When our conceptual modes abandon us, we return to literature, where cognition, perception, and sensation cannot be wholly disentangled. The flight from the aesthetic is another symptom of our society's unconscious but purposeful forgetting of its dilemma, its slide toward another Theological Age. Whatever Woolf may have repressed at one time or another, it was never her aesthetic sensibility.

That books are necessarily about other books and can represent experience only by first treating it as yet another book, is a limited but real truth. Certain works lift the limitation entirely: *Don Quixote* is one, and Woolf's *Orlando* another. The Don and Orlando are great readers, and only as such are surrogates for those obsessive readers, Cervantes and Woolf. In life history, Orlando is modeled upon Vita Sackville-West, with whom Woolf was, for a time, in love. But Sackville-West was a great gardener, a bad writer, and not exactly a reader of genius, as Woolf was. As aristocrat, as lover, even as writer, Orlando is Vita and not Virginia. It is as a critical consciousness, encountering English literature from Shakespeare to Thomas Hardy, that Orlando is the uncommon common reader, the author of his/her book.

All novels since *Don Quixote* rewrite Cervantes' universal masterwork, even when they are quite unaware of it. I cannot recall Woolf mentioning Cervantes anywhere, but that scarcely matters: Orlando is Quixotic, and so was Woolf. The comparison to *Don Quixote* is hardly fair to *Orlando;* a novel far more ambitious than, and as well executed as, Woolf's playful love letter to Sackville-West would also be destroyed by the comparison. The Don lends himself endlessly to meditation, like Falstaff; Orlando certainly does not. But it helps to set Woolf against Cervantes in order to see that both books belong to Huizinga's order of play, which I expounded in the discussion of *Don Quixote*. The ironies of *Orlando* are Quixotic: they ensue from the critique that organized playfulness makes of both societal and natural reality. "Organized playfulness" in Woolf and Cervantes, in Orlando and the Don, is another name for the art of reading well, or in Woolf's case for "feminism," if you must have it so. Orlando is a man, or rather a youth, who suddenly becomes a woman. He is also an Elizabethan aristocrat who, with no more fuss made about it than about his sexual change, is pragmatically immortal. Orlando is sixteen when we meet him, thirty-six when we leave her, but those twenty years of literary biography span more than three centuries of literary history. The order of play, while it prevails, triumphs over time, and in Woolf's *Orlando* it persists without travail, which may be one reason why the book's one flaw is its too-happy conclusion.

Love, in *Orlando*, is always the love of reading, even when it is disguised as the love for a woman or for a man. The boy Orlando is the girl Virginia when he is represented in his primary role, as a reader:

> The taste for books was an early one. As a child he was sometimes found at midnight by a page still reading. They took his taper away and he bred glow-worms to serve his purpose. They took the glow-worms away, and he almost burnt the house down with a tinder. To put it in a nutshell, leaving the novelist to smooth out the crumpled silk and all its implications, he was a nobleman afflicted with a love of literature.

Orlando, like Woolf (and quite unlike Vita Sackville-West), is one of those people who substitute a phantom for an erotic reality. His/her two grand passions, for the improbable Russian princess, Sasha, and for the even more absurd sea captain, Marmaduke Bonthrop Shelmerdine, can best be regarded as solipsistic projections: there is really only one character in *Orlando*. Virginia Woolf's love of reading was both her authentic erotic drive and her secular theology. Nothing in *Orlando*, beautiful as the book is, equals the concluding paragraph of "How Should One Read a Book," the final essay in *The Second Common Reader:*

> Yet who reads to bring about an end however desirable? Are there not some pursuits that we practise because they are good in themselves, and some pleasures that are final? And is not this among them? I have sometimes dreamt, at least, that when the Day of Judgment dawns and the great conquerors and lawyers and statesmen come to receive their rewards—their crowns, their laurels, their names carved indelibly upon imperishable marble—the Almighty will turn to Peter and will say, not without a certain envy when He sees us coming with our books under our arms, "Look, these need no reward. We have nothing to give them here. They have loved reading."

Those first three sentences have been my credo ever since I read them in my childhood, and I urge them now upon myself, and all who still can rally to them. They do not preclude reading to obtain power, over oneself or over others, but only through a pleasure that is final, a difficult and authentic pleasure. Woolf's innocence, like Blake's, is an organized innocence, and her sense of reading is not the innocent myth of reading but the disinterestedness that Shakespeare teaches his deeper readers, Woolf included. Heaven, in Woolf's parables, bestows no reward to equal the blessedness of the common reader, or what Dr. Johnson called the common sense of readers. There is at last no other test for the canonical than the Shakespearean supreme pleasure of disinterestedness, the stance of Hamlet in act 5 and of Shakespeare himself in the most exalted moments of his sonnets.

Woolf has finer works than *Orlando,* but none more central to her than this erotic hymn to the pleasure of disinterested reading. The fable of dual sexuality is an intrinsic strand in that pleasure, whether in Woolf or in Shakespeare, or in Woolf's critical father, Walter Pater. Sexual anxiety blocks the deep pleasure of reading, and for Woolf, even in her love for Sackville-West, sexual anxiety was never far away. One senses that for Woolf, as for Walt Whitman, the homoerotic, though the natural mode, was largely impeded by solipsistic intensity. Woolf might have said with

Whitman, "To touch my person to someone else's is about as much as I can stand." We don't believe in Orlando's raptures, whether with Sasha or with the sea captain, but we are persuaded by his/her passion for Shakespeare, Alexander Pope, and the possibility of a new literary work. *Orlando* may indeed be the longest love letter ever penned, but it is written by Woolf to herself. Implicitly, the book celebrates Woolf's preternatural strength as a reader and a writer. A healthy self-esteem, well earned by Woolf, finds its accurate release in this most exuberant of her novels.

Is Orlando a snob? In current parlance, that would be a "cultural elitist," but Woolf herself has a candid essay, "Am I a Snob?" that she read to the Memoir Club, a Bloomsbury gathering, in 1920. Its self-mockery clears away the charge, while containing a fine phrase characterizing the Stephens: "an intellectual family, very nobly born in a bookish sense." Orlando's family is certainly not intellectual, but there can be few descriptions of Orlando so clarifying as "very nobly born in a bookish sense." The bookish sense is the book; no one need look for an underplot in *Orlando;* there is no mother-daughter relationship hidden in this spoof of a story. Nor does Orlando love reading differently after he becomes a woman. It is the female Orlando whose aestheticism becomes wonderfully aggressive and post-Christian:

> The poet's then is the highest office of all, she continued. His words reached where others fall short. A silly song of Shakespeare's has done more for the poor and the wicked than all the preachers and philanthropists in the world.

Disputable as that last sentence must be, Woolf stands behind it, in passion as well as humorously. What if we rewrite it slightly so as to fit our present moment: A silly song of Shakespeare's has done more for the poor and the wicked than all the Marxists and Feminists in the world.

Orlando is not a polemic but a celebration that cultural decline has made into an elegy. It is a defense of poetry, "half laughing, half serious," as Woolf remarked in her diary. The joke that goes on too long is its own genre, which has never had a master to rival Cervantes—not even Sterne, who is an authentic presence in

Woolf's novels. Don Quixote is far vaster than Orlando, yet even the Don cannot run away from Cervantes, as Falstaff perhaps got away from Shakespeare, and as Orlando, except for the book's weak conclusion, pulls away from Woolf. Neither Vita nor Virginia, Orlando becomes the personification of the aesthetic stance, of what it means for the reader to be in love with literature. Soon such a passion may seem quaint or archaic, and *Orlando* will survive as its monument, a survival Woolf intended: "Indeed it is a difficult business—this time-keeping; nothing more quickly disorders it than contact with any of the arts; and it may have been her love of poetry that was to blame for making Orlando lose her shopping list."

Timekeeping, as in Sterne, is antithetical to the imagination, and we are not expected to ask, at the book's conclusion: Can Orlando ever die? In this mockery of a book, this holiday from reality, everything is shamanistic, and the central consciousness exemplifies a poetry without death. But what can that be? The novel astutely defines poetry as a voice answering a voice, but Woolf avoids emphasizing that the second voice is the voice of the dead. Determined for once to indulge herself as a writer, Woolf removes every possibility of anxiety from her story. Yet she does not know how there can be poetry without anxiety, nor do we. Shakespeare is a presence throughout *Orlando,* and we wonder how he can be there without introducing something problematic into the novel, something that must be resisted as an authority, since every kind of authority except the literary variety is put into question or mocked in the course of the book. Woolf's anxiety about Shakespeare's poetic authority is subtly handled in *Between the Acts* but evaded in *Orlando.* Yet the evasiveness belongs to what I have called the novel's shamanism; it works, as nearly everything does in this testament to the religion of poetry, to the exaltation of sensation and perception over everything else.

THE IDIOSYNCRATIC in Woolf, the enduring strangeness of her best fiction, is yet another instance of this surprisingly most canonical of all literary qualities. Orlando is unlike Woolf in supposedly transcending the quest for literary glory, but a holiday is a holiday, and Woolf was unrelenting in her quest to join herself to Sterne and to Hazlitt, to Austen and to the hidden paradigm, Pater. Her aestheticism is her center, figured most richly in *A Room of One's Own* as a Shakespearean intimation that the art itself is nature: "Nature, in her most irrational mood, has traced in invisible ink on the walls of the mind a premonition which these great artists confirm; a sketch which only needs to be held to the fire of genius to become visible."

Personality, for Woolf as for Pater, is the highest fusion of art and nature and far exceeds society as the governing determination of the writer's life and work. At the conclusion of *To the Lighthouse,* the painter Lily Briscoe, Woolf's surrogate, looks at her canvas, finds it blurred, and "With a sudden intensity, as if she saw it clear for a second, she drew a line there, in the centre. It was done, it was finished. Yes, she thought, laying down her brush in extreme fatigue, I have had my vision."

Perhaps a time yet will come when we will all find our current political stances archaic and superseded, and when Woolf's vision will be apprehended as what it most centrally was: the ecstasy of the privileged moment. How odd it would seem now if we spoke of "the politics of Walter Pater." It will seem odd then to speak of the politics, rather than the literary agon, of Virginia Woolf.

20.

Kafka: Canonical Patience and "Indestructibility"

IF YOU WANTED to choose the single writer most representative of our century, you might find yourself wandering hopelessly through legions of the dispossessed. Presumably there will be a twenty-second century, and readers—if there are readers, in our sense—will sort out our Dante (Kafka?) and our Montaigne (Freud?). In this book I have chosen nine moderns: Freud, Proust, Joyce, Kafka, Woolf, Neruda, Beckett, Borges, and Pessoa. I do not assert that they are our century's best; they are here to represent all the others for whom a canonical status might rationally be asserted.

Except for Neruda and Pessoa, the poets of the era are not here: Yeats, Rilke, Valéry, Trakl, Stevens, Eliot, Montale, Mandelstam, Lorca, Vallejo, Hart Crane, and so many others. I myself would rather read poems than novels or plays, yet it seems clear that even Yeats, Rilke, and Stevens are less fully expressive of the age than are Proust, Joyce, and Kafka. W. H. Auden thought that Kafka was the particular spirit of our time. Certainly

"Kafkaesque" has taken on an uncanny meaning for many among us; perhaps it has become a universal term for what Freud called "the uncanny," something at once absolutely familiar to us yet also estranged from us. From a purely literary perspective, this is the age of Kafka, more even than the age of Freud. Freud, slyly following Shakespeare, gave us our map of the mind; Kafka intimated to us that we could not hope to use it to save ourselves, even from ourselves.

To demonstrate Kafka's central place in this century's canon, one must range widely in his writings, because no particular genre that he attempted holds his essence. He is a great aphorist but not a pure storyteller, except in fragments and in the very short stories we call parables. His longer narratives—*Amerika*, *The Trial*, even *The Castle*—are better in parts than as complete works; and his longer stories, even *The Metamorphosis*, begin more acutely than they tend to close. Besides his aphorisms and parables, the strongest of Kafka's imaginings are brief tales or fragments, remarkably full fragments such as "The Bucket Rider," "The Country Doctor," "The Hunter Gracchus," and "The Great Wall of China." His diaries are preferable to his letters, even his letters to Milena Jesenka, since few more catastrophic lovers than Franz Kafka can ever have existed, even in the fiction of his disciple Philip Roth. Freud, once dismissed by Kafka as "the Rashi of contemporary Jewish anxieties," would have had a rare revenge had he read and analyzed Kafka's love letters, which may well be the most anxious ever written. To know the deep self of the canonical literary genius of our age, you need to absorb him where he hopes to be the most objective and impersonal, vain as that hope has to be.

Knowing the deepest self rather than the fragmented psyche was Kafka's highly individual mode of negativity, appropriate to a writer whose mottoes included "Never again psychology!" and "Psychology is impatience." Impatience, Kafka insisted, was the only major sin, embracing all others. Yet I am never able to read Kafka without thinking of my favorite apothegm: "Sleep faster! We need the pillows," the essence of Jewish impatience. Yahweh is not a patient God, at least in the J writer, and perhaps Kafka, a self-professed New Kabbalist, took as his secret theurgical quest the project of making the God of the Jews a more patient person.

Gustav Janouch's *Conversations with Kafka,* which merit little credence despite their persuasiveness in catching the inflections we also hear in Kafka's writings, demonstrate what some people call Kafka's Jewish gnosticism, which is also evident in Gershom Scholem and Walter Benjamin, both of whom Kafka influenced profoundly. That gnosticism, like any other, is impatient with time, yet in his writings and in his conversations Kafka always counseled patience above all.

Paradoxes are what his readers expect from Kafka, but a patient gnosticism is more than a paradox. Gnosis, by definition, is a timeless knowledge, both of the self within the self and of the alien God whose spark remains in that innermost self. Patience may be the pragmatic path to gnosis, as it evidently was for Kafka, but it has little to do with the abrupt negativity of any gnosticism whatsoever. And there is a clue to this dilemma; patience, Kafka's way of knowing, did not lead to his dualistic negations or his new Kabbalah. Although we tend to relate or ally gnosis and gnosticism, Kafka kept them separate. Gnosis he calls "patience," and gnosticism, "the negative"; the first is infinitely slow, the second, astonishingly rapid because it acknowledges a dualism that Kafka finds exists at the heart of everything and everyone. Kafkan "patience" finds something very different:

> There is no need for you to leave the house. Stay at your table and listen. Don't even listen, just wait. Don't even wait, be completely quiet and alone. The world will offer itself to you to be unmasked; it can't do otherwise; in raptures it will writhe before you.

"The world must not be cheated of its victory," while Kafka seeks no victory for himself. Yet he does not know defeat, "for nothing has yet happened." If you are convinced that nothing has yet happened, you cannot be farther from Jewish tradition. Jewish memory is like Freudian repression: everything has already happened, and there can never be anything new. Despite his dread of his own family romance, Kafka resolved to write as if "nothing has yet happened." To the Jews, the primary happening was the Covenant of Abraham, and for Kafka Abraham is a figure to be

distrusted. Perhaps Abraham's role as the hero of Kierkegaard's
Fear and Trembling provoked Kafka to his negative reflections.
They are certainly antithetical to Jewish and Christian tradition
alike:

> But take another Abraham. One who wanted to perform the
> sacrifice altogether in the right way and had a correct sense in
> general of the whole affair, but could not believe that he was
> the one meant, he, an ugly old man, and the dirty youngster
> that was his child. True faith is not lacking to him, he has this
> faith; he would make the sacrifice in the right spirit if only he
> could believe he was the one meant. He is afraid that after
> starting out as Abraham with his son he would change on the
> way into Don Quixote.
>
> *(translated by Clement Greenberg)*

In some dark ways, this Abraham is Kafka's Quixotic precursor.
In terms of literary influence, Goethe was the Abraham from
whom Kafka shrank; in spiritual terms, the Law or positive Judaism was incarnate in Abraham. Kafka, forsaking the Law for
his own Negative, abandoned also an Abraham who had misin-
terpreted the world:

> Abraham falls victim to the following illusion: he cannot stand
> the uniformity of this world. Now the world is known, however,
> to be uncommonly various, which can be verified at any time
> by taking a handful of world and looking at it closely. Thus
> this complaint at the uniformity of the world is really a com-
> plaint at not having been mixed profoundly enough with the
> diversity of the world.

Kafka was too intelligent an ironist to believe that either his art
or his life mixed profoundly enough with the world's diversity.
His wry rebellion against Abraham is a protest against his own
self and its evasions, including his evasions of Judaism and of the
principal literary tradition of the German language, from Goethe
on. Kafka's word for evasion was "patience," a preparatory trope
or metaphor for the practice of his art as a writer. That art, more

than the work of any other author of comparable powers, exists in a dialectical tension with the possibility of commentary. Joyce is at the opposite extreme: he welcomes interpretation and helpfully tries to guide it. Beckett—who had the temerity and the genius to combine Joyce, Proust, and Kafka—resembles Kafka rather than Joyce or Proust in this relation to commentary; but Kafka was less of a shadow for the author of *Murphy, Molloy,* and *Watt* than were Joyce and Proust.

Criticism is defeated by Kafka whenever it falls into the trap he invariably sets for head-on interpretation, the trap of his idiosyncratic evasion of interpretability. In his kind of irony, every figure he gives us is and is not what it might seem to be. So in the late story "Investigations of a Dog," which attains an extraordinary climax when a beautiful hunting dog manifests itself to the narrator, who is a poor dog lying on the ground soaked by its own blood and vomit, we are unable to interpret just who the hunting dog is, or what it represents. At least one distinguished Kafka commentator has had the audacity to say that the beautiful hound is God, but like all critical identifications of the divine that intrude into Kafka's work, this is the victim of another Kafkan irony. It is safe to say that there are not intimations, let alone representations, of divinity in Kafka's stories and novels. There are plenty of demons masking as angels and as gods, and there are enigmatic animals (and animal-like constructs), but God is always somewhere else, a long way off in the abyss, or else sleeping, or perhaps dead. Kafka, a fantasist of almost unique genius, is a romance author and in no way a religious writer. He is not even the Jewish Gnostic or Cabalist of Scholem's and Benjamin's imaginings, because he has no hope, not for himself or for us anyway.

Everything that seems transcendent in Kafka is truly a mockery, but uncannily so; it is a mockery that emanates from a great sweetness of spirit. Although he worshiped Flaubert, Kafka possessed a much gentler sensibility than that of the creator of Emma Bovary. And yet his narratives, short and long, are almost invariably harsh in their events, tonalities, and predicaments. The dreadful is going to happen. The essence of Kafka can be conveyed in many passages, and one of them is his famous letter to the extraordinary Milena. Agonizing as Kafka's letters frequently are,

they are among the most eloquent of our century. (I use here Philip
Boehm's translation.)

It's a long time since I wrote to you, Frau Milena, and even
today I'm writing only as the result of an incident. Actually, I
don't have to apologize for my not writing, you know after all
how I hate letters. All the misfortune of my life—I don't wish
to complain, but to make a generally instructive remark—derives, one could say, from letters or from the possibility of
writing letters. People have hardly ever deceived me, but letters
always—and as a matter of fact not only those of other people,
but my own. In my case this is a special misfortune of which I
won't say more, but at the same time also a general one. The
easy possibility of letter-writing must—seen merely theoreti-
cally—have brought into the world a terrible disintegration of
souls. It is, in fact, an intercourse with ghosts, and not only with
the ghost of the recipient but also with one's own ghost, which
develops between the lines of the letter one is writing and even
more so in a series of letters where one letter corroborates the
other and can refer to it as a witness. How on earth did anyone
get the idea that people can communicate with one another by
letter! Of a distant person one can think, and of a person who
is near one can catch hold—all else goes beyond human strength.
Writing letters, however, means to denude oneself before the
ghosts, something for which they greedily wait. Written kisses
don't reach their destination, rather they are drunk on the way
by the ghosts. It is on this ample nourishment that they multiply
so enormously. Humanity senses this and fights against it and
in order to eliminate as far as possible the ghostly element between people and to create a natural communication, the peace
of souls, it has invented the railway, the motor car, the aero-
plane. But it's no longer any good, these are evidently inventions
being made at the moment of crashing. The opposing side is so
much calmer and stronger; after the postal service it has invented
the telegraph, the telephone, the radiograph. The ghosts won't
starve, but we will perish.

It is difficult to conceive of sentences more eloquent than "Written
kisses don't reach their destination, rather they are drunk on the

way by the ghosts" or "The ghosts won't starve, but we will perish."

Kafka's attitude toward his own Jewishness is perhaps the largest of his paradoxes. There are some unfortunate traces of Jewish self-hatred in his letters to Milena, but they seem accountable enough, and they are surface irritants at worst. In endlessly complex ways, nearly everything Kafka wrote turns on his relation to Jews and to Jewish traditions. One should start with some clear realizations of this, if only because often they are not recorded. Kafka, a religious sensibility of rare genius, did not believe in God, not even in the infinitely remote God of the Gnostics. He shares this unbelief with Freud, Woolf, Joyce, Beckett, Proust, Borges, Pessoa, and Neruda—the other canonical figures I have selected from our age—but no one would find in that octet anything like Kafka's spiritual preoccupations, not even in Beckett, who was affected by Kafka. Heine, the major Jewish writer in German before Kafka, said that God's name was Aristophanes, a remark admirably exploited by Philip Roth in *Operation Shylock*. Heine was a tormented believer; Kafka, an unbeliever, gave God no name, but if the servitors of Kafka's Court and Castle have a god, it might well be Aristophanes.

Kafka speaks for and to a number of readers, Gentile and Jewish, who depart from Freud in declining to regard religion as an illusion, but who agree with Kafka that they have been born too late to assert the validity for themselves of Christian and Jewish traditions. Kafka did not know whether he was an end or a beginning, nor do we. One of the best informed of Kafka scholars, Ritchie Robertson, sensibly notes that for the author of *The Castle* "the imagery of religion is valid as the expression of the religious impulse, but misleading as an interpretation of this impulse." Since Kafka evades interpreting the impulse and will not sanction any of the received interpretations, the reader is abandoned to the Kafkan representations of the impulse, which sometimes follow familiar imageries and sometimes desert them. This makes it fairly important that we learn precisely what Kafka's own stance was, insofar as he allows us to do so.

I agree with Robertson on the starting point: the crucial texts are the aphorisms composed in 1917–18, now most readily available in English as *The Blue Octavo Notebooks* (1991, translated by Ernst Kaiser and Eithne Wilkins). Nietzsche, as powerful an aphorist as Emerson, Kierkegaard, and Kafka, denounced a consistent reliance on aphoristic writing as a kind of decadence. Nietzsche's most powerful single work may be *On the Genealogy of Morals*, three closely argued essays, but even they take most of their force from aphorisms, while the rhapsodic fiction of *Thus Spake Zarathustra* is now unreadable. The rest of Nietzsche is aphorism, and all the better for it. Kafka is a highly original crossbreed of an aphorist and a teller of parables, oddly akin to Wittgenstein as well as to Schopenhauer and Nietzsche. Behind all of them is Goethe in his role as wisdom writer, with the Aristophanic Heine adding a note of Jewish skepticism, which found its way into Kafka. But Kafka is not to be called a Jewish anything, be it skeptic, Gnostic, or heretic. He is, as he said, a Jewish end or a Jewish beginning, perhaps both.

Despite all his denials and beautiful evasions, he quite simply *is* Jewish writing, more even than Freud can be said to be. I once thought that this came about through the strength of usurpation: Kafka and Freud through their rival strengths redefining Jewish writing, because retrospectively they have become Jewish writing for us. But that view, although it exemplifies the vagaries of the canonical, underestimates the incessant Jewish concerns of Freud and Kafka, both of whom did become Rashis of contemporary Jewish anxieties. Freudian and Kafkan negation, as I have written before, differs profoundly from Hegelian negation by accepting the primacy of fact. Idealist philosophy, however dialectical, does not suit the Jewish respect for the literal. Despite his power of fantasy, Kafka is as empirical as Freud or Beckett. The Jewish condition of exposed marginality is very close by in nearly everything of Kafka's; it is there in "The Great Wall of China," which might as well be entitled "The Tower of Babel," and it is there when we least expect it, in the animal fables.

Is there something fundamentally Jewish in or about Kafka's indubitable spiritual authority? I agree with Ritchie Robertson that the spiritual center in Kafka is his concept of "indestructibility," though I find it more idiosyncratic and less in the spirit of the age than Robertson does. Here is a cento of the crucial aphorisms that dwell upon "the indestructible":

Believing means liberating the indestructible element in oneself, or more accurately, being indestructible, or more accurately, being.

Man cannot live without a permanent trust in something indestructible in himself, though both the indestructible element and the trust may remain permanently hidden from him. One of the ways in which this hiddenness can express itself is through faith in a personal god.

The indestructible is one: it is each individual human being and, at the same time, it is common to all, hence the incomparably indivisible union that exists between human beings.

If what is supposed to have been destroyed in Paradise was destructible, then it was not decisive; but if it was indestructible, then we are living a fake belief.

Believing is being, because something in deepest being cannot be destroyed. But belief is a redundancy, because a personal god is only a metaphor for one's sense of indestructibility, a sense that unifies us despite ourselves. Nor have we fallen, or lost a pragmatic immortality, since we remain, in our essential being, indestructible. Is this only another exaltation of Schopenhauer's will to live as the thing-in-itself, akin to Freud's Eros, or is Kafka getting at something more properly subtle and evasive? Robertson, tracking Kafka's rather diffuse relation to Kabbalah, finds a version of Isaac Luria's *tikkun,* the restitution of the broken vessels of our being, in this Kafkan aphorism:

There is nothing besides a spiritual world; what we call the world of the senses is the Evil in the spiritual world, and what we call Evil is only the necessity of a moment in our eternal evolution.

This hovers somewhere between Lurianic Kabbalah and the great German vitalistic mystic, Meister Eckhart. What startles me is the surprise I feel with all of the greater aphorisms in *The Blue*

Octavo Notebooks: how can Kafka, of all spiritual meditators, sound so hopeful? The evident answer is that he isn't; as he once said to Max Brod, there is plenty of hope for God, *but not for us.* Hope belongs to consciousness, which is destructible, not to indestructible being. You can't tell stories however short about being, not even if you are Count Leo Tolstoy, who came very close in *Hadji Murad,* where the hero almost fuses his being and his consciousness together. We have adopted Kafka as the most canonical writer of our century because all of us epitomize the split between being and consciousness that is his true subject, a subject he identified with being Jewish, or at least as being particularly exilic Jewish.

When the same split appears in Beckett, we sense that its deep root is Cartesian rather than Freudian, as it seems to be in Kafka. Jewish dualism is a kind of oxymoron, if by "Jewish" we mean Judaism or the normative tradition that it informs, which pulses on, however fitfully, in Freud and in Kafka. Freud certainly does not know of an "indestructible" in us; the will to live finally falters in him. And yet, like Nietzsche and Kafka, Freud believes that an innermost self can be strengthened, that Eros can be fortified against the death drive. Consciousness, for Freud, is as false and wrongly hopeful as it is in Nietzsche and in Kafka. Although Freud refuses the mystical concept of being (he dismisses it as "the oceanic sense"), he nobly and desperately substitutes for it his own benign authority and offers us a cure for false consciousness. Kafka refuses all authority (including Freud's) and offers himself, and us, no cure whatsoever. Yet he speaks for being, for the indestructible, in a way that is probably purely Jewish, a Jewish negation:

> I have brought nothing with me of what life requires, so far as I know, but only the universal human weakness. With this—in this respect it is gigantic strength—I have vigorously absorbed the negative element of the age in which I live, an age that is, of course, very close to me, which I have no right ever to fight against, but as it were a right to represent. The slight amount of the positive, and also of the extreme negative, which capsizes into the positive, are something in which I have had no hered-

itary share. I have not been guided into life by the hand of Christianity—admittedly now slack and failing—as Kierkegaard was, and have not caught the hem of the Jewish prayer shawl—now flying away from us—as the Zionists have. I am an end or a beginning.

"The extreme negative, which capsizes into the positive," must be a full-blown negative theology, whether Gnostic, Christian, or heretical Kabbalist (as in Nathan of Gaza, the prophet of the false Messiah, Sabbatei Zevi). Kafka's negative is subtler and more gradated, as fits the spirit of the age. To suggest both its outlines and its aura of shock, we can trace it in one of Kafka's masterpieces, the brief story called "A Country Doctor" (1917; I use the translation of J. A. Underwood). The abruptness of this first-person narrative is astonishing; most of it is told in the present tense, though its opening suggests a past anecdote. With an urgent call to make on a dangerously sick patient ten miles away, in harsh winter weather, the country doctor is without a horse, or so he thinks. Uncannily, an abandoned pigsty on the doctor's property opens to reveal a brutal, animalistic groom and two extraordinary, powerful horses. The groom, even before he harnesses them to the doctor's cart, makes an initial assault on Rosy, the doctor's maid, by savagely biting her cheek. As the doctor is swept away, half involuntarily, by the giant horses, the groom smashes through the door of the house to continue his rape of the terrified Rosy, whose name will recur as the description of the wound the doctor must soon confront, yet cannot hope to heal. The patient, a peasant boy, is no less uncanny and unpleasant than his wound. Unreality is everywhere; the peasants strip the doctor, sing threats to him, and lower him naked into the boy's bed. Left alone with his patient, the doctor, after being threatened by the boy, makes his escape on horseback, with the other horse, the cart, and the doctor's clothes all loosely following along, but now with a terrible slowness as compared to the preternatural speed of the journey there:

I shall never get home like this; my flourishing practice is lost; a successor is robbing me, but to no purpose since he cannot replace me; in my house the loathsome groom wreaks his havoc; Rosy is his victim; I refuse to imagine it. Naked, exposed to the frost of this most wretched of times, with an earthly cart and unearthly horses, I roam about, an old man. My fur coat is hanging from the back of the cart but I cannot reach it, and no one from the agile rabble of patients lifts a finger. Duped! Deceived! One response to a mis-ring of the night-bell—and there's no making amends.

The country doctor ends up, as do other Kafkan protagonists—the bucket rider, the hunter Gracchus, most of all K. the land surveyor—neither alive nor dead, neither in true motion with a purpose nor in stasis. Expectations—theirs and ours—are thwarted by the literal, the realm of fact. We do not know whether Kafka is or is not allegorizing the Jewish condition in his time and place, or his own situation as a writer. Somehow we apprehend that Kafka gets away with his own mode of negation: cognitively there is a release from repression, and the country doctor's fate is exemplary in a Jewish way, or has some relation to the experiential cost of Kafka's confirmation as an author.

Intellectually these identifications are possible, even suggestive, but emotionally they carry no conviction whatsoever. There is a weird lack of affect in the country doctor's fate, indeed in his entire story. Repression persists so far as the reader's transference is concerned; no one anywhere in Kafka is likable or sympathetic, or at least any more or less likable than someone else in Kafka. As a thought form, the country doctor's dilemma can be assimilated to our own, but fellow feeling with him is denied to us. What happens to him is both fantastic and inevitable. It could and sometimes does in transmuted ways happen to us, but no one will share our pathos, even as we cannot share his. An arbitrary beginning—our response to a mis-ring of the night bell—has teleological consequences in a narrative of an eternally present tense, and there is no way of making amends. The category of the Kafkaesque constitutes a new form of what was once called the literary "grotesque," and comes upon us as much in life as in literature. "A Country Doctor" has something close to daemonic force as a story and reminds us that the authentically daemonic or uncanny always achieves canonical status. Nietzsche insisted that only pain could ensure memorability. In literary terms, this translates into the lasting shock effect of "A Country Doctor," where the pain centers upon the absence of affect. It is Kafka's most peculiar and original gift that his stories seem to have returned from our forgetfulness, leaving us always with the sense that we continue to forget what it was that we felt as we experienced these strangenesses.

ALMOST SEVENTY years after his death, Kafka seems more than ever the central writer of Vico's Chaotic Age, as we whirl on toward millennium and the likelihood that a new Theocratic Age will engulf us. *The Trial* and *The Castle* are certainly nowhere close to the aesthetic eminence of *In Search of Lost Time* or *Ulysses* and *Finnegans Wake*. But the fragmentary best of Kafka—stories, parables, aphorisms—goes beyond Proust and Joyce in arming us with a spirituality in no way dependent on belief or ideology. There are no indestructibles for Proust and Joyce, as there were not for Flaubert or Henry James, all of them priests of the novel itself and as much celebrants of perception and sensation as Walter Pater was. If there is a mystery concerning Kafka, it is why he and his writing now have a spiritual authority for many among us, as Wordsworth and Tolstoy once had but have no more. Presumably Kafka's curiously religious aura will someday fade away also, but it still holds on. There are no theophanies in Kafka as we have seen; the only covenant he believed in was the one he had made with writing.

I once thought that Kafka's apparent spiritual position was largely the product of our critical retrospectiveness, akin to the processes that established Dante as *the* Catholic author despite his private gnosis of Beatrice, and Milton as *the* Protestant poet despite his Mortalist heresy and his monistic aspirations toward becoming a sect of one. Similarly Kafka, for all his uneasiness with Judaism, seemed *the* Jewish writer, more than any other since the Hebrew Bible. But that description underestimates Kafka's universalism in and for our century. He is our icon of the writer's vocation as a spiritual quest, and his aphorisms linger in us with the reverberations of authority. Is this more a commentary upon us than it is upon Kafka?

It comes down to Kafka's metaphor of "the indestructible."

Tolstoy's personal vitalism led to an immensely impressive rage for survival, Homeric and therefore archaic and bound to vanish. There is a quiet strength of persistence in Kafka, but like his own hunter Gracchus, he made no protest against mortality. Whatever constitutes "the indestructible," we need not find any images of immortality in it. There is something Biblical in Kafka's lack of interest in an afterlife, hardly a preoccupation for the Yahwist or for most of the prophets. If Kafka has any notion of the blessing, as a gift that he felt was withheld from him, he does not permit us to know what it is. Certainly the Court and the Castle cannot bless, even should they wish to, which is unlikely. Nor can any father bless any son whatsoever in Kafka. More life, into a time without boundaries, does not exist in his cosmos.

If neither immortality nor blessedness attends indestructibility, what does? There is no spiritual authority in Schopenhauer's will to live or in Freud's domain of the drives, and I have already expressed doubts about whether Kafkan "indestructibility" had roots in Lurianic Kabbalah. For all of his negations, Kafka had some interest in our religious beliefs. He did not accept the Freudian reduction that religious impulses merely betrayed a yearning for the father. But his aphorisms never clearly expose his concept of "the indestructible," and even his most sensitive critics have difficulty expounding it. In a letter to Milena, Kafka defended his sense of indestructibility as having "a hold in real ground" and being anything but a private obsession. For him, it was the true link between people, and it expressed their innermost secret being. I hardly know what to call this perception except a gnosis, but it is certainly not a gnosticism, since it repudiates any idea of a God, however remote, however hidden away in the primal abyss. What Kafka affirms is a primal human attribute, godlike but secular, a knowing in which indestructibility is known.

But Kafka was not a saint or a mystic; he is rightly not included in Aldous Huxley's beautiful if idealizing anthology, *The Perennial Philosophy*. Like Freud, Kafka was a literalist of the Negative, but his mode of negation was more dialectical than Freud's. The authority of the fact, repudiated by Hegel, was deeply respected by both Jewish writers, but Kafka allowed himself a larger sense of fact than Freud could. Kafka's sense of an indestructibility at the center was for him a fact, identical with his vocation as a writer. Perhaps that is the clue to Kafka's status as our canonical icon of spirituality: he was not a religious writer, but he transmuted writing into a religion.

In such a transformation, there need not be any peculiarly Romantic or Modern element, as I suggested in my discussion of Dante. The inescapable writers elect themselves to the Canon partly by wagering on their writing, much as Pascal made his wager on faith. Is Shakespeare again the grand exception? I would say just the opposite: he prepared the way for Milton and for Goethe, for Ibsen and for Joyce, by implicitly placing his entire pragmatic trust in his own art. Christianizing Shakespeare the playwright is a vain enterprise. Whatever the man Shakespeare believed or doubted, Hamlet is hardly a Christian hero, and the cosmos of *Othello, Lear,* and *Macbeth* is more shamanistic than Christian. Iago, Edmund, and Macbeth convey to us the weird yet persuasive impression that each of them is the genius of his place, perfectly embodying all of the world's darkest potential. The shadow side of Hamlet's nature sets the paradigm for Shakespearean tragedy. The world is disjointed, and so is Hamlet, its destined righter.

Kafka, perhaps by way of Goethe's influence, inherits the German sense of Hamlet as the hero too intricate and sensitive to prevail in a botched cosmos. The Kafkan swerve away from Goethe's Hamlet converts the protagonist's delicacy into an antipathetic aggressiveness, the stance toward Court and Castle of Joseph K. and K. the land surveyor. Such a conversion is halfway on the road to *Endgame,* where Samuel Beckett revises Hamlet in Kafka's mode. His Ham is far closer to Joseph K. than to Goethe's charming Hamlet, who is in no way guilty, unlike Shakespeare's Hamlet, and is incapable of feeling guilt for his very real crimes: the manslaughter of the prying Polonius, the gleeful dispatch to their executions of the wretched Rosencrantz and Guildenstern, and, worst of all, the sadistic hounding of Ophelia to her madness and suicide.

Hamlet suffers guilt only for the murder he has not yet performed. Shrewder in this regard than Goethe, Kafka seems to have understood that guilt, in Shakespeare, is not to be doubted and precedes all actual crimes. Not Christian original sin but the Shakespearean-Freudian unconscious sense of guilt is the law of Kafka's cosmos also. Guilt has priority in Kafka because it is the payment exacted by our "indestructibility"; indeed, for Kafka, we are guilty precisely because our deepest self is indestructible. I suspect that Kafkan evasiveness and allusiveness alike are defenses for his sense of the indestructible, a sense bequeathed by him to Beckett at his best, in *Endgame, Krapp's Last Tape, Malone Dies,* and *How It Is.*

The indestructible is not a substance in us that prevails, but in Beckett's terms is a going-on when you can't go on. In Kafka, going on almost always takes ironic forms: K.'s unrelenting assault on the Castle, Gracchus's endless voyagings upon his death ship, the bucket rider's flight into the ice mountains, the country doctor's wintry ride to nowhere. The "indestructible" resides within us as a hope or quest, but by the grimmest of all Kafka's paradoxes the manifestations of that striving are inevitably destructive, particularly self-destructive. Patience becomes not so much the prime Kafkan virtue as the only resource for survival, like the canonical patience of the Jews.

21.

Borges, Neruda, and Pessoa: Hispanic-Portuguese Whitman

TWENTIETH-CENTURY Hispanic American literature, possibly more vital than North American, has three founders: the Argentine fabulist Jorge Luis Borges (1899–1986); the Chilean poet Pablo Neruda (1904–1973); and the Cuban novelist Alejo Carpentier (1904–1980). Out of their matrix a host of major figures has emerged: novelists as varied as Julio Cortázor, Gabriel García Márquez, Mario Vargas Llosa, and Carlos Fuentes; poets of international importance in César Vallejo, Octavio Paz, and Nicolás Guillén. I center on Borges and Neruda, though time may demonstrate the supremacy of Carpentier over all other Latin American writers in this era. But Carpentier was among the many indebted to Borges, and Neruda has the same founder's role for poetry that Borges occupies for both fictional and critical prose, so I examine them here both as literary fathers and as representative writers.

Borges was a remarkably literary child; his first published work came at the age of seven, a translation of Oscar Wilde's story

"The Happy Prince." Yet had he died at forty, we would not remember him, and Latin American literature would be very different. He began writing Whitmanian poetry when he was eighteen, and aspired to become the bard of Argentina. But he came to understand that he was not to be the Spanish-language Whitman, the role powerfully usurped by Neruda. Instead he took to writing Kabbalistic and Gnostic essay-parables, perhaps under Kafka's influence, and from there his characteristic art flowered. The crossing point was a terrible accident he suffered near the close of 1938. Always afflicted by poor eyesight, he slipped on a badly lit staircase and fell, sustaining a severe head injury. Seriously ill for two weeks in the hospital, he had fearful nightmares and then a painfully slow convalescence, in which he began to doubt his mental condition and his ability to write. And so, at thirty-nine, he tried to compose a story, to reassure himself. The hilarious consequence was "Pierre Menard, Author of the *Quixote*," the forerunner of "Tlön, Uqbar, Orbis Tertius" and all the other brilliant short fictions with which we associate his name. His Argentine reputation for fiction began with *The Garden of Forking Paths* (1941); in 1962 two collections, *Labyrinths* and *Ficciones*, were published in the United States and instantly gathered in the discerning.

Of all Borges' stories, the one I loved best thirty years ago is still my favorite: "Death and the Compass." Like almost all of his work, it is intensely literary: it knows and declares its belatedness, the contingency that governs its relationship with previous literature. Borges' paternal grandmother was English; his father's library was large and centered on English literature. In Borges we have the anomaly of a Hispanic writer who first read *Don Quixote* in English translation, and whose literary culture, though universal, remained English and North American in its deeper sensibility. Still Borges, oriented toward a literary career, was haunted by the military glory that had dominated both his father's and his mother's families. Inheriting the poor eyesight that had kept his father from becoming an officer, Borges seems to have inherited also his father's flight into the library as a refuge in which dreaming could atone for an impossible life of action. What Ellmann said of the Shakespeare-obsessed Joyce, that he was anxious only to incorporate as many influences as possible, seems much truer of Borges, who overtly absorbs and then deliberately reflects the entire canonical tradition. Whether this open embrace of his precursors finally curtailed Borges' achievement is a difficult question, which I hope to begin to answer later in this chapter.

Master of labyrinths and of mirrors, Borges was a profound student of literary influence, and as a skeptic who cared more for imaginative literature than for religion or philosophy, he taught us how to read such speculations primarily for their aesthetic value. His curious fate as a writer, and as the foremost inaugurator of modern Latin American literature, cannot be separated from either his aesthetic universalism or what I suppose must be called his aesthetic aggressiveness. Rereading him now, I am both charmed and cheered, more even than I was thirty years ago, because his political anarchism (of his father's rather mild variety) is so refreshing at a time when the study of literature has become wholly politicized, and one fears the increasing politicization of literature itself.

"Death and the Compass" is an instance of what is both most valuable and most enigmatic in and about Borges. This twelve-page story traces the conclusion of a blood feud between the detective Erik Lönnrot and the gangster chief Red Scharlach the Dandy, in the visionary Buenos Aires that is so frequently the context for Borges' characteristic phantasmagoria. Mortal enemies, Lönnrot and Red Scharlach are obvious, if antithetical doubles, as the red color that they share in their names indicates. Borges, a fierce philo-Semite who sometimes played with the fancy that he might be of Jewish origin (a charge frequently made against him by the Fascist followers of his enemy, the dictator Perón), writes a Jewish gangster story that would have delighted Isaak Babel, the author of the splendid *Tales of Odessa,* which center upon the legendary mobster Benya Krik, like Red Scharlach a great dandy. Borges wrote an article on the life of Babel, whose work (indeed whose very name) should have fascinated him, and even a rapid summary of "Death and the Compass" suggests Babel.

The rabbinical scholar Dr. Marcel Yarmolinsky is murdered at the Hôtel du Nord. His body, the chest split by a knife, is accompanied by a note saying "The first letter of the Name has been uttered." Lönnrot, a severe reasoner like Poe's August Dupin, deduces that the reference is to the Tetragrammaton, the Secret Name of JHVH, the God Yahweh. Another body is found, constituting the second letter of the Name. These murders are mystical sacrifices, as Lönnrot works it out, of what he takes to be a deranged Jewish sect. A supposed third murder takes place, but no body is discovered, and step by step we come to understand that Lönnrot is falling into Scharlach's trap. At last the entrapment is complete at the abandoned villa called Triste-le-Roy, on the outskirts of the city. Red Scharlach explains his intricate plot, which turns upon the three images he has used to ensnare Lönnrot's mind: mirrors, the compass, and the labyrinth in which the detective has been caught. Confronting Scharlach's pistol, Lönnrot shares in the gangster's impersonal sadness and coolly criticizes the labyrinth as having redundant lines, while urging that, in the next incarnation, he be killed again by his enemy with a more elegantly designed labyrinth. The story ends with Lönnrot's execution, to the music of Scharlach's "The next time I kill you, I promise you that labyrinth, consisting of a single line which is invisible and unceasing." This is the emblem of Zeno the Eleatic, and for Borges the emblem of Lönnrot's quasi-suicide.

Borges said of "Pierre Menard, Author of the *Quixote*," his real origin as a writer, that it gives a sensation of tiredness and skepticism, of "coming at the end of a very long literary period." That is the irony or allegory of "Death and the Compass," where Lönnrot and Scharlach weave their murderous labyrinth of literature in an amalgam of Poe, Kafka, and multiple other instances of doubles facing off in a duel of secret sharers. Like so many Borges stories, the tale of Lönnrot and Scharlach is a parable, which demonstrates that reading is always a kind of rewriting. Scharlach subtly controls Lönnrot's reading of the clues that the gangster supplies and thus anticipates the detective's interpretative revisions.

In "Tlön, Uqbar, Orbis Tertius," another famous story, Borges begins with the direct statement, "I owe the discovery of Uqbar to the conjunction of a mirror and an encyclopedia." For the imaginary land of Uqbar, you can substitute any of the persons, places, and things of Borges' fiction; in all of them a mirror and an encyclopedia come together, for, to Borges, any encyclopedia, existent or surmised, is both a labyrinth and a compass. Even if Borges were not the prime founder of Hispanic American literature (as he is), even if his stories did not possess authentic aesthetic value (as they do), he would still be one of the canonical writers of the Chaotic Age because, more than any other writer except Kafka, whom he deliberately emulates, he is the literary metaphysician of the age. His cosmological stance is professedly chaotic; he is imaginatively a professed Gnostic, though intellectually and morally he is a skeptical humanist. For Borges the ancient Gnostic heresiarchs, Basilides of Alexandria in particular, are true precursors. The brief essay "A Vindication of Basilides the False" (translated by Andrew Hurley) concludes with a marvelous general defense of Gnosticism:

> Throughout the first centuries of our era, the Gnostics disputed with the Christians. They were annihilated, but we can imagine their possible victory. Had Alexandria triumphed and not Rome, the extravagant and muddled stories that I have summarized here would be coherent, majestic, and perfectly ordinary. Pronouncements such as Novalis's "Life is a sickness of the spirit," or the despairing one of Rimbaud, "True life is absent; we are not in the world," would know the conditional assent of the pious laboratories. In any case, what better gift can we hope for, than to be insignificant? What greater glory for a God, than to be absolved of the world?

For Borges as for the Gnostics, Creation and Fall of both the cosmos and humankind are one and the same event. The primordial reality was the Pleroma or fullness, which is called Chaos by normative Jews, pious Christians, and Muslims, but was revered as Foremother and Forefather by the Gnostics. In his imaginings, Borges returns to that reverence. Does he share it? Like Beckett, Borges read Schopenhauer with intense sympathy, but Borges interpreted him as insinuating "that we are fragments of a God who, at the beginning of time, destroyed himself in his desire for nonexistence." A dead or vanished God or, in

Gnosticism, an alien God, withdrawn from this false creation, is the only trace of theism left in Borges. His metaphysics, when he does not play at Idealism, also follows Schopenhauer and the Gnostics. We live in a phantasmagoria, a distorted mirror-image of Eternity, which Borges conveyed with considerable gusto. "The lower order is a mirror of the higher order; the earth's aspects correspond to those of Heaven; the blotches of the skin are a map of the incorrigible constellations; Judas somehow reflects Jesus," he wrote in "Three Versions of Judas," where the doomed Danish theologian Runeberg works out his theory that Judas, not Jesus, was the Incarnate God, thus adding to "the concept of the Son, which seemed exhausted, . . . the complexities of evil and misfortune."

Since the Valentinians had taught the doctrine of Divine degradation, Borges is being quite Gnostic, though more drastic perhaps than any Gnostics since the Ophites, who celebrated the snake in the story of the Fall. Borges' perfection in this mode comes in his story "The Theologians," in which two learned doctors of the early church, Aurelian of Aquileria and John of Pannonia (both Borgesian inventions), are rivals in refuting esoteric heresies. Borges charmingly sums up their competition, stressing that Aurelian, the less gifted and therefore the more resentful, is obsessed with John: "Both served in the same army, coveted the same guerdon, warred against the same Enemy, but Aurelian did not write a word which secretly did not strive to surpass John." At the story's close, Aurelian instigates the burning of John at the stake on a conviction of heresy, and then dies himself in precisely the same fashion in an Irish forest set ablaze by a lightning bolt. In the afterlife, Aurelian discovers that, for God, he and John "formed one single person," even as Lönnrot and Red Scharlach formed a single person. Borges is ruefully consistent: in the labyrinth of his universe we are confronted by our images in the mirror, not just of nature but also of the self.

As all critics have noted, the labyrinth is Borges' central image, the convergence of all his obsessions and nightmares. His literary precursors from Poe to Kafka are drawn upon to furnish this emblem of chaos, for almost anything at all can be transmuted into a labyrinth by Borges: houses, cities, landscapes, deserts, rivers, above all ideas and libraries. The ultimate labyrinth was the palace designed by the fabulous artificer Daedalus, both to protect and to imprison the Minotaur, half-bull, half-man. I have never quite understood why Joyce took the name for his younger self; true, Dublin is one labyrinth, and *Ulysses* is another, and the cyclic *Wake* is labyrinthine, but Joyce is both too comic and too naturalistic to exalt an image of chaos as such, unlike Kafka, Borges, Beckett. Joyce had his Manichean tendencies, but he did not immerse himself in Schopenhauer or Gnosticism or develop a Gnostic vision all his own.

Although in Borges the labyrinth is an essentially playful image, its implications are as dark as in Kafka. If the entire cosmos is a labyrinth, then Borges' favorite image is linked to death, or to a view of life that is essentially Freudian, the myth of the death drive. Hence we encounter irony; the two modern writers most exasperated by Freud were Nabokov and Borges. Both were petulant and unpleasant on Freud. Here is Borges at his least impressive:

> I think of him as a kind of madman, no? A man laboring over a sexual obsession. Well, perhaps he didn't take it to heart. Perhaps he was just doing it as a kind of game. I tried to read him, and I thought of him either as a charlatan or as a madman, in a sense. After all, the world is far too complex to be boiled down to that all-too-simple scheme. But in Jung, well, of course, Jung I have read far more widely than Freud, but in Jung you feel a wide and hospitable mind. In the case of Freud, it all boils down to a few rather unpleasant facts.

Those few rather unpleasant facts, in the matter of Borges, include a first and only marriage, entered into at sixty-eight and ending three years later in divorce, and an astonishing closeness (and continued residence with) his mother, who died in 1975, aged ninety-nine. Neither these facts, nor Borges' distaste for Freud, are of particular use to his readers, except insofar as they may help to illuminate both his stance toward literary tradition and the economical nature of his art. The particular delight of Borges on literature is its reversal of the older accounts of influence, as in the analysis of Kafka's effect on Browning in "Kafka and his Precursors":

> Kafka's idiosyncrasy, in greater or lesser degree, is present in each of these writings, but if Kafka had not written, we would not perceive it; that is to say, it would not exist. The poem "Fears and Scruples" by Robert Browning is like a prophecy of Kafka's stories, but our reading of Kafka refines and changes our reading of the poem perceptibly. Browning did not read it as we read it now. The word "precursor" is indispensable in the vocabulary of criticism, but one should try to purify it from every connotation of polemic or rivalry. The fact is that each writer *creates* his precursors.
>
> *(translated by Ruth L. C. Simms)*

Borges would not allow himself to see that polemic and rivalry guide that creation of the precursor. In *Dreamtigers* (*The Maker,* in Spanish), he identified as his prime precursor among Argentine writers the poet Leopoldo Lugones, who killed himself in 1938. The book's dedication to Lugones conveniently forgets the ambivalence about the older poet that Borges and his generation had manifested, though Borges had been characteristically ambivalent about his ambivalence. As he grew older, Borges began to favor the view that canonical literature is more than a continuity, is indeed one vast poem and story composed by many hands through the ages. By the 1960s, when Borges had become what his biographer Emir Rodriguez Monegal called "the old guru," this literary idealism began to be an absolute, surpassing the more skeptical versions of communal authorship that Borges had found in Shelley and in Valéry.

A curious pantheism, applied primarily to authors, swept through Borges: not just Shakespeare but all writers were at once everyone and no one, a single, living labyrinth of literature. Like Lönnrot and Red Scharlach, like the theologians Aurelian and John, Homer and Shakespeare and Borges blend into one author. Contemplating this nihilistic idealism, I recall the best sentence I have read about Borges, by Ana María Barrenechea: "Borges is an admirable writer pledged to destroy reality and convert man into a shadow." That breathtaking project, had Shakespeare pledged himself to it, would have been beyond even his resources. Borges can wound you, but always in the same way, so that one arrives at Borges' prime flaw: his best work lacks variety, even though it draws upon the entire Western Canon and more. Perhaps sensing this, Borges attempted a movement back to naturalistic realism in the later 1960s, but the result in *Doctor Brodie's Report* (1970) is still essentially phantasmagoria.

What is at the center of Borges' labyrinth? The tales he tells are like romance fragments, and yet Borges, unlike Hawthorne, whom he greatly appreciated, does not write romance, which depends on enchantment and imperfect knowledge. Borges is skeptical, very knowing, and deliberately lacks the extravagance of the romance, its sense of wandering beyond limits. His art is very carefully controlled and sometimes rather evasive. Neither Borges nor his reader can get lost in the stories, where everything is calculated. A dread of what Freud called the family romance and of what might be termed the family romance of literature confines Borges to repetition, and to overidealization of the writer–reader relationship. That may be precisely what made him the ideal father for modern Hispanic-American literature—his infinite suggestiveness and his detachment from cultural tangles. Yet he may be condemned to a lesser eminence, still canonical but no longer central, in modern literature. A comparison of his stories and parables to Kafka's, read side by side, is not at all flattering to him but seems inevitable, partly because Borges so frequently invokes Kafka, both overtly and implicitly. Beckett, with whom Borges shared an international prize in 1961, at his best sustains intense rereading as Borges does not. Borges' cunning is adroit but does not sustain a Schopenhauerian vision as powerfully as Beckett is able to do.

Nevertheless Borges' position in the Western Canon, if it prevails, will be as secure as Kafka's and Beckett's. Of all Latin American authors in this century, he is the most universal. Except for the strongest modern writers—Freud, Proust, and Joyce—Borges has more power of contamination in him than nearly anyone else, even when their gifts and the scale of their work far exceed his. If you read Borges frequently and closely, you become something of a Borgesian, because to read him is to activate an awareness of literature in which he has gone farther than anyone else.

This awareness, at once visionary and ironical, is hard to describe because it breaks down discursive antitheses between individuality and the communal. It is related to the realization that all literature is plagiaristic to some degree, an insight that Borges owes to Thomas De Quincey, English Romantic essayist, exuberantly self-conscious plagiarist, and probably the most crucial of all of the Borgesian precursors. De Quincey wrote a High Romantic prose, almost baroque in its sinuous emotional intensity and rhapsodic, frequently incantatory drive. Borges' prose style is almost a reaction-formation to De Quincey's, but Borges' procedures and obsessions are very near those of the author of *Confessions of an English Opium-Eater* and the unfinished *Suspiria de Profundis*. De Quincey is most original and subtle as an expounder of his own dreams, some of which are transmuted into stories by Borges. One of these, "The Immortal," is the uncanniest of all Borges' achievements, a condensation into fourteen pages of nearly all of his creative obsessions. It is one of the handful of sublime instances of fantastic literature in our century.

Most of "The Immortal" is first-person narration by Flaminius Rufus, the tribune of a Roman legion stationed in Egypt during the reign of Emperor Diocletian. His identity is a surprise from the start; the manuscript, found in 1929 in London, was tucked away in the last volume of Alexander Pope's six-volume *Iliad* (1720). Written in English, supposedly sometime in the 1920s, the story is presumably the work of an antique dealer, Joseph Cartaphilus of Symrna, "a wasted and earthen man, with gray eyes and gray beard, of singularly vague features," who speaks French, English, and "an enigmatic conjunction of Salonika Spanish and Macao Portuguese." We surmise, at the story's end, that the singularly vague features are those of the Immortal, the poet Homer himself, who has merged with the Roman tribune and finally (by implication) with Borges himself, even as the story, "The Immortal," merges Borges with his originals: De Quincey, Poe, Kafka, Shaw, Chesterton, Conrad, and several more.

"The Immortal" could be entitled "Homer and the Labyrinth,"

since those two entities, the author and the ruined, labyrinthine City of the Immortals, constitute the story. Rufus the tribune, who goes on a quest to find the City of the Immortals, sees his double in the rather frightening figure who turns out to be Homer, first of the immortal poets. Ronald J. Christ (a Borgesian name!) in *The Narrow Act: Borges' Art of Illusion* reads the story as a Conradian-Eliotic journey to the symbolic Heart of Darkness. The analogue is useful if we discount the moral element in Conrad, which finds no place in "The Immortal" and is only rarely central in Borges, whose greatness is allied to his heroic aestheticism, which repudiates conventional moral and societal concerns and even plays ironically at devaluing Homer, as though his epic art was commonplace.

Homer, like Shakespeare, is for Borges the Maker or archetypal poet, but also the archetypal man, like Blake's Albion or Joyce's Earwicker (Here Comes Everyone), which must be why Borges, with whatever irony, could describe "The Immortal" as the "outline of an ethic for immortals." This ethic turns out to be only Borges' customary evasion of the family romance of literature, his idealization of influence relationships. All writers are equal; originality is unlikely. Homer and Shakespeare, being everyone and anyone, render individuality impossible, so personality is an outmoded myth. We all live forever, so there will be time to read everyone and everything, as there is in Shaw's *Back to Methuselah,* one of the prime sources of "The Immortal."

This literary idealism, if it were not laced with savage irony, would render Borges insipid and make "The Immortal" a kind of parody-prophecy of a multiculturalist manifesto. No need to fear: the story is Borges' bleakest and most chilling nightmare, and the idealization of literature is reduced by Swiftian irony to a nihilistic pessimism, in which immortality is seen as the greatest nightmare of all, a dream architecture that can only be labyrinthine. Of all Borges' phantasmagorias, the City of the Immortals is the most dismaying. Rufus the tribune, exploring it, finds it to be "so horrible that its mere existence . . . contaminates the past and the future and in some way even jeopardizes the stars."

The crucial word there is "contaminates," and the dominant affect of "The Immortal" is an anguish of contamination. Homer, when he first identifies himself, is a mute, wretched, snake-eating troglodyte, and the much sought River of Immortality is only a sandy rivulet. Like the other Immortals, Homer has been all but destroyed by a life of "pure speculation." If Hamlet indeed thought not too much but too wisely, then Borges' Homer (who is also Shakespeare) has thought not too well, but too endlessly. Partly Borges is satirizing *Back to Methuselah,* but he is also savaging his own literary idealism. Without rivalry and polemic between the Immortals there is, paradoxically, no life, and literature dies. For Borges, all theology is a division of fantastic literature. In "The Immortal" he observes with superb irony that despite their professed belief in immortality, Jews, Christians, and Moslems venerate only this world because they truly believe only in it and bind future states to it only as rewards or punishments. In a note of 1966, Borges made a marvelous observation on the status of ontotheology and speculative metaphysics:

> I compiled at one time an anthology of fantastic literature. I have to admit that the book is one of the few that a second Noah should save from a second flood, but I denounce the guilty omission of the major and unexpected masters of the genre: Parmenides, Plato, John Scotus Erigena, Albertus Magnus, Spinoza, Leibniz, Kant, Francis Bradley. In fact, to what do the prodigies of Wells or Edgar Allan Poe amount—a flower that comes to us from the future, a corpse subjected to hypnosis— confronted with the creation of God, with the laborious theory of a being that in some way can be three and solitarily endures everlastingly *without time?* What is the bezoar compared to the notion of a pre-established harmony? What is the unicorn before the Trinity? Who is Lucius Apuleius before the Great Vehicle's proliferators of Buddhas? What are all the Arabian nights of Scheherazade paired with a Berkeley argument? I have venerated the gradual invention of God; also of Heaven and Hell (an immortal remuneration, an immortal punishment). They are admirable and curious designs of man's imagination.

The key terms, ironic and exact, are "venerated" and the repeated "immortal." God, gradually invented, is perhaps the greatest work of fantastic literature. The Yahwist did not invent Yahweh, but the God worshiped by Jews, Christians, and Moslems is the literary character Yahweh, whom the Yahwist did create; and whoever wrote the Gospel of Mark created the literary character Jesus, worshiped by all Christians. The "immortal remuneration" of heaven includes those literary characters as part of the payment, and that returns us to "The Immortal," where Borges leaves us with only words. Images, even of God, fade in the memory; words remain, and they are always the "words of others," because none among us can have his own words.

If "The Immortal" is, as I suspect, a self-punishment for excessive literary idealism, what does it and the rest of Borges give us? Is it an aesthetic fulfillment sufficiently vivid to overcome its own apparent nihilism? Borges sees himself as the celebrator of things in their farewell; his later poetry and stories frequently portray the experience of doing something for the last time, seeing someone or some place as a valediction. Loss was always Borges' creative emphasis: one can only lose what one never had, is a refrain throughout his work.

No one else in Western tradition has subverted the idea of literary immortality as relentlessly as Borges. He returns his readers to his initial motive for metaphor, for desiring to be different, for finding oneself someplace else, for choosing to become a writer. A lost military vocation is substituted for by the calling of literature, and yet Borges, as an Argentine gentleman, could never reconcile himself to any agonistic truths about the nature of poetic autonomy and originality. Personality and individuality could be expressed by military leadership and heroism, particularly by his ancestors, several of whom had died in lost causes. Courage was the province of his maternal grandfather, Isidoro de Acevedo Laprida, who had fought in his youth in Argentina's civil wars, lived a long retirement, and died in a phantasmagoria of the visionary defense of his nation: "he rounded up an army of Buenos Aires ghosts / so as to get himself killed in the fighting."

There are also Borgesian poems addressed to two other heroic ancestors, one killed by rebels in an earlier civil war, the other the victor at the battle of Junín during Argentina's war of independence. In comparison to these family warriors, Homer and

Shakespeare are ambiguously portrayed by Borges. Their principal spiritual attribute for him is a certain vagueness of outline; the blurred features of their identity partly reflect our lack of biographical knowledge but resulted primarily from Borges' need to merge them back into literature. There is a great love for them in Borges, as there is also a passion for Dante, Cervantes, Whitman, Kafka, and others; but there is a great ambivalence as well. The sense of belatedness that made Borges realize he resembled his own Pierre Menard more than he did Cervantes was transferred by him to all other authors, Homer and Shakespeare included. "I want time made into a plaza," one of his poems gently laments. It was a triumph of Borges' cunning that in "Everything and Nothing" he could interpret Shakespeare's retirement to Stratford as a weariness of "that controlled hallucination," his ability to create "the surfeit and the horror" of a myriad of characters. Such a Shakespeare is an exhausted Immortal, like Borges' Homer. It is a tribute to Borges to observe that he began and ended as another weary Immortal and founded an authentic aesthetic dignity upon his ambivalent entry into the labyrinth of canonical literature.

WALT WHITMAN, less the North American Homer (his aspiration) than he was a great original, seems to me a refutation of Borges' labyrinthine vision of literature as a blurring of authorial identities, even though Whitman himself frequently proclaimed his desire to absorb all other identities into his messianic largeness, his capacity for containing multitudes. That, as the chapter on Whitman revealed, was the proclamation of "Walt Whitman, an American, one of the roughs," and not of the most authentic Whitman, the "real me" or "me myself." Diverse as Whitman was in his poetry, he has been even more diverse in his influence on other poets, whether North American or Hispanic. His most important effect upon his heirs is almost always a repressed one, as in the poetry of T. S. Eliot and Wallace Stevens. Crucial as Whitman was for them, and for Ezra Pound (in despite of all three), and for Hart Crane (much more willingly), it could be argued that Whitman's most vital influence has been upon Hispanic America: Borges, Neruda, Vallejo, and Paz.

Borges, who began as a Whitmanian, recoiled from this early influence yet went on to develop a mature and subtle understanding of Whitman, perhaps best evidenced by his translation of selections from *Leaves of Grass* in 1969. During the 1920s, Borges had attacked the Latin American Whitmanians for making their hero the center of a personality cult; he also denigrated the poet of *Song of Myself* for his supposed belief that naming objects would suffice to make them into originals mounted upon Emerson's stairway of surprise. But in 1929 Borges repented, though only by turning Whitman into the impersonal Borges as another rather laconic Modernist. Too intelligent to rest in this Whitman, Borges went on to a second and better interpretation in "A Note on Walt Whitman," now included in *Other Inquisitions*. Here Borges distinguished nicely between the persona or mask, Walt Whitman, and the person or author, Walter Whitman, Jr.: "The latter was chaste, reserved, and somewhat taciturn; the former, effusive and orgiastic . . . it is more important to understand that the mere happy vagabond proposed by the verses of *Leaves of Grass* would have been incapable of writing them."

But Borges' best and most clarifying tribute to Whitman came in an interview of 1968:

Whitman is one of the poets who has most impressed me in the whole of my life. I think there's a tendency to confuse Mr. Walter Whitman, the author of *Leaves of Grass*, with Walt Whitman, the protagonist of *Leaves of Grass*, and that Walt Whitman does not provide us with an image so much as a sort of magnification of the poet. In *Leaves of Grass*, Walter Whitman wrote a species of epic whose protagonist was Walt Whitman—not the Whitman who was writing, but the man he would like to have been. Of course, I'm not saying this in criticism of Whitman; his work should not be read as the confessions of a man of the nineteenth century, but rather as an epic about an imaginary figure, a utopian figure, who is to some extent a magnification and projection of the writer as well as of the reader. You will remember that in *Leaves of Grass* the author often merges himself with the reader, and of course this expresses his theory of democracy, the idea that a single unique protagonist can represent a whole epoch. The importance of Whitman cannot be overstated. Even taking into account the versicles of the Bible or of Blake, Whitman can be said to be the inventor of free verse. He can be looked at in two ways: there is his civic side—the fact that one is aware of crowds, great cities, and America—and there is also an intimate element, though we can't be sure whether it is genuine or not. The character Whitman has created is one of the most lovable and memorable in all literature. He is a character like Don Quixote or Hamlet, but someone no less complex and possibly more lovable than either of them.

To compare Walt Whitman, the protagonist of *Leaves of Grass*, to Don Quixote or Hamlet is accurate and exciting; Whitman is indeed his greatest (and only) literary character, his strong creation. Hamlet is not really very lovable, charismatic though he be; but Don Quixote is, and so is Walt Whitman. The matter is even more complex than Borges allows: who was the unpaid male nurse who served the wounded and dying so selflessly during the Civil War in Washington, D.C.? Was it not both Walt Whitman the poetic hero and Walter Whitman, Jr., who in that context had merged? The image of Walt Whitman the wound dresser is as overwhelming as the image of the martyred Abraham Lincoln, and perhaps more lovable. The elegist of "When Lilacs Last in the Dooryard Bloom'd" earned the authority to lament Lincoln by his service in life and literature alike. There is something uncanny and overwhelming about Whitman in his best poems, but also as an image of America, evidently both South and North, as the Hispanic American poets have demonstrated.

Pablo Neruda is by general consent the most universal of those poets and can be regarded as Whitman's truest heir. The poet of *Canto general* is a worthier rival than any other descendant of *Leaves of Grass,* a difficult statement for me, as a lover of Hart Crane and Wallace Stevens, to make. I am skeptical whether Neruda, for all his variety and intensity, truly was of Whitman's eminence, or of Emily Dickinson's, but no Western hemisphere poet of our century can sustain a full comparison to him. His unfortunate Stalinism is frequently an excrescence, a kind of wart on the texture of his poems, but except in a few places it does not greatly mar *Canto general*. Neruda, in his relationship to Whitman, followed Borges' pattern: initial discipleship, followed by denunciation, culminating in a complex revision of Whitman in the poet's later works. In an interview in 1966 with Robert Bly, Neruda distinguished the poetry of Hispanic America (his own and Cesar Vallejo's) from that of the modern Spanish poets, so many of whom had been his friends: Lorca, Hernández, Alberti, Cernuda, Aleixandre, Machado. They had behind them, in the Spanish Golden Age, the great poets of the Baroque—Calderón, Quevedo, Góngora—who had named everything that mattered. The appeal of Whitman was that he taught how to see and name what had not been seen or named before:

> Poetry in South America is a different matter altogether. You see there are in our countries rivers which have no names, trees which nobody knows, and birds which nobody has described. It is easier for us to be surrealistic because everything we know is new. Our duty, then, as we understand it, is to express what is unheard of. Everything has been painted in Europe, everything has been sung in Europe. But not in America. In that sense, Whitman was a great teacher. Because what is Whitman? He was not only intensely conscious, but he was open-eyed! He had tremendous eyes to see everything—he taught us to see things. He was our poet.

That seems to be more Neruda's idealization of Neruda than an apt description of the nuanced and evasive Whitman. Still, Neruda goes on to say that "he is not so simple—Whitman—he's a complicated man and the best of him is when he is most complicated." Whitman's complexities are endless; Neruda's, perhaps not. Borges and Neruda disliked each other; the humane Borges was not about to embrace Stalinism, and the Communist Neruda snorted that Borges did not live in the real world, which consisted of workers, peasants, Mao, and Stalin. There is a deft decapitation of Neruda by Borges, who was not a man anyone should have wanted to take on in a verbal quarrel:

I think of him as a very mean man. . . . he wrote a book about
the tyrants of South America, and then he had several stanzas
against the United States. Now he knows that that's rubbish.
And he had not a word against Perón. Because he had a law
suit in Buenos Aires, that was explained to me afterwards, and
he didn't care to risk anything. And so, when he was supposed
to be writing at the top of his voice, full of noble indignation,
he had not a word to say against Perón. And he was married
to an Argentine lady, he knew that many of his friends had been
sent to jail. He knew all about the state of our country, but not
a word against him.

The book is *Canto general* (1950); Borges, speaking in 1967,
could have been slyly thinking of what Enrico Mario Santi suggests
was his prophetic satire against Neruda in the grand story, "The
Aleph," written in 1945, first published in 1949, a year before
Neruda's encyclopedic epic. *Canto general* actually consists of
about three hundred separate poems, arranged in fifteen sections
and written across the span of 1938–50. The book was well pub-
licized in advance by Neruda and the Chilean Communist party,
and Borges certainly knew what was coming. In "The Aleph"
Neruda is satirized as Borges' rival, the fatuous Carlos Argentino
Daneri, a poet of a badness not to be believed and an obvious
imitator of Whitman. Total demolition of Neruda's work in progress charmingly takes place; *Canto general* attempts to chant all
of Latin America: topography, trees and flowers, birds and beasts,
villains both native and from abroad, heroes including Pablo Neruda, the Communist Party, and the Great Punisher Stalin, of
whose murders Neruda appears to approve: "punishment is
needed." Blandly, Borges offers literary punishment in advance:

> Only once in my life have I had occasion to look into the fifteen
> thousand alexandrines of the *Polyolbion,* that topographical
> epic in which Michael Drayton recorded the flora, fauna, hy-
> drography, orography, military and monastic history of En-
> gland. I am sure, however, that this limited but bulky production
> is less boring than Carlos Argentino's similar vast undertaking.
> Daneri had in mind to set to verse the entire face of the planet,

and, by 1941, had already dispatched a number of acres of the State of Queensland, nearly a mile of the course run by the River Ob, a gasworks to the north of Veracruz, the leading shops in the Buenos Aires parish of Concepción, the villa of Mariana Cambaceres de Alvear in the Belgrano section of the Argentine capital, and a Turkish baths establishment not far from the well-known Brighton aquarium. He read me certain long-winded passages from his Australian section, and at one point praised a word of his own coining, the color "celestewhite," which he felt "actually *suggests* the sky, an element of utmost importance in the landscape of the continent Down Under." But these sprawling, lifeless hexameters lacked even the relative excitement of the so-called Augural Canto. Along about midnight, I left.

At its worst, *Canto general* does dispatch the vegetation, beasts, birds, rivers, and even the minerals of South America. In a 1970 commentary on "The Aleph," Borges disowned the notion that Daneri was intended to be a Dante imitator (the verses quoted clearly parody Neruda and lesser Whitman imitators) after paying another shrewd tribute to the almost Homeric cataloger of *Leaves of Grass:*

> My chief problem in writing the story lay in what Walt Whitman had very successfully achieved—the setting down of a limited catalog of endless things. The task, as is evident, is impossible, for such chaotic enumeration can only be simulated, and every apparently haphazard element had to be linked to its neighbor either by secret association or by contrast.

In Borges' own summary, the Aleph itself, the story's Kabbalistic fetish or talisman, is the spatial equivalent to eternity, where "all time—past, present, and future—coexists simultaneously. In the Aleph, the sum total of the spatial universe is to be found in a tiny shining sphere barely over an inch across." In relation to *Leaves of Grass* and *Canto general,* that is a good description of the fifteen-page story, "The Aleph," which is, amid much else, a critique of poetic sprawl. Borges, I venture, had far more in common, intellectually and formally, with Emerson than with Whitman.

For Neruda, Whitman was an idealized father, who replaced Neruda's actual father, the railwayman José del Carmen Reyes. "Pablo Neruda" was a pen name, a more drastic one than the shortening of Walter Whitman, Jr. into "Walt Whitman." Just as Whitman could not begin writing *Leaves of Grass* until he knew that his father, the alcoholic Quaker carpenter Walter Whitman, Sr. was dying, so Neruda could not begin *Canto general* until he was divested of "My poor hard father . . . virile in friendship, his glass full." An idealized father is best misunderstood, if you are a poet, and Neruda may have understood Whitman all too well. Neruda's creative misreadings of Whitman were highly deliberate, as is nicely caught by Doris Sommer, when she says that Neruda attempted to "destroy his teacher by resuscitating older models that never even tempted the reader with a promise of equality and the like of whom Whitman had kissed off in the preface to his poems." That may be, yet at his best Neruda dares direct comparison with Whitman.

The best section in *Canto general,* everyone agrees, is the second one, a sublime sequence of twelve chants, "The Heights of Macchu Picchu." Eighty miles away from Cuzco, Peru, which had been the capital of the Incan Empire, an abandoned city rests upon the heights of Macchu Picchu, a peak of the Andes. Returning to Chile in the autumn of 1943, after three years as Chilean consul-general in Mexico City, Neruda stopped in Peru and made his ascent to the heights. Two years passed, and "The Heights of Macchu Picchu" came into being. Superbly translated by John Felstiner, it is now probably the best introduction to Neruda for readers who need assistance with poetry written in Spanish.

Felstiner remarks that Whitman informs the pathos of Neruda's voice in the poem: "the plasmic human sympathy, the welcoming of materiality and sensuousness, the awareness of common lives and labor, the openness toward the human prospect, the poet's volunteering himself as a redeemer." I regard that last image as the most crucial, though in Neruda one of the most troublesome, because Whitman's Emersonian gnosis is very different from Neruda's Manichaean Communism. A direct juxtaposition of the

close of "The Heights of Macchu Picchu" and *Song of Myself*
presents both poets at their strongest, and does not favor Neruda:

> *(tell me everything, chain by chain,*
> *link by link, and step by step,*
> *file the knives you kept by you,*
> *drive them into my chest and my hand*
> *like a river of riving yellow light,*
> *like a river where buried jaguars lie,*
> *and let me weep, hours, days, years,*
> *blind ages, stellar centuries.*
> *Give me silence, water, hope.*
> *Give me struggle, iron, volcanoes.*
> *Fasten your bodies to me like magnets.*
> *Hasten to my veins to my mouth.*
> *Speak through my words and my blood.)*

> *I depart as air. . . . I shake my white locks at the runaway sun,*
> *I effuse my flesh in eddies, and drift it in lacy jags.*

> *I bequeath myself to the dirt to grow from the grass I love,*
> *If you want me again, look for me under your boot-soles.*

> *You will hardly know who I am or what I mean,*
> *But I shall be good health to you nevertheless,*
> *And filter and fibre your blood.*

> *Failing to fetch me at first keep encouraged,*
> *Missing me one place search another,*
> *I stop somewhere waiting for you.*

Both poets address multitudes, with Neruda's metaphors a blend
of High Baroque Quevedo and magical realism or surrealism: river
of riving yellow light, buried jaguars, and the "struggle, iron,
volcanoes" that animate the dead workmen, who in turn mag-
netize both Neruda's language and his desires. That is credible
pathos, intense and strenuous, but less persuasive than the gentle
authority of Whitman's lines, which are uncannily patient and

receptive. There is an anxiety of belatedness in Neruda, even as he nobly urges the dead laborers to speak through his words and his blood. Whitman asks us if *we* will speak before he is gone, if *we* will be too late to catch up, even though he waits for us. Neruda elsewhere learned Whitman's lesson, in the conclusion to his poem "The People" (translated here by Alastair Reid), which is a superb complement to the two closing tercets of *Song of Myself:*

> *(So let no one be perturbed when*
> *I seem to be alone and am not alone;*
> *I am not without company and I speak for all.*
>
> *Someone is hearing me without knowing it,*
> *but those I sing of, those who know,*
> *go on being born and will overflow the world.)*

That Neruda, who had translated Whitman, alludes to him here, I do not doubt, and the fusion of father and son is nearly complete, at least for this moment. Neruda appears to have agreed with the Mexican poet-critic Octavio Paz, who defied Borges and sought to merge the public and the private Whitman in the concluding appendix of *The Bow and the Lyre* (1956):

Walt Whitman is the only great modern poet who does not seem to experience inconformity vis-à-vis his world. Or even loneliness; his monologue is a vast chorus. Doubtless there are, at least, two persons in him: the public poet and the private person, who conceals his real erotic inclinations. But his mask—the poet of democracy—is something more than a mask: it is his true face. Despite certain recent interpretations, the poetic dream and the historic one coincide in him completely. There is no break between his beliefs and the social reality. And this fact is higher—I mean, broader and more significant—than any psychological circumstance. Now, the singularity of Whitman's poetry in the modern world can only be explained in the light of another, even greater singularity, which encompasses it: the singularity of America.

(translated by Ruth L. C. Simms)

This is beautifully mistaken. It both misunderstands Borges ("certain recent interpretations") and underestimates Whitman's poetic complexity. "Real erotic inclinations" and "psychological circumstance" are not the issue; what matters is Whitman's own map of the mind, a cartography in which he sets forth two opposed selves and a soul distinct from either. The true face of Whitman is neither democratic nor elitist; it is hermetic, as Neruda, despite himself, seems to have understood. Perhaps Hispanic Whitman is so bewildering a problem in reception because the principal figures involved—Borges, Neruda, Paz, Vallejo—all failed to read *Song of Myself* and the *Sea-Drift* elegies closely enough.

As a foil to the Latin American poets I offer the amazing Portuguese poet, Fernando Pessoa (1888–1935), who as a fantastic invention surpasses any creation by Borges. Pessoa, born in Lisbon and descended on the paternal side from Jewish *conversos*, was educated in South Africa and, like Borges, grew up bilingual. Indeed, until he was twenty-one, he wrote poetry only in English. In poetic eminence Pessoa matches Hart Crane, whom he closely resembles, particularly in *Mensagem* ("message" or "summons"), a poetic sequence on Portuguese history that is akin to Crane's *Bridge*. But powerful as many of Pessoa's lyrics are, they are only one part of his work; he also invented a series of alternative poets—Alberto Caeiro, Alvaro de Campos, Ricardo Reis among them—and proceeded to write entire volumes of poems for them, or rather *as* them. Two of them—Caeiro and Campos—are great poets, wholly different from each other and from Pessoa, not to mention Reis, who is an interesting minor poet.

Pessoa was neither mad nor a mere ironist; he is Whitman reborn, but a Whitman who gives separate names to "my self," "the real me" or "me myself," and "my soul," and writes wonderful books of poems for all three of them as well as a separate volume under the name of Walt Whitman. The parallels are close enough not to be coincidences, particularly since the invention of the "heteronyms" (Pessoa's term) followed an immersion in

Leaves of Grass. Walt Whitman, one of the roughs, an American, the "myself" of *Song of Myself,* becomes Alvaro de Campos, a Portuguese Jewish ship's engineer. The "real me" or "me myself" becomes the "keeper of sheep," the pastoral Alberto Caeiro, while the Whitmanian soul transmutes into Ricardo Reis, an Epicurean materialist who writes Horatian odes.

Pessoa provided all three poets with biographies and physiognomies and allowed all of them to become independent in regard to him, so much so that he joined Campos and Reis in proclaiming Caeiro as his "master" or poetic precursor. Pessoa, Campos, and Reis were all influenced by Caeiro, not by Whitman, and Caeiro was influenced by no one, being a "pure" or natural poet with almost no education who died at the High Romantic age of twenty-six. Octavio Paz, one of Pessoa's champions, summed up this fourfold poet with a fine economy: "Caeiro is the sun in whose orbit Reis, Campos, and Pessoa himself rotate. In each are particles of negation or unreality. Reis believes in form, Campos in sensation, Pessoa in symbols. Caeiro doesn't believe in anything. He exists."

The Portuguese scholar Maria Irene Ramalho de Sousa Santos, who has emerged as Pessoa's canonical critic, interprets the heteronyms as his "reading, half in complicity, half in disgust with Whitman, not only of Whitman's poetry, but also of Whitman's sexuality and politics." Pessoa's barely repressed homoeroticism emerges in Campos' furious masochism, which is hardly Whitmanian; and the democratic ideology of *Leaves of Grass* was unacceptable to a Portuguese visionary monarchist.

Although Ramalho de Sousa Santos attempts to evade Pessoa's anguish of contamination in regard to Whitman, influence anxieties are not easily mocked. Like D. H. Lawrence in *Studies in Classic American Literature,* Pessoa-Campos manifests an enormous ambivalence toward Whitman's ambitious embraces of the cosmos and everyone in it; and yet Pessoa seems to know, far better than his idealizing critics, how impossible it is to sever his poetic selves from Whitman's, despite the marvelous fiction of the heteronyms. Even Ramalho de Sousa Santos, after attempting a Feminist evasion of the burdens of influence, brilliantly returns to the harsh realities of temporal filiation, of the poetic family romance:

From the implicit dialogue in Whitman between the me and the *Me Myself*, Pessoa carved two explicitly distinct images of voice. Whitman, earlier, by virtue of a connective, organic consciousness, was able to weave these two voices together into one dynamic whole. Pessoa, coming half a century later, immersed in currents of contemporary thought and well-acquainted with Nietzsche, Marinetti, and especially Pater, whom he had translated in part, would have to discover a new strategy for expressing the Self in Whitmanian fashion, both technically and philosophically. In detecting two potentially opposing selves in *Leaves of Grass*, and particularly in *Song of Myself*, Pessoa found the means for poetically inscribing the perpetual flux of a single consciousness, darting back and forth between two essential attitudes towards Being. Caeiro and Campos, together, re-sing the *Song of Myself* as a duet, with the main voice of the soloist forever shadowed by the impalpable presence of the other. Reading one persona as an essential part of the other provides a new reading of the heteronyms.

According to this view, with which I concur, Pessoa accepts his role in the drama of poetic influence but brings the reading of Whitman to a greater degree of consciousness by externalizing his precursor's psychic cartography as the interaction of two fictive poets. I want first to apply this reading to poems by Caeiro and Campos and then leap back to Neruda, whose poetic diversity has exercised so much critical comment. When Ricardo Neftalí Reyes assumed the pseudonym Pablo Neruda and adopted Walt Whitman as foster father, he took his own first step toward Pessoa's heteronymic principle. Whether or not *Canto general* is confirmed by time as the general song of America, displacing *Leaves of Grass*, as some of its admirers prophesy, there is also an enormous body of poetry by Neruda that is distinct from his encyclopedic epic. The relation between volumes and phases of his very varied career is highly Whitmanian in that very different Nerudan selves manifest themselves in the poems, just as Caeiro and Campos are highly diverse and yet still Whitmanian selves. Caeiro, like Whitman's "real me," is both in and out of the game and watching and wondering at it:

One way or another,
The moment permitting,
Able to say what I think at times,
And otherwise saying it poorly and jumbled,
I keep writing my poems without wanting to,
As if writing weren't something made up of gestures,
As if writing were something that happened to me
Like the sun outside shining on me.

I try saying what I feel
Without thinking about what I feel.
I try fitting words to the idea
Without going down a corridor
Of thought to find words.

I don't always succeed in feeling what I know I should feel.
My thought swims the river only quite slowly,
Heavily burdened by clothes men have made it wear.

I try divesting myself of what I've learned,
I try forgetting the mode of remembering they taught me,
And scrape off the ink they used to paint my senses,
Unpacking my true emotions,
Unwrapping myself, and being myself, not Alberto Caeiro,
But a human animal that Nature produced.
            (translated by Edwin Honig and Susan Brown)

Whitman's real me did not write *Leaves of Grass* and mocked the rough Walt in "As I Ebb'd with the Ocean of Life," after suffering his masturbatory rape in *Song of Myself.* Pessoa's intuition taught him what sort of poem the Whitmanian me myself could have written: involuntary, the expression of the human animal or natural man, with learning, remembering, and past representations of the senses all cast off. Can there be such a poem? Clearly not, and Pessoa, of course, knows it; but the poems of Caeiro are a fascinating attempt to write what cannot be written. At the other limit of expression—the self-celebratory rhapsody of the demonic, rough Walt—Pessoa stations the outrageous Campos, as here in his "Salutation to Walt Whitman":

Infinite Portugal, June eleventh, nineteen hundred and
*   fifteen . . .*
A-hoy-hoy-hoy-hoy!
From here in Portugal, with all past ages in my brain,
I salute you, Walt, I salute you, my brother in the Universe,
I with my monocle and tightly buttoned frock coat,
I am not unworthy of you, Walt, as you well know,
I am not unworthy of you, my greeting is enough to make
*   it so . . .*
I, so given to indolence, so easily bored,
I am with you, as you well know, and understand you and
*   love*
*   you,*
And though I never met you, born the same year you died,
I know you loved me too, you knew me, and I am happy.
I know that you knew me, that you considered and explained
*   me,*
I know that this is what I am, whether on Brooklyn Ferry ten
*   years before I was born*
Or strolling up Rua do Ouro thinking about everything that
*   is not Rua do Ouro,*
And just as you felt everything, so I feel everything, and so
*   here we are clasping hands,*
Clasping hands, Walt, clasping hands, with the universe
*   doing a dance in our soul.*

O singer of concrete absolutes, always modern and eternal,
Fiery concubine of the scattered world,
Great pederast brushing up against the diversity of things,
Sexualized by rocks, by trees, by people, by their trades,
Itch for the swiftly passing, for casual encounters, for what's
*   merely observed,*
My enthusiast for what's inside everything,
My great hero going straight through Death by leaps and
*   bounds,*

Roaring, screaming, bellowing greetings to God!

Singer of wild and gentle brotherhood with everything,
Great epidemic democrat, up close to it all in body and soul
Carnival of each and every action, bacchanalia of all
  intentions,
Twin brother of every sudden impulse,
Jean-Jacques Rousseau of the world hell-bent to produce
  machinery,
Homer of all the insaisissable *of wavering carnality,*
Shakespeare of the sensation on the verge of steam
  propulsion,
Milton-Shelley of the dawning future of Electricity!
Incubus of all gestures,
Spasm penetrating every object-force,
Souteneur of the whole Universe,
Whore of all solar systems . . .
                    (translated by Honig and Brown)

This fantasia of 1915 surges on for more than two hundred lines and is accompanied by two longer Whitmanian extravaganzas, "Ode" and the thirty-page *Maritime Ode,* Campos' masterwork and one of the major poems of the century. Except for the best parts of Neruda's *Residence on Earth* and *Canto general,* nothing composed in Whitman's wake compares to the *Maritime Ode* as exuberant invention. The "Salutation to Walt Whitman," with its sublime ambivalence outdoing D. H. Lawrence as a Whitmanian reaction-formation ("Whore of all solar systems"), concludes by blessing Whitman as the "Impotent and ardent lover of the nine muses and the graces."

Federico Garcia Lorca, saluting Whitman fifteen years later (in 1930, the year Hart Crane's *The Bridge* was published), writes an "Ode to Walt Whitman" in his surrealistic *Poet in New York* that compares poorly to Campos' chants; but then Lorca, unlike Pessoa, knew Whitman only at second hand and imagined a "lovely old man" with "your beard full of butterflies." Pessoa-Campos, steeped in Whitman and ignited by him, fights back for his poetic life, partly by the Borgesian strategy (in advance of

Borges) of *becoming* Walt Whitman, even as Borges' Pierre Menard became Cervantes in order to usurp the authorship of *Don Quixote.*

Neruda understood, at least in his own Whitmanian poems, that the poet of *Leaves of Grass* was evasive, shy, defensive, invariably metamorphic. As Frank Menchaca has observed, "Neruda also must have understood that the self which claims to be everywhere freely available in Whitman's poetry is nowhere to be found." Death is perhaps part of that "nowhere" in both Whitman and Neruda, but it is one of the subjects in Neruda's work in which Whitman the wound dresser tends to hover. *Residence on Earth,* the culmination of his earlier poetry, displays Neruda confronting bleakness in the mode of the elegiac Whitman contemplating himself as part of the sea-drift. Neruda remarked that "It's poetry with no way out," and insisted he had emerged from despair only through his activities on behalf of the doomed Republican side in the Spanish Civil War. Leo Spitzer, one of the double handful of scholarly modern critics who matter, described *Residence on Earth* as a "chaotic enumeration," which would be the darker Whitman out of control, the Whitmanian creative process reduced to what Spitzer called "disintegrating activities," or Whitman ebbing with the ocean of life.

In terms of Pessoa's heteronyms, the *Residence on Earth* poems are written by the Caeiro element locked in Campos, a Whitman trapped inside himself. Perhaps this is caught best in the conclusion of the dead-end "Walking Around," as superbly translated by W. S. Merwin:

> *For this reason Monday burns like oil*
> *at the sight of me arriving with my jail-face,*
> *and it howls in passing like a wounded wheel,*
> *and walks like hot blood toward nightfall.*
>
> *And it shoves me along to certain corners, to certain damp*
>   *houses,*
> *to hospitals where the bones stick out of the windows,*
> *to certain cobblers' ships smelling of vinegar,*
> *to streets horrendous as crevices.*

There are birds the color of sulfur, and horrible intestines
hanging from the doors of the houses which I hate,
there are forgotten sets of teeth in a coffee-pot,
there are mirrors
which should have wept with shame and horror,
there are umbrellas all over the place, and poisons, and
  navels.

I stride along with calm, with eyes, with shoes,
with fury, with forgetfulness,
I pass, I cross offices and stores full of orthopedic appliances,
and courtyards hung with clothes hanging from a wire:
underpants, towels and shirts which weep
slow dirty tears.

Canto general at its strongest is the ultimate antidote to this suicidal version of Whitmanianism in Neruda. Roberto González Echevarria called *Canto general* a "poetics of betrayal," grimly prophetic of the terrible pathos of Neruda's death on September 23, 1973, twelve days after the massacres that commenced with the assassination of his friend, President Salvador Allende, by the Chilean military. Betrayal is only a minor theme in Whitman, whose political involvements are much overemphasized at our bad moment in criticism, when everything has been politicized. But betrayal, whether of the Spanish Republic or of Chile by the military, was a poetic liberation for Neruda, emancipating him from the dark side that he shared with Whitman without the preternatural Whitmanian capacity for sending forth, now and always, a sunrise from himself. The ultimate lesson of Whitman's influence—on Borges, Neruda, Paz, and so many more—may be that only an originality as outrageous as Pessoa's could hope to contain it without hazard to the poetic self or selves.

22.

Beckett ... Joyce ...
Proust ... Shakespeare

Richard Ellmann in his definitive biography, *James Joyce*, has a lovely vignette of the friendship between Joyce and Beckett, respectively fifty and twenty-six at that moment:

> Beckett was addicted to silences, and so was Joyce; they engaged in conversations which consisted often of silences directed towards each other, both suffused with sadness, Beckett mostly for the world, Joyce mostly for himself. Joyce sat in his habitual posture, legs crossed, toe of the upper leg under the instep of the lower; Beckett, also tall and slender, fell into the same gesture. Joyce suddenly asked some such question as, "How could the idealist Hume write a history?" Beckett replied, "a history of representations."

Ellmann's source was an interview with Beckett in 1953, more than twenty years later, but Beckett had a clear memory. Joyce died in 1941, not yet sixty; Beckett in 1989, at eighty-three.

Beckett always loved Joyce as a second father and began as a total disciple of the master. Of all Beckett's books I love best *Murphy*, his first published novel, written in 1935, not issued until 1938, but the book is as Joycean as any novel by Anthony Burgess and certainly has little overtly in common with the mature Beckett of the Trilogy (*Molloy*, *Malone Dies*, *The Unnamable*), of *How It Is*, or of the major dramas (*Waiting for Godot*, *Endgame*, *Krapp's Last Tape*). I choose *Murphy* as a starting point for discussion partly because of the delight it always gives me, and partly to examine Beckett at his most Joycean. Joyce himself liked *Murphy* enough to have memorized the description of the final disposal of Murphy's ashes:

> Some hours later Cooper took the packet of ash from his pocket, where earlier in the evening he had put it for greater security, and threw it angrily at a man who had given him great offence. It bounced, burst, off the wall on to the floor, where at once it became the object of much dribbling, passing, trapping, shooting, punching, heading and even some recognition from the gentleman's code. By closing time the body, mind and soul of Murphy were freely distributed over the floor of the saloon; and before another dayspring greyened the earth had been swept away with the sand, the beer, the butts, the glass, the matches, the spits, the vomit.

This amiable shocker, through its mention of "body, mind and soul," intends to remind us of Murphy's will, read out six pages earlier:

> With regard to the disposal of these my body, mind and soul, I desire that they be burnt and placed in a paper bag and brought to the Abbey Theatre, Lr. Abbey Street, Dublin, and without pause into what the great and good Lord Chesterfield calls the necessary house, where their happiest hours have been spent, on the right as one goes down into the pit, and I desire that the chain be there pulled upon them, if possible during the performance of a piece, the whole to be executed without ceremony or show of grief.

What might be called the negative high spirits of *Murphy* are, happily, incessant. The beauty of the book is its exuberance of language: it is Samuel Beckett's *Love's Labour's Lost*. It is not very Beckettian, partly because it is unabashedly Joycean, partly because it is Beckett's only substantial work that is part of a history of representations, the novel as written by Dickens, Flaubert, and early Joyce, rather than the more problematic "anatomy" form (as Northrop Frye liked to call it) of Rabelais, Cervantes, and Sterne. *Murphy* has a surprisingly continuous narrative, and when my two favorite characters, the Dublin Pythagoreans Neary and Wylie, are at hand, sometimes in the company of "Miss Counihan's hot buttered buttocks," Beckett gives them conversations whose vivacity and high good humor he was not to allow us, or himself, again:

"Sit down, the two of you, there before me," said Neary, "and do not despair. Remember there is no triangle, however obtuse, but the circumference of some circle passes through its wretched vertices. Remember also one thief was saved."

"Our medians," said Wylie, "or whatever the hell they are, meet in Murphy."

"Outside us," said Neary. "Outside us."

"In the outer light," said Miss Counihan.

Now it was Wylie's turn, but he could find nothing. No sooner did he realise this, that he would not find anything in time to do himself credit, than he began to look as though he were not looking for anything, nay, as though he were waiting for it to be his turn. Finally Neary said without pity:

"You to play, Needle."

"And do the lady out of the last word!" cried Wylie. "And put the lady to the trouble of finding another! Reary, Neally!"

"No trouble," said Miss Counihan.

Now it was anybody's turn.

"Very well," said Neary. "What I was really coming to, what I wanted to suggest is this. Let our conversation now be without precedent in fact or literature, each one speaking to the best of his ability the truth to the best of his knowledge. That is what

I meant when I said you took the tone, if not the terms, out of my mouth. It is high time we three parted."

Neary has given only the first, optimistic half of Beckett's favorite tag from Saint Augustine, which will center the ethos of *Waiting for Godot*: "Do not despair—one of the thieves was saved; do not presume—one of the thieves was damned." Beckett once remarked, "I am interested in the shape of ideas even if I do not believe in them . . . that sentence has a wonderful shape. It is the shape that matters." The shape of divine forgiveness is both antithetical and arbitrary in Protestant Christianity, which looks back to Augustine; and Beckett, a firm unbeliever, was Irish Protestant by upbringing. *Murphy,* deliciously unbelieving, is the purest comedy that Beckett ever wrote. Its darker overtones are omnipresent, but a continuous verve holds them to the periphery. Joyce is tempered throughout the book by the only other novelistic influence that ever affected Beckett: the very different Proust, about whom Beckett had published a brief, lively book in 1931. It culminates in a vision of Proust that perhaps only a disciple of Joyce would have written:

> For Proust the quality of language is more important than any system of ethics or aesthetics. Indeed he makes no attempt to dissociate form from content. The one is the concretion of the other, the revelation of a world. The Proustian world is expressed metaphorically by the artisan because it is apprehended metaphorically by the artist: the indirect and comparative expression of indirect and comparative perception.

If you substituted "Joyce" or "Beckett" for "Proust," this passage would be at least as cogent. Early in *Proust,* Beckett speaks of "our smug will to live," and he joins Proust in a Schopenhauerian resistance to this will. His own creed as a writer emerges from the monograph in two lucid sentences that form a bridge between Joyce and Proust:

> The only fertile research is excavatory, immersive, a contraction of the spirit, a descent. The artist is active, but negatively, shrink-

ing from the nullity of extracircumferential phenomena, drawn into the core of the eddy.

This descent into the abyss of the self is more the art of the Beckett trilogy than of *Wake* or *Search*. Joyce fascinated Beckett most, all love aside, because of the preternatural mastery he perpetually manifested. At no time did Beckett choose to see Joyce as being overwhelmed by the *materia poetica* that he transmuted into *Ulysses* and *Wake*. In contrast, Beckett's Proust is presented as an antithetical literary father, with the courage to be victimized and imprisoned by his material, to accept it with Romantic anxiety. Joyce's name is not mentioned anywhere in Beckett's monograph, but he appears as the classical artist as opposed to the romantic Proust (and Beckett), who will write as they have lived, in Time, unlike Joyce:

The classical artist assumes omniscience and omnipotence. He raised himself artificially out of Time in order to give relief to his chronology and causality to his development. Proust's chronology is extremely difficult to follow, the succession of events spasmodic, and his characters and themes, although they seem to obey an almost insane inward necessity, are presented and developed with a fine Dostoievskian contempt for the vulgarity of a plausible concatenation.

That is closer even to *Murphy* than to *Search,* and is already a defense of the trilogy. "The more Joyce knew, the more he could"; the alternate way is "working with impotence, ignorance." Those words should be taken as metaphors for some very acute states of consciousness, out of which ensued *Waiting for Godot,* the trilogy, the magnificent *Endgame,* and the authentic shocker, *How It Is.* I tend to doubt that these states are essentially different degrees of consciousness—of consciousness of consciousness, as it were—which is the post-Cartesian allegory of Hugh Kenner, whose Beckett is essentially the last of the High Modernists, the comic epilogue to Pound, Eliot, Joyce (and Wyndham Lewis!), and so a final witness to the destruction of the West by the Enlightenment.

Beckett's sense of our malaise was more a post-Protestant re-alization, stemming from Schopenhauer rather than Descartes. Self-consciousness is one element in Beckett's vision of our vertigo, but only as another fruit of the ravening will to live. Even Scho-penhauer, obsessed and eloquent on the drive beyond the pleasure principle, is only another latecomer in representing it, as Freud also was, after him. The masters of the will to live include Falstaff and Macbeth, or rather Falstaff as master and Macbeth as victim. Hamlet, who necessarily haunted Beckett despite his professed preference for Racine, is master and victim, and as such pervades Beckett's canonical drama, *Endgame*. Beckett's Hamlet follows the French model, in which excessive consciousness negates action, which is at some distance from Shakespeare's Hamlet. T. S. Eliot, who would like to have preferred the French Hamlet, opined that "The Hamlet of Laforgue is an adolescent; the Hamlet of Shake-speare is not, he has not that explanation and excuse." Beckett's Hamm, like Laforgue's Hamlet, is an adolescent blown up into a ruined god or demiurge. But self-consciousness is not Hamm's burden; the will to live, in horribly decayed form, abides in him, and that always remains the daemon for Beckett. If you are an artist, you suffer your vocation's peculiar augmentation of the will to live, a craving for recognition initially and ultimately for im-mortality. Beckett seems to have been as good and decent a human being as any strong writer ever, and much more so than most: infinitely compassionate, endlessly kind though even more infi-nitely withdrawn. But as writer qua writer, he suffered as all writers suffer; the stronger the writer, the stronger the suffering, and Beckett was a very strong writer, more than Borges or Pynchon the last (to date) unassailable author in the Canon.

After he made the transition to writing first in French and then translating himself back into English, he was free of Joyce sty-listically and fairly well untroubled by Proust's vision, despite their common ancestry in Schopenhauer. No one, confronting *Endgame* or *How It Is,* will find Beckett deficient in strangeness, in palpable originality. His shadow lies heavily upon the plays of Pinter and Stoppard; his prose fiction seems to have been a dead stop: no one can extend or deepen that mode. *Endgame* may be the end-game of the Western Canon's last major phase, while we uneasily find ourselves waiting for Godot, who will turn out to be the demiurge of a new Theocratic Age, as unwelcome to Beckett as to anyone else among us. What can our burgeoning covens of Cultural Studies do with *Endgame* or *How It Is,* except perhaps point to them as the culmination, together with *Search, Wake,* and Kafka, of the bad old days, the lost paradises of the aesthetes? Beckett, like Joyce, presupposes a reader who knows Dante and Shakespeare, Flaubert and Yeats, and all of the other great, ever-living dead men and women, to borrow Coleridge's praise of Shakespeare. The theater has its own traditions and its own continuity, and the Beckett of the dramas will survive as long as Shakespeare and Molière, Racine and Ibsen, in performance more than in readership. The Beckett of the prose narratives faces the same eclipse as his precursors, Joyce and Proust, since the new theocrats will enforce their quasi-literate, multicultural noncanon. What chance has *Malone Dies* or *How It Is* against Alice Walker's *Meridian* or all of the other correct prescribed readings? As an elegist, I am resigned and realistic enough to center Beckett's canonical survival on *Waiting for Godot, Endgame,* and *Krapp's Last Tape,* and sadly neglect the nondramatic later Beckett in what follows.

ALTHOUGH BECKETT's protagonists manifest surprising variety, nearly all of them share one feature: repetition, being doomed to tell and act out a story over and over again. They follow in the wake of the Wandering Jew, Coleridge's Ancient Mariner, Wagner's Flying Dutchman, Kafka's Hunter Gracchus. Beckett's genre is tragicomedy (the overt designation of *Waiting for Godot*); however dark the affect, the mode is not tragic, except in *Endgame. Waiting for Godot,* properly directed and acted, is not precisely a romp; but I always look forward to seeing it again, whereas I have to toughen myself in order to face even a good production of *Endgame,* a greater yet more savage work. Hamm, the irascible Hamlet of *Endgame,* is an almost perfect solipsist, and Beckett's powers of representation in the play can be hard to endure. The lasting popularity of *Godot* has something to do with the wistfulness of its clowns, Gogo and Didi. But the drama, though gentler than *Endgame* and less apocalyptic, is finally about as cheerful as late Ibsen in its implications. While waiting for Godot, you might as well be waiting for when we dead awaken.

Endgame moves out from a Shakespearean paradigm that grafts elements of *Lear, The Tempest, Richard III,* and *Macbeth* onto *Hamlet;* but *Waiting for Godot,* as all its critics recognize, takes its models from vaudeville, mime, circus, music hall, silent-film comedy, and ultimately from their origins: farce, medieval and later. *Godot* seems as archaic as *Endgame* seems prophetic: the older Theocratic Age meets the one always newly rushing toward us. Again, as all critics have agreed, *Godot* is haunted by the Protestant Bible: Cain and Christ hover nearby, but Godot is no more God than the dreadful Pozzo is. His name is arbitrary and meaningless, whatever its source, whether in Balzac (whom Beckett detested) or in Beckett's own life. As for Christianity and *Waiting for Godot,* Beckett was brutally definitive: "Christianity is a mythology with which I am perfectly familiar, and so I use it. But not in this case!" It is always worth remembering that Beckett more than shared Joyce's distaste for Christianity and for Ireland. Both men chose unbelief and Paris, and Beckett's explanation for why Ireland produced so many important modern writers was that a country so buggered by the British and the priests was compelled to sing. Salvation, hardly an option for Beckett, is also not available for Vladimir and Estragon in this least Augustinian of plays, the parable of the two thieves notwithstanding.

Beckett feared that *Waiting for Godot* might some day seem a period piece. I still remember the first performance I saw of it, in New York City in 1956, with Bert Lahr as Estragon and E. G. Marshall as Vladimir, both of them upstaged by Kurt Kaznar as Pozzo and Alvin Epstein as Lucky. Beckett, who declined to attend, condemned it as "a dreadfully wrong and vulgar production." Rereading the play in 1993, some of its aspects do have a period flavor, but that may be because the world of forty years ago, on the other side of the Sixties, now seems to be a century or so back in the abyss of time. What startled me then makes me nostalgic now, which is certainly not true of *Endgame.* Hamm is both a chess king, always about to be taken, and a poor player, though it is unclear just who his opponent can be except for ourselves, the audience. Estragon and Vladimir, who play only a waiting game, need to be played as and by grand entertainers and enjoy an amiable rapport with the audience. Beckett evidently did not wish his vagrants to charm us, but then he should have composed them differently. Hamm, the least charming of solipsists, could not be played by the late Bert Lahr, but then no one (I hope) would have cast Lahr as Pozzo, Hamm's precursor.

I first saw *Waiting for Godot* before I had read it, and I remember being startled at hearing Lahr quote Shelley when the moon rises: "Pale for weariness . . . of climbing heaven and gazing on the likes of us." Beckett, like Joyce, did not share Eliot's professed distaste for Shelley (it turned out that Eliot did not share it either). The fragment addressed to the moon by Shelley is in effect the epilogue to the first act:

> *Art thou pale for weariness*
> *Of climbing heaven and gazing on the earth,*
> *Wandering companionless*
> *Among the stars that have a different birth—*
> *And ever changing, like a joyless eye*
> *That finds no object worth its constancy?*

Shelley, a somewhat Humean skeptic despite his Platonic reputation, may have been playing an ironic game here with Bishop Berkeley; in any case I suspect that is how Beckett read this fragment, which explains why Estragon quotes it. Since for Berkeley objects in themselves did not exist but resided only in our minds as we perceived them, the Shelleyan moon parodies the Berkeleyan subjective consciousness, joyless and mutable, because no human being is a worthy candidate for object constancy. "The likes of us" are not worthy of the moon's regard, so we do not achieve existence.

As companionless wanderer, Shelley's moon is the emblem of Estragon's anxiety that Vladimir may abandon him, which he tends to express by threatening to leave Vladimir. The anxiety is related to Estragon's suicidal mania, which is allied to his comparison of Christ to himself. Beckett's biographer, Dierdre Bair, tells us that Estragon was originally called "Levy," and perhaps

we can surmise that Beckett first conceived of him in the image
of his Jewish friends, like his fellow Joycean Paul Léon, who were
murdered by the Germans. There is some tenuous but perpetually
disturbing link between the "waiting" for Godot and the anxious
waiting that was so much a part of Beckett's quietly heroic work
for the French Resistance. Mortality is the overt burden of *Waiting
for Godot,* and its ironic parody of Berkeley's evasion of the reality
principle, of death's finality, is one of the aspects that keep it from
falling into a period piece.

Soon after the beginning of act 2, Shelley returns when Estragon
adopts the Shelleyan figure of dead leaves for "all the dead voices,"
for all Beckett's losses of friends and lovers. Pozzo's subsequent
hysteria augments the lament for mortality: "They give birth
astride of a grave, the light gleams an instant, then it's night once
more." Earlier, in Lucky's amazing litany, Bishop Berkeley suffers
a dialectical refutation: "in a word the dead loss per head since
the death of Bishop Berkeley being to the tune of one inch four
ounce per head." Objectified by death, we lose existence, and
worry in advance if we ever had it. So Vladimir worries that he
may be only a dream projection of Estragon's, that someone may
be staring at him even as he stares at the sleeping Estragon.

At such a moment, Beckett as a dramatist achieves an effect
richly strange out of all proportion to its actual originality. Phil-
osophic drama abounds, and Beckett overtly goes back to Calderón's *Life Is a Dream,* as he does in his book on Proust. But
the pathos of Beckett's tramps is weirdly original, though behind
them are the shadows of Shakespeare's fools, culminating in the
Feste of *Twelfth Night.* Beckett oddly resembles Dr. Johnson in
his attitudes toward mortality, which may account for his early
desire to write *Human Wishes,* which would have brought Johnson in his proper person on the stage. Like Johnson, Beckett obsessively associates the early taste of mortality in the mind with
the conviction that love is lost early, or never could be. That is
the emphasis of *Krapp's Last Tape,* which regards Beckett's assumption in his fortieth year of his own aesthetic vision as being
ironically one with the shadow of the object falling upon the ego,
to cite Freud at his most cunning in "Mourning and Melancholia."
If the ultimate models for Estragon and Vladimir were Beckett

and his eventual wife, Suzanne, then their long march of a month's duration from Paris to southeast France in November 1942, in flight from the Gestapo, could be considered the *materia poetica* out of which *Waiting for Godot* was formed. So intense was the crucible of Beckett's dramatic imagination that, half a century later, we have great difficulty in absorbing this information about the play's origins. Its aesthetic dignity remains absolute and confounds any effort to link Beckett's experiential anxieties with the achieved anxiety of his dramatic art.

BECKETT'S FAME has little to do with his prose narratives (to call them that); his international reputation was and is founded on his plays, *Waiting for Godot* in particular. Remarkable as his quasi-novels are, his masterpiece is undoubtedly *Endgame,* and the theater is where he achieved an art almost entirely his own. Joyce's one play, *Exiles,* is an exercise in Ibsenism, and a play by Proust would have been as much a catastrophe as the plays of Henry James proved to be. The uncanny affinity with Kafka, unwelcome to Beckett, can be sensed in the plays but is limited by the Kafkan sense of "indestructibility," which, as we have seen, Beckett did not share. Joyce was something of a Hermeticist and a Manichaean; Beckett was not. He did not confuse himself with either God or Shakespeare, although *Hamlet, The Tempest,* and *King Lear* are all revised in *Endgame,* which has as great a relationship to Shakespeare as *Finnegans Wake* did.

It is difficult to find an equal to Beckett among the best dramatists of our Chaotic Age: Brecht, Pirandello, Ionesco, García Lorca, Shaw. They have no *Endgame;* to find a drama of its reverberatory power, you have to return to Ibsen. The author of *Murphy* still hovers while we wait for Godot but has vanished when we enter Hamm's rattrap, his version of Hamlet's mousetrap, which itself revised the putative *Murder of Gonzago.* I cannot think of any other twentieth-century work of literature composed as late as 1957 that is nearly as original an achievement as *Endgame,* nor has there been anything since to challenge such originality. Beckett may have forsworn "mastery" as not being possible after Joyce and Proust, but *Endgame* reaches it. After he turned fifty, in 1956, Beckett had five extraordinary years of creativity, a span that starts with *Endgame* and includes *Krapp's Last Tape* and *How It Is*, which with *Endgame* set a new standard that even he never quite touched again.

The earliest dramatic work we have by Beckett is the single scene that survives of a projected play on the relations of Dr. Johnson and Mrs. Thrale. Marked act 1, under the title *Human Wishes*, the scene is set in Dr. Johnson's strange household of vanities and charitable cases: Mrs. Williams, Mrs. Desmoulins, Miss Carmichael, the cat Hodge, and Dr. Levett. As the ladies quarrel, we are suddenly nearly twenty years later in Beckett's career as a writer: Levett enters drunk and staggers upstairs, and the ladies react:

> *Between the three women exchange of looks.*
> *Gestures of disgust. Mouths opened and shut.*
> *Finally they resume their occupations.*

Mrs. W. Words fail us.

Mrs. D. Now this is where a writer for the stage would have us speak no doubt.

Mrs. W. He would have us explain Levett.

Mrs. D. To the public.

Mrs. W. The ignorant public.

Mrs. D. To the gallery.

Mrs. W. To the pit.

Mrs. C. To the boxes.

It is only a step from this to *Waiting for Godot,* and a step after that to *Endgame*. Beckett's stance from the start looks out from the actors at the audience, and never vice versa. In *Endgame,* we get radical internalization; the entire play is like a play within a play, but there is no audience on the stage, and we might as well be inside the mind of the bizarre solipsist Hamm, Hamlet in the final ditch, who is also Prospero after the drowning of his book, and might even be Lear in his all-but-final madness. Like Joyce before him, Beckett takes on Shakespeare, but not at all in Joyce's mode. Overt allusions to Shakespeare are very few in *Endgame*. Beckett rethinks the crises of all three plays. Clov is Caliban and Ariel in relation to Prospero; Horatio and the Gravedigger caught in dialogue with Hamlet; the Fool and Gloucester horrified by Lear. There are a myriad of transpositions; Gloucester/Clov is not blind; Lear/Hamm is. Hamm/Lear demands love from Clov/the Fool; bitter as Lear's Fool is, he loves Lear as though he were Lear's own and only son. Hamlet at the end is disinterested and transcendent; Hamm is always pragmatically monstrous, but not nearly so dangerous as Hamlet. Clov is a very unloving Horatio, but like Horatio he represents the audience in regard to Hamm/ Hamlet. Prospero has practiced the rarer action of forgiveness; Hamm is churlish and vengeful toward all life. Clov in his resentments is more Caliban than Ariel but cannot want to leave, because there is nowhere to go.

Beckett, with awesome economy, cuts away all context from Shakespeare and concentrates the three most powerful Shakespearean protagonists into one actor. As every critic has noted, *Endgame* is even more knowingly theatrical than *Waiting for Godot*: Hamm is a playwright-performer giving a performance while conducting a contest (like a game of chess) with the audience, except that the performance turns out to be the contest. But the actor is hateful; *Endgame* is beyond any alienation effect. There are no wistful clown-tramps in front of us: Hamm is like Pozzo but endowed with creative talent, which he botches in a false creation. Clov is scarcely more sympathetic, and Nagg and Nell seem the remnants of parents altogether worthy of Hamm. Reading the play or watching it in performance, I always marvel that characters so antipathetic can engross me with something strangely parallel to the charismatic force of Hamlet, Prospero, Lear, and something more that compensates for the best pathos of Horatio, Caliban, the Fool, and Gloucester. The canonical challenge of *Endgame* is that it comes close to the ending of the Canon; it is our moment of literature's last stand, if literature means

Shakespeare, Dante, Racine, Proust, Joyce. Beckett, who might not have cared (though I doubt that), is the prophet of the silence just before the Viconian *ricorso*. It is almost as though he foretells the time when Dante, Proust, and Joyce will have no more deep readers, and Shakespeare and Racine will at last cease to be performed. That will be endgame indeed, and many who are now alive may live to see it.

Were you to perform *Hamlet* as if the chess player Beckett had written it, or even directed it, you could conceive of it as a match between Hamlet and Claudius in which the endgame of act 5 finally cleaned your stage except for Horatio, a forlorn knight, and Fortinbras, a king brought in from off the board after checkmate. In *Endgame,* there is no mighty opposite for the white-eyed Hamm; either he plays chess with himself, and loses, or his match is with the audience, and there is no winner. There is fierce lovemaking going on behind the scenes in *Hamlet* between Claudius and Gertrude; whether it counts as adulterous is disputable, for Shakespeare does not clarify exactly when it began. The romance of Nagg and Nell is grotesquely reduced, in comparison; that seems to be why they are in the play, which strictly speaking does not require them. I suspect that *Macbeth* is also shrewdly appropriated by Beckett; the small boy outside who causes Hamm disquiet is the play's Fleance, ancestor of a line of kings that yet may reign in what seems the rubble of a destroyed world.

Clov's relation to Hamm has reminded some critics that Beckett, in his youth, played the faithful Horatio to Joyce's solipsistic Hamlet. I don't know how to exclude that from *Endgame,* it being one of the play's powers that its rugged destitution universalizes it, so that no Shakespeare, including *Richard II* and *Richard III,* seems wholly unaffected by it. One way of recognizing *Endgame*'s interpretive power is to see the difference between the illuminations it bestows on Shakespeare's work and the failure of any backwards illumination in *Ulysses* and *Finnegans Wake,* Shakespeare-soaked epics. The difference is formal in the first place; Beckett has shaped our century's stage equivalent of Shakespeare. I did not much enjoy watching *King Lear* staged as *Endgame,* or *Hamlet* staged as *Waiting for Godot,* in Tom Stoppard's Beckett-obsessed *Rosencrantz and Guildenstern Are Dead.* It would be more imaginative, and more in Beckett's spirit, to direct *Lear* as *Godot* and *Hamlet* as *Endgame,* and even *The Tempest* as *Prospero's Last Tape.*

But however we apply *Endgame* as a critique of Shakespearean drama, Shakespeare remains scripture, and *Endgame* remains commentary. It is an Anglo-Irish-French interpretation of Shakespeare, with some ironic philosophical outrides: the Cartesian analytics, well expounded by Kenner, and Schopenhauer's nightmare send-up of the will to live, employed by the young Beckett in his monograph on Proust. Himself in *Endgame,* Beckett (on what level of conscious intention we cannot know) writes the drama of Hamm's consciousness, a challenge not taken up by Ibsen, though it flickers on and off in Emperor Julian in *Emperor and Galilean.*

However you read *Hamlet,* the prince bewilders you even as he bewilders himself. No dogmatic approach to the largest Western representation of consciousness has ever worked. Shakespeare himself experimented so radically with Hamlet that we do not know how to reconcile the boyish prince of act 1 with the purged stoic of act 5, who seems fifteen years older after a time span of only a likely month or two. Beckett, like Joyce, seems to lose interest in Hamlet after the graveyard scene, except that he has captured Hamlet's dying words, "The rest is silence." As the Western hero (or hero-villain) of consciousness, Hamlet is the portrait of a charismatic. His strong parody, Hamm, is anything but that; all that he definitely preserves of Hamlet is the play doctor and director of the play within the play; and yet that is a considerable part of Hamlet, the portion that convinces us that, uniquely among Shakespearean characters, the Prince of Denmark could have been the author of his entire play.

All of Shakespeare's plays, as everyone always has known, are on one level about playing, at least from *Love's Labour's Lost* on. "That's too long for a play," Berowne protests when Rosaline tells him he must put in a year and a day among the sick and dying, if he is to win her. Theatrical metaphors abound in the four great domestic tragedies of blood—*Hamlet, Othello, Macbeth,* and *King Lear*—as though even Shakespeare has to fall back on what he knows best in order to summon up the inventiveness that abounds upon the heights of his achievement. The playwriting impulse, in Shakespeare, Hamlet, and everyone else, is expressed perfectly by Hamm: "Then babble, babble, words, like the solitary child who turns himself into children, two, three, so as to be together and whisper together, in the dark."

It is true that Beckett at first seems more stylized than Shakespeare; Beckett admired the Noh-like, very stageable dramas of William Butler Yeats, and his extreme stylization picks up hints from Yeats. But reflection on *Hamlet* reveals that stylization—whether in Racine, late Ibsen, Yeats, or Beckett—cannot go farther than *Hamlet,* the play rather than the prince, who retains much spontaneity in himself, but who is propelled onward in the embassy of death with increasing stylization, until the black mass of the sword-and-poison ritual that closes the work.

Hamm's rhetorical violence is prompted by Hamlet's, and it would be difficult to judge which of the violences is the more stylized. Hamm, too, is mad only north-northwest, and responds with sharp distinctions when the wind blows from the south. No one could be charmed by Hamm's melancholy, as the centuries have been charmed by Hamlet's, but no one need undervalue Hamm's wounded intelligence, which inherits from Hamlet's. The best critical observation yet made about *Endgame* is by Hugh Kenner, who reads it as stoic comedy (as I do not) and who proposes that we are inside Hamm's skull from start to finish.

Hamm is a blunderer and evidently a poor chess player, but his obsessive force has an intellectual component, and he is a figure of capable gusto. He is not just played by an actor; he is an actor, again following Hamlet, who tends to accuse himself of being a player even when he wills otherwise. Joyce, in the years when Beckett served him faithfully, played Joyce all the time, which means he played at being Shem the penman, Hamlet, Shakespeare, Stephen, and Mr. Bloom. Beckett, by all reports, had nothing of the ham actor in him. Belacqua, his early surrogate in his short stories, is an Oblomov but not a Hamm. We never will know whether Shakespeare got into Hamlet (though it seems quite likely), but we know for certain that Beckett kept himself outside his finest dramatic protagonist, as opposed to the remarkable Krapp, where the barrier between dramatist and character gives way, with very effective results.

Hamm stands clear, as much the central man of twentieth-century drama as Hedda Gabler is the central woman of the drama's turn into our century. This is disconcerting and should be: we have a female Iago and a dethroned king (of sorts) down to one servant who cannot sit, while he himself is blind and cannot stand. He has, in his rhetoric, delusions of identity with both Oedipus and Christ, who were seen by W. B. Yeats as both being antithetical to, and in cycle with, each other. Hamm would like to be a cruel dictator, but we are never certain whether this may not be a mere stage desire, an actor's fancy, rather than a really vicious desire. Despite the clarity of his representation, Hamm may not belong to the imitative order of representation, which would permit us ethics and psychology by which he might be both judged and analyzed. Shakespearean mimesis allows Hamlet both to play himself and to be himself; Hamm perhaps can only play himself.

Since Hamlet is his paradigm, and we think of Hamlet as a poet, how do we exclude Hamm from the category of literary artist? The question, ably expounded by Sidney Homan, disturbs me, because we have lived (as Beckett did) through an age of destructive "artists," Hamms on a giant scale: Hitler, Stalin, Mussolini. Hamm owes something to them, and more to Alfred Jarry's *Ubu Roi*. What he owes to the blind Milton and the nearly blind Joyce is unclear. Homan disconcertingly insists on Hamm as a creator, and I am afraid he is right, even when Homan carries it to the point of invoking Shakespeare: "Hamm's lot, the playwright's lot—and the very condition about which Shakespeare complains in his Sonnets—is to express everything, to prostitute inner emotions before an audience." This again separates Hamm from Beckett, who refuses to be that Shakespearean a playwright. But whose play is it anyway, Beckett's or Hamm's—or, to state the point most harshly, Beckett's or Shakespeare's? Joyce quoted the elder Dumas as saying that, after God, Shakespeare had created most. Is not *Endgame* part of Shakespeare's creation?

Ancient Gnosticism, the most negative of heretical theologies, featured a false creator, the Demiurge (a parody of Plato's artisan in the *Timaeus*) whose blunders made Fall and Creation a single, simultaneous event. Palpably, as many critics have shown, the Biblical reference of *Endgame* is the story of Noah and his son

Ham, who was cursed for witnessing the Primal Scene reenacted between his father and his mother, perhaps indeed for a more serious outrage against Noah. We do not know (because Beckett won't tell us) whether Hamm's blindness was caused by this Oedipal curse, nor can we say how relevant Noah and the Flood are to *Endgame*. To the Gnostics (as I think Beckett knew) the Flood was the work of the Demiurge, the Hamm-like false creator, who desired to destroy all life: human, animal, natural. Borges, in his early story "Death and the Compass," remarks that, to the Gnostics, mirrors and fathers were alike abominable, because they multiplied the numbers of men. That is very much the Macbeth-like stance of Hamm, who dreads the surviving boy seen outside the window as a "potential procreator."

Clov, like Horatio, represents the audience, mediating Hamm and Hamlet for us. *Endgame* must close if Clov leaves, but though he declares his departure he still stands there silently, dressed for the road, staring at Hamm as the curtain comes down. Evidently Clov does not leave, and more than the handkerchief—"Old stancher!"—and the audience remain with Hamm. Caliban and Prospero prove finally to be inseparable, because they are adopted son and adoptive father-teacher, and the audience is left uncertain whether Clov can separate from Hamm. Horatio, in what I always find the most surprising moment in *Hamlet,* wishes to attempt suicide when he recognizes that Hamlet is dying. Hamlet, with astonishing fury and force, considering his repetition of "I am dead," wrests the poison away from Horatio, not out of affection, but so that Horatio will survive to tell Hamlet's story to Fortinbras and the other survivors. Hamm does not need Clov to tell his chronicle, and I rather doubt that the boy seen outside is going to replace Clov, as some critics have suggested.

Nothing in *Endgame* is more problematical than the Hamm–Clov relationship; to call it a variant on Hegelian master–slave dialectics is rather unhelpful. If you amalgamate Hamlet-Horatio with Prospero-Caliban, you are bound to have a volatile, contradictory mix. Since Hamm is the maker, Clov can only be a creation, and Clov is very unfond of the rest of the creation. Beckett famously said of *Endgame* that it was "Rather difficult and elliptic, mostly depending on the power of the text to claw, more inhuman than *Godot.*" The entire play is an ellipsis, and what it deliberately leaves out is any foregrounding, unlike *Godot.* Shakespeare always practices an art of foregrounding, without which we could never understand Hal's turn against Falstaff, which precedes the opening of *Henry IV, Part One,* or why the Fool bitterly pushes Lear into madness. Beckett refuses us any foreground, but if I am at all meaningful when I credit Shakespeare as the coauthor of *Endgame,* it ought to be possible to surmise the foreground of this amazing and canonical drama.

Adorno interpreted *Endgame* as an agon between consciousness and death. Kenner saw the play as carrying the conviction of despair. Neither of these judgments feels right to me; anxious expectations dominate, and anxiety is neither despair nor a wrestling with death. Freud notes that anxiety is a reaction to the danger of object loss, and Hamm fears the loss of Clov. I like Freud's observation that anxiety is only a perception, but a perception of the possibility of anxiety. While you wait for Godot, you are in the *kenoma;* the foreground for *Endgame* is *Godot,* and we are back in the *kenoma,* a dry flood, a vastation into emptiness. When Hamlet cries out against Rosencrantz and Guildenstern, he sets the stage for the endgame of his revenge against himself: "O God, I could be bounded in a nutshell, and count myself a king of infinite space—were it not that I have bad dreams." Here is existence in the nutshell, in the entropy of Hamlet's consciousness:

> HAMM:
> Go and get the oilcan.
> CLOV:
> What for?
> HAMM:
> To oil the castors.
> CLOV:
> I oiled them yesterday.
> HAMM:
> Yesterday! What does that mean? Yesterday!
> CLOV (*violently*):
> That means that bloody awful day, long ago, before this bloody

awful day. I use the words you taught me. If they don't mean anything any more, teach me others. Or let me be silent.
(Pause.)

HAMM:

I once knew a madman who thought the end of the world had come. He was a painter—and engraver. I had a great fondness for him. I used to go and see him, in the asylum. I'd take him by the hand and drag him to the window. Look! There! All that rising corn! And there! Look! The sails of the herring fleet! All that loveliness!
(Pause.)

He'd snatch away his hand and go back into his corner. Appalled. All he had seen was ashes.
(Pause.)

He alone had been spared.
(Pause.)

Forgotten.
(Pause.)

It appears the case is . . . was not so . . . unusual.

CLOV:

A madman? When was that?

HAMM:

Oh way back, way back, you weren't in the land of the living.

CLOV:

God be with the days!
(Pause. Hamm raises his toque.)

HAMM:

I had a great fondness for him.
(Pause. He puts on his toque again.)

He was a painter—and engraver.

CLOV:

There are so many terrible things.

HAMM:

No, no, there are not so many now.

Hamm and Clov, Prospero and Caliban, combine here as a reverse Macbeth, with the two "yesterdays" belonging to all those yesterdays that have lighted fools, the way to dusty death. Ignoring

Clov's violence, Hamm invokes a revised William Blake, who was never in an asylum but was thought a madman by many. Blake, painter and engraver, was an apocalyptic visionary, who saw through nature to the ashes of a Gnostic Creation-Fall. The crucial line, one of the most essential in the play, is Hamm saying of Blake, "He alone had been spared."

There is the Gnostic or Schopenhauerian argument of *Endgame,* insofar as it can be isolated. Hamm's perspective is now Blake's: to be spared is not to be saved, but at least you are not deceived, whether by nature or by the self. Like Lear, Hamm has lost a kingdom but gained a contempt for the appearances of an illusory world. As he proceeds toward endgame, things are not so terrible precisely because they are seen and acknowledged as being increasingly terrible. The authentic foreground of *Endgame* is some version of *King Lear,* even as what lies beyond its conclusion is likely to be a variant on *The Tempest.* In between, we are in Hamm's play, a second play within the play of *Hamlet* and a permanent epiphany of what Ruskin called "stage fire."

Endgame's coda, if it exists at all in Beckett's subsequent dramatic works, is in the biographical stage monologue, *Krapp's Last Tape* (1958). Kenner subtly finds in this work the Protestant heritage of the atheistic Beckett, who learned from Schopenhauer to distrust the will to live but could not escape the Protestant will, with its fierce emphasis on the inner light as the individual version of the candle of the Lord. Krapp is another scholar of one candle, but in a tramp version, not in an Emersonian or Stevensian guise. Watching Patrick Magee (for whom the part was written) chant Krapp in at least three separate tonalities, for three ages of man, one came to a new understanding of Beckett's aesthetic economy, a celebrated lessness that had the power to diminish itself into a fiction of infinity.

Intended as a replacement for *Act Without Words I,* to conclude a bill featuring *Endgame, Krapp's Last Tape* is almost too strong for that function, because not even *Endgame* outshines it. Presumably because it was composed for the English-speaking Magee, *Krapp's Last Tape* was Beckett's first return to an initial writing in English after twelve years. There is an aura of release in the language, and a Proustian, almost a Wordsworthian return to the personal past, to Ireland, the death of the mother, and what may have been an abandonment of a great love, presumably for his cousin, Peggy Sinclair, who had died in 1933. And yet what we hear on the tapes is revelation, the moment when Beckett's particular light broke in upon him. The gentlest and best moment recorded on the tapes is played twice, conveying the memory of a magical sexual fulfillment, but at the close we hear what I would suppose is not an irony:

> Perhaps my best years are gone. When there was a chance of happiness. But I wouldn't want them back. Not with the fire in me now. No, I wouldn't want them back.

There is nothing else like this in Beckett, early or late. Whether pathos or irony, or a mingling of the two, it is amazingly direct. As a coda to *Endgame,* the *Hamlet* of our elegiac era, it baffles the imagination. This is not Hamm, and is and is not Beckett. Whether that fire can be categorized in terms drawn from artistic tradition is not clear either. Kenner concluded one of his studies of Beckett by assuring himself, and us, that the author of the early *Proust* and the mature *Endgame* was not a believer in "the religion of art," and therefore was somehow at one with T. S. Eliot. I suppose I could worry that the New Theocrats to come might go beyond Kenner and convert Beckett posthumously, but *Endgame*'s achieved strangeness will save it from that.

PART V

CATALOGING THE CANON

23.

Elegiac Conclusion

I AM NOT presenting a "lifetime reading plan," though that phrase has now taken on an antique charm. There always will be (one hopes) incessant readers who will go on reading despite the proliferation of fresh technologies for distraction. Sometimes I try to visualize Dr. Johnson or George Eliot confronting MTV Rap or experiencing Virtual Reality and find myself heartened by what I believe would be their ironical, strong refusal of such irrational entertainments. After a lifetime spent in teaching literature at one of our major universities, I have very little confidence that literary education will survive its current malaise.

I began my teaching career nearly forty years ago in an academic context dominated by the ideas of T. S. Eliot; ideas that roused me to fury, and against which I fought as vigorously as I could. Finding myself now surrounded by professors of hip-hop; by clones of Gallic-Germanic theory; by ideologues of gender and of various sexual persuasions; by multiculturalists unlimited, I realize that the Balkanization of literary studies is irreversible. All of these

Resenters of the aesthetic value of literature are not going to go away, and they will raise up institutional resenters after them. As an aged institutional Romantic, I still decline the Eliotic nostalgia for Theocratic ideology, but I see no reason for arguing with anyone about literary preferences. This book is not directed to academics, because only a small remnant of them still read for the love of reading. What Johnson and Woolf after him called the Common Reader still exists and possibly goes on welcoming suggestions of what might be read.

Such a reader does not read for easy pleasure or to expiate social guilt, but to enlarge a solitary existence. So fantastic has the academy become that I have heard this kind of reader denounced by an eminent critic, who told me that reading without a constructive social purpose was unethical and urged me to re-educate myself through an immersion in the writing of Abdul Jan Mohammed, a leader of the Birmingham (England) school of cultural materialism. As an addict who will read anything, I obeyed, but I am not saved, and return to tell you neither what to read nor how to read it, only what I have read and think worthy of rereading, which may be the only pragmatic test for the canonical.

I suppose that once you have "cultural criticism" and "cultural materialism," you must also entertain the notion of "cultural capital." But what is the "surplus value" that has been exploited in order to accumulate "cultural capital"? Marxism, famously a cry of pain rather than a science, has had its poets, but so has every other major religious heresy. "Cultural capital" is either a metaphor or an uninteresting literalism. If the latter, it simply relates to the current marketplace of publishers, agents, and book clubs. As a figure of speech, it remains a cry partly of pain, partly of the guilt of belonging to the intellectuals spawned by the French upper middle class, or of the guilt of those in our own academies who identify with such French theorists and pragmatically have forgotten in what country they actually live and teach. Is there, has there ever been, any "cultural capital" in the United States of America? We dominate the Age of Chaos because we have always been chaotic, even in the Democratic Age. Is *Leaves of Grass* "cultural capital"? Is *Moby-Dick*? There has never been an official American literary canon, and there never can be, for the aesthetic in America always exists as a lonely, idiosyncratic, isolated stance. "American Classicism" is an oxymoron, whereas "French Classicism" is a coherent tradition.

I do not believe that literary studies as such have a future, but this does not mean that literary criticism will die. As a branch of literature, criticism will survive, but probably not in our teaching institutions. The study of Western literature will also continue, but on the much more modest scale of our current Classics departments. What are now called "Departments of English" will be renamed departments of "Cultural Studies" where *Batman* comics, Mormon theme parks, television, movies, and rock will replace Chaucer, Shakespeare, Milton, Wordsworth, and Wallace Stevens. Major, once-elitist universities and colleges will still offer a few courses in Shakespeare, Milton, and their peers, but these will be taught by departments of three or four scholars, equivalent to teachers of ancient Greek and Latin. This development hardly need be deplored; only a few handfuls of students now enter Yale with an authentic passion for reading. You cannot teach someone to love great poetry if they come to you without such love. How can you teach solitude? Real reading is a lonely activity and does not teach anyone to become a better citizen. Perhaps the ages of reading—Aristocratic, Democratic, Chaotic—now reach terminus, and the reborn Theocratic era will be almost wholly an oral and visual culture.

In the United States, "a crisis in literary study" has the same peculiarity as a religious revival (or Great Awakening) and a crime wave. They are all journalistic events. Our country has been in a perpetual religious revival for two centuries now; its addiction to civil and domestic violence is even more venerable and incessant, and in the nearly half-century since first I immersed myself in literary study, such activity has been questioned endlessly by society and generally held to be irrelevant. English and related departments have always been unable to define themselves and unwise enough to swallow up everything that seems available for ingestion.

There is a dreadful justice in such voraciousness having proved to be self-destructive: the teaching of poems, plays, stories, and novels is now supplanted by cheerleading for various social and political crusades. Or else, the artifacts of popular culture replace the difficult artifices of great writers as the material for instruction. It is not "literature" that needs to be redefined; if you can't recognize it when you read it, then no one can ever help you to know it or love it better. "A culture of universal access" is offered by post-Marxist idealists as the solution to "crisis," but how can *Paradise Lost* or *Faust, Part Two* ever lend themselves to universal access? The strongest poetry is cognitively and imaginatively too difficult to be read deeply by more than a relative few of any social class, gender, race, or ethnic origin.

When I was a boy, Shakespeare's *Julius Caesar,* almost universally part of the school curriculum, was an eminently sensible introduction to Shakespearean tragedy. Teachers now tell me of many schools where the play can no longer be read through, since students find it beyond their attention spans. In two places reported to me, the making of cardboard shields and swords has replaced the reading and discussion of the play. No socializing of the means of production and consumption of literature can overcome such debasement of early education. The morality of scholarship, as currently practiced, is to encourage everyone to replace difficult pleasures by pleasures universally accessible precisely because they are easier. Trotsky urged his fellow Marxists to read Dante, but he would find no welcome in our current universities.

I am your true Marxist critic, following Groucho rather than Karl, and take as my motto Groucho's grand admonition, "Whatever it is, I'm against it!" I have been against, in turn, the neo-Christian New Criticism of T. S. Eliot and his academic followers; the deconstruction of Paul de Man and his clones; the current rampages of New Left and Old Right on the supposed inequities, and even more dubious moralities, of the literary Canon. The very rare, strong critics do not extend or modify or revise the Canon, though they certainly attempt to do so. But, knowingly or not, they only ratify the true work of canonization, which is carried on by the perpetual agon between past and present. There is no socioeconomic process that has added John Ashbery and James Merrill, or Thomas Pynchon, to the vague, nonexistent, and yet still compelling notion of an American canon that yet may be. The poetry of Wallace Stevens and of Elizabeth Bishop has chosen its inheritors in Ashbery and Merrill, even as the poetry of Emily Dickinson selected Stevens and Bishop. Pynchon's best work can be said to marry S. J. Perelman and Nathanael West, but the canonical potential of *The Crying of Lot 49* depends more on our uncanny sense that it is being imitated by *Miss Lonelyhearts*.

Shakespeare and Dante are invariably the exceptions to the descents of canonicity; we never come to believe that they have read too deeply in Joyce and in Beckett, or in anyone else. That is another way of repeating what I have been moved to say throughout this book: the Western Canon *is* Shakespeare and Dante. Beyond them, it is what they absorbed and what absorbs them. Redefining "literature" is a vain pursuit because you cannot usurp sufficient cognitive strength to encompass Shakespeare and Dante, and they are literature. As for redefining them, good fortune to you. That enterprise is now considerably advanced by "the New Historicism," which is French Shakespeare, with Hamlet under the shadow of Michel Foucault. We have enjoyed French Freud or Lacan, and French Joyce or Derrida. Jewish Freud and Irish Joyce are more to my taste, as is English Shakespeare or universal Shakespeare. French Shakespeare is so delicious an absurdity that one feels an ingrate for not appreciating so comic an invention.

Precisely why students of literature have become amateur political scientists, uninformed sociologists, incompetent anthropologists, mediocre philosophers, and overdetermined cultural historians, while a puzzling matter, is not beyond all conjecture. They resent literature, or are ashamed of it, or are just not all that fond of reading it. Reading a poem or a novel or a Shakepearean tragedy is for them an exercise in contextualization, but not in a merely reasonable sense of finding adequate backgrounds. The contexts, however chosen, are assigned more force and value than the poem by Milton, the novel by Dickens, or *Macbeth*. I am not at all certain what the metaphor of "social energies" stands or substitutes for, but, like the Freudian drives, such energies cannot write or read or indeed do anything at all. Libido is a myth, and so are "social energies." Shakespeare, scandalously facile, was an actual person who contrived to write *Hamlet* and *King Lear*. That scandal is unacceptable to what now passes for literary theory.

Either there were aesthetic values, or there are only the over-determinations of race, class, and gender. You must choose, for if you believe that all value ascribed to poems or plays or novels and stories is only a mystification in the service of the ruling class, then why should you read at all rather than go forth to serve the desperate needs of the exploited classes? The idea that you benefit the insulted and injured by reading someone of their own origins rather than reading Shakespeare is one of the oddest illusions ever promoted by or in our schools.

The deepest truth about secular canon-formation is that it is performed by neither critics nor academies, let alone politicians. Writers, artists, composers themselves determine canons, by bridging between strong precursors and strong successors. Let us take the most vital contemporary American authors, the poets Ashbery and Merrill and the prose writer of epic fictions, Pynchon. I am moved to pronounce them canonical, but one cannot altogether know as yet. Canonical prophecy needs to be tested about two generations after a writer dies. Wallace Stevens, who lived from 1879 to 1955, is clearly a canonical poet, perhaps the major American poet after Walt Whitman and Emily Dickinson. His only rivals appear to be Robert Frost and T. S. Eliot; Pound and William Carlos Williams are more problematic, together with Marianne Moore and Gertrude Stein (when considered strictly for her verse), and Hart Crane died too soon. Stevens helped engender Merrill and Ashbery as well as Elizabeth Bishop, A. R. Ammons, and others of real achievement. But it is too soon to know if enduring poets are emerging from *their* influence, though I myself so believe. When one or more very clearly has emerged, that will help confirm Stevens, but not as yet Merrill or Ashbery, at least not to the same degree.

It is a curious process, and I tend to challenge my own sense of it by asking: What about Yeats? The Anglo-Irish poets after him are enormously wary of his influence and seem to have fought him off. The answer again is that it takes some time even to *see* influence accurately. Yeats died in 1939; after more than half a century, I can see his influence upon those who denied it, Eliot and Stevens; and their influence has been fecund, as in their joint effect upon Hart Crane, whose idiosyncratic accent, though disputed, floats almost everywhere. Eliot and Stevens had cultural stances fiercely opposed to one another, while Crane's relation to Eliot in particular was almost wholly antithetical. But sociopolitical considerations can be turned inside out by canon-producing influence relations. Crane rejected Eliot's vision but could not evade Eliot's idiom. Great styles are sufficient for canonicity because they possess the power of contamination, and contamination is the pragmatic test for canon formation.

Immerse yourself, say for several days together, in reading Shakespeare and then turn to another author—before, after, or contemporary with him. For experiment, try only the highest in each grouping: Homer or Dante, Cervantes or Ben Jonson, Tolstoy or Proust. The difference in the reading experience will be one of kind as well as of degree. That difference, universally felt from Shakespeare's time until now, is expressed alike by ordinary and sophisticated readers as having something to do with our sense of what we want to call "natural." Dr. Johnson assured us that nothing could please for long except just representations of general nature. That assurance still seems unassailable to me, though much of what is now exalted each week could not pass the Johnsonian test. Shakespearean representation, its supposed imitation of what is held to be most essential in us, has been felt to be more natural than anyone else's mirroring of reality ever since the plays were first staged. To go from Shakespeare to Dante or Cervantes or even Tolstoy is somehow to have the illusion of suffering a loss in sensuous immediacy. We look back at Shakespeare and regret our absence from him because it seems an absence from reality.

The motives for reading, as for writing, are very diverse and frequently not clear even to the most self-conscious readers or writers. Perhaps the ultimate motive for metaphor, or the writing and reading of figurative language, is the desire to be different, to be elsewhere. In this assertion I follow Nietzsche, who warned us that what we can find words for is already dead in our hearts, so that there is always a kind of contempt in the act of speaking. Hamlet agrees with Nietzsche, and both might have extended the contempt to the act of writing. But we do not read to unpack our hearts, so there is no contempt in the act of reading. Traditions tell us that the free and solitary self writes in order to overcome mortality. I think that the self, in its quest to be free and solitary, ultimately reads with one aim only: to confront greatness. That confrontation scarcely masks the desire to join greatness, which is the basis of the aesthetic experience once called the Sublime: the quest for a transcendence of limits. Our common fate is age, sickness, death, oblivion. Our common hope, tenuous but persistent, is for some version of survival.

Confronting greatness as we read is an intimate and expensive process and has never been much in critical vogue. Now, more than ever, it is out of fashion, when the quest for freedom and solitude is being condemned as politically incorrect, selfish, and not appropriate to our anguished society. Greatness in the West's literature centers upon Shakespeare, who has become the touchstone for all who come before and after him, whether they are dramatists, lyric poets, or storytellers. He had no true precursor in the creation of character, except for Chaucerian hints, and has left no one after him untouched by his ways of representing human nature. His originality was and is so easy to assimilate that we are disarmed by it and unable to see how much it has changed us and goes on changing us. Much of Western literature after Shakespeare is, in varying degree, partly a defense against Shakespeare, who can be so overwhelming an influence as to drown out all who are compelled to be his students.

The enigma of Shakespeare is his universalism: Kurosawa's film versions of *Macbeth* and *King Lear* are thoroughly Kurosawa and thoroughly Shakespeare. Even if you regard Shakespearean personages as roles for actors rather than as dramatic characters, you are still unable to account for the human persuasiveness of Hamlet or Cleopatra when you compare them to the roles provided by Ibsen, surely the principal post-Shakespearean dramatist that Europe has brought forth. When we move from Hamlet to Peer Gynt, from Cleopatra to Hedda Gabler, we sense that personality has waned, that the Shakespearean daemonic has ebbed into the Ibsenite trollishness. The miracle of Shakespeare's universalism is that it is not purchased by any transcending of contingencies: the great characters and their plays accept being embedded in history and in society, while refusing every mode of reduction: historical, societal, theological, or our belated psychologizings and moralizings.

Falstaff possesses most of the squalid flaws that scholars, following Hal's lead, find in him, but Falstaff, at once great wit, powerful thinker, and true humorist, nevertheless matches Hamlet as an original consciousness. It is inadequate to say of Falstaff that he provides a magnificent role; he is a cosmos, not an ornament, and holds up the mirror not so much to nature as to our outermost capacity for fresh life. Blake said that exuberance was beauty, and by such an equation no other dramatic character is as beautiful as Sir John Falstaff. The exuberance of Rabelais' Giant Forms is matched by Sir John, who must perform within the confines of a stage while Panurge surges across a visionary France. What William Hazlitt named *gusto,* "power or passion defining any object," and found foremost in Shakespeare, he assigned to Boccaccio and Rabelais above all other prose writers. Hazlitt also urged us to realize that the arts are not progressive—a realization that belated ages, like our own, attempt to resist.

What use can it be for an individual critic, so belated in the tradition, to catalog the Western Canon as he sees it? Even our elite universities now are supine before oncoming waves of multiculturalists. Still, even if our current fashions prevail forever, canonical choices of both past and present works have their own interest and charm, for they too are part of the ongoing contest that is literature. Everyone has, or should have, a desert island list against that day when, fleeing one's enemies, one is cast ashore, or when one limps away, all warfare done, to pass the rest of one's time quietly reading. If I could have one book, it would be a complete Shakespeare; if two, that and a Bible. If three? There the complexities begin. William Hazlitt, one of the few critics definitively in the Canon, has a splendid essay, "On Reading Old Books":

I do not think altogether the worse of a book for having survived the author a generation or two. I have more confidence in the dead than the living. Contemporary writers may generally be divided into two classes—one's friends or one's foes. Of the first we are compelled to think too well, and of the last we are disposed to think too ill, to receive much pleasure from the perusal, or to judge fairly the merits of either.

Hazlitt expresses a wariness proper to the critic in an age of gathering belatedness. The overpopulation of books (and authors) brought about by the length and complexity of the world's recorded history is at the center of canonical dilemmas, now more than ever. "What shall I read?" is no longer the question, since so few now read, in the era of television and cinema. The pragmatic question has become: "What shall I not bother to read?"

As soon as one accepts any part of the dogma of the School of Resentment and admits that aesthetic choices are masks for social and political overdeterminations, such questions quickly become easily answerable. By a variant on Gresham's Law, bad writing drives out good, and social change is served by Alice Walker rather than by any author of more talent and disciplined imagination. But where will the social changers find the guidelines for *their* choices? Politics, to our common sorrow, rapidly stales like last month's newspaper and only rarely remains news. Perhaps literary politics are always at work, but political stances have little effect in the strangely intimate family romance of the great writers, who are influenced by one another without much regard for political resemblances and differences.

Literary influence is "the politics of the spirit": canon formation, even if it necessarily always reflects class interests, is a highly ambivalent phenomenon. Milton, rather than the two greatest English poets—Chaucer and Shakespeare—is the central figure in the history of the Anglo-American poetic canon. In the same way, the crucial early writer in the history of the entire Western literary Canon is not one of the greatest poets—Homer, Dante, Chaucer, and Shakespeare—but Virgil, the great link between Hellenistic poetry (Callimachus) and the European epic tradition (Dante, Tasso, Spenser, Milton). Virgil and Milton remain poets who provoke immense ambivalences in those who come after them, and those ambivalences define centrality in a canonical context. A canon, despite its idealizers from Ezra the Scribe through the late Northrop Frye, does not exist in order to free its readers from anxiety. Indeed, a canon is an *achieved anxiety,* just as any strong literary work is its author's achieved anxiety. The literary canon does not baptize us into culture; it does not make us free of cultural anxiety. Rather, it confirms our cultural anxieties, yet helps to give them form and coherence.

Ideology plays a considerable role in literary canon-formation if you want to insist that an aesthetic stance is itself an ideology, an insistence that is common to all six branches of the School of Resentment: Feminists, Marxists, Lacanians, New Historicists, Deconstructionists, Semioticians. There are, of course, aesthetics and aesthetics, and apostles who believe that literary study should be an overt crusade for social change obviously manifest a different aesthetic from my own post-Emersonian version of Pater and Wilde. Whether this is a difference that makes a difference is unclear to me: the social changers and I seem to agree on the canonical status of Pynchon, Merrill, and Ashbery as the three American presences of our moment. The Resenters throw in alternative canonical candidates, African-American and female, but not very wholeheartedly.

If literary canons are the product only of class, racial, gender, and national interests, presumably the same should be true of all other aesthetic traditions, including music and the visual arts. Matisse and Stravinsky can then go down with Joyce and Proust as four more dead white European males. I gaze in wonder at the crowds of New Yorkers at the Matisse exhibition: are they truly there because of societal overconditioning? When the School of Resentment becomes as dominant among art historians and critics as it is among literary academics, will Matisse go unattended while we all flock to view the daubings of the Guerrilla Girls? The lunacy of these questions is plain enough when it comes to the eminence of Matisse, while Stravinsky is clearly in no danger of being replaced by politically correct music for the ballet companies of the world. Why then is literature so vulnerable to the onrush of our contemporary social idealists? One answer seems to be the common illusion that less knowledge and less technical skill is required for either the production or the comprehension of imaginative literature (as we used to call it) than for the other arts.

If we all talked in musical notes or in brush strokes, I suppose Stravinsky and Matisse might be subject to the peculiar hazards now suffered by canonical authors. Attempting to read many of the works set forth as resentment's alternatives to the Canon, I reflect that these aspirants must believe they have spoken prose all their lives, or else that their sincere passions are already poems, requiring only a little overwriting. I turn to my lists, hoping that literate survivors will find some authors and books among them that they have not yet encountered and will garner the rewards that only canonical literature affords.

APPENDIXES

A.

The Theocratic Age

Here, as in the following lists, I suggest translations wherever I have derived particular pleasure and insight from those now readily available. There are many valuable works of ancient Greek and Latin literature that are not here, but the common reader is unlikely to have time to read them. As history lengthens, the older canon necessarily narrows. Since the literary canon is at issue here, I include only those religious, philosophical, historical, and scientific writings that are themselves of great aesthetic interest. I would think that, of all the books in this first list, once the reader is conversant with the Bible, Homer, Plato, the Athenian dramatists, and Virgil, the crucial work is the Koran. Whether for its aesthetic and spiritual power or the influence it will have upon all of our futures, ignorance of the Koran is foolish and increasingly dangerous.

I have included some Sanskrit works, scriptures and fundamental literary texts, because of their influence on the Western Canon. The immense wealth of ancient Chinese literature is mostly a sphere apart from Western literary tradition and is rarely conveyed adequately in the translations available to us.

THE ANCIENT NEAR EAST
Gilgamesh, translated by David Ferry
The Egyptian Book of the Dead
The Holy Bible, *Authorized King James Version*
The Apocrypha
Sayings of the Fathers (Pirke Aboth), translated by R. Travers Herford

ANCIENT INDIA (SANSKRIT)
The Mahabharata
There is an abridged translation by William Buck, and a dramatic version by Jean-Claude Carrière, translated by Peter Brook
The Bhagavad-Gita
The crucial religious section of *Mahabharata,* Book 6, translated by Barbara Stoler Miller
The Ramayana
There is an abridged prose version by William Buck, and a retelling by R. K. Narayan

THE ANCIENT GREEKS
Homer
The Iliad, translated by Richmond Lattimore
The Odyssey, translated by Robert Fitzgerald
Hesiod
The Works and Days; Theogony, translated by Richmond Lattimore

Archilochos, Sappho, Alkman
translated by Guy Davenport

Pindar
The Odes, translated by
Richmond Lattimore

Aeschylus
The Oresteia, translated by
Robert Fagles
Seven against Thebes, translated
by Anthony Hecht and Helen
H. Bacon
Prometheus Bound
The Persians
The Suppliant Women

Sophocles
Oedipus the King, translated by
Stephen Berg and Diskin Clay
Oedipus at Colonus, translated
by Robert Fitzgerald
Antigone, translated by Robert
Fagles
Electra
Ajax
Women of Trachis
Philoctetes

Euripides
(translated by William
Arrowsmith)
Cyclops
Heracles
Alcestis
Hecuba
The Bacchae
Orestes
Andromache
Medea, translated by Rex
Warner
Ion, translated by H. D. (Hilda
Doolittle)
Hippolytus, translated by Robert
Bagg
Helen, translated by Richmond
Lattimore
Iphigeneia at Aulis, translated by
W. S. Merwin and George
Dimock

Aristophanes
The Birds, translated by William
Arrowsmith
The Clouds, translated by
William Arrowsmith
The Frogs
Lysistrata
The Knights
The Wasps
The Assemblywomen (also called
The Parliament of Women)

Herodotus
The Histories

Thucydides
The Peloponnesian War

**The Pre-Socratics (Heraclitus,
Empedocles)**

Plato
Dialogues

Aristotle
Poetics
Ethics

HELLENISTIC GREEKS

Menander
The Girl from Samos, translated
by Eric G. Turner

"Longinus"
On the Sublime

Callimachus
Hymns and *Epigrams*

Theocritus
Idylls, translated by Daryl Hine

Plutarch
Lives, translated by John Dryden
Moralia

"Aesop"
Fables

Lucian
Satires

THE ROMANS

Plautus
Pseudolus
The Braggart Soldier
The Rope
Amphitryon

Terence
The Girl from Andros
The Eunuch
The Mother-in-Law

Lucretius
The Way Things Are, translated
by Rolfe Humphries

Cicero
On the Gods

Horace
Odes, translated by James
Michie
Epistles
Satires

Persius
Satires, translated by W. S.
Merwin

Catullus
Attis, translated by Horace
Gregory
Other poems translated by
Richard Crashaw, Abraham
Cowley, Walter Savage Landor,
and a host of English poets

Virgil
The Aeneid, translated by
Robert Fitzgerald
Eclogues and *Georgics,*
translated by John Dryden

Lucan
Pharsalia

Ovid
Metamorphoses, translated by
George Sandys
The Art of Love
Epistulae heroidum or *Heroides,*
translated by Daryl Hine

Juvenal
Satires

Martial
Epigrams, translated by James
Michie

Seneca
Tragedies, particularly *Medea;*
and *Hercules furens,* as
translated by Thomas
Heywood

Petronius
Satyricon, translated by William
Arrowsmith

Apuleius
The Golden Ass, translated by
Robert Graves

THE MIDDLE AGES: LATIN, ARABIC, AND THE VERNACULAR BEFORE DANTE

Saint Augustine
The City of God
The Confessions

The Koran
*Al-Qur'an: A Contemporary
Translation* by Ahmad Ali
*The Book of the Thousand Nights
and One Night*
The Poetic Edda, translated by Lee
Hollander

Snorri Sturluson
The Prose Edda

The Nibelungen Lied

Wolfram von Eschenbach
Parzival

Chrétien de Troyes
Yvain: The Knight of the Lion,
translated by Burton Raffel
Beowulf, translated by Charles W.
Kennedy
The Poem of the Cid, translated by
W. S. Merwin

Christine de Pisan
The Book of the City of Ladies,
translated by Earl Richards

Diego de San Pedro
Prison of Love

B.

The Aristocratic Age

It is a span of five hundred years from Dante's *Divine Comedy* through Goethe's *Faust, Part Two,* an era that gives us a huge body of reading in five major literatures: Italian, Spanish, English, French, and German. In this and in the remaining lists, I sometimes do not mention individual works by a canonical master, and in other instances I attempt to call attention to authors and books that I consider canonical but rather neglected. From this list onward, many good writers who are not quite central are omitted. We begin also to encounter the phenomenon of "period pieces," a sorrow that expands in the Democratic Age and threatens to choke us in our own century. Writers much esteemed in their own time and country sometimes survive in other times and nations, yet often shrink into once-fashionable fetishes. I behold at least several scores of these in our contemporary literary scene, but it is sufficient to name them by omission, and I will address this matter more fully in the introductory note to my final list.

ITALY

Dante
  The Divine Comedy, translated
    by Laurence Binyon in terza
    rima, and by John D. Sinclair
    in prose
  The New Life, translated by
    Dante Gabriel Rossetti

Petrarch
  Lyric Poems, translated by
    Robert M. Durling
  Selections, translated by Mark
    Musa

Giovanni Boccaccio
  The Decameron

Matteo Maria Boiardo
  Orlando innamorato

Ludovico Ariosto
  Orlando furioso

Michelangelo Buonarroti
  Sonnets and Madrigals,
    translated by Wordsworth,
    Longfellow, Emerson,
    Santayana, and others

Niccolò Machiavelli
  The Prince
  The Mandrake, a Comedy

Leonardo da Vinci
  Notebooks

Baldassare Castiglione
  The Book of the Courtier

Gaspara Stampa
  Sonnets and *Madrigals*

Giorgio Vasari
  Lives of the Painters

Benvenuto Cellini
  Autobiography

Torquato Tasso
Jerusalem Delivered

Giordano Bruno
The Expulsion of the Triumphant Beast

Tommaso Campanella
Poems
The City of the Sun

Giambattista Vico
Principles of a New Science

Carlo Goldoni
The Servant of Two Masters

Vittorio Alfieri
Saul

PORTUGAL

Luis de Camoëns
The Lusiads, translated by Leonard Bacon

António Ferreira
Poetry, in *The Muse Reborn*, translated by T. F. Earle

SPAIN

Jorge Manrique
Coplas, translated by Henry Wadsworth Longfellow

Fernando de Rojas
La Celestina, translated by James Mabbe, adapted by Eric Bentley

Lazarillo de Tormes, translated by W. S. Merwin

Francisco de Quevedo
Visions, translated by Roger L'Estrange
Satirical Letter of Censure, in J. M. Cohen's *Penguin Book of Spanish Verse*

Fray Luis de León
Poems, translated by Willis Barnstone

St. John of the Cross
Poems, translated by John Frederick Nims

Luis de Góngora
Sonnets
Soledades

Miguel de Cervantes
Don Quixote, translated by Samuel Putnam
Exemplary Stories

Lope de Vega
La Dorotea, translated by Alan S. Trueblood and Edwin Honig
Fuente ovejuna, translated by Roy Campbell
Lost in a Mirror, translated by Adrian Mitchell
The Knight of Olmedo, translated by Willard F. King

Tirso de Molina
The Trickster of Seville, translated by Roy Campbell

Pedro Calderón de la Barca
Life Is a Dream, translated by Roy Campbell
The Mayor of Zalamea
The Mighty Magician
The Doctor of His Own Honor

Sor Juana Inés de la Cruz
Poems

ENGLAND AND SCOTLAND

Geoffrey Chaucer
The Canterbury Tales
Troilus and Criseyde

Sir Thomas Malory
Le Morte D'Arthur

William Dunbar
Poems

John Skelton
Poems

Sir Thomas More
Utopia

Sir Thomas Wyatt
Poems

Henry Howard, Earl of Surrey
Poems

Sir Philip Sidney
*The Countess of Pembroke's
    Arcadia*
Astrophel and Stella
An Apology for Poetry

Fulke Greville, Lord Brooke
Poems

Edmund Spenser
The Faerie Queene
The Minor Poems

Sir Walter Ralegh
Poems

Christopher Marlowe
Poems and *Plays*

Michael Drayton
Poems

Samuel Daniel
Poems
A Defence of Ryme

Thomas Nashe
The Unfortunate Traveller

Thomas Kyd
The Spanish Tragedy

William Shakespeare
Plays and *Poems*

Thomas Campion
Songs

John Donne
Poems
Sermons

Ben Jonson
Poems, Plays, and *Masques*

Francis Bacon
Essays

Robert Burton
The Anatomy of Melancholy

Sir Thomas Browne
Religio Medici
Hydriotaphia, or Urne-Buriall
The Garden of Cyrus

Thomas Hobbes
Leviathan

Robert Herrick
Poems

Thomas Carew
Poems

Richard Lovelace
Poems

Andrew Marvell
Poems

George Herbert
The Temple

Thomas Traherne
Centuries, Poems, and
    Thanksgivings

Henry Vaughan
Poetry

John Wilmot, Earl of Rochester
Poems

Richard Crashaw
Poems

**Francis Beaumont and
John Fletcher**
Plays

George Chapman
Comedies, Tragedies, Poems

John Ford
'Tis Pity She's a Whore

John Marston
The Malcontent

John Webster
The White Devil
The Duchess of Malfi

**Thomas Middleton and
William Rowley**
The Changeling

Cyril Tourneur
The Revenger's Tragedy

Philip Massinger
A New Way to Pay Old Debts

John Bunyan
The Pilgrim's Progress

Izaak Walton
The Compleat Angler

John Milton
Paradise Lost
Paradise Regained
Lycidas, Comus, and the *Minor Poems*
Samson Agonistes
Areopagitica

John Aubrey
Brief Lives

Jeremy Taylor
Holy Dying

Samuel Butler
Hudibras

John Dryden
Poetry and Plays
Critical Essays

Thomas Otway
Venice Preserv'd

William Congreve
The Way of the World
Love for Love

Jonathan Swift
A Tale of a Tub
Gulliver's Travels
Shorter Prose Works
Poems

Sir George Etherege
The Man of Mode

Alexander Pope
Poems

John Gay
The Beggar's Opera

James Boswell
Life of Johnson
Journals

Samuel Johnson
Works

Edward Gibbon
The History of the Decline and Fall of the Roman Empire

Edmund Burke
A Philosophical Enquiry into . . . the Sublime and Beautiful
Reflections on the Revolution in France

Maurice Morgann
An Essay on the Dramatic Character of Sir John Falstaff

William Collins
Poems

Thomas Gray
Poems

George Farquhar
The Beaux' Stratagem
The Recruiting Officer

William Wycherley
The Country Wife
The Plain Dealer

Christopher Smart
Jubilate Agno
A Song to David

Oliver Goldsmith
The Vicar of Wakefield
She Stoops to Conquer
The Traveller
The Deserted Village

Richard Brinsley Sheridan
The School for Scandal
The Rivals

William Cowper
Poetical Works

George Crabbe
Poetical Works

Daniel Defoe
Moll Flanders
Robinson Crusoe
A Journal of the Plague Year

Samuel Richardson
Clarissa
Pamela
Sir Charles Grandison

Henry Fielding
Joseph Andrews
*The History of Tom Jones, a
Foundling*

Tobias Smollett
*The Expedition of Humphry
Clinker*
*The Adventures of Roderick
Random*

Laurence Sterne
*The Life and Opinions of
Tristram Shandy, Gentleman*
*A Sentimental Journey through
France and Italy*

Fanny Burney
Evelina

Joseph Addison and **Richard Steele**
The Spectator

FRANCE

Jean Froissart
Chronicles

The Song of Roland

François Villon
Poems, translated by Galway
Kinnell

Michel de Montaigne
Essays, translated by Donald
Frame

François Rabelais
Gargantua and Pantagruel,
translated by Donald Frame

Marguerite de Navarre
The Heptameron

Joachim Du Bellay
The Regrets, translated by
C. H. Sisson

Maurice Scève
Délie

Pierre de Ronsard
Odes, Elegies, Sonnets

Philippe de Commynes
Memoirs

Agrippa d'Aubigné
Les Tragiques

Robert Garnier
Mark Antony, translated by
Mary (Sidney) Herbert,
Countess of Pembroke
The Jewesses

Pierre Corneille
The Cid
Polyeucte
Nicomède
Horace
Cinna
Rodogune

François de La Rochefoucauld
Maxims

Jean de La Fontaine
Fables

Molière
(translated by Richard Wilbur)
The Misanthrope
Tartuffe
The School for Wives
The Learned Ladies
(translated by Donald Frame)
Don Juan
School for Husbands
Ridiculous Precieuses
The Would-Be Gentleman
The Miser
The Imaginary Invalid

Blaise Pascal
Pensées

Jacques-Bénigne Bossuet
Funerary Orations

Nicolas Boileau-Despréaux
The Art of Poetry
Lutrin

Jean Racine
(translated by Richard Wilbur)
Phaedra
Andromache
(translated by C. H. Sisson)
Britannicus
Athaliah

Pierre Carlet de Marivaux
Seven Comedies

Jean-Jacques Rousseau
The Confessions
Émile
La Nouvelle Héloïse

Voltaire
Zadig
Candide
Letters on England
The Lisbon Earthquake

Abbé Prévost
Manon Lescaut, translated by
Donald Frame

Madame de La Fayette
The Princess of Clèves

Sébastien-Roch Nicolas de Chamfort
*Products of the Perfected
Civilization,* translated by
W. S. Merwin

Denis Diderot
Rameau's Nephew

Choderlos de Laclos
Dangerous Liaisons

GERMANY
Erasmus, a Dutchman living in
Switzerland and Germany,
while writing in Latin, is
placed here arbitrarily, but
also as an influence on the
Lutheran Reformation.

Erasmus
In Praise of Folly

Johann Wolfgang von Goethe
Faust, Parts One and Two,
translated by Stuart Atkins
Dichtung und Wahrheit

Egmont, translated by Willard
Trask
Elective Affinities
The Sorrows of Young Werther,
translated by Louise Bogan,
Elizabeth Mayer, and W. H.
Auden
Poems, translated by Michael
Hamburger, Christopher
Middleton, and others
*Wilhelm Meister's
Apprenticeship*
*Wilhelm Meister's Years of
Wandering*
Italian Journey
Verse Plays and *Hermann and
Dorothea,* translated by
Michael Hamburger and
others
*Roman Elegies, Venetian
Epigrams, West-Eastern
Divan,* translated by Michael
Hamburger

Friedrich Schiller
The Robbers
Mary Stuart
Wallenstein
Don Carlos
*On the Naïve and Sentimental
in Literature*

Gotthold Lessing
Laocoön
Nathan the Wise

Friedrich Hölderlin
Hymns and Fragments,
translated by Richard Sieburth
Selected Poems, translated by
Michael Hamburger

Heinrich von Kleist
Five Plays, translated by Martin
Greenberg
Stories

C.

The Democratic Age

I have located Vico's Democratic Age in the post-Goethean nineteenth century, when the literature of Italy and Spain ebbs, yielding eminence to England with its renaissance of the Renaissance in Romanticism, and to a lesser degree to France and Germany. This is also the era where the strength of both Russian and American literature begins. I have resisted the backward reach of the current canonical crusades, which attempt to elevate a number of sadly inadequate women writers of the nineteenth century, as well as some rudimentary narratives and verses of African-Americans. Expanding the Canon, as I have said more than once in this book, tends to drive out the better writers, sometimes even the best, because pragmatically none of us (whoever we are) ever had time to read absolutely everything, no matter how great our lust for reading. And for most of us, the harried young in particular, inadequate authors will consume the energies that would be better invested in stronger writers. Nearly everything that has been revived or discovered by Feminist and African-American literary scholars falls all too precisely into the category of "period pieces," as imaginatively dated now as they were already enfeebled when they first came into existence.

ITALY

Ugo Foscolo
On Sepulchres, translated by
    Thomas G. Bergin
Last Letters of Jacopo Ortis
Odes and The Graces

Alessandro Manzoni
The Betrothed
On the Historical Novel

Giacomo Leopardi
Essays and Dialogues, translated
    by Giovanni Cecchetti
Poems
The Moral Essays, translated by
    Howard Norse

Giuseppe Gioacchino Belli
Roman Sonnets, translated by
    Harold Norse

Giosuè Carducci
Hymn to Satan
Barbarian Odes
Rhymes and Rhythms

Giovanni Verga
Little Novels of Sicily, translated
    by D. H. Lawrence
Mastro-Don Gesualdo,
    translated by D. H. Lawrence
The House by the Medlar Tree,
    translated by Raymond
    Rosenthal
The She-Wolf and Other Stories,
    translated by Giovanni
    Cecchetti

SPAIN and PORTUGAL

Gustavo Adolfo Bécquer
Poems

Benito Pérez Galdós
Fortunata and Jacinta

Leopoldo Alas (Clarín)
La Regenta

José Maria de Eça de Queirós
The Maias

FRANCE

Benjamin Constant
Adolphe
The Red Notebook

François-Auguste-René de Chateaubriand
Atala and René, translated by
Irving Putter
The Genius of Christianity

Alphonse de Lamartine
Meditations

Alfred de Vigny
Chatterton
Poems

Victor Hugo
The Distance, The Shadows:
Selected Poems, translated by
Harry Guest
Les Misérables
Notre-Dame of Paris
William Shakespeare
The Toilers of the Sea
The End of Satan
God

Alfred de Musset
Poems
Lorenzaccio

Gérard de Nerval
The Chimeras, translated by
Peter Jay
Sylvie
Aurelia

Théophile Gautier
Mademoiselle de Maupin
Enamels and Cameos

Honoré de Balzac
The Girl with the Golden Eyes
Louis Lambert
The Wild Ass's Skin

Old Goriot
Cousin Bette
A Harlot High and Low
Eugénie Grandet
Ursule Mirouet

Stendhal
On Love
The Red and the Black
The Charterhouse of Parma

Gustave Flaubert
Madame Bovary, translated by
Francis Steegmuller
Sentimental Education
Salammbô
A Simple Soul

George Sand
The Haunted Pool

Charles Baudelaire
Flowers of Evil, translated by
Richard Howard
Paris Spleen

Stéphane Mallarmé
Selected Poetry and Prose

Paul Verlaine
Selected Poems

Arthur Rimbaud
Complete Works, translated by
Paul Schmidt

Tristan Corbière
Les Amours jaunes

Jules Laforgue
Selected Writings, translated by
William Jay Smith

Guy de Maupassant
Selected Short Stories

Émile Zola
Germinal
L'Assommoir
Nana

SCANDINAVIA

Henrik Ibsen
Brand, translated by Geoffrey
Hill

Peer Gynt, translated by Rolf
    Fjelde
Emperor and Galilean
Hedda Gabler
The Master Builder
The Lady from the Sea
When We Dead Awaken

August Strindberg
To Damascus
Miss Julie
The Father
The Dance of Death
The Ghost Sonata
A Dream Play

GREAT BRITAIN

Robert Burns
Poems

William Blake
Complete Poetry and Prose

William Wordsworth
Poems
The Prelude

Sir Walter Scott
Waverley
The Heart of Midlothian
Redgauntlet
Old Mortality

Jane Austen
Pride and Prejudice
Emma
Mansfield Park
Persuasion

Samuel Taylor Coleridge
Poems and Prose

Dorothy Wordsworth
The Grasmere Journal

William Hazlitt
Essays and Criticism

Lord Byron
Don Juan
Poems

Walter Savage Landor
Poems
Imaginary Conversations

Thomas De Quincey
*Confessions of an English
    Opium Eater*
Selected Prose

Charles Lamb
Essays

Maria Edgeworth
Castle Rackrent

John Galt
The Entail

Elizabeth Gaskell
Cranford
Mary Barton
North and South

James Hogg
*The Private Memoirs and
    Confessions of a Justified
    Sinner*

Charles Maturin
Melmoth the Wanderer

Percy Bysshe Shelley
Poems
A Defence of Poetry

Mary Wollstonecraft Shelley
Frankenstein

John Clare
Poems

John Keats
Poems and Letters

Thomas Lovell Beddoes
Death's Jest-Book
Poems

George Darley
Nepenthe
Poems

Thomas Hood
Poems

Thomas Wade
Poems

Robert Browning
Poems
The Ring and the Book

Charles Dickens
*The Posthumous Papers of the
    Pickwick Club*
David Copperfield
The Adventures of Oliver Twist
A Tale of Two Cities
Bleak House
Hard Times
Nicholas Nickleby
Dombey and Son
Great Expectations
Martin Chuzzlewit
Christmas Stories
Little Dorrit
Our Mutual Friend
The Mystery of Edwin Drood

Alfred, Lord Tennyson
Poems

Dante Gabriel Rossetti
Poems and *Translations*

Matthew Arnold
Poems
Essays

Arthur Hugh Clough
Poems

Christina Rossetti
Poems

Thomas Love Peacock
Nightmare Abbey
Gryll Grange

Gerard Manley Hopkins
Poems and *Prose*

Thomas Carlyle
Selected Prose
Sartor Resartus

John Ruskin
Modern Painters
The Stones of Venice
Unto This Last
The Queen of the Air

Walter Pater
*Studies in the History of the
    Renaissance*
Appreciations

Imaginary Portraits
Marius the Epicurean

Edward FitzGerald
The Rubáiyát of Omar Khayyám

John Stuart Mill
On Liberty
Autobiography

John Henry Newman
Apologia pro Vita Sua
A Grammar of Assent
The Idea of a University

Anthony Trollope
The Barsetshire Novels
The Palliser Novels
Orley Farm
The Way We Live Now

Lewis Carroll
Complete Works

Edward Lear
Complete Nonsense

George Gissing
New Grub Street

Algernon Charles Swinburne
Poems and *Letters*

Charlotte Brontë
Jane Eyre
Villette

Emily Brontë
Poems
Wuthering Heights

William Makepeace Thackeray
Vanity Fair
The History of Henry Esmond

George Meredith
Poems
The Egoist

Francis Thompson
Poems

Lionel Johnson
Poems

Robert Bridges
Poems

Gilbert Keith Chesterton
Collected Poems
The Man Who Was Thursday

Samuel Butler
Erewhon
The Way of All Flesh

W. S. Gilbert
Complete Plays of Gilbert and Sullivan
Bab Ballads

Wilkie Collins
The Moonstone
The Woman in White
No Name

Coventry Patmore
Odes

James Thomson (Bysshe Vanolis)
The City of Dreadful Night

Oscar Wilde
Plays
The Picture of Dorian Gray
The Artist as Critic
Letters

John Davidson
Ballads and Songs

Ernest Dowson
Complete Poems

George Eliot
Adam Bede
Silas Marner
The Mill on the Floss
Middlemarch
Daniel Deronda

Robert Louis Stevenson
Essays
Kidnapped
Dr. Jekyll and Mr. Hyde
Treasure Island
The New Arabian Nights
The Master of Ballantrae
Weir of Hermiston

William Morris
Early Romances
Poems
The Earthly Paradise

The Well at the World's End
News from Nowhere

Bram Stoker
Dracula

George Macdonald
Lilith
At the Back of the North Wind

GERMANY

Novalis (Friedrich von Hardenburg)
Hymns to the Night
Aphorisms

Jacob and Wilhelm Grimm
Fairy Tales

Eduard Mörike
Selected Poems, translated by Christopher Middleton
Mozart on His Way to Prague

Theodor Storm
Immensee
Poems

Gottfried Keller
Green Henry
Tales

E. T. A. Hoffmann
The Devil's Elixir
Tales

Jeremias Gotthelf
The Black Spider

Adalbert Stifter
Indian Summer
Tales

Friedrich Schlegel
Criticism and *Aphorisms*

Georg Büchner
Danton's Death
Woyzeck

Heinrich Heine
Complete Poems

Richard Wagner
The Ring of the Nibelung

Friedrich Nietzsche
The Birth of Tragedy
Beyond Good and Evil
On the Genealogy of Morals
The Will to Power

Theodor Fontane
Effi Briest

Stefan George
Selected Poems

RUSSIA

Aleksandr Pushkin
Complete Prose Tales
Collected Poetry, translated by
    Walter Arndt
Eugene Onegin, translated by
    Charles Johnston
Narrative Poems, translated by
    Charles Johnston
Boris Godunov

Nikolay Gogol
The Complete Tales
Dead Souls
The Government Inspector,
    translated by Adrian Mitchell

Mikhail Lermontov
Narrative Poems, translated by
    Charles Johnston
A Hero of Our Time

Sergey Aksakov
A Family Chronicle

Aleksandr Herzen
My Past and Thoughts
From the Other Shore

Ivan Goncharov
The Frigate Pallada
Oblomov

Ivan Turgenev
A Sportsman's Notebook,
    translated by Charles and
    Natasha Hepburn
A Month in the Country
Fathers and Sons
On the Eve
First Love

Fyodor Dostoevsky
Notes from the Underground
Crime and Punishment
The Idiot
The Possessed (The Devils)
The Brothers Karamazov
Short Novels

Leo Tolstoy
The Cossacks
War and Peace
Anna Karenina
A Confession
The Power of Darkness
Short Novels

Nikolay Leskov
Tales

Aleksandr Ostrovsky
The Storm

Nikolay Chernyshevsky
What Is to Be Done?

Aleksandr Blok
The Twelve and Other Poems,
    translated by Anselm Hollo

Anton Chekhov
The Tales
The Major Plays

THE UNITED STATES

Washington Irving
The Sketch Book

William Cullen Bryant
Collected Poems

James Fenimore Cooper
The Deerslayer

John Greenleaf Whittier
Collected Poems

Ralph Waldo Emerson
Nature
Essays, first and second series
Representative Men
The Conduct of Life
Journals
Poems

Emily Dickinson
Complete Poems

Walt Whitman
Leaves of Grass, first edition
Leaves of Grass, third edition
The Complete Poems
Specimen Days

Nathaniel Hawthorne
The Scarlet Letter
Tales and Sketches
The Marble Faun
Notebooks

Herman Melville
Moby-Dick
The Piazza Tales
Billy Budd
Collected Poems
Clarel

Edgar Allan Poe
Poetry and Tales
Essays and Reviews
The Narrative of Arthur Gordon Pym
Eureka

Jones Very
Essays and Poems

Frederick Goddard Tuckerman
The Cricket and Other Poems

Henry David Thoreau
Walden
Poems
Essays

Richard Henry Dana, Jr.
Two Years before the Mast

Frederick Douglass
Narrative of the Life of Frederick Douglass, an American Slave

Henry Wadsworth Longfellow
Selected Poems

Sidney Lanier
Poems

Francis Parkman
France and England in North America
The California and Oregon Trail

Henry Adams
The Education of Henry Adams
Mont Saint Michel and Chartres

Ambrose Bierce
Collected Writings

Louisa May Alcott
Little Women

Charles W. Chesnutt
The Short Fiction

Kate Chopin
The Awakening

William Dean Howells
The Rise of Silas Lapham
A Modern Instance

Stephen Crane
The Red Badge of Courage
Stories and *Poems*

Henry James
The Portrait of a Lady
The Bostonians
The Princess Casamassima
The Awkward Age
Short Novels and Tales
The Ambassadors
The Wings of the Dove
The Golden Bowl

Harold Frederic
The Damnation of Theron Ware

Mark Twain
Complete Short Stories
The Adventures of Huckleberry Finn
The Devil's Racetrack
Number Forty-Four: The Mysterious Stranger
Pudd'nhead Wilson
A Connecticut Yankee in King Arthur's Court

William James
*The Varieties of Religious
Experience
Pragmatism*

Frank Norris
The Octopus

Sarah Orne Jewett
*The Country of the Pointed Firs
and Other Stories*

Trumbull Stickney
Poems

D.

The Chaotic Age:
A Canonical Prophecy

I am not as confident about this list as the first three. Cultural prophecy is always a mug's game. Not all of the works here can prove to be canonical; literary overpopulation is a hazard to many among them. But I have neither excluded nor included on the basis of cultural politics of any sort. What I have omitted seem to me fated to become period pieces: even their "multiculturalist" supporters will turn against them in another two generations or so, in order to clear space for better writings. What is here doubtless reflects some accidents of my personal taste, but by no means wholly represents my idiosyncratic inclinations. Robert Lowell and Philip Larkin are here because I seem to be the only critic alive who regards them as overesteemed, and so I am probably wrong and must assume that I am blinded by extra-aesthetic considerations, which I abhor and try to avoid. I would not be surprised, however, could I return from the dead half a century hence, to discover that Lowell and Larkin are period pieces, as are many whom I have excluded. But critics do not make canons, any more than resentful networks can create them, and it may be that poets to come will confirm Lowell and Larkin as canonical by finding them to be inescapable influences.

ITALY

Luigi Pirandello
  Naked Masks: Five Plays,
    translated by Eric Bentley
    and others

Gabriele D'Annunzio
  Maia: In Praise of Life

Dino Campana
  Orphic Songs, translated by
    Charles Wright

Umberto Saba
  Stories and Recollections,
    translated by Estelle Gilson
  Poems

Giuseppe Tomasi di Lampedusa
  The Leopard, translated by
    Archibald Colquhoun

Giuseppe Ungaretti
  Selected Poems, translated by
    Allen Mandelbaum
  *The Buried Harbour: Selected
    Poems,* translated by Kevin
    Hart

Eugenio Montale
  (translated by William
    Arrowsmith)
  *The Storm and Other Things:
    Poems*
  The Occasions: Poems
  Cuttlefish Bones: Poems
  (translated by Jonathan Galassi)

Otherwise: Last and First
Poems
The Second Life of Art:
Selected Essays

Salvatore Quasimodo
Selected Writings: Poems and
Discourse on Poetry,
translated by Allen
Mandelbaum

Tommaso Landolfi
Gogol's Wife and Other Stories

Leonardo Sciascia
Day of the Owl
Equal Danger
The Wine-Dark Sea: Thirteen
Stories

Pier Paolo Pasolini
Poems, translated by Norman
MacAfee with Luciano
Martinengo

Cesare Pavese
Hard Labor: Poems, translated
by William Arrowsmith
Dialogues with Leucò, translated
by William Arrowsmith and
D. S. Carne-Ross

Primo Levi
If Not Now, When? translated
by William Weaver
Collected Poems
The Periodic Table

Italo Svevo
The Confessions of Zeno
As a Man Grows Older

Giorgio Bassani
The Heron, translated by
William Weaver

Natalia Ginzburg
Family

Elio Vittorini
Women of Messina

Alberto Moravia
1934, translated by William
Weaver

Andrea Zanzotto
Selected Poetry

Italo Calvino
Invisible Cities, translated by
William Weaver
The Baron in the Trees,
translated by Archibald
Colquhoun
If on a Winter's Night a
Traveler, translated by
William Weaver
t zero, translated by William
Weaver

Antonio Porta
Kisses from Another Dream:
Poems, translated by Anthony
Molino

SPAIN

Miguel de Unamuno
Three Exemplary Novels,
translated by Angel Flores
Our Lord Don Quixote,
translated by Anthony
Kerrigan

Antonio Machado
Selected Poems, translated by
Alan S. Trueblood

Juan Ramón Jiménez
Invisible Reality: Poems,
translated by Antonio T. de
Nicolas

Pedro Salinas
My Voice Because of You,
Poems, translated by Willis
Barnstone

Jorge Guillén
Guillén on Guillén: The Poetry
and the Poet, translated by
Reginald Gibbons

Vicente Aleixandre
A Longing for the Light:
Selected Poems

Federico García Lorca
Selected Poems
*Three Tragedies: Blood
Wedding, Yerma, The House
of Bernarda Alba*

Rafael Alberti
The Owl's Insomnia: Poems,
translated by Mark Strand

Luis Cernuda
Selected Poems, translated by
Reginald Gibbons

Miguel Hernández
Selected Poems

Blas de Otero
Selected Poems

Camilo José Cela
The Hive

Juan Goytisolo
Space in Motion, translated by
Helen R. Lane

CATALONIA

Carles Ribá
Selected Poems

J. V. Foix
Selected Poems

Joan Perucho
Natural History, translated by
David H. Rosenthal

Merce Rodoreda
The Time of the Doves,
translated by David H.
Rosenthal

Pere Gimferrer
Selected Poems

Salvador Espriú
La Pell de Brau: Poems,
translated by Burton Raffel

PORTUGAL

Fernando Pessoa
The Keeper of Sheep, translated
by Edwin Honig and Susan
M. Brown
Poems, translated by Edwin
Honig and Susan M. Brown
Selected Poems, translated by
Peter Rickard
*Always Astonished: Selected
Prose,* translated by Edwin
Honig
The Book of Disquiet, translated
by Alfred Mac Adam

Jorge de Sena
Selected Poems

José Saramago
Baltasar and Blimunda

José Cardoso Pires
Ballad of Dogs' Beach

Sophia de Mello Breyner
Selected Poems

Eugénio de Andrade
Selected Poems

FRANCE

Anatole France
Penguin Island
Thaïs

Alain-Fournier
Le Grand Meaulnes

Marcel Proust
*Remembrance of Things Past (In
Search of Lost Time),*
translated by C. K. Scott
Moncrieff, revised by Terence
Kilmartin

André Gide
(translated by Richard Howard)
The Immoralist
Corydon
(translated by Dorothy Bussy)
*Lafcadio's Adventures (The
Caves of the Vatican)*
The Counterfeiters
The Journals

Colette
Collected Stories
Retreat from Love

Georges Bataille
Blue of Noon

Louis-Ferdinand Céline
Journey to the End of the Night

René Daumal
Mount Analogue, translated by
Roger Shattuck

Jean Genet
(translated by Bernard
Frechtman)
Our Lady of the Flowers
The Thief's Journal
The Balcony

Jean Giraudoux
Four Plays, translated by
Maurice Valency

Alfred Jarry
Selected Works, translated by
Roger Shattuck and Simon
Watson Taylor

Jean Cocteau
*The Infernal Machine and Other
Plays*

Guillaume Apollinaire
Selected Writings, translated by
Roger Shattuck

André Breton
Poems, translated by Jean-Pierre
Cauvin and Mary Ann Caws
Manifestoes of Surrealism,
translated by Richard Seaver
and Helen R. Lane

Paul Valéry
The Art of Poetry
Selected Writings

René Char
Poems, translated by Jonathan
Griffin and Mary Ann Caws

Paul Éluard
Selected Poems

Louis Aragon
Selected Poems

Jean Giono
The Horseman on the Roof

Michel Leiris
Manhood, translated by Richard
Howard

Raymond Radiguet
Count d'Orgel's Ball

Jean-Paul Sartre
No Exit
Nausea, translated by Lloyd
Alexander
Saint Genet
The Words, translated by
Bernard Frechtman
*The Family Idiot: Gustave
Flaubert*

Simone de Beauvoir
The Second Sex

Albert Camus
The Stranger, translated by
Matthew Ward
The Plague
The Fall
The Rebel

Henri Michaux
Selected Writings, translated by
Richard Ellmann

Edmond Jabès
The Book of Questions,
translated by Rosmarie
Waldrop
Selected Poems, translated by
Keith Waldrop

Saint-John Perse
Anabasis, translated by T. S.
Eliot
Birds, translated by Robert
Fitzgerald
Exile and Other Poems,
translated by Denis Devlin

Pierre Reverdy
Selected Poems

Tristan Tzara
Seven Dada Manifestos,
translated by Barbara Wright

Max Jacob
Selected Poems

Pierre-Jean Jouve
Selected Poems

Francis Ponge
Things: Selected Writings,
translated by Cid Corman

Jacques Prévert
Paroles

Philippe Jaccottet
Selected Poems, translated by
Derek Mahon

Charles Péguy
*The Mystery of the Charity of
Joan of Arc*

Benjamin Péret
Selected Poems

André Malraux
The Conquerors
The Royal Way
Man's Fate
Man's Hope
The Voices of Silence

François Mauriac
(translated by Gerard Hopkins)
Therese
The Desert of Love
The Woman of the Pharisees

Jean Anouilh
Becket
Antigone
Eurydice
The Rehearsal

Eugène Ionesco
The Bald Soprano
The Chairs
The Lesson
Amédée
Victims of Duty
Rhinoceros

Maurice Blanchot
Thomas the Obscure, translated
by Robert Lamberton

Pierre Klossowski
The Laws of Hospitality
The Baphomet

Raymond Roussel
Locus Solus

Antonin Artaud
Selected Writings, translated by
Helen Weaver

Claude Lévi-Strauss
Tristes Tropiques

Alain Robbe-Grillet
(translated by Richard Howard)
The Voyeur
Jealousy
In the Labyrinth
The Erasers
*Project for a Revolution in
New York*
For a New Novel

Nathalie Sarraute
The Use of Speech, translated by
Barbara Wright
The Planetarium, translated by
Maria Jolas

Claude Simon
(translated by Richard Howard)
The Grass
The Wind
The Flanders Road

Marguerite Duras
The Lover, translated by
Barbara Bray
Four Novels, translated by Sonia
Pitt-Rivers and others

Robert Pinget
(translated by Barbara Wright)
Fable
The Libera Me Domine
That Voice

Michel Tournier
The Ogre
Friday

Marguerite Yourcenar
Coup de Grace
Memoirs of Hadrian

Jean Follain
*Transparence of the World:
Poems,* translated by W. S.
Merwin

Yves Bonnefoy
  Words in Stone, translated by
    Susanna Lang

GREAT BRITAIN and IRELAND

William Butler Yeats
  The Collected Poems
  Collected Plays
  A Vision
  Mythologies

George Bernard Shaw
  Major Critical Essays
  Heartbreak House
  Pygmalion
  Saint Joan
  Major Barbara
  Back to Methuselah

John Millington Synge
  Collected Plays

Sean O'Casey
  Juno and the Paycock
  The Plough and the Stars
  The Shadow of a Gunman

George Douglas Brown
  *The House with the Green
    Shutters*

Thomas Hardy
  The Well-Beloved
  The Woodlanders
  The Return of the Native
  The Mayor of Casterbridge
  Far from the Madding Crowd
  Tess of the d'Urbervilles
  Jude the Obscure
  Collected Poems

Rudyard Kipling
  Kim
  Collected Stories
  Puck of Pook's Hill
  Complete Verse

A. E. Housman
  Collected Poems

Max Beerbohm
  Zuleika Dobson
  Seven Men and Two Others

Joseph Conrad
  Lord Jim
  The Secret Agent
  Nostromo
  Under Western Eyes
  Victory

Ronald Firbank
  Five Novels

Ford Madox Ford
  Parade's End
  The Good Soldier

W. Somerset Maugham
  Collected Short Stories
  The Moon and Sixpence

John Cowper Powys
  Wolf Solent
  A Glastonbury Romance

Saki (H. H. Munro)
  The Short Stories

H. G. Wells
  The Science Fiction Novels

David Lindsay
  A Voyage to Arcturus

Arnold Bennett
  The Old Wives' Tale

Walter De la Mare
  Collected Poems
  Memoirs of a Midget

Wilfred Owen
  Collected Poems

Isaac Rosenberg
  Collected Poems

Edward Thomas
  Collected Poems

Robert Graves
  Collected Poems
  King Jesus

Edwin Muir
  Collected Poems

David Jones
  In Parenthesis
  The Anathemata

John Galsworthy
  The Forsyte Saga

E. M. Forster
Howards End
A Passage to India

Frank O'Connor
Collected Stories

D. H. Lawrence
Complete Poems
Studies in Classic American
Literature
Complete Short Stories
Sons and Lovers
The Rainbow
Women in Love

Virginia Woolf
Mrs. Dalloway
To the Lighthouse
Orlando: A Biography
The Waves
Between the Acts

James Joyce
Dubliners
Portrait of the Artist as a Young
Man
Ulysses
Finnegans Wake

Samuel Beckett
Murphy
Watt
Three Novels: Molloy, Malone
Dies, The Unnamable
Waiting for Godot
Endgame
Krapp's Last Tape
How It Is

Elizabeth Bowen
Collected Stories

J. G. Farrell
The Siege of Krishnapur

Henry Green
Nothing
Loving
Party Going

Evelyn Waugh
A Handful of Dust
Scoop

Vile Bodies
Put Out More Flags

Anthony Burgess
Nothing like the Sun

G. B. Edwards
The Book of Ebenezer Le Page

Iris Murdoch
The Good Apprentice
Bruno's Dream

Graham Greene
Brighton Rock
The Heart of the Matter
The Power and the Glory

Christopher Isherwood
The Berlin Stories

Norman Douglas
South Wind

Aldous Huxley
Collected Essays
Antic Hay
Point Counter Point
Brave New World

Lawrence Durrell
The Alexandria Quartet

William Golding
Pincher Martin

Doris Lessing
The Golden Notebook

Mervyn Peake
The Gormenghast Trilogy

Jeanette Winterson
The Passion

W. H. Auden
Collected Poems
The Dyer's Hand

Roy Fuller
Collected Poems

Gavin Ewart
Selected Poems

Basil Bunting
Collected Poems

William Empson
  Collected Poems
  Milton's God
  Some Versions of Pastoral

George Wilson Knight
  The Wheel of Fire
  The Burning Oracle

R. S. Thomas
  Poems

Frank Kermode
  The Sense of an Ending

Stevie Smith
  Collected Poems

F. T. Prince
  Collected Poems

Philip Larkin
  Collected Poems

Donald Davie
  Selected Poems

Geoffrey Hill
  Collected Poems

Jonathan Spence
  The Death of Woman Wang
  *The Memory Palace of Matteo
    Ricci*

Elizabeth Jennings
  Selected Poems

Keith Douglas
  The Complete Poems

Hugh MacDiarmid
  Complete Poems

Louis MacNeice
  Collected Poems

Dylan Thomas
  The Poems

Nigel Dennis
  Cards of Identity

Seamus Heaney
  Selected Poems: 1969–1987
  Field Work
  Station Island

Thomas Kinsella
  Peppercanister Poems

Paul Muldoon
  Selected Poems

John Montague
  Selected Poems

John Arden
  Plays

Joe Orton
  The Complete Plays

Flann O'Brien
  The Dalkey Archive
  The Third Policeman

Tom Stoppard
  Travesties

Harold Pinter
  The Caretaker
  The Homecoming

Edward Bond
  The Fool
  Saved

George Orwell
  Collected Essays
  1984

Edna O'Brien
  A Fanatic Heart

GERMANY

Hugo von Hofmannsthal
  Poems and Verse Plays,
    translated by Michael
    Hamburger and others
  Selected Prose, translated by
    Mary Huttinger and Tania
    and James Stern
  Selected Plays and Libretti,
    translated by Michael
    Hamburger and others

Rainer Maria Rilke
  Selected Poetry, translated by
    Stephen Mitchell (includes the
    Duino Elegies)
  The Sonnets to Orpheus,
    translated by Stephen Mitchell
  *The Notebooks of Malte Laurids
    Brigge,* translated by Stephen
    Mitchell

New Poems: First Part and Other Part, translated by Edward Snow

Hermann Broch
The Sleepwalkers
The Death of Virgil
Hugo von Hofmannsthal and His Time

Georg Trakl
Selected Poems

Gottfried Benn
Selected Poems

Franz Kafka
Amerika
The Complete Stories
The Blue Octavo Notebook
The Trial
Diaries
The Castle
Parables, Fragments, Aphorisms

Bertolt Brecht
Poems, 1913–1956
The Threepenny Opera, translated by Desmond Vesey and Eric Bentley
The Good Woman of Setzuan, translated by Eric Bentley
Mother Courage and Her Children, translated by Eric Bentley
Galileo, translated by Charles Laughton
The Caucasian Chalk Circle

Arthur Schnitzler
Plays and *Stories*

Frank Wedekind
Lulu Plays
Spring Awakening, translated by Edward Bond

Karl Kraus
The Last Days of Mankind

Günter Eich
Moles

Thomas Mann
The Magic Mountain
Stories of Three Decades
Joseph and His Brothers
Doctor Faustus
Confessions of Felix Krull, Confidence Man

Alfred Döblin
Berlin Alexanderplatz

Hermann Hesse
The Glass Bead Game (Magister Ludi)
Narcissus and Goldmund

Robert Musil
Young Törless
The Man Without Qualities

Joseph Roth
The Radetzky March

Paul Celan
Poems, translated by Michael Hamburger

Thomas Bernhard
Woodcutters

Heinrich Böll
Billiards at Half-Past Nine

Ingeborg Bachmann
In the Storm of Roses, translated by Mark Anderson

Hans Magnus Enzensberger
Poems for People Who Don't Read Poems

Walter Benjamin
Illuminations

Robert Walser
Selected Stories, translated by Christopher Middleton, et al.

Christa Wolf
Cassandra

Peter Handke
Slow Homecoming

Max Frisch
I'm Not Stiller
Man in the Holocene

Günter Grass
The Tin Drum
The Flounder

Friedrich Dürrenmatt
The Visit

Johannes Bobrowski
Shadow Lands, translated by
Ruth and Matthew Mead

RUSSIA

Anna Akhmatova
Poems, translated by Stanley
Kunitz and Max Hayward

Leonid Andreyev
Selected Tales

Andrey Bely
Petersburg

Osip Mandelshtam
Selected Poems, translated by
Clarence Brown and W. S.
Merwin

Velimir Khlebnikov
The King of Time

Vladimir Mayakovsky
The Bedbug and Selected Poetry,
translated by Max Hayward
and George Reavey

Mikhail Bulgakov
The Master and Margarita

Mikhail Kuzmin
Alexandrian Songs

Maksim Gorky
*Reminiscences of Tolstoy,
Chekhov, and Andreev*
Autobiography

Ivan Bunin
Selected Stories

Isaac Babel
Collected Stories

Boris Pasternak
Doctor Zhivago
Selected Poems, translated by
Jon Stallworthy and Peter
France

Yury Olesha
Envy

Marina Tsvetayeva
Selected Poems, translated by
Elaine Feinstein

Mikhail Zoshchenko
*Nervous People and Other
Satires*

Andrei Platonov
The Foundation Pit

Aleksandr Solzhenitsyn
*One Day in the Life of Ivan
Denisovich*
The Cancer Ward
The Gulag Archipelago
August 1914

Joseph Brodsky
A Part of Speech: Poems

SCANDINAVIA

**Isak Dinesen (Danish, but wrote in
English)**
Winter's Tales
Seven Gothic Tales

Martin Andersen Nexo
Pelle the Conqueror

Knut Hamsun
Hunger
Pan

Sigrid Undset
Kristin Lavransdatter

Gunnar Ekelöf
Guide to the Underworld,
translated by Rika Lesser

Tomas Tranströmer
Selected Poems

Pär Lagerkvist
Barabbas

Lars Gustafsson
Selected Poems

SERBO-CROAT

Ivo Andrić
The Bridge on the Drina

Vasko Popa
Selected Poems

Danilo Kis
A Tomb for Boris Davidovich

CZECH

Karel Čapek
War with the Newts
R. U. R.

Vaclav Havel
Largo Desolato

Milan Kundera
The Unbearable Lightness of Being

Jaroslav Seifert
Selected Poetry

Miroslav Holub
The Fly

POLISH

Bruno Schulz
The Street of Crocodiles
Sanatorium Under the Sign of the Hourglass

Czeslaw Milosz
Selected Poems

Witold Gombrowicz
Three Novels

Stanislaw Lem
The Investigation
Solaris

Zbigniew Herbert
Selected Poems

Adam Zagajewski
Tremor

HUNGARIAN

Attila József
Perched on Nothing's Branch

Ferenc Juhasz
Selected Poems

Laszlo Németh
Guilt

MODERN GREEK

C. P. Cavafy
Collected Poems

George Seferis
Collected Poems

Nikos Kazantzakis
The Greek Passion
The Odyssey: A Modern Sequel

Yannis Ritsos
Exile and Return

Odysseas Elytis
What I Love: Selected Poems

Angelos Sikelianos
Selected Poems

YIDDISH

Sholem Aleichem
Tevye the Dairyman and *The Railroad Stories*, translated by Hillel Halkin
The Nightingale, translated by Aliza Shevrin

Mendele Mokher Seforim
The Travels and Adventures of Benjamin the Third

I. L. Peretz
Selected Stories

Jacob Glatstein
Selected Poems

Moshe-Leib Halpern
Selected Poems

H. Leivick (Leivick Halpern)
Selected Poems

Israel Joshua Singer
The Brothers Ashkenazi
Yoshe Kalb

Chaim Grade
The Yeshiva

S. Ansky
The Dybbuk

Mani Leib
Selected Poems

Sholem Asch
East River

Isaac Bashevis Singer
Collected Stories
In My Father's Court
The Manor, The Estate, The
  Family Moskat
Satan in Goray

HEBREW

Hayyim Nahman Bialik
Shirot Bialik: The Epic Poems

S. Y. Agnon
In the Heart of the Seas
Twenty-one Stories

Aharon Appelfeld
The Immortal Bartfuss
Badenheim 1939

Yaakov Shabtai
Past Continuous

Yehuda Amichai
Selected Poetry, translated by
  Stephen Mitchell and Chana
  Bloch
Travels, translated by Ruth
  Nevo

A. B. Yehoshua
A Late Divorce

Amos Oz
A Perfect Peace

T. Carmi
At the Stone of Losses,
  translated by Grace Schulman

Nathan Zach
Selected Poems

Dalia Ravikovitch
A Dress of Fire

Dan Pagis
Selected Poems

David Shahar
The Palace of Shattered Vessels

David Grossman
See Under: Love

Yoram Kaniuk
His Daughter

ARABIC

Najib Mahfuz
Midaq Alley
Fountain and Tomb
Miramar

Adunis
Selected Poems

Mahmud Darwish
The Music of Human Flesh

Taha Husayn
An Egyptian Childhood

LATIN AMERICA

Rubén Dário
Selected Poetry

Jorge Luis Borges
The Aleph and Other Stories
Dreamtigers (The Maker)
Ficciones
Labyrinths
A Personal Anthology

Alejo Carpentier
Explosion in a Cathedral
The Lost Steps
Reasons of State
The Kingdom of This World

Guillermo Cabrera Infante
Three Trapped Tigers
View of Dawn in the Tropics

Severo Sarduy
Maitreya

Reinaldo Arenas
The Ill-Fated Peregrinations of
  Fray Servando

Pablo Neruda
Canto general, translated by
  Jack Schmitt
Residence on Earth, translated
  by Donald Walsh
Twenty Love Poems and a Song
  of Despair, translated by
  W. S. Merwin
Fully Empowered, translated by
  Alastair Reid

Selected Poems, translated by
Ben Belitt

Nicolás Guillén
Selected Poems

Octavio Paz
The Collected Poems
The Labyrinth of Solitude

César Vallejo
Selected Poems, translated by
H. R. Hays
Spain, Take This Cup from Me

Miguel Angel Asturias
Men of Maize

José Lezama Lima
Paradiso

José Donoso
The Obscene Bird of Night

Julio Cortázar
Hopscotch
All Fires the Fire, translated by
Suzanne Jill Levine
Blow-up and Other Stories,
translated by Paul Blackburn

Gabriel García Márquez
One Hundred Years of Solitude,
translated by Gregory Rabassa
Love in the Time of Cholera,
translated by Edith Grossman

Mario Vargas Llosa
*The War of the End of the
World*

Carlos Fuentes
A Change of Skin
Terra Nostra

Carlos Drummond de Andrade
Travelling in the Family,
translated by Elizabeth Bishop,
et al.

THE WEST INDIES

C. L. R. James
The Black Jacobins
The Future in the Present

V. S. Naipaul
A Bend in the River
A House for Mr. Biswas

Derek Walcott
Collected Poems

Wilson Harris
The Guyana Quartet

Michael Thelwell
The Harder They Come

Aimé Césaire
Collected Poetry

AFRICA

Chinua Achebe
Things Fall Apart
Arrow of God
No Longer at Ease

Wole Soyinka
A Dance of the Forest

Amos Tutuola
*The Palm-Wine Drinkard and
His Dead Palm-Wine Tapster
in the Dead's Town*

Christopher Okigbo
*Labyrinths, with Path of
Thunder*

John Pepper Clark (-Bekederemo)
Casualties: Poems

Ayi K. Armah
*The Beautyful Ones Are Not Yet
Born*

Wa Thiong'o Ngugi
A Grain of Wheat

Gabriel Okara
The Fisherman's Invocation

Nadine Gordimer
Collected Stories

J. M. Coetzee
Foe

Athol Fugard
A Lesson from Aloes

Léopold S. Senghor
Selected Poems

INDIA (in English)

R. K. Narayan
The Guide

Salman Rushdie
Midnight's Children

Ruth Prawer Jhabvala
Heat and Dust

CANADA

Malcolm Lowry
Under the Volcano

Robertson Davies
The Deptford Trilogy
The Rebel Angels

Alice Munro
*Something I've Been Meaning to
 Tell You*

Northrop Frye
Fables of Identity

Anne Hébert
Selected Poems

Jay Macpherson
Poems Twice Told

Margaret Atwood
Surfacing

Daryl Hine
Selected Poems

AUSTRALIA and NEW ZEALAND

Miles (Stella) Franklin
My Brilliant Career

Katherine Mansfield
The Short Stories

A. D. Hope
Collected Poems

Patrick White
Riders in the Chariot
A Fringe of Leaves
Voss

Christina Stead
The Man Who Loved Children

Judith Wright
Selected Poems

Les A. Murray
*The Rabbiter's Bounty:
 Collected Poems*

Thomas Keneally
The Playmaker
Schindler's List

David Malouf
An Imaginary Life

Kevin Hart
Peniel and Other Poems

Peter Carey
Oscar and Lucinda
Illywhacker

THE UNITED STATES

Edwin Arlington Robinson
Selected Poems

Robert Frost
The Poetry

Edith Wharton
Collected Short Stories
The Age of Innocence
Ethan Frome
The House of Mirth
The Custom of the Country

Willa Cather
My Ántonia
The Professor's House
A Lost Lady

Gertrude Stein
Three Lives
*The Geographical History of
 America*
The Making of Americans
Tender Buttons

Wallace Stevens
Collected Poems
The Necessary Angel
Opus Posthumous
*The Palm at the End of the
 Mind*

Vachel Lindsay
Collected Poems

Edgar Lee Masters
Spoon River Anthology

Theodore Dreiser
Sister Carrie
An American Tragedy

Sherwood Anderson
Winesburg, Ohio
Death in the Woods and Other Stories

Sinclair Lewis
Babbitt
It Can't Happen Here

Elinor Wylie
Last Poems

William Carlos Williams
Spring and All
Paterson
Collected Poems

Ezra Pound
Personae: Collected Poems
The Cantos
Literary Essays

Robinson Jeffers
Selected Poems

Marianne Moore
Complete Poems

Hilda Doolittle (H. D.)
Selected Poems

John Crowe Ransom
Selected Poems

T. S. Eliot
The Complete Poems and Plays
Selected Essays

Katherine Anne Porter
Collected Stories

Jean Toomer
Cane

John Dos Passos
U.S.A.

Conrad Aiken
Collected Poems

Eugene O'Neill
Lazarus Laughed
The Iceman Cometh
Long Day's Journey into Night

e. e. cummings
Complete Poems

John B. Wheelwright
Collected Poems

Robert Fitzgerald
Spring Shade: Poems

Louise Bogan
The Blue Estuaries: Selected Poems

Léonie Adams
Poems: A Selection

Hart Crane
Complete Poems and *Selected Letters and Prose*

Allen Tate
Collected Poems

F. Scott Fitzgerald
Babylon Revisited and Other Stories
The Great Gatsby
Tender Is the Night

William Faulkner
As I Lay Dying
Sanctuary
Light in August
Absalom, Absalom!
The Sound and the Fury
The Wild Palms
The Collected Stories
The Hamlet

Ernest Hemingway
Complete Short Stories
A Farewell to Arms
The Sun Also Rises
The Garden of Eden

John Steinbeck
The Grapes of Wrath

Zora Neale Hurston
Their Eyes Were Watching God

Nathanael West
Miss Lonelyhearts
A Cool Million
The Day of the Locust

Richard Wright
Native Son
Black Boy

Eudora Welty
Collected Stories
Delta Wedding
The Robber Bridegroom
The Ponder Heart

Langston Hughes
Selected Poems
The Big Sea
I Wonder as I Wander

Edmund Wilson
The Shores of Light
Patriotic Gore

Kenneth Burke
Counter-statement
A Rhetoric of Motives

Joseph Mitchell
Up in the Old Hotel

Abraham Cahan
The Rise of David Levinsky

Kay Boyle
Three Short Novels

Ellen Glasgow
Barren Ground
Vein of Iron

John P. Marquand
H. M. Pulham, Esquire

John O'Hara
Collected Stories
Appointment in Samarra

Henry Roth
Call It Sleep

Thornton Wilder
Three Plays

Robert Penn Warren
All the King's Men
World Enough and Time
Selected Poems

Delmore Schwartz
Selected Poems: Summer
  Knowledge

Weldon Kees
Collected Poems

Elizabeth Bishop
The Complete Poems

John Berryman
Collected Poems

Paul Bowles
The Sheltering Sky

Randall Jarrell
Complete Poems

Charles Olson
The Maximus Poems
Collected Poems

Robert Hayden
Collected Poems

Robert Lowell
Collected Poems

Theodore Roethke
Collected Poems
Straw for the Fire

James Agee
Permit Me Voyage
Let Us Now Praise Famous Men
  (with Walker Evans)

Jean Garrigue
Selected Poems

May Swenson
New & Selected Things Taking
  Place
In Other Words

Robert Duncan
Bending the Bow

Richard Wilbur
New and Collected Poems

Richard Eberhart
Collected Poems

M. B. Tolson
Harlem Gallery

Kenneth Koch
Seasons on Earth

Frank O'Hara
Selected Poems

James Schuyler
Collected Poems

James Baldwin
The Price of the Ticket

Saul Bellow
Seize the Day
The Adventures of Augie March
Herzog

John Cheever
The Stories
Bullet Park

Ralph Ellison
Invisible Man

Truman Capote
In Cold Blood

Carson McCullers
The Ballad of the Sad Café
The Heart Is a Lonely Hunter

Flannery O'Connor
Complete Stories
The Violent Bear It Away
Wise Blood

Vladimir Nabokov
Lolita
Pale Fire

Gore Vidal
Myra Breckinridge
Lincoln

William Styron
The Long March

J. D. Salinger
The Catcher in the Rye
Nine Stories

Wright Morris
Ceremony in Lone Tree

Bernard Malamud
The Stories
The Fixer

Norman Mailer
Advertisements for Myself
The Executioner's Song
Ancient Evenings

John Hawkes
The Cannibal
Second Skin

William Gaddis
The Recognitions

Tennessee Williams
The Glass Menagerie
A Streetcar Named Desire
Summer and Smoke

Arthur Miller
Death of a Salesman

Edwin Justus Mayer
Children of Darkness

Harold Brodkey
*Stories in an Almost Classical
Mode*

Ursula K. Le Guin
The Left Hand of Darkness

Raymond Carver
Where I'm Calling From

Robert Coover
Spanking the Maid

Don DeLillo
White Noise
Libra
Running Dog
Mao II

John Crowley
Little, Big
Aegypt
Love and Sleep

Guy Davenport
  Tatlin!

James Dickey
  The Early Motion
  The Central Motion

E. L. Doctorow
  The Book of Daniel
  World's Fair

Stanley Elkin
  The Living End

William H. Gass
  *In the Heart of the Heart of the
    Country*
  Omensetter's Luck

Russell Hoban
  Riddley Walker

Denis Johnson
  Angels
  Fiskadoro
  Jesus' Son

Cormac McCarthy
  Blood Meridian
  Suttree
  Child of God

William Kennedy
  Ironweed
  The Albany Cycle

Toni Morrison
  Song of Solomon

Gloria Naylor
  The Women of Brewster Place

Joyce Carol Oates
  Them

Walker Percy
  The Moviegoer

Grace Paley
  The Little Disturbances of Man

Thomas Pynchon
  V.
  The Crying of Lot 49
  Gravity's Rainbow

Cynthia Ozick
  Envy, or Yiddish in America
  The Messiah of Stockholm

Ishmael Reed
  Mumbo Jumbo

Philip Roth
  Portnoy's Complaint
  My Life as a Man
  *Zuckerman Bound: A Trilogy
    and Epilogue*
  The Counterlife
  Patrimony
  Operation Shylock

James Salter
  Solo Faces
  Light Years

Robert Stone
  Dog Soldiers
  A Flag for Sunrise

John Barth
  The Floating Opera
  The End of the Road
  The Sot-Weed Factor

Walter Abish
  Alphabetical Africa
  How German Is It
  Eclipse Fever
  I Am the Dust Under Your Feet

Donald Barthelme
  Forty Stories
  The Dead Father

Thomas M. Disch
  On Wings of Song

Paul Theroux
  The Mosquito Coast

John Updike
  The Witches of Eastwick

Kurt Vonnegut, Jr.
  Cat's Cradle

Edmund White
  Forgetting Elena
  *Nocturnes for the King of
    Naples*

James McCourt
Time Remaining

James Wilcox
Modern Baptists

A. R. Ammons
Collected Poems
Selected Longer Poems
Sphere: The Form of a Motion

John Ashbery
The Double Dream of Spring
Houseboat Days
Selected Poems
Flow Chart
Hotel Lautréamont
And the Stars Were Shining

David Mamet
American Buffalo
Speed-the-Plow

David Rabe
Streamers

Sam Shepard
Seven Plays

August Wilson
Fences
Joe Turner's Come and Gone

Anthony Hecht
Collected Earlier Poems

Edgar Bowers
Living Together: New and
Selected Poems

Donald Justice
Selected Poems

James Merrill
From the First Nine
The Changing Light at Sandover

W. S. Merwin
Selected Poems

James Wright
Above the River: The Complete
Poems

Galway Kinnell
Selected Poems

Philip Levine
Selected Poems

Irving Feldman
New and Selected Poems

Donald Hall
The One Day
Old and New Poems

Alvin Feinman
Poems

Richard Howard
Untitled Subjects
Findings

John Hollander
Reflections on Espionage
Selected Poetry
Tesserae

Gary Snyder
No Nature: New and Selected
Poems

Charles Simic
Selected Poems

Mark Strand
Selected Poems
The Continuous Life
Dark Harbor

Charles Wright
The World of the Ten Thousand
Things

Jay Wright
Dimensions of History
The Double Invention of Komo
Selected Poems
Elaine's Book
Boleros

Amy Clampitt
Westward

Allen Grossman
The Ether Dome and Other
Poems: New and Selected

Howard Moss
New Selected Poems

James Applewhite
River Writing: An Eno Journal

J. D. McClatchy
The Rest of the Way

Alfred Corn
A Call in the Midst of the Crowd

Douglas Crase
The Revisionist

Rita Dove
Selected Poems

Thylias Moss
Small Congregations: New and Selected Poems

Edward Hirsch
Earthly Measures

Tony Kushner
Angels in America

Index

Boldface page numbers indicate main discussions